Oxford Studies in Lexicography and Lexicology

*Series editors*
Richard W. Bailey, Noel Osselton, and Gabriele Stein

# John Palsgrave as Renaissance Linguist

# John Palsgrave as Renaissance Linguist

## A Pioneer in Vernacular Language Description

GABRIELE STEIN

CLARENDON PRESS · OXFORD
1997

*Oxford University Press, Great Clarendon Street, Oxford* OX2 6DP
*Oxford New York*
*Athens Auckland Bangkok Bogota Bombay*
*Buenos Aires Calcutta Cape Town Dar es Salaam*
*Delhi Florence Hong Kong Istanbul Karachi*
*Kuala Lumpur Madras Madrid Melbourne*
*Mexico City Nairobi Paris Singapore*
*Taipei Tokyo Toronto*
*and associated companies in*
*Berlin Ibadan*





*Published in the United States*
*by Oxford University Press Inc., New York*



*British Library Cataloguing in Publication Data*
*Data available*

*Library of Congress Cataloging in Publication Data*
*John Palsgrave as Renaissance linguist: a pioneer in vernacular language description/Gabriele Stein.*
*(Oxford studies in lexicography and lexicology)*
*Includes bibliographical references and index.*
*1. Palsgrave, John, d. 1554. 2. Contrastive linguistics.*
*3. English language–Lexicon, Grammar, Comparative–French. 4. French language–Lexicon, Grammar, Comparative–English. I. Title. II. Series.*
*P85.P35S74 1997 410–dc20 96-43075*
*ISBN 0–19–823505–4*

1 3 5 7 9 10 8 6 4 2

*Typeset by Joshua Associates Ltd., Oxford*
*Printed in Great Britain on acid-free paper by*
*Bookcraft (Bath) Ltd., Midsomer Norton*

# Preface

The most conspicuous feature in the history of English is surely the way the vocabulary has undergone enormous change and expansion. Yet, doubtless because of the general neglect of lexicology by Anglophone scholars, even the best historical treatments of English deal with relatively restricted aspects of vocabulary only, often recycling the same familiar examples from generation to generation, and neglecting the quite extraordinarily rich resources available to scholars in medieval and Renaissance word books. In consequence, students find it impossible to learn about the overall structure or even size of the lexicon at key points in the history of English, let alone about lexical phenomena such as functional differentiation in specific subject fields or the stylistic differentiation that enabled users to respond to the varying situations of communication.

In *The English Dictionary before Cawdrey* (Tübingen, 1985), as well as in numerous papers before and since, I have sought to redress the position by drawing attention to the achievements of the many 'clerks' who compiled the first 'repositories' and word lists that gradually led to dictionaries as we now know them. In the detail of observation and depth of linguistic penetration, however, one work stands out as a foremost document and treasure trove of sixteenth-century French and English usage, inexhaustible in its wealth of linguistic and cultural information. This is John Palsgrave's *Lesclarcissement de la langue francoyse*. The stature, originality, and sheer scale of his work demanded a separate book-length treatment. In *Lesclarcissement* we have a unique achievement, presenting as it does the description of two major vernaculars, lexically and grammatically, and—what is still more remarkable—in explicit comparative and contrastive relationship one with the other. This is a pioneering achievement of breathtaking dimension, and expounding Palsgrave's achievement has been no light task.

Although the majority of my research time throughout an entire decade has been enjoyably and often excitingly devoted to establishing Palsgrave's pioneering analyses and approach, I am acutely aware that the present book can do little more than open the field of

Palsgrave studies and invite the attention of Anglophone and Francophone scholars. But if my efforts have even this degree of impact, the foundation will have been laid for a full recognition of John Palsgrave as a leading descriptive linguist and for a proper exploration of the wealth of data he provides on sixteenth-century French and English, clearly demonstrating the essential interdependence of lexicology and grammar.

Needless to say, this study was not completed without the help of my students and colleagues, to whom I would like to express my thanks. I am particularly indebted to Ellen Runte for her many searches and consistency checks. I gratefully acknowledge the help of my fellow editors, R. W. Bailey and Noel Osselton, which went far beyond the call of editorial duty. Indeed, Professor Osselton's meticulous reading of the whole manuscript at the final stages, together with his highly appreciated suggestions, greatly improved its overall structure.

The untiring competence and expertise of my secretary, Christa Schlumberger, in preparing a most difficult manuscript was not only a tremendous reassurance during the writing of the book but also an awe-inspiring experience. Thanks to her splendid work, Frances Morphy, Hilary Walford, and their colleagues at Oxford University Press were able to reproduce the original texts as closely as possible.

Finally, I find it difficult to express the gratitude I owe to my husband, Randolph Quirk. His enduring enthusiasm, wide learning, and percipient advice during the years of writing were an inexhaustible source of inspiration and support—most of all during the time when my health made me fear for the completion of my Palsgrave study. He helped me in every possible way, was always prepared to listen and discuss difficult points, to draw my attention to inconsistencies, to make my English style more lucid, to give his time for my work, and—not least—to welcome me with lovely cooked dinners after a day's work in the British Library. In deep gratitude I dedicate this book to him.

*Heidelberg*
*April 1997* G.S.

# Contents

# Note on the Text

Quotations from early texts reproduce the originals as closely as is consistent with accessibility. For my readers' convenience, the following changes have been made:

1. The long s 'ſ' in all texts is replaced by 's'.
2. *Promptorium parvulorum* (1440)
   Instead of the conventions adopted in the modern printed edition, I have in each case used boldface for the English lemma and italic for the Latin equivalent.
3. *Catholicon Anglicum* (1483)
   Instead of the conventions adopted by S. J. H. Herrtage, I have used boldface for English lemmata and italic for the Latin equivalents, with roman for pre- and postlemmatic expansions.
   All the parenthetical additions, including items in Add. MS 15, 562, have been silently omitted. The same holds for the parenthetical signs (†), indicating words not occurring in the **Promptorium parvulorum**, and (*), added to words annotated by A. Way.
4. *Promptorium parvulorum* (1499)
   In place of the practice of the early printed edition, I have used boldface for the English lemmata and roman for the Latin equivalents.
5. *Ortus vocabulorum* (1500)
   In place of the practice of the early printed edition, I have used boldface for Latin text and roman for English text.
6. *Lesclarcissement de la langue francoyse* (1530)
   Only two conventions need to be mentioned. I have replaced 'ȝ' by a normal roman 'z' where this is the common modern form, and I have introduced elision points (. . .) in place of certain postlemmatic expansions.

The following abbreviations are used in the text (full publication details are given in the Bibliography):

| | |
|---|---|
| *DNB* | *Dictionary of National Biography* |
| *EDD* | *The English Dialect Dictionary* |
| *FEW* | *Französisches etymologisches Wörterbuch* |
| *MED* | *Middle English Dictionary* |
| *OED* | *The Oxford English Dictionary* |

# 1

# John Palsgrave: Clerk, Royal Schoolmaster, and Chaplain

Within the history of English dictionary-making John Palsgrave is the first lexicographer whose name is known. Dictionary-making involving English began with bilingual word lists. By the early fifteenth century these lists had assumed the scale and nature of dictionaries, and some have been preserved. The oldest are the *Medulla grammatice* and the *Hortus vocabulorum*. Of these two Latin–English dictionaries it is only the *Hortus vocabulorum* that was ever printed (between 1500 and 1532). The earliest English–Latin dictionaries are the *Promptorium parvulorum* and the *Catholicon Anglicum*, and again, only one of them was printed: the *Promptorium parvulorum* (between 1499 and 1528). For none of these four early lexicographical works has the compiler been identified.

The year 1530 marks the date of publication of *Lesclarcissement de la langue francoyse*. The third book in this monumental work contains an English–French dictionary, which Palsgrave himself calls the 'frenche vocabuler' or the 'frenche vocabulyst' (the *OED* has no earlier use of either word). At that time, as we might have gathered from the fanciful titles of the first bilingual English dictionaries, the generic term 'dictionary' was not yet common in English. The first compiler of an English work who actually called his book a dictionary was Sir Thomas Elyot (1538). For Palsgrave's work, we may usefully adopt Palsgrave's term, *vocabulist*.

What do we know about the author of *Lesclarcissement de la langue francoyse*? The sources of information that we have are his works, records of some personal letters, references to him in the correspondence of his famous contemporaries Thomas More and Erasmus, and various official documents specifying the professional functions he held. They allow us glimpses of a life that in most of its phases still remains unknown to us. We shall pick up the few clues that we have to outline the main stages of his life and activities.

We do not know when Palsgrave was born. But we do know that he was born in London for he describes himself on the title-page of *Lesclarcissement de la langue francoyse* as 'maistre Jehan Palsgraue

Angloys natyf de Londres'. Here, as in his other work, his translation of William Fullonius' Latin comedy *Acolastus* into English,[1] he gives his name as 'Palsgrave', but in the earlier records his name also appears as *Paggrave*, *Palgrave*, *Palgrove*, *Paullsgrave*, *Polegrave*, *Polgrave*, and *Polygrave*.

The earliest mention we have of him is as a student in Cambridge. In the records of the University of Cambridge for 1503–4 we find, under the 'cauciones recepte post festum natalis domini', his name and that of a fellow student: 'Cauciones dominorum Schynner et paggraue est vna murra cum pecea argentea' (Bateson 1903: 188).[2] The same source tells us that 'D. Polgrave' received his BA in 1504 (ibid., 193). This then allows us to assume that he was born in the 1480s, which makes him younger than Erasmus (?1466–1536) and Thomas More (1478–1535), but older than King Henry VIII (b. 1491) and Henry's sister Mary (b. 1496), Palsgrave's future royal pupil. After Palsgrave's graduation at Cambridge we lose sight of him for a good number of years. When we encounter him again, we find him in a position of high distinction. In January 1513 the king paid him the sum of 6*l.* 13*s.* 4*d.* as a year's wages for his services as 'schoolmaster to my Lady Princess' (Brewer 1864/1965: 1459). Two months later, in March 1513, he received another 66*s.* 8*d.* as 'schoolmaster to the Princess of Castile' (ibid.: 1460). At that time Mary Tudor, Henry VIII's sister and Palsgrave's pupil, was often referred to as the 'Princess of Castile', because, according to a treaty signed in 1507, she was to marry Prince Charles of Castile (who later was to become Emperor Charles V). *Lesclarcissement de la langue francoyse* provides us with further information. From the dedicatory epistle to the king we learn that Palsgrave had been asked to instruct the king's sister, the 'queen Mary, dowager of France', in the French tongue. And on the title-page Palsgrave describes himself as a graduate of Paris. We may then assume that during the years not yet accounted for Palsgrave went to France and obtained an MA from the university of Paris. He must have spent quite some time in France to master the French language to such a degree that he became the author of its first comprehensive grammar and the first bilingual vernacular word list.[3] But at the time when he was entrusted by the king to instruct

[1] There is a modern text edition with an introduction and notes (Carver 1937); the introduction gives the best account of Palsgrave's life.

[2] The *DNB* and Carver give as the college he entered *Corpus Christus College*. Emden (1974: 429), however, has pointed out that Palsgrave is not included as a member of the college in J. Lamb's edition of R. Masters, *History of Corpus Christi College*.

[3] Since there is no generic term in English to cover such different lexicographical products as small word lists, glossaries, vocabularies and dictionaries, 'word list' will also be used as a generic term in this book.

his sister *Lesclarcissement de la langue francoyse* was not yet written. He must therefore have enjoyed a high reputation as an expert of French and a first-class teacher to have been appointed by the king.

How had it come about that the king's sister, the princess of Castile, had become the queen dowager of France? In the delicate balancing of power, Henry VII had made it his policy to form alliances with Spain and Burgundy to prevent a *rapprochement* between France and Spain that might result in an annexation of the Low Countries and thus a control of, or possibly even an end to, the flourishing wool and cloth trade between the countries on both sides of the Channel. At the same time he sought friendship with France and Scotland to deter them from joining their forces against England. The first step in the alliance with Spain was the marriage in 1501 between his eldest son Arthur, prince of Wales, and Catherine of Aragon, daughter of Isabella of Castile and Ferdinand of Aragon. Unfortunately, however, the heir to the British throne died one year after his marriage. Henry VII's second step was his marriage plans for his daughter Mary. On 21 December 1507 the future marriage between Mary Tudor and Charles, the prince of Castile, was agreed upon in the Treaty of Calais. Henry VII died in 1509. His successor, his second son, Henry VIII, continued his external policy by not only marrying Catherine of Aragon but also by renewing the marriage contract for his sister in October 1513. This amply accounts for the reference to the 'Princess of Castile' in the 1513 records of his Privy Purse expenses. The wedding was fixed for 1514, but as time drew near it became clear that the emperor had other plans for his grandson. The contract was officially renounced on 30 July 1514. Charles of Castile was to marry Isabella of Portugal, the daughter of Manuel I of Portugal. In the meantime, however, Henry VIII had prepared another move for his sister Mary in the complicated European game of marriage chess. In January 1514, the French queen, Anne of Brittany, had died. The French king, Louis XII, gout-stricken and ailing at the age of 52, had two daughters and no male offspring. Mary was then only 18 years of age and emotionally attached to Charles Brandon, the duke of Suffolk. She agreed to marrying Louis XII on condition that, should she outlive the French king, she would then have the husband of her choice. A fortnight after the official renunciation of the marriage contract with the prince of Castile a new contract was signed at the royal manor of Greenwich, with the duke of Longueville acting as the French king's proxy (13 August 1514). The actual marriage took place on 9 October that year, and we know from the records that Palsgrave accompanied the young queen to France as her secretary (Brewer 1920: 1408–9).

The marriage was not to last long. Louis XII died on 1 January 1515, and the queen dowager of France then had her own choice: she married Charles Brandon, the duke of Suffolk.

The sequence of events that we have established leaves no doubt that Palsgrave became schoolmaster to the Princess Mary when she was still engaged to Charles, prince of Castile. We do not know the exact date of his royal appointment. All we can go by are the wage records for January and March 1513. The sum of 6*l.* 13*s.* 4*d.*, paid as a year's wages in January 1513, would suggest that he had been in royal service for a year, starting in 1512.

If Palsgrave had hoped to remain in the services of the queen of France as her schoolmaster or secretary, then, like many of the English officials and servants who had accompanied her to Abbéville and assisted her at the splendid royal wedding, he was to be disappointed. From the complaints dispatched by Mary three days after the royal wedding to Wolsey and her brother, King Henry VIII, we learn that on the morning after her marriage she found that all her servants had been discharged. Fortunately, however, Palsgrave was not without means at that time. Earlier in the year (29 April 1514) he had been admitted to the prebend of Portpool in the church of St Paul in London, a position which he was to hold until his death (Le Neve 1854: 428).

The queen of France, however, had not forgotten her French instructor. In a letter sent from Paris to Wolsey on 13 November 1514 she begged his favour on behalf of John Palsgrave (Carver 1937: pp. xiii–xiv).[4]

The preferment requested seems not to have been granted, and some months later (3 April 1515) Mary, then queen dowager of France, sent another letter to Wolsey. In it she pointed out that she had heard that Dr Nicholas West, one of the English ambassadors in Paris, was to become bishop of Ely. She asked that her servant, John Palsgrave, might be appointed to the living of 'Egylsfeld' in the diocese of Durham, or the archdeaconry of Derby, both positions being vacated by West's promotion (Brewer 1864/1965: 93). Again, Wolsey did not comply.

About one and a half years later we hear again of Palsgrave's activities. Our source is Sir Thomas More's correspondence with Erasmus. From the letters exchanged in 1516 it becomes clear that Palsgrave had become a friend of Sir Thomas More.[5] When and where this friendship started, we do not know. More's letter in which

[4] The letter from the *State Papers*, I, vol. 9, fo. 158, is summarized in Brewer (1920: 1444–5).

[5] There are very few surnames in Palsgrave's example sentences, one of them is Moore: '*I neuer knewe none harpe so well as mayster Moore dothe/and yet he is blynde*' (III, fo. cc.lviii).

he talks about Palsgrave dates from 4 December 1516. The English translation of the relevant part in the Latin original reads as follows:

MORE TO ERASMUS, GREETING

My friend Palsgrave, whose attachment to you is, as you know, of long standing, is off to Louvain to devote himself to the law, but on the understanding that he means to add to his stock of the humanities in Latin and Greek, as is his way. He has heard that you will be living there, and in view of his old acquaintance with you reckons that he can count on you for anything; but all the same . . . he has asked me with some urgency to be sure to add my own recommendation to the good will he thinks he already enjoys with you on his own account; he wants to be allowed to enjoy your advice and help in his pursuit of a liberal education. I know, my dear Erasmus, I need waste few words in asking you to assist the studies of a man who is devoted to good literature, full of promise, known to be a hard worker, and his progress hitherto is already familiar to you; one moreover who is both my friend and yours, which means yours twice over . . . I have given him for delivery to you all the letters which were sent to you some time ago by your friends in Basel and have been lying in my hands all this time. This has turned out very conveniently; for no more reliable person could offer himself to carry them, nor could he himself wish for anything more likely to secure him a welcome than a large bundle of letters from very dear and learned friends, awaited for so long and almost despaired of. I have, however, instructed him not to hand them over except against a formal undertaking from you to accept them solely on condition that he is agreeable to you in every respect . . . (Mynors and Thomson 1977: 162–3)[6]

Thus armed with a letter of recommendation from More and the precious letters Erasmus had received from his friends in Basle, Palsgrave must have set off for Louvain because, in a letter to Erasmus dated 15 December 1516, More assumes that Palsgrave had successfully completed his mission (ibid.: 169).

For 1517, we have evidence that Palsgrave spent some time in Louvain as well as in England. In a letter of 17 July to his friend Cuthbert Tunstall, Erasmus mentions that Palsgrave has returned to England, acting again as a messenger (Mynors and Thomson 1979: 31). This may suggest that Palsgrave stayed in Louvain from December 1516 to July 1517. He spent at least a month in England, for on 19 August More explains the delay of an answer to a letter from Erasmus as follows:

The belated and long-postponed departure of my friend Palsgrave, who is daily expected to leave, has meant that you should receive my letter and other people's much later than either I desired or you deserved. For I thought that my answer could most conveniently be carried by the man who had brought me yours. (ibid.: 67–8)

We know that More's letter reached Erasmus in Louvain, but it is not clear whether the carrier was John Palsgrave or someone else. In a

[6] For the Latin text, see Allen (1910: 412–13). Another English translation is that in Rogers (1961: 83–4).

letter to Erasmus, dispatched from Calais (25 October), More sends his 'cordial greetings' to his 'friend Palsgrave if he has returned' (ibid.: 157).

We do not know how long Palsgrave stayed in Louvain on this occasion. Our next point of reference is his appointment to the benefice of the church of Asfordby in the county of Leicester (Carver 1937: p. xvii). He was instituted on 2 June 1518 and resigned from it in April 1525. His successor, Master Richard Brokesbye, was instituted on 9 April 1525, 'reserving an annual pension of 3*l.* 6*s.* 8*d.* to the same Master John resigning' (ibid.: p. xvii).

During the Asfordby period we find him in 1520 with the king in Calais. On 10 July of that year the emperor, Charles V, and Henry VIII met in Calais to renew their treaties. Among the noblemen, officials, and other subjects appointed to attend upon the king was 'the Palsegrave' who was paid 14*s.* 4*d.* for his services to the king (Brewer 1867/1965: 327).

Journeys between England and the continent must have become quite a regular experience for Palsgrave, since they presented themselves so readily to his mind when he was looking for example sentences to illustrate the meaning of a number of verbs in his English–French dictionary. *Dover* and *Calais* figure most prominently in these examples, in one case one might even think of the 1520 journey:

> **I Am within syght as a shyppe is that cometh within the kennyng/** Ie blanchis, iay blanchy, blanchir. secunde coniuga. **We were within syght towardes the coste of Douer two houres byfore daye:** Nous blanchissons vers le coste de Douer deux heures deuant le iour.
>
> (III, fo. c.xlviii$^{r-v}$)

> **I Come to lande as a shyppe or mã doth after he hath sayled a iournaye/** Ie arriue. prime coniuga. **We departed from Calays at syxe of the clocke in the mornyng and we came to Douer by noone:** Nous partismes de Calays a six heures de matin, et nous arriuasmes a Doure sur le point de mydy.
>
> (III, fo. cc.ii$^{r-v}$)

But there are also references to other ports (such as *Bordeaux* and *Dunkirk*) and one may well wonder whether the examples provided relate to other personal experiences of the author:

> **I Freyght a shyppe or suche lyke** Ie charge vne nauire. prime coniuga. and ie esquippe. pri. con. **My shyppe was freyghted to go in to Bordeaulx more than fourtene dayes passed:** Ma nauire estoyt chargée, or esquippée pour aller a Bordeaulx plus de quatorze iours passez.
>
> (III, fo. cc.xlii$^{v}$)

> **I Go to wrake as a shyppe dothe on the see whan she is in daũger of lesynge/** Ie naufrage, prime cõiuga. **Our shyppe wente to wrake open vpon Donkyrke:** Nostre nef se naufragea deuant Donkyrke, or se laissa perir tout deuant Donkyrke.
>
> (III, fo. cc.liii$^{v}$)

Palsgrave's stay in the Low Countries also seems to have left some imprint on his mind, as suggested, for instance, by the example given to illustrate the meaning and use of the verb *to slide*:

> **I Slyde as one dothe vpon the yse or any slypper place/** Ie glisse. prime cõiu. **I haue sene one in Hollande slyde as faste vpon the yse as a bote dothe in the water whan it is towed:** Iay veu en Hollande vng hõme glisser sur la glace aussy viste qung batteau peult aller per ses auirons.
>
> (III, fo. ccc.lxiii$^{v}$)

The year 1520 also marks a year in which Palsgrave obtained another benefice. In August he became rector of Alderton in Suffolk, a position which he seems to have kept until 1525 (Carver 1937: p. xviii). Yet this was not to be the only time that Thomas More exercised his patronage. Palsgrave also owed to Sir Thomas the rectorship of Holbrook near Ipswich (obtained in May 1523) (Morley 1936: 68; Carver 1937: p. xviii) and the living of St John Baptist, Keyston in Huntingdonshire (18 July 1524) (Noble 1914: 136). But, while Holbrook became the living of T. Foster (Morley 1936: 51) in 1533, Palsgrave held the rectorship of Keyston for thirty years until his death, just as the prebend of Portpool in St Paul's Cathedral contributed to his income for forty years.

Preferment in the Church during the years 1523 and 1524 thus seems to have improved Palsgrave's financial and social situation. For these years we have further documentary evidence. Of prime importance are the drafts of a contract between Richard Pynson, the printer, and John Palsgrave for the printing of 750 copies of a book entitled *Lesclarcissement de la langue francoyse* (Brewer 1867/1965: 1522–3; Brewer 1870/1965: 16). The first two draft contracts date from 1523, and the third, in Cromwell's hand, is dated 18 January 1524. The first two contracts have been edited by F. J. Furnivall (1867: 362–74) and all of these will be discussed in more detail in Chapter 2. We do not know when exactly Palsgrave started his work on *Lesclarcissement de la langue francoyse*, but the draft contracts make it clear that in 1523–4 the work was to comprise 'iij sondrye bokes' (ibid.: 368) and that there was concern about its completion. In the first draft Pynson is expected to 'make all his diligence in hym̃ possible to furnysshe and made [*sic*] an end of the forsaid worke w*i*th*o*ut any further delay' (ibid.: 367) and the second draft specifies the rate of speed in the printing:

Farder more hyt ys agreed betwene the saide master Johñ Palsgraue and Richard Pensoñ, that the sayde Richard schall imprint euery hoole workyng day, for the more speding off the saide work, a schete off paper on bothe the sides, and not to cesse for none occasion (except the Kyng*es* grace haue any thyng*es* to be pryntyd) tyll the saide hole worke be full fynyshyd. the said Rychard to begyñ to print the saide worke as to-morowe, whyche schalbe the day off Januarye in the yere off o*ur* Lord as ; and the saide master John Palsgraue byndith hym, that other he or hys assignes schall so from tyme to tyme deliuer hys copye correctid to the saide Richard, or hys compositours, that the saide worke schall not be stopped on hys behallff. (ibid.: 369)

Provision, however, was made for a possible delay on the part of the author. From this we learn that at that time Palsgrave was still in the king's and in Wolsey's service:

Also prouyded that yf yt fortune or chaunce the forsayd M*aster* John Palsgrave to be absent by occasioñ or attendaunce by hym̃ to be gevyñ by the King*es* grace, my Lorde Cardinall*es* co*m*maundement, or by co*m*maundement of the Kyng*es* Counsayll, by the space of iiij [or] v dayes, mo or lesse, by reaso*n* of his s*er*uyce duely proved, that thañ that matter shalbe no cause of letche of this bargayñ. (ibid.: 367–8)

There was to be another royal appointment in 1525 which undoubtedly delayed the completion of *Lesclarcissement*. It must have raised great hopes in Palsgrave, who, as we learn for the first time from two different sources, seems not to have had all the financial means he needed. For 1524 there is an inventory account of Thomas Cromwell's documents. Among the documents listing bills and acquittances, mention is made of a 'bill of Mr Palsgrave for 26*l.* 7*s.* "4 acquittances for this my house"' (Brewer 1870/1965: 414). The other source is the draft of a letter from Palsgrave to the Lord Cardinal and Chancellor petitioning the Court of Chancery. Palsgrave complains that, when he was presented to the benefice of Asfordby in the county of Leicester, he found the parsonage in ruins. The executors of his predecessor had been ordered to pay Palsgrave 68*l.* for repairs. In the seven years of his rectorship he had received only 23*l.* 6*s.* 8*d.* and John Wilcocks, the executor, refused to pay the remainder (Brewer 1867/1965).[7]

What then was the new position he came to hold in 1525? Catherine of Aragon had borne Henry VIII only one child, Princess Mary. The king's first male offspring was Henry Fitzroy, whose mother, Elizabeth Blount, had been a lady-in-waiting to the queen. He was born in 1519 and Cardinal Wolsey became his godfather and took special care of the young prince and his mother. At the age of 6,

[7] The entry is placed under the year 1523, but Carver (1937: p. xvii) argues that the petition must have been drawn up later, closer to the time when Palsgrave resigned the living.

on 7 June 1525, he was made a knight of the Garter. A few days later he was created earl of Nottingham and duke of Richmond and Somerset 'with precedence over all dukes except the king's lawful issue' (Stephen 1889: 204; see also Childe-Pemberton 1913: 133). The official installation ceremony took place at Bridewell on 18 June 1525. A month later, the young prince was to be made the recipient of further honours and duties. He 'received a patent as Lord High Admiral of England, Wales, Ireland, Normandy, Gascony, and Acquitaine, for life, with the appointment of Commissioners, Lieutenants, Vice-Admirals, &c.' (Childe-Pemberton 1913: 140). A few days later still more was to come: 'the great office of Warden General of all the Marches towards Scotland, namely, the Eastmarch, the Westmarch, and the Middlemarch, with powers of array extending to the counties of Cumberland, Westmoreland, and Northumberland, for the defence of the Marches, and for the rescue and safe custody of the towers and castle of Berwick and Carlisle in time of danger' (ibid.: 141). The seat of the administration of the northern parts of England was Sheriff Hutton in Yorkshire. With these responsibilities and duties the duke of Richmond's court at Sheriff Hutton had to be run by a number of principal officers and a council. The income and the lands of the duke of Richmond were estimated at a yearly value of over 4,000*l.* (Stephen 1889: 204) and 245 servants were on the Duke's payroll (Childe-Pemberton 1913: 145).

John Palsgrave was awarded a double appointment. He became schoolmaster to the little prince, the duke of Richmond, and was at the same time made a member of the duke's Council (Stephen 1889: 204; Childe-Pemberton 1913: 145; see also Nichols 1855: p. xxiii). All the principal officers were allocated a number of servants to help them to carry out their duties. Palsgrave—like Dr Buttes, the physician, Mr Woodhall, the secretary, Mr Walter Luke, the general attorney, Mr Fairfax, the sergeant-at-law, and Dr Tate, the almoner—was given three servants. His wages were 13*l.* 6*s.* 8*d.* (Nichols 1855: p. xxiv). In terms of salary, he was as high in position as the general attorney and the sergeant-at-law, above the secretary and the solicitor, but below the physician (ibid.: p. xxiv).

In 1525, Palsgrave thus moved to Yorkshire and it is interesting to note that York is one of the few places in England he refers to in his examples:

> **I Peplysshe I fyll or store with people/** Ie peuple. prime coniu. **The towne is nat all thynge so bygge as is yorke but it is better peoplysshed:** La ville nest pas du tout si grant

quest yorke, mays elle est mieulx peu-
plée.

(III, fo. ccc.xvii = ccc.xv)

Other cases in point are the example sentences for the verbs *abyde* (III, fo. c.xxxvi), *kepe resydence* (III, fo. cc.lxxii), and *make a house* (III, fo. cc.lxxxvii).

The years from 1525 to 1530 are the period of Palsgrave's life that is documented best, probably because it was not only the hardest and most controversial but also the least happy one. On various occasions between 29 August 1525 and 25 December 1526 we encounter him as a co-signatory in the correspondence on behalf of the duke of Richmond, thus fully sharing the collective responsibilities of the duke's Council.

Henry VIII as well as the duke of Richmond's mother, who three years after the birth of Henry Fitzroy had become Lady Tailboys, took considerable interest in the education of their son. This becomes evident from the documents preserved. The king, for instance, asked the opinion of Thomas More and a Dr Stevyns whether the duke of Richmond should learn Greek and Latin (Brewer 1876: 2593), and a letter from Palsgrave to Lady Tailboys makes it clear that the duke's mother and his schoolmaster corresponded on his educational progress.

Palsgrave's appointment as Henry Fitzroy's Latin schoolmaster seems to have come to an end in February 1526, when Dr Richard Croke took over his duties. We learn from Palsgrave's letter to Thomas More (and the king) that he was totally committed to his task and that he consulted the educational authorities of his time and of the past for guidance. Yet the new educational ethos of the Renaissance was far from being shared by the Duke's immediate entourage. Here is an extract from the letter; Palsgrave has already thanked More for sharing his opinion that the little duke of Richmond should be taught Latin and Greek:

I haue not oonly demanded the opinions off Horman, Gonnell, Ryghtwise and all syche as I thowght cowld any thyng instruct me, howe I schould best aquite me in the charge commytted vnto me, but I haue all so diligently redde Quintiliane, Maphes Vegius, Otho Moguntinus, Baptista Guarinus, and especially Herasmus, whyche all, as you knowe, agree in that thing.

But I remember that you schewyd me oones how a lytyll Latine schould serue so the saide Duc myght haue Frenshe, and to be playne with you, me thynketh that our schavyn folk wold in no wyse he schoulde be lernyd. Whyche I assure you were a great pytye; for on my faithe I knewe neuer a more singular wytt, nother ryche or power, than he hathe, and all be hyt that he hathe all redye and euery day schall haue more and more sondry callers vpon hym to bring hys mynde from lernyng, som to here a crye at a hare, somm to kyll a bucke with hys bow, somtyme with grayhowndes and somtyme with buckehow(n)des, and that yt ys not lefull to depart tyll he haue takyn the same, somm to se a flyght with a hawke, some to ryde a hors, whyche yett he ys not gretly combryd with by cause off hys youthe, bysydes many other diuises fownde within the howse . . . (Rogers 1947: 404)[8]

The real obstacle to Palsgrave's endeavours were thus attendants and officials around the duke, bent on distracting and discouraging the young boy from his studies. We might therefore assume that it was neither Palsgrave's method of teaching nor the tasks set which were at issue, but rather the moot question of whether a prince's education should be confined to 'hunting, hawking and jousting' or include letters and learning. That our assumption is correct becomes manifest from the various long letters which Palsgrave's successor, Dr Richard Croke, wrote to Cardinal Wolsey, asking him repeatedly to intervene. In a letter of 1527 Croke bitterly complained about George Cotton,[9] whom he described as 'exhibiting a general enmity towards the duke's literary studies, and especially to his prosecution of Latin' (Nichols 1855: p. xxxvii).

This then accounts for the unexpectedly difficult circumstances which Palsgrave had to face in his new position. But let us return to the letter he wrote to Thomas More and look more closely at his first explicit description of his teaching method. Having beseeched More to come to Sheriff Hutton to judge for himself whether his [Palsgrave's] report was correct he continues:

And to make the chylde loue lernyng, I neuer put ⟨him⟩ in fere off any maner correction, nor neuer suffer hym to continu at any tyme tyll he schould be weryed, but diuise all the wayes I can possible to make lernyng playsant to hym, in so myche that many tymes hys officers wott not whyther I lerne hym or playe with hym, and yett haue I all redye browght hym to haue a ryght good vnderstanding in the principles off the grammars bothe off Greke and Latine and I haue redde hym an egloga (the fyrst) of Virgile and ii of the fyrst scenes off *Adelphorum*, whyche he can pronownce ryght pretyly, but I fynde Quintiliane and Herasmus trewe, for the barbarus tong off hym that tawght hym hys mattens ys and hath bene a great hindrance to me. (Rogers 1947: 405)

From a similar letter to the king himself we learn that Palsgrave had also tried to get a painter to support him in his teaching—an interesting idea at a time when there were no picture books for

[8] Rogers, who is quoting from the R.O. State Papers of Henry VIII queries the date conjectured, 1529, and suggests a redating in her later book (1961: 83). This also holds for Carver (1937: p. xxix), who believes that the bundle of Palsgrave's letters which in Brewer (1876: 2593–6) is entered under the year 1529 was written earlier. In one particular case, the letter addressed to Sir William Stevynson, he adduces proof that the letter was composed in 1525.

[9] George Cotton's brother Richard was comptroller of the duke of Richmond's household (Nichols 1855: p. xlvi).

schoolchildren to show them which objects the new 'names' they were learning related to (Brewer 1876: 2594).

Palsgrave reiterates to More that he will do his best to bring the duke up in learning and all such qualities that should become a nobleman in spite of 'som here whych be hyghe schavyn [i.e. tonsured] murmur agaynst yt' and think 'that lernyng ys a great hyndrance and displeasur to a nobyll man' (Rogers 1947: 405).

The gravity with which he then presses More ('I do therfore most instantly require you' (ibid.: 405)) to reassure the king that he was teaching the duke of Richmond as requested shows us a deeply worried Palsgrave. Rumours to the contrary might have come to the king's ears. How much he feared and suffered from jealous calumniators becomes manifest from a letter written at about the same period to the duke's mother, Lady Tailboys:

> Madame, I have sustayned, synce my coming into Yorkshire a great dele more displeasure than you wold know off, and that, not only in wantyng off these things that were requisite for me to have, but allso both for my necessity and honesty by reason off my povertye am malynych agaynst. I am sore dispicet [despised] at, in so myche [in-so-much] that not so lytyll as VI sundrye matters have been contryved agaynst me . . . (Childe-Pemberton 1913: 165)

Palsgrave then recalls the occasion in Hampton Court (Brewer 1876: 2594) when the king commissioned him and gives voice to his fears that the personal relation between the duke of Richmond and himself is being undermined:

> But, Madame, to be playne with you, on my conscience my lorde of Richemont ys off as good a nature as mych enclyned to all manner vertuous and honorable inclination, as any babe lyvyng. Now ys my roome undoutyd great about hym, for the Kynges Grace said unto me/in the presence of Master Parre and Master page [Page] I deliver q he [quoth he] unto you iij [three], my worldly jewell, you twayne to have the guyding off hys bodye, and thou, Palsgrave, to bring hym uppe in vertu and learnyng, wherefore yff there be not a fayth and a trewth and honestye in me, and, by sydes that, a sufficient dyscretion, the Kynges Grace ys hyghly beguyld in me, and the chyldes manners shall at the lengthe be corrupted by me as many a great yong Princes hath beene . . . unto theym in lyke roume, and on the othersyde yff I be as I ought to be, and other folkes imagyne and conceyve matters agaynst me that I woulde never [have] thought or wrought, and bring me in disputation before hym as thoughe I were gyltye . . . (Childe-Pemberton: 1913: 166–7).

Emphasizing that it is not in his nature to make accusations about other people, Palsgrave asks Lady Tailboys to come to Sheriff Hutton and judge for herself. His letter includes three such requests, two being in the manner of polite invitations, the third expressing the same urgency that we had in the letter to Thomas More. These appeals to More and the duke's mother reveal an honesty of character and Palsgrave's readiness to offer his resignation should the lady regard this as necessary:

As for me, yt ys not my natuer to accuse no parson, but yett for feare hys good qualities shall be marryd [marred] by any about hym, come hyther, Madame, and yff [if] after you could secret wysdom trye [try] every man and parson about hym, yff I be worthye to be expulsyd from hym, lett me; for on my conscience yt hadd beene better that I hadde never bene borryn [born] than so excellent a creature should by me be corrupted in hys maners—and yff ytt be others (as you may well parceyve that I thynke by my playne writyng) assaye yff you can trye theyr evyll conditions. (ibid.: 168)

These two personal letters to Thomas More and Lady Tailboys show us John Palsgrave as a committed and deeply worried schoolmaster, as an honest and fair-minded cleric even in personally difficult circumstances, and as a vulnerable human being asking for help. A man with ample means would not have taken these adversities at Sheriff Hutton too much to heart. But Palsgrave was at that time in a precarious financial situation as he admits in both letters. The appeal to Thomas More speaks for itself:

I beseech you off your goodnesse, for your accustumyd goodnesse to continu vnttyll syche tyme that I may oones trede vnder fote thys horrible monster pouerty, whyche hytherto hath benne so homely wyth me, that sche hath made me aschamyd off my sellff, and many a hundred tymes to forbere to do my dutye to you by cause I was lothe to cum to your howse with empty hand*is*. (Rogers 1947: 403; cf. Brewer 1876: 2593)

He was indeed in dire straits. He had not only resigned one of his livings, Asfordby—the rectory he had found in ruins when he was presented to it and which had made him petition the Court of Chancery to obtain the roughly £45 which his predecessor's executor still owed him for repairs. In resigning he had also managed to arrange for his successor in Asfordby, Master Richard Brokesbye, to pay him an annual pension of 3*l.* 6*s.* 8*d.* How desperate his situation was can be seen from the following letter to a certain Sir William Stevynson, showing that he had attempted to sell another of his benefices to the highest bidder:

Instructions for Syr Willm Stevynson what he schall do for me John Palsgrave w[t] the frenche quenes grace and the Duc off Suffolk her espowse.
Fyrst that all that I haue nowe to lyue by to paye my dettys and to mayntayne my poor mother ys but lityll aboue l li; for Alderton and Holbroke be but xx li Kayston xviii li, my prebend in Polles iiij li, and my wages xx[ti] markes, and was indettyd viij[xx] & xij li. Item, that I haue resigned Aschefordeby and receyuyd afore the hande Holbroke and all my wages to apparaill me and to bere my charges in my journay.

Item, that Master Humphrey Wyngfeld tolde me hym sellf that he wold gyue me but xx[ti] li for Holbrok, where as I haue hadde all redy, and shall haue aboue l iij li off Syr John Maxwell, and cowld haue more than l. for Holbroke, yff Master Humphraye hadde not the aduousion. Item, that yff I schoulde resigne Alerton and Holbroke, and haue for theym but l li, I shoulde be in a great danger other to fall all at ones, and nother be abyll to helpe my sellf nor my poore mother, or ellys to be compellyd to resigne Kayston to, for yff it should be a yere or their abowte, or euer I hadd any promocion by the Kyng or my lorde Cardinall, yf wold be a yere after or euer I hadde any profites off that benefice.

Item, you schall deuys all the meanes you can, bothe w[t] the Dukes Grace and the queenes, to borowe me xl markes at the leste xxx li and you can and beseeche hys grace to take Aldyrton and Holdbroke in to hys owne hand vnto he be payed. (Carver 1937: pp. xxix–xxx; see also H. Ellis 1846: 212–13; Brewer 1876: 2596)

In Brewer's *Letters and Papers, Foreign and Domestic, of the Reign of Henry VIII* Palsgrave's letter to Sir William Stevynson is entered under the year 1529. The content, however, suggests in several points 1525–6 as the more likely time of composition. First, the resignation from Asfordby, then the reference to Keyston, which he had obtained only in 1524, and finally his hopes for Cawston, which became vacant in 1525 and was given to Chrystopher Lynham (Rye 1898: 45; see also Carver 1937: p. xxix; Gunn 1988: 100).

Apart from documenting that Palsgrave found himself in dire financial straits the letter also tells us something more about Palsgrave's personal circumstances. For the first time we hear that his mother was still alive and that he was supporting her. In further instructions given to Sir William he wants him to make sure that the sum of £20 is paid to his mother in London at Easter (Brewer 1876: 2596). In addition, we learn that his contacts with his former pupil, the king's sister, and her husband, the duke of Suffolk, were still such that he could hope the latter would come to his financial rescue. The duke of Suffolk had helped him before: he had presented him to the living of Alderton in 1520 (Gunn 1988: 87), and two of his people had provided for Palsgrave 'iiii pec[es] of green say for the anging of ys chambre' (ibid.: 122). And Palsgrave showed his gratitude to the duke and the queen of France in the dedication of *Lesclarcissement de la langue francoyse* for 'their manyfolde benefyts' (Aii[v]).

Palsgrave's membership of the duke of Richmond's council seems to have ended in 1526. The last evidence of his acting for the council dates from 25 December 1526 (Brewer 1872/1965: 1217). Whether the total of debts mentioned in the letter to Sir William Stevynson ('viij[xx] + xij li') included a debt to Thomas Cromwell which was still unsettled in February 1529 or whether by that time he had run into new ones is difficult to establish (Brewer 1876: 2344).

A very specific entry in the French vocabulist might suggest that Palsgrave had further worries, a case against a certain Bulkyn (III, fo. c.lxxix[v]: **I Call vpon a man**).

After the rather unfortunate and personally unsatisfactory experience in Yorkshire, Palsgrave may have concentrated his efforts on finishing the book for which he had signed a contract with Richard Pynson, the printer. There is for the same period some evidence of his continued private tutoring. We know from Richard Croke's letters to Cardinal Wolsey that the young duke of Richmond was taught in a group of boys of roughly his age. According to W. S. Childe-Pemberton, Lady Tailboys's younger brothers George and William Blount lived at her son's court and were educated with him (Childe-Pemberton 1913: 148). It is thus reasonable to assume that they had also been taught by Palsgrave. From Andrew Baynton's epistle in *Lesclarcissement de la langue francoyse* we learn that Palsgrave had been teaching another little group of illustrious sons before 1530. The epistle is addressed to 'the ryght noble and excellent yong gẽtilmen/ my lorde Thomas Hawarde/ my lorde Geralde/ and maister Charles Blont/ sonne and heyre to the lorde Montioye/ his late scole felowes'.

Andrew Baynton was the son of Sir Edward Baynton, one of Henry VIII's favourite courtiers and the vice-chamberlain to three of the queens (Stephen 1885: 457). Thomas Howard was the son of the third duke of Norfolk, one of the most powerful noblemen of the realm and Cardinal Wolsey's strongest enemy. The identity of 'Lord Geralde' is not clear.[10] Charles Blount, a distant relative of Lady Tailboys, was the son of the fourth Lord of Mountjoy, one of the great patrons of the age. These were, however, not the only young sons of the nobility Palsgrave was teaching. The name of another pupil at that time is known from a letter by a certain John Chekyng to Thomas Cromwell, the earl of Essex and Cardinal Wolsey's secretary. In 1528, John Chekyng was private tutor to Cromwell's son Gregory, and on 27 July he sent the father a progress report to the following effect:

> His son Gregory is not now at Cambridge, but in the country, where he works and plays alternately. He is rather slow, but diligent. He had been badly tutored, and could hardly conjugate three verbs when committed to Chekyng's care, though he repeated the rules by rote. If this is Palsgrave's style of teaching, does not believe he will ever make a scholar. Will have to unteach him nearly all he has learned. He is now studying the things most conducive to the reading of authors and spends the rest of the day in forming letters. The plague, happily, is abating. (Brewer 1872/1965: 1988–9)

Again, this assessment of Palsgrave's qualities as a teacher by a rival must be taken with caution. Chekyng may have been explaining the son's slow progress or excusing his own failure by blaming the

[10] Carver (1937: p. xlii) thinks he might have been one of the third duke of Norfolk's children. Add. MS 24493 fo. 93 suggests that he might have been the brother of Geraldine.

teaching method of his predecessor. It is known that Gregory Cromwell was not the brightest of boys (Stephen 1888: 195).

Brewer's *Letters and Papers, Foreign and Domestic, of the Reign of Henry VIII* enable us to retrace several events in Palsgrave's life for the years 1528–9, but for some of them there is considerable doubt as to whether the dating is correct. As to Palsgrave's financial matters, he tried to get a papal bull to unite 'the parish church of Alderton, Norwich dioc., to the prebend of Portpole, in St Paul's Cathedral, London, before next Ascension Day.' (Brewer 1876: 2596). For this he was under an obligation of 7*l.* 6*s.* 8*d.* to Thomas Cromwell. He was not successful in procuring the bull and then seems to have resigned the living, since, according to the Diocesan Registry of Norwich, his successor in Alderton was instituted in December 1525 (Carver 1937, pp. xxxiv–xxxv).

The dating for the second series of events is equally doubtful. It very much looks as if, during the period of Cardinal Wolsey's fall, in a clearing-out attempt, the documents relating to John Palsgrave were all bundled together and entered under the year 1529. Although the exact nature of these events is not clear, they seem to give John Palsgrave a place in English history with respect to the fall of the king's First Minister, Cardinal Wolsey.

Let us first look at the facts available. For 1 July 1529 we have the records of three documents in the hand of Lord Darcy, one of Cardinal Wolsey's strongest opponents, beginning 'Hereafter followeth by protestation articles against the cardinal of York, shewed by me Thomas Darcy, only for to discharge my oath and most bounden duty to God and the King, and of no malice' (Brewer 1876: 2548–55). They are followed in Brewer's *Letters and Papers, Foreign and Domestic, of the Reign of Henry VIII* by three papers, two of which are reported as 'signed: Jo. Palsgrave', the last described as 'The last matter found in Palsgrave's coffer' (ibid.: 2555–62). But at the end of each paper there is more to learn: after the two pages headed by 'Here followeth a brief remembrance how the affairs of this realm have been conducted since it pleased our Sovereign to make my lord Cardinal's grace the chiefest and only councillor', there is a note 'This leeff of papir was ffurste founde at the furste serche' (ibid.: 2556). After the four and a half pages beginning with 'A brief remembrance how our Commonwealth hath been ordered since my lord Cardinal had the chief authority', a similar note states: 'These 2½ leaves were found at the second search like as they be marked with A.B.C. by Master Palsgrave's own hand' (ibid.: 2561). The last document, in the form of a letter, is incomplete and is said to have been found in Palsgrave's 'coffer'. The three sets of drafts were thus recovered by searching

Palsgrave's rooms. There were at least two searches, but the recovery of the unfinished draft of a letter seems to suggest that it was seized on a separate search, not on the second.

So much for the tangible factual evidence. We do not know when the three drafts were composed. It is not known who authorized the searches and when they were undertaken. Scholars have therefore tried to get more insight into the events by studying the content of the papers. Scrutinizing some of the items on the list of indictments drawn up against Wolsey, Carver has shown that the date of composition must have been earlier than 1529. This would tie in with another instance calendered in the public records to which S. J. Gunn has directed Peter Gwyn's attention (Gwyn 1990: 614). In his monograph *The King's Cardinal: The Rise and Fall of Thomas Wolsey*, Gwyn discusses Palsgrave's list of charges against Wolsey, arguing that Palsgrave seems not to have kept his grievances to himself, for 'on 11 April 1528 he was formally bound "to demean and behave himself discreetly, soberly and wisely in his words towards the king's highness and his most honourable Council, and not to use or to speak any seditious words against them"' (ibid.: 614).

In the literature, it is generally assumed that Palsgrave nursed a grievance against Wolsey because he resented his replacement as the duke of Richmond's schoolmaster by Richard Croke, believed to have been Wolsey's choice. And this grievance is regarded as the driving force behind his attack. Since Palsgrave's account of the cardinal's deeds is not drawn up in the form of a legal document, Gwyn interprets it as 'an essentially private and therapeutic exercise' in which Palsgrave 'let off steam by working upon a very literary attack upon the king's leading minister, in which ironic praise was the main weapon' (ibid.: 614). This 'therapeutic' interpretation seems to make Palsgrave a rather small-minded, emotion-ridden cleric—a view for which there is no factual basis and which a thorough study of his work totally contradicts. J. K. McConica, who sees Palsgrave as a member of the More–Erasmus circle, finds it 'interesting as additional light on the temper of this group to discover that an extended satire on Wolsey, headed "A brief remembrance how our Commonwealth hath been ordered since my Lord Cardinal had the chief authority", is endorsed "The last matter found in Palsgrave's coffer"' (McConica 1965: 121). He regards the three drafts as a 'satirical dialogue on Wolsey's career' (ibid.: 121). Such a view moves another aspect into the foreground: was the second draft written after the first had been found and taken away, and similarly, was the third, incomplete and more cautious version composed after the second draft had been discovered and confiscated? Why should Palsgrave have been so keen on compiling charges against Wolsey, taking a rather high personal risk? The first search should and would have been a warning and would surely have prevented him from drafting a new, longer, and still more dangerous account. There is another, in my view, more plausible possibility. The drafts were written at about the same time and were discovered on different searches. But why were there different searches? From the picture of Palsgrave's personality—honest, circumspect, sharp-witted, and balanced—as it emerges from his letters and his published work, above all the French vocabulist, it is inconceivable that his rooms were searched because he had the reputation of an impudent hothead. Searches might, however, have been repeated because it was known or rumoured that something specific had been written. Since this was not found the first time, a further searching was undertaken. In the intellectual and social circle in which Palsgrave was moving, open criticism of Wolsey's 'good deeds' might have taken the form of ironic praise (not least to deceive double-dealing intruders reporting back to the opponent). It might have been known in this circle that Palsgrave had experimented with composing a satirical dialogue on the merits of Cardinal Wolsey in different forms. It might have further been known that the versions differed not only in length and form, but also in the seriousness of accusations. The following enumeration, for instance, is taken from the first draft:

> We have begun to put in use the grant of resumption.
>
> We have begun to execute the statute of enclosing.
>
> We have begun to reform the abusions of the temporal law, especially concerning calumniation and recoveries. (Brewer 1876: 2555)

Compare these with some of the much stronger ironies of the second draft:

> We have begun to punish liberal speaking against us by nailing of men's ears, and set up new posts at the Standard in Chepe for that use. (ibid.: 2557)
>
> We have begun to encourage the young gentlewomen of the realm to be our concubines by the well marrying of Besse Blont, whom we would yet by sleight have married much better than she is, and for that purpose changed her name. (ibid.: 2558)
>
> We have begun to attempt to be Pope when the Pope was dead. (ibid.: 2559).
>
> Yet have we brought to end and finished some few things since we were in authority, to the honour of the realm. For we have overthrown the army of the king of Scots, and slain the King and the most part of his nobles spiritual and temporal, when he invaded the realm, the King being absent, contrary to the tenor of the league between us. (ibid.: 2559)

In the ambiance of the circle, the more outspoken charges of the diatribe, as for instance those on the punishment of liberal speaking or the young gentlewomen of the realm, might have been quoted and become common knowledge and thus, by an ambitious member, been reported to the opposite party.

This then takes us to the third record for 1529, the dating of which also needs some explaining. There is a letter by a Stephen Vaughan, written from Antwerp on 13 April 15.., to Thomas Cromwell, which reads as follows:

> Right worshipfull Sir, I humblye commende me vnto youe, and praye youe, that whereas I am muche desirous tatteyne the knowlage of the Frenche tonge, which is to me so muche the more difficulte as neyther by any sufficient instructer, ne any treatise heretofore made I maye be easely lede to the knowlage of the same, and at my beyng at London made not a letle labour to m^r^ Palsgraue to haue one of his books, whiche he made concernyng the same, whiche in no wise he wolde graunt for no price, that ye wilbe so good m^r^ to me as to healpe me to haue one of them, not doubtyng but, though he vnkyndly denyed me one, he will not denye youe one. I perceyue that Palsgrave hathe willed Pynson to sell none of them to any other ꝑson then to suche as he shall comaunde to haue them, lest his proffit by teching the Frenche tongue myght be mynished by the sale of the same to suche ꝑsons as, besids hym, wern disposed to studye the sayd tongue. If I had one I wolde no lesse esteme it then a iewell, wherfore I hartely praye youe to healpe me to one, and for the same I shall sende some other thing to youe of muche more value. If it please youe to cause Willyamson to bring the same to my brother, William Pratt, he will convey it to me at all tymes.
>
> Syr, I humbly com̃ende vnto yo^r^ goodness, the memory of my louyng frende, Willyam Claye, who intendith on thisside Whitsuntyde to departe towards Ingland, and wyll resorte vnto youe, for to desire you to be good maister vnto hym in his right, and none otherwise, I departed from london vpon the Tewysday, and cam to Andwerpe the Saturdaye then next following, where I remayn yo^r^ most humble and obedyent seruant. And thus I hartely praye for the contynuance of y^r^ health and prosperete. At Andwerpe, the xiij daye of Aprell.
>
> Syr, I remember m^r^ Palsgraue gaue youe one of his books, whiche if it please you to geue me, I wer muche bounde to youe. (*State Papers*, I, vol. 53, fo. 199)[11]

Vaughan's letter specifies the day and the month of writing, but not the year. On the basis of the persons and movements referred to in the letter itself, Brewer attributes it to the year 1529, and Carver argues in the same way. This leaves us with a considerable problem. We know the completion date of the printing of *Lesclarcissement*. It was 18 July 1530. Vaughan says that Palsgrave gave Thomas Cromwell 'one of his books', suggesting thus that Cromwell owned a copy of the book more than one year before its printing was actually completed. How

[11] Summarized in Brewer (1876: 2403); see also Furnivall (1867: 370–1); Carver (1937: p. xliii–xliv).

can we account for this patently contradictory situation? Carver's suggestion is as follows:

> The probability is that Palsgrave had supplied his pupils, including Gregory Cromwell, with a set of spare proofs and manuscript notes, serving as a provisional text-book, and that Vaughan, who was on visiting terms with the Cromwell family, saw just enough of Gregory's studies to mislead him into the belief that the book was in print. If, acting on this assumption, he went to Palsgrave and asked for a copy of the book which Master Gregory Cromwell was using, we cannot be surprised that the request should have been refused. It is only by some such reconstruction as this that we can explain the remark that Cromwell already, in April 1529, had a copy of the book in his possession. It is impossible that Cromwell should have had a complete copy, though he may have had somewhere in the house the set of printed sheets which we may imagine Gregory to have left behind when he went to Cambridge in charge of John Chekynge. (Carver 1937: p. xlv)

Carver's explanation thus hinges on Cromwell's son Gregory. I think we should seek another possible answer which does not rely on one of John Palsgrave's former pupils, all the more so since we do not know whether the pupil concerned was taught French or Latin by Palsgrave.

We know that *Lesclarcissement* consists of three books, the first basically dealing with pronunciation, the second with grammar, and the third including the English–French dictionary. In the dedication to Henry VIII Palsgrave tells us that the composition of *Lesclarcissement* went through two phases. He had finished 'two sondrie bookes'. Since he did not think that his endeavours would be worthy enough to come to the king's notice, he offered them to the duchess and the duke of Suffolk. With their encouragement he was then going to offer his work, enriched by a third part setting forth English words explained in French, to the king himself.

Palsgrave's contract with the printer Pynson leaves no doubt that he was aware of the great value of his linguistic enterprise. It was only human that he would hope for official recognition by the king. In view of the ways in which patronage and social advancement worked at that time, it would be natural for Palsgrave to arrange for a copy of the two books representing the first stage in the composition of *Lesclarcissement* to go through the hands of Cromwell, Cardinal Wolsey's secretary. The second draft of the contract with Richard Pynson provides us with some evidence of just this. Towards the end, the contract stipulates that Pynson restrict the print run to 750 copies and that he is not allowed to print parts of the work 'sauff oone off the fyrst [the following words are difficult to decipher] of the saide worke . . . to geue to my Lord Cardinall' (Furnivall 1867: 369).

We also know from Palsgrave's contract with Pynson and from the dedication to *Lesclarcissement de la langue francoyse* that the writing of the work took a very long time. Would it then not be quite natural that the (assumed) completion of a long awaited work to teach the French language, presented in the form of two books to the most important people in the kingdom, would be talked about? And Stephen Vaughan was one of those who had heard the news. Because of the keen interest in the work and the demand for copies, details of the contract between Palsgrave and Pynson will have become known. And that is what Stephen Vaughan also learned.

This concludes the events for the late 1520s. For 1530, there is only one outstanding document: the publication of *Lesclarcissement de la langue francoyse*, for which the king, in recognition of its outstanding quality, on 2 September, granted Palsgrave a privilege for seven years. The royal patent as well as the contract signed earlier with Pynson will have restricted the sale and the distribution of the book. It is not clear whether the king, in recognition of the unparalleled achievement, conferred any other honour on the author. Carver regards it as possible that the king made him one of his chaplains (Carver 1937: p. xlvi), admitting, however, that no record of the appointment has been found. The basis of this assumption is Anthony Wood's assertion that, in 1531, Palsgrave was chaplain to Henry VIII (Wood 1813/1967: col. 122; cf. Newcourt 1708: 200). Anthony Wood provides us with a date, whereas in Charles Dodd's *Church History of England* Palsgrave is merely described as 'also one of king Henry VIII's chaplains' (Dodd 1737–42: i. 228). Carver then thinks it probable that 'the king, when conferring the honour, suggested that an Oxford degree in Divinity would be a suitable accompaniment' (Carver 1937: p. xlvi).

The first factual evidence we have after the publication of *Lesclarcissement de la langue francoyse* dates from 1532. Palsgrave, who held two arts degrees, a BA from Cambridge and an MA from Paris, went back to university to obtain a degree in divinity from Oxford. In February 1532 he supplicated for incorporation and for the degree of Bachelor of Divinity. He was incorporated on 19 June (Boase 1885: 168; Emden 1974: 430),[12] and admitted to the degree on 27 June. From a letter, dated 28 October 1532, we learn that he intended to continue his studies and to become a Doctor of Divinity:

> The causes that moue me to goo to the vniuersite be thysse: yt ys greatly to my hyndrance to lyue off an vnyuersite seeyng that I am all redy bachelor off Diuinite and trust yett by goddes grace ones to be Doctor. Fardermore I myght in an vniuersite haue a substanciall man vnder me whyche myght ease me greatly off my paynes whyche nowe be intollerable more for the cõtinuall attendance . . . than for my

[12] The date 17 June in Carver (1937: p. xlvi) is a mistake.

labours . . . which intollerable attendance ys greatly hurtfull to my helth. (Gairdner 1880: 621).

This long letter to the father of one of his private pupils, Master William Saint Lowe, is very informative on Palsgrave's situation and movements as well as his private plans for the autumn of 1532 and the spring of 1533. He was still teaching private pupils, but at the age of about 50 he found it tiresome to have to attend constantly to his pupils and was therefore thinking of finding a student or graduate to help him in his task. The three rectorships he held at that time, Portpool in London, Holbrook near Ipswich, and Keyston in Huntingdonshire, thus clearly did not provide enough for a living. We get an insight into his financial situation from accounts made for Thomas Cromwell on 2 September 1532. In the 'true pie or catalogue of all my master's obligations, bills obligatory, and all other escripts, remaining in the custody of John Williamson, his servant', Palsgrave is mentioned in the 'Inventory of the desperat bills': 'A bill from the abbot of St Benet's, stating that he had sent my master 5*l.* in part payment of 10*l.* for which he stands bound for Mr. Palsgrave' (ibid.: 556). The John Williamson who described himself as Cromwell's servant seems to have been Cromwell's brother-in-law.[13]

Who were his private pupils in 1532? Palsgrave mentions some of them in his letter, undoubtedly his most notable ones to impress his standing on Mr Saint Lowe:

This Monday . . . your servant Thos. Fowlkes informed me you had commissioned him to fetch home your son, Master Will. Sayntlowe, as the mortality in London was so great, and you supposed I had gone over sea with the King; but as I was not gone, and there is no other danger of sickness, he left it to me to write. I have promised to serve Mr. Baynton and Mr. Dominico, in the house of the latter, till Candlemas, when I mean to go to the university of Cambridge, and keep house at the Blackfriars. There I could have with me your son, Mr. Russell's son, a younger brother of Andrew Baynton, and Mr. Noryce's son, of the King's privy chamber, for whom I have been spoken to my means, though he hath not as yet spoken to me himself. (ibid.: 621–2).

We do not know the affiliations of Mr Dominico, who so kindly offered his house as the location for the tutoring, but those of the other gentlemen are well known. Andrew Baynton and his younger brother were the children of Sir Edward Baynton, a favourite courtier of Henry VIII. Master Russell was Frances Russell, the only son of Sir John Russell, the ancestor of the dukes of Bedford, one of the most

[13] This is suggested by the entry for Thomas Cromwell in the *DNB*, where we read (p. 195): 'In July 1529, being then in very prosperous circumstances, he made a draft will . . . with bequests to his son Gregory, his sisters Elizabeth and Catherine, and his late wife's sister Joan, wife of John Williamson . . .'

important noblemen during the reign of Henry VIII, and Sir Henry Norris was another of the king's favourites who was later executed, suspected as having been Ann Boleyn's lover. The rather unhappy experience as schoolmaster of the king's son, the duke of Richmond, had manifestly thus not affected Palsgrave's reputation as a teacher to be sought after as a private tutor by the nobility of the time.

We also learn from the same letter that Palsgrave planned to go on teaching until 'Candlemas' and then to re-enter university. Although he had only just received his Bachelor of Divinity from Oxford, he intended to become Doctor of Divinity at Cambridge, explaining 'I go to Cambridge rather than Oxford, because I have a benefice 16 miles off' (ibid.: 622).

The last important point in the letter to which I would like to return is Saint Lowe's assumption that Palsgrave might have gone abroad with the king. It reflects the image in which Palsgrave was held: he was in the service of the king. This is given further support from the third piece of evidence we have for 1532.

It is connected with 'the king's matter'—his divorce from Catherine of Aragon, who had not given him the expected heir. During the year 1530 there was talk in the court circles that a book in favour of Henry VIII's cause was being printed to explain his case to the people in order to win their support. Reports even spread that its author was the king himself. And the publication of a little treatise, produced by the king's printer Berthelet, entitled *A Glasse of the Truthe* was proof that the rumours had some substance. The work has the form of a dialogue between a divine and a lawyer and purports to justify the king's pleas that it is unlawful to marry a deceased brother's wife and that therefore he ought not to be cited to Rome. The date of printing is not certain. In the *Letters and Papers, Foreign and Domestic, of the Reign of Henry VIII* the date for the printing is 1531 (ibid.: 250). The two different versions of the dialogue that have been preserved, both printed by Berthelet, are entered as [1532?] in the *Short Title Catalogue* (Pollard and Redgrave 1976–91: i, nos. 11918, 11919).[14]

This work, which brought all the arguments and scholarly opinions together to support the king's case against the pope, was written in the language of his subjects, English. But not all the officials and others that the king was keen to reach and convince were familiar with English. Home consumption was not the only aim of the enterprise. Translations were called for. The archbishop of Ely,

[14] A modern edition is found in Pocock (1870: 385–421). See also Haas (1979: 353–62) and Dowling (1986: 52).

Nicholas Hawkins, was entrusted with preparing a Latin version. He reported twice to the king on the progress of his translation. On 21 November 1532, half of the dialogue had been translated (Gairdner 1880: 656), and on 24 December 1532 the Latin translation was completed (ibid.: 688). In his report Hawkins gives us an interesting insight into the Latin chosen:

> For your English dialogue, I send you 'a dialogue for my small eloquence Latinised'. I could if it pleased you, have 'conversed' it into English or French Latin, but I perpended that for England that in English was sufficient, and for France that which you have commanded to be transposed into French; and men, I trust, will by little and little acknowledge the truth. The difficulty is in the Italians, who are so curious and delicate, that if the writing please them not, they abject it, and for this cause very many of them 'fastide' the study of Scripture. I have, therefore, accommodated it to their tastes. (ibid.: 688)

We do not know whether Hawkins' Italianized Latin version was ever printed, since no copy has been located. But one copy of the French translation has been preserved. It is kept in Lincoln Cathedral (Pollard and Redgrave 1976–91: i, no. 11919, 5). The translator is not known. Some scholars have regarded Palsgrave as a likely translator on the basis of a passage in a letter by John Wylliamson to Cromwell, dated 20 October 1532. The relevant passage reads: 'I have sent you 100 books, entitled *le Myrouer de Verite*, received from Mr. Palsgrave' (Gairdner 1880: 615). Carver initially shared this opinion (Carver 1937: p. xlix), but when he learnt that a unique copy of the French version had survived, he made further enquiries. The 'transcription of the colophon reads as follows: "Imprime a Londres, par Thomas Berthelet, Imprimeur du roy, nostre souuerayn Sire. Lan delincarnation de nostre Seigneur, 1532. Le 19 jour Doctobre"' (ibid.: addenda). This, according to Carver, 'proves that the hundred copies received by Wylliamson from Palsgrave on the 20th October, 1532, and transmitted to Cromwell on the same day, were, as we should have supposed, fresh from the press' (ibid.: addenda). This leaves us wondering why the 100 pristine copies of *le Myrouer de Verite* were first delivered to Palsgrave, who then sent them off to Cromwell's assistant.

There is no evidence that Palsgrave put into action his intention, expressed in the letter to Mr Saint Lowe, to return to Cambridge University and study for a Doctorate of Divinity. For Carver the reason for his staying on in London was his translation of the *Glasse of Truthe* (ibid.: p. xlix). Yet the dates contradict this view. As we have seen, the printing of the French version of the *Glasse of Truthe* was completed on 19 October 1532, and Palsgrave made sure the 100 copies received were with John Wylliamson on 20 October. The letter to Mr Saint Lowe was written a good week later, on 28 October 1532.

The following year was to become one of major vocational advancement for Palsgrave, but there is no evidence that his preferment in church was a royal reward for his translation of the *Glasse of Truthe* into French. He then held the benefices of Portpool and Keyston, and resigned from Holbrook. His clerical status was that of a deacon. His progress within the church hierarchy, for reasons unknown, had hitherto been very slow.[15] On 17 December 1513 he had been ordained acolyte in the parochial church of Fulham, within the London diocese.[16] The following year he was presented to his first benefice, Portpool in St Paul's. We do not know when he took the next step on the echelon and became subdeacon, but it is clear that the appointment did not occur within the London diocese. Towards the end of 1529, the year of Cardinal Wolsey's fall, Palsgrave was ordained deacon, on 17 December, in Holy Trinity, London.[17] And then, nearly twenty years after his ordination as an acolyte, on 23 September 1533, he was ordained priest in his native city London.[18] Ten days later, on 3 October 1533, he was collated to the church of St Dunstan-in-the-East by Cranmer, who only half a year earlier had been consecrated archbishop of Canterbury (West [1923]: 97). The benefice was in the archbishop's gift and the rectorial stipend was 60*l.* 8*s.* 3*d.*, 'larger than any in London except St Magnus the Martyr' (ibid.: 17; see also Gairdner 1882: 529).

The size of the stipend seems at last to have put an end to Palsgrave's financial worries. There is one further letter which provides us with some details of his pecuniary predicament, written a fortnight after his collation and addressed to the archbishop of Canterbury with a reply by Thomas Cranmer.[19] The dire straits must have been temporary, for after 1533 there are no records of any financial difficulties.

Material on the next six years of Palsgrave's life is scarce. In April 1534 he intervened in the contest between the earl of Oxford and a canon of Royston, one Richard Britten (or Breten), by writing to Cromwell (Gairdner 1883: 206, 217, 293, 336, 338, 598). Britten became prior of Royston and Palsgrave's intervention was thus successful.

[15] Cf. in this respect the examples given in Ch. 10 referring to a summons to appear at a court.

[16] Diocese of London, bishops' registers, Guildhall Library MS 9531, vol. 9, fo. 166$^{v}$.

[17] Ibid., vol. 10, fo. 163$^{v}$.

[18] Ibid., vol. 11, fo. 129$^{v}$.

[19] British Library, MS Harley 6, 148, fo. 37. Summarized in Gairdner (1882: 529).

Four years later he tried to help in another complicated matter by writing to Seigneur de Gouy at Amiens (Gairdner 1892/1967: 533). The case does not become totally clear from the letter, but what matters for our account of his life is that this letter of 24 July 1538 is the last of the few personal letters of Palsgrave that have been preserved.

Then in 1540, ten years after the publication of *Lesclarcissement de la langue francoyse*, the appearance of *The Comedy of Acolastus* gave further proof of his deep educational concern and commitment. The comedy narrates the story of the prodigal son, and the original is by the Dutchman, William Fullonius. It was written in Latin and was first published in 1529. Palsgrave translated it into English and on the title-page describes the setting-out of the text as follows:

> The Comedye of Acolastus translated into oure englysshe tongue, after suche maner as chylderne are taught in the grammer schole, fyrst worde for worde, as the latyne lyeth, and afterwarde accordynge to the sence and meanyng of the Latin sentences: by shewing what they do value and counteruayle in our tongue, with admonitions set forth in the margyn . . .[20]

The double-text edition of 1540 is the only known version of Palsgrave's translation.[21] It is dedicated to the king, and we note an interesting change in what Palsgrave says about himself. On the title-page of *Lesclarcissement de la langue francoyse* he had styled himself as 'Angloys, natyf de Londres/ et gradue de Paris'. In the 1540 work he describes himself in the dedication to Henry VIII as 'his moste humble and most obeysaunt Chapleyn . . . bacheler of diuinitie'. This is solid confirmation that Palsgrave was a chaplain of the king, but, as pointed out earlier, we still lack the evidence as to when exactly he was appointed.

The dedication comprises nine pages in which Palsgrave sets out the immediate educational background for his translation. He explains his choice of text and gives us an impressive, rather unadorned picture of contemporary schooling.

Let us begin with the historical educational background. A Latin grammar was being prepared (in due course to become known as Lily's grammar) which by the king's authority was to be prescribed for all the schools throughout the realm. Palsgrave welcomed this

[20] Quoted from the copy in the British Library (C. 34. f. 2).

[21] According to the *STC* (no. 11470) there was no other edition, and the number of copies known to exist is very small. As to Britain, there are copies in the British Library (3), the Bodleian Library (2), Gloucester Cathedral, and Ripon Cathedral. The following libraries in the USA hold a copy: Folger Shakespeare Library, Washington, DC, Harvard University, Cambridge, Mass., Huntington Library, San Marino, Calif., New York Public Library, New York City, University of Illinois, Urbana, Ill. A modern edition was produced by P. L. Carver (Carver 1937).

development because of its positive effect on teachers and pupils alike:

Nowe shal the great varietie vsed afore tyme in the techyng of the grammatical rules of the latyn tonge in this realm, wherby hytherto no smal hynderãce hath ensued, herafter vtterly cesse and be put to sylence. Wherby vndoubtedly shall ensue a great cõmoditie and furtheraunce, bothe to the maysters, and alsoo to the yonge begynners, whyche shall hereafter succede.[22]

Palsgrave, however, was thinking further ahead. One Latin grammar for all would surely improve the teaching of Latin, but was the reform movement really taking into account what was going on in the classrooms? Teacher and pupils were reading Latin texts. And this is the area where his translation of Fullonius' *Acolastus* was to set an example:

But as yet vnto my poore iugement . . . for the more effectuall and spedy furtherance of your graces sayd youth, I wyshed, that vnto this moch expedient reformation of your schole maisters vnstayd libertie, which hytherto haue taught such grammers, and of the same so dyuers and sondry sortes, as to euery of theym semed best . . . myght therto also folowe and succede one stedy and vnyforme maner of interpretation of the latyn authours into our tonge, after ỷ the latyn principles were by your graces youth ones surely conned and perceyued.[23]

What Palsgrave means by a 'vnyforme maner of interpretation of the latyn authours' becomes clear from his description of how Latin texts were customarily explained to the pupils. Drawing from his long teaching experience he distinguishes three typical forms of behaviour shown by the Latin schoolmasters:

[1] For some instructers of youre hyghnes youth, for want of a perfyte iudgement in this behalfe, so much desyre to seme affectately curiouse, that hauyng no due consyderation to the tender wyttes, whiche they take vnder theyr charge to teache in the stede of pure englyshe wordes and phrases, they declare to their chylderne one latyne worde by annother, and confounde the phrases of the tongues: And thus not a lytell do hynder their yong scholers, while they wold seme for their own partes to haue a knowledge and erudition aboue the common sort.[24]

[2] And som other ageyne there be, whiche hauynge vndoubtedly, lernyng ynoughe, vaylable and sufficiente, yet whyle they by sondry wayes and maners of speakynge vsed in our tongue, labour to expresse such latyn auctours myndes, as they do take vppon them for the tyme to interprete, and for to seme therin more dilygent, than the cõmon sorte, dyspende in maner hole forenoones and afternoones, in the declarynge of a fewe lynes of suche latyne authours, as they for the season haue in hande (as to confesse the very truthe, the schole maisters hole dilygence tendeth in maner chiefely to that

[22] British Library (C. 34. f. 2) A ii$^{v}$.

[23] Ibid. A ii$^{v}$–A iii.

[24] Ibid. A iii.

effecte and purpose) they do by that meanes not only ryght lytell for the tyme further their yong audience, but also by that wayes do oppresse and ouerlaye the tender wyttes, the whiche they wold so fayne further, with their multitude of sondry interpretations, confusedly by them vttered.[25]

[3] And somme other furthermore there be, whiche thoughe they haue by their greatte studye, at youre graces Unyuersyties, soo moche prouffyted in the Latyne tongue, that to shewe an euydente tryalle of theyr lernynge, they canne wryte an Epistle ryght latyne lyke, and therto speake latyne, as the tyme shall mynyster occasyon, very well, yea and haue also by theyr diligence atteyned to a comly vayne in makynge of verses: yet for all this, partely bycause of the rude language vsed in their natyue countreyes, where they were borne and firste lerned (as it happened) their grammer rules, ⁊ partely bycause that commyng streyght from thense, vnto some of your graces vniuersities, they haue not had occasions to be conuersaunte in suche places of your realme, as the pureste englysshe is spoken, they be not able to expresse theyr conceyte in theyr vulgar tonge, ne be not suffycyente, perfectly to open the diuersities of phrases betwene our tonge and the latyn (whiche in my poore iudgemente is the veray chiefe thynge that the schole mayster shulde trauayle in). In so moche that for want of this sufficient perfection in our owne tongue, I haue knowen dyuerse of theym, which haue styl continued theyr study in some of your graces vniuersities, that after a substanciall encrease of good lernynge, by theyr great and industrious study obteyned, yet whan they haue ben called to do any seruice in your graces cõmen welthe, eyther to preach in open audience, or to haue other administration, requiringe theyr assiduous conuersantynge with your subiectes, they haue then ben forced to rede ouer our englyshe auctours, by that meanes to prouyde a remedy vnto their euident imperfection in that behalfe. And when it hath fortuned any suche for theyr good name or estimation to be called from your vniuersities, to instructe any of your graces noble mennes chyldren, then euidently hath appered their imperfection in that case to be notable, and that to no smal detriment and hinderaunce of suche as they haue taken charge to enstruct and brynge forwarde.[26]

We may all, at various times of our education, have come across and experienced teachers of the types (1) and (2), and they may perhaps be to some extent endemic to the teaching profession; type (3), however, is less familiar today, and may therefore be regarded as more characteristic of Palsgrave's time.

In (3) Palsgrave is drawing our attention to a situation that must have been very widespread at a time when a widely understood standard form of English was not yet in existence but rather in the process of gradual development. Young men from the different parts of England, having been brought up in the regional dialect of their home parish, went to the universities in Oxford and Cambridge to take a degree. Teaching and studying were done in Latin, in which they became more or less fluent. But when, after graduation, they entered a career, they were expected to speak to and deal with the

[25] British Library A iii–A iii$^{v}$.
[26] Ibid. A iii$^{v}$–[A iiii].

ordinary people. For these purposes, their need was to be conversant in the 'vulgar tongue', not a learned language. It was a challenge for which their years at university had not prepared them. We thus have open criticism of the educational system, and Palsgrave, who held three university degrees and who had gone back to university at a mature age, had ample experience of the system. The important point Palsgrave is making here is that all academic study has to be accompanied by education in the mother tongue. He draws a distinction between 'the rude language vsed in their natyue countreys' and 'places of your realme, as the pureste englysshe is spoken'. We are not told where these places are, but it seems to be implicit in (3) that the 'purest form of English' is spoken in the court circles. Competence in this model form of English will have been second nature to Palsgrave, being a native of London who was moving and teaching in these very circles and who, as we shall see when we look more closely at the French vocabulist, knew the 'englyshe auctours'.

The second crucial point which Palsgrave makes in (3) concerns the aim of language teaching. His view strikes us as eminently modern. At a time when teaching the foreign language of the age, Latin, consisted in explicating the rules of Latin grammar and in reading and interpreting good Latin authors, Palsgrave advocated that the 'chiefe thynge' of a schoolmaster was 'to open the diuersities of phrases betwene our tonge and the latyn', or, in more general terms, to characterize and contrast the mother tongue and the foreign language. And again, we note the emphasis on the preconditional competence in the teacher's mother tongue.

By translating a Latin text into English and having both versions printed next to each other, Palsgrave was providing schoolmasters with a textbook that not only assisted them in their interpretations of the text itself, but offered them also word by word and then more idiomatic English renderings, thus helping them in their mother tongue.

On the selection of *Acolastus* for his purpose, Palsgrave tells us:

> I haue chosen for my latten authour, to be Ecphrastes vppon, the comedie entiteled *Acolastus*, not onely forbycause that I esteme that lyttell volume to be a very curiouse and artificiall compacted nosegay, gathered out of the moche excellent and odoriferouse swete smellynge gardeynes of the moste pure latyne auctours, but also bycause that the maker therof (as farre as I can lerne) is yet lyuing, wherby I wold be glad to moue into the hartes of your graces clerkes of whiche your noble realme was neuer better stored, some lyttell grayne of honeste and vertuous enuye, whiche on my partie to confesse the verye truthe vnto your grace, hath contynually in all the tyme of these my poore labours takyng, accompanyed me, and styred me onwardes to achieue this matter, on this wise by me attemted.[27]

[27] Ibid. b$^{v}$.

Fullonius' real Dutch name was Willem de Volder or van de Voldergraft. In the humanist tradition he had not only a Latin but also a Greek name, and, since he was born in The Hague (1493), he is also referred to as Gulielmus Gnapheus Hagiensis. He had a BA from Cologne and became principal of the grammar school in his native town. He was twice imprisoned for his Lutheran sympathies and then left The Hague in 1528 to teach in Elbing and Königsberg.

He wrote *Acolastus* for his pupils in The Hague. The parable of the prodigal son lent itself well to composing a work in which a style of colloquial Latin could be combined with Christian morals. No wonder that this didactic play became during the sixteenth century 'the most celebrated play in Northern Europe and one of the most frequently printed among all the literary works of its time' (Atkinson 1964: 1). W. E. D. Atkinson gives the following account of its printings:

> *Acolastus* was first published in Antwerp in 1529. It immediately became a best-seller. Within five years it was reprinted eleven times, not only in Antwerp but also in Paris, Cologne, Leipzig and Basel. It remained in steady demand for about fifty years: at fairly regular intervals there appeared in Cologne between 1530 and 1577 a dozen editions; in Antwerp during the same period, thirteen; in Paris up to 1584, ten. It was also translated, paraphrased and otherwise adopted into German, French and English. (ibid.)

The play was first translated into German. Georg Binder's *Acolastus. Ein Comoedia von dem Verlornē Sun* was printed in Zurich five years before Palsgrave's translation. The great popularity of the play on the continent and Palsgrave's personal contacts with the Low Countries and Paris, as well as with the Erasmus circle (Erasmus himself died in 1536) may have brought Fullonius' work to his attention. Whereas Binder's text is a translation only, Palsgrave's particular contribution was the two-language text for the specific school needs of England as he perceived them.

Palsgrave concludes his dedication to the king with a detailed account of how his proposed method, supported by one concrete sample text, will reform teaching in schools. He sees the foremost effect in the following—and this highlights again his deep concern for the state of the mother tongue, English:

> Fyrst, for if this kynde of interpretation maye take effecte, and be put in execution, not onely the speache of your graces subiectes shoulde be that meane haue a great aduauntage to waxe vniforme, throughe out all your graces domynions, but also the englysshe tonge, whiche vnder your graces prosperouse reygne is comme to the hygheste perfection that euer hytherto it was, shulde by this occasion remayne more stedy and parmanent in his endurance, not onely by the well kepynge of his perfection already obteyned, but also haue a great occasion to come to his most hyghest estate, and there, by that meanes longe be preserued.[28]

[28] British Library b ii$^{r+v}$.

The claim that 'the englysshe tonge . . . is comme to the hygheste perfection' might be linked to the Renaissance debate of the *questione della lingua*, the gradual coming of age of the vernaculars. Yet it was not the recognition of English as a medium of expression equal in precision and beauty to the classical languages that preoccupied Palsgrave's mind. He was a Latin and Greek scholar, it is true, but his main concern was a vernacular of the time, sixteenth-century French. Trying to teach a living language at a time when there were no textbooks and when a uniform or supraregional form was not yet in existence necessarily raised the question as to which form of the language to take as a model. Palsgrave was fully aware of the problem and repeatedly addressed it in *Lesclarcissement*.

For the period after 1540 we have very little knowledge of Palsgrave. On 7 November 1545 he was presented with another living (Whalley 1791: ii. 390), and became rector of Wadenhoe in the county of Northampton. The benefice was in the gift of the Lord of Mountjoy, who in 1545 was Charles Blount, the fifth baron of Mountjoy, Palsgrave's former pupil. A year later, on 6 December 1546, Palsgrave was granted a lease of lands in Wadenhoe that had been held by his predecessor but were in the possession of Lord Mountjoy.

The exact date of Palsgrave's death is not known. But we know that he died in 1554, when all the rectorships he had held became vacant. His successor in Wadenhoe, for instance, was one Richard Pulchers, who was instituted on the 3 August 1554, thus suggesting that Palsgrave died before August in 1554 (ibid.: ii. 390).

The documents from which we have drawn our account of Palsgrave's life and activities do not contain very much that is of a more private nature. That the duke of Suffolk, the husband of his former royal pupil, Princess Mary, the dowager queen of France, and Charles Blount, Lord Mountjoy, acted as his patrons could be taken as an expression of their appreciation of his linguistic and moral instruction in their younger years. On the basis of our present knowledge—the new recently discovered letters by Thomas More (see Schulte-Herbrüggen 1965; 1966; 1967; 1983; 1990*a*; 1990*b*) do not provide us with any further insights into the relationship between the two men—More was the only one of his patrons to whom he was not bound by any services. More's letter to Erasmus tells us something of the high esteem in which More held his friend Palsgrave. From this letter, as well as from the one written by Palsgrave ('and many a hundred tymes to forbere to do my dutye to you by cause I was lothe to cum to your howse with empty hand*is*'), emerges something of the social relations between them.

The only reference to Palsgrave's family that we have comes from his letter to Sir William Stevynson of [1529], revealing that his mother was still alive, living in London, and that he had to support her.

Carver, when editing Palsgrave's translation of *Acolastus* for the Early English Text Society, put considerable effort into elucidating Palsgrave's family background. He brings to our attention an ancient Norfolk family that derives its name from the village of Pagrave. Suspecting a possible family connection, he argues as follows:

Henry Pagrave, or Palgrave, the head of the family in the reign of Henry VII, and the grandson of that John Pagrave whose name occurs occasionally in the *Paston Letters*, had married Anne Glemham, daughter of Sir John Glemham of Glemham, Suffolk, and grand-daughter of the first Sir William Brandon. The Glemhams, though themselves important in the county, were insignificant beside the Brandons, who already approached ducal grandeur and were soon to be of ducal rank. In the church of Barningham Northwood, Norfolk, may still be seen the effigies of Henry and Anna Pagrave, with those of their five sons and seven daughters arranged in two groups. The eldest son was named John, and acted in 1518, jointly with his mother, as executor of his father's will. May we identify John Palsgrave, the grammarian, of unknown parentage, with the contemporary John Pagrave whose name and parentage constitute his only title to historical existence? (Carver 1937: p. x)

Apart from the close similarities in the name and lifetime, the death of that possible father Henry Pagrave in 1516 is an additionally intriguing aspect. We do not know when Palsgrave's father died, but his death must have occurred before Palsgrave wrote his pleading letter to Sir William Stevynson. And while, of course, example sentences are doubtless usually fictitious, this does not exclude their having some possible foundation in real life and personal experience, so it is interesting to note examples in *Lesclarcissement* which actually specify the day when 'my father' died. For example (and see p. 34 below):

**I Lette my lyfe I departe out of the worlde/** Ie trespasse. prime cõiu. **and** ie desuie. prime cõiuga. **Romãt. My father let his lyfe vpon saynte Bartylmewes euyn:** Mon pere trespassa, **or** alla de vie a trespas, **or** desuia la veille saint Bartholmieu.

(III, fo. cc.lxxix$^{r-v}$)

One of the attractions of the parentage postulated by Carver concerns the daughter Frances of Henry and Anne Pagrave, the Norfolk family. She was at some time a member of the household of the king's sister, Princess Mary, and could thus have been instrumental in John Palsgrave's appointment as royal schoolmaster. The only difficulty in this parental theory is the fact that Henry and Anne

Pagrave's son John is said to have died young, though Carver did not regard this as an insuperable obstacle:

This belief, whether correct or not [that he died young] probably originated in a fact mentioned in Parkin's continuation of Blomefield's *History of Norfolk*: 'In 1524, Sir *William Paston* presented to this church, being guardian of *Clement*, son of *Henry Pagrave*, Esq. by which it appears that his eldest brother *John*, was then dead.' This, though strong evidence, does not amount to proof, for it is possible that John had exceptional reasons for his inaction. Let us suppose that John was a clergyman and schoolmaster with duties in the Royal household and at St Paul's; that he was soon to leave for Yorkshire on the King's business, and that, in the meantime, he was arranging for the publication of an important book. In such a situation, which was that of John Palsgrave, the grammarian, in 1524, he might well have divested himself of his responsibilities in Norfolk in favour of a younger brother. (ibid.: pp. x–xi)

D. A. Kibbee and S. J. Gunn in their publications accept Carver's hypothesis, but, attractive though it is, I do not regard it as wholly plausible for the following reasons. First, Palsgrave's date of birth has been conjectured for something like 1480–5. As a member of the Pagrave family of Norfolk, he would have been the eldest son. Next in line would have been brother Clement. This Clement Pagrave of Northwood Barningham died in 1583; his date of birth is not known, but his father died in 1516. After their two sons John and Clement, Henry and Anne Pagrave had ten further children. The number of children born to the family does not suggest major intervals between the births. So, if we give John Palsgrave a relatively late date of birth and then make some allowance for a generous interval, letting Clement be born in 1490, Clement would still have been 93 when he died—a very high and rather unlikely age for the sixteenth century. Secondly, the only family member mentioned by Palsgrave in his letters is his mother. From the evidence we have, it looks pretty much as if the Palsgrave household consisted of himself, the priest, and his mother. He seemed to have suffered prolonged phases of great poverty. If he had had eleven brothers and sisters—Frances, for instance, was married to Sir William Pennington of the North, ancestor of the Lords Muncaster—would it then not have been more acceptable for the mother and her well-being to have stayed with one of the better-off children? With the necessary caution given to examples in a dictionary, his mother could easily—during his absences from London—have experienced situations like the one described under the verb entry for *to cry out* in the French vocabulist:

**I Crye out as one dothe that is**
**in daunger/** Ie mescrie, ie me suis es-
crié, escrier. verbĩ mediũ. prime con.
**He kryed out a loude:** Il sescria haul

> tement. **My mother was a frayde there had ben theues in her house/ ⁊ she kryed out haroll alarome:** Ma mere auoit paour quil ny eust des larrons a la mayson, et elle sescria harol alarme.
>
> (III, fo. cc)

Finally, though he would have been the oldest brother in that huge family of twelve children, would it not have been quite natural that one or other of the brothers and sisters could have helped, or indeed would have presented himself or herself to his mind when he was sitting in his study looking for example sentences to illustrate the meaning of verbs? There is not really anything.

This then takes us to the French vocabulist to see whether it can give us some more clues on Palsgrave's life. As pointed out earlier, Palsgrave illustrates the meaning of many words with example sentences, and we shall investigate these in more detail in Chapters 9 and 10. Some of these illustrations are taken from good authors, but the majority are invented. For these freely contrived examples it is often very difficult to assess what is fictitious and what may have some anchorage in the author's life. Cases like the following are exceptional:

> **I Am called/ I am named/** ie me fais appeller. **I am called Johan/** ie me fays appeller Iehan.
>
> (III, fo. c.xli$^{v}$)

It is the precision of reference that in some cases makes one suspect that Palsgrave is referring to actual personal experience. A case in point is the example under *to let one's life* which mentions the precise day of the father's death. The death of one's father is an event in one's life that one will not easily forget. It is interesting that there is another example in the dictionary in which father and St Bartholomew co-occur:

> **I Sekyn I waxe sycke or fall sicke/** Ie deuiens malade. **My father syckened first vpon saynte Bartylmewes euyn:** Mon pere deuint malade premier la veille saynct Bartholomy . . .
>
> (III, fo. ccc.liiii)

Another, even more striking example is the one we have under the verb entry *to carve*:

> **I Carue afore a lorde or a great man at his borde/** Ie trenche. prime cõiuga. **And in this sence I fynde somtyme vsed/** Ie sers descuier trenchant, **and howe** Ie sers, **is cõiugate shall here after apere in I serue: I fynde also in this sence** ientame. prime cõiuga. **My father was chefe caruer with kyng Henry the seuenth:** Mon pere estoyt premier escuyer trenchant au roy Henry septiesme.
> **I carue byfore my mayster to day:** Ie trenche deuãt mon maistre a iourdhuy. **Carue or breake this capon:** Entames ce chapon.
>
> (III, fo. c.lxxxii)

It has been worth quoting the entry in full so as to show that, although the head verb is given in the first person and could thus trigger off example sentences in the first person, Palsgrave's examples vary with respect to the first, second, and third person as subject.

There is another more humorous instance where Palsgrave's example contains a reference to the occupation of 'my father'—and to what 'my mother' was doing:

> **I Heckell flaxe/** Ie cerance. prime cõiu. **and** ie habille du lyn, iay habillé, habiller. prime cõiu. **Am nat I a great gentylman my father was a hosyer and my mother dyd heckell flaxe:** Ne suis ie pas vng grãt seignieur, mon pere estoyt vng chaussetyer et ma mere habilloyt du lyn, **or** cerancoyt du lyn.
>
> (III, fo. cc.lx^v^)

and later, under the letter *S,* more about 'my mother':

> **I Spynne threde/** Ie fille. prime cõiu. **And you wyll speake with my mother she spynneth nowe at home:** Si vous voulez parler a ma mere elle fille mayntenant a la mayson.
>
> (III, fo. ccc.lxix)

Other interesting examples with respect to a father's death and will are to be found under **I Regyster** (III, fo. ccc.xxxv^v^) and **I Resume** (III, fo. ccc.xl^v^). There is even one for a dignity by birth (**I Am borne to lyuelodde** (III, fo. c.xli)).

I conclude this chapter with a picture of Palsgrave given by J. Pits.

It dates from 1619 and is part of Pits's descriptions of famous sixteenth-century authors (Pits 1619: 703–4). F. Génin, who translated it into French for his 1852 critical French reprint of *Lesclarcissement*, has pointed out that Pits did not disclose the source of his assessment (Génin 1852). For me it excellently captures the personality of Palsgrave as it seems to emerge on every page of *Lesclarcissement de la langue francoyse*:

> Jean Palsgrave, Anglais, natif de Londres. La nature lui avait libéralement départi ses dons: heureux génie, mémoire imperturbable, élocution facile, une modestie et une modération d'âme dignes d'éloges. Parvenu à l'âge mur, il se distinguait du commun des hommes par la gravité, la prudence et une dignité de maintien qu'il savait allier avec le charme des manières et une merveilleuse affabilité. (ibid.: 4)

# 2

# *Lesclarcissement*: Composition, Production, and Structure

From the letters and documents that relate to Palsgrave's life we learn very little about the composition of *Lesclarcissement de la langue francoyse*. Our only sources of information are his contract with Richard Pynson for the printing of the work and Stephen Vaughan's letter to Thomas Cromwell. Both precede the actual date of publication, 1530, and might enlighten us on stages of the work. In this chapter we shall look at them more closely and assess how far they are in line with what Palsgrave tells us about his work, its beginnings, its progress, and its difficulties, as well as his aim in *Lesclarcissement de la langue francoyse* itself.

## PRINTING, PRICE, AND PRESERVATION

Several copies of the *Lesclarcissement* have been preserved, but it has always been pointed out in the literature that Palsgrave's masterpiece was a very precious and rare work. T. F. Dibdin in his enlarged edition of Joseph Ames's *Typographical Antiquities* describes it as follows: 'This seems to be the FIRST GRAMMAR OF THE FRENCH LANGUAGE in our own country, if not in Europe . . . It is undoubtedly a noble performance, and reflects equal credit upon the author and the age' (Ames 1816/1969: 364). Since he had found that 'it is by no means of common occurrence', Dibdin gives us an account of the copies known to exist:

> Mr. Bliss considers it a volume of peculiar rarity; as Anthony à Wood knew of only one copy of it, which was Selden's, now in the Bodleian library. *Athen. Oxon. vol.* i. col. 122, edit. 4to. [this refers to the seventeenth century] Mr. Bliss discovered another copy (at Bristol); and I have seen and examined not fewer than five copies; in the libraries of Earl Spencer, Mr. R. Wilbraham, Mr. Dobree, senr. Mr. Douce, and Mr. Heber. They are usually in fine condition. (ibid.)

Sir Henry Ellis, in his *Original Letters* of 1846, writes 'Very few copies of this work are now known to exist, probably not more than seven or eight' (Ellis 1846: 211). A slightly higher figure is given by William T. Lowndes in *The bibliographer's manual of English literature*. Here we are given not only the names of owners but also the prices of purchase:

| | | | |
|---|---|---|---|
| Walley, Bishop of Ely | 7*l.* 17*s.* 6*d.* | Singer part iii | |
| Hibbert | 30*l.* 9*s.* | 17 leaves wanting | 5*l.* 17*s.* 6*d.* |
| Heber part ii | 25*l.* | Another copy, wanting | |
| another part vi | 13*l.* 13*s.* | title, dedication and | |
| Bright | 17*l.* | introduction | 7*l.* 2*s.* 6*d.* |

For the copies in Lord Spencer's library and the Shelden and Douce collections no prices are given (Lowndes 1861: 1769).

From a French source we learn that copies had also made their way beyond England: 'Il faut ajouter aux sept exemplaires cités par Dibdin, et dont il indique les possesseurs . . . celui de lord Haddington, pair écossais, et celui de la bibliothèque Mazarine, à Paris' (*Biographie universelle ancienne et moderne* n.d.: xxxii. 55) and Magnin assures us that 'Le travail de Jehan Palsgrave n'eut pas seulement un grand succès en Angleterre, il fut assez estimé en France pour avoir mérité à son auteur une place honorable et, pour ainsi dire, son droit de cité, dans la *Bibliothèque françoise* de la Croix du Maine, qui parut en 1584' (Magnin 1849: 116).

For the nineteenth century we can thus retrace fourteen copies and R. C. Alston's enquiry for the twentieth century produced sixteen copies in the libraries around the globe. Most of the copies are held in English and American libraries:

British Library, London—2 copies
Bodleian Library, Oxford
University Library, Cambridge
University Library, Manchester
Shrewsbury School, Shrewsbury
Cathedral Library, Canterbury
Cathedral Library, York
University of Texas, Austin
University of Illinois, Urbana
Yale University, New Haven
Library of Congress, Washington, DC
Folger Shakespeare Library, Washington, DC

The only copy known to be held in France is still the one in the Bibliothèque Mazarine in Paris. Two further privately owned copies have found their way into the Kongelige Bibliotek in Copenhagen and the Stadsbibliotheek in Antwerp.

According to Magnin, sixteenth-century Frenchmen knew about *Lesclarcissement de la langue francoyse* and its incomparable value. Later bibliophile and scholarly generations must have lost sight of it, for the *Biographie universelle* describes it as an 'ouvrage . . . très-rare et peu connu en France' (*Biographie universelle ancienne et moderne* n.d.: 55). In order to remedy this situation the Comité des Publications Historiques decided to provide the scholarly world with a critical modern edition. The task was entrusted to F. Génin and this only French edition of the work appeared in 1852 as part of the *Collection de documents inédits sur l'histoire de France publiés par les soins du ministère de l'instruction publique*. Because of the greatly improved technological means of text reproduction in the twentieth century, we now also have two facsimile reprints, one produced in 1969 by Scolar Press in England and the other published in 1972 by Slatkine in Geneva. A microfiche version has been made available in Paris as number 309 of the Archives de la linguistique française (Goyens and Swiggers 1989: 160) and an electronic version is being prepared by Professor Ian Lancashire at the University of Toronto.

One may well wonder why *Lesclarcissement de la langue francoyse* never went through a second edition. The only English dictionaries printed before 1530 were the English–Latin *Promptorium parvulorum* and the Latin–English *Ortus vocabulorum*. The *Promptorium parvulorum* had six editions, the first printed by Pynson in 1499, the second by Notary in 1508, and the last four by de Worde in 1510 [1511], 1512, 1516, and 1528. All in all, twenty-six copies of these editions have been located. According to our present-day knowledge, the number of editions of the *Ortus vocabulorum* was more than double that number, fifteen altogether. Editions were printed not only in London, but also in York and Rouen. Almost fifty copies are to be found in scholarly libraries all over the world. Both dictionaries are much smaller than *Lesclarcissement de la langue francoyse* and they were used in the schools. That the *Ortus vocabulorum*, a dictionary that was used for translating Latin texts into English, was more in demand than the *Promptorium parvulorum*, which was needed for composing Latin texts, is not surprising for a time when the emphasis in teaching was more on reading and translating than on text production. If we compare the three works with respect to their number of editions and the number of copies known to exist, the preservation record of *Lesclarcissement de la langue francoyse* is relatively good.

Palsgrave's masterpiece is one of the very few early books of which the size of print run is known. In the early days of printing, decisions as to how many copies to print of one particular work were dangerous guesswork for the printer. Haebler estimated that between 1480 and 1490, on the continent, 400–500 copies of an ordinary book were a fair average (Bennett 1970: 224). Information on the size of editions of books printed in England is scanty. One of the few sources is Pynson's lawsuits. From these we know, for instance, that five books which he had printed and which included *Dives and pauper* and the *Fall of princes* had an edition of at least 600 copies. From the little evidence there is, Bennett concluded that 'very special reasons were required to persuade a printer to print more than 600–700 copies of any ordinary work in the first seventy-five years of printing in England' (ibid.: 228). With the increasing demand for books, editions went up, but from a regulation issued by the Stationers' Company in 1588 we learn that

> no booke to be printed excede the number of 1250 or 1500 at one ympression except any book whatsoeuer of the non pareille letter [i.e. size of type] and the brevier letter, and also except iiij ympressions yerely of the *grammer* and lykewise iiij ympressions yerely of the *Accidence* seuerall [y] in $4^{to}$ or $8^{uo}$ and also all *prymers* and *Catechisms.* and that euery of th[e] impressions of *grammers Accidences prymers* and *Catechisms* and of all bookes of the none pareill letter and brevier letter be not aboue 2500 or 3000 at the most and except also *the statutes* and *proclamacons*. (Arber 1875–94: ii. 43)

This background helps us to assess Pynson's contracts with William Horman and John Palsgrave and the importance which the printer must have attributed to the two works. In 1519, Pynson and Horman agreed that Pynson was to print 800 copies of the *Vulgaria*, a book of eighty-two sheets.[1] The three drafts of the contract between Pynson and Palsgrave give the number of copies to be printed of *Lesclarcissement de la langue francoyse* as 750.

The severe restrictions imposed on the sale of *Lesclarcissement* may have slowed down interest and reduced circulation, which in turn may have affected demand. In the first draft of 1523 it is stipulated that the books 'shall rest and remayne in the custody and possessioñ vnder lok and key, at the will and pleasure of the aboue-said *Master* John Palsgraue/ Prouyded alleway that the forsaid Richard Pynsoñ may at all tymes haue sufficient book*es* to sell' (Furnivall 1867: 367). These conditions do not seem to have satisfied Palsgrave, for the later draft of 1524 is more specific in details. After the completion of printing and binding, Pynson and Palsgrave were to count the number of copies produced independently and, having established that there were indeed 750 copies, these would

> Remayn in the hand*es* of the sayd Richard Pynson, to be solde at suche pryce or prycys as the sayd Maister Palsgraue and the saide Richard schall indifferently sett apoñ the bokes,—after the iust nombers off quayres that every off theym̃ sc[h]all contayne, Sett vppoñ everay boke—the saide bokes to remayn in a chamber w*ith*in the saide Richard*es* howse, where-off the kay schall be in the custodye off the said Master

[1] The contract was edited by Furnivall (1867).

Johñ Palsgraue or his assignes, whyche froñ tyme to tyme schall reckyñ howe many off the hoole saide soñ off vij^c^ & ł bokes they take owt & the same nomber expresse in wryghtyng, to whyche eyther off theyñ or theyr assignes schall signe, for the avoyding of all manner dowt*es* that myght ryse apon forgettfullness. (ibid.: 368–9)

By means of these restrictions on the free sale of his book, Palsgrave was trying to protect his own professional interests as a teacher of French. As long as other teachers of the French language were not in possession of his grammar and his dictionary, their insight into the working of the French (and English) language was bound to be inferior to his. It was the best teachers of French that the nobility were seeking to instruct members of their family.

*Lesclarcissement de la langue francoyse* is an impressive book of 91 sheets or nearly 1,100 pages, much bigger than the *Promptorium parvulorum* or the *Ortus vocabulorum*. One may therefore wonder how much the price of a single copy was and who would have been able to afford such a work. The contract drafts tell us that Palsgrave was to pay Pynson for the paper, his servants' labour, and the printing the sum of 6*s*. 8*d*. per ream. In the 1523 draft it was assumed that 'the sayde book*es* . . . by estimacioñ wyll amount to Thre skore Reames of paper' (ibid.: 367). The cost of sixty reams to be paid by John Palsgrave would thus have been £20.

One ream contained 500 sheets. In 1523 it was thus estimated that for the production of 750 copies of *Lesclarcissement de la langue francoyse* 30,000 sheets were needed. This would have been equivalent to forty sheets per copy—much less than what the ultimate book turned out to be.

When *Lesclarcissement de la langue francoyse* was completed and published, its size was more than double what the estimate had been in 1523. Assuming that the price per ream was unchanged, the total cost for Palsgrave would have been 45*l*. 10*s*. In order to assess what a sum of £20 or £45 was worth at the time, we may recall that, in 1513, Palsgrave was paid 6*l*. 13*s*. 4*d*. as a year's wages for his services as schoolmaster to the princess of Castile. Richard Pynson received a salary of 40*s*. per year when he became the royal printer, a salary that was later increased to 4*l*. (Plomer 1900: 40). And in 1525, as schoolmaster to the little duke of Richmond, Palsgrave's salary was 13*l*. 6*s*. 8*d*.. The same amount was paid to the general attorney and the sergeant-at-law in the duke's household.

The question of how much a copy of *Lesclarcissement de la langue francoyse* may have sold for is much more difficult to answer. Very little is known about early book prices. What we can go by are the rare cases in which a price was printed on the volume or written down in a contemporary hand somewhere in the book. Other guides are prices occasionally mentioned by stationers when a book changed hands or inventories of books drawn up for various purposes. That there was some cause to worry about excessive prices charged for books becomes evident from an ordinance passed by the Stationers' Company on 19 January 1598. It required

> That all book*e* beinge newe copies w$^{che}$ hereafter shalbe printed w$^{th}$out/ pictures, in the pica. the Romane, the Italica, the Englishe letter & the Romane & Italica to the same and the breviere and longe prȳmers letters shall not be sold aboue these rat*e* folowinge viž
>
> Those of the pica, Roman. Italica, the Inglishe. and the Romane & Italica to the same, to be sold, not aboue a penny for twoo sheet*e*
>
> Those of the brevier and the longe prymer letters not to be sold for aboue a penny for one sheete & a half (Greg and Boswell 1930: 58–9)

Book prices were thus predominantly determined by the age of edition (new or old edition), the size of the volume, the printing types used and whether it contained illustrations or not.

The largest part of *Lesclarcissement de la langue francoyse* is the English–French dictionary. Of the few sources available to estimate the selling price of dictionaries at Palsgrave's time, the book inventories are most informative.

An interesting case is that of Henry Bynneman, a master printer, publisher, and bookseller. Under Queen Elizabeth I, various printing monopolies were introduced—that is, individual master printers were granted special patents for the exclusive printing of certain types of books. Thus Master Flower, the printer of the Latin tongue, was granted the monopoly to print the 'Grammar, and accidens for the instruction of youth', and Master Seres the monopoly for the 'booke of common prayer' (Arber 1875–94: i. 116). At the suit of the earl of Leicester and Sir C. Hatton, on 28 April 1580, Henry Bynneman obtained a licence to print not only Cooper's famous dictionary but 'all *Dictionaries* in all tongues, all *Chronicles* and *histories* whatsoever' (ibid.: 116).

The end of Bynneman's life seems to suggest that the dictionary monopoly was not without its dangers. These were in their implications and consequences foreseen by Christopher Barker, who, in December 1582, voiced them as follows in his report on the printing patents granted between 1558 and 1582:

> In this patent is conteyned all *Dictionaries* in all tongues, all *Chronicles* and *histories*. This generality carieth a great shewe, and in deed to be executed with commendacon doth requyer a stock of ten thowsand pounde at the least: But if the printer should print many of the said volumes, he must needes stande betwixt two extremes, that is, if he print competent nombers of each to mayntayne his charges, all England Scotland and much more, were not able to vtter [dispose of] them; and if he

should print but a few of each volume, the prices should be exceading greate, and he in more Daunger to be vndone, then likely to gayne . . . (ibid.: 116)

Barker who had the best monopoly—he held the Bible patent (Handover 1960: 34)—assessed the difficulties created by the dictionary patent very realistically. Bynneman appears to have taken his privilege very seriously and in preparation for its exercise he had borrowed money. He owed Richard Hutton £1,000; when he failed to pay his debt he was ordered to prison, and Richard Hutton was to get his London estate and goods. Bynneman died before the sentence came into force.

In order to assess the value of his estate an inventory of his property and books was made in 1583. In it a number of dictionaries are itemized with their estimated prices. Under the circumstances, the sheriffs will have marked the prices down rather than up:

| | |
|---|---|
| 15. Item one olde Coopers diccionary | viij$^{s}$ |
| 16. Item one olde Morelius diccionary | iij$^{s}$ viij$^{d}$ |
| 17. Item Junius his nomen Clator | xvj$^{d}$ |
| 19. Item one olde verens diccionary | xij$^{d}$ |
| 20. Item one olde Ricechling diccionarie hebreue | ij$^{s}$ iiij$^{d}$ |

(Eccles 1957: 83)

With the exception of Hadrianus Junius' *Nomenclator*, the prices quoted are given for old editions of these works.

In Bennett's study 'Notes on English retail book-prices, 1480–1560' we are given prices for the two Latin–English/English–Latin dictionaries that preceded the publication of *Lesclarcissement de la langue francoyse* as well as for Sir Thomas Elyot's dictionary, which was the fourth printed dictionary involving English published in England. In all three cases, it is old editions for which prices are indicated. In the day-book of John Dorne (1520) the price given for a 1514 reprint of the *Ortus vocabulorum* is 1*s.* 2*d.* and that for an unbound copy of the 1516 edition of the *Promptorium parvulorum* is 5*d.* The inventory of his library which Sir William More compiled in 1556 contains a bound copy of the 1548 edition of the *Bibliotheca Eliotae* for 3*s.* 4*d.* In the case of the unbound *Promptorium parvulorum*, the buyer got four sheets for a penny, whereas the price, including the binding, of the *Ortus vocabulorum* was two and a half sheets per penny. In the case of the *Bibliotheca Eliotae*, one penny would not have bought a sheet (again including the binding). The price per sheet of the typographically more sophisticated *Bibliotheca Eliotae* amounted to about 1.2*d.*

Francis R. Johnson provides us with further data on dictionary prices during the sixteenth century. A 1559 edition of the *Bibliotheca*

*Eliotae* was priced at 5*s*. by the Cambridge stationer John Denys in 1578 (Johnson 1950: 101). Copies of the 1578 and 1584 editions of Thomas Cooper's *Thesaurus* were sold by Thomas Chard for 21*s*. in 1583–1584 and priced at 20*s*. by a Cambridge physician in 1595 (ibid.: 99). A bound copy of the 1580 edition of John Baret's *Alvearie* appeared as worth 8*s*. in Bennet Waulker's inventory of his stock in 1588 (ibid.: 96).

With respect to the founts used and their variation within the dictionary text, Thomas Cooper's monumental *Thesaurus linguae romanae et britannicae* comes closest to *Lesclarcissement de la langue francoyse*. We might therefore base our estimate of the price of Palsgrave's work on the *Thesaurus*. The first edition of Cooper's *Thesaurus* dates from 1565. The prices quoted thus relate to later editions. The discrepancy between the price given by John Denys in 1578, 21*s*., and that put down for Bynneman's copy by the sheriffs assessing his estate in 1583, 8*s*., is striking, but in view of the circumstances not at all surprising. On the assumption that the *Thesaurus* contains about 150 sheets, the selling price per sheet (including the binding) would have amounted to 1.68*d*. For the ninety-one sheets of *Lesclarcissement de la langue francoyse*, this would have yielded a price of about 12*s*. 8*d*. The purchasing price of *Lesclarcissement* calculated on the basis of the 1556 price quoted for the *Bibliotheca Eliotae* (1.2*d*. per sheet) would have been slightly more than nine shillings.

All in all then, Palsgrave's masterpiece was a rather expensive treasure at the time—a scholarly work to be held in a library or on a reference shelf, not a book to carry around to wherever a group of young pupils were privately tutored in French. This distinguished it clearly from the smaller-sized *Ortus vocabulorum* and *Promptorium parvulorum* used in schools and the polyglot vocabularies which became very popular from the middle of the sixteenth century (Stein 1988*a*, *b*). In the *Authours Epistell to the kynges grace*, Palsgrave tells us that with his book he had wanted to 'do some hũble seruice vnto the nobilite of this victorius realme' (A ii). At the end of the book he emphasizes again the English nobility as the envisaged users of *Lesclarcissement de la langue francoyse*, but the scope is widened to include anyone interested in acquiring the French language:

> Besechyng god that these my labours maye not onely be commodyouse and profitable vnto the nobylyte of this realme (the more soner by the meanes herof in their tender age to attayne vnto ỹ knowledge of this tonge) but also maye bc moche vayllable vnto all other persones of this noble realme/ of what estate or condyscions so euer they be: for than shall I nat onely thynke my labours well bestowed/ but also take it for a recompence of my displeasurs endured otherwyse. (III, fo. cccc.lxxiii$^{v}$)

Palsgrave also identified who these 'other persons' might be who would be desirous to learn French: those for whom the command of French was a professional necessity. In *The Introduction of the authour* he informs us:

> But if any of our nation be desyrous to be exquisyt in the french tong/ and by trayct of tyme/ couyte to come vnto suche parfyte knowledge therin/ that he may be able to do seruyce in the faict of secretarishype or other wyse in to those partyes to haue farther charge/ or to vse amõgest thẽ the fait of marchandyse/ let hym rede ouer all yͤ thre bokes by order/ and he shall euidently parceyue that the fruyt of his labour shall farre passe any traueyle/ which shalbe nedefull or requisyte to be there about employed. (C [vi])

The fact that *Lesclarcissement de la langue francoyse* did not have a second edition may be accounted for by Palsgrave's control of its sale and the relatively high price. In its scholarly achievement it is comparable to Sir Thomas Elyot's *Dictionary* and Thomas Cooper's *Thesaurus linguae romanae et britannicae*, but the demand for Latin was far more pervasive than the demand for French. In addition, Elyot's and Cooper's dictionaries helped the learned Englishman not only to read the classical texts but also to be part of the scholarly community, to share and understand the new learning published in texts couched in Latin. By contrast, *Lesclarcissement*, above all its dictionary part, was not a help to read French texts, but to produce correct French, in a spoken or a written form. It was more a reference book than a textbook, an excellent guide for the more advanced student. The demand for more elementary introductions to the French language was met by smaller books (see below). Their very compilation during the first half of the sixteenth century is indicative of the increased interest in learning French. What the nobility, the gentry, the merchants, and the travellers needed were booklets instructing them how to pronounce French properly, and what to say in specific situations—for example, when meeting someone, when requesting a service, when taking leave, and so on. A certain degree of communicative ease and fluency in speaking French were the keys to successful commerce in these classes of society.

## EARLY PRINTED BOOKS TEACHING FRENCH

In the early days of printing the introductory textbooks for French seem to have developed at intervals of about twenty years, and there is the obvious question whether those published before 1530 were consulted by Palsgrave when he was compiling his book. At the earliest stage, the three leading printers in England, William Caxton,

Wynkyn de Worde, and Richard Pynson, must have thought it profitable to print a little treatise contrasting English and French.

The first in date is the one printed by William Caxton (*c.*1483) 'Tres bonne doctrine pour aprendre briefment francoys et engloys/ Ryght good lernyng for to lerne shortly frenssh and englyssh'. Since it did not have a title-page, early bibliographers referred to it by different names, e.g. 'Instructions for Travellers' or 'A Vocabulary in French and English' (Bradley 1900: p. v; Lambley 1920: 42). Henry Bradley in his modern adaptation calls it 'Dialogues in French and English' and Jean Gessler in his reprint of 1931 uses 'Caxton's Dialogues' and 'Dialogues in French and English'. J. C. T. Oates and L. C. Harmer in their facsimile reprint returned to 'Vocabulary in French and English' (1964). The book is derived from a French–Flemish *manuel de conversation* whose author is not known and which was compiled about 1340.[2] It is generally assumed that Caxton translated the French text into English and adapted the content to an English context. The Flemish text was replaced by an English version, thus keeping French in the first position. This assumption has been challenged by N. F. Blake, who, on the basis of external and internal factors, as well as a comparison with other works by Caxton, argues that *The Vocabulary in French and English* 'was translated by a mercer in 1465–66. Later the book came into Caxton's hands and he printed it straightaway' (Blake 1965–6: 15). For the English student, this was a foreign-language text provided with a mother-tongue translation. In order to achieve fluency in speaking French, learners would have had to convert their understanding (or receptive) knowledge into a productive one.

The language arrangement in the little textbooks printed by Wynkyn de Worde, Caxton's successor, and Richard Pynson was more favourable to the needs of English learners because the source language was English, the learners' mother tongue. Pynson's text has no title, whereas de Worde's title-page informs us that 'Here begynneth a lytell treatyse for to lerne Englysshe and Frensshe'. Under the headline there is a woodcut representing a schoolmaster seated in a large chair and at his feet three small boys holding their books. Both texts[3] are undated and very similar in content.[4] They seem to have been printed during the last years of the fifteenth

[2] *Le Livre des Mestiers* was first edited by Michelant (1875). An evaluation of Michelant's edition with a correction of his errors is found in Gessler (1931).

[3] The British Library, London, has a unique copy of each. Wynkyn de Worde's text has been reproduced: *A lytell treatise for to lerne Englisshe and Frensshe* (*Westmynster*, (*1497?*) (The English Experience no. 630; Amsterdam and New York: Da Capo Press, 1973).

[4] See Gessler (1941*a*) (this is an illustrated and revised extract of Gessler (1941*b*)).

century and scholars differ as to which should be regarded as the earlier version.[5]

Unlike Caxton's *Dialogues in French and English*, the two texts are for the most part not printed in parallel columns but in lines where English precedes French. Gessler in his edition has rearranged the text and printed it in opposing columns. The text can be seen as falling into three major parts. Part one provides model dialogues for such interactive situations as salutations, buying and selling, asking one's way, and conversation at an inn. Longer dialogue sequences alternate with vocabulary sections. Here the author/printer seems to have hesitated between which typographical arrangement would be best for the users. The predominant order is that the French translation equivalent is printed under the English headword—for example:

My hede
Ma teste

Yet occasionally, display in opposite columns takes over, e.g.

| | |
|---|---|
| My throte | Ma gorge |
| My face | Mon visage |
| My armes | Mes bras |

An odd mixture of these two types of arrangement occurs at the end of part one:

| | |
|---|---|
| Mondaye | Tuesdaye |
| Lundy | Mardy |
| Wednesdaye | Thursdaye |
| Mercredy | Jeudy |
| Frydaye | Satyrdaye |
| Vendredy | Samedy |
| Sondaye | Dimenche |

In addition, the vocabulary sections show an interesting variation in use of the possessive pronouns (for parts of the body as illustrated above), the indefinite article (as in *A keye/Vng clef*, *A shoo/Vng soulier*), and the definite article (as in *The Sonne/Le soleil*, *The sterry/Lestoile*) preceding the noun in question.

Part two is a bilingual little book of courtesy and part three contains two models of commercial letters.

With these four components—dialogues for typical situations encountered by travellers and merchants, a little bilingual English–French vocabulary, a booklet on how to behave properly, and an

[5] Lambley (1920: 47–8) regards Pynson's edition as the first. Gessler (1941*a*: 10–11) thinks that the priority of printing cannot be established and makes de Worde's text the basis of his edition because de Worde's printing career started before Pynson's. Alston (1985) has the date [1497] for de Worde's edition and [1500?] for Pynson's.

epistolary section—these 'little treatises for to lerne Englisshe and Frensshe' must have met the specific needs of their users. (For a more detailed account, see Lambley 1920: 46–55.) What was still missing was more information on how to pronounce the French words and phrases properly, and how to vary the words and phrases given, and how to string them together in a grammatically correct way. The changed external conditions which called for such a fuller and more detailed knowledge of, and instruction in, French have been well summarized by Lambley:

> In the early part of the sixteenth century, however, French began to be studied with more thoroughness in England. Communication with France and the tour in France were no longer fraught with the same dangers and difficulties, and favoured the use of a purer form of French. Fluent speaking was no longer sufficient without correct pronunciation and grammar. The standard of French taught was also raised by the arrival of numerous Frenchmen, who made the teaching of their language the business of their lives. Further, the spread of the art of printing had rendered French literature more accessible, and supplied a rich material from which the rules of the language might be deduced. (ibid.: 56–7)

Some twenty years into the century, a new generation of teachers of French was intent on supplying introductions to the French language that covered these aspects. All three of them, just like Palsgrave himself, had been encouraged by members of the nobility to write the book. As a good and conscientious scholar, Palsgrave knew the work that had been done on the French language by his contemporaries. In the *Authours Epistell* of *Lesclarcissement de la langue francoyse* he acknowledges the work of his predecessors:

> nowe sithe yͤ beginnyng of your most fortunate and most ꝓsperous raigne/ the right vertuous and excellent prince Thomas late duke of Northfolke/ hath cõmanded the studious clerke Alexãdre Barkelay/ to embusy hym selfe about this excercyse/ and that my sayd synguler good lorde Charles duke of Suffolke/ by cause that my poore labours required a longre tracte of tyme/ hath also in the meane season encouraged maister Petrus Uallensys/ scole maister to his excellent yong sonne the Erle of Lyncolne/ to shewe his lernynge and opinion in this behalfe/ and that the synguler clerke/ maister Gyles Dewes somtyme instructour to your noble grace in this selfe tong/ at the especiall instaũce and request of dyuers of your highe estates and noble men/ hath also for his partye written in this matter. (A iii$^{v}$)

The authors and works referred to by Palsgrave are in chronological order: Alexander Barclay's introduction described as 'Here begynneth the introductory to wryte and to pronounce frenche', published in 1521 and printed by Robert Coplande, Pierre Valence's *Introductions in frensshe*, published in 1528 and printed by Wynkyn de Worde, and Giles du Wes's *An introductorie for to lerne to rede to prononce/ and to speke Frenche trewly*, published in 1532–3 and printed by Thomas Godfray.

Of these manuals du Wes's *Introductorie* was the most interesting and comprehensive one for the students, providing them with information on pronunciation, grammatical rules, a little vocabulary, and practical exercises in the form of letters and dialogues. These contemporary works will be dealt with in more detail in the context of Palsgrave's sources. What matters here is that it was du Wes's more practical *Introductorie* that became the leading French textbook of the 1530s and 1540s. It was in demand, and, unlike *Lesclarcissement de la langue francoyse*, it went through several editions. Alston lists four different printings.[6]

With the 1550s we enter the third phase. The textbooks and books for the teaching of French in England are not only more varied in scope but there are also more serious attempts at describing the grammar and the lexicon, as though the time for these more scholarly studies had come. Palsgrave had simply been ahead of his time. The anonymously published *A very necessarye boke bothe in Englishe & in Frenche wherin you mayst learne to speake & wryte Frenche truly in a litle space* . . . (1550) and Pierre du Ploiche's *A treatise in Englishe and Frenche right necessary and proffitable for al young children* . . . (1553) continued the type of textbook of the second phase. Du Ploiche's *Treatise* seems to have replaced du Wes's *Introductorie*. Like its predecessor it went through several editions (1553, 1554?, 1578). The grammar of French was tackled by Louis Meigret in *Le tretté de la grammere françoeze* (1550),[7] and after *Lesclarcissement de la langue francoyse* a second full-length dictionary became available when Jean Veron provided Robert Estienne's Latin–French dictionary with English equivalents. The trilingual edition appeared in 1552 as the *Dictionariolum puerorum tribus linguis latina anglica & gallica conscriptum*.[8] Next in date we have Gabriel Meurier's *Traicte pour apprendre a parler Francoys et Angloys*, published in 1553. For the further history of the teaching of French in England see Lambley (1920) and Kibbee (1991).

[6] For none of the editions of du Wes's *Introductorie* do we have exact dates. Those given by Alston (1985) are: [1533?], [1540?] printed by Nicolas Bourman for John Reyns, [1546?] printed by N. Hill for H. Smyth, [1546?] printed by John Waley, and [1546?] printed by J. Herford and N. Hill for J. Waley. Kibbee (1991) has slightly earlier dates: 1532?, 1539?, 1540?, 1545?

[7] There are two modern editions. The first, by Wendelin Foerster, dates from 1888; the second is Hausmann (1980*a*).

[8] There is a facsimile reprint (The English Experience no. 351, New York: Da Capo Press, 1971).

## COMPOSITION

Let us now, on the basis of this brief historical and educational background, come back to the composition of *Lesclarcissement de la langue francoyse.* Palsgrave tells us in *The Authours Epistell to the kynges grace* that he began his great work after he had been appointed French tutor to Mary Tudor, the king's sister—that is, in 1512, at a time when the little treatises printed by Caxton, Pynson, and de Worde were available as bilingual textbooks to students of French. His intention was that 'the frenche tonge may herafter by others the more easely be taught/ also be attayned vnto by suche/ as for their tymes therof shalbe desyrous'. We learn that he approached his task in a rather scholarly way by investigating and studying what had been done before him. Finding that his predecessors' work had concentrated on how 'the Frenche tong ought to be pronounced/ and to shewe wherin their trewe Analogie dyd rest', he too decided to tackle these two aspects of the French language, and duly produced 'two sondrie bookes'. As a token of gratitude he offered them to the king's sister and her husband, the duke of Suffolk. Both, after having 'thorowly visyted' the two books, encouraged him, suggesting that the king himself might accept his work. We do not know what the original version of the first two books was like—the existing version contains a good number of cross-references to the third book and thus obviously has been revised to make it agree with the added third book—but one might wonder whether Mary Tudor, the dowager queen of France, and her husband had sensed the exceptional character and quality of the work. After all, Palsgrave had been Mary's teacher and she might have glimpsed his intellectual potential, and she will most certainly have had experience of his assiduity and perseverance. Her shrewd assessment of Palsgrave's linguistic faculties may thus have given rise to one of the greatest vernacular achievements in sixteenth-century Europe. He describes how he tried to meet the new challenge as follows:

> [S]o I on my ꝑtie to make my pore gyfte some lytell thing more acceptable/ wolde yet in this mater take a farther dilygence/ and wolde assay/ if I coulde by the order of the letters fyrst set forthe in our tonge/ and than declared in Frenche/ sette out worde for worde ⁊ phrasis for phrases/ affyrmynge that though my labours were some thynge cõmodious for an Introduction towardes the better attaynyng of this langage. yet were they nat fully sufficient for any of our nation/ by his owne study to attayne the Frenche tonge by/ except after their trewe ꝓnunciation and arte Grãmaticall ones knowen/ we myght haue plenty of frenche wordes also/ to expresse our myndes withall. . . . But most especially/ aboue all other thynges/ desyrous to leaue some lytell monument vnto your noble graces posterite/ . . . I haue nat onely assayde so to mary our tonge ⁊ the frẽch togider/ that there shulde fewe wordes in comparison of

bothe the tonges be wantyng/ nor phrases where the tonges diffre/ ⁊ haue nat worde for worde be vnsetforthe/ and by examples expressed/ But farthermore/ folowyng the order of Theodorus Gaza/ in his grãmer of the Greke tonge/ I haue also added vnto my former labours a thirde boke/ whiche is a very cõment and exposytour vnto my seconde. So that the accidentes/ vnto the partes of reason in the Frenche tong/ and other preceptes grãmaticall/ whiche I haue but brefely and in a generaltee touched in my secõde boke/ and so/ as vnto an Introduction dothe suffise. In my said thirde boke cõsequently ⁊ in due ordre be declared/ dilated/ ⁊ sette forthe at the length. (A ii$^v$–A iii$^r$)

Palsgrave thus added a third book which expands the grammatical treatment given in the first two books and which includes an English–French dictionary. From the passage quoted we also learn that he regarded the first two books as a general introduction and the third as a detailed outline of French grammar.

We do not know when the manuscript version of the first two books was completed to be offered to the duchess and the duke of Suffolk. By 1523, however, some ten years after the idea of writing a French grammar had first occurred to him, Palsgrave had conceived the plan and even the title of the work. In the second contract draft of 1523, we have the first mention of the title of the work. From the original of the draft in the Public Record Office we learn that, after the specification of the title, the content of the book was then added between the lines. The envisaged structure in 1523 was:

iij sondrye bokes, where-in ys schewyd howe the saide tong schould be pronownsyd in reding & spekyng, and all-so syche grammatical rules as concerne the p*er*fection of the saide tong, w*ith* ij vocabulist*es*, oone begynnyng w*ith* Englishe nownes & verbes expowndyd in frenshe, and a general vocabulist contaynyng all the word*es* off the frenshe tong expownd in Englishe. (Furnivall 1867: 368)

According to this second contract draft, *Lesclarcissement* was to include two vocabulists: an English–French dictionary listing nouns and verbs and a general French–English dictionary containing all the words of the French language. In the third draft, which is in Cromwell's hand and exists in manuscript only, the book to be printed is also called *Lesclarcissement* and its structure is specified as having three books in one volume. The manuscript shows two additions in lighter ink and a different hand which Brewer regards as corrections by Palsgrave. Each of them is inserted to specify the content of the three books. The first reads 'wyth certayn tabylls and a frenshe vocabulyst', the second 'tabylls ⁊ a vocabulist'. The elaborate care taken over the wording of the title and the content of the work to be printed, together with the explicit specification of the print run (750 copies), the number of presentation copies (6) and the precise conditions for the storing of the printed copies, the accounts of sale, and the printing of further copies, make the contract between Pynson and Palsgrave a most precious document for the history of printing. For S. H. Johnston (1977: 153–4), it is the first copyright granted to an author in England. Such a privilege was first granted in Italy, in 1491, to Peter of Ravenna.

Two points in the second and third contract drafts are noteworthy: the first is the French title of the book. Palsgrave was an Englishman and the language in which his *magnum opus* is written is English. It was meant for English people seeking to perfect their knowledge of French. The actual title-page does not only have its title in French but it also describes the author in French: 'compose par maistre Jehan Palsgraue Angloys natyf de Londres/ et gradue de Paris'. Could this already have been an early market strategy to attract the attention of a French-speaking public?

The second point is the 'French vocabulist'. The last contract draft that has been preserved leaves no doubt that there was going to be only *one* word list. This, as we know, has the language order English–French. To refer to this as a 'French' vocabulary may seem unusual, but it is not so in its historical context. At the beginning of dictionary-writing involving English, the reading community's perception seems to have been more caught by the existence of a (particular) dictionary rather than its specific language arrangement. Thus the *Promptorium parvulorum*, the first English–Latin dictionary was also referred to as the *Medulla grammatice*. The *Medulla grammatice*, however, was a dictionary compiled much earlier with the opposite language order: Latin–English (Stein 1985*a*: 77–8). In the case of Palsgrave's English–French dictionary, the salient factor simply was that it was a word list for the learning and teaching of the French language, and this justified its being called a 'French vocabulist'.

We do not know how much of *Lesclarcissement* had been written by the time the contract with the printer was set up. Since the contract draft even specifies the printing speed 'that the sayde Richard schall imprint euery hoole workyng day, for the more speding off the saide work, a schete off paper on bothe the sides. and not to cesse for none occasioñ (except the Kyng*es* grace haue any thyng*es* to be pryntyd) tyll the saide hole worke be full fynyshyd. the said Rychard to begyñ to print the saide worke as to-morowe' (Furnivall 1867: 369), we might conclude that a good part of the work was ready in manuscript, possibly the revised first two books and part of the third book. In 1523–4, the whole work was estimated to come to about forty sheets, when in fact it amounted to some ninety sheets in its completed stage. This makes it very likely that the bulk of the English–French dictionary was far from being finished in 1524. The manuscript may not even have been completed by 1529, for Pynson died before the total work was printed.

Pynson printed the first two books only. Book I is composed of the gatherings A–D, book II has the gatherings F–K. We do not know why there is no gathering E. Book III, the main part of *Lesclarcissement*, was printed by the 'mysterious printer' John Haukins, whom S. H. Johnston in his study of the career and publications of Richard Pynson (1977: 3) has identified as Pynson's son-in-law. The third book starts with the gathering M, so that gathering L, too, is missing. One may wonder whether the missing gatherings between book I and book II, and between book II and book III, indicate that Palsgrave was still in the process of writing while the work was at press. Gathering E and gathering L might have been reserved for a table of contents to each book to be added and inserted after the completion of the work. Book I starts with a table of contents.

That the printing was in progress while Palsgrave was still trying to finish his work is confirmed by a number of passages in *Lesclarcissement* itself (see III, fos. l, v; ccc.lxxxxiii).

The compilation, writing, and printing of *Lesclarcissement de la langue francoyse* thus stretched over a period of eighteen years, and its major part, the third book with the English–French vocabulist, was printed in 1529 and 1530. We remember from the contract drafts that there was a very keen interest in the completion of the work. But six years elapsed between the contract of 1524 and the actual publication of the work in 1530. Palsgrave himself tells us in the *Authours Epistell* that the delay in finishing his work caused the duke of Suffolk to ask a fellow teacher to write a little introduction to the study of French. Pierre Valence obliged and produced a booklet called *Introductions in frensshe*, published in 1528, but he begins his introduction with apologies for the work, because he had made it 'ĩ haste and without grete layser'. At the end of his booklet he tells his readers that circumstances had obliged him to bring his book to an end. He had planned to include a small vocabulary listing everyday words. But, in view of the work prepared by Palsgrave, he regarded the omission as acceptable. Thus Palsgrave's contemporary Pierre Valence explicitly refers to the work Palsgrave was compiling (Q [iii$^{v}$]).

Palsgrave's book is of a totally different scholarly nature which, as we shall see in the chapters to follow, because of its original and comprehensive character, could not have been written in a short span of time. In addition, its setting—with, for instance, three different founts (in major parts), for three different languages (English for the headwords, French for the equivalents, and Latin for grammatical specifications), and their variation within entries, as well as the spacing and arrangement of the entries themselves—required meticulous skill and attention by the printers, their assistants, and the proof-readers. *Lesclarcissement* includes a number of complaints about printers and their work. But printing errors are not the only signs that indicate that serious efforts were made to bring the book to completion.

The word lists include a good number of items for which there are no French equivalents. Cases in point include:

> **Blode worte herbe**
> **Gredy worme that is in a dogges tong**
> **I Pytche a bottell or shyppe with.**

In some cases the omission of the French equivalent may have been caused by lack of space. For example, there may have been no space left in the line because the headword was too long, as in the case of *Dressar where meate is serued out at*, or the entry may have occupied two full lines, as in the following headword:

> **Goulfe of corne / so moche as may lye by**
> **twene two postes/ otherwyse a baye.**

Alternatively these 'gaps' in the dictionary may have been caused by Palsgrave having to supply copy for the printer when the manuscript was not quite ready. Yet equally well, the missing French equivalents may not be accidental oversights but instances for which the author was unsure of the corresponding French word. The oversights might also reveal something about Palsgrave's lexicographical sources, which we shall deal with in detail in Chapters 4 and 5.

The long vocabulary lists for nouns and verbs are arranged alphabetically, but we have to remember that alphabetical order in early dictionary-making was far from being consistently alphabetical. There are word lists where all the words beginning with a letter are put together irrespective of the internal order of the letters (e.g. *bread, bath*, etc.). This stage of alphabetical arrangement is also referred to as 'first-letter order'. When the second letter was taken into account, 'second-letter order' had been achieved, and so on. Following the lexicographical tradition of the time, a subheading was given for each letter of the alphabet, highlighting the beginning of another second letter in the lemma. The substructure has the following form in *Lesclarcissement*: B before A, B before E, etc. Occasionally, such a subheading is missing, so that, for instance, *Cr*-words are immediately run onto *Co*-words. In the case of verbs beginning with the letter *E*, there are no subheadings at all. For a number of letters (*F, G, H, I, R*), subheadings 'before U' are missing in the verb section, suggesting that there might have been pressure to finish that particular letter so that work became slightly rushed towards the end of the section. There are instances where whole batches of items seem to have been misplaced—for instance, the twenty-seven *Com*-entries between the verbs *cuffe* and *cure*. The alphabetical sequencing of *Sc*-, *Sh*-, *She*-, *Shi/ o/ r*-, *Scl*-, *Sco*- is rather muddled. And finally, for the interestingly odd case of *There*-entries under verbs beginning with the letter *I*, an explanation suggests itself: at the end of *Is*-items Palsgrave lists impersonal expressions beginning with *It* or *It is*. These are then followed by impersonal expressions with *There*.

## THE STRUCTURE OF *LESCLARCISSEMENT*

I shall conclude this chapter by outlining in some more detail the overall structure of *Lesclarcissement de la langue francoyse*. So far I have concentrated on its inception, and the various stages in its composition and production. We have seen it develop from a small treatise into a monumental volume of more than 1,000 pages, containing a comprehensive description of the pronunciation, the grammar and the lexicon of the French language. The work is divided into three parts which are called books and reflect the genesis of the work. The main interest of the present study lies in the English–French vocabulist and Palsgrave's contribution to English–French, and to sixteenth-century vernacular lexicography. The vocabulist constitutes the essential part of the third book, and all three books are interrelated.

Palsgrave tells us in the *Authours Epistell* (A iii) that in the structuring of his work he had followed the example of Theodorus Gaza. Gaza's grammar of the Greek language had been printed in Venice in 1495, and it had become one of the leading textbooks by the early sixteenth century. Parts of it were translated by Erasmus. The third book of Gaza's Greek grammar takes up points of the second book and develops them in more detail. When Palsgrave decided to expand his work to make it a worthy gift for the king, Gaza's method may have offered itself as an adequate model to avoid a complete recasting of the first two books.

He gives explicit credit to contemporary 'French specialists' with whose work he was familiar. These were, as we have seen, in the chronological order of their publication: Alexander Barclay's *Introductory to wryte and to pronounce frenche* (1521),[9] Pierre Valence's

[9] According to the STC, the Bodleian Library, Oxford, and Christ College, Cambridge, each holds a copy of the work. The parts which relate to pronunciation are reprinted in Ellis (1871*a*, 804–14). See also Lambley (1920: 77–80) and Kibbee (1991).

*Introductions in frensshe* (1528),[10] and Giles du Wes's *An introductorie for to lerne to rede to pronounce/ and to speke Frenche trewly* (1532–3).[11] The two Frenchmen, du Wes and Valence, and the translator of Sebastian Brant's famous *Narrenschiff*, Barclay, were all teachers of French at the time. The most outstanding by far was du Wes, who had been in the service of Henry VII, who had been named the king's librarian and who had been French tutor to the king's sons, the princes Arthur and Henry. He continued his services under Henry VIII and became French tutor to his daughter, the Princess Mary. All three, like Palsgrave, had been encouraged by their employers/patrons to produce a textbook for the teaching and learning of French: Barclay by the duke of Norfolk, Valence by Charles Brandon, the duke of Suffolk, whose son, the earl of Lincoln, was his pupil, and du Wes by his pupil, the Princess Mary. The first descriptive treatises on the pronunciation, the grammar and the lexicon of modern French, printed in a vernacular, thus owe their existence to the English court's keen interest in speaking French well.

As far as we know, Palsgrave, beginning in 1512, was the first to tackle the task. But while he was still at work, Barclay's *Introductory* appeared in 1521 and seven years later Valence's hastily produced *Introductions*. Although du Wes's book was not published before 1532, that is after the publication of *Lesclarcissement de la langue francoyse*, there is some reason to assume that a first manuscript version of du Wes's *Introductorie* was available in court circles before 1530. Génin (1852: 16–17) has drawn attention to the dialogue *Confabulacion betwene the lady Mary/ her seruant Gyles/ touchyng the peace*, suggesting 1527–30 as a composition date for the dialogues (see also Schmitt 1979: 5). Kibbee (1991: 194), referring to the peace treaty of 1525 between England and France as well as Princess Mary's stay at Tewkesbury, regards 1524–7 as the period when du Wes compiled his work, thus accepting Lambley's argument (Lambley 1920: 93–4). Palsgrave himself tells us in the *Authours Epistell* that he was familiar with what du Wes had written on the subject. All this amply illustrates the competitive spirit in the endeavours to produce an acceptable French textbook for the English aristocracy and it also accounts for the fact that, quite suddenly, within a span of twelve years, four such books were printed.

So Palsgrave was fully aware of what his predecessors and contemporary competitors had attempted to do. He approached the task

[10] Alston (1967*a*) is a facsimile reprint. See also Alston (1964), as well as Ellis (1871*a*: 814–16), Lambley (1920: 80–2), and Kibbee (1991).

[11] The work was re-edited in Génin (1852). Alston (1972*b*) is a facsimile reprint. See also Lambley (1920: 86–91), Schmitt (1979), and Kibbee (1991).

of describing the French language of his time in a completely different way. He was an Englishman, with an excellent command of French, but with respect to that language a foreigner. As such, he was superbly qualified to outline the linguistic and cultural areas where both languages were similar and where they differed. But what was he, the foreigner, going to take as the basis for his description? Linguistically this was the time when speakers of the vernaculars in Europe were challenging the pre-excellence and predominance of Latin and developing the grammar and vocabulary of their mother tongue to equal the expressive beauty and precision of Latin. So those professionally concerned with the language—probably more than ever before—will have been struck and preoccupied by the concurring changes on all linguistic levels. Norms in grammatical use were not yet in existence, still less in spelling; they were in the process of developing. Faced with this transitional indeterminate period during which Middle French and Middle English were gradually changing into their modern forms, Palsgrave chose to complement his personal knowledge of French with a meticulous study of works by such authors as he felt 'to be most excellent in the frenche tonge' (1, fo. xxi$^{v}$). Among these we encounter the names of Jean Lemaire de Belges (1473–*c.*1520), Jean Meschinot (*c.*1420–91), Guillaume Alexis (d. 1486), Alain Chartier (*c.*1385–1433) and Jean Froissart (*c.*1333–*c.*1410). He refers to specific works he has studied closely, such as Jean Lemaire de Belges's *Epître de l'amant vert* or his *Illustrations des Gaules*, or Alain Chartier's *Quadrilogue*, or the *Roman de la rose*, for, as we shall see, his command of the French language had a historical dimension. Occasionally, he quotes from these works, but in most cases he assumes the role of an observant language recorder, specifying which forms are used by which French author. The role of the linguistic observer and interpreter permeates the whole *Lesclarcissement*, and in the French vocabulist it becomes most prominent in the stereotyped phrase 'I finde . . .'. In performing his task in a scholarly way, basing the description of French on a detailed study of 'good' French literary works, Palsgrave gave his work unparalleled authority. With this methodological approach he was simply generations ahead of his age, but no doubt this working method is one of the reasons why the completion of *Lesclarcissement de la langue francoyse* took so long.

When a living language has been little studied, so that few clerics, scholars, or schoolmasters have jotted down their analyses, where is one to start in describing it? One has to observe and study language use and deduce from it regular occurrences, patterns, rules. Rules explain its functioning, and, if explicitly formulated, they will assist and accelerate the learning process. Reducing French to rules is exactly what Palsgrave regards as the joint achievement of his fellow authors Barclay, Valence, and du Wes, and himself. Here is what he says in the *Authours Epistell to the kynges grace*:

> If any one of vs all/ whiche syns ẏ begynnyng of your said well fortuned raygne of this thyng haue written/ or we all amongest vs/ haue by our diligent labours nowe at the last/ brought the frenche tong vnder any rules certayn ⁊ preceptz grãmaticall/ lyke as the other thre ꝑfite tõges be/ we haue nat onely done the thyng whiche by your noble graces progenitours/ of all antiquite so moche hath ben desyred/ that besydes all other maner polycies by them essayd/ whiche myght serue to the aduaũcement and fordrance of that purpose/ they neuer cessed to encorage suche clerkes as were in theyr tymes/ to proue and essay what they by theyr dyligence in this matter myght do. (A iii$^{v}$)

But this is not all. Just as Palsgrave had related the structure of his work to Gaza's Greek grammar, so he put his scholarly achievement in the context of a great contemporary Frenchman's work: Geofroy Tory de Bourges and his *Champ fleury auquel est contenu lart et science de la deue et vraye proportion des lettres*, published in Paris in 1529. Tory's major contribution to the French language, such as the introduction of the *accent aigu* and the *ç*, is well known. Ferdinand Brunot (and with him Gustave Cohen, who has produced the modern edition of the *Champ fleury* (Cohen 1931)) has stressed that Tory's work has much more comprehensive merits, especially with respect to French dialectology.

Palsgrave was familiar with the *Champ fleury* and the concern voiced by Tory with respect to the state of his mother tongue:

> O Deuotz Amateurs de bonnes Lettres. Pleust a Dieu que quelque Noble cueur semployast a mettre & ordõner par Reigle nostre Lãgage Francois . . . Sil ny est mys & ordonne/ on trouuera que de Cinquante Ans en Cinquante Ans la langue Francoise, pour la plus grande part, sera changee & peruerte. Le Langage dauiourd-huy est change en mille facons du Langage qui estoit il y a Cinquante Ans ou enuiron . . . (Tory 1529: Aux Lecteurs)

'Mettre & ordõner par Reigle' the French language was what Palsgrave claimed he and his fellow writers had achieved: 'we haue here within the lymitz of your most fortunat obeyssance and domynions/ done the thynge whiche by the testimony of the excellent clerke/ maister Geffray Troy de Bourges . . . in his boke intituled Champ Fleury/ was neuer yet amongest them of that contrayes selfe hetherto so moche as ones effectually attempted' (A iii$^{v}$).

Tory himself did not produce the grammar of French he so fervently wished to see realized, but he excelled in describing how French was spoken in the different regional areas of France, and, in doing so, he provided a most valuable picture of sixteenth-century

French dialects. He includes in the prefatory matter to the *Champ fleury* an extensive table of authors referred to in the book. In it Palsgrave discovered the names of those writers he had made the linguistic basis of his description of French (see A iii$^{v}$-iiii). Finding his choice thus confirmed by an outstanding contemporary Frenchman, he could not but highlight this in the *Authours Epistell*, for it lent still greater authority to his work.

As we have seen from the passages quoted, Palsgrave includes Barclay, Valence, and du Wes in his claim to have brought the French tongue under certain rules and precepts, thus fully recognizing his debt to his predecessors. This did not prevent him from voicing his criticism when he disagreed with a point made by any of them. A case in point is his outspoken criticism of Barclay's treatment of the consonant *k* (1, fo. xii$^{v}$). Yet it is very unlikely that any of his named predecessors would have appreciated Palsgrave's assessment of their joint efforts. The prevailing teaching method for a vernacular advocated long and persistent exercise in the speaking and reading of the language. The common belief was that it was impossible to 'reduce a vernacular to rules', and, since little credence was given to rules that were rarely observed, learning rules by heart was regarded as interfering with the natural way. This widely held view is amply reflected in du Wes's little-disguised attack on Palsgrave. Though mostly written before 1530, du Wes's *An Introductorie for to lerne and to rede to pronounce/ and to speke Frenche trewly* was not printed before 1532, which gave du Wes enough time to make his view of *Lesclarcissement de la langue francoyse* publicly known (A ii$^{v}$-iii). Palsgrave had not only sinned against the widely held opinions of scholars, clerics, schoolmasters, and educationalists; he had also committed the linguistic crime of having the audacity to reduce another nation's mother tongue to rules and principles. The age during which the European vernaculars were beginning to emancipate themselves was not yet ready to accept that what generations of writers and grammarians had done for Greek, Latin, and Hebrew—describe the functioning of these languages—could and would be achieved for the vernaculars. Individual authors like Geofroy Tory in France or, years later, Richard Mulcaster in England called for vernacular grammars and dictionaries to be compiled, but, in general, their voices remained unheard for a long time. Moreover, the fact that the first comprehensive linguistic description of French was so successfully undertaken by an Englishman remains something with which French scholarship has not always felt at ease. In this context, Hausmann's factual assessment and position, which corrects the balance and gives credit to the individual scholar's achievement, is particularly welcome: 'nous avons, en ce qui concerne la grammaire française, trois "premières": la première grammaire du français (rédigée en anglais), la première grammaire française (rédigée en latin) et enfin la première grammaire française rédigée en français!' (Hausmann 1980*a*: 133).

## THE TREATMENT OF FRENCH PRONUNCIATION

As one might have expected, none of the early treatments of French pronunciation that have come down to us could avoid attempting to describe what the author assumed to be general tendencies or rules in the pronunciation of French. The common feature in the characterization of French pronunciation in such treatises as the *Tractatus orthographiae* by T.H., the student of Paris, the *Tractatus orthographiae* by M. T. Coyfurelly, and the *Orthographia gallica*, as well as in Barclay, Valence, Palsgrave, and du Wes, is that pronunciation is seen in its relation to spelling. Usually, a distinction is made between three types of letters: vowels, semi-vowels (*i* and *u*), and consonants. These are then described in more detail, but the actual phenomena singled out and their order of presentation vary greatly from work to work. In a number of cases elision is mentioned—as, for example, by du Wes, who deals with it in his third rule (B. ij.). The rule, like the others, is illustrated by examples, but the value of du Wes's treatment of pronunciation has been well summarized by Ch. Thurot: 'Il donne sept règles de prononciation . . . qui ne nous aprennent pas grand' chose' (1881–3/1966: i, p. xxvi). Thurot credits Palsgrave with having formulated 'Les règles de prononciation les plus anciennes que nous possédions' (ibid. 13), but he may have been unaware of both T.H.'s and Canon Coyfurelly's *Tractatus orthographiae*, made accessible in editions in 1910 and 1879. The same holds for the *Orthographia gallica*, edited by Stürzinger in 1884. Yet he is right when he regards the first book of *Lesclarcissement de la langue francoyse* as 'le traité le plus développé sur la matière qui ait été composé avant le XVII^e^ siècle' (ibid.). The superior quality of descriptive depth and comprehensiveness in Palsgrave's treatment of French pronunciation can be illustrated with the letter/sound *H*. In T.H.'s *Tractatus orthographiae* which was composed around 1300, *H* is described as follows:

> *H* vero non est litera set aspiracionis nota, ut in hiis diccionibus: ***heitez, haiez, huis, hors, hounte, honye, hopeland, herd, harde, aherder***, in quibus *h* semper sonabitur, set in hiis diccionibus ***huit, huie, hier, heyer, heur, hostiller, he, helas, honour*** in istis *h* non debet asspirari et sic de huius modi. (Pope 1910: 190)

Coyfurelly's description, which is based on T.H.'s *Tractatus orthographiae*, reads as follows:

*H* vero non est litera, sed aspirationis nota, ut in hiis diccionibus: ***huis***, ***hors***, ***hounte***, ***hony***, ***hault***, ***hopelande***, ***herde*** a ***herder***, ***Jehan***, ***hard***, in quibus *h* semper sonabitur. Sed in hiis diccionibus: ***hinc*** (?), ***huy***, ***hier***, ***heure***, ***le hostel***, ***helas***, ***huisseux***, ***regehir***, *h* non debet aspirari et sic de huiusmodi. (Stengel 1879: 17)

Alexander Barclay, in his *Introductory*, has the following to say:

H. is no letter but a tokyn of asperacion or sharpynge of a worde, as in these wordes, hors, out, dehors, without, honte, shame, haut, hye, *and* in other lyke in whiche wordes and lyke .h. is sounded. other wordes be in whiche .h. is wryten and not soundyd as here. an houre, helas, alas, ho*m*me. a man, w*ith* other lyke. (Ellis 1871*a*: 809)

The similarities are evident. The oldest text, T.H.'s, is the fullest and has the longest list of examples. Canon Coyfurelly did not take over all the examples and at the same time added new ones: ***hault***, ***Jehan***, ***huisseux***, and ***regehir***, two of them showing *h* in non-initial position. Barclay further reduced the lists of his predecessors.

We do not know whether Palsgrave was familiar with the little treatises by the Paris student and the canon and doctor of law from Orleans, but the circumspection and care he took in compiling his book strongly suggest that he was. *Lesclarcissement de la langue francoyse* includes two passages which make it clear that he knew old manuscripts on the subject. Assessing Barclay's booklet, he stresses:

I haue sene an olde boke written in parchement in maner in all thynges like to his sayd Introductory: whiche/ by coniecture/ was nat vnwritten this hundred yeres. I wot nat if he happened to fortune vpon suche an other: for whan it was commaunded that the grãmar maisters shulde teche te youth of Englande ioyntly latin with frenche/ there were diuerse suche bokes diuysed: whervpon/ as I suppose began one great occasyon why we of Englade soũde the latyn tong so corruptly/ whiche haue as good a tonge to sounde all maner speches ꝑfitely/ as any other nacyon in Europa. (1, fo. xii$^{v}$–xiii)

What then did Palsgrave make of the descriptions of French *h* that had been attempted before him? Here is what he has to say:

The soundynge of this letter h/ whan he hath his aspiracion/ and whan he hath it nat/ and what is ment by aspiration. Cap. xx.

C This letter h/ where he is written in frenche wordes/ hath somtyme suche a soũde as we vse to gyue hym in these wordes in our tong/ haue/ hatred/ hens/ hart/ hurt/ hobby/ and suche lyke: and than he hath his aspiration/ and somtyme he is written in frenche wordes/ ⁊ hath no soũde at all/ no more than he hath with vs in these wordes/ honest/ honour/ habundaunce/ habitacion/ and suche like: in whiche h is written/ and nat sounded with vs. whiche thynge also happenneth in the frenche tonge in all suche wordes as be deducted out of latin wordes/ whiche be written with h/ and sounde hym nat in that tong/ as in these wordes ***habit***, ***hérbe***, ***homicíde***, ***hóste***, ***húmble***, the h shall nat haue his aspiration: for the latin wordes that they come of/ though they writte h sounde it nat/ as apereth by *habitus*, *herba*, *homicida*, *hospes*, *humilis*, and so of all suche other. (1, fo. vii)

Palsgrave explains the phenomenon of *h aspiré* by drawing the learner's attention to the similar situation in his mother tongue: in English too, initial *h* is pronounced in some words and in others it is not. He illustrates both types of pronunciation with French and English examples. But he does not stop there: he provides an explanation for those words in which *h* is not pronounced. They are derived from Latin, in which *h* was not pronounced. He thus gives his treatment of *h* a historic perspective. Having first outlined the dual

TABLE 2.1. *Initial aspiration of* h *in French words*

| | | | | |
|---|---|---|---|---|
| H ante a. | hardý | H ante e. | hÿérre | hovssér |
| | hardillón | | hýre | hovssévre |
| Háche | harénc | Heaúlme | | hovx |
| hachér | harengiére | hemée | | |
| hachét | haréngve | helás | H ante o. | |
| hacqvenée | hariás | hennýr | | H ante v. |
| háye | haricót | heraúlt | hobér | |
| háyne | hariér | herbergiér | hobreáv | hván |
| hayneúx | harnoýs | hérce | hobbýn | húche |
| haÿr | haró | hercér | hochette | huchér |
| háyre | hárpe | hercié | hocqvetón | huchiér |
| hayt | harpýe | herciér | hoyáv | hucqve |
| haytÿér | harpóy | hérdre | hollétte | huée |
| haytÿé | hart | hericón | hongnér | huér |
| hále | hasárt | herissón | honnýr | hviboúst |
| halebarde | háste | herissér | hónte | hviér |
| halér | hastér | herón | hovrs | humér |
| halettér | haterél | hérpe | hontér | húne |
| hallér | hastereáv | héstre | hótte | húppe |
| hamassón | hatíf | hévre **a boris** | hovllér | huppér |
| hameáv | havbáns | **heed.** | hóve | húre |
| hameúx | havberión | hevrt | hovér | hurlér |
| hanáp | havbért | hevrtér | hovlétte | hurtér |
| hánche | háue | hévse | hóvppe | hurtebillér |
| hanettón | háure | hevsér | hovppe-lánde | hutýn |
| hánte | hãnýr | | hóvrt | heurt |
| hantér | havít | | hovs | hutynér |
| hantíse | haultévr | H ante i. | hovseáv | |
| happér | hazárd | | hovsétte | |
| harás | hazardér | hybóv | hovspaillér | |
| harcellér | | hydévx | hóvsse | |

character of *h* in French, he then goes on to specify which is the regular pronunciation and which the exception: in general, *h* is not sounded in French. In order to help the learner he then provides a list of those French words in which initial *h* is aspirated. The list is headed by a further rule stating that *h* in proper names is sounded, as in *Henry*, *Huét*, *Húges*. The list is arranged alphabetically, and, as we can see from Table 2.1, it is of a totally different order from those of his predecessors. Having discussed the basic sound values for the letter *h*—no correspondence in sound or *h* aspiré—and equipped the learner with a list of words that sound the *h*, Palsgrave then proceeds to more specialized issues. This is the general pattern adopted in the description of letter/sound correspondences. First an attempt is made to establish the basic value and then this is formulated as a rule, with a discussion of special or more complex cases. Palsgrave's next rule for *h* deals with what happens when an item from this list becomes the basis of a word-formation process: 'it is to be noted/ that nat only these wordes aboue rehersed giue ther h his aspiration but also all the wordes/ whiche after the formation of verbes in the frenche tonge be deriued of them' (1, fo. vii^v). In the cases of prefixation and compounding where a free morpheme is premodifying the basic *h*-word, *h* is no longer word-initial. The treatment of *h* is thus expanded to cover the cases in which *h* occurs in the second or later syllable of the word:

[1] Whan so euer composicion is made with any of these wordes aboue rehersed ⁊ the preposiciōs in the frenche tong/ the *h* shall kepe his aspiration styll/ as in these wordes *ahontér, dehontér, enhantér, enhazardér, dehovsér, dehórs* . . .

[2] Also whan so euer suche a worde is compoūde with any preposicion as soūdeth his h in latine. or whan so euer h is written in the mean sillables/ nat cōmyng before a perfect worde of the frenche tong/ but onely beyng a part of a worde/ in all suche wordes h shall haue his aspiratiō. Example of suche wordes/ where the latine worde kepeth his aspiratiō/ as *enhortér, adherénce, comprehensión*. Example where h is writtē afore a syllable onely or .ii. whiche be of no signification/ as *trahýr, esbahír, behóvrs, chathván, bahús*, and suche lyke/ in all whiche h shall haue his aspiration.

[3] But whan there is cōposicion made of prepositions/ and suche wordes as haue h written for the kepyng of true orthographie/ bycause the latine worde is written with h/ and yet in frenche they sounde hym nat/ all suche wordes comyng in composition/ leaue theyr h vnsoūded also/ as *enhabitér, surhahunder, deshonéste*, and all suche lyke. (1, fo. viii)

I have dwelt in some detail on Palsgrave's description of *h* to bring out the contrast between his treatment and that of his predecessors. With Palsgrave we enter a totally different world of linguistic analysis: an attempt is made to embrace the language phenomenon under investigation in its entirety as well as in its many aspects, to differentiate between its various manifestations, to describe them and their interrelations, and to interpret the linguistic facts. Research on his contribution to the description of sixteenth-century French pronunciation (see especially Ellis 1871*a*; Lütgenau 1880; Thurot 1881–3/1966; Brunot 1906/1967) has concentrated on his accounts of individual sounds and words, sound-spelling relations, and sound sequences. These have been studied, together with other sources, to establish the historical development of French pronunciation, and their accuracy as well as their progressive or conservative nature have been discussed. Yet this scholarly assessment will have to be complemented by taking into account another aspect of his work which is at least equally essential: his superb overall grasp of French pronunciation as such compared to other phonological systems (for instance, English, his mother tongue), and his meticulously systematic presentation.

The basic parts of book I, which deals with pronunciation, are a brief introduction, a detailed list of contents, and the description itself. Palsgrave begins with a general articulatory and acoustic characterization of French pronunciation. What strikes non-native learners when they hear French, what is it that they have to notice and to practise to sound 'French'? For Palsgrave, the French 'in theyr pronunciation do chefly regarde and couet thre thynges'. These are:

1. 'To be armonyous in theyr spekyng' (*The Introduction of the authour*, A [vi$^v$]). The most characteristic feature of French pronunciation is *nasalization*. Being 'harmonious in their speaking' is explained as follows:

   they vse one thyng which none other nation dothe/ but onely they/ that is to say/ they make a maner of modulation inwardly/ for they forme certayne of theyr vowelles in theyr brest/ and suffre nat the soũde of them to passe out by the mouthe/ but to assende frõ the brest straight vp to ẙ palate of the mouth/ and so by reflection yssueth the sounde of them by the nose. (ibid).

   L. Geschiere (1968: 182) has rightly pointed out that Palsgrave is the first writer to have described the pronunciation of the nasalized vowels in French. He discusses the contribution which Palsgrave's description makes to a better understanding of the origin and development of the phonological opposition between nasalized and non-nasalized vowels in French.

2. 'To be brefe and sodayne in soundyng of theyr wordes/ auoydyng all maner of harshnesse in theyr proñciation' (*The Introduction of the authour*, A [vi$^v$]). The feature which Palsgrave is trying to capture is that French *consonants in consonant clusters tend not to be all sounded.* Here is his explanation:

what consonantes so euer they write in any worde for the kepyng of trewe orthographie/ yet so moche couyt they in redyng or spekyng to haue all theyr vowelles and diphthongʒ clerly herde/ that betwene two vowellʒ whether they chaunce in one worde alone/ or as one worde fortuneth to folowe after an other/ they neuer sounde but one consonant atones/ in so moche that if two different cõsonantes/ that is to say/ nat beyng both of one sorte come together betwene two vowelles/ they leue the fyrst of them vnsounded/ and if thre consonantes come together/ they euer leue two of the fyrst vnsoũded/ puttyng here as I haue sayd no difference whether the consonantes thus come together in one worde alone/ or as the wordes do folowe one another/ for many tymes theyr wordes ende in two consonantes/ bycause they take awaye the last vowell of the laten worde/ as *Corps*/ cõmeth of *Corpus*/ *Temps*/ of *Tempus*/ and suche lyke/ whiche two consonantes shalbe lefte vnsounded/ if the next worde folowyng begyn with a consonant/ as well as if thre cõsonantes shuld fortune to come together in a worde by hym selfe. (ibid.: B i$^{v}$–B ii)

Exceptions to this tendency are given. By pointing out this second feature, that there is a lack of correspondence between the spelling and the sounding of consonants in French, Palsgrave hoped to help the 'hunderdes in this realme/ whiche with a lytell labour employed and by the ayde of latyn/ do so parfytly vnderstande this tonge/ that they be able to translate at the fyrst syght/ any thyng out of the frenche tong/ in to ours/ yet haue they thought ẏͤ thing so strange to leue the consonantes vnsounded/ whiche they sawe written in suche bokes as they studyed/ that they haue vtterly neglected the frenche mẽnes maner of pronunciation/ and so rede frenche as theyr fantasy or opinion dyde lede them' (ibid.).

3. 'to gyue euery worde that they abyde and reste vpon/ theyr most audible soũde' (ibid.: A [vi$^{v}$]). The third characteristic feature of French pronunciation, as the explanation reveals, is the position of the *accent on the last syllable*. Palsgrave here contrasts French, Greek and Latin:

where as in the Greke tong/ the accent hath thre dyuers places/ that is to say/ the last syllable/ the last saue one/ and the thyrde syllable from the ende/ and in the latin tong/ at the leest hath twayne/ that is to say/ the last syllable saue one/ or the thyrde syllable from thende/ the frenche men iudgyng a worde to be most parfaytly herde/ whan his last end is sounded hyghest/ vse generally to gyue theyr accent vpon the last syllable onely/ except whan they make modulation inwardly . . . (ibid.)

Among the exceptions to this rule are words whose last syllable ends in *e*. In such cases 'the syllable next afore him must haue the accent/ and yet is nat this rule euer generall/ for if a frenche worde ende in Te/ or haueʒ/ after E/ or be a preterit partyciple of the fyrst coniugation/ he shall haue his accent vpon ẏͤ last syllable' (ibid., B ii^v). The descriptive basis is obviously the final *e* which carries stress only in the surroundings *-té* (as in *bonté, fierté*), *-ez* (as in the second person plural, present tense, e.g. *allez, tenez*), or as past participle (*allé, travaillé*). Yet Palsgrave is aware not only of word stress but also of sentence stress and the fact that this overrules the former. For, though he maintains on the one hand that the French tend to give every word its most audible sound, he also draws attention to the fact that

> there is no worde of one syllable whiche with them hath any accent/ or that they vse to pause vpon/ and that is one great cause why theyr tong semeth to vs so brefe and sodayn and so harde to be vnderstãded whan it is spoken/ especially of theyr paysantes or cõmen people/ for thoughe there come neuer so many wordes of one syllable together/ they pronouce them nat distinctly a sonder as the latines do/ but sounde them all vnder one voyce and tenour/ and neuer rest nor pause vpon any of them/ except the cõmyng next vnto a poynt be the cause therof. (ibid.)

How did a scholar, long before the era of phonological theory, bring order into the bewildering mass of pronunciation facts he was to record? The distinction between letter and sound was not yet generally made. The letter alphabet therefore served as an organizational thread after a first differentiation between vowels and consonants. We have this basic ordering pattern in the orthographic treatises and in Barclay's *Introductory*. Palsgrave uses it, too. His superior intellectual grasp manifests itself fully in the overall coverage and, particularly, in the systematic and consistent execution. In addition, he incorporated into this basic structuring pattern generalizations on accent, vowel quantity, and prosody, progressing from smaller linguistic units (syllables) to bigger ones (words, phrases, sentences). The description of the consonants, for instance, is preceded by four chapters outlining the pronunciation of French consonants in general, as they occur, in the first, the middle, and the last syllable of a word. After all the consonants have been described, we have a number of chapters on the 'trewe redyng of french wordes', tackling elision phenomena which affect pronunciation as well as spelling. From there we proceed to a discussion of stress and its position in French. He describes stress as follows: 'Accent in the frenche tonge is a lyftinge vp of the voyce/ vpon some wordes or syllables in a sentence/ aboue the resydue of the other wordes or syllables in the same sentence/ so that what soeuer worde or syllable as they come toguyder in any sentence/ be sownded higher than the other wordes or syllables in the same sentence vpon them/ is the accent' (I, fo. xviii). There is a special chapter (ch. lix) on words 'whiche in writtynge by lyke/ and by reason of dyuerse accent haue diuerse significations'. We know from the early textbooks and word lists that have been preserved that the differentiation of homonyms was a traditional topic in the teaching of Latin. Two of the four manuscripts of the *Orthographica gallica*, MS Ee. 4.20 in the University Library of Cambridge, and MS 188 in Magdalene College, Oxford, contain a list of French words which differ in spelling but are said to be similar in pronunciation (Stürzinger 1884: 14–15; see also Génin 1852: 30–3).

By contrasting and listing items differentiated by stress, Palsgrave joins the pedagogical tradition and draws the learner's attention to this particular area. Following the Latin tradition (or else drawing on his experience as a teacher), he not only lists the items concerned, as did the author of the *Orthographia gallica*, but matches them with translation equivalents. He uses the acute accent to indicate the position of the stress:

*peché* syn—*péche* a peche a kynde of fruite
*costé* a syde—*cóste* a rybbe
*pasté* a pasty—*páste* paaste to baake with
*fossé* a dytche aboute a towne—*fósse* a pytte
*conté* an erledome—*cónte* an erle
*cúre* a cure a personage—*curé* a curate a parson
*bále* a bale of any marchandise—*balé* a bales of a precioustone
*márche* a bondes or a marke betwene contrey ⁊ cõtrey—*marché* a bargen or a marketstede or cheepe, as good cheepe *bon marchié*
*parenté* a kyndred—*parénte* a kynswoman
*clére* cleere—*cleré* clary a kynde of wyne
*pére* a father—*peré* pery a kynde of drynke
*pie* a pye byrde—*pié* a foote, whiche I wolde writte *pied*
*plánche* a planke a brydge—*planché* the florth of any thyng that is bourded
*ápres* sharpe *in plurali*—*aprés* afterwarde
*fille* a daughter—*fillé* a spyndel with threde vpon it, or a haye for coonys (I, fo. xix)

In the concluding sections of book I, Palsgrave puts all his abstract rules and generalizations into practice. He quotes four passages from those French authors whom he regards as the 'most excellent in the frenche tongue' (Alain Chartier, Jean Lemaire de Belges, and the thirteenth century Guillaume de Lorris), two samples in prose and two samples in verse. Under each line of text he gives a transcription of the pronunciation, so that the learners can practise the reading of the text for themselves. Palsgrave repeatedly stresses the usefulness of *Lesclarcissement* for self-study purposes. I do not know of any other language treatise before 1530 in which the author attempts to transcribe French pronunciation. Here is the first line of Alain Chartier's *Quadrilogue* and its transcription to illustrate Palsgrave's 'transcription system':

*A la tres haulte et excellente maieste des princes*
Alatrehåutoeevzsellåntomaiestédeprínsos

Palsgrave was, of course, aware that learners would have difficulties in understanding a transcribed text that looked like an endless unreadable string of symbols. The first such transcribed passage is therefore followed by detailed explanations, taking up individual points that might have startled learners. They cannot all be discussed here, but some may suffice to show their quality. Why is the transcription an uninterrupted string with no indication of word-division? This is meant to reflect 'the brefnesse that the frenche tonge vseth in soundyng of theyr wordes/ whiche in redynge and spekynge neuer cesse or pause/ tyl they come at suche worde/ where the poynt shulde be' (I, fo. xxii$^{v}$). The *s* of *tres* does not appear in the transcription 'bycause that h/ hauyng his aspiration hath the power of a consonant'. The *l* in *hault* 'is left vnwritten/ to declare/ that l/ so comyng before a nother consonant/ is left with them vnsoũded'. Why a sign over the *a* of *haut*? There 'is a stryke aboue the hed of au/ bycause the accent of yͤ worde is there'. And, finally, we note the explanation of an *o* after *haut*: 'the e of haulte is written like an o/ bycause that e/ beynge the last letter shalbe sounded almost like an o/ and moche in the noose'. The o is thus Palsgrave's attempt at transcribing a *schwa*-sound. Each explanation is followed by a cross-reference to that section in book I where the phenomenon is described in detail.

In the analysis, interpretation, and description of individual sounds and such things as phonotactic aspects, a sixteenth-century scholar like Palsgrave was bound to err from time to time. His methodological thoroughness and consistency, and his pedagogical presentation, however, are exemplary.

## THE TREATMENT OF FRENCH GRAMMAR

It is for these characteristics that he has been repeatedly praised by scholars assessing his achievement for French grammar. And, also repeatedly, they have expressed their regret that his example was not followed. In 1848 Francis Wey wrote in his *Histoire des révolutions du langage en France*:

Palsgrave, exception brillante au milieu de nos grammatistes, ou plutôt grammatophobes, a tracé un tableau limpide et suffisamment complet de la langue française au seizième siècle. Ce traité, à considérer chaque œuvre isolément dans son siècle, est à la fois la première et la plus essentiellement française de nos grammaires; un modèle à consulter et à suivre encore aujourd'hui.

Le livre de Jean Palsgrave, dirigé par une méthode solide, indépendante et claire, eût dû servir de modèle à nos grammairiens, qui n'en eurent souci, et procédèrent d'un principe tout opposé. Or celui de Palsgrave était juste. Son but était d'enseigner notre langue à ceux qui l'ignorent: nos Français ont, dans leurs travaux, supposé le problème résolu, et disserté sur la grammaire française en vue des savants contemporains, et à seule fin de prouver qu'ils entendaient le latin, le grec, l'hébreu même, autant qu'hommes de France. (Wey 1848: 262, 275)

A similar assessment was made by H. Breitinger (1868: 2, 3) when he contrasted Palsgrave's method as a linguistic observer, collector, interpreter, and recorder with that of his contemporaries whose preoccupations with the ideals of Latin and Greek grammar precluded them from looking at the French language in an unprejudiced way. And another German scholar, Johann Wildermuth (1857: 38), argued that descriptions of French grammar would have been thorough, comprehensive, and scholarly if grammarians had followed Palsgrave's lead.

The fact that Palsgrave was an Englishman and not a native speaker of French meant that he had had, of course, to learn the language himself. We have seen that, at the time when he will have gone through this practical stage of learning French, there were extremely few textbooks in existence. During his language-acquisition process, he will thus have had to make his own generalizations from the French he heard around him and from the French he encountered in the works of good French authors. His study in Paris had clearly exposed him to the French language for some years. His knowledge of Latin and Greek will have helped him in understanding and analysing a living language, at least to the extent of providing him with some kind of grammatical framework. The various references to, and comparisons between, French, Latin, and Greek in *Lesclarcissement* suggest that concrete experience will have shown him where the Latin and Greek language systems were of no help, and where he had to start making his own analyses and generalizations of French. Practical experience in the endeavour to master the French language will thus have been at the basis of what has been referred to as his break with tradition. L. Kukenheim's comparative study on the history of grammar in Italy, Spain, and France during the Renaissance period is of interest in this connection. In discussing the distinction of parts of speech, he draws attention to Palsgrave's progressive position: 'Les grammairiens français se recommandent, comme leur confrères en Italie et en Espagne, des auteurs classiques, avec cette différence qu'ils suivent leur antiques de plus près. Et—chose remarquable—celui qui écrit la première grammaire sérieuse, un Anglais, se montre indépendant de la tradition . . .' (Kukenheim 1932: 100). So too, in his *Recherches sur le français des XV^e^ et XVI^e^ siècles et sur sa codification par les théoriciens de l'époque*, one of the most thorough studies of

Palsgrave's contribution to French grammar, Sven Gösta Neumann writes: 'Palsgrave fut le premier, en ce qui concerne le français vulgaire, à rompre avec ce préjugé si répandu parmi les grammairiens scolastiques du moyen âge et parmi beaucoup d'humanistes de la Renaissance, et cela constitue peut-être son plus grand mérite . . .' (Neumann 1959: 21).

What we then have in Palsgrave's grammar (books II and III) is a description of grammar that follows classical tradition to a certain degree, and, at the same time, breaks away from it when linguistic facts call for a different approach. All this has added to the adequacy of his treatment and prompted the highest praise from Francis Wey: 'son *Esclarcissement de la langue francoyse* . . . est, parmi toutes nos grammaires, la seule d'après laquelle on puisse se représenter la situation, les allures et la physionomie du langage, au temps où elle a été écrite. Les autres sont fixes, décõbrées, immobiles comme des corps morts; parcequ'elles furent façonnées sur le modèle d'une langue morte' (Wey 1848: 274).

Let us now look at Palsgrave's description of French grammar in more detail. If we compare Palsgrave's grammar part again with the work of his predecessors such as du Wes, we are immediately struck by the more thorough analysis, the more comprehensive grasp and treatment, but, most of all, by the clearer and more consistent structure of the grammatical framework. In Pierre Valence's *Introductions* and Giles du Wes's *Introductorie* one looks in vain for an ordering principle. Valence, for instance, first deals with the tenses and forms of the verb, then with negation, pronouns, questions, impersonal verbs, irregular verbs, demonstratives, adverbs, and so on. Du Wes's grammar section begins with pronouns, after which the author discusses prepositions, conjunctions, adverbs, and finally the verb with its tenses and forms. In the eyes of their authors both these books were conceived as introductions to the study of French, and the presentation seems to be made up of unsystematic and arbitrary changes from one grammatical topic to another. Palsgrave impresses us with the systematical approach of his treatment. As Kukenheim has shown (1932: 143), most Renaissance grammarians of the vernaculars were influenced by the Latin grammarians, few by Greek sources—as, for instance, Antonio de Nebrija and John Palsgrave. As we have seen, Palsgrave tells us in the *Authours Epistell* that he followed 'the order of Theodurus Gaza/ in his grãmer of the Greke tonge' (A iii). His reason for comparing the external structure of *Lesclarcissement* to that of Gaza's grammar may have been less the fact that Gaza, too, had added a third book to his grammar than to impart more authority to his work (Chevalier 1968: 135; Padley 1985–

8: ii. 357–8). Gaza's Greek grammar was very highly considered at the time, and had, as J.-C. Chevalier (1968: 66–70) has shown, six reprints during 1511–31 in Paris alone. In England, it was referred to in the works of such eminent scholars of Greek and Latin as Thomas Linacre. Linacre was the king's physician, and Palsgrave's quoting of Gaza may reflect the high esteem in which the latter's work was held in court circles.

Grammar, as we have seen, is dealt with in three places, in each of the three books of *Lesclarcissement*. This is not to be taken as an indication of Palsgrave's preoccupation with the number three and its mystique believed to be working in the French language (*The Introduction of the authour*, B [i]). The many specific cross-references between these three books make it clear that the original first two books had been revised, and that the distribution of the grammatical description over three books manifests the pedagogical concern shared by many authors of early grammatical works. They begin with *rudimenta* for the beginning student and then the subsequent, more detailed treatment takes up and expands the issues of the rudiments, in the order of the elementary introduction.[12] Palsgrave clearly differentiated between different types of learners and their needs (ibid.: C v$^{v}$).

The introduction to the second 'book' in book I, which we may regard as the grammatical *rudimenta* of *Lesclarcissement*, is divided into two parts. The first is a brief outline of the grammar in the order in which it will be dealt with; the second is called 'Of the differences of Phrasys betvene our tong and the frenche tong', in which the author gives an ingenious characterization of the main grammatical differences between English and French as perceived by a native speaker of English.

The structural basis of Palsgrave's grammar of French is the grammatical framework then commonly used in Latin grammars. As with Donatus in his *Ars minor*, the *partes accidentes* are described for each part of speech. Contrary to the Latin tradition, Palsgrave does not, however, distinguish eight parts of speech but nine. The normal eight were: *nomen*, *pronomen*, *verbum*, *adverbium*, *participium*, *coniunctio*, *praepositio*, and *interiectio*—that is, nouns and adjectives were not different word classes but subcategories of the noun class. Palsgrave's ninth word class is the article for which, as he tells us, he borrowed the name from the Greeks. Scholars have properly credited Palsgrave for this first clear perception and description of the definite and indefinite article in French (in this respect see also Julien 1988).

[12] It is of some interest to note that an analogous triple cycle is explicitly adopted in Quirk *et al.*'s grammar (1985).

Within the traditional order of the parts of speech, nouns and verbs were central. Where in this order would one expect Palsgrave to integrate his ninth part of speech? Close to the class of pronouns, because it functions like demonstrative pronouns? In fact, Palsgrave puts it at the head of the parts of speech, thus reflecting the fact that the article not only precedes the noun but that it is a noun-phrase element, and both article and noun are followed by the pronoun which functions as their substitute.

In the rudimentary introduction to French grammar in book I, the following parts of speech and accidents are distinguished:

- the article
- the noun substantive, gender, number, person,
- the noun adjective, gender, number, comparison,
- the pronouns, three types of declination
- the verb
- the participle.

As to grammatical tenses, W. Ayres-Bennett and J. Carruthers (1992: 223–4) have recently drawn attention to the occurrence of double compound forms in *Lesclarcissement.* In the first book there is no basic introduction to the adverb, the participle, the conjunction, the preposition, the interjection and their respective accidents. They are, however, addressed in the second part of the grammatical introduction to book II, the section which is called 'Of the differences of Phrasys betvene our tong and the frenche tong'. The chapter leading to it deals with questions of concord and thus provides a welcome link between morphology and more syntactical aspects. The overall grammatical comparison of English and French recalls Palsgrave's lucid characterization of French pronunciation for a foreign student. And, again, we are deeply impressed by this sixteenth-century English scholar's grasp of French grammar and his insights into its functioning. Here are some of his perspicacious observations. In English, nouns are semantically subclassified by premodifying the noun; in French the order is reversed: 'where as we adde any wordes for a difference to any substantyue we put the difference before/ and say a wynde myll/ a wedder cocke a fyer pan/ and suche lyke they torne the order contrary/ and adde this preposytion A/ as *Vng cochet au vent. Vng moulyn au vent. Vne poille a feu*' (*The Introduction of the authour*, C iiii$^{v}$).

As to adjectives, he draws the learner's attention to two striking differences between his mother tongue, English, and French. One is the position of the adjective with respect to the noun it modifies: 'Where we put our adiectiue before the substãtyue whan he is put to hym bycause of a difference/ ⁊ say a whyte hors/ a rounde cappe/ a long gowne/ they torne ẏͤ order and say *Vng cheual blanc. Vng bonet rond. Vne robbe longue*' (ibid., C iiii$^{v}$–C [v]). The other concerns comparison. John Barton in his *Donait francois*, the first attempt at writing a grammar of French, viewed the grammatical pattern as follows:

> Quantz degrés de comparison est il? Trois. Quelx? le positif, si come *bon, mauveis, bel, lait, haut, bas* et ainsi des aultres, le comparatif, si come *plus bon, plus mauveis, plus hault, plus bas* et . . . ainsi des aultres, le supellatif, si come *tres bon, tres mauveis* et ainsi des autres . . . Ci endroit il fault sçavoir que le comparatif en françois est le mesmes mot que est son positif ovecque cest mot *plus*, si come *plus bon, plus mauveis*; et le suppellatif est le mesmes mot que est son positif ovec cest mot *tres*, si come *tres bon, tres mauveis*. Mais quant on veult fair un excellent suppellatif, donque l'en ajoint cest mot *plus* ovec cest mot *tres* ou le positif, si come *tres plus bon, tres plus mauveis*. (Städtler 1988: 132)

Palsgrave is the first grammarian to recognize that the pattern is *plus* for the comparative and *le plus* for the superlative: 'also where as we make cõparison by addyng of certayne letters to the ende of our posytiues/ as whyte/whyter/whytest/blacke/blacker/blackest/ they kepe the adiectyue vnchanged/ and adde *Plus* or *le plus* before hym . . .' (*The Introduction of the authour*, C [v]).

With respect to the use of personal pronouns, he contrasts such sentences as *I loue hym—Ie le ayme; he beteth me—Il me bat; I defende her—Ie la deffens*. Thus, he says, the French put 'the pronowne of the accusatyue case before the verbe that gouerneth hym' (ibid.). He was also aware of differences in the use of the possessive pronoun. In certain sentence types in which the English use the possessive pronoun with a noun denoting a part of the body, the French have to use the personal pronoun as object and put the definite article before the part of the body concerned. Palsgrave explains the construction as follows:

> Also where as we vse our pronownes possessyues whan we betoken an acte or hurte to be done to a parson/ as he hath hurte my hande/ thou burnest thy here he shall breke his necke/ they torne the possessyue into his primityue ⁊ in his stede vse the article *Le*/ as *Il ma blesse la mayn. Tu te brusles les cheueulx. Il se rompera le col.* vsyng in the thyrde parson reciprocation/ which in this tong is moche more precisely vsed than in latin . . . (ibid.)

The last example from Palsgrave's insightful observations on major grammatical differences between the two languages concerns the use of the *ne explétif* in French:

> Whan they vse any aduerbe of comparation with *Que*/ folowynge hym sygnifiyng than/ theyr verbe must haue *Ne*/ before hym/ though we vse nat in our tong to put Nat/ before our verbe/ as for more than I say/ lesse than I deserue/ better than he

doth/ they say *Plus que ie ne dis/ moins que ie ne merite/ mieulx quil ne fait.* (ibid., C [v$^v$])

We now come to book II, which deals with grammar alone. I shall illustrate the more detailed treatment and its still greater specialization and comprehensiveness in book III with one example, the noun and one of its accidents. In book I, Palsgrave outlined three accidents for the substantive: gender, number, and person. In book II, he introduces and discusses three more: derivation (the fourth accident), composition (the fifth accident), and declination (the sixth accident). For the non-native speaker of French, gender is probably the most difficult aspect of the grammar of the noun. In the rudimentary introduction in book I, Palsgrave tells us something about gender in French (ibid., B iii$^v$-[iiii]).

He recognizes three genders in French, the masculine, the feminine, and the common gender which is both masculine and feminine. Which of these genders a noun takes depends on three factors: meaning, ending, or origin. A noun that betokens 'any name belõgyng onely to man/ or be ẙ name of any he beest/ or be the name of any tree' is of the masculine gender. The semantic classes are exemplified by *roy*, *cheual*, and *chesne*. A noun which betokens 'any name that belongeth onely to women/ or be ẙ name of any she beest/ or the name of any frute' is of the feminine gender as *royne*, *iument*, and *poyre*. Endings that cause the Frenchman to regard a noun as masculine 'be in a generalte all/ sauyng onely E/ so that if a substantiue in the frenche tong ende in any vowell/ diphthong/ or cõsonant/ except onely E/ he shalbe of the masculyne gender/ and the exceptions be but fewe as appereth in the secõde boke/ but chefly in the thyrde'. The corresponding rule of thumb for nouns ending in *-e* is that they are feminine. An exception to this rule are nouns ending in *-e* that 'cõe out of a latin substantyue endyng in vm' as *consile*, *edifice*, and *domicile*, which go back to Latin *consilium*, *edificium*, and *domicilium*. They are masculine. As to the common gender, we learn that there are only six nouns of this gender in French: *veufue*, *adultere*, *esclaue*, *guyde*, *garde*, and *hoste*.

In book II, gender, the first accident of nouns, is dealt with in one chapter taking up only about three-quarters of a page (II, fo. xxxi$^{r-v}$). What new insights are provided? The expansions on book I are:

1. The semantic class of nouns becomes more specified. The previous general class of names denoting men and women is broken down into such names as well as names for dignities, offices and crafts that are sex-specific.

2. The general rule on ending-related gender allocation is reformulated and refined:

   By reason of terminatiõ. for all other substãtiues/ whose gender can nat be knowen by his signification endyng in any vowel or diphthong/ except e. And also the most parte of substantiues endyng in any consonant/ be of the masculine gender/ except endyng in vowelles/ *mercý* and *uertú*, and in diphthonges *laý*, *peáv*, *foy*, and *loy*.

   In addition, nouns ending in a consonant may be feminine, but examples are not yet provided.

3. A fourth type of gender is introduced which Palsgrave calls 'doubtful gender'. The reason for it is that, apart from the six nouns of common gender, he finds a further 'sixe vsed of their auctours incertaynly/ sometyme as masculynes/ sometyme as femynines: and therfore I calle theym of the doutfull gendre'. We here have a clear instance of Palsgrave observing actual language use, recording it, and admitting that he cannot explain the findings.

In book III, the treatment of the gender of nouns assumes a different dimension: it is discussed in forty-nine chapters which amount to about nineteen pages. I shall outline the overall structure of this account and draw attention to the more interesting expansions, revealing Palsgrave's struggle to expose the semantic and orthographic/phonological rules that determine gender distribution in French.

There is an overall progression in content and coverage from book I to book II and book III inasmuch as the treatment becomes more detailed and specialized and more comprehensive at the same time. The categories distinguished previously are taken up again and more fully explained and exemplified. The linguistic analysis is pushed further and new categories are introduced. The more advanced description of French grammar in book III includes—and this is a distinguishing feature compared to books I and II—many interesting expositions and discussions of the language use in the French literary works read and consulted by Palsgrave.

All four gender classes are dealt with, and the only one for which there is a mere restating of the earlier account is the common gender. In a similar way, of the three factors regarded as determining gender distribution in French—meaning, ending, and word origin—the latter is not pursued any further, whereas the former two are explored at great length and in great detail. The order in which the various aspects of gender are tackled is as follows. The masculine and feminine gender are studied with respect to their semantic correlates.

Then the class which includes both the masculine and the feminine gender, common gender, is outlined, after which we have a full description of the so-called uncertain or doubtful gender. The last part is an extensive investigation into word endings and their influence on gender allocation.

Let us first look at Palsgrave's class of uncertain or doubtful gender and then at the semantic and formal conditions that may make a noun in French masculine or feminine. Whereas nouns of common gender like *guide* may be masculine or feminine according to the context of situation, nouns of uncertain gender, according to Palsgrave, are 'somtyme of the masculyne gendre and somtyme of the feminyne. And therfore I wyll nat take vpon me to name them of any certayne gendre, no more than suche as haue written grãmars in the latyn tonge do *Talpá* and *damá*, and .xxi. suche lyke/ whiche they haue therfore named *Dubii generis*' (III, fo. iiii[v]). He lists six such nouns: *affayre*, *evangille*, *mevrs*, *navire*, *val*, and *gent*, and justifies his description by providing text examples from French literature.

We come to meaning and its relation to gender in French. The three semantic groups of nouns distinguished so far were: (1) names for human beings with the subgroups (*a*) dignitaries, (*b*) office-holders, and (*c*) craftsmen; (2) male or female beasts; (3) trees and their fruit. The group of nouns based on natural sex (1) is extended further to include (*d*) nouns denoting 'kynred or cognation spirituall' as in *père/mère* and *parrain/marraine*. Palsgrave then focuses on the morphological relationship between nouns denoting male human beings and female ones. He describes a number of formal-semantic correlates and patterns, specifying the formal constraints as well as the meaning involved. Examples are:

| | |
|---|---|
| verb: | *broder*—derived noun in *-eur* m: *brodeur*<br>the feminine noun derived from it in *-esse* is *broderesse*;<br>similarly, *tenceur/tenceresse*. |
| *-ier/-ière*: | *coûturier/coûturière* |
| *-ois/oise:* | *François/Françoise* |
| *-art/-arde:* | *bastart/bastarde.* |

Further example pairs like '*compaignón* a man felowe/ *compaígne* a woman felowe' are added, of which he says that he 'can nat comprehende [them] vnder any generall rule' (III, fo. ii).

The line of argument is continued in group (2), which comprises animals. It is subdivided into (*a*) beasts, and (*b*) fowls, and for each group he enumerates items 'whiche haue a distyncte name for their male and another for their female', as for instance:

| | | | | | |
|---|---|---|---|---|---|
| | *Lyon* | a lyon | / | *lyonésse* | a lyonesse |
| | *cerf* | a harte | / | *byche* | a hynde |
| | *cheual* | a horse | / | *ivment* | a mare |
| and | *pan* | a pecocke | / | *pannésse* | a pehen |
| | *cocq* | a cocke | / | *geline* | a henne |
| | *gars* | a gander | / | *óÿe* | a goose. |

For the semantic group (3), trees and their fruit, some exceptions are given.

In addition, he singles out further semantic groups, all illustrated with examples: nouns denoting months (m), seasons (m), feasts (f), towns (f), big (m) and small (f) rivers. In the case of diminutives like *cheualét* and *maysonette* we have another semantic subgroup of nouns, but one which is based on a word-formational pattern. According to Palsgrave's rule, 'nownes dimynutiues folowe the gendre of the substãtyue that they be fourmed of' (III, fo. ii$^{\mathrm{v}}$).

If we go one step further with respect to grammaticalization, we get mere grammatical conversion: substantivized adjectives and infinitives like *le/mon possible*, *le/mon penser* to which Palsgrave rightly attributes the masculine gender.

The part that deals with meaning as a factor that influences gender in French concludes with a long alphabetical list of nouns which 'beyng all one in writyng/ by reason of their dyuers signification/ alter their gendre', as for example '*vng livre*, a boke to lerne on, *vne livre*, a pounde in weight or in money' (III, fo. iii$^{\mathrm{r-v}}$).

How far does the ending of a noun have a bearing on its gender? The possibly relevant letters/sounds discussed in the earlier books: a vowel, a diphthong, a consonant, *e* are taken up in this order and systematically investigated. Palsgrave's unparalleled analytic understanding of French and his mastery in describing it manifest themselves again in the systematic way in which he observes the object of his investigation. One example may illustrate this. He comes to deal with the ending *-e*. He realizes the number of French nouns ending in *-e* is huge. So he needs another ordering principle and he takes into account the consonant preceding *-e*, tackling the sequences in alphabetical order. He arrives at *-le*, which, again, is quite common in French. So the letter preceding *-le* is taken into account (*-ble*, *-cle*, *-fle*, *-gle*, etc.).

At the end of his description of gender assignment for French nouns, Palsgrave addresses the question of gender in compounds. He sets out a classification of noun compounds which is very much indebted to Latin grammar and he illustrates the different types of compounds with French examples. H. Lewicka (1978) has studied the nominal compounds in *Lesclarcissement*, but Palsgrave's treatment of word-formation in French and in English deserves a fuller investigation.

Let me summarize. We have looked at one particular area of French grammar, nouns, and their first accident, gender, to bring out the compositional structure between books I, II, and III, and to exemplify the progression in content and depth of linguistic analysis. The treatment of a particular part of speech is then completed by an alphabetical word list in which English words are matched with French translations. In our specific case, nouns, grammar, and the 'Frenche vocabulist' of nouns become interlinked by Palsgrave's indication of gender (as well as the plural) after the French translation equivalent.

# 3
# Linguistic Provenance: What are the Languages Palsgrave is Describing?

Having outlined the compilation, the production, and the overall structure of *Lesclarcissement de la langue francoyse*, we shall now look at the kind of English and French which Palsgrave describes in his grammar and his dictionary. At the time when he was compiling *Lesclarcissement*, English and French, like other European vernaculars, were still in the process of establishing themselves on a par with the classical languages, Latin and Greek. Supraregional prestige norms, in the spoken as well as the written vernacular, were gradually emerging, and the printing press played a considerable role in the development and spread of a particular social and regional form of the language. There is a concurrent crucial factor for the period which we have to bring back to our minds: there were no agreed rules for spelling and there was wide variation. Apart from having no existing word lists to hand from which to compile their own word lists, the early vernacular lexicographers were thus faced with the further burden of selecting the spellings for words. The users of these early vernacular dictionaries, on the other hand, had to be imaginative and flexible enough to check in different places of the dictionary (still only imperfectly alphabetical) when the spelling which they had assumed for a word did not coincide with that chosen by the lexicographer.

## DIFFERENCES BETWEEN ENGLISH AND FRENCH

Palsgrave was competent in several foreign languages, one of which was the vernacular of a growing political power in Europe, France. His keen observational and linguistic powers made him note down a good number of challenging and insightful differences between the use of French and the use of English, his mother tongue. These embrace all the different levels of contrast when two languages are compared, as can be seen from the following few illustrations.

Anyone who has learnt a foreign language knows that the lexicon relating to cultural and administrative institutions is rarely matched with the lexical adequacy in another language, because each speech community has different such institutions. Palsgrave repeatedly draws our attention to differences in the legal system:

**Justyce of peace or quorum/ they haue no such offycers.**

(III, fo. xlii[v])

**I Indyte a man by indytement/ they haue no suche processe in their lawe.**

(III, fo. cc.lxvi[v])

Where given institutions are said not to exist in France, we are not provided with French equivalents or paraphrases explaining the English words.

A further area where the professional culture varies according to Palsgrave is brewing:

**Grout that serueth to brewyng/ in Fraunce there is none vsed.**

(III, fo. xxxviii)

Another case is where a thing is said not to occur in a speech community:

**Stocke fysshe they haue none.**

(III, fo. lxvii[v])

From this we have to distinguish the cases where one language has lexicalized a concept and the other has not. Examples are:

**Whit mete they haue no suche worde.**

(III, fo. lxxiiii[v])

**I Fetche a thyng that I or other haue nat/ for this worde they haue no propre verbe but vse to ioyne the tenses of** Ie men vas, **coniugate in the secõde boke to** querir, **as/** ie men vas querir, ie men suis allé querir, ie men iray querir, aller querir . . .

(III, fo. cc.xxxv)

Differences in the meaning of words are also pointed out:

**I Smyte/** Ie frappe, **and** ie fiers, nous fierons, ie ferus, iay feru, ie ferray, que ie fierè ferir. &c. **you smyte to harde:** Vous frappez trop fort, **but** frapper, **is properly with the hande or with a thing that dothe me great hurte/** ferir, **is to stryke with a weapon or to gyue a greuouse stroke/ but I fynde them ofte confounded.**

(III, fo. ccc.lxiiii[v])

In addition, Palsgrave draws attention to differences in grammar, the use of the verb *to do* in particular:

> **I Do/ is a verbe moche comenly vsed in our tonge to be put byfore other verbes: as it is all one to say/ I do speke/ I do thynke/ I do write I do coniecture/ and suche lyke/ and I speake/ I thynke/ I write/ I coniecture: but in the frẽche tonge they vse neuer to put any verbe that coũtreuayleth/ I do/ in this sence/ but vse the verbe selfe onely lyke as for I dyd speake/ I dyd thynke/ I dyd write/ I dyd cõiecture/ they vse euer the preter imperfyte tence or the indiffynite tence of the verbes selfe in their tõge and neuer vse to put any verbe that countreuayleth I dyd in this sence . . .**
>
> (III, fo. cc.xvi$^{\text{v}}$–cc.xvii)

Occasionally, reference is made to the extralinguistic situation which prompts a different use of language in English and in French:

> **I Speke/** Ie parle. prime coniu. **I speke to him of my busynes:** Ie luy parle de mes affaires, ⁊ ie parolle. prime coniu. **but I fynde for I speke nat a worde/ as they do nat that by thretnyd if they speke or make any noyse to be corrected or that be commandyd to kepe a matter secret:** Ie ne sonne mot, ie nay sonné mot, sonner mot. prime cõiuga.
>
> (III, fo. ccc.lxviii)

The examples quoted provide us with fascinating insights into the working of sixteenth-century English and French and into differences of use between the two languages. There were no comparable descriptions of English or French available showing that depth of linguistic penetration, and Palsgrave's exceptional linguistic faculties are therefore all the more striking. The contrast focuses on individual items or uses, and these, each of them taken on its own, do not in general presuppose a comprehensive understanding of the whole language system. We know this ourselves from our own experience of learning a foreign language: we may have grasped a specific instance of contrast between our mother tongue and the language we are attempting to learn without being able to give a complete description of our mother tongue or the foreign language. In Palsgrave's case, however, we have seen in the previous chapter that he had a much deeper and more comprehensive grasp and command of French. Was Palsgrave also aware of regional and social differences in the French he was describing? Since he meant his book to teach those who wished to learn the French language, did he say anything about the model of French he had chosen? If so, did he give reasons for his choice?

The issues raised are central to one of the most intricate and complex areas of the linguistic history of English and French: the emergence, evolution, and dissemination of a standard form. Linguists are far from having exhausted all the textual evidence available and from having satisfactory answers to the many problems involved. Our account of the attitude adopted and the evidence provided by Palsgrave may therefore contribute to seeing a further side of the multifaceted linguistic situation of the time. I shall first outline what Palsgrave has to say about the forms of English and then focus on the situation of sixteenth-century French.

## THE COMMON SPEECH AND ENGLISH REGIONALISMS

What then was Palsgrave's position with respect to English? There is no explicit statement that characterizes the form of English which he uses in his work. This is not surprising at all, for several salient points spring to mind. Palsgrave was a Londoner born, and, as far as one can establish, he spent a considerable part of his life in London. At his time the form of English used in London was already widely regarded as the standard form to be followed. Of the five major Middle English dialects, the Northern, the West Midland, the East Midland, the Southern, and the Kentish dialects, it was the East Midlands form that was to become the basis for the modern standard. In their book on the history of the English language, A. C. Baugh and T. Cable summarize the rise of the standard form as follows:

> Out of this variety of local dialects there emerged toward the end of the fourteenth century a written language that in the course of the fifteenth won general recognition and has since become the recognized standard in both speech and writing. The part of England that contributed most to the formation of this standard was the East Midland district, and it was the East Midland type of English that became its basis, particularly the dialect of the metropolis, London. (Baugh and Cable 1978: 191–2)

Of the factors which contributed to this development the following are probably the most important. The dialect area of the East Midlands had a border with each of the other dialect areas, and it was thus a dialect area where the extreme differences between the dialects of the North and the South could most easily be bridged, mediated, and levelled. Of all the five dialect areas, that of the East Midlands was the most populated. Most importantly, this was the district that included London: not only the capital, the political and commercial centre of England, but also the seat of the highest legal institutions, and of the court. As such it was the centre of social and intellectual life. And when the printing press was introduced in England, it also became the centre of book publishing. The first English printer, William Caxton, as well as his successors, used the form of English current in London for the books that were printed and which were then distributed and read in other parts of the realm. For more detailed accounts of the powers and personalities that shaped the English language, see Fisher (1977), Cable (1984), and McIntosh *et al.* (1986). Dobson's description of standard spoken English (1956) begins with *Lesclarcissement* (but the date is misprinted as 1532).

In such a linguistic context, a well-regarded scholar and schoolmaster, a royal tutor, born and living in London itself, may have taken his use of his own English mother tongue for granted. This may account for Palsgrave's frequent references to English as 'our comen spetche'. Yet, though he does not describe in any detail within the book the form of English which enjoyed the highest esteem and which he used himself, he made sure that there could not be any doubt about the authority of his work: the title-page portrays him as a 'natyf de Londres' to provide the credentials for his English, just as the other attribute 'gradue de Paris' is meant to guarantee them for French.

*Lesclarcissement* includes evidence that Palsgrave was aware of regional differences in the English of his time. The French vocabulist contains a number of entries which are clearly marked as northernisms. One may, of course, wonder why there are no lexical items listed from other regional areas. A rather self-evident explanation would be that the items recorded are based on personal experience. We remember that as tutor to the duke of Richmond and member of the duke's Council of the North, Palsgrave had spent some time in Yorkshire, and his perceptive mind may well have registered and retained the different use of words in the northern regions. He seems to distinguish between 'northerne' and 'farre northerne', but there is no evidence that 'farre northerne' may refer to Scottish usage; from the point of view of a Londoner, 'farre northerne' may refer to the north of England and 'northern' simply to the Midlands lying north of London. The lexical items characterized as northern (or far northern) are: *to blente* 'to let, hinder', *to carpe*, *to clepe*, *to sye* 'to sieve', *to sperre* 'to shut', *to spere* 'to ask', *to spurre* 'to ask', *to stye* 'to ascend', *to threche* 'to thrutch', *to threpe* 'to threap', *to twhyte* 'to thwite', *to twyst*, *to warrye*, *to wynne*, and *ylke*.

How reliable was Palsgrave in his assessment of these regional differences? The examples below are checked against J. Wright's *English Dialect Dictionary* (*EDD*) and the second edition of the *OED*.

> **I Blente I lette or I hynder/** Ie empesche. prime cõiuga. **This terme is to moche northerne.**
>
> (III, fo. c.lxvii)

The *EDD* does not list the verb, and the *OED* reveals that the only record of the item is Palsgrave's entry.

> **I Carpe (Lydgat)** Ie cacquette, prime. **this is a farre northern verbe.**
>
> (III, fo. c.lxxxi$^{v}$)

The *EDD* lists the verb for Scotland and Lancashire but as obsolete. In the *OED* it is listed as obsolete in the intransitive sense of 'to speak, talk' and in the transitive sense of 'to speak, utter, say, tell'. Palsgrave's entry is given under the equally obsolete vituperative sense 'to talk much, to prate, chatter'. The *OED* describes the senses 1–3 as used 'chiefly in northern poetry'.

The next verb is 'farre northerne' by Palsgrave:

> **I Clepe I call/** Ie huysche. prime. **This terme is farre northerne . . .**
>
> (III, fo. c.l.xxxix)

The *EDD* records the use of this verb in the spelling given by Palsgrave for Scotland, Ireland, Northumberland, Yorkshire, and East Anglia. The *OED*, on the other hand, lists the intransitive meaning of the verb 'to cry, to call' as having fallen out of common use towards the second half of the sixteenth century. The entry from *Lesclarcissement* is the last but one.

The verb to **sye, sie** is, like to **blente**, described as being 'to moche northerne':

> **I Sye mylke or clense/** Ie coulle du laict. prime cõiu. **this terme is to moche northerne.**
>
> (III, fo. ccc.lxi)

The *EDD* lists it as a dialect word common in the north and the Midlands. The *OED* regards the verb as obsolete except in dialects and includes among its citations the entry from *Lesclarcissement*.

For the next verb we have three entries in the *OED*, one in the form *to spar v.*[1], another under *to spare v.*[2] and finally *to spear v.*[1]:

> **I Sperre I shytte/** Ie ferme. pri-
> me coniu. **⁊ ie clos, coniugate in I**
> **close. This verbe is of yͤ northyrne**
> **langaige and nat commynly in vse.**
>
> (III, fo. ccc.lxviii[v])

The *EDD* informs us that the verb occurs not only in the north and the Midlands but also in the southern and south-western regions. The rather puzzling treatment in the *OED* is as follows: *to spar* is regarded as now archaic and the quotations for the sense 'to fasten (a door or gate) with a bar or bolt; to shut or close firmly or securely' end with the close of the sixteenth century; *spare* with the transitive meaning 'to bar, bolt, or secure (a door or gate)' describes the verb as northern and obsolete in Scotland, and *to spear* with the meaning 'to shut or close' is marked as obsolete.

The verb *to speer* has two entries in *Lesclarcissement*:

> **I Spere I aske/** Ie demande. pri
> me con. **This terme is also fare nor-**
> **thyrne ⁊ nat vsed in cõmyn speche.**
>
> (III, fo. ccc.lxviii[v])

The other spelling under which it is listed is *spurre*:

> **I Spurre I aske a questyon/** Ie
> demande vne question. **this terme is**
> **farre northerne.**
>
> (III, fo. ccc.lxx[v])

The *EDD* confirms the use for the north and Midland areas. The *OED* lists the entry from *Lesclarcissement* under the intransitive use, and the verb itself is described as chiefly Scottish and northern.

For the following verb:

> **I Stye I assende or I go vp-**
> **warde/** Ie monte. **a farre northerne**
> **terme.**
>
> (III, fo. ccc.lxxiiii[v])

there is no record in the *EDD*. The *OED*'s citations do not include the entry from *Lesclarcissement*. For the later stages of its use, citations do not go beyond the seventeenth century.

> **I Treche I pynche/** Ie pynce.
> prime cõiuga. **This is a farre nor-**
> **thren terme.**
>
> (III, fo. ccc.lxxxix)

The *EDD* records its occurrence in the North Country, Westmoreland, Yorkshire, Lancashire, Cheshire, Staffordshire, Derbyshire, and Nottinghamshire. The verb *to thrutch* is regarded as now dialectal by the *OED*. So again, Palsgrave was right in describing it as a northernism.

We come to the verb *to threap*:

> **I Threpe a mater vpon one/ I beare one in hande ỷ he hath doone or said a thing a mysse**: Ie luy fays ac croyre, **or** ie luys mets sus. **this terme is also farre northren . . .**
>
> (III, fo. ccc.lxxxix)

For the *EDD*, *to threap* is a general dialect word common in Scotland, Ireland, and in northern and Midland English. The *OED* describes it as now occurring in Scotland and the northern dialects.

The next northernism in Palsgrave's list of verbs is *to thwite*:

> **I Twhyte one I caste hym in the tethe or in the nose/** Ie luy reprouche. prime cōiu. **This terme is also northren.**
>
> (III, fo. ccc.xxxxv[v])

The *EDD* records the use of this verb not only for Scotland, the North Country, and areas in the Midlands, but also for Devon in the south-west. According to the *OED*, the verb is, with the exception of dialectal uses, obsolete.

> **I Twyst threde I twyne threde/ this terme is northren . . .**
>
> (III, fo. ccc.xxxxv[v])

The description in the *EDD* is very general and Palsgrave's description as a northernism is not supported by the *OED*.

For the verb *to wary* Palsgrave's entry reads as follows:

> **I Warye/ I banne or curse/** Ie mauldis, **coniugate in** ie dis, **I saye. This is a farre northren terme.**
>
> (III, fo. cccc.i[v])

The verb is regarded as obsolete by both the *EDD* and the *OED*. The *EDD* records its use for Lancashire only.

With respect to the use of *to win* (*to win to*):

> **I Wynne to a thing I retche to it/** Ie attayns, **cōiugat in** attayne/ **this terme is farre northren.**
>
> (III, fo. cccc.ix)

the *EDD* records the dialect use also for areas of the Midlands and Sussex. The *OED* writes (senses **12.a.** and **d.**) that it was 'formerly chiefly *Sc.* and *n. dial*', which would confirm Palsgrave's assessment.

We conclude our review of Palsgrave's northernisms with the well-known northern form of *each*, confirmed by the *EDD* and *OED*:

> **That ylke day/ Northerne:** Ce mesmes iour.
>
> (III, fo. cccc.xxvi$^{v}$)

To summarize then: in the majority of cases Palsgrave appears to have been accurate in his assessment. This makes him the first English lexicographer to have recorded and correctly identified dialect words in his dictionary. Future historical accounts of English dialects will have to incorporate the findings from this early lexicographical work.[1]

## DIFFERENCES IN USE, ARCHAISMS, NEOLOGISMS, BORROWINGS

Explicit statements on the currency of a good number of words in sixteenth-century English amply demonstrate that Palsgrave's linguistic awareness with respect to his mother tongue embraced further parameters. The verb *to apparel*, for instance, is said to be better English than the form *to reparel* (**I Reparell** . . . (III, fo. ccc.xxxviii)), which the *OED*, in the meaning 'to fit up, to array, to apparel', describes as rare, giving Palsgrave's entry as the last citation for the verb use.

He was aware of linguistic borrowings entering English:

> **I Surmoũte I ouer passe or excede a nother thynge:** Ie surmonte. prime cõiu. **and** ie passe. prime coniu. **and** ie surpasse. **This is a frenche verbe but of late taken in vse in our tonge.**
>
> (III, fo. ccc.lxxx)

The 'of late' is rather vague. Records of the word in the *OED* date from the last quarter of the fourteenth century. This temporal parameter, which will be dealt with in Chapter 5, gives *Lesclarcissement* a

[1] James Milroy's account of Middle English dialectology in the second volume of the *Cambridge history of the English language* is rather disappointing in this respect. He does not go beyond a cursory mention of the two well-known explicit comments on Middle English dialects by John Trevisa and William Caxton (Milroy 1992: 166).

historical dimension. Associated with this parameter are accounts on the frequency of occurrence of certain words. The latter will have an impressionistic basis, but we shall consult the *OED* to see how adequate Palsgrave's judgements were. We thus learn that the verb *to thrill* is 'nowe lytell vsed' (III, fo. ccc.lxxxiv). The *OED* lists Palsgrave's entry, and the last citation for the sense 'to pierce' dates from 1661. With respect to the now obsolete verb *to warish* in the intransitive sense of 'to recover from sickness or trouble', there is an interval of about 300 years in the *OED*'s citations from Palsgrave to W. Carr (1828).

When a word is little used, it may be replaced by another one. This is the case of

> **I Gynne to do a thyng for whiche**
> **we vse nowe/ I begyn/ as I begyn**
> **to laughe/ to speake/ to eate/or suche**
> **lyk . . .**
>
> (III, fo. cc.xlviii)

A surprising number of items listed is said to be out of use or no longer (for which Palsgrave used the phrase *nat yet*[2]) used. Many of them are attributed to Lydgate or Chaucer, and we shall look at these more closely in Chapter 5. Among the archaisms not identified with a particular writer we find: *to depaint*, *to disconsolate*, *to quake*, *quoth*, *to rubify* as well as the northernisms *to spar* (*spare*, *spear*) and *to speer*. Again, we may wonder how reliable Palsgrave's assessments were. Let us begin with the verb to *depaint*:

> **I Depaynte I coloure a thynge**
> **with colours/** Ie depaings . . .
> **This terme as yet is nat admytted**
> **in comen spetche.**
>
> (III, fo. cc.viii$^{v}$)

The *OED* lists the verb as obsolete or archaic. It includes Palsgrave's entry, after which two other citations are given, the last dating from 1706.

The verb *to disconsolate* does not seem to have ever been current at all. Palsgrave's entry

> **I Disconsolate I bringe out of**
> **comfort/** Ie desconsolate. prime con.
> **this terme is nat yet comenly vsed . . .**
>
> (III, fo. cc.xii$^{v}$)

is the first entry in the *OED* and there is only one other citation.

[2] See sense **II. 2. b.** of yet in the *OED*: *not yet* = no longer; two citations from Palsgrave are given. D. A. Kibbee was not aware of this now obsolete use of *yet* (see 1992: 54; 1991: 123).

Palsgrave's description of *to quake* is not supported by the evidence from the *OED*, whereas that of the form *quoth* (**I Quod** . . . (III, fo. ccc.xxxi)) is, and this basically holds for *to rubify*:

> **I Rubyfye I make reed/** Iecshaufe
> ⁊ ie rubifie. prime cõiu. **this terme is**
> **nat yet admytted in comen spetche.**
> (III, fo. ccc.xliiii^v)

The *OED* records Palsgrave's entry and has a few later citations.

Thus we see Palsgrave clearly identifying an implicit norm.

## THE EMERGENCE OF A STANDARD FORM IN FRENCH

We can now turn our attention to French and pursue more closely the stages of development in the formation of a standard norm. As several scholars have pointed out, it is simplistic to assume that the language form of the Île de France gradually supplanted the other regional forms, and, in doing so, made them dialects with respect to itself. Following a distinction made by M. Delbouille in 1939 and then elaborated on by other linguistic historians, C. Marchello-Nizia (1979: 18–19) has stressed that any understanding of the dialect situation in medieval France has to distinguish between the spoken language of a region (the spoken local dialect) and the *scripta* of that area. A *scripta* is understood as a written form with more or less dialect features which, and this is crucial, remains legible throughout the domain of the French language. From very early on, then, the written language was a unifying factor. The earliest texts in the vernacular that have come down to us reveal that in the north the basis of these regional scriptas was already the spoken form of the language of Paris. The main reasons for this, as Marchello-Nizia has pointed out (1979: 19–23), were political. Under the Capetians, the court became more stationary, and, with the eleventh century, Paris began to prosper as the capital of the realm. With the political power located in one area, the whole administrative and legal state machinery had to be developed and run efficiently from there. Scholars have also drawn attention to another important factor, one which reminds us of the situation in England: the manner of using the language in and around the capital occupied an intermediary position with respect to the other regional forms. The dialect features of *Francien* were less pronounced (François 1959: 95). In the process of establishing a centralized government and of gradually 'incorporating' provinces which until then had enjoyed relative autonomy, the development of the legal system was to play an important role. Latin as the language of the legal statutes and documents was gradually replaced by French, and, once the vernacular had entered this administrative domain, there was no return. The beginnings of this change go back to the thirteenth century, and, in the fourteenth century, the replacement became quite common. We see again a certain parallel with respect to the situation in England: in the wake of the Norman Conquest French had replaced Latin in the legal procedures of the country.

So, whereas in France the vernacular had to overcome Latin in legal practice, in England the vernacular had to replace French. In 1362 a decisive step was taken to restore English in the law courts (and with it also in the country). The *Statute of Pleading* was introduced because

> it is often shewed to the king by the prelates, dukes, earls, barons, and all the commonalty, of the great mischiefs which have happened to divers of the realm, because the laws, customs, and statutes of this realm be not commonly known in the same realm; for that they be pleaded, shewed, and judged in the French tongue, which is much unknown in the said realm; so that the people which do implead, or be impleaded, in the king's court, and in the courts of others, have no knowledge nor understanding of that which is said for them or against them by their serjeants and other pleaders . . . the king . . . hath ordained . . . that all pleas which shall be pleaded in his courts whatsoever . . . shall be pleaded, shewed, defended, answered, debated, and judged in the English tongue, and that they be entered and enrolled in Latin. (Baugh and Cable 1978: 148–9)

The French kings may have had similar concerns for the injustice their subjects might or did encounter through not understanding the language used in the law courts. But they might equally well have been driven by the urge to centralize and strengthen their political power by instituting a legal system that was to be observed throughout the realm. From the last decade of the fifteenth century onwards, several statutes were issued to ensure that the accused as well as the witnesses understood what was said against them or in their favour. The earliest were the *Ordonnances de Moulins*. In the first of 1490 Charles VIII decreed 'que les "dits et depositions" de témoins dans les cours de justice du Languedoc "seront mis ou redigés *en langage françois ou maternel*"' (Rickard 1968: 22). Twenty years after this first interference in the legal matters of the Languedoc area, Louis XII (who was to marry Palsgrave's royal pupil, Henry VIII's sister Mary) gave order that 'tous les procès criminels et les dites enquestes en quelque maniere que ce soit seront faites *en vulgaire et langage du pays* où seront faits les dits procès criminels et enquestes . . .' (ibid.).

The interesting part in both these decrees is that there is not yet an attempt to impose one particular form of French. But the coordinated noun phrases *en langage françois ou maternel* and *en vulgaire et langage du pays* are open to interpretation: are these appositive expressions or do they refer to different forms of language? Is it the vernacular as the language of the country or does the formulation leave an option to those involved between the vernacular, French, and the language of the area, the local manner of speaking?

In the *Ordonnances d'Is-sur-Tille* issued in 1535 with respect to the reform of justice in the Provence (Rickard 1968, 22), the two options—the use of French or of the local vernacular of the region—are still admitted, though with an explicit weighting in favour of the superregional form. In the *Ordonnances*, François I insists 'que doresenavant tous les procès criminels et les enquestes seront faictz en francoys ou a tout le moins en vulgaire du dict pays'.

The last step in the series of royal decrees to reform and centralize the legal system were the famous *Ordonnances de Villers-Cotterets* of 1539. The articles 110 and 111 stipulated that for all legal actions the language had to be French (Brunot 1906/1967: 30).

During the fourteenth and fifteenth centuries, the linguistic development in the country had already been moving towards a more uniform use of the language in the scriptas. In addition, the Hundred Years War (1337–1453) had produced a considerable national feeling. The royal interventions thus gave more impetus and vigour to a process which was well on its way.

At the same time, the *Zeitgeist* of the Renaissance, which, from Italy, had spread north and sought to make all human knowledge widely accessible, called for the use of the vernacular. In order to make the works of learning accessible to the people who were not versed in the classic languages, scholars had to translate them into the vernacular and in doing so to expand and refine the vernacular itself. A massive translation work began—and it was able to reach a wider readership because at that crucial time of history the printing press had been invented. P. Rickard provides us with a good picture of the various factors at work and concurring to spread one form of French throughout the country:

> Outre les ordonnances royales intervenant directement dans l'état linguistique du Midi d'autres facteurs, naturellement, travaillaient pour la diffusion du français. Le protestantisme, amenant à sa suite la Bible française, les cadets de Gascogne rentrant chez eux après avoir appris la langue du nord du pays, les nouveaux collèges transmettant, d'abord en latin mais ensuite en français, les idées de la Renaissance et les trésors de la culture nationale, l'imprimerie introduisant partout des ouvrages scientifiques et littéraires en français, et enfin et surtout l'absence d'une culture locale

capable d'étayer les langues régionales—tout conspirait à rendre le français indispensable à ceux qui savaient lire et écrire. (Rickard 1968: 23–4)

But surely it was the all-pervading influence of printing that was the most important force. C. T. Gossen (1957: 450) has stressed this role. It was in 1469 that the first printing press was set up in Paris.

## FRENCH AND ITS REGIONAL FORMS GROWING LANGUAGE AWARENESS IN SCHOLARLY WORKS

All these far-reaching and consequence-laden changes which mark the transition from the Middle Ages into the Renaissance period were still going on in West European countries during Palsgrave's lifetime. Let us look specifically at what can be regarded as the rising consciousness of a French language. Serge Lusignan's book *Parler vulgairement. Les intellectuels et la langue française aux XIII^e^ et XIV^e^ siècles* (1986) is a close study of major thirteenth- and fourteenth-century works tracing the growing awareness of the French language and its various regional forms with the intellectuals of the time. Thus we learn that Thomas Aquinas, in his comments on the gospel of St Matthew, points out that there are different ways of speaking Hebrew 'sicut patet in Francia, et Picardia, et Burgundia, et tamen una loquela est', that is, just as in French, in Picardian, and in Burgundian, though they represent one language. Roger Bacon's description of French dialects (1266) is not only richer but also slightly subtler. He maintains in his work that one and the same language may have several *idiomata* (Lusignan 1986: 67). In his *Opus majus* he puts forward the view that it is not possible to translate all the nuances of one language into another because each has its own characteristics and he argues as follows:

Nam et idiomata ejusdem linguae variantur apud diversos, sicut patet de lingua Gallicana, quae apud Gallicos et Picardos et Normannos et Burgundos multiplici variatur idiomate. Et quod proprie dicitur in idiomate Picardorum horrescit apud Burgundos, immo apud Gallicos viciniores: quanto igitur magis accidet hoc apud linguas diveras? (Bacon, *Opus majus* iii. 66)

Robert Belle Burke, who translated the *Opus majus* into English, clearly softened the attitude said to characterize interdialectal behaviour when he rendered Bacon's *horrescit* by 'is out of place':

For even dialects of the same tongue vary among different sections, as is clear from the Gallic language, which is divided into many dialects among the Gauls, Picards, Normans, Burgundians, and others. A fitting and intelligible expression in the dialect of the Picards is out of place among the Burgundians, nay, among the nearer Gallic neighbors; how much more then will this be true as between different languages? (Burke 1928/1961: 75)

St Thomas Aquinas had mentioned *Francia*, *Picardia*, and *Burgundia*. Bacon, in his explanatory comparisons, had seen linguistic variation within French (*lingua Gallicana*), occurring with the *Gallicos*, *Picardos*, *Normannos*, and *Burgundos*. Lusignan has rightly drawn our attention to a striking characteristic in the early description of the different regional forms of French: the name for the people in one of the regional areas, the neighbours of those in Picardy, is *Gallici*, the very name which is also applied to the inhabitants of the whole geographical area where the *lingua Gallica* (or *Gallicana*) is used. Lusignan interprets this as a first instance of the beginning predominance of the Francien form of French: 'les *Gallicos*, voisins des Picards, ne peuvent être que les habitants de l'Île de France. On constate là un premier indice du début de la prédominance du français parisien . . .' (Lusignan 1986: 69).

In the *Compendium studii philosophiae*, Bacon's description of the different regional forms of French is further differentiated. Parisian French is mentioned (Brewer 1859: 438), and, when he returns to the question of translatability from one language into another Bacon even uses the phrase 'puros Gallicos':

Nam proprietas unius non concordat cum alia, et quod optime sonat in una, pessime vel nihil sapit in altera, sicut manifestum est illis qui Latinum et maternas linguas noverunt, et se exercitaverunt in hac parte. Nos etiam videmus, quod cum eadem lingua sunt diversa idiomata, id est, modi et proprietas loquendi, ut in Anglico apud boreales, et australes, et orientales, et occidentales; in Francia apud Picardos, et Normannos, et *puros Gallicos*, et Burgundos, et alios; tamen quod bene sonat et proprie apud homines unius idiomatis, male sonat et improprie apud alios. (Brewer 1859: 466–7) (emphasis added)

The 'Gallici' of the *Opus majus* have become the 'puri Gallici', as if the real French language in the middle of the thirteenth century was already the language of the Île de France (Lusignan 1986: 69).

So far, we have followed Lusignan and looked at some medieval works by leading intellectuals to see how aware they were of the regional linguistic variation within the areas of the langue d'oïl and the langue d'oc. Let us now turn to works of literature.

## LANGUAGE AWARENESS IN LITERARY WORKS

Medieval French literature includes quite a number of instances that reflect the gradually shifting relation between the different forms of

French with respect to each other. Conon de Bethune's complaint, made around 1180, about the royal family's criticism of his work—it included some Picard features—seems to be the first sign of the court's attitude towards forms of French which differed from their own (Rothwell 1985: 41; François 1959: 93). And towards the end of the twelfth century the poet Aymon de Varenne from Lyon preferred French to his local variant, maintaining

> Chanson ne estoire ne plait
> As Franceis se il ne l'ont fait.
>
> (François 1959: 94)

But it was not only the Picard or Lyon version of French which was not fully appreciated in the capital. M. D. Legge cites the following with respect to the relation between the language of Paris and the Norman form. A certain Gui, writing in the thirteenth century, had translated the Life of St Catherine from Latin into French, but his Norman French did not please the French:

> Un clerc translatee l'avoit
> Mes, por ce que normant estoit,
> La rime qui fu faite ençois,
> Si ne pleisoit mie aus François.
>
> (Legge 1963: 69; Rothwell 1985: 41)

Such literary evidence led W. Rothwell to conclude that from 'the closing years of the twelfth century onwards most of those who wrote French (as distinct from the vast majority who only spoke it), when using it for purposes other than purely local communication and record, were to try to model their language on *francien*' (Rothwell, 1985: 41).

What was the contemporary name for the language form characteristic of the Paris area? Roger Bacon had used the Latin term for the inhabitants of the area: *Gallici* or *puri Gallici*. Authors writing in French used the terms *langue*, *langage*, and *parler* with a specifying attribute or postmodification, according to H.-G. Koll, who investigated the use of the French words *langue* and *langage* in the Middle Ages in his 1958 dissertation. In the preface to his translation of Boethius' *De consolatio philosophiae*, Jean de Meung uses *langage*, *parler*, and *Paris* in his apologetic lines:

> Si m'escuse de mon langage,
> Rude, malostru et sauvage:
> Car nés ne suis pas de Paris,
> Ne si cointes com fu Paris;
> Mais me raporte et me compère
> Au parler que m'aprist ma mère,

A Meun, quant je l'alaitoie,
Dont mes parlers ne s'en desvoie;
Ne n'ay nul parler plus habile
Que cellui qui keurt à no ville.

(Lusignan 1986: 71)

Towards the middle and the later part of the fourteenth century other well-known translators like Pierre Bersuire, who translated Livy into French, and above all Nicole Oresme, who had been asked by Charles V to provide a French version of Aristotle's *Politics* and his *Nicomachean Ethics*, wrote in their prefatory lines that they were translating these works into 'français'.

With one regional form of French becoming recognized as dominant to write in and to imitate, the forms of other areas diminished in prestige. No wonder, therefore, that varying regional language forms were stylistically exploited in the *théâtre comique* of the fifteenth and sixteenth centuries (Lewicka 1961).

To what extent were the linguistic changes evolving in France known in England? One of the most famous passages in English literature in this respect is Geoffrey Chaucer's comment on the form of French spoken by the Prioress in his *Canterbury Tales*:

And Frenssh she spak ful faire and fetisly,
After the scole of Stratford atte Bowe,
For Frenssh of Parys was to hire unknowe.

(Robinson 1983: 18)

So Chaucer was well aware of the differences at least between Parisian French and the insular French largely common in England. In an interesting study, William Rothwell has shown that Chaucer was far from being the first to compare the differing uses of French on both sides of the Channel. Comments on the differences between continental French and insular French have a much longer history (Rothwell 1985: 39). This is not surprising if we recall the early external history of French in England. For some time, the English territorial possessions in France had been extensive and therefore members of the higher classes of society would have been exposed to a variety of regional forms of French. If we keep in mind that the successful running of such estates called for a means of communication understandable on both sides, we might wonder whether there may not be a point in distinguishing between the oral and the written use of French when we are trying to assess its nature and quality. Rothwell, for instance, reminds us that

far from being a fairly obscure dialect in a state of rapid decline, the French used in England from the early thirteenth century to the end of the fourteenth is the only variety to be on a par with *francien* in the sense of being an official language of record widely used by the dominant classes in a vigorously developing nation. Not only does it have to its credit works on various aspects of science, medicine, history, agriculture, law (both of land and sea)—just as authoritative as those in continental French and often in advance of the continental works. (ibid.: 47)

To the latter category belong the linguistic treatises written to teach French to native speakers of English.

## FRENCH AND ITS REGIONAL FORMS IN PEDAGOGICAL WORKS

To these we shall now turn our attention. As pedagogical works which preceded the publication of *Lesclarcissement* and which could have set an example for Palsgrave, we shall investigate the following aspects. Do the authors of these treatises say anything about a particular form of French to which their work provides an introduction? If they do, which regional form is this? Is there a gradual change in the regional form of French selected? If these authors are silent on a particular model of French, which are the first treatises in which the authors explicitly comment on this matter? Having investigated these issues we shall then be in a position to assess Palsgrave's position. He will have been aware of the preferred form of French at the courts in Paris and in London, but very little is known about his sources. It may be that the close study of his predecessors' work with respect to the model of French adopted and the regionalisms mentioned will provide us with some helpful insight.

The classic work on the teaching of French in England during the relevant period is Kathleen Lambley's book *The teaching and cultivation of the French language during Tudor and Stuart times* (1920). A more recent monograph is D. A. Kibbee's work *For to speke frenche trewely* (1991), which investigates the status, description, and teaching of French in England from 1000 to 1600. Closest to our concern, though not addressing Palsgrave's achievement, are the studies by Lusignan and Andres Max Kristol. In chapter III of his book, Lusignan turns to England and reviews the status of French in the grammatical treatises and manuals teaching Englishmen the French language. His focus of research is thus more sociolinguistic in nature than intrinsically linguistic. This latter aspect, the close linguistic study of the language used in these pedagogical works, is more fully explored in Kristol's paper 'Le début du rayonnement parisien et l'unité du français au moyen âge: le témoignage des manuels d'enseignement du français écrits en Angleterre entre le XIII$^{e}$ et le début du XV$^{e}$ siècle' (1989). Kristol's article is a challenging contribution to the complex history of the unification of written French. His investigation focuses on the actual language used in the treatises, and not so much on the explicit metalinguistic statements made by the compilers as to which particular form of French they were teaching. It shows that the degree to which these texts reflect Anglo-Norman French usage changes during the period under consideration (ibid.: 361). Kristol furthermore stresses that the continental influence on written French in England during the fourteenth century is not only that of Parisian French. The written French in England also shows Picard features, Picard influence thus lagging behind the impact it had on the continent during the thirteenth century (ibid.: 365).

Which of the authors specifies the French he is describing? The oldest treatise that has come down to us, believed to have been composed around the middle of the thirteenth century, is Walter de Bibbesworth's *Traité sur la langue française*. The form of French used by Bibbesworth reflects the Anglo-Norman tradition of the time, though the author himself refers to the two languages in his treatise as simply French and English. In two instances, however, the manuscripts show a more interesting wording (Kibbee 1991: 46).

In the *Tractatus orthographiae* specific regional features are identified. The author, a student of Paris, is believed to have composed the little treatise around 1300. All we know about him is that his initials are T.H. He tells us at the beginning that he intends to describe French and explain its rules 'secundum usum et modum modernorum tam in partibus transmarinis quam cismarinis'. He identifies two areas where Anglo-Norman French differs from continental French, but the differences pointed out are not unique to the French used in England. They also occur in some regions of France, which thus use French not 'secundum dulce gallicum'. The first Anglo-Norman feature is the *e*-spelling in certain future tense forms of the verb. This characteristic is said to be also common in Picard French and Breton French: 'Item iste dicciones: *aura*, *en array* sine *e* in medio [scribi debent et] sonari, secundum dulce gallicum, sine *v* ut sic: *aray*, *en array* que indifferenter sic scribi possunt. Tamen Romanici, Britannici et Anglii scribunt easdem dicciones cum *e* in medio ut *aueray*, *j'aueray* et sic de similibus' (Pope 1910: 189).

The other Anglo-Normanism is a *t*-spelling in certain words, a feature which Anglo-Norman French is said to share with the French common in Gascony: ' Item secundum gallicum *t* omittatur in istis diccionibus, *liz*, *pounz*, *porpoinz*, et sic cetera cum *z* vel *s*. Tamen Vasconi et Anglici scribunt cum *t*, *ut amy sount noz litz faitz*, *sount noz porpointz prestez* quod non est gallicum immo Vasconium' (Pope 1910: 192).

The earliest manuscripts of the *Donat*, *Donat B*, *Donat G*, and the *Donats* $M^1$ and $M^2$ (see Städtler 1988), as well as the *Orthographia gallica* in its various manuscripts, which cover the period from the end of the thirteenth century to the early fifteenth century (see Stürzinger 1884), do not include any explicit comments of the regional forms of French. The same holds for the *Nominale sive verbale*, which dates from about 1340 and was edited by W. W. Skeat.

This takes us to the *Tractatus orthographie gallicane* by Canon M. T. Coyfurelly, believed to have been composed between 1377 and 1399. In his concluding lines Coyfurelly makes it clear that his work is based on that of the Paris student T.H. The work is not only far more expansive but provides us with further interesting insights into the varying use of French towards the close of the fourteenth century. First of all, we note that with Canon Coyfurelly we no longer have a claim to describe French usage on both sides of the Channel. The complex noun phrase of the earlier work 'tam in partibus transmarinis quam cismarinis' has been reduced to 'in partibus transmarinis': 'sermones gallicanos et formam scripture cum regulis in eisdem intendo propulsare et secundum usum in partibus transmarinis dulciter sonare . . .' (Stengel 1879: 16).

How can we account for this striking contrast between the two treatises? If we assume with W. Rothwell (1968: 41) that T.H. was an Englishman who had studied at Paris and who was intent on helping his countrymen to acquire the French language, we might argue as follows. Around 1300 T.H. was aware that there were basically two forms of French, one in England (Anglo-Norman) and one in France. Having been to France himself and having been exposed to the French of the country and the capital, he knew that French was the native language of those born in France and that the French in England did not have the same mass of native users. From an Englishman's point of view then, the *transmarine* French was the form to select for teaching and learning. This is reflected in his use of 'tam in partibus *trans*marinis quam *cis*marinis' and not 'tam in partibus *cis*marinis quam *trans*marinis'. The predominant form of French he is describing is the transmarine (i.e. continental) form. We might even go further. Since he identifies some Picardisms, Bretonisms and Gasconisms, we might assume that the form of language described by him is a transmarine form of French which is not marked by such regionalisms: one which, by implication, may be the form that is associated with his credentials 'student of *Paris*'. Almost a century later, at a time when French had clearly become a foreign language in England, Coyfurelly must have seen no sense in outlining a cismarine (i.e. insular) French and thus he dropped the part 'quam cismarinis'. The only form of French to be discussed was the continental one. The difference in goals which T.H. and Coyfurelly set themselves thus reflect the change in linguistic status held by French in fourteenth-century England.

The greater number of regionalisms pointed out by Coyfurelly made E. Stengel (1879: 23) stress the treatise's value for a history of French dialectology. Coyfurelly does not mention the form of French used by the Bretons, but refers to that used by the Picards, the Burgundians, and the 'Leodii' (people of Liège). He briefly discusses aspects of Gascon French and his work is a much richer source for fourteenth-century Picard usage (ibid.: 23). When he refers to the pronunciation of *qu* in Scotland and England, he is, of course, considering the Scottish and English pronunciation of Latin, not the pronunciation of French. But what are the regional features of French which are not 'secundum dulce gallicum' (ibid.: 18)?

Contrary to French use, the Picards, Burgundians, and 'Leodii' are said to pronounce *u* after certain consonants (*q*, *g*, *s*): 'Tamen Picardi, Burg' et Leodien post predictas tres literas quoque sonant *u*, quod indecens et irregularis est, ut *quatre*, *quarrant*' (ibid.: 21). We note that Coyfurelly is not as purely descriptive as T.H. In using 'indecens', and 'irregularis' he voices his attitude towards such *u*-pronunciations.

As for the specific features that characterize Gascon use of French, T.H. had drawn attention to a spelling convention by which words ending in *t* are spelled *tz* in the plural (*litz*, *faitz*), whereas *t* is usually dropped before *z* in French. Coyfurelly also discusses this peculiarity (ibid.: 20), but, in addition, he attributes to Gascon French the use of *e* in such verb forms as *averai*, *enaverai*. For Coyfurelly this particular feature is Gascon as well as Picard (ibid.: 17).

He concedes that there may be 'alii', but in the corresponding passage T.H. had mentioned Breton French and Anglo-Norman French, not Gascon French at all.

With this we come to the linguistic features described as being peculiar to the *Romanici* (Picards).[3] Those mentioned relate chiefly to pronunciation and spelling. Thus we learn on the pronunciation of *a*:

[3] In the context of Coyfurelly's aim to describe French 'secundum usum in partibus transmarinis', it is not clear why S. Lusignan identifies *romanicus* with Anglo-Norman: 'Il est particulièrement attentif à toutes les différences qui existent entre le français (*gallicus*) et l'anglo-normand, qu'il désigne curieusement par le terme *romanicus*. Il s'agit bien pourtant de l'anglo-normand, comme le suggère l'analyse de la lettre *K*' (Lusignan 1986: 102). A. M. Kristol (1989: 364) equals *romanicus* with *Picard*.

Et sciendum est quod *a* fere debet sonari sicut *e* literam verbi gracia: *Savez . . . vous faire un chancon. Savez vous trair del arc. Pierre remaint al hostel. Saint Jaques est un tresnoble saint. J'en ai un bonne hopelande de pearce. J'en ai grand paour. Je l'ay achivee.* Et sic de similibus simile sit iudicium. Romanici vero proprie et plena voce sonant *a*, ut *faire*, *traire*, et huiusmodi. (ibid.: 16)

Two consonants are mentioned as having a particular use in Picard French. In a very detailed paragraph the different pronunciations for the spellings *l* or *ll* are outlined, ending with the statement 'Romanici vero presertim *l* sonant in omni loco nullo obstaculo impediente' (ibid.: 18). In a similarly detailed description of the sounding of the letter *s* or *ss* we learn that the Picards in most cases 'semper sonant *s* in medio diccionis ut *dont estee bons, je m'en iray al ostel et je revenrey tantost, qu'est la droite au Liege*' (ibid.: 19). This is then said to be also common in French.

Picard spellings are *ei* instead of *ie* in the following cases:

Unde errant, qui dicunt quod *i* vel *e* in huiusmodi diccionibus sonum penitus amittere debent tam in Gallicis quam eciam in romanicis, quia Gallici et Romanici *i* et *e* semper sonant in huiusmodi, sed non simili modo scribunt in sermonibus Romanici. Namque scribunt sic videlicet: *beins*, *ceins*, *leins*, *meins*, *reins*, *seins* et *bein* . . . et *ieo*, ubi Gallici scribunt *biens*, *liens*, et *ie* . . . (ibid.: 17)

A special case is the plural of words ending in *p*. The general rule given is that *p* in final position is not sounded when followed by a consonant. This has its reflections in spelling too: 'Item ista nomina *dras*, *tens*, *cors* sine *p* sunt scribenda, prout rectus sonus exigit in hac parte. Tamen Romanici non tenent illam regulam, quia pro majori parte *p* in huiusmodi semper scribunt. Et in gallico bene potest itaque scribi, ut *draps*, *temps*, *corps*' (ibid.: 18).

Under the letter *k*, two completely different linguistic phenomena are discussed. The first concerns the spelling and sounding of *k*/*ch*, the other a particular spelling for *nomina dignitatis*. What is spelled *ch* in French, is spelled *k* or *q* in Picard, and the corresponding spelling for *c* is *ch*:

*K* eciam in lingua romanica, non autem in lingua gallicana, nomine et loco *c* et *h* scribi debet et sonari, ut *kival* i. gallice *chival*, *kien* i. *chien*, *vake* i. *vache* et aliquando *q*, ut *quesne* i. *chesne*, nec non loco *C* debent scribi *c* et *h* secundum Romanicos, ut *pour chou* vel *pour cheu* i. gallice *pource* vel *pourceu*, *decha* i. *deca*, *tresdouche* i. *tresdoulce* et sic de aliis consimilibus. (ibid.: 17)

We may finally remark that nouns denoting dignitaries or offices are said to have a plural *s*, the assumed normal singular use in French being not only shorter but also regarded as more beautiful:

Item Romanica . . . nomina dignitatis (a)ut officii, que sunt singularis numeri, scribunt pluraliter in effectu, ut *lui papes de Rome*, *l'empereurs d'Alemaigne*, *lui rois d'Engleter et de France, lui chauncellers du saint peres, lui tresorerers mons. lui duques de Launcastre, lui recevours madame la roign*[e], *lui sainz esperes vous garde*; ubi vero Gallici sine *s* scribunt huiusmodi nomina singulariter, quod pulcrius et brevius est, ut *le pape de Rome, l'empereur de R., le Roy de l'Engleterre* et sic de ceteris. (ibid.: 17)

Quite obviously, Canon Coyfurelly was not aware of the two-case system of Old French which was retained longer in Picard, the nominative forms for masculine nouns ending in *-s*.

The next texts, also dating from the end of the fourteenth century, are dialogues. As such, unlike the treatises of orthography stating rules, they do not include explicit references to regional differences of French. The anonymous author of the *Petit livre pour enseigner les enfants* of 1399 is content with stating in the opening line 'Cy comence un petit livre pour enseigner les enfantz de leur entreparler comun francois' (ibid.: 10). In the *Manières de langage*, the language to be taught is not only described as the French of France but French itself is given the same attribute which we have already encountered in T.H.'s *Tractatus orthographiae*: '*dulce gallicum*': 'Ci comence la maniere de language que t'enseignera bien à droit parler et escrire doulz françois selon l'usage et la coustume de France' (Gessler 1934: 43).

The praise of the French language is sung more fully in the following lines from the *Manière de langage* of 1396 edited by P. Meyer:

. . . doulz françois, qu'est la plus bel et la plus gracious language et plus noble parler, après latin d'escole, qui soit au monde, et de tous gens mieulx prisee et amee que nul autre; quar Dieux le fist si doulce et amiable principalment a l'oneur et loenge de luy mesmes. Et pour ce il peut bien comparer au parler des angels du ciel, pour la grant doulceur et biaultee d'icel. (Meyer 1873: 382; cf. Gessler 1934: 44–5).

Entering now the fifteenth century, we find that the earliest pedagogical texts that have been preserved are grammatical treatises. Of these *Donats* (MSS Oxford All Souls 182, Cambridge University Library D.d.XII.23, and *Donat soloum doulce franceis de Paris*, BL Sloane 513), John Barton's is the most interesting for our purposes.[4] In the opening paragraph Barton outlines the purpose of his treatise, enlightens us on why the French language should be studied, and tells us who his envisaged learners are. In earlier literary sources, poets had offered apologies for their local use of French, pointing out that they had not been born in Paris, thus implying that the French of Paris was the form of language that enjoyed most prestige. In Barton's *Donat* we have for the first time an explicit statement that

[4] There are a number of recent editions of the various *Donat* manuscripts: Swiggers (1986); Städtler (1988); and an edition of the manuscript in the University Library, Cambridge, D.d.XII.23 is in preparation by Brian Merrilees.

what is being taught is the 'droit language de Paris' and even a reference to the regional area in which this form of French is used: 'Paris et de païs la d'entour':

Pour ceo que les bones gens du roiaume d'Engleterre sont enbrasez a sçavoir lire et escrire, entendre et parler droit françois, a fin qu'ils puissent entrecomuner bonement ové lour voisins, c'est a dire les bones gens du roiaume de France, et ainsi pour ce que les leys d'Engleterre pour le graigneur partie et aussi beaucoup de bones choses sont misez en françois, et aussi bien pres touz les seigneurs et toutes les dames en mesme roiaume d'Engliterre volentiers s'entrescrivent en romance, tres necessaire je cuide estre aus Engleis de sçavoir la droite nature de françois. A le honneur de Dieu et de sa tres doulce miere et toutz les saintez de paradis, je, Johan Barton, escolier de Paris, nee et nourie toutez voiez d'Engleterre en la conté de cestre, j'ey baillé ans avant diz Anglois un Donait françois pur les briefment entreduyr en la droit language du Paris et de païs la d'entour, la quelle language en Engliterre on appelle 'doulce France'. Et cest Donait, je le fis la fair a mes despenses et tres grande peine par pluseurs bons clercs du language avantdite. Pur ce, mes chiers enfantz et tres doulcez pusellës que avez fain d'apprendre cest Donait, sçachez qu'il est divisé en belcoup de chapiters . . . (Städtler 1988: 128)

From this passage we also learn that John Barton was an Englishman from the Chester area who had been a student at Paris and who had engaged several French literati ('*clercs*') for the compilation of the work.

It is Parisian French that is also singled out in the *Femina* (*nova*), a pedagogical work related to Walter de Bibbesworth's rhymed vocabulary treatise. The date given for the manuscript which was edited by W. A. Wright is about 1415 (Wright 1903). The name *Femina* (or *ffemina nova*) (ibid.: 118) is derived from the function of the work which the unknown author explains at the beginning: 'Lyber iste vocat*ur* fe*min*a q*ui*a sicut fe*min*a doc*et* infa*n*tem loq*ui* mate*rn*a*m* s*ic* doc*et* iste liber Iuvenes rhetorice loq*ui* gallicu*m*' (ibid.: 1). The presentation of the material offers a number of interesting aspects: homonyms are contrasted, the French words included are listed in three columns—the first giving the correct spelling, the second the pronunciation of the French item, and the third the meaning in English—and, closely related to our present concern, there are some references to varying regional forms of French. In these the language of Picardy is contrasted with the French of Paris (ibid.: 106).

In a manuscript of about the same time, the *doux Français de Paris* appears in the opening line: 'Cy comence le donait solon douce franceis de paris' (MS Sloane 513, fos. $136^{v}$–$137^{v}$; cf. Stürzinger 1884: 5). The manuscript contains a list of verbs; the Latin verb is given in the left-hand margin and the corresponding French verb is given in all its (irregular) forms. In other manuscripts of the early fifteenth century, the authors go straight to their task of describing dialogues (see the *Dialogues français* composed in 1415 and edited by Paul Meyer) or grammatical and orthographic rules (see the *Liber Donati* of about 1415 for which B. Merrilees is preparing an edition). The Add. MS 17.716, fos. 88$^{r}$–91$^{r}$, has parallels with T.H.'s *Tractatus orthographiae*, for instance the passage 'secundum usum et modum modernorum tam in partibus transmarinis quam cismarinis'. For the following years a number of grammatical manuscripts have been preserved (*Donat S* (before 1436), *Gram M*$^{1}$, *Gram M*$^{2}$, *Gram M*$^{3}$, *Gram M*$^{4}$, *Gram M*$^{5}$ (fifteenth century) in Städtler 1988) which do not advance our issue.

With this we come to the end of the fifteenth century and the appearance of several works containing dialogues. The MS I i. 6.17 of the University Library in Cambridge, referred to as *Dialogues in French and English* (Gessler 1934: 27), has been edited as 'Une manière de parler' by Södergård (1953). In addition, we have, of course, William Caxton's *Dialogues in French and English*, and the two similar works by Wynkyn de Worde ('Here begynneth a lytell treatyse for to lerne Englysshe and Frensshe') and Richard Pynson (see Chapter 2).

What the study of the early pedagogical works for the teaching of French in England reveals is that, not unexpectedly, the conversation books, whether they are called 'manières' or 'dialogues', contain very little if anything that may be taken as an explicit statement on the different forms of French used in France (or England). They simply teach French or the French of France. The more linguistically oriented works, however, the treatises on orthography and/or grammar, are better sources and they provide us with metalinguistic comments on early regional differences in French.

## THE FRENCH DESCRIBED BY ALEXANDER BARCLAY AND PIERRE VALENCE

We now come to the first decades of the sixteenthth century and Palsgrave's immediate predecessors and contemporaries. Let us see whether and how they tackle the question of linguistic variation in early sixteenth-century French and how they describe the French they are teaching.

The first work in chronological order is Alexander Barclay's *Introductory to wryte and to pronounce frenche* of 1521 (see Ellis 1871*b*).[5] It

[5] An early reference that Alexander Barclay was indebted to Canon M. T. Coyfurelly's *Tractatus* is found in the *Athenaeum* of 5 Oct. 1878, no. 2658, p. 433.

includes several references to regional differences in sixteenth-century French. This has been noted by K. Lambley:

> On the back of folio 4 he begins his 'introductory of orthography or true wrytynge wherby the diligent reder may be informed truly and perfytely to wryte and pronounce the Frenche tunge after the dyvers customes of many contrees of France'. Barclay, then, does not adopt an exclusive attitude towards provincial accents; he rather calls attention to them, though probably merely stating facts and drawing distinctions with no intention of teaching provincial forms. (Lambley 1920: 78)

Of all these references to varying regional French use, only one is specific in identifying particular regions within France. After discussing the co-occurrence of the vowels *I* and *E*, Barclay adds: 'Also in true frenche these wordes. Ie. ce. are. wryte*n* without o. in theyr ende but in pycard, or gascoygne, they are wryten with o. at *th*e ende, as thus ieo ceo' (Ellis 1871*b*: 809). Barclay here clearly goes beyond the *Orthographia gallica.* Three of its manuscripts, the British Library MS Harley 4971, and the MSS Cambridge University Library Ee. 4.20 and Oxford, Magdalene College 188, mention variation in spelling but do not give regional specifications (Stürzinger 1884: 5).

Barclay is otherwise not dialect-specific: 'But in some cou*n*trees .A. is sou*n*ded with full sou*n*de in lyke maner as it is wryten as, rayre, *and* suche other whan this lettre .A. is put for a worde it betokeneth as moche i*n* englysshe as this worde .hath. But some frenche men than adnex .d. withall as, ad. as il ad, he hath' (Ellis 1871*b*: 807). The passage is not without a predecessor. In Canon Coyfurelly's *Tractatus orthographie* the addition of a *d* after the third person singular of the verb *avoir* is regarded as erroneous (Stengel 1879: 16–17).

We have already earlier encountered the next phenomenon: the spelling and pronunciation of the future tense of *avoir*:

> Also in true frenche these wordes, auray, I shal haue. and, auroy, I had: be wryten w*ith*out e in myddes of the worde, *and* in lykewyse be they sou*n*ded w*ith*out, e but in certayne countrees of fraunce in suche maner of wordes this lettre e is sounded *and* wryten in the myddes as thus, aueroy, aueroie: whiche is contrary bothe in the true wrytynge, *and* also to the true p*ro*nuncyacion of perfyte frenche. (Ellis 1871*b*: 807)

Whereas Barclay here speaks of 'certayne countrees of fraunce', the Paris student T.H. in his *Tractatus orthographiae* had attributed this particularity to the Picards, the Bretons, and the Anglo-Norman speech in England. Canon Coyfurelly for his part maintained that this feature was common in Picard and Gascon.

The varying uses between *k*, *ch*, and *c* are illustrated by Barclay but not identified with any particular region:

This letter .k. in dyuerses speches is put for .ch. As kiual. kien. vak. but in true frenche it is not, but these wordes and suche lyke be wryte*n* with ch. as cheual. a hors, chien. a dogge, vache. a cowe, Also in certaynes countres of Frau*n*ce for c. is wryte*n* ch. as piecha. for a pieca, a whyle ago, tresdoulche for tresdoulce. ryght svete . . . (ibid.: 809).

The order of the examples *cheval*, *chien*, and *vache* immediately recalls the same sequence of words in Canon Coyfurelly's *Tractatus*. Coyfurelly, however, had identified the use of *k* instead of *ch*, and of *ch* instead of *c* as a Picardism (lingua romanica):

*K* eciam in lingua romanica, non autem in lingua gallicana, nomine et loco *c* et *h* scribi debet et sonari, ut *kival* i. gallice *chival*, *kien* i. *chien*, *vake* i. *vache* et aliquando *q*, ut *quesne* i. *chesne*, necnon loco *c* debent scribi *c* et *h* secundum Romanicos, ut *pour chou* vel *pour cheu* i. gallice *pource* vel *pourceu*, *decha* i. *deca*, *tresdouche* i. *tresdoulce* et sic de aliis consimilibus. (Stengel 1879: 17)

So far, we have been able to show that four of the variant uses within France described by Alexander Barclay had had a precedent in Canon Coyfurelly's *Tractatus orthographie*. There is further evidence that Barclay must have had access to a copy of Coyfurelly's work. In some areas of France, Barclay says, nouns denoting dignitaries or offices appear with a plural *s* when used in the singular: 'In lykewyse in some countrees of Fraunce names of dygnyte *and* offyce whiche are the synguler nombre are wryten plurell w*ith*, s, at the ende, as luy papes de Rome, luy roys de france, luy sains esperis: but in true frenche these names be wryten w*ith*out, s . . .' (Ellis 1871*b*: 809).

The next feature singled out by Barclay concerns the variation between final *r* and final *z* in some words. In T.H.'s *Tractatus orthographiae* there is a brief mention '*R* vero aliquando in fine diccionis retinebit sonum *r* et aliquando sonum *z*, ut *vuilez vouz aler* ou *voilez vous alez* et sic de similibus' (Pope 1910: 191). Coyfurelly draws attention to the same phenomenon, and, like the Paris student T.H., he does not associate it with a particular French region. Yet his examples are completely different:

*R* autem in fine diccionis indifferenter potest sonari quasi *z* vel *r*, ut *j'en ay grand mal ou cuer*, *j'en ay bon quer*. Set dulcior est sonus quasi *z* in lingua gallica quam quasi *r*. Tamen hec regula non tenet in omnibus ut in hiis diccionibus *quar*, *querir*, *ferir* et *ferrer*, in quibus et proprie debet sonari et sic de similibus. (Stengel 1879: 18)

Here is what Barclay says about this variation:

This letter .R. put in the ende of a worde shall kepe his owne full sounde, as cueur, as thus Iay grant mal au cueur, I haue graet dysease at my herte: Ie vous prie pour me consailler, I pray you counsell me: but in some cou*n*tres .r. is soundyd, as this letter .z. as compere, a gossyp, is somtyme soundyd thus compez, and so of other wordes endynge in this letter .R. . . . (Ellis 1871*b*: 811)

Some parts of Barclay's treatment look like Coyfurelly's, the example *compere/compez*, however, occurs in neither T.H.'s nor Coyfurelly's *Tractatus*.

The proper plural spelling of words ending in *t* (as in *les lits*, *les pots*) is a recurrent issue with T.H. and Canon Coyfurelly, and, following them, also with Alexander Barclay. According to T.H. Anglo-Norman and Gascon French preserved the final *-t* in the plural contrary to the general French use. Coyfurelly had attributed this particularity to Gascon usage (Stengel 1879: 20).

Again, Barclay uses the same examples given by his predecessors but does not follow their description in identifying the differing use with particular areas within France:

> . . . but it accordeth not to reason to wryte these wordes thus saintz toutz marcha*nt*z in *the* plurell no*m*bre, all if they be wryten w*ith* t. in *th*e synguler no*m*bre. for in *th*e plurell nombre they ought nat to be writen with t. for ony of these two letters s. or z. in fre*n*che stande for as moche as ts. or tz. But for a co*n*clusion though suche wordes in certayne countres of Fraunce be wryten with ts. or w*ith* tz. in *th*e ende. as thus mon amy sont no*us* litz faitz, my frende are our beddes made. Beau sir so*n*t mez pourpointz faitz, faire sir be my doublettes made. yet after true ortography of frenche these wordes and other suche muste be bothe wryten and sou*n*dyd without t. as lis fais pourpoins. (Ellis 1871*b*: 812)

To sum up, it is quite evident that Barclay used the earlier treatises on orthography when he compiled his *Introductory*. What is striking is that, while his various sources identified a number of regionalisms, he did not repeat their findings. This may mean that Barclay had had no personal experience with the regional features outlined by his predecessors and did not want to commit himself merely to copying what he found in his sources. He was satisfied with pointing out that usage differed within France. Another explanation could be that the actual copies of T.H.'s and Coyfurelly's treatises which he consulted were versions of these manuscripts which did not include explicit statements with respect to regional differences in French.

The second work in chronological order is Pierre Valence's *Introductions in frensshe* of 1528. It includes one single reference to a French regionalism—the negative particle *mie* (see Alston 1967*a*: E ii$^{v}$).

## TORY'S DESCRIPTION OF FRENCH REGIONALISMS

We come now to the most important work that preceded John Palsgrave's *Lesclarcissement*: Tory's *Champ fleury*. Tory provides us with a more complex picture of sixteenth-century linguistic variation in France. He follows the discussion of the form of each letter in alphabetical order with an indication of how the letter in question is (or should be) pronounced, identifying not only specific French regionalisms but also social variants and drawing particular attention to the ways of pronunciation introduced or cultivated by women. If we rearrange his descriptions to gather together the linguistic features outlined for specific regional areas, we get an interesting picture. In our arrangement, vowels are discussed before consonants. We begin with the Picardy.

*The letter E*

. . . ie treuue en oultre que le Picard dit V. pour E. et le pronũce cõme aspire, en disant. Chu garchon. pour Ce garcon . . . (fo. xxxix)

For the letter *C* Tory compares the pronunciation by the Italians, the Romans, and the French:

*The letter C*

Les Italiens de leur bonne costume pronuncent le C. mol, & quasi comme si la syllabe ou il est, estoit escripte auec aspiration H. tant en Latin quen leur vulgar . . . La quelle chose nous ne regardons pas en nostre pronunciation de lãgage Frãcois, ne de Latin. Toutefois les Picards y sont fort bien vsitez en beaucop de vocables de leur langage. Comme quant ilz veulent dire Cela, Cecy. ils pronuncẽt Chela, & Chechy, comme syl y auoit en lorthographe vne aspiration. H. deuãt la vocale E. et deuant I. Au contraire, la ou le bon Frãcois escript & pronunce la dicte aspiration H. deuant C. & O. comme en disant Chanoine, & Chose. le Picard dit. Canoine, & Cose. Le Francois dit, vng Chien, vng Chat, & vne Mouche, et le Picard pronunce, vng Quien, vng Cat, & vne Mouque. Le dict Picard pronunce le C. deuant V, comme nous. en disant. Cuydez vous q̃ ie soye Crapot deaue? sans y faire signe daspiration. Toutesfois il dit De chu monde, en escripuant & pronunceant laspiration H. deuãt le dict V. En latin il pronunce le C. myeulx que ne faisons, car il le pronũce gras/ & comme aspire, mais il ne lescript pas aspire. Il dit Amiche, & Sochie, Chichero erat pater eloquentiæ. mais il escript bien Amice & Socie, Cicero erat pater eloquentiæ. Entre toutes les nations de France, le Picard pronũce tresbien le C . . . (fo. xxxvii)

The passage not only shows us that the distinctive features in Picard pronunciation, the retention of /k/ before an original stressed *a* in Latin (e.g. *canis*) which had developed into /tʃ/ and later /ʃ/, and the assibilation of /s/ to /ʃ/ as in *ceci*/*chechy*, were commonly known by contemporaries (see Coyfurelly's treatment of *k*); it also reveals that in precision and clarity of description Tory far outdoes earlier writers. He attempts to identify linguistic conditions for the differences in pronunciation: *c* is pronounced *ch* when followed by *e* or *i*. He contrasts the pronunciations of *cuydez* and *de chu monde*, but does not yet account for the fact that the *u* in *chu* is a secondary feature and as such different from a primary *u* in a *C* + *u* context. We would have to assume the following stages in the pronunciation: *Ce* becomes *che* in Picard according to the rule outlined above, and, in addition, according to the description given under the letter *e*, (unstressed) *e* is rendered as *u*.

*The letter G*

. . . Les picards au cõtraire dessusdits Alemans qui pronuncent I. consone pour G. en lieu de le I. cõsone/ pronuncent le .G. en aucunes dictions. comme en lieu de dire. Ma iambe sest rompue en nostre iardin, & y ay perdu mon chapeau iaulne. Ilz disent. Me gambe sest/rompue en noz gardin, & y ay perdu men capiau gaulne . . . (fo. xlii)

When he was dealing with the letter *C*, Tory expressed his admiration for the pronunciation of *C* by the Picards. He reiterates this praise under the letter *H*.

*The letter H*

. . . les Picards, comme iay cy dessus dict, la pronuncent moult bien auec le C. & sans icelluy C. Et ie ne cognois Nation en France qui aye la langue plus apte & diserte a bien pronuncer Grec, Latin, & Francois, que Picards . . . (fo. xlv)

The last feature described as a Picard particularity is the dropping of *t* in final position after a nasal. The example provided by Tory is as delightful as the earlier example *Ma iambe sest rompue en nostre iardin, & y ay perdu mon chapeau iaulne*, incorporating three instances (*jambe*, *jardin*, and *jaune*) of the contrast under consideration. The example under *t* has not only a rhythmical structure but also a rhyme:

*The letter T*

. . . Pareilleement aucuns Picards laissent celluy T. a la fin de aucunes dictions en Francois. comme quant ilz veulẽt dire Comant cela comant? Monsieur cest vne iument. Ilz pronuncent. Coman chela coman? Monsieur chest vne iumen. (fo. lviii$^{v}$)

We also note that Tory is consistent within his own description by giving *cela* and *cest* in the Picard pronunciation *chela* and *chest*.

The other regional variants are not as extensively dealt with as language use in Picardy, which has not only salient characteristics but also Tory's admiration.

From Picardy we move on to Normandy. Tory singles out two features. The Normans are said to pronounce an *e* where there should be an *oy*, but no examples are provided.

The people from Brittany, the Le Mans area, and Lorraine are recognizable by their pronunciation of *R*:

*The letter R*

Ie treuue dauantage trois aultres Nations qui pronuncent le .R. tresmal. Les Manseaulx, les Bretons, & les Lorains. Les Manseaulx adiouxtent S. auec R. car si vouloient dire Pater noster, or Tu es Magister noster, Ilz pronunceroient Paters nosters, Tu es magisters nosters. Les Bretons ne pronuncent que vne R. ou il en ya deux escriptes. Comme en disant Homo curit. pour Homo currit. Au contraire les Lorains en pronuncent deux/ ou il ny en a que vne. Car silz veulent dire, Saincte Marie, vecy grande moquerie, & dure dyablerie, Ilz pronuncent. Saincte Marrie, vecy grãde mocquerrie, & durre dyablerrie. Ce sont les Lorains contre lesquelz le

Prouerbe. Sept cents cinquante & trois de la Segonde Chiliade Derasme peult estre allegue . . . (fo. lv)

The speakers of Brittany are identified by another particularity, their voiceless pronunciation of intervocalic *s* (fo. lviii). For the Lorraine speakers, however, Tory also describes a characteristic way of pronouncing the French of the region:

*The letter E*

. . . Les Lorains, & les Ecossois en parlant en langage Francois, au moings en y cuidãt parler, laissent quasi tousiours a pronuncer le E, quant il est a la fin des dictions. Les Lorains disent. Sus lherbet, De ma muset, Vne chansonet, Ay dict mon comper, ma comer, Ioliet, Et frisquet, quen dictes vous? en lieu de dire. Sur lherbete, de ma musete, vne chansonnete, Ay dict mon compere, Ma comere ioliete, Et frisquete, Quen dictes vous? Item si veulent dire Simone, ils pronuncẽt Simon. Lione, Lion. Bone, Bon qui est vice en Frãcois . . . (fo. xxxix)

From Lorraine we turn to Burgundy. Coyfurelly had told us that the Burgundians tended to pronounce the *u* after a *q*, as in *quatre*, *quarrant* (Stengel 1879: 21). According to Tory, Burgundians, or more precisely the young students who went to the university of Paris, substituted an *r* for an *l* when speaking Latin (fo. xlix).

With this we come to Tory's home town, Bourges. He observes two tendencies of pronunciation among his fellow townsmen. *G* is said to resemble *C* in cases like *lignum*, and *Z* tends to be realized as *SD* or SS, as in Gaza (fos. xlii, xliiii).

From Bourges we move further south. Tory gives us an interesting picture of Lyon: the fairs and banks of the town are well frequented by Italians and their linguistic habits seem to have had an influence on the women's pronunciation:

*The letter A*

A. veult estre pronunce apertement . . . La quelle chose les Italiens obseruent tresbien, tant en Latin quen leur vulgaire, au quel la pluspart de leurs dictions est terminee en A. Comme quãt ilz disent vna charta, vna bella dona, mya sorella, & daultres vng millier. A la cause de quoy, pour la frequentation des dicts Italiens, qui est aux ferez & bancquez de Lion, les dames Lionnoises pronuncent gracieusement souuent A. pour E. quant elles disent. Choma vous choma chat affeta. & mille aultres motz semblables . . . (fo. xxxiii$^{v}$)

This is the second instance of Tory indicating the social group of speakers who use a particular form of language. Young students from the Burgundy and Forest regions had been described as substituting *r* for *l* in Latin. In the case of Lyon, it is the women whose pronunciation is marked. And we shall see that the women from Paris are another social group distinguishing themselves by a particular pronunciation.

The other characteristic which Tory noted with people from Lyon is that they drop *t* in certain circumstances—for instance, in the third person plural form of Latin verbs, e.g. *amaverun* instead of *amaverunt* (fo. lviii$^v$).

The southernmost areas for which Tory identified some regional characteristics are Toulouse and Gascony. Both regions are said to use a prosthetic *e* before *s* (plus consonant) (fo. lviii).

The more interesting feature, however, is the substitution of *b* by *v*, which, according to Tory, accounts for the Latin name *Vascones* instead of *Gascones*:

*The letter B*

. . . Nous pronũceõs, ou debuons pronũcer le B. de noz lefres sentre-ouurans de la force de lyssue de nostre alaine .B. en Grec, est dict vita, & y est ꝓnũce cõme vng V. cõsone . . . La quelle pronũciation les Gascons tiennent en leur langage en beaucop de dictions. comme quantz ilz veulent dire. Iay beu de bon vin, Ilz disent. Iay veu de von bin. Pareillement en Latin. Nõ in solo pane bibit homo, pour, viuit homo. Et en ce disant le sens est bien souuãt peruerty selon le bon francois, & selon le Latin, comme voyez aux dits exemples alleguez, ou il ya pour iay beu, iay veu. & pour viuit, bibit. Ilz font beaucop dautres incongruytes, comme quãt ils disent, Vng veau bieillard, pour, vng beau vieillard. En lieu de le V. consone ilz disent. B, & en lieu de B., V. cõsone . . . Les Gascons ne pronũcent seullement B. pour V, consone, en francois, mais pareillement en Latin, comme quantz ilz disent. Vona dies. pour. Bona dies. . Bibat Faustus, pour Viuat Faustus. Beni ad me & viues, pour, Veni ad me/ & bibes. a loccasion de ce quilz ont le V. consone en si frequẽte locution. Il semble que les Latins les appellent plustost vascones par V. que Gascones. pour en dõner secretemẽt quelque intelligence. (fo. xxxv$^v$)

We now return to the capital Paris. Here, it is interesting to note that Tory becomes more argumentative in his description—and also critical: the nouns *abus* and *vice*, and the adverb *abusivement* are conspicuous. And again, as in the case of the women of Lyon, *les dames de Paris* are a social group of language users who do not follow what is regarded as the normal way of speaking:

*The letter A*

. . . Au contraire les Dames de Paris, en lieu de A pronuncent E. bien souuent, quant elles disent. Mon mery est a la porte de Peris, ou il se faict peier. En lieu de dire. Mon mary est a la porte de Paris ou il se faict paier. Telle maniere de parler vient dacoustumence de ieunesse. (fo. xxxiii$^v$)

Thus, whereas the ladies of Lyon tend to lower *e* to *a*, those of Paris are said to raise *a* to *e*. This habit of pronouncing, says Tory, goes back to a childhood habit. With respect to the dropping of *s* in final position Tory thinks that it would be excusable if it were not for the fact that the female way of speaking was passed on to men (fos. lvi$^v$–lvii).

We conclude our summary of Tory's assessment of regional variation in sixteenth-century French with a linguistic feature which was common not only in Paris but also in Bourges, Tory's home town. Having pointed out that the Romans often wrote and pronounced an *s* instead of an *r*, as in *Valerius*/*Valesius*, *Furius*/*Fusius*,[6] Tory continues:

> *The letter R*
> La quelle mode de ꝓnuncer est auiourdhuy en abus tant en Bourges, dou ie suis natif, quen ceste noble Cite de Paris, quãt pour R. bien souuãt y est pronunce S. & pour S. R. Car en lieu de dire IESVS, MARIA. ilz ꝓnuncẽt IERVS MASIA. Et en lieu de dire au cõmãcemẽt du Premier liure de Eneides de Virgile. Musa mihi causas memora que numine læso, Ilz pronuncent abusiuement. Mura mihi cauras memosa quo numine læro. (fo. lv)

The substitution of *r* by *z* had been mentioned by T.H. and by Canon Coyfurelly. Both had drawn attention to the phenomenon as such (see p. 105), whereas Alexander Barclay in his *Introductory* had made it a regionalism by pointing out that it occurred in some 'countries'. His example had been *compere*/*compez*, which clearly differs from those examples provided by Tory. The common characteristic of Tory's examples is the fact that the substitution occurs in intervocalic position.

*Lesclarcissement de la langue francoyse* tells us that Giles du Wes had taken Palsgrave to the library of the Guildhall in London (I, fo. xiii$^{v}$), that Palsgrave had seen 'an olde boke written in parchement in maner in all thynges like to his [Barclay's] sayd Introductory' (I, fo. xii$^{v}$),[7] that he knew Alexander Barclay's *Introductory* (and disagreed with his description of French usage), that he was familiar with Tory's *Champ fleury*. Palsgrave was also aware of the work undertaken by his teaching colleagues and competitors Pierre Valence and Giles du Wes. We might, therefore, reasonably assume that Palsgrave tried to inform himself as best as he could on the work that had been done on French pronunciation, grammar, and vocabulary. At the same time, he had been in Paris at a time when the French of Paris was imposing itself more and more and when it was becoming the model to be imitated by those seeking professional advancement. He frequented the court circle. He had taught the king's sister as well as the king's son. Did Palsgrave take his linguistic model for French for granted, as he did with respect to his mother tongue, or did he explicitly comment on it?

[6] These are the very examples we find in Erasmus (1973: 45). See also Erasmus (1981: 128).

[7] For S.-G. Neumann, this old book was a manuscript of John Barton's *Donait*. According to him, Barclay's *Introductory* 'était une réproduction du *Donait Barton*' (Neumann 1959: 20).

## THE 'RIGHT' FRENCH: PALSGRAVE'S MODEL

We recall that on the title-page of *Lesclarcissement* Palsgrave is described as 'gradue de Paris'. In providing the users of his book with this item of information, Palsgrave as a non-native speaker of French seems to be assuring them that he had not only been in the country but had even received a university degree from there. So his authority was established. Palsgrave here followed a practice established by earlier writers. T.H. had described himself as a student of Paris, Canon M. T. Coyfurelly made sure that his name as well as his doctorate in law from the university of Orleans were mentioned at the end of his *Tractatus*. John Barton, in the first paragraph of his *Donait*, introduces himself as an 'escolier de Paris'. In view of the fact that the French use of Paris had a much higher prestige by 1530 than during the preceding centuries, the qualifying specification 'gradue de Paris' may have fulfilled a double function. It advertised the author not only as someone who had been to France, who knew French, and who had a French degree, but also as someone who had a qualification in Paris, such that one might assume that he was an expert in the French of Paris.

The introductions to the first and the second book of *Lesclarcissement* do not say anything about the variety of French which Palsgrave takes as his model for the pronunciation and grammar for which he is trying to formulate rules. Nor does the first part of the first book itself 'wherin the true sowndynge of the frenche tonge resteth'. Yet, at the very point at which Palsgrave sensed a difference between what he regarded as the prestige form of French and a specific local feature of that area, he feels it necessary to make his overall approach explicit. The specific local feature in question is the one which had already been mentioned by Tory: the substitution of *r* by *s*. Palsgrave describes the sounding of the letter *R* as follows:

> R in the frenche tonge shalbe sounded as he is in latyn/ without any exceptyon/ so that where as they of Parys sounde somtyme R lyke z/ Sayng Pazis for Paris/ pazisien for parisyen/ chaize for chayre/ Mazy for Mary/ and suche lyke: in that thyng I wolde nat haue them folowed. Albeit that in all this worke I moost folowe the Parisyens/ and the coũtreys that be conteygned bytwene the ryuer of Seyne and the ryuer of Loyre/ which the Romayns called somtyme Gallya Celtica: for within that space is contayned the herte of Fraunce/ where the tonge is at this day moost parfyte/ and hath of moost auncyente so contynued/ so that I thynke it but superfluous/ and vnto the lernar but a nedelesse confusyon/ to shewe the dyuersite of pronuncyacion of the other frontier countreys/ seyng that besydes the thousandes that haue written sythe Alayn Charters dayes/ which in maner haue left none auctours written in the latyn tonge vntranslated. (I, fo. xiii$^{v}$)

The statement is the most explicit that we have come across in the various texts consulted. John Barton had described his model as 'la droit language du Paris et de païs la d'entour', including the area around Paris. Palsgrave, however, is more specific: he tries to delimit the area by giving as its borders the Seine and the Loire. D. Trudeau quotes this very passage from *Lesclarcissement* in support of her characterization of early sixteenth-century French as '[a]u début du XVIe siècle, la prééminence linguistique de Paris et de ses environs est un fait déjà établi' (Trudeau 1992: 23). Palsgrave provides us with a reason for describing the French of this area: it is the most perfect and has been so for a long time. He also justifies his decision not to describe the pronunciation current in the regions stretching beyond these limits: too much diversity would confuse the learner. Palsgrave then describes the social impact of this form of French which he regards as the most perfect:

> There is no man of what parte of Fraunce so euer he be borne/ if he desyre that his writynges shulde be had in any estymacion/ but he writeth in suche language as they speke within the boundes that I haue before rehersed. Nor there is no man that is a mynister of their cõmon welth/ outher as a capitayne/ or in offyce of Indicatoure/ or as a famous preachour/ but where soeuer his abyding be/ he speketh the parfyte frenche: In somoche that the Heynowers/ and they of Romant/ Brabant/ and all other nacyons vsynge the kynde of speche/ nowe called Uallon or Romant/ thoughe in pronũciacion they folowe moche the said olde Romant tonge/ lyke as the Pycardes/ liegeoys/ and Ardenoyes do yet in writynge/ as well concernyng their iudiciall causes/ as any other thyng made by any of them of their owne inuencyon/ or in the letters missyues/ of suche as be secreatores in the sayd countreis/ they folowe in writyng as nere as they may/ the very true ortography and congruite of the parfyte frenche tonge: and onely suche be had in estymacion/ and haue charge cõmytted to them as be able to do so. (I, fo. xiii[v])

As we can see, Palsgrave clearly distinguishes between the spoken and the written language, and the passage quoted confirms the convergence towards one uniform written use of French and different spoken regional forms discussed earlier.

Yet in the programmatic statements under the pronunciation of the consonant *R*, Palsgrave not only outlines the social influence of 'perfect French' on the other coexisting forms of French; he also introduces his readers to historically different stages of the language:

> But if there were dyuersite in writyng amõgest them of the frenche tonge/ lyke as there were sõtyme among the Grekes *Dialecta*/ so that euery man wrote in his owne tonge/ lyke as the grekes somtyme dyd. Or that the Romant of the Rose/ whiche vndouted is a syngnler [*sic*] auctour/ were nowe at these dayes imprinted in the olde Romant tong wherin it was made/ as dothe appere by a boke in the library of Gyldehall in London/ whiche mayster Gylles somtyme scole mayster to our souerayne nowe raygning/ in the frẽche tong shewed me I coude than be contẽted: and it

were for that auctours sake onely/ to shewe the differẽce bitwene tholde Romant tong ⁊ the right french tong. (I, fo. xiii$^{v}$-xiiii$^{r}$)

Palsgrave here opposes the 'right' French tongue and the 'old Romant' which S.-G. Neumann (1959: 38, 43) takes to mean the French before 1400, crediting Palsgrave with having used a special term, 'olde Romant', for this earlier stage of French.

Having defined the regional boundaries of the area in which the 'right' or 'true' French was used and made this form of French his model, Palsgrave then faced the concrete task of describing this form or reducing it to rules. There were no precedents for the study of French, but there were, of course, precedents for the classical languages: linguistic authority came from those who were believed to have made the best use of the language, the good authors. The next step in Palsgrave's approach, then, was to establish who these best authors were for the French language. Having found out which French authors were most highly regarded at his time, he would then have to read their works.

In the first book of *Lesclarcissement*, towards the end when Palsgrave quotes some pieces of literature and indicates how they should be sounded, he describes the authors from whom he quotes as 'auctors/ as I estyme to be most excellent in the frenche tonge' (I, fo. xxi$^{v}$). Alain Chartier and Jean Lemaire de Belges are the most frequently quoted by Palsgrave. Others are: Guillaume de Lorris, Jean de Meung, Jean Froissart, Gaston Foix, Guillaume Alexis, Octovien de Saint-Gelais, and Jean Meschinot.

The compilation of *Lesclarcissement de la langue francoyse* took Palsgrave about twenty years, so that he will have had to make his choice of authors long before Tory engaged on his *Champ fleury*. We recall that Tory had drawn up a list of those authors whom he regarded as the best in the French language. Palsgrave felt elated when he discovered that the eminent Frenchman's choice was very similar to his own. He highlighted this near-coincidence in the *Authours Epistell* of his book and, in doing so, evidently tried to give his own work still greater authority.

The oldest text referred to in *Lesclarcissement* is the *Roman de la Rose*, so greatly admired by Palsgrave. The works of French literature which Palsgrave was familiar with and which he occasionally mentioned thus span a period of more than 200 years. This has led to some criticism that the language he describes was not the current French of his time. Such criticism reveals a very superficial knowledge of Palsgrave's work. Nowhere does he claim to describe contemporary French use. And what would 'contemporary' refer to? The period of his life, the first part of the sixteenth century? S.-G. Neumann has pointed out that Palsgrave's approach was not unusual for the sixteenth century:

Si notre grammarien a néanmoins utilisé ces vieux textes, la raison en fut sans doute l'immense prestige *littéraire* dont ils jouissaient en son temps. Palsgrave avait besoin d'autorités pour étayer sa doctrine, et ils prenaient celles qu'ils trouvaient, quitte à mettre ses lecteurs en garde contre leurs archaïsmes. C'est là un procédé qui peut nous paraître étrange aujourd'hui, mais qui n'avait rien de choquant au XVIe siècle. On n'a qu'à se rappeler que dans son *Champ Fleury* de 1529, Geofroy Tory donne une liste d'auteurs dont il recommande l'étude au futur codificateur du français. Dans cette liste figurent non seulement les grands auteurs du XVe siècle et le *Roman de la Rose*, mais aussi Chrétien de Troies, Pierre de Saint-Cloud, Arnoul et Simon Graban . . . (Neumann 1959: 43–4).

And let us not forget the literary tastes of the time. As someone employed by the king, Palsgrave would have been well advised to take note of the court's literary preferences. These, especially their Burgundian origins, are admirably described in a most enlightening study by Gordon Kipling (1977). The Tudors, we learn, followed the literary tastes and educational attitudes of the dukes of Burgundy. These preoccupations go back to the court of Edward IV and Queen Elizabeth Woodville. When Henry VII created the office of king's poet, Bernard André became its first holder. He then progressed to becoming the king's chronicler, and his literary models were Georges Chastellain, Jean Molinet, and Jean Lemaire de Belges. Any English poet hoping to make a career for himself had to follow these Burgundian tastes. According to Kipling, it was the marriage of the king's sister, Mary Tudor, to the French king, Louis XII, in 1514, that made Jean Lemaire de Belges popular in England:

In preparation for this event, John Palsgrave had been hired to tutor the future queen in French, and judging by his *Esclarcissement*, which was based on his experience, Palsgrave designed a reading programme for Mary grounded heavily in the works of Lemaire's poetry, particularly the two *Épistres de L'Amant Vert*. This emphasis was only natural, for Lemaire currently held the position of chief chronicler and poet at the French court, and Mary's predecessor as Queen of France, Anne of Brittany, had been particularly fond of *L'Amant Vert*. (ibid.: 24–5)

The literary tastes of the English court would, of course, also be reflected in the king's library. Their first keepers were mostly of Flemish origin, as, for instance, Giles du Wes, Palsgrave's contemporary, who became the king's librarian in 1509. Catalogues of the king's library reveal not only that Jean Froissart, Alain Chartier, and Christine de Pisan were court authors; they also 'testify conclusively to the predominantly Burgundian and Flemish orientation of the Royal library' (Kipling 1977: 40; see also Casley 1734; Omont 1891).

### FRENCH REGIONALISMS IN *LESCLARCISSEMENT*

Let us now investigate *Lesclarcissement* itself. Palsgrave had argued that an indication of regional variations would confuse learners. He was, therefore, going to concentrate on describing the 'true' and 'right' French, and this is what he does. It might be worthwhile to mention that under the nouns in the dictionary Palsgrave has a lemma *Good frenche speche* which is translated as *francoys*. Yet occasionally he does indeed draw attention to regional variants. We shall review these instances and compare them with those pointed out in the earlier texts which we have studied. The actual number of translation equivalents that are explicitly marked as regionalisms is relatively small.

In four cases we have Normanisms:

> **I Fare well or yuell concernyng the helthe of my body or otherwyse concernyng yͤ quyete of my mynde/** Ie me porte, ie me suis porté, porter, verbũ medium. prime cõiuga.
>
> . . . . . . .
>
> **Fare you well:** Vous est il bien. **I haue fared yuell sythe I** sawe you: Il ma esté mal depuis que ie ne vous vis. **Howe farest thou:** Cõment te va, **is normante/ and so is/ Howe do you:** Comment vous va. . . .
>
> (III, fo. cc.xxx.iii)

The second instance is the verb *mehaigner* in the sense of 'to maim'. Palsgrave's entry reads as follows:

> **I Mayne or I mayne one I take the vse of one of his lymmes from hym/** Iaffolle, or ie mutille, **and** ie mehaigne. prime cõiu. . . . **but** mehaigner, **is normante.**
>
> (III, fo. cc.lxxxvi$^{v}$)[8]

The third item is listed under the adverbs answering a question *Howe long*:

> **Hence ouer a yere:** Dicy a vng an passé **and** douen danten. **Normant.**
>
> (III, fo. cccc.liii$^{v}$)

[8] See also the treatment of *mehaing, mehaingnié, mehaigner* in G. Roques (1982: 96–7); see Sainéan's (1922–3: ii. 103) discussion of Rabelais's use.

and the fourth is an adverbial phrase answering a question *why*:

> **ye trewly**: Voyre vrayement. **but as for** voyre vraymecques, **is but a cou trefayte terme for nycenesse/ lyke as** ouy en da, ⁊ non en da, **lyke as** ouy dea, **is vsed of the normannes.**
>
> (III, fo. cccc.lx$^{r\text{-}v}$)

From Normandy we move on to Picardy. For the verb *to rent* in the meaning of 'to tear' Palsgrave gives us four French equivalents, one of which is described as *Romant*, and 'nowe out of vse in comen spetche', and another as *Pycarte*:

> **I Rent I teare a thyng asonder/** Ie dessire, prime. **and** ie arrable, Romant. prime cõiuga. **and** ie deschire. prime cõiu. **and** ie despece. pri. cõiu. **He hath rent my gowne**: Il a dessiré ma robbe, il a deschiré, **is Pycarte/ and** il a despecé ma robbe, **as for** arrabler, **is nowe out of vse in comen** spetche.
>
> (III, fo. ccc.xxxviii)

In the parallel entry for the English verb *to tear*, Palsgrave includes *dechirer*, but marks it as *Romant* (III, fo. ccc.lxxxiii).

Next we have two adverbial phrases answering a question *whan*:

> **Ryght nowe**: Or ayns. **Pycart/ as/** Pource que ie le vis orayns, **but the frenche men vse rather** Tout asteure, **or** Tout mayntenant.
>
> (III, fo. cccc.xxvi)

> **Whyle eere**: Orayn. **and** Ores. **but** orayn, **is Pycarte**. Ores, **as/** Aynsi comme ores les vistes.
>
> (III, fo. cccc.xxvii)

In the case of the only Gasconism, we have a repetition of the same French equivalent under the different spellings of the noun *horse*:

> **Horse in Gascoyne speche** roucyn [*sic*] s.ma.
>
> (III, fo. xl$^{v}$)
>
> **Hoorse in gascoyne speche** roncyn s.ma.
>
> (III, fo. xli)

These occurrences of clearly marked French regionalisms sharply differ from those encountered in the earlier texts studied. Whereas compilers writing before the publication of *Lesclarcissement* had concentrated on differences in pronunciation and spelling, Palsgrave adduces individual lexical items as well as colloquial expressions—for example, *cõment te va*, *douen danten*, *ouy dea*, and *or ayns*.[9]

We return to the capital. We recall that Palsgrave had drawn attention to the substitution of *r* by *z* in Paris speech. He had illustrated the phenomenon with the examples *Pazis* for *Paris*, *pazisien* for *parisyen*, *chaize* for *chayre*, and *Mazy* for *Mary*. Yet the description of the pronunciation of the letter *R* is not the only instance where he mentions this feature. There are two other occurrences in the French 'vocabulist':

> **I Blaber as a chylde dothe or he can speake/** Ie gasouille. prime cõiu. **the right worde after yͤ latyn shulde be/** ie garrouille, **but the parysyens tourne R/ in to S/ whiche bytwene two vouels hath the sounde of Z** . . .
>
> (III, fo. c.lxvii)

> **I Chatter as byrdes do or they begyn to speake or parfetly to synge their note:** Ie gariolle. prime coniu. **but the parisyens chaunge R/ in to S/ or Z/ and saye** ie gasoille, **as I haue in the first boke touched.**
>
> (III, fo. c.lxxxv)

All the examples provided by Palsgrave illustrate the substitution of /r/ by /z/ in intervocalic position. His formulation 'but the parysyens tourne R/ in to S/ whiche bytwene two vouels hath the sounde of Z' appears to combine spelling and pronunciation: the letter *S* is substituted for *R*, and an *S* in intervocalic position becomes voiced. Palsgrave thus seems to have been aware of the phonological conditions of the substitution. Tory in his *Champ fleury* does not include such a specification. Tory gives two examples which are not only different from Palsgrave's, but also exemplify a two-way substitution: *s* for *r*, as in *Maria*/*Masia*, and *r* for *s*, as in *Iesus*/*Ierus*.

Tory had, like Erasmus, pointed out that *s*/*r*- substitutions were not unknown in Latin. Scholars differ on the origin and spread of this pronunciation fashion in French. It had attracted F. Diez's attention in 1874, but Fought is right to argue (1961–2) that the phenomenon has still not received satisfactory treatment.[10]

We come to the last group of items singled out by Palsgrave as not

[9] Dialect words in French dictionaries of the sixteenth to the eighteenth centuries are the subjects of two monographs by W. Heymann (1903) and J. Leip (1921) respectively. Unfortunately, both authors take Robert Estienne's *Dictionnaire Francois–Latin* of 1539 as their starting-point, thus disregarding Palsgrave's earlier work. We note, however, that two of Palsgrave's regionalisms are listed as dialect words in Cotgrave (1611/1968): the Normandism *douen d'antan* and the Picardism *orayn* (Heymann 1903: 6, 33; 7, 96; see also Heymann 1909).

[10] See also the earlier treatments in Diez (1856), Joret (1875), Meyer (1875; 1876), Thomas (1877), Nyrop (1904), Bloch (1927), Dauzat (1930), Bourciez (1946), F. Bruneau (1955). L. Sainéan (1922–3: ii. 147–8) has drawn attention to Palsgrave's description and actual language use by Rabelais, Robert Estienne and Montaigne. Of interest, too, is Jacques Dubois's mention of the inverse substitution of *r* for voiced /z/ (Dubois 1531/1971). See also J. H. Sledd (1947: 272–5), who discusses the sources and analogues for Baret's description of *R* and *Z*.

belonging to 'parfyte frenche' usage. He uses the terms *Wallon* and *Romant* to refer to a kind of French that is spoken in Burgundy (III, fo. xxxv) or used by 'Heynowers' and those of 'Romant Brabante' (I, fo. xiii$^{v}$). There is one instance of a word being described as a Wallonism:

> **Hemy, is vsed rather in the doutche lande ꝛ where they speake rõmant and wallon than in France.**
>
> (III, fo. cccc.lxxiii)[11]

*Rõmant* and *wallon* are here coordinated by means of *and*. In the only other passage where they co-occur, they are linked by the conjunction *or*:

> Nor there is no man that is a mynister of their cõmon welth/ outher as a capitayne/ or in offyce of Indicatoure/ or as a famous preachour/ but where soeuer his abyding be/ he speketh the parfyte frenche: In somoche that the Heynowers/ and they of Romant/ Brabante/ and all other nacyons vsynge the kynde of speche/ nowe called Uallon or Romant/ thoughe in pronũciacion they folowe moche the said olde Romant tonge/ lyke as the Pycardes/ liegeoys/ and Ardenoyes do yet in writynge . . . they folowe in writyng as nere as they may/ the very true ortography and congruite of the parfyte frenche tonge. (I, fo. xiii$^{v}$)

'*Uallon or Romant*' suggests that the one can be substituted for the other, so that Palsgrave seems to oppose *perfect French* (used between the Seine and the Loire, the former *Gallia celtica*) and *Romant/ Walloon* (used in the regions specified).

Palsgrave here evidently adopts the view of one of his admired authors: Jean Lemaire de Belges. In his *Illustrations de Gaule et singularitez de Troye* of 1510–13 Lemaire de Belges lauds the sovereign and the princes 'des deux nations citramontaines. Cestassauoir francoise ꝛ gallicane qui dominẽt auiourduy sur pluiseurs aultres'. In these two nations, different languages are used: 'Cestassauoir germanique et thyoise: vualõne/ ou rõmande/ et francoise. Toutesuoies la derniere nommee est maintenãt la plus elegante/ cogneue et vsitee les nobles cours de nosditz princes' (bk. I, C ij$^{v}$).

When he comes to the description of the foundation of Gaule, Lemaire not only dwells on the different languages used in the realm but also delimits the geographical area in which Walloon or Romant is spoken:

> Si succeda ou Royaume de Gaule. Son filz nomme Romus xvj$^{e}$. Roy. Lequel funda vnd peuple nõme Rõmandz . . . Ce son ceulx/ que Ptolemee descript en sa

[11] This use of *doutche lande* predates that given for John Minsheu's *Ductor in linguas* (1617) by the *OED*. *Wallon* in this quotation is clearly nominal, and a revised third edition of the *OED* should therefore credit Palsgrave with the first use of the noun *Walloon* in the sense of the language, and not James Howell (1642).

cosmographie/ en la Gaule Belgicq̃. Et les appelle Romãdissos. Nous disons encoires auiourduy/ la ville de Niuelle estre situe ou Romãbrabant/ a cause de la differẽce du langaige. Car les autres Brabãsons parlẽt Thiois/ ou Teuthonicq̃. Cestadire bas allemãt. Et ceulx cy parlẽt le viel lãgaige Gallicque que nous appellõs Uuallõn ou Rõmãd. Et les vieulx liures en ladicte lãgue nous les disons Rommãdz. Sicõme le Rõmãd de la Rose. Et de ladicte anciẽne lãgue Uualonne/ ou Rõmande Nous vsons en nostre Gaule Belgicq̃. Cestadire en Haynnau Cãbresis Artois Namur/ Liege Lorraine/ Ardẽne ꝛ le Rõmãbrabant. Et est beaucop differẽte/ du Frãcois. Leq̃l est plus/ moderne/ ꝛ plus gaillart. (bk. I, ch. 16, e vi$^{v}$–vii)

In the third book, Lemaire de Belges describes the realm of the dukes of Burgundy, specifying that 'Ledit royaume participoit de toutes les trois Gaules. Cestassauoir/ belgicque/ celtique/ ꝛ acqtanicque'. This realm is further characterized by the use of 'troys lãgues principalles et differentes lune de lautre. Cestassauoir: germanicq̃/ rõmande/ ou vualõne/ ꝛ ytaliẽne' (bk. III, le secõd traictie, f vi).

*Romant* or *Walloon* is here understood as the *langue d'oïl*, the French language spoken in the areas of the Low Countries ruled by the dukes of Burgundy. This may account for Palsgrave's entry in *Lesclarcissement* (III, fo. xxxv):[12]

**Frenche spoken in Burgondy** wallon s fe.

This has been commented upon by A. Henry: '. . . par *Burgondy*, Palsgrave veut dire les Pays-Bas. Le terme Bourgogne fut employé pour désigner tout le faisceau de principautés rassemblées par Philippe de Bon' (Henry 1965: 24). Quoting P. Bonenfant, Henry also pointed out that the 'dénomination persistera après la perte du duché de Bourgogne et même après celle de la Comté: l'expression *langue bourguignonne* «servit dans les Pays-Bas jusqu'au XVIII$^{e}$ siècle» pour dire «le français»' (ibid.: 24).

## 'OLDE ROMANT'

Yet Palsgrave does not only use the terms *Wallon* and *Romant*. In addition, there is *olde Romant*, by which he refers to the older stage of the French language (before 1400, in Neumann's view (Neumann 1959: 38, 43)). The bilingual dictionary thus has a historical perspective both for English as well as for French. Chaucer and Lydgate are quoted for English, and Palsgrave's high admiration for the *Roman de la Rose* is manifest on a good number of pages of *Lesclarcissement*. He had a profound knowledge of those French texts which he regarded as

[12] See in this respect the lemma **Wallon tonge** which is rendered by *romant* (III, fo. lxxiii$^{v}$). For the very complex history of the terms 'wallon' and 'Wallonie', see also Piron (1964), Legros (1965–7), Henry (1973), and Heim (1984).

exponents of good French. This made him occasionally quote a passage from a specific author when he agreed or disagreed with a certain grammatical usage. In the dictionary, French equivalents for an English headword sometimes include an Old French word as well. Such instances are more frequent for verbs than for other parts of speech:

> **I Dye I ꝑte my lyfe/** Ie me meurs . . ., **and in this sence I fynde also** ie vas de vie a trespas, . . .. **as for** ie deuie, **is olde Romãnt.**
>
> (III, fo. cc.x$^{v}$)

> **I Take parte or holde of a mans syde/** Ie prens part . . . **and** ie tiens de cousté . . . **I fynde also** ie adheres . . . **but** ie adhers, **is olde Romant.**
>
> (III, fo. ccc.lxxxv$^{v}$)

If we remind ourselves that the dictionary was meant for productive use by an English learner, the fact that Palsgrave supplied French equivalents of contemporary and earlier use is rather impressive. Some of the lexical items or grammatical constructions common during the older period of French must have been so inscribed in Palsgrave's mind that they came up whenever a corresponding semantic item occurred. We can illustrate this with the two examples given. *Deuier* is mentioned as an equivalent of English *to die*. When he has to provide French equivalents for the English items *to decease* and *to let one's life*, we are first given contemporary French verbs and then the archaic *devier*, *desvier*:

> **I Decease I dye or departe out of the worlde/** Ie decede. prime cõiu. **and** ie vas de vie en trepas, **and** ie deuie. Romant . . .
>
> (III, fo. cc.v$^{v}$)

> **I Lette my lyfe I departe out of the worlde/** Ie trespasse. prime cõiu. **and** ie desuie. prime cõiuga. **Romãt.** . . .
>
> (III, fo. cc.lxxix$^{r-v}$)

*Aherdre* is listed not only under *to take part* but also under *to apply*:

> **I Applye or cleaue a thyng harde togyther as glue dothe to a tree or thynges that be glued/** Ie adhers, . . . aherdre. tercie cõiugationis. **a verbe vsed of the Romante formed out of** adhereo, **but it is nat nowe vsed/ thoughe it be moche vsed of Johan de Meun.**
>
> (III, fo. c.li)

The additional examples for *devier/desvier* and *aherdre/adherdre* reveal that Palsgrave was not always consistent in his use of language labels. In the first examples the older forms are said to be characteristic of *olde Romãnt*, in the later ones he is content with *Romãnt*. The term *Romãnt* used in *Lesclarcissement* is thus ambiguous: it either refers to Walloon or, more often, to *olde Romant*. All in all, the dictionary has about three scores of instances described as belonging to an earlier period of French. One of the most interesting entries in this respect is the verb **I Begyle**:

> **I Begyle by craftes and wyles/** Ie ruse. prime coniu. **and in olde Romant/** ie lobe. prime. **I fynde also in this sẽce** iaffine. prime. **He begyleth no mo than he medleth with**: Il ne trompe non plus de gens que ceulx a que il a affaire
>
> . . . . . . .
>
> **And** ie barratte. prime coniuga. **I fynde also** ie boulle. prime coniuga. Romãt **I fynde also** ie cautelle. prime cõiu. **and** ienguyne. pri. **but** ie lobe ie baratte, **and** ie boule, **be olde romant wordes and nowe waxe out of vse** . . .
>
> (III, fo. c.lix$^{v}$)

For one single English verb, *to beguile*, Palsgrave provides eight French equivalents: *ruser*, *affiner*, *tromper*, *cauteller*, *enguyner*, and three archaisms *lober*, *barratter*, and *bouller*. The wealth of French equivalents prompted Neumann to investigate them in more detail and to assess the reliability of Palsgrave's attributions:

> Palsgrave cite trois synonymes de «tromper» qui selon lui seraient sortis de l'usage: *lober*, *baratter* et *bouller*. Nous avons contrôlé cette information sans trouver rien qui la contredise. Nous avons en outre examiné trois synonymes de *tromper* qui, au dire de Palsgrave, s'employaient au XVI$^{e}$ siècle, à savoir *affiner*, *cauteler* et *enguy(n)gner*. Notre examen a montré que les verbes *cauteler* et *enguy(n)gner* sont extrêmement rares dans les textes; c'étaient probablement des formations de circonstance. . . . (Neumann 1959: 43)

Neumann's conclusion is

> Il serait facile de citer d'autres passages du 3$^{e}$ livre de *Lesclarcissement* qui montrent chez Palsgrave une préoccupation de délimiter le français de son temps par rapport à la langue ancienne. Voilà ce qu'il faut retenir lorsqu'on reproche à notre grammairien d'utiliser le *Roman de la Rose* et le *Quadrilogue* d'Alain Chartier comme témoignages de l'usage. Ces vieux textes risquaient d'induire Palsgrave en erreur et de lui faire admettre comme encore usités des mots qui en réalité étaient obsolètes. Mais jusqu'à un certain point, ce risque fut éliminé, précisément par le fait que Palsgrave, loin d'être toujours dupe des archaïsmes offerts par les vieux textes, a pris soin d'avertir son lecteur de leur caractère désuet. (ibid.)

In this chapter we have looked at the forms of English and French which Palsgrave made the basis of his linguistic descriptions. As a native Englishman, he was aware of regional differences in his mother tongue, yet, himself a Londoner, he recorded only some 'northernisms'. His keen observation of language use made him also note differences in the currency of words, thus introducing a diachronic dimension into the description of English as we shall see especially in Chapter 5 when discussing the archaisms explicitly attributed to Geoffrey Chaucer and John Lydgate.

He was aware not only of regional differences in French, but also, and more importantly, of their differing social and professional relevance. The French of Paris and the area between the Seine and the Loire had become the most prestigious form of the language. It was this form which he chose as his model. As a responsible and dedicated teacher he deliberately excluded regional variants from his description of French, because he felt that their inclusion would confuse the learner. The very few dialect words—marked as such—confirm this deliberate strategy. Our close study of the treatment of regional variants in earlier and contemporary works dealing with grammar, spelling, and pronunciation has revealed that he was quite independent of these treatises.

In order to provide his analysis of French with the necessary authority, he had read the works of many highly esteemed authors writing in French and he had recorded their use of the language. These records include older uses of French, which he marks as such.

Yet Palsgrave's linguistic awareness went far beyond regional and temporal differences in English and French. He also discusses differences in the medium—that is, differences between the spoken and the written language, and, within the latter, between prose and poetry. We also find interesting examples showing that language use differed also with respect to the social status of its speakers. All these instances will be investigated in Chapter 9. Our next concern will be the word list of the dictionary.

# 4
# The Word List

In this chapter we shall study the word list in Palsgrave's English–French dictionary. He himself never calls it a 'dictionary'; he uses the terms 'vocabular', 'vocabuler', and 'vocabulyst' and characterizes it as the 'frenche vocabular', thus highlighting what he regarded as its most salient feature. The earliest date we have for the use of 'dictionary' in English is 1526,[1] and we know that the first dictionary including English as one of the languages described is the *Dictionary of Syr Thomas Elyot*, published in 1538. In using 'vocabular', 'vocabulyst', Palsgrave strikes us as more factual than other earlier and later compilers of English word lists, who described their collections of words and phrases for want of a generic term metaphorically as a *Medulla*, a *Promptorium*, a *Hortus vocabulorum*, a *Catholicon*, an *Abecedarium*, a *Thesaurus*, a *Manipulus vocabulorum*, an *Alvearie*, a *Sylva synonymorum*, a *Bibliotheca*, or simply a *Worlde of Words* (see Stein 1985*a*).

### *Coverage and word-formation*

We begin with what Palsgrave himself tells us about the compilation of his word list and its arrangement. We shall then look at the order in which the words are actually listed in the dictionary and see how far there is agreement between plan and execution.

The French vocabulist is part of the third book of *Lesclarcissement*. As we have seen in Chapter 2, there is a progression in the depth of treatment from books I and II to book III. The third book resumes the grammatical description of the different parts of speech given earlier and provides us with a more specialized analysis of the accidents (of the different word classes). Palsgrave continues his introductory account in book III as follows:

[1] There is an earlier use of the word *dictionary* in English than the one given in the *OED* to which J. F. Huntsman has drawn attention in his edition of the *Medulla grammatice* (1973: p. xlv). The date conjectured for MS Pepys 2002' is 'the last quarter of the fifteenth century, perhaps about 1480' (ibid.: p. xxxii).

After euery of whiche partes so cōpletely entreated of/ shall folowe certayne tables/ cōtayning *all the wordes in our tong*/ after the order of a/b/c/ with the frenche wordes ioyned vnto them/ To thentent that after the lernar can by the helpe of the sayde first boke/ pronounce this frenche tong truely/ and by the meanes of the seconde/ with the frēche vocabulyst (whiche shall folowe whan the thirde boke with his tables is completely finisshed) vnderstande any authour that writeth in the sayd tong by his owne study/ without any other teacher. (III, fo. I) (emphasis added)

After his further discussion of nouns, he tells his readers:

And nowe that I haue here in this thirde boke declared at length/ what accidentes and properties belong vnto all the substātyues in the frenche tong/ I shall here cōsequently set forthe/ what and howe many substantyues there be in the same tong/ whiche to thentent they may of euery lernar the more easely be foūde/ whan he hath any sentence or mater to be made out of our tong in to the frenche/ I shall set forthe all the englysshe substantyues in our tong/ after the order of a/b/c/ and in the same lyne shewe what substantyues in the frenche tonge is of lyke signification. (III, fo. xvi)

For each part of speech, there is thus a word list (or table, as Palsgrave calls it) in which the items are arranged in alphabetical order. Palsgrave's claim to list 'all the wordes' of the English language seems to be more an expression of aspiration than achievement. His intention, however, is noteworthy for two reasons. One of the traditionally held views in English lexicography is that it began with the explanation of 'hard' English words by simpler English words and that only with J.K. and Dr Johnson did 'common' English words become part of an English dictionary. But in fact, more than seventy years before Robert Cawdrey published his *Table Alphabeticall, conteyning and teaching the true writing, and understanding of hard usuall English wordes* . . . (1604), Palsgrave had already conceived the idea of an English dictionary that was to list *all the words* of the language. We may even go further. Since the names of the authors of the first English dictionaries, the *Medulla grammatice*, the *Promptorium parvulorum*, the *Catholicon Anglicum*, and the *Ortus vocabulorum*, cannot be established with certainty, we can say that the first known lexicographer to have the idea of compiling a dictionary registering all the words of the English language was John Palsgrave.

But towards the end of his book he bows to the impossibility of this task:

Nowe haue we by goddes fauoure brought our worke hyther to in whiche though any fewe wordes amongest so many thousandes shall fortune in their dewe places to be wantyng/ with moste humylyte I beseche all maner persones whiche shall take pleasure or delyte in these my poore labours to cōsyder the ample largenesse of the mater whiche I here entreate/ and the great diffyculte of myne entrepryse/ whiche if I haue for the chefe effecte brought to passe that is to say redused the frenche tonge vnder a rule and grammer certayne/ the wantynge somtyme of a worde is nat of so great importance/ for it may soone be gotten/ and ones had /maye easyly be set in his dewe place/ so the lerner be ones acquaynted with these tables/ but yet tyll he be somthyng well acquaynted with them/ the thynge maye parchaunce be in dede in his place/ whiche he for wante of dewe knowledge shall suppose to be wantyng. But in effecte if any suche worde be wantyng in dede/ if it shall than lyke hym to seke out an other of lyke signyfycacion or nere vnto it/ than may he be satysfyed/ and this booke vnto hym shall be a great deale bothe the more profytable and also pleasant. (III, fo. cccc.lxi$^{v}$)

Word-formations occupy an intermediate position between words and phrases. One of the vital issues for every lexicographer is the question of whether all the word-formations of a language should be recorded in the dictionary. After dealing with the formation of nouns under the fourth accident of substantives, Palsgrave wants his readers to note:

that it is moche requisyte for the learnar/ to haue regarde to these rules/ wherby I declare the ryght formation of substantyues in the frenche tonge/ for the better vnderstandyng of my frenche vocabular /wherby if any of these substãtiues whiche after my rules be formed of other/ happen to be lafte vnwritten/ if he call to mynde my sayd rules/ he maye forme all suche hymselfe: and therfore to putt all suche in the vocabular I reken it but superfluous. (III, fo. xv$^{v}$)

He was thus not going to list all the word-formations coined in English.

The other issue in word-formation is where compounds should be listed within a dictionary. Here he seems to shift ground. He does not argue from the point of view of English, which is the source language in his vocabulist, but seems to have taken French as his starting-point. *Bec de favlcon* would be listed after *bec*, and similarly *chavldron de mer* after *chavlderon*:

And here it is to be noted that in the frenche vocabular/ euery substãtyue whiche is expressed by thre wordes/ of whiche the myddle worde is a preposition/ shalbe sette forthe in the worde that cometh before the preposytion: as *Bec de favlcon*, shall folowe after *bec*, and *chavldron de mer*, shall folowe after *chavldron*: ⁊ therfore whan the lernar hath founde out *bec* and than *favlcon*, and yet can nat fynde out any worde of suche sence as he loketh for/ let hym tourne backe agayne to *bec*, and there folowynge he shall fynde the sayde thre wordes expressed . . . (III, fo. xv$^{v}$)

*Bec* is the bill of a bird, and *becq de faulcou* [*sic*] is the French equivalent for 'polaxe a weapen'. The question of bringing *bec* and *becq de faulcon* together does not arise for the English headwords *bill* and *poleaxe*. The same holds for the other examples. One might wonder whether the point as such was valid and the examples wrongly chosen. The compound type of the structure sb + prep + sb is much more common in French than in English, and this fact may have been uppermost in Palsgrave's mind when he was looking for examples to illustrate the point. Yet, from some random checks of such true English compounds as *brother-in-law*, *man-of-war*, it emerges that Palsgrave was not consistent in listing these words immediately after their bases *brother* and *man*.

We shall focus on two aspects of the word list. First, we shall look at its arrangement. This may throw some light on Palsgrave's working method, and it will also help us to assess the degree to which Palsgrave was innovative. Secondly, we shall address the very difficult question of Palsgrave's sources.

## ARRANGEMENT

The guiding principle for the tables is word-class membership and this makes sense in the context of the genesis and overall structure of *Lesclarcissement*. Yet one might wonder whether the incorporation of the different word lists of nouns, verbs, adjectives, and so on into *one* single alphabetical word list would have impaired the structural unity of the book. Palsgrave was well aware of the alphabetical arrangement of word lists, so we may wonder what might have kept him from producing a bilingual dictionary consisting of one alphabetical word list from A to Z. We might address this question from different points of view: (1) the 'tradition' of compiling word lists as it had been established by then; (2) the actual process of compilation, and (3) the user perspective.

### *The tradition*

We do not know whether Palsgrave was familiar with the great Latin dictionaries of the Middle Ages. But, given his education and his professional status, we might reasonably assume that he had access to one or other of these lexicographical works. The lexicon in Papias' *Elementarium doctrinae rudimentum*, an introduction to education, written around the middle of the eleventh century, has a third-letter alphabetical order—that is, the first three letters of the word have been taken into account (Angelis 1977–80; Weijers 1989: 140; Merrilees 1990: 285). Compared to Isidore of Seville's much earlier *Etymologiae* (seventh century), alphabetization is much more stringent.[2] Alphabetical order in book ten of the *Liber ethimologiarvm*, which deals with the 'vocabvlis hominvm per alfabetvm distinctis', means only first-letter order: within the groups of *a*-words, *b*-words, etc., which are written as a continuous text, there is no further attempt at ordering. Yet the whole text is not printed in one block with

[2] For an excellent account of alphabetization see Daly (1967).

occasional paragraphs but in two columns, and a big red initial, standing out from the text, guides the user to each new letter of the alphabet. The following books (book 11: *De homine et partibvs eivs*, book 12: *De peccoribvs et ivmentis*, etc.) have a display according to subject fields. Isidore's *Etymologiae* thus offers a combination of an alphabetical and a topical arrangement.

In Osbern of Gloucester's *Panormia*, a very interesting word list of the twelfth century,[3] there is a different interplay of two principles of arrangement, one alphabetical, the other derivational. In the block entry under the Latin noun *arbor*, for instance, we find the morphologically related nouns and adjectives *arborcula*, *arborcus*, *arborinus*, *arbustum*, *arbuteus*, *arbutus*, *arbutetum*. They are given a brief grammatical description and their meaning is paraphrased in Latin.

In the *Repetitiones*, the items are then listed in alphabetical order. Mai, in his edition of the work, has omitted all those words which are explained in the more comprehensive derivational treatise. The order of the remaining 'new' (that is, previously not listed) words seems to be a sequence of clusters in which the second letter of the alphabet was taken into account. Thus there is a group of *Am*-items which is followed by *Ar*-words, *Al*-words, *Aq*-words, and so on.

The next important work in chronological order is Hugutio's *Derivationes*, compiled about the last decade of the twelfth century. As the title of the work indicates, the overall arrangement is derivational.

From the late thirteenth century we have Johannis Balbus' *Catholicon*, which was to become one of the most influential lexicographical works of the Middle Ages. It was printed at Mayence as early as 1460, and Palsgrave may have seen a copy of it. The lexicographical advance on the preceding works lies above all in the richness of linguistic information provided for the headwords. Besides the explanation of the meaning, users are also given information on aspects of pronunciation and grammar, and the (supposed) origin of the word. In addition, derivatives may be listed. The work does not, however, have any really new features with respect to the ordering principles of the word list.

Of more interest in this respect is a work compiled in the fifteenth century: Guarinus Veronensis' *Vocabularius breviloquus* of 1485–6. In the words of its author, this vocabulary has three alphabets: the word list has a grammatical subdivision into nomina (nouns, pronouns, adjectives), verbs, and, as a third group, adverbs, prepositions, conjunctions, and interjections listed together. The first two groups

[3] The work was first edited by A. Mai in 1836. See also Goetz (1923: 196-215), R. W. Hunt (1958), and Riessner (1965).

are the grammatical classes of *declinabilia*, the third the grammatical class of *indeclinabilia*. Each group is arranged in broadly two-letter alphabetical order. The lists are displayed in two columns per page, and alphabetization sometimes proceeds beyond the second letter. The beginning of a new second letter of the alphabet is highlighted by title headings of the type *A ante B*, *A ante C*, *A ante D*. These headings are repeated at the top of the page to guide the vocabulary user. The two-colour contrast (red and black) is carried further than in earlier works. In some word lists, red was used to highlight the beginning of each different letter of the alphabet (e.g. Isidore's *Etymologiae*), or the capital initial of the lemma. In Balbus' *Catholicon* a red and a blue capital even alternate. In the *Vocabularius breviloquus*, up to the letter sequence *Li*, not only are the lemmata touched with red, but some sections of the entry also have red underlinings. It looks as if an attempt has been made to signal different types of information (examples, quotations, synonym discriminations) with a different colour or combination of colours, just as later printers have used different founts to distinguish headwords from explanations and illustrative examples.

So far as Latin works are concerned, it thus emerges from our review of leading lexicographical works that Guarinus' *Vocabularius breviloquus* is the only vocabulary in which word-class membership was made a distinctive principle of lexicographical arrangement.

Let us now turn to the treatment of vernaculars. As to English, the first of the dictionaries compiled before 1530 was the *Medulla grammatice*, a Latin–English alphabetical word list which was never printed. The *Ortus vocabulorum* is the first printed Latin–English dictionary, and the entries, as in the *Medulla*, are arranged alphabetically. The two English–Latin dictionaries compiled before *Lesclarcissement*, the *Promptorium parvulorum*, and the *Catholicon Anglicum*, are lexicographically more interesting than the Latin–English counterparts. The compiler of the *Promptorium parvulorum* listed the lexical items for each letter in two sequences: the first alphabetical list includes nouns, adjectives, participles, adverbs, pronouns, and prepositions; the second alphabetical list has verbs only. The *Catholicon Anglicum* has one A-to-Z list for all the items listed. Yet the lemma proper of the entry does not always begin the line, as can be seen from the following examples, though it is distinguished from prelemmatic matter by an initial capital:

an **Halle**; *Aula, Atrium, castrum,*
*palacium, regia.*

. . . . .

**Happy**; *beatus, faustus, felix,* &
cetera; *vbi* blissed.
to mak **Happy**; *vbi* blissed.
vn **Happy**; *Acharis, infaustus, infelix, in vna re, jnfortunatus, miser, in omni re.*

(Herrtage 1881: 171, 174)

Besides these full-size dictionaries, there were of course smaller bilingual word lists, arranged either alphabetically or topically or as lists of synonyms. The grammatical principle often correlated with this classification. Word class was not criterial for word lists with an overriding alphabetical order. A good example is the fifteenth-century vocabulary preserved in the Library of Trinity College, Cambridge, reproduced in Wright (1884/1968: cols. 560–621). MS Harley 1002, fos. $137^{v}$–$138^{v}$, in the British Library is a small list of synonyms covering various parts of speech (Stein 1985*a*: 64). Topical word lists were mostly collections of nouns, as, for instance, the so-called *Mayer-Nominale*, reproduced in Wright (1884/1968: cols. 673–744; see also Stein 1985*a*: 53–65). The part of the *Tractatus sinonimorum* that has come down to us also has a nominale–verbale arrangement. Yet medieval clerks and schoolmasters did not only compile groups of nouns to refer to things or to cover certain subject areas; there are also lists of verbs, as in the *Nominale sive verbale*, a bilingual French–English word list, the manuscript of which is believed to date from about 1340 (Skeat 1906). I have traced three further manuscripts in the British Library which contain verbs only (Stein 1985*a*: 58–9). The actual verbs included in these verbales differ greatly as does their lexicographical treatment, and such variation may suggest that the vocabulary type of the verbales was less well established than that of the nominales. Finally there were collections of adjectives, adverbs, and conjunctions (ibid.: 64). So, from the manuscripts that have been preserved, we see that the compilation of words according to word classes had a certain precedent by Palsgrave's time.

## *Compilation*

We know that Palsgrave excerpted lexical items from books he had read. In addition, he may have used existing word lists, deleting items he regarded as no longer in use, and adding others which the compilers had overlooked or which had become current. If he had had a good English headword list as his master source, he might have been content with just identifying deletions in it and marking the spaces for additions. The additions themselves could have been collected on separate leaves headed in the then common second-letter manner 'A ante B', 'A ante C', etc. If he had used the English word list of the *Promptorium parvulorum*, he would have had to set up two different lists: one for verbs, one for the other parts of speech. If he had had a manuscript of the *Catholicon Anglicum*, he might have disagreed with that compiler's lexicographical approach: the examples provided above, for instance—*happy*, *to make happy*, *unhappy*—illustrate the lexicographical principle of bringing word families together and of listing them in one place within the dictionary. The practical compilation of additions to such a word list would have become quite a complicated process. On each separate leaf allocated to a particular letter of the alphabet, enough space would have had to be left for potential members of the word family. Since lemmatization seems to have been guided by the target language, such potential members of a word family would be unpredictable. That is, for an English lexicographer, entries for the English headwords *a calf* and *to calve* (Latin *vitulus* and *fetare*) could have been predictable (so a space could have been left after *calf* or *calve*, whichever turned up first). But an unlexicalized entry 'with calfe', for instance, rendering the Latin adjective *fetosus*, could not have been anticipated. The same holds for such English entries as *to be childish* with respect to the Latin verbs *puerare*, *repuerare*, *puerascere*, *repuerascere*, or *to make with childe* with respect to Latin *gravidare*, *pregnare*, *impregnare*. This may be why in *Lesclarcissement de la langue francoyse* Palsgrave did not adopt the lexicographical principle of registering and clustering word families.

In view of the size of the enterprise, where thousands of lexical items had to be recorded and then matched with French equivalents (or English translations found for French items), a breakdown into more manageable groups of words, according to parts of speech, for instance, might have presented itself as an easier process of compilation. A checking of one's work, of whether certain basic items had been covered, was equally more feasible.

There is then also the question of whether Palsgrave intended to provide the same lexicographical treatment for all kinds of words.

### *The user perspective*

Palsgrave's tables are word lists for English users learning French—that is, they are lists for productive language use. The passage quoted earlier (p. 125) tells us that Palsgrave envisaged his learners to be teacher-independent, to make progress through self-study. As an experienced teacher, he knew that different words behave differently in a language, and that he had to provide as much guidance as possible in his dictionary if he wanted its users to become successful learners. Palsgrave's introduction into English dictionary-making of the grammatical part-of-speech arrangement as an overriding classificatory principle could therefore be taken as further proof of a deep pedagogical commitment to his task.

At a time when the foundation of all language-teaching and learning consisted in a clear and detailed discrimination of the different parts of speech and their accidents, at a time when dictionary-making was still in its infancy and learners therefore not yet experienced in consulting books with thousands of words arranged in only rudimentary alphabetical ordering, at such a time, the compilation of word tables according to word classes must have been regarded as a highly sensible and user-oriented approach. For the correct and appropriate use of words, there has to be a grammatical basis. This becomes clear from Palsgrave's teaching of French—and indirectly then also for English, since the English user, keen on translating something into French, would have had to analyse his mother-tongue expression before being able to put it into French. With the number of Englishmen trained in this way being relatively small, this may well have explained the small number of copies sold.

### *Nouns*

We come to the tables of nouns, adjectives, verbs, etc. in the French vocabulist. How much does Palsgrave's lexicographical treatment vary for the different parts of speech? For nouns, there is only one ordering principle and this is alphabetical. Alphabetization is carried through to varying degrees. Some sections of the table of substantives are consistently alphabetical throughout; in others it is only the first two or three letters of the word that have been taken into account. This is also reflected in the column headings. In order to make the consultation of the tables easier—there are two columns per page—the beginning of a new second letter is marked by a title heading. In the printed editions of the *Promptorium parvulorum* these guiding titles within the *A*-words have the form *AB*, *AC*, *AD*, etc.—that is, before the beginning of the section of words sharing the first two letters, *a* and *b*, we have a title heading highlighting these two letters as juxtaposed capitals. In the *Ortus vocabulorum* these guiding titles have the form *A ante B*, *A ante C*, etc.—that is, the two letters are printed as capitals and linked by the preposition *ante*, indicating at the same time that the lexicographical metalanguage is Latin.

In the 1511 edition of the *Ortus vocabulorum*, the title headings are slightly more adjusted to the dictionary text. In the lemma itself, it is only the initial that is printed as a capital letter to highlight it. The second and following letters are given in lower case: *A ante b*, *A ante c*, *A ante d*, etc. Palsgrave's title headings in the table of substantives have the form *A. before B.*, *A. before C.*, etc.—that is, the pattern is the one used in the *Ortus vocabulorum*, but Palsgrave's metalanguage is English and not Latin. In addition, the first lemma under such a heading is often preceded by an attention-catching 'new paragraph sign' C, as for instance in

| | |
|---|---|
| C **Arage an herbe** | aroche s fe. |
| **Araye of men in a felde** | ranc z ma. |

For the letters *Q* and *S* Palsgrave deviates from his practice. In the case of the former, the heading gives three letters: *Q. before U A.*, *Q. before U E.*[4] Words beginning with that most copious letter *S* naturally gave Palsgrave difficulty, as we can see from the sequences of headings:

| | |
|---|---|
| S before A. | |
| S before C H A. | (none of the items listed, however, has an initial sequence *scha*, all are *sca*-items) |
| S before C H. | (these are basically *scha*-words) |
| S before C H E. | (the last third of the nouns are *she*-nouns) |
| S before C H I. | (the majority of items begins with an *sh*-spelling) |
| S before C H O. | (here too, there are a number of *sh*-spellings) |
| S before C H R. | |
| S before C L.[5] | |

With 'S before E', we are back to the common style of indicating the second letter only. The guiding headings, the paragraph signs, and the capital initials for the lemmata are visual markers in the lexicographical presentation of linguistic information.

### *Adjectives, numerals, and pronouns*

The overall arrangement for adjectives is also alphabetical. Yet there are no title headings at all. When a new letter of the alphabet begins, it is usually highlighted before the first one or two indented items of that letter by an oversized capital letter. Paragraph signs occur in some cases, just as an oversized capital had occasionally appeared among

[4] In the *Ortus vocabulorum* (1511 edition) *Q*-headings are *Q u ante a*, *Q u ante e*, *Q u ante i*, *Q u ante o*.

[5] Here too we have a precedent in the earlier *Promptorium parvulorum*. In the 1508 edition, for instance, the title heading *Sc* for nomina includes *Sch*-items and *Sh*-items. There is no *Sh*-heading. For verbs, however, the compiler distinguishes between an *Sc*-heading and an *Sh*-heading, which precedes the sequence *Se*-.

the nouns. In addition, the whole column is separated from the preceding one by some space. Here is an example:

> R **Agged** ma. et fe. dechiré s.
> **Raynisshe/belongyng to rayne**
> ma. pluuial x. fe. pluuialle s.

The criteria used for the arrangement of the tables of numerals are completely different. There are two brief tables for cardinal numbers and one for ordinal numbers. The common feature of all three lists is that French has become the language of the headwords. The first little table of cardinal numbers is tripartite: the French number is followed by its English equivalent and the third column gives the Roman numerals:

| | | |
|---|---|---|
| *Ung* | **One** | i. |
| *Deux* | **Twayne** | ii. |
| etc. | | |

An English user who would start from the Roman numeral on the right-hand side would then, proceeding towards the left, get first the mother-tongue word and then the French equivalent. The second table of cardinal numbers is longer and is monolingual only, illustrating in more detail the French way of counting; Palsgrave obviously took for granted counting in English. As to there being two tables of cardinal numbers, Palsgrave explains the difference between the two tables as follows: the first (the tripartite list) gives 'all suche nombres as the lerned men in France vse to sõme or reken thynges by/ and by what names and fygures they be expressed' (III, fo. c.xiiii$^{v}$). The list includes *septante* (70), *octante* (80), and *nonante* (90). Palsgrave maintains that the 'vulgar people' never use *septante*, *octante*, and *nonante*, and his second table of numerals is, therefore, headed by the statement:

> Here foloweth wherin ẏ voulgar people marchate men/ and suche as write hystories dyffer from the maner of nombring here afore rehersed. (III, fo. c.xv$^{v}$)

The interesting part of this list are the figures from 70 upwards: 'Soixante dix, Quatre vingtz, Quatre vingtz et dix, Cent, Six vingtz, Sept vingtz, Huict vingtz, Neuf vingtz', etc. This way of counting is then described in more detail:

> And note that from four score they recken by scores to .xx. score and from four hundred where they cease to reken by scores they recken by hũdredes or thousandes/ they name them as ẏ lerned men do sayeng/ *cent, deux cens, troys cens, quatre cens, mille, deux mille.*
>
> Note also that suche lyke maner of accountyng by scores and hundredes as they vse from fourscore to two thousande/ suche lyke maner of reckenyng they vse

bytwene two thousande ⁊ two millions/ and bytwene two millions and two millions of millions/ in all other thynges they agre with the lerned men. (III, fo. c.xvii^v)

Next we have the tables of pronouns (which should have preceded the treatment of the numerals). Here, too, there are two tables. Both are arranged alphabetically, that is, all the pronominal items beginning with one particular letter of the alphabet have been collected under that very letter which is also given as a title heading. The first is an English–French table of pronouns, which includes references to the relevant chapters in the grammar section:

W
**We our selfe.** nous mesmes. ca.xvi.
regula prima.
**We.** nous. capi. x. regu. i
(III, fo. c.xix)

The second list looks like gleanings from French authors which Palsgrave had read in preparation of his book. French phrases are mostly translated into English:

T
Tant estoit paris agreable a vng chascun, **so moche was Paris agreable to euery man** Capi. xxix. re. v.
Tel maistre tel valet, **suche maystre suche man.** Capi. xxxij. regu. j.
(III, fo. c.xx^v)

*Verbs*

The centrepiece of the French vocabulist is Palsgrave's list of verbs, which takes up more than 550 pages. The ordering principle is alphabetical and we have title headings for the first two letters of the word which are similar to the ones used with nouns: *A/ byfore C.*, *A/ byfore D.*, and so on. The new element is the paragraph sign in the title heading. Yet it is not the first letter of the lemma, given with a capital initial, that starts the first line of verb entries. For verb entries, early lexicographers have used two different forms as citation forms. Latin verbs are predominantly listed in the first-person singular, present tense. In bilingual verb lists for Latin and English we encounter a varying practice. In the Royal MS 17. C. XVII in the British Library the verb list on fo. 4^r to fo. 17^v pairs a Latin infinitive with an English infinitive (e.g. *Obstruere to stop*). In the other two manuscript verb lists (ADD MS 34, 276 and MS Harley 1002 in the British Library (Stein 1985*a*: 58–9), the Latin citation form is the first person singular, present tense, which is matched with an English infinitive. This also holds for the Latin–English *Medulla grammatice* and the *Ortus vocabulorum*. As for the English–Latin dictionaries, the *Promptorium parvulorum* merely adopts in reverse the practice in the Latin-English dictionaries: the English infinitive form is followed by Latin verb equivalents in the first-person singular, present tense. In the *Catholicon Anglicum* the English infinitive form is preceded by the element *to* and the Latin equivalent is also given in the infinitive form:

to **Arme**: *Armare, accingere*

A capital initial for the English lemma ensures its appropriate place within the alphabetical structure of the word list.

So the practice for English was clearly to list verbs either in the bare infinitive or in the infinitive form with *to*. This style was not adopted by Palsgrave. He adduces English verbs in the first-person singular, present tense (**I Adde**, etc.) which are then matched by the same grammatical form in French. In view of the paucity of inflectional forms for verbs in English, this decision may not strike us as very sensible, but in French verb forms vary considerably with respect to person and tense, and it may thus well be that Palsgrave's decision to list English verbs in the first-person singular, present tense, was prompted by the complexity of the corresponding forms in the target language, French. None the less, the dogged insistence on the first person results in some absurdities like **I Laye an egge as a henne or any other foule dothe**.

Yet Palsgrave was fully aware that some verbs occur in the third person only. So among the entries for *to draw* we also have instances reflecting this use:

> **It Draweth towarde day**/ Il ad-
> iourne, il a adiourné, adiourner. ver-
> bũ imparsonale. prime cõiu. . . .
>
> (III, fo. cc.xx)

Impersonal and existential expressions seem to have caused Palsgrave lexicographical problems. They are either, as the example above, listed under the section of the first two relevant letters of the verbs, or under the letter *I*. Towards the end of the letter *I*, after **I Yssue**, when *It*-verbs should begin, we find a whole string of entries where the element *it* seems to have counted as the lemma:

> **It yrketh me I waxe wery or dis-**
> **pleasaunt of a thyng/** Il me ennuyt . . .
>
> (III, fo. cc.lxviii$^{v}$)

The *it*-entries are then followed by existential *there*-entries, e.g.:

> **There is difference bytwene thyn ges/ the one differeth from yͤ other /** Il y a dire. . . .
>
> (III, fo. cc.lxx)

But the recording of impersonal expressions was only one of the lexicographical problems confronting Palsgrave. Others were the many verb entries beginning with **I Am** . . ., **I Get** . . ., **I Make** . . ., and so on. Alphabetization for the letter *S* proved to be as difficult as for nouns.

As we shall see in Chapters 9 and 10, there is another respect in which Palsgrave's treatment of verbs differs from that of nouns, adjectives, and numerals: he illustrates the appropriate use of verbs with illustrative examples—for example:

> **I Knele vpon one knee/** Ie me agenouille sur vng genouil, **or** ie me mets sur mon genouil. **The men of this countray knele vpon one knee whan they here masse/ but yͤ frenche men knele vpon bothe:** Les gens de ce pays icy sagenouillent sur vng genouyl, mais les francoys sagenouillẽt sur tous les deux.
>
> (III, fo. cc.lxxiii)

*Prepositions*

Palsgrave seems well aware that prepositions, like verbs, are a very tricky area for learners, and he sees the need to illustrate their use in example sentences. He emphasizes this lexicographical treatment in the introductory remarks to the table of prepositions:

> The table of Preposycions in our tonge declared by exemples in the frẽche tonge where euery exemple is as vayllable to yͤ lerner as thoughe I gaue a rule. Notyng first yͭ for so moche as yͤ preposycions in bothe our tonges maye waxe somtyme aduerbes and somtyme be vsed as coniunctions I shall gyue example of al their dyuersytes . . . (III, fo. cccc.xv)

The prepositions are listed in alphabetical order with the English headword functioning as a title heading. The user is then given a list of all the possible French equivalents, which are taken up one by one and illustrated in example sentences. A good case in point is the treatment of the preposition *with*:

> **With.**
>
> Auec. Auecques. A tout. A. De. Ensemble.

> Auec, or auecques, **bytwene whiche I fynde no difference nother in signyfycacion nor in vse. As/** Voulez vous coucher auec moy, **or** auecques moy. Et par grant curiosité auec reuerẽce. Mays iuuenille honte ioincte auec rusticité. Pour prendre soulas auecques les creatures mortelles. Et faire icy sõ gracieux seiour auecques moy ton hũble seruiteur. **as for** auec du pain, auec du vin, auec du sel, **for a courtesy of breed. &c.**[6]
>
> A tout, **as** Il partit Degipte a tout vne grosse armée. Et a tout ceste proye se partit dillecques. . . .
>
> A, **as/** voulez vo⁹ iouer a moy. Et luy a ces motz cõmenca a se eschauffer . . .
>
> De, **as/** Venus daigna bien saccointer de luy. Il le frappa dung marteau de mareschal et loccist de ses mayns . . .
>
> Ensemble, **as/** Et Hercules au contrayre ensemble tout leur sequelle. Iay receu voz lettres ensemble vostre enseigne, **but** enseigne, **maye be englished and also.**
>
> (III, fo. cccc.xvi$^{v}$)

As we can see from this example, Palsgrave occasionally makes metalinguistic comments on individual points of usage or meaning. Contrary to his lexicographical practice for verbs, there is no English version for the French example sentences and phrases.

### *Adverbs*

Palsgrave did not regard a mere alphabetical arrangement of adverbs as satisfactory. It emerges from the introduction to the table of adverbs that he was preoccupied with how best to structure their presentation and how to make this structure transparent for the user. He decided on an overall semantic framework that was superimposed on alphabetical order. Here is his explanation for the dictionary user:

> For so moche as it is harde to a lerner to discerne the difference bytwene an aduerbe and the other partes of spetche and that as well in our awne tonge as in the frẽche tonge/ therfore whan so euer they here any worde or wordz whiche may serue to make answere vnto any of these twelue questyons folowyng/ demaundynge of the cyrcumstaunce of a dede/ let the lerner resorte vnto this table and seke out the

[6] According to the *OED*, *a courtesy of* in the sense of 'a 'mannerly' or moderate quantity' is first recorded by Palsgrave (*courtesy n.* 10).

questyon that the worde or wordes serue to make answere to/ and vnder it after the order of A. B. C. he shall fynde out the same answere set forthe. (III, fo. cccc.xviii[v])

The twelve questions are: *Whan—Quant*, *Where—Ou* or *Oue*, *Whyter—Ou* or *oue*, *Howe—Comment*, *Howe moche—Combien*, *Howe longe—Combien*, *Howe often—Quantesfoys*, *Howe many—Combien*, *Howe farre forth—Combien auant*, *From whence—Dou*, *Sythe whan—Despuis quant*, *Whye—Pour quoy*.

Having outlined his general policy, Palsgrave then takes the user, step by step, through the exercise of finding a French equivalent for the adverb *tomorrow*: 'if a lerner shall stande in doute what parte of spetche is to morowe/ let him loke if the worde serue to make answere to any of these twelue questyons demaũded of a dede' (III, fo. cccc.xviii[v]). Since the reply to such questions as 'When will you come?', 'When will you pay me?', etc. could be *tomorrow*, it will be listed in the table of adverbs answering the question *when*.

But what if the user cannot find the item in that list? Then, Palsgrave continues, 'seke out euery worde by hymselfe'. A question like 'When will you come?' could have a reply like 'Every day come summer', so *every*, *day*, etc. would have to be checked individually. Palsgrave tells his users why some adverbials are listed and others, like *every day*, are not:

If I shall nat/ that signyfyeth that the frenche tonge hath no different wordes nor dyuerse maner of phrasys to expresse those wordes by/ so that than I must seke out/ Euery/ amongest the pronownes/ and Daye amongest the substantyues/ ⁊ come amongest the verbes/ and Sõmer/ amongest ẏ substantyues/ and saye. Chascun iour mays que lesté viengne. yet for the more ease of the lerner I haue set out a great nombre of answers whiche myght be made takyng euery worde by it selfe. (III, fo. cccc.xviii[v])

He then explains how the French equivalents are arranged:

And note that whan the frensche tonge hathe many aduerbes that cõtreuaile one aduerbe in englyshe I shall fyrst reherce howe many sõdry wordes they haue in frenshe ⁊ than gyue an exemple for euery one of thẽ whiche shalbe to the lernar worth a lure to knowe howe he shulde vse the same aduerbe. (III, fo. cccc.xviii[v])

The presentation is similar to the one used for verbs and prepositions. Palsgrave is ahead of his time when he says that 'in case that I gyue none exemple at all that signifieth ẏI suppose it is not requisyt' (III, fo. cccc.xviii[v]).

We are given further instances of the circumspection with which Palsgrave went about his task when he admits the limits of his knowledge:

**In ẏ owle flyght: they haue no maner of suche speakyng ẏI wotte of.**

(III, fo. cccc.xxiii[v])

or when he explicitly discusses differences of meaning and usage as in the following example listed under the table of adverbs answering the question *where* (similarly, a good example illustrating Palsgrave's handling of adverbs):

> **Amongest.**
> Entre. Parentre. Parmy. Entremy.
> Entre, **as/** Mettez vous hardimẽt entre eulx.
> Par entre. **as/** Le vent se bouta par entre ses vestemens, **and** Et men iray iouer par entre les herbes ioliettes.
> Parmy, **as/** Le vent se bouta parmy ses vestemens, ⁊ Et ilz alloyent coyemẽt parmy les buyssons. ⁊ Elle alloyt a la chasse parmy les boys et forestz, **and** Et des belles espices parmy.
> Entremy, **as/** Nous meslerõs les roys gallicques entremy les troyans, **but as for** A entre. **as/** Et voulõs notifier a entre vous femmes. **that I fynde of none auctour: and** Emmy, Et mener les leuriers emmy les boys, **signyfyeth rather in ỷ woddes than amongest the woddes.**
>
> (III, fo.cccc.xxviii$^{r-v}$)

*Conjunctions*

The remaining parts of speech for which there are word lists are conjunctions and interjections. The table of conjunctions is arranged in alphabetical order and includes 'suche other partes of spetche as be twyse vsed bothe in our tong and in the frẽche tonge/ with all suche differences of phrasys as is bytwene the tonges' (III, fo. cccc.lxxii$^{v}$). The presentation is similar in style to that used for adverbs. When there are several possible French translation equivalents, they are all first listed, and then, one by one, differentiated. A good case in point is the English conjunction *but*, which may be rendered by French *que*, *sinon*, *fors*, *ayns*, *ayncoys*, *mays*, and *si*. The differentiation between these various possibilities is often detailed and illustrated with a number of examples. In not being satisfied with mere translation equivalents and usage examples, Palsgrave is a very modern lexicographer. And, as a modern lexicographer, he is one of the innovators. He provides us with what metalexicographers nowadays call functional definitions for closed-category items. We find these in some modern monolingual English dictionaries, above all when a mother-tongue ready-made equivalent or paraphrase is not easily available. Palsgrave is the first English lexicographer to attempt such functional descriptions in bilingual dictionaries. They are often at the same time precious little gems of contrastive analysis. The whole of Palsgrave's description of *but* and its French renderings is too extensive to be quoted. I shall therefore confine myself to the overall differentiation and one translation equivalent. *Que*, *sinon*, *fors*, *ayns*, *ayncoys*, *mays*, and *si* as possible translations of English *but* are characterized as follows:

> Of the whiche seuen *que*, *sinon*, and *fors*, maye be vsed in a sentence a lone/ whiche nouther dependeth of any sentence goynge byfore/ nor bringeth in no sentence to folowe/ but with this difference. For *que*, is vsed whan we vse but/ after a verbe byfore any one parte of spetche a lone. As for he is but a foole/ she is but a beest/ my wyfe is but blacke/ I aske but the/ I haue but foure/ they saye: *Il nest que vng fol. Elle nest que vne folle, Ma femme nest que noyre, Ie ne demande que toy, Ie nay que quattre.* So that *que*, causeth his verbe to haue *ne*, byfore hym/ though our verbe haue nat not/ byfore hym in our tonge/ accordynge as I haue touched in the secõde rule vpon the accydentes partyculer of aduerbes in the seconde booke. (III, fo. cccc.lxv)

The user is then given very explicit metalinguistic descriptions of the use of these seven conjunctions:

> *Mays*, whan he signyfyeth but/ is euer the firste worde of a sentence/ whiche hath respecte to the sentence nexte goynge byfore in suche wyse that if the chiefe verbe of the sentence byfore the affyrmatyue thanne the verbe folowynge *mays*, muste be negatyue: And contrarye wyse/ if the verbe in the formore sentẽce be negatyue/ than the verbe also where *mays*, is muste be negatyue/ or at the leste the verbes muste be of contrarye sence: as/ *Ie ne lay pas faict encore mays ie le feray tantost.* and *En vostre presence Il resẽble a vng aigneau mays arriere de vous il fait le deable.* (III, fo. cccc.lxv$^{r-v}$).

## *Interjections*

We come finally to the table of interjections. Here, Palsgrave decided against alphabetical order and for a semantic grouping. He thus assembles into separate groups the interjections of calling, those of asking, those of warning, etc. Within these groups, he follows the pattern which we have encountered before: when there are several French possibilities, he first lists them all and then illustrates each with an example—for example:

> **Interiections betokenyng kepyng of sylence**: Houische. Mom. Payx.
> Houische. **as**/ Houische ne sõnez mot.
> Mom. **as**/ Mom ne parlez plus.
> Paix. **as**/ Payx paix monsieur vient.
>
> (III, fo. cccc.lxxiii)

As we may infer from these examples, Palsgrave does not list English interjections. That is, there are no English headwords apart from the general semantic heading.

To summarize: Palsgrave's lexicographical treatment of the different parts of speech varies considerably. These differences do not only manifest themselves in the ordering of the headwords within the tables. They also pervade other sections of the dictionary entries, as we shall see in the chapters that address the structure of the English lemmata and the French equivalents. The only generalization that one might venture so far is that, the further Palsgrave progresses in his bilingual dictionary, the more the lexicographical practice of illustrating headwords in example sentences or phrases becomes integral to his lexicographical method.

## SOURCES

We now come to the very difficult question of Palsgrave's sources. As a non-native speaker of the French language, he felt that he had to base his analyses and statements on authentic linguistic data. This is why he first sought to identify those literary texts and authors that might be regarded as the best exponents of good French usage. As we have seen, he was pleased to find that his choice very closely resembled that of Geofrey Tory.

For his mother-tongue English, the language of his headwords, he obviously did not feel a need to do likewise. He was a native user of it, and, as he moved in the circle of the court and the nobility, he seems to have taken its use and standard for granted. Yet his word list discloses that he also drew upon literary sources of English. He attributes a good number of his headwords to either Geoffrey Chaucer or John Lydgate. Since he is the first English lexicographer to quote English literary works or authors in his work, we shall deal with these in detail in a separate chapter and investigate their function in the dictionary.

The circumspection and scholarly thoroughness with which he undertook his task made him assess as non-literary sources the work that had been done before him (A ii$^{v}$). Palsgrave thus acknowledges that he consulted earlier and contemporary studies but we are not given any specific titles of works or names of authors with the exception of three colleagues and rivals: 'the studious clerke Alexãdre Barkelay', 'maister Petrus Uallensys', and the 'synguler clerke/ maister Gyles Dewes'. But none of these equals Palsgrave in scholarly depth and comprehensiveness, nor did any of them attempt a dictionary on the scale of Palsgrave's.

For the methodology of presenting his grammar in three successive parts, he had referred us to Theodore Gaza as his model. There is no passage in *Lesclarcissement* comparable to that at the beginning of the *Promptorium parvulorum*: 'Isti sunt autores ex quorum libris collecta sunt vocabula huius libelli', followed by a list of names and works. For his lexicographical model, Palsgrave has left us in the dark. Our review of word list arrangements in earlier medieval Latin reference works has yielded few clues as to his possible sources.

### *French and English texts: the functional identification of adverbials and conjunctions*

Palsgrave may have compiled his word lists from literary works and other reading material by carefully excerpting words, phrases, and examples, allocating them to the respective tables kept separate during the practical process of item collection. In the case of word classes that consist of relatively small sets of items, this could have been a plausible method of work. In the case of interjections, for instance, he might have had separate leaves headed by such titles as 'interjections betokening lamenting', 'interjections betokening abhorring', and then filled them from his reading, copying *helas* and such examples as *Helas que ferons nous poures gens darmes*, and so on.

To some extent this may also have been his method of compilation for the units and phrases which he lists under the table of adverbs and conjunctions. Again, he would have had twelve different leaves (and piles of leaves) according to the guiding questions (*when*, *where*, *whither*, *how*, *how much*, *how long*, *how often*, *how many*, *how far forth*, *from whence*, *since when*, *why*), and then have entered lexical items as they turned up during his reading. These lexical units could have been gleaned from French books or from English ones. Let us speculate about the following entry:

> **Strayght ouer agaynste/ as one house or place is strayght ouer an other or as persons syt at the borde:** Vis a vis, **as/** Il demeure vis a vis des cordeliers. **and** Puis que nous sõmes assis vis a vis lung de lautre beuuons ensemble.
>
> (III, fo. cccc.xxxii)

It seems plausible that Palsgrave first noted the French item *vis-à-vis*, and then rendered it into English. To have isolated from some English text source a lemma *strayght ouer agaynste* appears rather unlikely. There is no entry for the more idiomatic English corresponding item *opposite* in *Lesclarcissement*. In the prepositional sense in which *vis-à-vis* is used here, *opposite* was not yet common in English according to the *OED*.

A similar case might be *chez*. It does not occur on its own as a preposition, presumably because English *at* as a headword was considered not satisfactory to match it. We find it under the following entry:

> **At home with you/ at home $\overset{t}{w}$ me / the/ vs/ thẽ: at my house/ thy house / our house/ your house/ their house/** : Chez moy, chez toy, chez luy, **or** elle, chez nous, chez vous, chez eulx, **or** elles, **and in lyke wyse/** chez monsieur, chez mon pere.
>
> (III, fo. cccc.xxviii$^{v}$)

The French series reveals that Palsgrave was carried away by the grammatical pattern, starting with the first-person singular and ending with the third-person plural. The English headword unit *At home with you* strikes us as a match for the French expression, not as an authentic example from an English text. With the other additions *at home with me*, etc., Palsgrave then explains the use of *chez*.[7]

As instances that Palsgrave collected items of his word list from actual English text bases we might adduce

> **Atwene** (Lyd) Entre. **as/ Atwene vs bothe**: Entre nous deux.
>
> (III, fo. cccc.xxviii$^{v}$)

where he actually refers to his source, Lydgate, or the entry *Farre wyde*, for which there is no French equivalent. In the case of *in the owl flight*, he even admits that he does not know the French equivalent:

> **In $\overset{e}{y}$ owle flyght: they haue no maner of suche speakyng $\overset{t}{y}$ I wotte of.**
>
> (III, fo. cccc.xxiii$^{v}$)[8]

[7] There is another entry where Palsgrave also gives the forms for all the grammatical persons in English: 'In my house/ thy house/ his house/ her house: In our house/ in your house/ their house: in my lordȝ house in my maysters house: Chez moy, chez toy, chez luy, chez elle, chez no$^{9}$ chez vous, chez eulx, chez elles, chez monsieur, chez mon pere. &c. **as/** Allons boyre chez margot la librayre' (III, fo. cccc.xxx$^{v}$).

[8] There is, however, an entry *At The owle flyght* which is glossed as *A la volée du hybou*. It is not clear to me whether this is an example of a double entry. There are instances where an entry is listed twice in different places, suggesting that Palsgrave did not have enough time for checking or revision. The difference between *at* and *in* might correlate with different meanings (at a point of time, during a period of time).

All the adverb examples given lead us to another important issue: the distinction between the different parts of speech. In the introductions to the table of prepositions, adverbs, and conjunctions, Palsgrave repeatedly draws the learner's attention to the difficulties of differentiating between these three classes. When dealing with prepositions, he points out that they may also function as adverbs or conjunctions (III, fo. cccc.xv). To show what he regards as adverbs, he provides his users with twelve adverbial question types. The '*lytell proheme . . . for the better vnderstandyng of the table of coniunctions*' puts three rules with examples at the users' hands how to identify conjunctions. He apologizes for the length of his explanations, but they are meant

> to helpe suche as be nat lerned in the laten tonge: that they myght by some generall meanes deserne a Coniunction from an other parte of spetche: but vnto suche as be lerned in fewe wordes to expresse this mater here consequently shall folowe the table of coniuctyons/ nat so precysely as the latynes vse them/ for I haue reduced a great meyny of them vnder the generall questyons/ but specyally copulatyues/ and disiunctyues/ causales/ collectyues/ aduersatyues. ⁊c. remyttyng the lerner chefely to the exemples to knowe howe those coniunctions shulde be vsed. (III, fo. cccc.lxii$^{v}$)

Palsgrave thus assumed that *Lesclarcissement* would be used by people coming from different educational backgrounds and that the range of knowledge of Latin grammar would vary greatly. During the Middle Ages grammar knowledge was acquired through Latin, and at the time of the Renaissance grammar-teaching had not changed to a noticeable degree. Until then, no scholar had deemed a vernacular worthy of a serious grammatical analysis. The predominant concept of a vernacular did not lend itself to such an analysis. In this intellectual climate, Palsgrave, as we have seen, attempted to reduce a vernacular to rules. This vernacular was French. The challenge to discover the regularities operating within the French language made him compare it to his mother tongue. In working out the differences between the two languages, he subjected a second vernacular, English, to the same linguistic analysis—not, admittedly, in all the areas he investigated for French in the three books of *Lesclarcissement* that deal with pronunciation and grammar; and not to the same degree of depth, if we think of the tables of nouns, verbs, and adjectives in the dictionary part, where he indicates the gender and plural forms for nouns and adjectives in French, as well as the basic tense forms and conjugation classes for verbs. The grammatical identification of nouns, verbs, adjectives, numerals, and pronouns might be regarded as relatively unproblematic, and the medieval bilingual nominales, verbales, and adjectivales may have contributed to sharpen, or indeed to establish, the perception of the classes of words. These easily recognizable grammatical units of language make up a large part of anything spoken or written. But how about the rest? How can we delimit and classify the remainder into sensible grammatical units? It is well known within grammatical metatheory that the class of adverbs has been the *fourre-tout par excellence* for many very disparate linguistic elements. With their distinction of adjuncts, conjuncts, disjuncts, and subjuncts, Quirk *et al.* (1985) bring substantial structure into this highly complex field of grammatical analysis. Yet this is an achievement of twentieth-century linguistic theory and description. Some 450 years earlier, John Palsgrave set himself the same task. In addressing this task he was a pioneer. The rules which he set out for his learners to distinguish an adverb from a conjunction are the very rules which he himself will have applied to decide for each lexical unit in which table to place it. In order for his learners to understand his rules, he formulated them in English, not in Latin, and he provided examples. All this makes him a very early pioneer in the history of English grammar-writing.

How did he tackle the analysis of his mother tongue? If we disregard one-word representatives of the form class adverb like *already*, *always*, etc., there was no precedent, no tradition of lemmatization. His method of analysis consisted in setting up twelve questions to elicit sequences of linguistic elements, syntactic units which could take the place of an adverbial in a sentence—for example:

Where did it happen?
- Here.
- Euery where.
- On euery syde.
- On the syde towardes ẏ medowes.

Or among the syntactic units answering the question *when* we find such a range of elements as *never*, *At The poynt of dethe*, *As sone as it may be done*, *In lesse whyle than I haue tolde you ẏ tale*. The table of adverbs thus includes members of the grammatical form class adverb (*here*, *never*, *playnly*), prepositional phrases as well as clauses. Palsgrave's insight that all these sequences showed the same syntactical behaviour made him classify them together. Just as his table of 'adverbs' subsumes adverbs as form classes and adverbials as functional units, so his 'conjunctions' include what Quirk *et al.* regard as conjunctions and conjuncts. That the first attempt at classifying these grammatical units will include inconsistencies and mistakes is no surprise.

In assigning part-of-speech membership (which may be a form or a function class) to all the headword units included in his dictionary, Palsgrave is still unparalleled as an English lexicographer at the end of the twentieth century. Modern English dictionaries, whether of the general-purpose type such as *Collins English Dictionary*, or the EFL type such as the *Advanced Learner's Dictionary of Current English* or the *Longman Dictionary of Contemporary English*, and also the *OED*, are based on word-class distinctions. Idiomatic phrases and expressions, with the exceptions of phrasal verbs and word-formations, in general, are not given any grammatical specification or headword status. Let us look at the expressions *by little and little*, *by no means*, and *in good faith*. All three are described as adverbs by Palsgrave. Where would we find them in modern English dictionaries? The *OED* lists *by little and little* as sense 7 of the *absolute* and *substantive* use of *little*, describing it as a phrase with a preposition. *By no means* appears under number 14 of *mean sb.*[2], which covers adverbial, prepositional, and conjunctional phrases. *In good faith*, registered under number 12 of the noun entry *faith*, is described as an asseverative phrase. For lexical units larger than the word, the *OED* thus uses the term phrase, which may be further specified according to its constituents or its semantic function.

*Collins English Dictionary* lists *by no means* and *in good faith* as run-on entries under the nouns *means* and *faith* respectively. The same holds for the two EFL dictionaries. Collins varies between no further specification (*by no means*) for the expression and calling it a phrase (*in good faith*). Longman does not say anything about the formal or grammatical nature of the units, and the *Advanced Learner's Dictionary of Current English* stresses their fixed formal and special semantic status by calling them idioms. So none of these reference works takes into account the level of syntactic function as Palsgrave did.

### *Word lists including English and/or French*

If we accept that a fair part of the lexical units listed as headword units may have their source in a variety of English and French texts which Palsgrave read and studied for his great enterprise, we are still left with the problem of accounting for other sources which he might have used. The central question is whether he used other reference books. The advantages of consulting the lexicographical works of other compilers would have been enormous. He would not have had to start from scratch. He could have chosen one such word list as his working basis, and then added, expanded, deleted, rearranged items, meanings, examples. But were there word lists, and were they substantial enough to determine his overall working method? We have some knowledge about the beginning of dictionary-making for English and French, but the existing inventories taking stock of the glossaries, vocabularies, and dictionaries known to exist or have existed, or to have been printed, are in need of updating and revision. Manuscript fragments and whole manuscripts that have been brought to scholarly notice are still awaiting careful editing. For both languages the foundations of lexicographical research were laid in the last decades of the nineteenth century. A still earlier attempt at drawing up an inventory of word lists is W. Marsden's *Catalogue of dictionaries, vocabularies, grammars, and alphabets* of 1796. From the second half of the nineteenth century we have three surveys of dictionaries involving English which complement each other. The first is the list of dictionaries included in the introduction to J. E. Worcester's *Dictionary of the English language* of 1860. It was followed five years later by H. B. Wheatley's paper in the *Transactions of the Philological Society* 'Chronological notices of the dictionaries of the English language', which W. W. Skeat complemented with 'A bibliographical list of the works that have been published, or are known to exist in ms., illustrative of the various dialects of English'. The most comprehensive account of English dictionaries from the beginning of printing up to 1800 is R. C. Alston's excellent bibliography. The best collection of edited vocabulary manuscripts is still that by T. Wright. Substantial research work in identifying, describing, and investigating the interrelations between a great number of early word lists has been done by D. T. Starnes, J. Schäfer, and G. Stein.

For Palsgrave, word lists with English as the headword language would have been the most helpful. The most widely accessible English headword list would have been that in the *Promptorium parvulorum*, which by the time when Palsgrave began work on *Lesclarcissement* had already run through four editions. From the manuscripts that have come down to us we conclude that he could also have used a dictionary-sized manuscript copy of the *Catholicon Anglicum* or the much smaller *tractatus sinonimorum*. More laborious would have been the use of bilingual Latin-English word lists and dictionaries, because he would have had to reorder their English equivalents into an alphabetical list. Since English dictionary-making began with Latin–English glossaries and vocabularies, more Latin–English manuscripts would have been available. Topical vocabulary lists as we find them in Wright's edition would have helped him to ensure that certain vocabulary areas had been covered in his work. The first Latin–English dictionary, the *Medulla grammatice*, was in circulation, and so were the printed editions of the *Ortus vocabulorum*.

An early account of the various glossaries and vocabularies compiled for Old and Middle French is that by E. Littré in volume 22 of the *Histoire littéraire de la France*. To this we have to add the biographical lists of dictionaries involving French compiled by R. Schwartze (1875) and C. Beaulieux (1904/1972). But from a review of the lexicographical works known to exist, it is still a major step to making manuscripts accessible to a wider scholarly public by editing them. This was a project envisaged as early as the late 1860s by Gaston Paris. The enterprise seems to have been too ambitious, for, though begun according to his pupil Mario Roques, it was abandoned. Yet the master's vision had left its imprint on the pupil's mind. In 1936 Roques outlined the plan of a comprehensive research undertaking to edit all the known medieval word lists including French, and in the following years he published the first fruits of his work as the *Recueil général des lexiques français du moyen âge*. Yet again, the work was halted. The two volumes of 1936–8 did not have any successors. Individual scholars have contributed to the advancement of medieval French lexicography, but there still is no bibliographical handbook filling this dearly felt gap for medieval French scholarship. This state of research was sadly noted by Mario Rocques some forty years after the publication of his *Recueil*, at the fourth International Colloquium on Middle French, held at Amsterdam in 1982. The remark was then addressed to M. Lindemann, who had drawn the participants' attention to a French dictionary of 1511 that had escaped scholarly notice: the *Vocabularius nebrissensis latin-français*. And this time, the remark was heeded. M. Lindemann has now produced a monumental account of the early lexicographical works involving French in her book *Die französischen Wörterbücher von den Anfängen bis 1600* (1994).

All we can do, therefore, from the literature on the subject, is draw up a list of works that Palsgrave might have consulted for the French part of his dictionary. Since we might assume that Palsgrave would have concentrated on fifteenth- and early sixteenth-century word lists, I shall confine myself to this period.

There were word lists with French as the source language. We know about three fifteenth-century manuscripts. One is the MS Paris BN lat. 7684 (Diez 1865: 4; Littré 1895: 30–2; Merrilees 1990: 287; Lindemann 1994: 136, 152). The other, in the possession of Professor A. W. B. Simpson, contains a French-Latin topical vocabulary and was published by J. H. Baker in 1989. The third, MS Lille BM no. 147, fos. 313–16, pairs French lemmata with a range of Latin synonyms (Lindemann 1994: 154, 156).

There is one manuscript in which French precedes Latin, but

French is not the headword language. This is the manuscript version of Jean Lagadeuc's trilingual Breton–French–Latin dictionary. The manuscript is in the Bibliothèque Nationale, Paris, and the date given for it is 1464 (Lindemann 1985: 78).

The number of word lists preserved with Latin as the headword language is higher. Most of these have an alphabetical arrangement and are bilingual derivatives of Johannes Balbus's *Catholicon*. They belong to the *Aalma* group, their first word usually being the item *aalma*. Mario Roques's *Recueil* gives an account of these manuscripts, and the most recent description of the various affiliations is that by Lindemann (1994: 202–50). Others belong to the *Abavus* group, bilingual derivatives of Brito's *Expositiones vocabulorum Biblie*. For the interrelations between the manuscripts that have been preserved, see Roques, but above all Lindemann (1994: 176–201). That topical vocabularies were also common is evidenced by two manuscripts: the first, MS Paris BN lat. 8426, has not been edited (ibid.: 129, 134–5), the other, MS Lille BM no. 147, fos. 1–12, $310^{v}$-$12^{v}$, has been edited by A. Scheler[9] (ibid.: 129, 132–4).

Some of the Latin–French word lists that have come down to us are of dictionary size. The MS H 110 in the Medical Faculty of Montpellier, for instance, covers 292 folios with approximately 13,500 entries (see Nobel 1986; Merrilees 1990; Lindemann 1994: 247–50). The MS 78 in the Royal Library of Stockholm is said to have a similar coverage (Merrilees 1990: 287). The biggest is the MS Paris BN nouv. acq. française 1120. We know its date of completion, 1440, and the name of its compiler, Firmin Le Ver, who spent some twenty years producing this monumental dictionary of 466 folios (Merrilees 1988*b*; Merrilees and Edwards 1989; Lindemann 1994: 240–7). An edition of Le Ver's *Dictionarius* has been prepared by B. Merrilees and his colleagues (1994).

The first *printed* dictionaries involving French are all works where French is not the language of the lemmata. Before 1530, three different dictionaries had been printed, all of which had several editions. The earliest is the so-called *Catholicon abbreviatum*, printed in Paris between 1482 and 1484. According to Lindemann's account (1985: 58–62; 1994: 222–40), more than twenty editions had appeared before 1530. The great popularity which this dictionary enjoyed at the time is further demonstrated by its being printed in six different places: Paris, Rouen, Rennes, Caen, Lyon, and Geneva.

9 This is a highly interesting topical vocabulary which deserves more scholarly attention. Some of its groupings are unmatched in the nominales known to me, as is the systematicity in the recording and coverage of words.

The second printed dictionary is Jean Lagadeuc's *Catholicon en troys langaiges scavoir est breton franczoys et latin* of 1499. A second edition was printed by Corre and the third, in 1521, by Quillivéré (Lagadeuc 1499/1975; Lindemann 1985: 78–9; Lindemann 1994: 278–84). And finally, there was the *Vocabularius nebrissensis*, printed for the first time in 1511,[10] based on Antonio de Nebrija's famous Latin–Spanish dictionary of 1492 with French equivalents replacing the Spanish ones. Though the second edition did not appear before Palsgrave had begun work in 1516 on *Lesclarcissement de la langue francoyse*, there were seven further editions before 1530.

With the exception of Lagadeuc's Breton–French–Latin dictionary, all the bilingual glossaries, topical vocabularies, and full-size dictionaries discussed so far matched Latin and French. Since the first bilingual dictionaries for English as well as French derive from medieval Latin dictionaries, the compiler of an English–French or French–English dictionary could have used them side by side to select his word list and to supply the appropriate equivalents in the other vernacular. Balbus's *Catholicon* was seminal in this respect. The Latin headwords in the *Catholicon abbreviatum* and the *Ortus vocabulorum*, for instance, show many similarities. But before investigating these possibilities in more detail, we have to look at what works there were pairing both our vernaculars in some kind of word list.

The most obvious little booklets of the late fifteenth century which Palsgrave might have exploited are, of course, William Caxton's 'Tres bonne doctrine pour aprendre briefment francoys et engloys', Wynkyn de Worde's 'Here begynneth a lytell treatyse for to lerne Englysshe and Frensshe', printed by Richard Pynson. Alexander Barclay's *Introductory* and Pierre Valence's *Introductions* would not have been helpful. How familiar Palsgrave may have been with the content of du Wes's *Introductorie* before its publication in 1532–3 is not clear.

Other printed vernacular word lists involving French, above all as the language of the headwords, could have been used. But the earliest dictionary with French lemmata according to our present-day knowledge is the 1529 edition of Hieronymus Cingularius' *Tersissima latini eloquii synonymorum collectanea*, in which French is matched with Flemish and Latin—that is, we have a combination of a vernacular bilingual dictionary with Latin equivalents (Lindemann 1994: 458–60). The publication date of this version of Cingularius' dictionary, 1529, is too late to have been used by Palsgrave for the compilation of *Lesclarcissement*.

[10] See Lindemann (1985: 64–71; 1994: 250–6) for an account of the various editions of the work.

Finally, we might turn our attention to monolingual French word lists in which 'hard' or more specialized vocabulary was explained in simpler French. That they were already compiled towards the end of the fifteenth century has been shown by G. Hasenohr (1984).

From our review of the lexicographical activities going on in England and in France during the second half of the fifteenth century and the early sixteenth century, it emerges that there were indeed works which Palsgrave could have consulted. We shall now look in more detail at some that I have been able to check with this in mind.

## Catholicon Anglicum *and* Promptorium parvulorum

Assuming that it would have been more likely for Palsgrave to have used a printed version of the *Promptorium parvulorum* than a manu-

TABLE 4.1 *A comparison of* P-*nouns in the* Catholicon Anglicum *and* Lesclarcissement

| *Catholicon Anglicum* | *Lesclarcissement* |
|---|---|
| **a Paciens** | **Pacyence vertue** |
| **a Pacoke** | **Pecocke a byrde** |
| **a Paddokstole** | — |
| **a Page** | **Page a seruaunt** |
| **a Paiande** | **Pagiant in a playe** |
| **a Payere** | — |
| **a Paynyme** | **Panym an infydele** |
| **Paynymery** | — |
| **a Payne** | **Payne desease/ tourment in payne** |
| **a Payntynge** | **Payntyng with colours** |
| **a Payntour** | **Paynter** |
| **a Payre** | **Payre of any thing** |
| **a Palace** | **Palays** |
| **a Palace staffe** | — |
| **a Palace of a mouthe** | **Palate of the mouthe** |
| **an Palenes** | **Palenesse** |
| **a Palfray** | **Palfray a beest** |
| **a Palmer** | — |
| **a Palmare of þe scole** | — |
| **Palme sonday** | **Palme sonday** |
| **a Palme tre** | **Palme tree** |
| **a Pamentt** | **Pament of a strete** |
| **a Panne** | **Panne a vessell** |
| **a Pancake** | **Pancake** |
| **a Panne of a howse** | **Pane of a wall** |

script, we begin with the *Catholicon Anglicum* the manuscript of which is older than the first edition of the *Promptorium parvulorum*. We may consider the likelihood of Palsgrave's using the *Catholicon Anglicum* by comparing some items as they appear in both books (see Table 4.1).

Of the twenty-five headwords listed in the *Catholicon Anglicum*, six do not appear in *Lesclarcissement*, and one might argue that they were omitted because they represent more specialized vocabulary items. In *Lesclarcissement* the alphabetical section from *P* to *Pane of a wall* includes seventy-nine headwords. Palsgrave's list is thus three times that of the *Catholicon Anglicum*. One, *pace a goyng*, occurs as *a pase* in the *Catholicon Anglicum*. Palsgrave seems to have had a particular interest in expressions with *a pair of*. There are a further twenty-six entries (*payre of indentures*, *payre of hose from one kne vp*, *payre of beedes*, *payre of bootes*, etc.),[11] which he may deliberately have collected to focus on the contrast between the English and the French expression.

Let us now look at the beginning of this same letter *P* in the printed edition of the *Promptorium parvulorum* (1499). There are numerous nouns which are common to all the three works, but here are the nouns which do not occur in the *Catholicon Anglicum*, but are listed in the *Promptorium parvulorum* and *Lesclarcissement* (see Table 4.2).

There are five lemmata which are unmatched in *Lesclarcissement*: *Page of a stabyll* could already have been covered by Palsgrave's *page a*

TABLE 4.2. *A comparison of* P-*nouns in the* Promptorium parvulorum *and* Lesclarcissement

| *Promptorium parvulorum* (1499) | *Lesclarcissement* |
|---|---|
| **Pacyens herbe** | **Pacyence an herbe** |
| **Patche clowte to sett to a thinge** | **Patche or clout** |
| **Pay or payment** | **Payment of money** |
| **Payle or mylke stoppe** | **Payle a vessell** |
| **Payne mayne** | **Payne mayne** |
| **Packe** | **Packe** |
| **Pale of a parke** | **Pale of a parke or suche lyke** |
| **Palme** | **Palme of the hande** |
| **Palsye** | **Palsey a disease** |
| **Paltok** | **Paltocke of lether** |
| **Pane of furrowe** | **Pane of furre** |

[11] See in this respect Woledge (1956), where he discusses Palsgrave's list of nouns of the type *unes paces* 'a pair of pastes for the attire of a woman's head'.

*seruant*; *Palet armowre of the hede* (Lat. *pellitis*) is rendered as 'helme of lether' in the *Ortus vocabulorum*; *Paly or bryn* in the meaning of 'bran', according to the *OED*, is recorded only for the *Promptorium parvulorum*; *Pane or party* (in Mayhew's edition we have *pane of parte of athynge*) and finally, *pan of the hede*.

Some *P*-nouns occur in the *Catholicon* but not in the *Promptorium*. These are:

a **Palace staffe**
a **Palmer**
**Palme sonday**
a **Palme tre**
a **Panne of a howse**

What emerges from our comparison so far is that Palsgrave may indeed have consulted both the *Catholicon Anglicum* and the *Promptorium parvulorum* and selected his headwords from these two dictionaries. But, in view of the fact that he was intent on compiling all the words of the language with some allowance made for the omission of word-formations, it is not easy to account for his presumed rejections. He might either have consulted another still unidentified source or added selected items from it. In Palsgrave's *P*-section of nouns the following entries occur that do not appear in either the *Catholicon* or the *Promptorium*. The additions are substantial:

| | | |
|---|---|---|
| **Pacyentnesse** | | pacience s fe. |
| **Pacyent a sicke body** | | pacient s ma. |
| **Pacquet of letters** | | pacquet de lettres. &c. z ma. |
| **Packe sadyll** | } the item is listed twice | batz, bas ma. |
| **Packe sadell** | | bast z ma. |
| **Pagyll a cowsloppe** | | no equivalent given |
| **Payment by driblettes**[12] | | entreneve poyement. |
| **Payment of dette**[12] | | solution s fe. |
| **Payne of sickness** | | agonie s fe. |
| **Payntyng of ones face** | | farcement s ma. |
| **Payre of indentures** | | endenturez fe. |
| **Payre of hose from the kne vp** | | demy chausses fe. |
| **Payre of beedes** | | paternostres ma. |
| **Payre of botes** | | bottes fe. |
| **Payre of sloppe hoses** | | braiettes a marinier s fe. |
| **Payre of burlettes** | | une paces fe. |

[12] There is only one entry *pay or payment* in the *Promptorium*. Palsgrave has three entries for *payment* which are more specialized: *payment of money*, *payment by driblettes*, and *payment of dette* matching three different French equivalents. As to the noun *driblette*, the *OED* needs revision. Its first quotation for the sense 'a small sum, odd money in a sum' dates from 1632; Palsgrave's use thus predates it by 100 years. The earliest record for the word is from 1591 in the sense 'a small or petty debt'.

| | |
|---|---|
| **Payre of brigandyns** | brigandines fe. |
| **Payre of curates** | curace s fe. |
| **Payre of tonges** | tenailles fe. |
| **Payre of fettars** | ceps ma. |
| **Payre of sycers**[13] | ciseletz ma. forces fe. |
| **Payre of belowes** | soufflетz ma. |
| **Payre of pynsons** | pinces fe. estriquoires fe. |
| **Payre of spectacles** | lunettes fe. |
| **Payre of golde weyghtes** | poix, trebuchet z ma. |
| **Payre of wynding blades** | tournettes fe. |
| **Payre of pastes** | unes pases fe. |
| **Payre of tables** | unes tables fe. iev de tables fe. |
| **Payre of smythes tonges** | greffes fe. |
| **Payre of startoppes** | hovssettes fe. |
| **Payre of lytell sheres** | forcettes fe. |
| **Payre of cardes to playe with** | cartes fe. |
| **Payre of writyng tables** | tablettes fe. |
| **Payre of clarycordes** | monocorde fe. |
| **Payre of balances** | unes balances fe. |
| **Paytrell for a horse** | poictral x ma. |
| **Pale before a dore** | palis ma. |
| **Pale a fence** | tavldis ma. |
| **Pale or a stake** | piev x ma. claie s fe. |
| **Palfray man** | palefronier s ma. |
| **Paleron a pece of harnesse** | espalleron s ma. |
| **Palme for palme sonday** | rameau x ma. |
| **Palmus christi an herbe** | no equivalent given |
| **Palme/ the yelowe that groweth on wyllowes** | chatton s ma. |
| **Palmers scrippe** | escharpe s fe. |
| **Paltocke a garment** | halcret z ma. |
| **Paltocke a patche** | palleteau x ma. |
| **Panche a belly** | pance s fe. |
| **Pancy floure** | menve pencee s fe. |
| **Pane of gray furre** | panne de gris fe. |

Let us now turn from nouns to adjectives. Table 4.3 includes all the adjectives beginning with *P* listed in the *Catholicon Anglicum*, the *Promptorium parvulorum*, and *Lesclarcissement*. As we have seen earlier for nouns, spelling differed considerably, and I have therefore included in the table an item that occurs in one dictionary in a *pa*-spelling and in another in a *pe*-spelling, etc.

Comparing these lists shows some salient features: the *Catholicon Anglicum* has the lowest number of adjectives, and nearly all of them occur in one or other of the two dictionaries. The *Promptorium parvulorum* has about a dozen adjectives not included in either of the other two dictionaries. And similarly, about half of Palsgrave's

[13] The item is listed without *a pair of* as *sysowre* in the *Promptorium parvulorum*.

TABLE 4.3. *Table of adjectives beginning with* P

| *Catholicon Anglicum* | *Promptorium parvulorum* (1499) | *Lesclarcissement* |
|---|---|---|
| Pacient | Paciens | Pacyent |
| un Pacient | — | — |
| Paynfulle | — | Paynefull/ that may endure payne |
| | | Paynefull |
| Palde as Ale | Palted as drynke | — |
| Pale | Pale of colowre | Paale of colowre |
| Parellos | — | Peryllouse/ full of peryll |
| Passynge transient' | — | — |
| — | Payed of dette | — |
| — | Payed or quemed ꝛ pleased | [pleased is listed] |
| — | Paraffed | — |
| — | Parboyled | — |
| — | Parceyued | — |
| — | Parchyd as pesyn and benys | — |
| — | Parcyall | — |
| Perfyte | Parfight | Parfyte |
| — | Parfourmed | — |
| — | Partable | — |
| — | Parted asonder | — |
| | Parted or deuyded or daft aboute | — |
| Pesabylle | Pecible | Paysible/ full of peace or rest |
| — | — | Palpable/ apte or mete to be felte |
| — | — | Pardurable |
| — | — | Parochyall/ belongyng to a parysshe |
| — | — | Parpetuell |
| — | — | Passyng measure |
| — | — | Passyng other of the same sorte |
| — | — | Passed as the tyme is |
| — | — | Passyonate/ inclyned sone to be in a passyon |
| — | — | Patrymonyall/ belongyng to a mannes enherytaũce or patrymony |

adjectives are unique to *Lesclarcissement*. If we assume that Palsgrave consulted the *Promptorium parvulorum*, we would have to explain his ignoring such adjectives as *parboiled*, *parched*, *paraphed*, *partial*, etc. The adjectives listed in the *Promptorium parvulorum* differ from the others in often constituting past participles, and Palsgrave may have entered the verb in its place and ignored the past participle. This holds, for instance, for *to parboil*, *to part*, *to perceive*, *to perform*, *to parch*, the latter even having three entries ('*I Parche I drye . . .*', '*I Parche pesyn as folkes vse in lent*', '*I Partche by heate of the sonne*'). *Paraffed* 'divided into paragraphs' appears only in the *Promptorium parvulorum* and might have been regarded as rare or old by Palsgrave. But this does not explain the omission of *partial* which was current at the time.

### *Word groups: fingers*

Instead of looking at alphabetical sequences of items or words belonging to the same part of speech, we might also consider semantic sets of words to find out whether the words recorded by Palsgrave follow one particular source. The first example will be a small set: the words for the five fingers of the hand. Fifteenth-century vocabularies provide us with the data given in Table 4.4 (the examples are taken from Wright (1884/1968)).

We may now look at the terms used in the *Promptorium parvulorum*, the *Catholicon Anglicum*, the *Ortus vocabulorum* and *Lesclarcissement de la langue francoyse*, given in Table 4.5.

What emerges from the two tables is that the terms for thumb and the little finger have a relatively stable history in English, whereas words for the three fingers in between have varied. The *forefinger* has also been called the *lickpot* (*finger*), a more imaginative purpose-oriented designation than the enumerative *second finger*. Words for the *middle finger* common in fifteenth- and sixteenth-century English were the *longman* or the *long finger* and *middle finger*. The use of the *third finger* for ring finger instead of the more common *leech finger* or just *leech* is rather interesting if we compare it with the earlier alternative for the *second finger*. *Second finger* for the forefinger suggests a counting that starts with the thumb; *third finger* for the ring finger begins with the forefinger, disregarding the thumb in the counting of fingers.

Palsgrave's use of *middle finger* is closest to MS Harley 1002 and the *Catholicon Anglicum*, but, unfortunately, there is no word for *index* in *Lesclarcissement* to invite further conclusions. A striking feature is Palsgrave's non-use of *leech* or *leech finger*. Of the nine

TABLE 4.4. *The nouns denoting fingers in fifteenth-century vocabularies*

| Latin | MS Harl. 1002, fol. 116v | BM MS Reg 17, C XVII., fol. 21r | *Mayer Nominale* | *Pictorial Vocabulary* |
|---|---|---|---|---|
| pollex | thombe | thowme | thome | thombe |
| index | forefynger | — | the secunde fynger | lykpot |
| medius | medulle fyngur | — | the longe fynger | the longman |
| medicus | leche fyngur | — | the therde fynger | the leche |
| auricularis | litylle fyngure | — | the lytyle fynger | the lythyl man |

TABLE 4.5. *Nouns denoting fingers in the first English dictionaries*

| Latin | *Promptorium parvulorum*, ed. Mayhew | *Catholicon Anglicum* | *Promptorium parvulorum* (1499) | *Ortus vocabulorum* (1500) | *Lesclarcissement* |
|---|---|---|---|---|---|
| pollex | thom[m]be | thome | thombe | thome | thombe |
| index | lykpote ffinger | lykpotte | lykpot finger | [no English equivalent] | — |
| medius | — | lang fynger<br>middis fynger | — | [not listed] | myddle fyngre<br>[no French equivalent] |
| medicus | — | rynge man fingur | — | leche | ryng fyngar<br>[no French equivalent] |
| auricularis | — | litille finger | — | lyttyll fynger | lytell fynger |

lists considered, *Lesclarcissement* is the only one to record *ring finger* and it is thus closest to the *Catholicon Anglicum*.

Palsgrave gives no French equivalent for *myddle fyngre* and *ryng fyngar*. This could merely be an oversight on his part, but on the other hand, we learn from the *Trésor de la langue française* that both the words *médius* and *majeur* for middle finger are first recorded for 1520. In the case of *annulaire*, the noun, the date is slightly later (1539). So Palsgrave might be excused for not listing them—but words relating to the human body are so common in early word lists that other designations for *medicus* and *auricularis* must have existed in French. The lack of French equivalents in *Lesclarcissement* might thus reveal something about Palsgrave's French sources.

The topical vocabulary in the Lille library which A. Scheler has edited, for instance, provides us with the following items:

Polex, pauch
Index, secundus digitus
Medius, le moyen doit
Medicus, le quart doit
Auricularis, le petit doit.

The 1492 edition of the *Catholicon abbreviatum* does not list *medius* and *medicus*. The other three French equivalents are:

| | |
|---|---|
| Pollex | • cest le gros doy de la main |
| Index | • second doy de la main demonstreur |
| Auricularis | • le petit doy |

Lagadeuc's trilingual dictionary lists *pollex* only (*le poulce de la main*). The *Vocabularius nebrissensis* of 1511 covers *pollex* and *index*:

| | |
|---|---|
| Polex licis. | le poux de la main . . . |
| Index cis. | q̃ demõstre: reuelant les secretz. d'r le doit second cestui pres le pousse: le doit indicatif . . . |

Three of the Latin–French word lists record the *index*, which could have induced Palsgrave to list *forefinger* as a headword, if he had used these lists during the compilation of the French part of his dictionary. Lagadeuc's dictionary does not list *index*, nor does Palsgrave have the English equivalent. Palsgrave's spelling of the French word for thumb is *poulce*, the same as in Lagadeuc's list, whereas the three other French sources have *pauch*, *le gros doy de la main*, *le poux de la main*. His French contemporary, François Rabelais, describes an interesting argumentation by means of signs between Panurge and Thaumaste, the 'grand clerc de Angleterre' (Rabelais 1962). In this context, Rabelais uses the following French terms for the fingers of the hand: *le poulce, le poulse; le doigt indice; le doigt meillieu, le doigt mylieu, le mylieu; le doigt auriculaire; le petit doigt, le doigt petit* (ibid.: 127–30, 132–3).

### *Word groups: kinship terms*

My second semantic group of nouns is kinship terms. Early word lists differ greatly in how many of these terms they record. Word lists that include Latin are usually richer, because of the highly differentiated system of relation in that language. I shall not compare all the nouns of relation listed in all the dictionaries consulted but concentrate on a basic core.

In Table 4.6 the respective terms recorded in the *Catholicon Anglicum*, the *Promptorium parvulorum* (printed edition of 1499), the *Ortus vocabulorum*, and *Lesclarcissement* are contrasted in order to show whether any of them could have been Palsgrave's source for the English headword list. Since the English term listed in Latin–English and English–Latin dictionaries may render different Latin words—*aunt*, for instance, may be the equivalent of Latin *amita* or Latin *matertera*—I have given Latin equivalents for the modern English words.

For the items *father-in-law* and *mother-in-law*, the *Catholicon Anglicum* still has *eldfader* and *eldmoder*. Both words are also given in the *Promptorium parvulorum*, but the modern equivalents are added: *fader in lawe, moder in lawe*. Palsgrave lists the *-in-law* words only.

Relationship by marriage is not yet lexically systematized in the *Catholicon Anglicum*, where *son-in-law* is paraphrased as *doghter husband*, *brother-in-law* as *syster husbande* (beside *broder in law*), and *sister-in-law* as *broder wyfe*. In the *Promptorium parvulorum* as well as in *Lesclarcissement*, the modern lexical system is in existence, and the term *sister-in-law* is the only one that needed further explanation (*husbondis syster, wyues syster* in the *Promptorium parvulorum*, *syster brothers wyfe* in *Lesclarcissement*). This supports the recording in the *OED*: *sister-in-law* is more recent as a term than *brother-in-law*; the first recording of the latter dates from about 1300, whereas *sister-in-law* is first documented in the *Promptorium parvulorum*. The *Ortus vocabulorum* is strikingly different: Latin *levir* and *sororius* are the only headwords with an English equivalent (*husbond brother* and *brother in lawe*). For all the other terms of relation by marriage, a Latin explanation is given.

There are further points worth commenting upon. The *Ortus vocabulorum* is the only dictionary that lists *grandfather*. The other three dictionaries give forms common in earlier use.

TABLE 4.6. *Kinship terms in English*

| Modern English | *Catholicon Anglicum* | *Promptorium parvulorum* (1499) | *Ortus vocabulorum* | *Lesclarcissement* |
|---|---|---|---|---|
| father [Lat. *pater*] | a fader | Fader | a fader | Fader |
| father-in-law [Lat. *socer*] | an Eldfader | Elfader<br>Fader in lawe | est pater vxoris vel mariti | Fader in lawe |
| mother [Lat. *mater*] | a modyr | Moder | a modyre | Mother |
| mother-in-lawe [Lat. *socrus*] | an Eldmoder | Elmoder<br>Moder in lawe | est mater vxoris | Mother in lawe |
| grandfather [Lat. *avus*] | a Grawnesire<br>a Gudsyre<br>a Bellsyre | Grauncer or faders fader<br>Belsyr faders or moders fader | granfader | Grauntsyre[a]<br>Belsyre |
| grandmother [Lat. *avia*] | a Grawnedame<br>a Gudame<br>a Beldame | Grādame or faders moder<br>Beldame faders or moders whether it be.<br>[Beldam moders moder. Bellona . . .] | grandame or an olde moder | Grandame[b]<br>Beldame |
| son [Lat. *filius*] | a son | Son | a sonne a chylde | Sonne a naturall chylde |
| son-in-law [Lat. *gener*] | a Doghter husbande | Son in lawe | est maritus filie | Sonne in lawe |

| | | | | |
|---|---|---|---|---|
| daughter<br>[Lat. *filia*] | a Doghter | Doughter | a doghtur | Doughter |
| daughter-in-lawe<br>[Lat. *nurus*] | — | Doughter in lawe | est vxor filij | Doughter in lawe |
| brother<br>[Lat. *frater*] | a Broder | Brother | a brother or frere | Brother |
| brother-in-lawe<br>[Lat. *levir*, *sororius*] | a Broder in law<br>a Syster husbande | Brother in lawe | a husbond brother or a brother in lawe | Brother in lawe |
| sister<br>[Lat. *soror*] | a Syster | Cyster<br>Syster | a syster | Syster |
| sister-in-law<br>[Lat. *glos*] | a Broder wyfe | Syster lawe/ as husbondis syster/ or wyues syster | femīa fratris | Syster brothers wyfe/Syster in lawe |
| aunt<br>[Lat. *amita*, *matertera*] | an Awnte | Aunte faders suster<br>Aunte moders suster<br>Mome or aunte faders suster<br>Mome or aunte moders syster | faders syster<br>an awnte | Aunt |
| uncle<br>[Lat. *avunculus*, *patruus*] | an Eme | Eme faders broder<br>Eme moders broder | myn eame | Eme vncle<br>Uncle by the father syde<br>Unkell |

[a] *Grandfather* does not occur on its own in *Lesclarcissement*. It is, however, used in the two entries that follow *Grauntsyre*: *Grauntfathers father* is translated as *aieul* and *Grantfather grantsyre* as *grant aieul* or *atave*.

[b] Though *grandmother* is not listed on its own, it occurs in the entry immediately following the headword *grandame*: *Graunt mothers mother*—aielle.

An interesting case is the item *aunt*. Whereas the *Catholicon Anglicum* adduces *awnte* as a headword for which it then supplies the translations *amita* and *matertera*, the *Promptorium parvulorum*, listing the older word *mome* and anticipating the different translations of *aunt* in Latin, differentiates the two uses of *aunt* by adding a paraphrase (*faders suster, moders suster*) after the headword itself. For the *Ortus vocabulorum* the word for father's sister is not yet lexicalized.

For the word *uncle*, the *Catholicon Anglicum* and the *Promptorium parvulorum* follow the descriptive approach for *aunt*. *Myn eame* in the *Ortus vocabulorum* is a rendering of *avunculus*, the possessive pronoun having no Latin basis. In *Lesclarcissement* we have three entries for *uncle*. Under the letter *E* we find *eme vncle*, and the fact that *vncle* is added after *eme* is noteworthy. It could be interpreted as an indication that *eme* was no longer recognized as the general term and needed more modern support. The most striking feature, however, is that Palsgrave is the only compiler to list the word that has become our modern use.

Let us now move a step further and look at the first printed dictionaries involving French to see whether it is likely that Palsgrave consulted them for his French equivalents. In Table 4.7 the English headword of *Lesclarcissement* is followed by its French equivalent, which is then contrasted with the corresponding items (if listed) in the *Catholicon abbreviatum*, Iehan Lagadeuc's *Catholicon*, and the *Vocabularius nebrissensis*.

The comparison of the French equivalents in *Lesclarcissement* with the other three dictionaries in Table 4.7 suggests that Palsgrave was not indebted to any of them. This is corroborated by another comparison.

### *Ortus vocabulorum, Catholicon abbreviatum, and Vocabularius nebrissensis*

Since Latin was the language mediating between vernaculars, Palsgrave could have used a Latin–English and a Latin–French dictionary or word list side by side and then excerpted the English and the French part. He could have done this with a copy of the *Ortus vocabulorum* and a copy of the *Catholicon abbreviatum* or a copy of the *Vocabularius nebrissensis*. His working method would thus have involved the following type of comparison:

*Ortus vocabulorum*

**Balare .i. clamare admodũ ouis.** to crye as a scheepe

*Catholicon abbreviatum*

**Balo/ as/ aui/ atum.** baaler . . .

or

*Ortus vocabulorum*
**Balare .i. clamare admodũ ouis.** to crye as a scheepe
*Vocabularius Nebrissensis*
**Balo as.** crier come les ouailles

*Lesclarcissement de la langue francoyse* could then have had an entry

**to crye as a scheepe**—baaler

or

**to crye as a scheepe**—crier come les ouailles

Palsgrave could have made this his overall working method, but he might also have used this method to expand a word list extracted from the *Promptorium parvulorum* by additional English headwords obtained from the *Ortus vocabulorum*.

On the other hand, a random check of items under the letter *F* suggests that this method was not employed for the three dictionaries under review (see Table 4.8). Lexical items listed in the *Ortus vocabulorum*, *Catholicon abbreviatum*, and the *Vocabularius nebrissensis* under the letter *F* are, for instance, *fababresa* (*fabafresa*), *faber*, and *fabre*. In each case there is an English or a French equivalent. Yet *Lesclarcissement* has no *sprotte bene*, nor a *smythe*, nor *craftely*.

In trying to trace Palsgrave's sources we have studied English–Latin as well as Latin–English word lists and dictionaries that preceded the publication of *Lesclarcissement*. The comparison suggests that none of them seems to have been used by Palsgrave as a master word list to which he added from other sources. Palsgrave's headword list looks more like a compilation of items from various sources, the *Promptorium parvulorum* figuring as a prominent possibility. Other headwords, above all phrasal units, have, to my knowledge, no precedents in earlier word lists and thus look like personal observation of the English around him or meticulous gleanings from the study of English texts. Some indeed, as we shall see in the next chapter, are attributed to John Lydgate and Geoffrey Chaucer. From cases like the entry *at home with you* for French *chez* it emerges that still other English entries owe their headword status to the existence of a lexical unit in French.

We have also looked at the first printed dictionaries involving French and explored some possible working methods. On the basis of these comparisons we may exclude some works as possible sources.

So far we have concentrated on reference works—that is, word lists. Palsgrave has told us himself that he read widely for his great enterprise. It was his aim to record the language use of those writers

TABLE 4.7. *Kinship terms in French*

| *Lesclarcissement* E | *Lesclarcissement* F | *Catholicon abbreviatum* | *Lagadeuc's Catholicon* | *Vocabularius nebrissensis* |
|---|---|---|---|---|
| Fader [Lat. *pater*] | pere<br>geniteur | pere | — | — |
| Fader in lawe as a man is to his doughters husbande/or to his sonnes wiyfe [Lat. *socer*] | beau pere | le pere de la femme/ ou du mari | — | le pere de la femme ou du mari: le sire ou le beau pere en socardie |
| Fader in lawe/as he is that maryeth a wyfe/ whiche hath chyldre by another man [step-father] [Lat. *victricus*] | parastre | — | — | — |
| Mother [Lat. *mater*] | mere | mere | — | — |
| Mother in lawe [Lat. *socrus*] | marrastre | la mere du mari/ou de la femme | — | la mere de la fẽme ou du mari |
| Grauntsyre [Lat. *avus*] | pere grant | ael<br>le pere d'la mere | — | — |
| Grandame[a] [Lat. *avia*] | mere grant | petite aelle | — | — |
| Sonne a naturall chylde [Lat. *filius*] | filz | filz | — | filz naturel |

| | | | | |
|---|---|---|---|---|
| Sonne in lawe [Lat. *gener*] | gendre | le mari de la fille gendre | — | le mari de la fille |
| Doughter [Lat. *filia*] | fille | — | fille | la fille naturelle |
| Doughter in lawe [Lat. *nurus*] | belle fille | bru. cest fẽme du fils | seronge ou bru | la femme du filz |
| Brother [Lat. *frater*] | frere | frere | — | frere germain |
| Brother in lawe [Lat. *levir*] | seurourge beav frere | le frere du mari/ou de la femme mariee | — | le mari de la soeur |
| Syster [Lat. *soror*] | sevr | soeur | — | seur la germaine |
| Syster brothers wyfe/ Syster in lawe [Lat. *glos*] | belle sevr | femme du frere | femme du frere | femme du frere |
| Aunt [Lat. *amita, matertera*] | tante or ante | tãte/seur de la mere | ante | la germaine de la mere |
| Eme vncle<br>Uncle by the father syde<br>Unkell [Lat. *avunculus patruus*] | oncle | oncle, fr̃ p̃ris | oncle | oncle, frere du pere |

[a] Though *grandmother* is not listed on its own, it occurs in the entry immediately following the headword *grandame*: *Graunt mothers mother*—aielle.

TABLE 4.8. *The relation of* Lesclarcissement *to the* Ortus vocabulorum, *the* Vocabularius nebrissensis, *and the* Catholicon abbreviatum: *a sample*

| *Ortus vocabulorum* | *Vocabularius nebrissensis* | *Catholicon abbreviatum* | *Lesclarcissement* |
|---|---|---|---|
| **Fabrica** . . . a smythye | **Fabrica** . . . fabrique ou lieu ou lon forge | | **Smethy** . . . forge |
| **Fabula** . . . a tale or a trufle | **Fabula** . . . fable, parler ioieulx | **Fabula** . . . fable | **Tale a storie** . . . compte |
| **Facinus** . . . treson in dede | **Facinus** . . . felõnie, meffait, forfait, mauuaistie | **Facinus** . . . pechie, desloyaute, mauuaistie | **Treyson** . . . trahison |

whom he (and others) regarded as the best. He refers to two literary authors, John Lydgate and Geoffrey Chaucer. Yet good writing is not restricted to literature. We may therefore safely assume that he will have consulted other texts. Since he was compiling a dictionary, he might have studied more specialized books on hunting, fishing, and husbandry. Herb and plant lore may also have been an area of knowledge to explore. And, since he was also a teacher, he may have exploited the English section of a good Latin–English textbook then used in the local schools. So the task of establishing more definite sources is quite substantial.

### *English headwords without French equivalents*

Early bilingual English dictionaries show a feature which is no longer acceptable in modern dictionaries: they list headwords for which the equivalent is missing. *Lesclarcissement* is no exception in this respect. There are more than 350 headwords for which there is no French equivalent. The majority of them are noun headwords. This could be related to the early lexicographical practice of compiling *nominales*. The recording of nominal elements thus had a longer tradition. It could equally suggest that Palsgrave consulted books on more specialized subject fields but lacked access to corresponding works in French.

One obvious explanation could, of course, be haste of production. The compiler had to hand in copy when the manuscript was not yet ready. Another possibility is an oversight on the part of the printer which was not corrected by the proof-readers. Such omission could easily occur when the headword itself occupied the whole of the line which was usually allocated to the lemma and the equivalent. An example from *Lesclarcissement* is:

> **Dressar where meate is serued out at/**
>
> (III, fo. xxx)

In *Lesclarcissement* we have a third possibility where Palsgrave explicitly explains why there is no French equivalent for the English lemma. He seems to distinguish between three different cases:

1. There is a difference in culture and administration between England and France. The following instance draws the reader's attention to differences in the legal institutions and processes:

> **I Indyte a man by indytement / they haue no suche processe in their lawe.**
>
> (III, fo. cc.lxvi)

A difference in the cultural customs is highlighted in the following example:

**Carde clothe for brides they vse none.**
(III, fo. xxii$^{v}$)

2. The object denoted by the English word is said not to occur in France:

**Stonde a vessell they haue none**
(III, fo. lxvii$^{v}$)

3. For the object denoted by the English word there is no lexicalized French item:

**Whit mete they haue no suche worde**
(III, fo. lxxiiii$^{v}$)

The fourth possibility is that the compiler simply did not know the equivalent in the other language, and that he had no source book at his disposal to find the corresponding item in the other language. As we know, Palsgrave had an excellent command of the French language. And yet, his English–French dictionary reveals that his knowledge of the French vocabulary had some gaps. For a foreigner, this is not at all surprising, we might argue. But we might go a step further. Which are the vocabulary areas where people in spite of a near-native-like command of the foreign language most easily detect the limits of their lexical knowledge? Those who have acquired a foreign language have discovered this for themselves: when it comes to the flora and fauna, one is often at a loss.

A closer study of all those English lemmata in *Lesclarcissement* for which there are no French equivalents yields some interesting results. There are three subject areas for which Palsgrave seems less familiar with the French vocabulary: names of plants, and their parts, names of animals and their parts, names of tools and their parts. Less striking but still noticeable are the following areas: colours, illnesses, and units of measure. These findings obviously prompt some speculations as possible sources he would seek: more specialized books, treatises dealing with these topics. It would thus be worthwhile to review the availability of such books at Palsgrave's time.

A more practical step would be to look up in the *OED* all Palsgrave's English headwords that lack a French equivalent. This check, one might assume, would reveal whether Palsgrave was the first (or even the last) to record a particular item or what other documentations there might be of the item in question.

The checks in the *OED* yielded some interesting points. First of all, for a good number of items, *Lesclarcissement* represents the first documentation of their use in English. Examples for plant names are: *Dogge brere* (*dog-brier*), *Herbe royall*, and *Rosecampyon a floure.* Names of animals that are first recorded by Palsgrave are for instance: *Cubbe a yong foxe* (*cub*), *Hoggerell a yong shepe* (*hoggerel, hogrel*), and *Morte a fysshe* (*mort*). The following items which denote an instrument or tool are also recorded for the first time in Palsgrave: *Formour or grublyng yron* (*former*), *Paryng yrone to pare a horse hofe with* (*paring-iron*), and *Stoppe of a lute.* Secondly, in some cases the mention in *Lesclarcissement* is (so far) the only attestation of the item at all. Examples are: *Lurke an herbe, Renger for a baker, Wakeworte an herbe.* Thirdly, there are lexical items for which the *OED* has not taken Palsgrave into account and gives a much later date of attestation. For *puffin*, a fish, which Palsgrave lists as *Puffyn a fysshe lyke a teele* (III, fo. lvii), the *OED* has John Florio (1598) as the first record. *Small guts* with the plural form of *gut* is first recorded for 1601 (Holland), though it appears in Palsgrave as *Small guttes* in 1530.

Fourthly, there are words for which the *OED* documentation preceding *Lesclarcissement* is restricted to vocabulary and dictionary sources. This may lend more plausibility to the assumption that Palsgrave consulted all the contemporary reference work(s). Examples are:

1. *Hornkecke a fysshe lyke a mackerell* (*OED*: garfish or hornbeak)
   The three attestations before 1530 are: *c.* 1425 Vocabulary (in Wright 1884/1968: 642/9), *c.* 1440 *Promptorium parvulorum*, *c.* 1475 *Pictorial Vocabulary* (in Wright 1884/1968: 765/12–13).
2. *Ribbe for flaxe* (*OED*: a flat iron tool used for cleaning flax after the breaking process)
   The three attestations before 1530 are: *c.* 1340 *Nominale sive verbale* edited by Skeat, *c.* 1440 *Promptorium parvulorum*, 1483 *Catholicon Anglicum.*
3. *Scheldrake a byrde* (*OED*: sheldrake)
   The *OED* attestations before 1530 are: *c.* 1325 *Glossary of W. de Bibbesworth*, *c.* 1340 *Nominale sive Verbale* edited by Skeat, *c.* 1475 *Pictorial Vocabulary.*

Fifthly, there are lexical items for which documentation in the *OED* begins with one of Palsgrave's contemporaries. The two herbs *southernwort* and *tussyllage* (*tussilago*), for instance, are first recorded for John Stanbridge's *Vocabula* of 1510. *Body* in the sense of 'the main stem, trunk . . . of a plant or tree' is attested in John Fitzherbert's

*A newe tracte or treatyse moost profytable for all husbande men* (1523). From the same work the noun *plough-ear* is recorded. These findings may suggest that the items were neologisms at the time and Stanbridge and Fitzherbert happened to record them first, or they may indicate that Palsgrave was familiar with their works. The fact that Palsgrave lists other items for which the contemporary documentation in the *OED* is Stanbridge's *Vocabula* (*Schuttell for a weuer* (III, fo. lxii)), or Fitzherbert's book on husbandry (*Nathe stocke of a whele* (III, fo. l); *Coccle a reede floure* (III, fo. xxv); *Fulmarde a beest* (III, fo. xxxv)) might lend more plausibility to this latter assumption. Yet *shuttle* is also listed in the *Catholicon Anglicum* and *cockle* in the *Promptorium parvulorum*.

This takes us to our last point. The consultation of the *OED* for those headwords in *Lesclarcissement* which lack a French equivalent was meant to provide us with some guidelines in the search of Palsgrave's sources. The documentation in the *OED* points in the direction of some contemporary works or works still commonly read at the time. Works which Palsgrave may thus have used for the compilation of *Lesclarcissement* according to their subject matter may be grouped as follows:

1. *Specialized treatises*
   The *Alphita*
   The *Book of St. Albans*
   John Fitzherbert, *A newe tracte or treatyse moost profytable for all husbande men*
   John Russell, *The book of nurture*
   *The Grete herball*

2. *Latin-English textbooks*
   William Horman, *Vulgaria*
   John Stanbridge, *Vocabula*
   John Stanbridge, *Vulgaria Stanbrigi*

3. *French sources*
   William Caxton, *Dialogues in French and English*
   John Bouchier (Berners), *The first volum . . . of Syr John Froissart, of the cronycles of Englande, France . . .*

4. *Contemporary writers*
   Alexander Barclay, *The shyp of folys*
   John Skelton, *Phyllyp Sparowe*

For a man of Palsgrave's erudition and social standing, it is not implausible to assume his knowledge of these works.

To sum up: so far as French sources are concerned, we can only speculate that he may have used word lists including French which I was unable to check and that he predominantly relied on his reading of literary texts and his personal knowledge of French. As regards English sources, it seems likely that he used a copy of the *Promptorium parvulorum*, as well as contemporary specialist books. Further additions come from his reading of literary works. These will be investigated in the next chapter.

# 5
# Literary Citations

As he was not a native speaker of French, Palsgrave tells us in *Lesclarcissement de la langue francoyse* which authors writing in French he had read to give his work the necessary linguistic authority. There is no corresponding list of authors writing in English. Yet his English–French dictionary provides us with some evidence that his reading programme also embraced English literary texts. In more than 100 cases a headword is identified as occurring in the works of either Geoffrey Chaucer or John Lydgate. This confirms the view expressed earlier when discussing his list of adverbs, prepositions, and conjunctions: when he compiled his word list, Palsgrave was not only using material from his own knowledge as a native speaker and from reference sources; he also added lexical items studiously collected from his own reading of authentic English texts. He is thus the first English lexicographer to refer within his work to English literature by named authors.[1]

He does not tell us why he refers to these two poets, Chaucer and Lydgate, and not to others, such as Gower. The introductory matter to the dictionary says nothing about his occasional indication of literary English sources. There is obviously the possibility that both writers may have been Palsgrave's favourite authors. But his acute awareness of the tastes and changing fashions at court, his shrewd assessment of which writers enjoyed most prestige—we have seen his excellent judgement with respect to French writers, confirmed by Geofrey Tory—suggest another wider, more adequate interpretation. Chaucer and Lydgate were the most highly regarded English poets of the fourteenth and fifteenth centuries. Sidney Lee's entry in the *DNB* even goes so far as to write that '[d]uring the Elizabethan period Lydgate's fame was at its zenith' (Lee 1893: 310). Lydgate's *Troy Book*, for instance, was printed by Pynson in 1513, at the very time that Palsgrave was beginning his work—a book which he was compiling for the king's sister. The references to Chaucer and

[1] To my knowledge the first English author referred to in an English dictionary is the *Venerable Bede* (?673–735), writing in Latin. He is mentioned in the *Ortus vocabulorum* under the entry *publicanus*.

Lydgate in a bilingual English–French dictionary of 1530 might thus be taken as a social document reflecting the literary tastes of the early sixteenth century.

The references to Chaucer and Lydgate occur in the latter part of the dictionary—that is, there are no such references among the nouns, adjectives, pronouns, and numerals. The references begin with the verbs and continue in the lists of adverbs and conjunctions. This may suggest that Palsgrave relied for nominal elements more on existing reference lists.

There are three references to Geoffrey Chaucer:

> **I Queme I please or I satysfye/**
> **Chauser in his Caũterbury tales/**
> **this worde is nowe out of vse.**
>
> (III, fo. ccc.xxxi)

An adverb answering the question 'Howe long' is

> **But a throwe (Chaucer)** Guayres,
> or que bien peu de temps.
>
> (III, fo. cccc.lii$^{v}$)

Among the conjunctions we find:

> **Nere that (Chaucer) for were nat**
> **that**: Ne fust cela, **as/** Si neust este
> cela ie fusse mort long temps a.
>
> (III, fo. cccc.lxviii$^{v}$)

The *Canterbury Tales* are the only named literary work in English and the Lydgate references specify only the author.

Of the 117 references to Lydgate, two are listed under the adverbs:

> **Atwene (Lyd)** Entre. **as/ Atwene**
> **vs bothe**: Entre nous deux.
>
> (III, fo. cccc.xxviii$^{v}$)

> **Atwyn (Lydgat)** Densemble.
>
> (III, fo. cccc.xxviii$^{v}$)

The rest are among the verbs. The references to Lydgate vary in form. There are three different spellings of the name: *Lydgate*, *Lidgate*, and *Lydgat*. In some cases the name is abbreviated as *Lyd* or *Lidga*, and in one case Lydgate is referred to as the *monk of Bury*:

> **I ennose I abuse (the monke of**
> **Berye Lydgate)** Ie abuse. pri. cõiu.
> **This terme is nat in vse.**
>
> (III, fo. cc.xxvi)

The citations of these English poets in Palsgrave's bilingual dictionary raise a number of questions. Are the lexical items identified as having been used by Chaucer and Lydgate really traceable back to both authors? How reliable are Palsgrave's citations? Since Palsgrave is the first English lexicographer to refer to English poets in a dictionary, which lexicographical form does he use to present these usage attributions? And, finally, what is the reason for his identifications of particular linguistic uses by Chaucer and Lydgate?

Let us begin with the first issue, the reliability of Palsgrave's attestations. For Chaucer's works there are two concordances, the hand-based work by J. S. P. Tatlock and A. G. Kennedy of 1927, and the computer-based concordance by A. Oizumi of 1991. In the whole of Chaucer's works the phrase . . . *but a throwe* occurs twice. Both instances belong to the *Canterbury Tales*, one occurs in the *Clerk's Tale*, the other in the *Man of Law's Tale* (Oizumi 1991: i, B. ML 953, E. CL 450).

The construction *nere that* (not *nere it that*, which also occurs) occurs four times: in the *Man of Law's Tale* (ibid.: ii, B. ML 132), the *Romaunt of the Rose* (ibid.: ix, RR B 2754, B 3855) and *The Legend of Good Women* (ibid.: viii, F 1920).

The verb *queme* 'to please' is said by Palsgrave to occur in the *Canterbury Tales* , but according to Oizumi's concordance there are only four occurrences of *queme* in Chaucer's works and none is in the *Canterbury Tales*. The form *quemen* is recorded in *Troilus and Criseyde* (ibid.: vii and x, TR II 803), the form *queme* in *Troilus and Criseyde* (Oizumi 1991I vii and x, TR V 6951), the *Romaunt of the Rose* (ibid.: ix and x, RR C 7268) and the poem *Gentilesse* (ibid.: x, Gent 20).

We come to John Lydgate. Since there is no Lydgate concordance, I have relied on the glossaries available for some of his works, the *Middle English Dictionary* (*MED*), and the *OED*. The results of these checks are most impressive. Out of the 117 references, more than 100 can be confirmed as correctly attributed to Lydgate. The use (or the use in the particular meaning given by Palsgrave) could not satisfactorily be clarified for the following items: *adioust* 'ioyne togyther', *bayte myne eares* 'apply them to herken a thynge', *betraysshe* 'go aboute the stretes of a towne or cytie', *darrayne* 'chaũge or alter a thing from one purpose to a nother', *diffigure* 'bring out of knowlege' (a misprint for *disfigure*?), *endrosse* 'multyplye' (one may wonder whether this is a misprint for *engrosse* or *encresse*), *enuoye* 'sende', *fende* 'defende', *fownce* 'dent a thyng', *imprint* 'borowe', *ouerslyppe*, *rauyne* 'take away by force'. In the case of *enflaunce* for French *enflamber*, one may have to do with a misprint of *enflamen*, *enflaumen*. In two cases the irregular past participle is listed instead of the verb (*dreynt*, *fordreynt* instead of *drench*, *fordrench*).

*Cyrcumspecte* 'loke rounde aboute', *ennose* 'abuse', and *mage colle* 'make false brayes aboute a towne wall' are all correctly attributed to Lydgate, and indeed dictionaries record them as all first used by Lydgate in his *Troy Book.* There they are used as an adjective or past participle, and the *MED* thus records them in this grammatical form only. What may have happened is that Palsgrave, when encountering these forms, extrapolated from them full verb forms which he then listed as headwords.

With the last three examples, we have taken the step from correct assignation and attestation to correct first attestation. There are further instances where Palsgrave has identified lexical items and phrases which happen to be first attested in the work of John Lydgate. A very striking case is the verb *enhaste* 'to cause . . . to make haste', 'to expedite', which, to judge from the *MED* and *OED*, is a Lydgatism. Lydgate indeed seems to be the only one to have used this verb. Most of the instances recorded are from the *Troy Book*; one is from *The Pilgrimage of the Life of Man.* There is thus definite proof not only of Palsgrave's close readings in the work of Lydgate but also that he excerpted words and phrases from his reading. We have here a superb example of Palsgrave's discriminating linguistic faculties. At a time when there was no index to Lydgate's work in existence, he correctly identified these uses of a verb to the point of recording them in his dictionary.

Another interesting case is the verb *to disappear.* Palsgrave's entry reads as follows:

> **I Disapere (Lydgate)** Ie dispars
> **coniugate lyke** ie appars, **I apere.**
> **The vysion disapered incontynẽt:**
> La vision disparut tout incontinent.
>
> (III, fo. cc.xii)

The *OED* entry for *disappear* begins with a note: 'In Palgr., but app. not in common use before 17th c. Not in Shaks., nor in Bible of 1611'. The reference to Lydgate was thus not noticed. The *MED*, however, notes that the verb *disappear* occurs in Lydgate's *Troy Book*, the *Siege of Thebes*, and the *Fall of Princes.* So, again, Palsgrave deserves the credit of having recorded the early and possibly the first use of an item.

One of the few Lydgate words that is not used in the *Troy Book* is the verb *exaltate*, which Palsgrave records as follows:

> **I Exaltate (Lydgate)** Ie me ex-
> alte, **and** ie exalce.
>
> (III, fo. cc.xxix$^{v}$)

The *OED* does not credit Lydgate with the first use, but the *MED* does, noting Lydgate's *Fabula duorum mercatorum.*

That Palsgrave picked up not only lexical items that were either characteristic of Lydgate's use or neologisms first recorded by Lydgate but also new senses of already existing words can be illustrated with the verb *to curtain*. The entry from *Lesclarcissement de la langue francoyse* reads as follows:

> **I Courtyne (Lydgat) I hyde vnder or behynde a courtayne/** Ie encourtine. prime coniu. **Wolde to god I were a mouse or yͭ I coulde courtayne my selfe yonder I shulde here many thynges:** Pleust a dieu que ie fusse vne souris ou que ie me puisse encourtiner la iorroys mayntes choses.
>
> (III, fo. c.xcix)

The usual sense of the denominal verb *to curtain*, attested from about 1300, is 'to furnish, cover, adorn with a curtain'. The additional sense 'to veil with a curtain, to conceal behind a curtain' is first recorded for Lydgate's *Troy Book.*

Idiomatic phrases were also noticed by Palsgrave. Cases in point are:

> **I Fagge from the trouthe (Lyd) this terme is nat in our comen vse.**
>
> (III, fo. cc.xxxi)

> **I Ronne in age (Lydgate)** Ie deuiens viel.
>
> (III, fo. ccc.xliii$^v$)

The *OED* adduces the entry from *Lesclarcissement* as the first attestation of the verb *to fag*, but the *MED* confirms with the citation 'Me list nat lye . . . what schulde I feyn or fage fro þe trou þe?' from the *Troy Book* (2. 7989) that the first record goes back to 1420. *Ronne in age* 'advanced in age' also goes back to the *Troy Book.*

The close study of all the headwords which Palsgrave assigned to Geoffrey Chaucer and John Lydgate reveals a commendable degree of accuracy. The scholarly approach which Palsgrave adopted for the description of the French language is thus also apparent in the description of his mother tongue. There is no doubt that he knew at least the *Canterbury Tales* of Chaucer and that he was very familiar with John Lydgate's *Troy Book* (recording some ninety items from it). The documentation of the verb *queme* and the construction *nere that* suggest that he might also have read Chaucer's *Romaunt of the Rose* or *Troilus and Criseyde.* In view of his great admiration of the French original of *le Roman de la Rose* I would regard the former more likely. As to the other identified Lydgate citations, he may have known the

*Fall of Princes*, the *Siege of Thebes*, the *Pilgrimage of the Life of Man*, and the fable of the two merchants.

Since Palsgrave is the first English lexicographer to cite English poets in his dictionary, we cannot expect him to have a fully consistent practice of inserting the reference always at the same place within the dictionary entry. A close investigation shows that the references themselves vary in content and in position. The various types are listed below in order of frequency:

1. The name of the poet is given immediately after the headword:

> **I Expowne (Lydgat)** Ie expose prime cõiu. **Expowne me this lesson and thou shalte do me a pleasure:** Exposez moy ceste lecon et tu me feras vng playsir.
>
> (III, fo. cc.xxx^v^)

2. The name of the author is given after the synonym or synonymic explanation provided for the headword:

> **I Gaste I feare (Lyd)** Ie baille belle paour. **I gasted hym as sore as he was these twelue monethes**: Ie luy baillay aussi belle paour quil eust de cest an.
>
> (III, fo. cc.xliiii)

3. The name of the author is given between the two synonyms or synonymic explanations provided for the headword:

> **I Enarme I serue with armour (Lydgate) or store with armoure/** Ienharnesche. prime cõiu. **He is very well enarmed with all sortes of armour**: Il est fort bien enharnesché de toutes sortes de armures.
>
> (III, fo. cc.xxiii)

4. The name of the author is given after all the synonyms or synonymic explanations provided for the headword:

> **I Combyne I ioyne I knyt thinges togyther (Lydgate)** Iennoue. prime coniu. **These thynges be combyned togyther**: Ces choses sont enouées ensemble, **and** ie combine.
>
> (III, fo. c.xci^v^)

5. The name of the author is given after the French equivalent:

**I Enbrowde as a broudrer dothe a garment/** Ie embrode. prime coniu. (Lydgate) (III, fo. cc.xxiii^v^)

More complex are those entries where a metalinguistic comment is added. For four of the five types outlined there is such a variant:

**I Carpe (Lydgat)** Ie cacquette, prime. **this is a farre northern verbe.** (III, fo. c.lxxxi.^v^)

**I Nomme I take (Lydgate)** Ie prens. **this terme is dawthe ⁊ nowe none Englysshe.** (III, fo. ccc.vii)

**I Ewre I make happye or fortunate (Lydgate)** Ie eure. prime cõiu. or ie fais eureux, **thoughe Lydgate vse this verbe it is nat yet comen.** (III, fo. cc.xxix^v^)

**I Dawnte I mate I ouercome/** Ie matte. prime coniuga. **(Lyngate** [*sic*]**) This terme is yet scarsly admitted in our comen spetche.** (III, fo. cc.v)

In some cases the reference to Lydgate is enclosed in the metalinguistic comment:

**I Adioust or ioyne togyther/** Ie adiouste. prime coniuga. **coiugate in I ioyne: and this terme is nat yet vsed in our comen speche though Lydgate haue it ofte tymes.** (III, fo. c.xxxviii^v^)

or it occurs twice, as with the verb *ewre* and the following example:

**I Warysshe I recouer my helth after a sycknesse or daũger (Lydgat)** Ie me garis, or ie me guaris. verbum mediũ. prime. **This terme is nowe lytel vsed/ thoughe Lydgate hath it often.** (III, fo. cccc.i)

These examples enable us to characterize Palsgrave's lexicographical method as follows: the references to Chaucer and Lydgate are justly regarded as separate pieces of lexicographical information. They are therefore given a separate lexicographical treatment: they are set between brackets and thus clearly set off from other elements of information. Metalinguistic comments on the use or currency of the item in question are placed at the end of the entry. Palsgrave thus anticipates the practice of authorial attestation as in Dr Johnson's dictionary. If the metalinguistic comment at the end does not explicitly refer to English, as in the example *nomme*, or to Chaucer or Lydgate, ambiguity may arise as to whether the comment relates to the English headword or the French equivalent. This is illustrated with the example *carpe*, where the specification 'this is a farre northern verbe' could refer to *carpe* or to *cacquetter*. The printing type might serve as a disambiguator. The fount used is the one in which the English headwords are cast, as well as the citations of the two English poets. Yet, as we shall see, the same black letter is also used for metalinguistic comments relating to the French equivalents.

What is the function of Palsgrave's literary citations? In recording Chaucer's and Lydgate's use of English, Palsgrave may have wanted to emphasize that what he listed in his dictionary had actually been used in the language. Mere documentation of general language use, however, would raise the question why he provided only very few items with such a specification. It might, therefore, be more appropriate to assume that he may have wanted to record a particular language use. Two types of language use seem to suggest themselves for such a documentation. Neither Geoffrey Chaucer nor John Lydgate was a contemporary of Palsgrave. He may, therefore, have been aware of differences between his own use of language and that of those two poets. On this assumption, we might expect him to have recorded old language use and/or also neologisms. The other type of language that Palsgrave might have wanted to document is 'good' language use. Chaucer and Lydgate were highly admired; the printing of the *Troy Book* in 1513 had made Lydgate's work more widely accessible and thus contemporary reading matter. So why not record what his envisaged dictionary users might encounter in their reading? In documenting 'good' language use, Palsgrave would have kept company with other lexicographers, in particular with the compilers of English dictionaries that included Latin. He would also have been consistent within his own framework: the lexicographical method adopted for French was also applied to English. Yet there is one important difference. For French he occasionally provides authentic quotations from the authors mentioned. There are no such literary citations for English. Palsgrave does not provide the dictionary user with example sentences taken from Chaucer or Lydgate to illustrate 'good' language use.

Palsgrave does not claim explicitly that by referring to Geoffrey Chaucer and John Lydgate he wanted to attest the use in English of a certain word, sense, or form. Yet I do not think that mere usage attestation can be excluded as one of the functions of his literary citations. One of the puzzling findings from the investigation of Palsgrave's 'Lydgatisms', for instance, is that some of the items

Table 5.1. A comparison of Palsgrave's 'Lydgatisms' with the *Promptorium parvulorum*

| *Lesclarcissement* | *Promptorium parvulorum* (1499) |
|---|---|
| **I Carpe (Lydgat) . . .** | **Carpen or talken . . .** |
| **I Growpe (Lydgate) sculpe or suche as coulde graue/ groupe/ or carue . . .** | **Growpyn . . .** |
| **I Nomme I take (Lydgate) . . .** | **Nymyn or take . . .** |
| **I Rewall I gouerne (Lydgate)** | **Rewlyn or gouernyn . . .** |
| **I Ryue I take lande at a porte or at a hauen (Lydgat)** | **Ryuyn to lond as shippes botys . . .** |

listed also occur in the *Promptorium parvulorum*. Examples are shown in Table 5.1.

A possible interpretation might be that the use of these verbs in the *Troy Book* predates their listing in the *Promptorium parvulorum*, both in its manuscript version of about 1440 and its first printed version. Other possible interpretations, however, might be that Palsgrave did not consult the *Promptorium parvulorum* while compiling his dictionary.

For the attestation of specific language use there is more evidence. The most frequent types of referring to Chaucer or Lydgate often correlate with a cross-reference:

**I Clymme (Lydgate) loke in I clayme.**

(III, fo. c.lxxxix$^{v}$)

**I Fley (Lydgate) loke in I flye.**

(III, fo. cc.xxxvii)

**I Dyrke I make dyrke (Lydgat) declared in I darke.**

(III, fo. cc.xi$^{v}$)

**I Enbelysshe I make fayre (Lyd) loke in I embelysshe.**

(III, fo. cc.xxiii$^{v}$)

It looks as if most of the cross-referred items are spelling variants used by Lydgate. Palsgrave's cross-reference practice is quite interesting and revealing in this context. We cannot yet expect a sixteenth-century English lexicographer to be entirely and unerringly systematic. If we make allowances for some inconsistencies, Palsgrave's practice can be described as follows. In general, the cross-referred item is not recorded again under the form listed as the more common spelling. That is, there are no entries of the type:

I Clayme, I clymme (Lydgate) . . .
I Darke, I dyrke, I make darke (Lydgate) . . .

Instead, the typical correlation of entries is as follows:

**I Appese (Lydgate) loke in I appayse.** Ie apaise. prime coniuga. **and there be also exemples.**

(III, fo. c.l[v])

**I Appayse or content or styll/** Ie appaise. prime coniu. **And he be ones angred you shall haue moche a do to appayse him:** Sil est vne foys cour rouce vous aures fort affaire de lap paiser.

(III, fo. c.l)

**I Appayse or quiet a person from his displeasure/** Ie desennuie. prime con. **He is appaysed nowe for al his anger:** Il est appaisé, or desennyié de son ire a steure non obstant son grant courroux.

(III, fo. c.l)

**I Coharte (Lydgat) loke in I coarct. In this worde ẏ printers haue corrupted the trewe orthographye.**

(III, fo. c.xc[v])

**I Coarcte I constrayne/** Ie coarcte. prime coniuga. **or** ie constraings, **cõiugate in I constrayne. He that wyll nat do his dutye with good wyll muste be corrected:** Qui ne veult faire son debuoyr de bon gré fault quon le coarcte, **or** quon le constraigne.

(III, fo. c.xc[v])

In general, there is a correspondence between the spelling of the item to which the entry cross-refers and the main entry for the cross-referred item itself; that is, *appese* refers to *appayse*, and *appayse* is the main entry for the more common spelling. The same holds for *coharte* and *coarcte*. There are some exceptions: *dreynt*, for instance, cross-refers to *drownde*, though the main entry spelling is *drowne*; *enbrace* cross-refers to *embrace*, which is spelled *embrase* as the main entry; *hamyne* cross-refers to *eyme*, where the main entry word is *ame*. The metalinguistic terms used for cross-reference vary. There is *look in* besides *coniugate in*, *declared in*, *for*, *in*, and *idem*. The entry with the more common spelling usually gives all the particulars on the word as well as examples. Since the spelling variant is not relisted after the more common spelling, the name *Lydgate* does not re-occur.

As is well known, in the early sixteenth century, English spelling did not yet have an established standard norm. If we assume that Palsgrave may have wanted to show that some of Lydgate's spellings differed from what he conceived of as the more common spellings of his own time, his motive may have been purely scholarly: to show that another prestigious author used a different spelling. There is, however, another possibility. Palsgrave did not adopt Lydgate's spellings. The very fact that Lydgate's forms are cross-referred to another spelling and that that form of the verb is given the full lexicographical treatment suggests that Palsgrave regarded his own spellings as reflecting contemporary usage more adequately. This would imply that he may already have had an implicit idea of a normative range of spellings for a word. Let us, therefore, look more closely at those headwords where there is a reference to Lydgate and at the same time a cross-reference to another spelling.

Are the spellings attributed to Lydgate really those that occur in his works? The astonishing fact is that the majority do. A striking case is the verb *to aim*. Palsgrave credits Lydgate with the spelling *hamyne*. The *OED* has no *h*-variant for the verb. The *MED*, however, lists three occurrences of the verb for Lydgate: two from the *Troy Book*, one from the *Sieges of Thebes*. The forms are: *TB* 1.884 *hame*, *TB* 3.784 *hamen*, *ST* 4326 *hamyng*. In some cases the spelling attributed to Lydgate is the only one actually used by Lydgate (*demene* for me. *demeinen*, *preyse* for *preisen*). In others, Lydgate has various spellings, and the one singled out by Palsgrave is the more frequent one. Lydgate's spelling of the verb *to embrace* is 15 times *enbrace*, 2 times *embrace*. *Lesclarcissement* duly gives *enbrace* as Lydgate's spelling. In two cases the cross-reference does not make sense:

**I Ordayne (Lidgate)** Ie ordonne, **declared in I ordayne.**

(III, fo. ccc.ix)

**I Seiourne (Lydgate) declared in I seiourne.**

(III, fo. ccc.lxvi)

The spelling of the headword and the cross-referred item is the same. But according to the *MED*, Lydgate's spellings for these two verbs are *ordeyn* and *soiourne*. So what may have happened is that the printers in setting the headwords anticipated the spelling of the cross-referred item.

Palsgrave's cross-reference practice thus seems to provide evidence that he was trying to record special language use when he cited Chaucer and Lydgate. The entries that provide us with the best insight into the function that Palsgrave himself attributed to his literary citations are those that include an explicit metalinguistic usage statement. In one instance the comment refers to a dialect feature:

**I Carpe (Lydgat)** Ie cacquette, prime. **this is a farre northen verbe.**

(III, fo. c.lxxxi$^{v}$)

Other interesting cases are instances in which he draws attention to borrowings from French:

**I Enuoye I sende/** Ienuoye. prime cõiu. **This terme is a mere frenche worde thoughe Lydgate vse it.**

(III, fo. cc.xviii)

**I Mage colle (Lydgat) I make false brayes aboute a towne wall/** Ie machecoulle. prime coniu. **whiche terme Lydgate borowed of ỷ frẽche tonge/ for they call** vng moche coulys, **a false bray/ but they vse nat the verbe.**

(III, fo. cc.lxxxvi)

Most frequently, however, his metalinguistic comment corresponds to a temporal label, as in the following examples (where Palsgrave's *not yet* seems usually to mean 'not now', i.e. 'no longer'):

**I Adioust or ioyne togyther/** Ie adiouste. prime coniuga. **coiugate in I ioyne: and this terme is nat yet vsed in our comen speche though Lydgate haue it ofte tymes.**

(III, fo. c.xxxviii$^{v}$)

**I Betraysshe (Lydgate) I go aboute the stretes of a towne or cytie/** Ie tracasse. prime coniu. **This verbe is nat yet taken in comen vse.**

(III, fo. c.lxiiii$^{v}$)

**I Cyrcumspecte/** Ie regarde a len tour. **I loke rounde aboute. These thre termes[2] go nere the latyn and be nat yet vsed in our tonge/ thoughe Lydgate haue them.**

(III, fo. c.lxxxviii)

**I Darrayne (Lydgat) I chaũge or alter a thing from one purpose to a nother/** Ie transmue. prime cõiuga. **This worde is nat yet admytted in our comen spetche.**

(III, fo. cc.iiii)

**I Dawnte I mate I ouercome/** Ie matte. prime coniuga. **(Lyngate) This terme is yet scarsly admitted in our comen spetche.**

(III, fo. cc.v)

**I Embellissh I make fayre (Lyd)** Ie embellys. secunde coniuga. **This terme is nat yet fully vsed in comen spetche.**

(III, fo. cc.xxii$^{v}$)

**I Encause (Lydgat) nat yet vsed comenly / but I cause.**

(III, fo. cc.xxiiii)

**I Ennose I abuse (the monke of Berye Lydgate)** Ie abuse. pri. cõiu. **This terme is nat in vse.**

(III, fo. cc.xxvi)

**I Ewre I make happye or fortunate (Lydgate)** Ie eure. prime cõiu. or ie fais eureux, **thoughe Lydgate vse this verbe it is nat yet comen.**

(III, fo. cc.xxix)

**I Fagge from the trouthe (Lyd) this terme is nat in our comen vse.**

(III, fo. cc.xxxi)

**I Fyche (Lydgat) I stedye or make ferme or stedfaste/** Ie fiche. prime cõiu. **this terme is nat yet admytted but for exemple. He that hath his purpose fyched vpon any one thyng may parchaunce bring it to passe:** Qui a son cueur fiché sur aul cun propos vnicque il le peult par ad uenture paracheuer.

(III, fo. cc.xxxv$^{v}$)

**I Fyne (Lydgat) I ende/** Ie parachieue. prime coniuga. **This terme is nat yet admytted.**

(III, fo. cc.xxxvi$^{v}$)

**I Fownce (Lyd) I dent a thyng/** Ie fonce, **this terme is nat yet in comen vse.**

(III, fo. cc.xlii)

**I Growpe (Lydgate) sculpe or suche as coulde graue/ groupe/ or carue. this worde is nat vsed in comen spetche.**

(III, fo. cc.lvi)

**I Kydde (Lydgate) I knowe/** Ie cõgnois. **this terme is nat yet in vse.**

(III, fo. cc.lxxii$^{v}$)

[2] The three verbs referred to are *cyrcuite, cyrcule,* and *cyrcumspecte.*

**I Kythe/ I shewe or declare a thyng/ as he kytheth from whence I am (Lydgate)** Ie demonstre, **this terme is nat vsed in comen spetche.**

(III, fo. cc.lxxii$^{v}$)

**I Nomme I take (Lydgate)** Ie prens. **this terme is dawthe ⁊ nowe none Englysshe.**

(III, fo. ccc.vii)

**I Queme I please or I satysfye/ Chauser in his Caũterbury tales/ this worde is nowe out of vse.**

(III, fo. ccc.xxxi)

**I Restytue I restore/** Ie restitue. prime cõiu. **(Lydgate) This worde is nat yet vsed in cõmen spetche.**

(III, fo. ccc.xl)

**I Warysshe I recouer my helth after a sycknesse or daũger (Lydgat)** Ie me garis, or ie me guaris, verbum mediũ. prime. **This terme is nowe lytel vsed/ thoughe Lydgate hath it often.**

(III, fo. cccc.i)

Palsgrave's metalinguistic statements embrace usage restrictions with respect to region, provenance, and currency. To judge from the *OED*, his assessments seem to be reliable. *To carp* is a northern term. The verb *to envoy* corresponds to French *envoyer*. The *OED* entry has two citations only. The first, covering the meaning 'to send', is from Caxton (1481); the second, in the meaning 'to write as an "envoy" or concluding stanza', is from Barclay's *Ship of Fools*. Palsgrave's entry would be the last documentation, but it is not listed in the *OED*. The verb *to machecole* is Old French *machecoller*. The four citations in the *OED* begin with one from Lydgate's *Troy Book* and end with the entry from *Lesclarcissement*.

We come to the temporal restrictions. A striking feature of the twenty entries is that, with the exception of two (*fyche* and *kythe*), no example sentences are provided.

Instead of discussing the reliability of Palsgrave's specifications in alphabetical order, I shall follow the scale of temporal restrictions as it emerges from his descriptions. At one extreme of the scale we have 'this terme is dawthe ⁊ nowe none Englysshe' (*nomme*). According to the *OED*, the verb *nome* is first attested for about 1225, and the last of the five quotations is from Palsgrave. 'Nowe out of vse' is said of *queme*. The verb was used by Chaucer as well as Lydgate. In the meaning recorded in *Lesclarcissement* 'of persons: to please, satisfy', the *OED* documentation confirms Palsgrave's judgement. His entry from 1530 is preceded by a citation from 1496 (*Dives & Pauper*) and 1374 (Chaucer). Quite a number of verbs are regarded as no longer in use. The checks provide the following picture:

*adioust* — *OED* † **adjoust** *v. Obs.*

In the meaning 'to put one thing to another, to add', the first quotation from Caxton dates from 1474, the last from Palsgrave.

*dawnte* *OED* **daunt** *v.*

The sense given by Palsgrave is already recorded for *c.*1300 in the *OED*. The last citation given dates from 1610.

*encause* *OED* † **encause,** *v. Obs.*

For this obsolete verb the *OED* has only two citations that precede the one from *Lesclarcissement*; one is from the fifteenth century, the other from 1527.

*ewre* *OED* † **eure,** *v. Obs.*

The last illustration given in the *OED* dates from 1526. Palsgrave's entry is not mentioned.

*fyche* *OED* † **ficche,** *v. Obs.*

The *OED* gives quotations for the fourteenth century, and both the *MED* and the *OED* have citations for the fifteenth century. The entry from *Lesclarcissement* is the last attestation in the *OED*.

*fyne* *OED* † **fine,** *v.*[1] *Obs.*

The intransitive use of the verb is last recorded for Lydgate's *Troy Book* and a fifteenth-century text. The transitive verb was used during the period beginning with Chaucer and ending with Shakespeare.

*kydde* *OED* † **kyd, kydde,** *v. Obs.*

The *OED* contains the following explanation: 'Evolved from ME. *kyd*, *i-kyd*, pa. pple of KITHE *v.* misunderstood by Palsgrave, and misused by Spenser'. The only citations recorded are the one from *Lesclarcissement* and a second from Spenser (1579).

*restytue* *OED* † **restitue,** *v. Obs.*

The earliest quotation is from Langland (1377) and the last from Palsgrave.

From 'no longer used' we move on to verbs described as 'not used' at Palsgrave's time.

*ennose* *OED* † **enose,** *v. Obs.*

The *OED* begins its entry as follows: '*trans.*? To choke. Only in Lydgate, in somewhat obscure fig.

senses; ? to baffle, perplex, hamper'. There are only fifteenth-century citations apart from Palsgrave's entry saying that the verb is not in use.

*fagge* — *OED* **fag**, *v.*

Palsgrave's entry is the only one in the *OED* to record the expression *to fag from the truth*.

*growpe* — *OED* † **groop**, *v. Obs.*

The first attestation for the sense 'to groove, hollow out, incise' (*OED*), 'to make a groove in wood' (*MED*), in both dictionaries stems from Lydgate. Fifteenth-century quotations are from the *Medulla* and the *Promptorium parvulorum*. The *OED* has only one sixteenth-century quotation (Palsgrave), and the last citation is from 1638.

*kythe* — *OED* **kithe, kythe**, *v.*

The earliest quotation for the sense 'to make known' is taken from the *Corpus Glossary* (.*c* 725), and the last one provided is the entry from Palsgrave.

*Warish* is said by Palsgrave to be 'lytel vsed'. In the *OED* the sense 'to recover from sickness or trouble' of the obsolete verb *to warish* is recorded from the fourteenth century. Quotations after 1530 are nineteenth-century ones. And, finally, there are verbs for which Palsgrave's 'not yet, not yet fully' used may mean relative neologisms:

*betraysshe* — *OED* † **betraise, betraish**, *v. Obs.*

The verb was used by Lydgate, but the sense recorded by Palsgrave is listed in neither the *MED* nor the *OED*.

*cyrcumspecte* — *OED* † **circumspect**, *v. Obs.*

Lydgate used only the adjective *circumspect*, and this is well recorded in the Lydgate glossaries and the *MED*. The *OED* does not list the entry from Palsgrave. It gives two citations for the verbal use, one from 1667 and the other from 1708.

*darrayne* — *OED* † **deraign**, *v.*$^{2}$ *Obs.*

The first quotation in the *OED* for the sense 'to put into disorder, to derange, disarrange' is from Dunbar (1500-20), the second from Palsgrave and the third and last dates from 1706.

*embellish* *OED* **embellish,** *v.*

The *OED* lists four quotations before 1530 in the sense given by Palsgrave. The earliest is from *c.*1340.

The references to Chaucer and Lydgate enable us to identify unambiguously some of the source texts which Palsgrave consulted for the compilation of his dictionary and from which he drew parts of his word list. Although we shall discuss his French equivalents in Chapter 8, it would be useful to bring all the literary citations together in this chapter and review the French ones here, comparing their lexicographical presentation to that of the English ones.

The most striking feature is the small number of explicit literary citations for French. There are less than twenty. We do, however, have to remember that the word list for each part of speech is preceded by a detailed grammatical treatment of the word class in question. The description of the verb, for instance, includes the formulation of a number of grammatical rules and in their discussion Palsgrave weighs the textual evidence from the *Roman de la Rose*, and the works of Alain Chartier and Jean Lemaire de Belges. In such discussion, Palsgrave occasionally refers not only to a particular work but to a particular part within that very work. With respect to the construction *aller* + infinitive, for example, he writes:

> whan they wyll expresse an acte to be in begynnyng they vse the tenses of *ie vas*, and the infynityue mode of ŷ verbe whose acte dothe begyn/ as I begyn to drinke to you/ *ie vas boyre a vous*, he begynneth to dye or he is at the poynte to dye/ *il va mourir*. Note that at all tymes whan ŷ tenses of *ie vas*, is ioyned to an infynityue/ that he dothe betoken inchoacion/ for many tymes *ie vas*, hath his owne signyfycacion/ as Johan le Mayre in the first epystle of the Lamant vert/ *elle va veoir la noble Germanie*, whiche is nat/ she begynneth to se/ but she goeth to se. (III, fo. c.xxx$^{v}$–xxxi)[3]

The verb list includes two such precise locations of where a phrase or construction occurs within a particular French work. Palsgrave's lexicographical treatment thus differs for French citations. The closest correspondence we have for English is the mention of the title of a literary work, the *Canterbury Tales*. Here are the two examples:

> **I Dare I haue boldnesse or hardynesse to do a thyng/** Ie ose. prime. **But I fynde in the epystell of Medea:** Tu as ausé, **but Johñ le Maire vseth** ose, **moste comenly/ thoughe**

> **I Shyne as any bright thynge shyneth/** Ie resplendis. secunde cõiu. **but Johñ le Mayre vseth/** ie resplẽs tu resplens, il resplend, aussi replend [*sic*] la ducalle baniere, **but all other ten-**

[3] The citation is confirmed by Stecher (1969: iii. 4, l. 34).

**one I fynde ause, vsed also of him,**
...

(III, fo. cc.iiii)

**ses be euer vsed of the seconde coniugacion/ ⁊ in his first booke. capi. xxii.** Et la noble cõqueste de Iason en Colcos prent son fondemẽt dung mouton a la toison dor qui resplend maintenant au ciel faisant lung des douze signes du zodiacque . . .

III, fo. ccc.l[v])

Where, with English, literary reference is only with verbs, the position with French citations is sharply different. The majority of instances relate to verbs, but there is one literary citation to a numeral, one to an adverb form, and one under the conjunctions. An answer to the question 'Howe many' might be

> **All that euer/** Tout tanque, **or** tout quanque (**Froissart**) **as/** Tous tant q̃ se tenoyent sur le pont sont noyez.
>
> (III, fo. cccc.lvi)

French equivalents for the English conjunction *yet* are *encores*, *ayncoys*, *non pour tãt*, *pour tant*, *toutesfoys*, *si*, and *mays*. Under the description of *encores* we find a reference to Jean Lemaire de Belges:

> Encores. **as/** Ie ne voys riens encores dont ie me doibs esbahir. **as/** Attendez ie nay pas fait encores. **as for** encor, **and** encore, **be vsed in ryme / and Johan le Mayre vseth** encoyres, **as/** Dauid encoyres exercant lestat de bergerie. **and** Or me dictez encoyres. &c.
>
> (III, fo. cccc.lxvii[v])[4]

As we can see from the examples quoted so far, the literary references to French authors may consist in a mere mention of the work or in a longer metalinguistic comment. Unlike the literary citations for English, the French ones may use both the founts found in the dictionary. The black letter highlights the citations within the text of the French equivalents. When the citation is accompanied by a metalinguistic comment, it is given in black letter only. Examples where the mention of the literary references is not emphasized and therefore only cast in the same fount as the French part of the dictionary are:

[4] *Encores* is quite common in *Les Illustrations de Gaule et Singularitez de Troye*: '. . . le Roy Dauid encores exerçant estat de bergerie . . .' (Stecher 1969: i. 228).

Cinquantiesme **fyftyth.**
**And** cinquantainier **vsed of** Gillaume
Dalexis en son blason

(III, fo. c.xvii^v^)

**I Set on the ryght hande of one/**
Ie luy adestre. Frossart. ꝛ ie adestre.
prime cõiu.

(III, fo. ccc.lix)

The French poets cited in the English–French word lists are: Jean de Meung, Jean Froissart, Alain Chartier, Guillaume Alexis, and Jean Lemaire de Belges. Most of the citations relate to Jean Lemaire de Belges, perhaps because he was a contemporary of John Palsgrave, and possibly an acquaintance. According to G. Doutrepont (1934: p. xi), Louis XII called Lemaire to his court and in 1513–15 Lemaire was a historiographer to the French king who also entrusted him with various missions to Italy. When Mary Tudor married Louis XII in 1514, Palsgrave accompanied her to France, and an encounter with the French poet may have occurred. At that time the three books of Lemaire's then much acclaimed *Illustrations de Gaule et Singularitez de Troye* had just appeared.

Next in order of frequency of citations comes Froissart. Here we might also recall that Pynson printed Lord Berners's translation of Froissart's *Chronicles of England, France*, etc. in 1522–3 (the first volume) and 1525 (the second volume), the very time when Palsgrave was compiling his *Esclarcissement*.

Without concordances for the works of the authors quoted, checks on the reliability of Palsgrave's literary citations for French can be carried out only with the help of the standard reference works, but a few such checks confirm Palsgrave's accuracy. Godefroy has citations for the use of *atourner* and *aherdre* in the *Roman de la Rose*, and he confirms Froissart's use of the verb *adestrer*. Huguet lists *encoires* as a variant of *encor*, *encore*, and includes a citation from Jean Lemaire de Belges. Latin *resplendere* has two forms in medieval French, *resplendre* and *resplendir*. Among the authors using the form *resplendre*, the *FEW* (x. 309b) lists Jean Lemaire.[5] And Lemaire is also one of the authors listed in the *FEW* (ix. 135a) as having used the adjective/past participle *pollu*.

Finally, there is the question of the function of Palsgrave's French literary citations. The examples quoted which refer to Guillaume

[5] That Palsgrave occasionally took Lemaire as his model is also suggested by the entry *up and down*:

> **Up and downe:** Amont et aual. **and**
> Ie me prommayne. **I walke vp and**
> **downe: and** Ius et sus, **as/** Qui ne le
> tournast ius et sus.
>
> (III, fo. cccc.xlvi)

The phrase *ius et sus* occurs in *Les Illustrations*, iv. 52, and Stecher (1969) has drawn attention to the fact that '[d]'ordinnaire néanmoins on trouve: *sus et jus*'.

Alexis and Jean Froissart illustrate cases of usage attestation. As with Lydgate, differences in spelling seem to be among Palsgrave's interests in the literary citations for French, and Palsgrave explicitly discusses (for example) the variants (*auser/oser* (III, fo. cc.liiii), *fuir/ fouir* (III, fo. cc.xxxvii$^{\mathrm{v}}$)).

Dialectal differences are not singled out in the citations, but temporal ones are, just as for English:

> **I Applye or cleaue a thyng harde togyther as glue dothe to a tree or thynges that be glued/** Ie adhers, nous adherdons, vous adherdez, ilz adherdent, ie adherdis, iay adhert, ie adherdray, que ie adherde, adhers aherdre. tercie. cõiugationis. **a verbe vsed of the Romante formed out of** adhereo, **but it is nat nowe vsed/ thoughe it be moche vsed of Johan de Meun.**
>
> (III, fo. c.li)

> **I Cleaue as a thynge dothe that styketh fast to an other/** Ie tiens, con iugate in I holde. **My shyrte cleaueth to my backe:** Ma chemise tient a mon dos, or ma chemise me tient au dos, **and** ie adhers, nous adherdons, ie adherdis, iay adhert, iadherderay, que iadherde, adherdre. tercie cõiu. **though I fynde it moche vsed in the Romante of the Rose it is an olde romant worde and nowe lytle vsed/ howe be it it maye stande with the tonge well ynoughe bycause of his latyn worde** adhereo . . .
>
> (III, fo. c.lxxxix)

The historical dimension is also manifest in the discussion of grammatical changes. There is no such focus on grammatical points in the literary citations of English authors. Attention may be drawn to changes in the conjugation class:

> **I Make blynde/** Ie aueugle. prime cõiu. **or** ie aueuglis. secunde cõiu. **so that in yͤ olde romant tonge they vse this verbe of their fyrste coniugacion/ but Johan le Mayre vseth hym of their seconde . . .**
>
> (III, fo. cc.lxxxxix = fo. cc.lxxxix)

so too with the active/reflexive dichotomy:

> **I Waxe reed/** Ie menrougis. verbũ mediũ. secũde cõiu. **Johan le Maire vseth him as an actyue/** Et rougist le fleuue panthus, **but whan the acte passeth nat from the doer they must nedes be al vsed lyke meane verbes** . . .
>
> (III, fo. cccc.v)[6]

[6] The full and correct version of the citation is: 'Et rougist souuentesfois le fleuue Xanthus, du sang des occis . . .' (Stecher 1969: i. 137, ll. 9–10).

Even a change in word-formation productivity is highlighted:

> **I Out beare one in his dede.** Ie supporte. prime coniu. **Who so euer saye the contrary/ I wyll out beare the.** Quiconques die le contraire, ie te veulx supporter. **But where as in som frenshe verbes I fynde** for ad- did **byfore them whiche cõtreualith owt/ whan he is thus cõpownde wͭ verbes in our tõg as where we saye I owt crye/ I owt eate/ I owttake/ I owt cept/ in Alayne Chartiers tyme they vsed** Ie forcrie Ie forman- gens Ie forprens Ie forcepte: **nowe yͤ frenshe tonge leueth syche maner of composition sauyng in one or two here expressed/ and for owt they vse** oultre/ **or** plus **as the sentence shall require.**
>
> (III, fo. ccc.xi)

The comparison and discussion of linguistic forms found in earlier French writers and works is further illustration of Palsgrave's awareness of historical differences in French and thus complements the picture provided in Chapter 3.

# 6
# Lemmatization and Headword Structure

We now come to the actual structure and presentation of Palsgrave's word list, and, as we can see from the following examples, his lexicographical method of presentation differs greatly from modern practice in bilingual English–French dictionaries. These differences will first be described and then interpreted in the lexicographical context of Palsgrave's time.

Since it is impossible to characterize Palsgrave's lemmatization *in toto*, I shall restrict myself to the three major parts of speech: the noun, the adjective, and the verb. Some examples from each in the letter *n* are listed in Table 6.1 to illustrate the contrast between lemmatization in *Lesclarcissement* and a modern English–French dictionary, the *Collins-Robert* in its second edition (1987).

There are some obvious differences, such as the indication of pronunciation, in the twentieth-century dictionary and the specification of the grammatical form class after the headword since its overriding principle of arrangement is alphabetical for the whole lexicon and not by grammatical classes as in *Lesclarcissement*. Of more importance in our context is a feature which they share: in each dictionary different founts are used to distinguish different types of information. The sixteenthth-century dictionary uses two types, the modern *Collins-Robert* three. In addition, the latter has broken down the linguistic information to be conveyed into smaller information units which are presented as such by means of a bracketing and numbering system. The modern dictionary thus looks much more compartmentalized.

In both dictionaries, the unit which is to be translated into French is set off from the rest of the text: it always starts a new line and it is given in the boldest type. The units themselves, however, vary considerably:

| | |
|---|---|
| **Nacyon** | **nation** |
| **Nagge a horse** | **nag** |

TABLE 6.1. *Lemmatization in* Lesclarcissement *and a twentieth-century English–French dictionary*

| *Lesclarcissement* | | *Collins-Robert* |
|---|---|---|
| Nouns | | |
| **Nacyon** | nacion s fe. | **nation** ['neɪʃən] 1 *n* nation f, peuple *m*. . . . |
| **Nagge a horse** | courtavlt z ma. | **nag** [næg] *n* (horse) cheval *m*.; (*pej*) canasson *m* (*pej*) |
| **Nayle of yron** | clov x ma. | **nail** [neɪl] 1 *n* (**a**) (*Anat*) ongle *m*. . . .<br>(**b**) (*Tech*) clou *m*. . . . |
| **Nayle of a fyngre** | vngle s fe. | |
| Adjectives | | |
| **Naked without clothes**<br>ma. neu s. fe. neue s.<br>ma. nu s. fe. nue s. ma.<br>nud. fe. nue. | | **naked** ['neɪkɪd] *adj* (**a**) *person* (tout) nu |
| **Narrow or strayte** ma.<br>estroict z. fe. estroicte s.<br>**Narrow as a passage** ma.<br>ague s. fe. ague s. | | **narrow** ['nærəʊ] 1 *adj* (**a**) *road, path* étroit; *valley* étroit, encaissé; *passage* étranglé, *garment* étroit, étriqué; *boundary, limits* restreint, étroit . . .<br>(**b**) (*fig*) *outlook, mind* étroit, restreint, borné; *person* aux vues étroites, à l'esprit étroit, borné; *existence* limité, circonscrit; *scrutiny* serré, poussé; *means, resources, income* limité, juste (*fig.*); *majorité* faible, petit; *advantage* petit . . . |
| Verbs | | |
| **I Nayle a thyng with a nayle/** Ie cloue, ⁊ ie affiche. pri. cõiu. . . . | | **nail** [neɪl] . . .<br>3 *vt* (**a**) (*fix with* ~ *s*) clouer . . . |
| **I Nayle in a thynge/** Ie encloue. prime cõiuga. . . . . . . | | (**b**) (*put* ~ *s* **into**) clouter |
| **I Name a person by his name/** Ie nomme. prime coniuga. **and** ie denomme . . . | | **name** [neɪm] . . .<br>2 *vt* (**a**) (*call by a* ~ , *give a* ~ *to*) nommer, appeler, donner un nom à . . . |
| **I Name one by his surname/** Ie surnõme. prime cõiuga. . . . | | (**b**) (*give* ~ *of; list*) nommer, citer (le nom de); (*designate*) nommer, désigner (par son nom de) |

| | |
|---|---|
| **Nayle of yron** | **nail** |
| **Nayle of a fyngre** | |
| **Naked without clothes** | **naked** |
| **Narrow or strayte** | **narrow** |
| **Narrow as a passage** | |
| **I Nayle a thyng with a nayle** | **nail** |
| **I Nayle in a thynge** | |
| **I Name a person by his name** | **name** |
| **I Name one by his surname** | |

Traditionally, the lexical unit in a dictionary for which a meaning explanation or a translation equivalent is provided is called the *lemma* or the *headword.* The contrast manifested between the units listed in *Lesclarcissement* and in the *Collins-Robert* calls for a more detailed identification and description of the *lemma.*

In a language dictionary, a dictionary entry typically consists of two constituents: a linguistic sign and the linguistic information supplied for it. Between both these constituents there is a predication relationship. If one wants to predicate something of something else, the linguistic unit of which something is to be predicated has to be given first. When a linguistic sign is thus mentioned lexicographically, the production of the sign itself disregards and at the same time encompasses all concrete realizations of the sign, such as the actual pronunciation, spelling, the number for nouns, tense, mood, aspect, and voice for the verb, etc. The linguistic sign thus mentioned is the lexicographical *lemma* or *headword.* The lemma is by definition a part of the dictionary entry. A dictionary entry as it has been described here bears through ordering a structural relationship to other dictionary entries and the whole of the dictionary proper. The ordering element is a property of the lemma. Thus, in an alphabetical dictionary, for instance, the order of the letters $n + a + g$ determines the place which the linguistic sign *nag* has within the whole of the dictionary and in relation to other dictionary entries. And, similarly, the final sound sequence [g] + [æ] + [n] will determine the item's place within a rhyming dictionary, or the semantic feature 'animal' or 'horse' will determine its position in a thesaurus.

The lexicographical mention of the lemma cannot be effected without an actual physical realization in sound or writing. The lexicographer-compiler uses this realization at the same time as a lexicographical comment on the pronunciation or spelling of the item in question. This is the reason why, in a dictionary based on the written language, for instance, the mention of the lemma is never followed by a presentation of the spelling as in

| | | | |
|---|---|---|---|
| **nag** | *nag* | /næg/ | *n* a small riding horse . . . |
| \| | \| | \| | |
| lemma | spelling | pronunciation | |

The total set of lemmata listed in a dictionary is the *word list.*

The raising of a linguistic sign to the status of a lemma in a dictionary implies that lexicographers strip it of all its actualizing, contextualizing features. They may rightly wonder, and this seems to have been particularly characteristic of the early stages of dictionary-making in England, whether their users would be able to grasp this 'artificial' use of the linguistic sign and correctly identify the latter in its decontextualized form.

Since the lemma or headword may be realized as a simple lexical item or as a more complex syntactic unit, the term *lemma entry* (or *headword entry*) is introduced. In all such cases in which the lemma (or headword) consists of a letter, an abbreviation, an affix, a simple word, a derivative, or a compound, lemma (or headword) and lemma entry (or headword entry) coincide. Palsgrave's *Nacyon*, for instance, is thus a lemma entry and at the same time the lemma. If the lemma (or headword) is syntactically expanded, the lemma (or headword) and lemma entry (or headword entry) do not coincide. The lemma (headword) will then be referred to as the *lemma* (*headword*) *proper*. Palsgrave's entry *I Name a person by his name* is thus a lemma entry where the first *Name* is the lemma proper. It determines the place of the lemma entry within the dictionary. The elements that precede and follow the lemma proper will be referred to as the *prelemmatic expansion* (*I* in the above example) and the *postlemmatic expansion* (*a person by his name*).

## NOUNS

### *Formal aspects and reference point*

Let us now after these preliminary clarifications look at Palsgrave's lemmatization of nouns. Within the lemma entry the lemma proper is identified by an initial capital. With very few exceptions (e.g. *Tonge tyed* - qui a le filet ma.) the lemma entries are nouns. In presenting a lemma, Palsgrave uses the unactualized form of the linguistic sign which is characteristic of any metalinguistic mention: the form without any article and the form which in English coincides with the singular, as, for instance, in

**Diall to knowe the houres by yͤ course**
**of the sonne** quadrant s ma.

Lemmata in plural form are rare and are usually nouns which are typically used in this form—for example:

| | |
|---|---|
| **Dregges** | lie de biere ou deuin s fe. |
| **Eymbres hote asshes** | brasiers fe. |

In a few cases the variant forms are listed next to each other, joined by the conjunction *or*. What may look like differences in spelling are alternative grammatical or dialect forms:

| | |
|---|---|
| **Eye or egge** | oevf. |
| **Frecken or freccles in ones face** | lentille s fe. or brand de iudas |

The more common case, however, is the listing of such items in their respective alphabetical places. Unlike in the verb list, there are no cross-references. The contrast in the lexicographical treatment of nouns and verbs is rather striking. Examples are:

| | |
|---|---|
| **Kichen** | cvisine s fe. |
| **Kytchen** | cvisine s fe. |
| **Roughe fysshe** | no equivalent |
| **Ruffe a fysshe** | no equivalent |

One may wonder why Palsgrave did not indicate any relation between the different spellings. A possible explanation might be that the cross-reference system which he devised for his verb entries was a rather late methodological development during his compilation process. Other factors suggest that he may not have had enough time to check and revise his word list. Among the nouns, we encounter a number of double listings where the entries are either identical or else the French equivalents vary:

| | |
|---|---|
| **Colte a yong horse** | pollayn s ma. |
| **Colte a yong horse** | povllain s m. |
| | (III, fos. xxv–xxvi$^{v}$) |
| **Hauthorne** | espine blanche s fe. |
| **Hauthorne** | aulbespin espine blãche s ma. Ro. dessoubz ung aulbespin gisant |
| | (III, fo. xxxix) |

The most striking instance of such double listings is the following:

| | |
|---|---|
| **Standert a baner** | estandart s ma. avriflame s fe. |
| | (III, fo. lxvi$^{v}$) |

and two items further

**Standart a baner** estandart s ma.
Auriflame s fe. **a standart whiche with**

**the Frenchmen was had/ in suche estymacion as with vs is saynt Cuthbertȝ baner/ whiche they lost in Flaunders.**

(III, fo. lxvii)

The linguistic reference point adopted by Palsgrave is the third-person singular. An exception with a first-person plural orientation is

**Hearyng/ the place wherby we here** ovye s fe.

(III, fo. xxxix^v)

As to the linguistically unmarked third-person singular orientation, there are two different forms. The dominant form seems to be *one* (with its correlating forms), as, for instance, in

| | |
|---|---|
| **Place to bathe one in** | thermes fe. |
| **Sight that disceyueth ones iugement** | illusion s fe. |

The other is *man* in the sense of 'a person' or 'someone' with its correlating forms:

| | |
|---|---|
| **Pymple on a mannes face** | pustule s fe. |
| **Place where a man is lodged** | herbegerie s fe. |

Headword status is typographically indicated by a capital initial letter for the lemma, and the lemma itself begins a new line. If the lemma entry takes up more than one line, the second line is indented so that the lemma is given a certain prominence. The noun list has main entries only. In many instances it is easy to identify the lemma because the lemma entry consists solely of a simple noun, a derivative, or a compound noun. Letters of the alphabet and affixes are not listed. Examples are:

| | |
|---|---|
| **Cake** | gasteav x ma. |
| **Carefulnesse** | sollicitude s fe. |
| **Cancker worme** | uers de chancre s ma. |

Sometimes the lemma is followed by an illustration of the item in question, as in

| | |
|---|---|
| **Sake/ as for goddes sake** | amovr s fe. |
| **Wyll as with my good wyll** | gre ma. |

### *Types of headword structure*

There are, however, many cases where we may wonder about the structure of the lemma entries and the function of the postlemmatic expansions. The following cases are among the most conspicuous occurrences:

1. The lemma is followed by a prepositional phrase:

| | |
|---|---|
| **Hafte of any tole** | manche s ma. |
| **Heed fro the sholders vp** | chief z ma. |
| **Iacket without sleues** | hocqueton s ma. |

2. The lemma is followed by a past participle (plus complement):

| | |
|---|---|
| **Phesycion named in derisyon** | merdefin s ma. |
| **Prayse made before a great man or preposition** | harengue s fe. |
| **Processe shewed by wordes** | proces uerbal x ma. |

3. The lemma is followed by a relative clause:

| | |
|---|---|
| **Hole that swete or heres cometh out at** | pore s ma. |
| **Hole where the meate gothe downe** | gavion s ma. |
| **Husbande that hath wedded a wyfe** | mary s ma. |

4. The lemma is followed by an infinitive (plus complement):

| | |
|---|---|
| **Diall to knowe the houres by yͤ course of the sonne** | quadrant s ma. |
| **Engyn to throwe stones** | martinet s ma. |
| **Goblet to drinke in**[1] | gobelet z ma. |

5. The lemma is followed by a clause of comparison introduced by *suche as* or *as*:

| | |
|---|---|
| **Father in lawe as a man is to his doughters hus-bande/ or to his sonnes wyfe** | beau pere s ma. |
| **Popple/ suche as ryseth whan water or any lycour setheth fast** | bovillon s ma. |

[1] Other instances where the noun denoting a vessel is followed by the infinitive *to drinke in* are, for instance: **Cruse to drinke in** pot de beavuais, **Cuppe to drinke in** covppe . . ., hanap . . ., **Pece to drinke in** tasse s fe. The *OED* mentions the construction under the absolute and intransitive senses (II, 10. absol. **a.**). The first and only quotation for the obsolete construction with *in* dates from 1634 and the first and only quotation for the construction *drink out of* + NP carries the date 1698. The documentation seems to suggest that *drink in* + NP is the older construction. Evidence from *Lesclarcissement* predates the *OED* by more than a century. Since the French is *on boit dans une bouteille*, one may wonder whether Palsgrave's instances could be gallicisms. Surprisingly, the *MED* has no attestations for the use of *drink in* + NP.

6. The lemma is followed by *or* and another noun phrase:

| | |
|---|---|
| **Gilde or brotherheed** | confrairie s fe. |
| **Hyebles or herbe that groweth in the water** | hiebles ma. |
| **Poppy sede or the herbe** | pauot z ma. |

The maximum number of noun phrases joined is three, as in:

| | |
|---|---|
| **Poysy/ deuyse/ or worde** | deuise s fe. |

7. The lemma is followed by an explanatory, usually appositional noun phrase, which may consist of a simple noun or of a noun followed by a complex postmodification. Within this type of lemma entry we may distinguish different groups:

(a) The noun phrase is 'a proper name'. Since *Lesclarcissement*, in general, does not list names of towns, rivers, mountains, people, etc., such instances are rare. Examples are:

| | |
|---|---|
| **Iohan a proper name** | Iehan. |
| **Mary a proper name** | marie s fe. |

(b) The names of the months are followed by the noun phrase 'a moneth':

| | |
|---|---|
| **Decembre a moneth** | decembre s ma. |
| **February a moneth** | fevrier s fe. |

(c) The noun phrase is 'an element':

| | |
|---|---|
| **Aire an element** | ayr s ma. |
| **Erthe an element** | terre s fe. |

(d) The noun phrase is '(a) metall':

| | |
|---|---|
| **Brasse metall** | arain s. ma. |
| **Coppar metall** | cviure, souldure s ma. |

(e) The noun phrase is '(a) precious stone':

| | |
|---|---|
| **Camuse precious stone** | chamahievx ma. |
| **Safyre a precious stone** | saphire s ma. |

(f) The noun phrase is the word 'colour'. Whether this item is part of the lemma or whether it is a postlemmatic expansion is difficult to decide:

| | |
|---|---|
| **Crane colour** | gris cendré ma. |
| **Kenet coloure** | cendré s ma. |

(g) The noun phrase is 'a measure':

| | |
|---|---|
| **Gallon a measure** | gallon s ma, pot s ma. |
| **Halfe pynt a measure** | demion s fe. choppine s. fe. |

(h) The noun phrase is '(a) beest':

| | |
|---|---|
| **Calfe beest** | ueav x ma. |
| **Cammell a beest** | chameav x ma. |

(i) The noun phrase is '(a) fysshe':

| | |
|---|---|
| **Carpe fysshe** | carpe s fe. |
| **Ceale a fysshe** | chavlderon de mer s ma. |

(j) The noun phrase is '(a) byrde':

| | |
|---|---|
| **Drake a byrde** | canart s ma. |
| **Finche a byrde** | pincon z ma. |

(k) The noun phrase is '(an) herbe':

| | |
|---|---|
| **Dandelyon an herbe** | dandelion s ma. |
| **Endyue an herbe** | endiue s fe. |

(l) The noun phrase is '(a) spyce':

| | |
|---|---|
| **Cynamome a spyce** | cinamome, canelle s fe. |
| **Cloue spyce** | clou de girofle x ma. |

(m) The noun phrase is 'an instrument':

| | |
|---|---|
| **Croude an instrument** | robecq z ma. |
| **Fyle an instrument** | lime s fe. |

(n) The noun phrase is 'a vessell' :

| | |
|---|---|
| **Kettyll a vessell** | chauderon s ma. |
| **Kylderken a vessell** | cacque s fe. |

(o) The noun phrase is '(a) disease, sickenesse':

| | |
|---|---|
| **Collyke a sickenesse** | colique s fe. |
| **Coughe disease** | tous s fe. |

(p) The noun phrase begins with 'a kynde of':

| | |
|---|---|
| **Cypres a kynde of wode** | cypres s ma. |
| **Date a kynde of frute** | datte s fe. |

(q) The noun phrase is an appositional noun:

| | |
|---|---|
| **Aide helpe** | aide s ma. |
| **Alyen straunger** | alien s ma. |

(r) The noun phrase is a complex noun phrase:

| | |
|---|---|
| **Cressent the newe mone as long as it is nat rounde** | cressant s ma. |

**Doulphyn the frenche kynges eldest sonne** doulphin s ma.

The preceding list is not exhaustive, but seeks to provide some insight into the complex variety of headword structures that we encounter among Palsgrave's noun lemmata. The lemma entries illustrated under 7(*a*)–(*p*) provide evidence that Palsgrave attempted a systematization of his noun entries. Yet not all the nouns belonging to one category have a postlemmatic expansion. *Bullock*, *Frogge*, and *Hogge*, for instance, are not described as beasts.

### *A comparison with the* Catholicon *and the* Promptorium

Let us briefly look at the headword structure in the *Catholicon Anglicum* and the *Promptorium parvulorum* before we discuss the syntactic–semantic relationship that holds between the lemma proper and the postlemmatic expansion in the seven types of lemma entries outlined above. Of these seven types, type 1 (the lemma is followed by a prepositional phrase) is the most common one in the *Catholicon*. Type 2 does not occur. Type 3 is represented by one single example:

a **Skyñ ỳ ỳ chylde is lappyd in jn ỳ moder wame**; himen genetiuo himenis, matrix.

Type 4 (the lemma is followed by an infinitive plus complement) occurs three times. An example is **a Mulde to cast in**; *duca*, *formula*, *effegies*, *patrona*. Type 5 (a clause of comparison introduced by *as*) occurs in a handful of instances. Type 6 (the lemma is followed by *or* plus a noun phrase) is the most common one after Type 1.

Of all the various types under 7, type (*a*) is the one that is handled most systematically. Unlike in *Lesclarcissement*, however, it is not the English first name that is followed by the specification 'proper name', but the Latin equivalent, as in

**George**; *georgius*, *nomen proprium*

This characteristic holds for all the other types that occur. Types 7(*i*), 7(*j*), and 7(*k*) are represented by a number of instances. The following examples illustrate each subgroup:

7(*i*) a **Loche**; *Alosa*, *fundulus*, *piscis est*.
7(*j*) a **Rayle**; *glebarius*, *Auis est*.
7(*k*) **Longdebefe**; *buglossa*, *herba est*.

Although the manuscript of the *Promptorium parvulorum* is older than that of the *Catholicon Anglicum*, the *Promptorium* is more independent of the Latin target language and also more advanced in its lexicographical method. This becomes manifest in the subtypes of type 7: specifications like 'proper name', 'metal', 'precious stone', 'measure', 'beast', and so on are given in English, after the lemma.

With the exception of the subtype 7(*p*) ('a kind of . . .'), all the seven types with their subtypes occur in the *Promptorium* (Mayhew, 1908), yet the frequency with which they occur differs. In addition, there are lemma entry types that are specific to the *Promptorium*.

Lemma entries with prepositional phrases (type 1) are very common. Headwords followed by a past-participle construction (type 2) occur, but their overall occurrence is low. An example is:

> **Grave**, solemly made or grauyn:
> *Mausoleum* . . . [2]

There are quite a number of instances illustrating type 3, the lemma being followed by a relative clause:

> **Play** þat begynnyþ with mornynge
> and sorow and endyth with merth:
> *Comedia* . . . [3]

Type 4, the lemma followed by an infinitive (plus complement) as in *Lesclarcissement*, occurs chiefly after nouns denoting artefacts to indicate their use or function:

> **Trap** to take with beestys, as borys
> or oder lyke: *Cenabulum, -li*:
> *venabulum* . . . [4]

Type 5, the lemma followed by a clause of comparison introduced by *as* is not very frequent:

> **ffundelyng**, as he þat ys fowndyn
> and noman wot hoo ys his ffader
> or moder: *Inuenticius* . . ., *Inuen-*
> *ticia* . . . [5]

Type 6, the lemma followed by *or* plus a noun phrase, occurs frequently in the *Promptorium*, which not only lists more spelling

[2] The entry in the first printed edition of 1499 reads as follows:

> **Graue solemly made and arayed.** Mausoleũ . . .

[3] In the 1499 edition the entry is not listed under *play*, but under *Ioy* we find a similar entry:

> **Ioy and myrthe that begynneth with sorow**
> **and endeth with gladnesse.** Comedia die . . .

[4] An example from the 1499 edition is

> **Nette to take fisshe.** Rethe this . . .

[5] There is no postlemmatic expansion in the 1499 edition.

variants conjoined by *or* than *Lesclarcissement* but also prefers to join synonyms by means of *or* to juxtaposing them as in type 7(*q*) (*Age, oldnesse*). As many as four noun phrases may be joined together:

> **Levte**, potte, or vessell, or mesure:
> *ffidelia* . . . [6]

Very often the conjunction is followed by a full explanation of the lemma in English:

> **Snyvlare**, or he þat spekyþ in his
> nose: *Nasitus* . . . [7]

It looks as if the author of the *Promptorium parvulorum* was intent on making agent–noun formations transparent by his explanatory paraphrases. Examples illustrating compound nouns are:

> **ffote man**, or he þat goth a-fot: *hic*
> *pedester, hec-tris, hoc-tre* . . .,
> *Pedes* . . . [8]
> **Horsman**, or he þat rydythe horsys:
> *Equester* . . . [9]
> **Ragman**, or he þat goþ with raggyd
> cloþys: *Pannicius* . . ., *Pannicia* . . . [10]

Examples for derivatives in *-ard*, *-er*, and *-ling* are:

> **Scabbarde**, or he þat ys scabbyd:
> *Scabidus* . . ., *Scabida* . . . [11]
> **Macere**, or he that beryth a mace:
> *Septiger* . . . [12]
> **Sokelyng**, or he þat sokyth: *Sub-*
> *uber* . . ., *Subibis* . . . [13]

As we can see from these examples, the reference point is the third person, but with *he* rather than Palsgrave's *one* to express generic reference.[14]

[6] The entry reads as follows in the 1499 edition:

> **Leute pot of mesure.** Fidelia lie. . . .

[7] The item is not listed in the 1499 edition.
[8] There is no postlemmatic expansion in the 1499 edition.
[9] There is no postlemmatic expansion in the 1499 edition.
[10] The item is not listed in the 1499 edition.
[11] There is no postlemmatic expansion in the 1499 edition.
[12] There is no postlemmatic expansion in the 1499 edition.
[13] The entry is not listed in the 1499 edition. Both versions of the *Promptorium* include the entry

> **Sokar or he that soketh** . . .

[14] This does not mean that there are no such lemma entries in *Lesclarcissement*, but the typical

We come to type 7. Subgroups (*a*) to (*o*) are conspicuous in *Lesclarcissement* and this is the reason why they were singled out. The *Promptorium parvulorum* is much more detailed than *Lesclarcissement.* Further groups that emerge from a perusal of the dictionary are for instance: 'bread', 'drink', 'fruit', 'sore', 'stone', 'tree', 'worm'. The *Promptorium* is thus more structured with respect to the explicit semantic classification of nouns, while *Lesclarcissement* is more refined in lexicographical form and style, using for example the indefinite article (see Table 6.2).

TABLE 6.2. *Lemmatization style in the* Promptorium parvulorum *and* Lesclarcissement

| *Promptorium* | | *Lesclarcissement* |
|---|---|---|
| 1440 | 1499 | |
| **Colyk**, sekenesse | **Colyk sekenesse** | **Collyke a sickenesse** |
| **Ketyl**, or chetyl, or caudron | **Ketyll or cawdron** | **Kettyll a vessell** |
| **Bottell**, vessell | **Botell** | **Bottell to kepe drinke in** |

We conclude this brief comparison by drawing attention to some further characteristics of the *Promptorium parvulorum.* There are some lemma entries where the postlemmatic expansion is a present participle clause:

> **Mos** growyng a-mong stonys: *Mus-cus . . .* [15]

*While*-phrases are exemplified by the following instances:

> **Corn**, whyl hit growyth: *Seges . . .* [16]

Similar instances, though with the conjunction *when*, occur in *Lesclarcissement*:

> **Sneuyll whan it hangeth at ones nose** rovpie z fe. boe s fe.

postlemmatic expansion is not 'he þat . . .', making the expansion an apposition; rather the postlemmatic expansion in *Lesclarcissement* is a relative clause, as in:

> **Driuelar that driueleth** baueux ma.
> **Lawyer that occupyeth the lawe** homme de loy s ma. homme de robe longue s ma.

[15] There is no postlemmatic expansion in the 1499 edition.
[16] The 1499 edition has the same lemma entry.

**Walnot whan he is cut out of the grene shell** cerneau x ma.

*Syntactic–semantic relationship between lemma and postlemmatic expansion*

Let us now look at the syntactic–semantic relationship that holds between the lemma proper and the postlemmatic expansion. All the types of lemma entries outlined so far can be subsumed under two basic relationships: semantic specification and apposition. A third relationship, alternative reference expressing polysemy, is realized only sporadically.

*Specification*

The postlemmatic expansion represents a semantic specification by grammatical postmodification that restricts the sense of the lemma to be translated into French. Restrictive postmodification is typically expressed in five ways:

1. Prepositional phrase, as in

   **Declaryng of a noble mannes stocke** genealogie s fe.

2. A past participle clause, as in

   **Detie made in ryme** rommant s ma.<br>diction s ma.

3. A relative clause, as in

   **Drake that is tame** anet z ma.

4. An infinitive clause, as in

   **Distaffe to spynne with** quenoille s fe.

5. A clause of comparison introduced by *as*, as in

   **Fader in lawe/ as he is that maryeth a wyfe/ whiche hath chyldre by another man** parastre s ma.

If the postmodification was omitted, the lemma would have a different sense, which would lead to a different French translation equivalent. Thus *Declaryng* might be rendered by 'declaration, ostentation', etc., *Drake* by 'canard', *Fader in lawe* by 'beau pere'.

*Apposition*

Although there are different types of an appositive relationship, they all share one characteristic: the apposition itself is non-restrictive. If it was omitted, the sense of the lemma would not change. Quirk *et al.* (1985: 1302ff.) distinguish between *partial* syntactic apposition and *full* syntactic apposition. Two of the criteria to distinguish between the two are: co-referentiality and omissibility without affecting acceptability. If we apply this distinction to lexicography, *partial* apposition would be realized by the lemma entries of the types 7(*a*)–(*p*) where the lemma proper is followed by a generic noun phrase. This can be illustrated as follows:

| | |
|---|---|
| **Anteloppe a beest** | **antelop z ma.** |

The omission of 'a beest' would not affect the translation of *anteloppe* by French *antelop*. The equation with the appositive

| | |
|---|---|
| **A beest** | antelop z ma. |

however, is unacceptable. This is the case of partial apposition. In the case of

| | |
|---|---|
| **Carre a lytell carte with two wheles** | char s ma. |

we have an instance of full apposition, since both of the following are acceptable:

| | |
|---|---|
| **Carre** | char s ma. |

and

| | |
|---|---|
| **A lytell carte with two wheles** | char s ma. |

We might pair the two terms with a semantic description: a *partial* apposition is *generic*—that is, the appositive noun phrase expresses a generic subclassification—and a *full* apposition is *specific*—that is, the appositive noun phrase is a specific explanation of the lemma.

Partial and full apposition are the extreme ends of a scale. Generic specification can become more specific. This scale can be illustrated with examples from *Lesclarcissement*:

| | |
|---|---|
| **Ratte a beest** | rat z ma. |
| **Mouse a lytell beest** | sovris fe. mousse s fe. |
| **Irchen a lytell beest full of prickes** | herison s ma. |

While 'a lytell beest' is more specific than 'beest', it is still not specific enough for a full apposition:

| | |
|---|---|
| **A lytell beest** | sovris fe. mousse s fe. |

By contrast, the following is acceptable:

| | |
|---|---|
| **A lytell beest full of prickes** | herison s ma. |

Full apposition is thus realized by the lemma entry type 7(*r*).

Type 7(*p*), the lemma followed by a noun phrase beginning with 'a kynde of', might be regarded as an intermediate type:

| | |
|---|---|
| **Prune a kynde of frute** | prune s fe. |

Type 7(*q*), as in

| | |
|---|---|
| **Aide helpe** | aide s. ma. |

as well as co-referential noun phrases linked by *or* (type 6), as in

| | |
|---|---|
| **Kyrnell or knobbe in the necke/ or other where** | glandre s fe. |

also exemplify full apposition. In the case of type 7(*q*) the asyndetic relation could be made syndetic without changing the meaning of the lemma entry, and type 6 could be changed respectively:

| | |
|---|---|
| **Aide or helpe** | aide s ma. |
| **Kyrnell knobbe in the necke/ or other where** | glandre s fe. |

*Polysemy*

When there is no co-reference between the lemma and the postlemmatic noun phrase linked by the conjunction *or*, the coordinative relationship expresses polysemy, as in the following example:

| | |
|---|---|
| **Poppy sede or the herbe** | pauot z ma. |

An example from the *Promptorium parvulorum* (1440) is:

**Levte**, potte, or vessel, or mesure: *ffidelia* . . .

What the lemma entries mean is that two different senses are rendered by the French or Latin equivalent. That is, *pavot* may mean 'poppy seed' and/or the plant, herb 'poppy', and *fidelia* has the two meanings 'a vessel' and 'a measure'.

Occurrences of a coordinating polysemous relationship between lemma and postlemmatic expansion are relatively rare.

Apposition, especially full apposition, in lemma entries makes the bilingual dictionary a double dictionary: lemmata with full appositions constitute part of a monolingual dictionary which is combined with a bilingual one. This is in itself a highly interesting phenomenon in the history of English lexicography. At a time when the monolingual English dictionary was not yet in existence, it was already in part contained in bilingual works. Partial or full appositions in lemma entries may therefore be regarded as postlemmatic glosses. This will undoubtedly have increased the educational value of early bilingual dictionaries.

The syndetic and asyndetic pairing of a lemma and a synonym, as in

| | |
|---|---|
| **Brere or hethe** | bruyere s fe. |

and

| | |
|---|---|
| **Batte a staffe** | baston s ma. |

would constitute the earliest stage of monolingual English lexicography, while a full explanatory paraphrase after the lemma would constitute a more advanced later stage. Here are some examples to show how closely some of Palsgrave's sophisticated headword entries anticipate the modern monolingual dictionary:

| | |
|---|---|
| **Bowe shotte/ the space that one maye shote** | archee s fe. |
| **Gossommer/ thynges that flye in sommar lyke copwebbes** | no equivalent |

That Palsgrave, as well as the unknown compiler of the *Promptorium parvulorum*, made serious attempts at describing the meaning of an English word in their word list, becomes manifest from lemma entries like the following:

| | |
|---|---|
| **Fote of a stole or of a bedde/ or of any other thyng** | pie z ma. |

The prepositional phrase 'of any other thyng' is a substitute for all the other possible objects to which *foot* might apply, but which cannot all be specified. Other examples reflecting the compiler's endeavour to narrow down or to generalize the application of a word are:

| | |
|---|---|
| **Box for medicyns/ or to put any other thyng in** | boite s fe. |
| **Case of lether to put a combe/ a recorder or any suche lyke thyng in** | estuy s ma. |

In the *Promptorium parvulorum* (1440 and 1499), there are some stereotyped expressions for this, of which 'or oder lyke' 'or other like' is the most common:

> **Leef**, of a boke or a tre, or odyre lyk: *ffolium* . . .
> **Syde** of a beeste or oþer thynge what so hyt be: *latus* . . .

*Postlemmatic expansions as indicators of lexicographical indebtedness*

Postlemmatic expansions obviously play an important role in establishing the sources of a dictionary. For example, the noun *suburb* has the following entry in the *Promptorium parvulorum* (1440):

> **Suburbe** of a cyte or a wallyd town:
> *Suburbanum* . . .: *Suburbium* . . .

By contrast, we find in *Lesclarcissement*:

> **Subburbes the houses without a cytie or towne** faulx bourgz s ma.

Clearly, the differences do not suggest that Palsgrave copied from the *Promptorium*, but it may be worth looking at a specific group of nouns, those denoting animals. Palsgrave's list of such nouns is much richer than those of either the *Promptorium* or the *Catholicon Anglicum*. If he had had a manuscript copy of the *Catholicon* in front of him while working on his dictionary, one would have expected him to include all the animal nouns listed in that dictionary. But the following nouns, for instance, from the *Catholicon* do not figure in *Lesclarcissement*: *barbel* (first documentation in the *OED c.*1386), *blindworm* (*c.*1450), *carthorse* (1398), *crane* (*c.*1000), *dragon* (*c.*1220), *midge* (*c.*725), *mouldwarp* (*c.*1325), and *scrayfish* (1309–10), to adduce some nouns of the animal list. Four items of that list are first documented in the *Catholicon Anglicum*: *Gabriel-rache*, *goldworm*, *hagworm*, and *snig*.

The list of nouns denoting animals in the *Promptorium parvulorum* is of more interest because of the postlemmatic expansions. Again, we are struck by the number of nouns listed in the *Promptorium parvulorum* and not admitted to *Lesclarcissement*. Examples are: *beaver* (*c.*1000), *dragon* (*c.*1220), *hake* (*c.*1310),[17] *porcupine* (?*c.*1400),[18] and *tortoise* (1398),[19] to name some. According to the *OED*, the following nouns denoting animals, not included in *Lesclarcissement*, are first documented in the *Promptorium parvulorum*: *chaffinch*, *dotterel*, *garfish*, *greenling*, *kingfisher*,[20] *polliwog*, *rain-fowl*,[21] *scarbot*, *shepherd's dog*, and *scut*.

Apart from the animals actually in the two dictionaries, the generic or specific appositions given for their names also differ considerably. Table 6.3 lists some instances. There are further differences that look

[17] The item occurs in the 1440 edition only.
[18] The item occurs in the 1440 edition only.
[19] The form in the 1499 edition is *Torcute beste*. Torcuta, te.
[20] The item occurs in the 1440 edition only.
[21] The item occurs in the 1440 edition only.

TABLE 6.3. *A comparison of postlemmatic appositions for nouns denoting animals in the* Promptorium parvulorum *and* Lesclarcissement

| *Promptorium parvulorum* (1440) | *Lesclarcissement* |
|---|---|
| **Byttyl** wyrme . . . | **Bettle a blacke flye** |
| **Catrypel**, a worme Amonge frute | **Caterpyllar worme** |
| **Doo**, wyld beest | **Doo a beest** |
| **ffowne**, beeste | **Fawne a yonge dere** |
| **Hecfore**, beest | **Hecforde a yong cowe** |
| **Mows**, beeste | **Mouse a lytell beest** |
| **Muskyyt**, bryd | **Musket a lytell hauke** |
| **Nyte**, wyrme | **Nyt in a mannes heed** |
| **Pyion**, yong dove | **Pygion a byrde** |
| **Prik[et]**, beest | **Pricket a yonge dere** |

more systematic and that may be related to the authors' concept of the animal kingdom or to linguistic changes that had occurred.

In the medieval topical vocabularies edited by T. Wright, we encounter different classifications of the animal kingdom. The fifteenth-century *English Vocabulary* (Wright 1884/1968: cols. 633ff.), for instance, distinguishes five subkingdoms:

- nomina animalium
- nomina animalium ferarum
- nomina avium
- nomina piscium
- nomina vermium.

The *Mayer Nominale* of the same century has a further subdivision for the *nomina avium* and a group of *nomina muscarum* (Wright 1884/1968: cols. 679ff.).

- nomina animalium domesticorum
- nomina ferarum
- nomina volatilium domesticorum
- nomina volatilium incomestilium
- nomina piscium
- nomina vermium et muscarum.

The classification in the *Pictorial Vocabulary* goes one step further and differentiates between different types of fish (Wright 1884/1968: cols. 757ff.):

- nomina animalium domesticarum
- nomina animalium ferorum
- nomina avium domesticarum
- nomina avium ferorum
- nomina piscium aquarum recencium
- nomina piscium marinorum
- nomina vermium
- nomina muscarum.

Neither the compiler of the *Promptorium parvulorum* nor Palsgrave classify all the animals listed in their respective dictionaries, but, from the animals listed and the appositions provided, we may derive the authors' idea of the animal kingdom. As to 'beests', both distinguish three types: beasts in general, wild beasts (very few are labelled), and water beasts. *Ootyr* is called a 'water beeste' in the *Promptorium* (1440); Palsgrave does not use the term as a generic classification, but his word list includes *a water leche* and a *water serpent*. The *Catholicon Anglicum* includes *watir edyr*. The description of birds shows some striking differences. Both specify a group that is characterized by their habitat, the sea or water. The items listed, however, differ: the *Promptorium* (1440) has *Doppare*, water byrde, and *Mowe*, bryd or see mowe, the *Catholicon Anglicum* has *Semawe*, and *Lesclarcissement* lists *See cobbe a byrde* as well as *water hen*. The generic term in the *Promptorium* is bird. 'Fowl' is used only in the following cases: *Gandyr*, byrd, or ffovle, *Storke*, bryd, or fowle, *Totte*, fowle. It looks as if the compiler was not quite sure with respect to the classification of the gander and the stork. *Reyne fowle* itself is also regarded as a bird. The 1499 edition has only *Gander*, *Storke*, birde, and *Reyne fowle*.

In *Lesclarcissement*, *fowl* as a generic noun is much more prominent, Table 6.4 lists some examples. Not all of the birds listed, however—for example, *eagle* and *heron*,—are domestic fowl.

'Fish' seems to be the most regularly applied generic term in the two dictionaries. We come to the *nomina vermium*. Here, again, there is a noteworthy difference between the *Promptorium parvulorum* and *Lesclarcissement*. The generic term in the *Promptorium* is *worm*, as in the medieval vocabularies, but Palsgrave uses *worm* and *serpent*, as can be seen from the examples in Table 6.5. Other serpents included in *Lesclarcissement*, but not included in the *Promptorium*, are *Aspycke* and *Basylike*.

'Flye' as a generic term is rare in the *Promptorium* (e. g. *Scarbote*, flye), but less so in *Lesclarcissement*: *Bettle a blacke flye*, *Brese a long flye*, *Drone bee flye*, *Flesshe flye*, *Flyeng dragon a long flye*, *Gadde bee a flye*, *Globerde a flye*, *Gnatte a flye*, etc.

TABLE 6.4. *A comparison of* bird *and* fowl *in postlemmatic apposition*

| *Promptorium parvulorum* (1440) | *Lesclarcissement* |
|---|---|
| — | **Dawe a foule** |
| **Egyl**, byrde (**Ogyll** [*sic*] 1499) | **Egle a foule** |
| **Gandyr**, byrd, or ffovle (**Gander** 1499) | **Gandre a foule** |
| **Goos** (also 1499) | **Gose a foule** |
| **Henne** (also 1499) | **Henne a foule** |
| **Heryn**, bryd (also 1499) | **Herne a foule** |
| **Ostrych**, bryd (also 1499) | **Hostryge a foule** |
| | **Ostrydge a byrde** |
| **Koke**, bryd (**Kocke** 1499) | **Kocke a foule** |

TABLE 6.5. *A comparison of* worm *and* serpent *in postlemmatic apposition*

| *Promptorium parvulorum* (1440) | *Lesclarcissement* |
|---|---|
| **Cocetryce** (also 1499) | **Cockeatrice a serpent** |
| **Kokatryce** (also 1499) | **Kockeatryce sarpent** |
| **Cryket** (also 1499) | **Cricket a worme** |
| **Pismere** (also 1499) | **Pysmyre a lytell worme** |
| **Scorpyon**, wyrme (also 1499) | **Scorpion a serpent** |

The generic terms discussed so far do not, however, exhaust the terms used in the *Promptorium* and *Lesclarcissement*. In both dictionaries an attempt is made to single out the young. The *Promptorium* (1440) specifies the young in the following cases: *Colt*, yonge hors, *Dowve*, yonge byrde, *ffoole*, yong hors, *Lam*, yong shepe, *Lombe*, yonge scheppe, *Pyion*, yong dove, *Pulte*, yonge henne, *Rabet*, ȝong cony. *Whelp* is defined as a 'lytyl hounde'. In *Lesclarcissement* we find: *Choughe a yong crowe*, *Colte a yong horse*, *Cubbe a yong foxe*, *Fawne a yonge dere*, *Foole a colte*, *Hecforde a yong cowe*, *Hoggerell a yong shepe*, *Poled a yonge tode*, *Pricket a yonge dere*, *Rabet a yong cony*, *Sokelyng a yong befe*, *Sokelyng a yong calfe*, and *Sorell a yonge bucke*. There is a total of twenty instances, and only three (*colt*, *foal*, and *rabbit*) are common to both.

Two further animals deserve our attention: the dog and the horse. Dogs are mostly classified by a generic term, and, again, there is an

TABLE 6.6. *A comparison of* dog *and* hound *in postlemmatic apposition*

| *Promptorium parvulorum* (1440) | *Lesclarcissement* |
|---|---|
| **Bycche** hounde (also 1499) | **Bytche a she dogge** |
| **Blode hownd** (also 1499) | **Blode hounde** |
| — | **Bucke hounde** |
| — | **Curre dogge** |
| **Dogge** (also 1499) | **Dogge a beest** |
| **Dogge**, schepherdis hounde (also 1499) | — |
| — | **Dogge a mischevous curre** |
| **Gresehounde** (also 1499) | **Gray hounde** |
| **Hownd** (also 1499) | **Hounde** |
| **Mastyf**, hounde | **Mastyfe dogge** |
| **Mestyfe**, hound (also 1499) | |
| **Ratch**, hound (also 1499) | **Rache hounde** |
| **Scheperdys doge** (also 1499) | — |
| **Spanyel**, hound (also 1499) | **Spanyell a dogge** |
| **Terryare**, hound (not in 1499) | **Taryer a dogge** |
| | **Terryer a dogge** |
| **Whelp**, lytyl hounde (1499 **Whelp** only) | **Whelpe** |

interesting linguistic difference between the two dictionaries (see Table 6.6). In the *Promptorium* the generic word is still *hound*, while in *Lesclarcissement* it is *dog*, *hound* being used when it forms part of the name itself, in compound words.[22]

'Horse' is also used as a generic term, but here it is not its use that is striking so much as the variety of horses named in *Lesclarcissement* (see Table 6.7).

The inclusion and the treatment of nouns denoting animals in *Lesclarcissement* reveal Palsgrave's overall independence of the two English–Latin dictionaries compiled before he began his work. Further support comes from the fact that Palsgrave's animal kingdom is occasionally explicitly described as one where there are male and female animals. Like *Lesclarcissement*, the *Catholicon* and the *Promptorium parvulorum*, it is true, list names of male and female animals—for examples, *cock* and *hen*, or *horse* and *mare*—but they do not attempt to define such instances as male and female pairs of a species.

[22] That *rache hound* must have been common besides *rache* is evidenced by the quotations in the *OED*.

TABLE 6.7. *A comparison of the names of horses listed in* Lesclarcissement, *the* Catholicon Anglicum, *and the* Promptorium parvulorum

| *Lesclarcissement* | *Catholicon Anglicum* | *Promptorium parvulorum* (1440) |
|---|---|---|
| Amblyng horse | an Ambler | Avmlar, hors (1499 Aumlinge hors) |
| Bayart a horse | — | — |
| Blacke horse | — | — |
| Capull a horse a | Capylle | Capulle, or capyl, hors (1499 Capull hors) |
| Colte a yong horse | a Colte | Colt, yonge hors (1499 Colte or fole) |
| Foole a colte | a Foyle | ffoole, yong hors (1499 Foole) |
| Coursar horse | a Cowrssor | Cowrcer, hors (also 1499) |
| Fore horse | — | — |
| Geldyng a horse | — | Geldyng, or gelt hors (also 1499) |
| Graye horse | — | — |
| Great horse a courser | — | — |
| Hackeney horse | an Haknay | Hakney, hors (1499 Hakeney) |
| Horse in Gascoyne speche | — | — |
| Horse a beest | an Horse | Hors, gelte or gelt hors (1499 Hors) |
| Iade a dull horse | — | — |
| Iustyng horse | — | — |
| Light horse | — | — |
| Mare a she beest | a Mare<br>a Mere | Mere, hors (also 1499) |
| Nagge a horse | a Nag | Nagge, a lytyl beeste (not in 1499) |
| Palfray a beest | a Palfray | Palfrey (also 1499) |
| Sompter horse | — | Somonour hors (also 1499) |
| Stallant a horse }<br>Stalume horse } | Sstaloñ | Stalyone, hors (also 1499) |
| Stede a horse | a Steed | Stede, hors (also 1499) |
| Stonde horse | — | — |
| Trotter a horse | a Trotter | Trottare, hors (also 1499) |

By contrast, Palsgrave uses the pronouns *he* and *she* to distinguish between the male and the female when this distinction is necessitated by the existence of two different words in French:

| | |
|---|---|
| **Asse a he beest** | asne s ma. |
| **Asse a she beest** | asnesse s. fe. |

In other cases he uses these pronouns to define the name of an animal that is specific to the male or the female kind:

| | |
|---|---|
| **Bytche a she dogge** | chienne s fe. |
| **Cocke a he byrde** | cocq s ma. |
| **Mare a she beest** | ivment s fe. |

Sometimes they are part of the lemma itself. There is a group of *she*-lemmata, but none for *he*-headwords (e.g. *Sche lyparde, Sche lyon, Sche beare, Sche ratte, Sche wolfe*).

Were there any precedents in earlier lexicographical works which Palsgrave might have followed? Explicit sex distinctions in the description of animals in fifteenth-century vocabularies are rare, and they vary from word list to word list. In the *English Vocabulary* (Wright 1884/1968: col. 640) the distinction is referred to in Latin:

*Hic pardus,* $A^{ce}$ leparde
*Hec parda, est femella*

In the *Mayer Nominale* (Wright 1884/1968: col. 698), we have an English equivalent as well as the specification 'uxor ejus' in Latin. The English item signalling the sex is the pronoun *she*:

*Hec caprella,* a sche gatt

An example for the Latin 'equivalent' is:

*Hic lupus,* $A^{cce}$ a wolffe
*Hec lupa, uxor ejus*

In the *Pictorial Vocabulary* (Wright 1884/1968: cols. 758 ff.), there are two instances of an English equivalent and three different Latin solutions:

*Hic caniculus,* a qwelpe
*Hic catulus, idem est*
*Hec catula,* a byche qwelpe

*Hic lupus,* $A^{ce}$ a wulfe
*Hec lupa,* $A^{ce}$ a femel wulfe

*Hic ursus,* $A^{ce}$ a bere
*Hec ursa, idem est*

*Hic columbus,* }
*Hec columba,* } a dowe

*The function of postlemmatic expansions*

Why did Palsgrave apparently feel the need to add some specification after the headword in so many cases? The easiest assumption would be that he was not responsible for these additions, but took them over from his sources. Since I have not come across an early English word list that resembles Palsgrave's in the style of postmodifications, I shall discard this possibility. We have to look for other explanations.

At the end of his introduction to the noun word list Palsgrave explains his lexicographical arrangement as follows:

> And nowe that I haue here in this thirde boke declared at length/ what accidentes and properties belong vnto all the substãtyues in the frenche tong/ I shall here cõsequently set forthe/ what and howe many substantyues there be in the same tong/ whiche to thentent they may of euery lernar the more easely be foũde/ whan he hath any sentence or mater to be made out of our tong in to the frenche/ I shall set forthe all the englysshe substantyues in our tong/ after the order of a/b/c/ and in the same lyne shewe what substantyues in the frenche tonge is of lyke signification. (III, fo. xvi)

From this we learn that the orientation chosen by Palsgrave in his bilingual dictionary was that from native-language English to the foreign-language French and that the work was intended as an encoding dictionary. We might, therefore, reasonably expect that one of Palsgrave's concerns will have been to make sure that his users would be able to find the English item they might want to express in French. An alphabetical organization of language makes words stand next to each other which do not usually co-occur in texts. This holds above all for words of similar or identical spelling. We know that Palsgrave was aware of homographs when writing *Lesclarcissement*, because the third book contains a list of French homographs. A mere listing of homographic lemmata in English with their French translation equivalents in the following fashion would be unsatisfactory:

| | |
|---|---|
| **Lydde** | paulpiere s fe. |
| **Lydde** | covueleque s fe. |

English learners of French would not have been able to pair the right words in order to exclude such sentences as **Elle couvrit le pot d'une paupière* (paulpiere) or **Elle était très nerveuse, ses couvercles* (*covueleques*) *tremblaient* . . . Nor would numerical differentiation by superscript figures have been of any value:

| | |
|---|---|
| **Lydde**$^{1}$ | paulpiere s fe. |
| **Lydde**$^{2}$ | covueleque s fe. |

The best means of helping users to identify headwords and their translations with no difficulty would obviously be an explicit disambiguation. This is exactly what Palsgrave achieves with his postmodifications. His listing of the items *lydde* reads as follows:

| | |
|---|---|
| **Lydde of the eye** | paulpiere s fe. |
| **Lydde of a cuppe or potte/** | covueleque s fe. |

The syntactic postmodifications 'of the eye' and 'of a cuppe or potte' literally spell out which *lydde* is lexicographically intended.

When I used the term 'homograph' earlier on, I did not explicitly define it, but used it in its commonly accepted meaning, which *Collins English Dictionary* gives as 'one of a group of words spelt in the same way but having different meanings'. This obviously raises the question of whether there are two different words *lid* in English or whether there is only one word *lid* with two different senses. The more central question, however, is what constitutes a word lexicographically. The traditional convention in modern dictionaries is to regard semantically relatable meanings of one linguistic form as different senses correlating with that form and to regard this form-multiple-meaning unit as a word. If, in the mind of the lexicographer, a semantic link cannot be established or at least not in a plausible way, different form-meaning units—i.e. different lexicographical words—are set up. Scholars have, of course, long noted that this conventional procedure is theoretically unsatisfactory. A mere glance at the varying practice in different modern English dictionaries will suffice to illustrate how arbitrary is the postulation of lexicographical words. When Palsgrave compiled his bilingual English–French dictionary, he could not fall back on an established tradition in vernacular dictionary-writing of what to treat as a lexicographical word and what as a mere sense of a word. Homographs and different senses of a word in the modern sense of the terms must, therefore, have been on the same theoretical level for Palsgrave and as such treated alike: the lexicographical identification is made unambiguous by syntactic postmodifications and all are treated as main entries. In actual practice, this does not mean for Palsgrave that each member of a homographic lemma set is provided with an identifying postmodification. There are many instances where one member of the set is left unspecified, as in:

| | |
|---|---|
| **Chest** | coffre s ma. |
| **Chest of a man** | fovrcelle, pis. |
| **Price estymation** | estime s fe. |
| **Price** | pris ma. |
| **Price of any thyng** | ualue s fe. |

The principle of disambiguating homograph sets can explain a substantial number of Palsgrave's complex lemma entries, but it does not account for all. We therefore have to look for other possible explanations. One could come from the life history of the items in question. As we have seen in Chapters 4 and 5, in a good number of cases Palsgrave explicitly recorded lexical items that were dropping out of general use. But the English language of his time was characterized by a tremendous expansion in vocabulary and so we might well expect that Palsgrave's word lists include relative neologisms. In recording such items he may have felt it necessary to provide the English word with some explanation before giving its French equivalent. Instances where this is plausible include:

**Dromslade/ suche as almayns vse in warre** bedons s ma.

The now obsolete item *drumslade, dromslade* in the meaning 'a drum, or some form of a drum' was certainly a neologism at Palsgrave's time and its first record in the *OED* dates from 1527, the entry from *Lesclarcissement* being only the second citation.

Consider also:

**Flappe that couereth the wynde pype** la loette de la gorge s fe.

In the anatomical sense of epiglottis, the noun *flap* is first recorded in the *OED* for *c.1550* but this is antedated by Palsgrave's entry.

The item *lavell* is given the same French translation:

**Lauell that standeth in the myddes of the throte** alovette s fe.

According to the *OED*, Palsgrave was the first to record the use of the item. The only other citation provided by the *OED* is from 1847.

A special London usage was also new in Palsgrave's time:

**Flete a prisone for gentylman** consergerie s fe.

The *OED* lists the entry from *Lesclarcissement* under sense 2 of the noun *fleet*, which provides an explanation for the term: '**the Fleet**: a run of water, flowing into the Thames between Ludgate Hill and Fleet Street, now a covered sewer; called also **Fleet ditch**; hence the prison which stood near it'.

For the noun *gag*, Palsgrave's entry, which reads as follows:

**Gagge to sette in ones mouthe** baillon s ma.

antedates the first *OED* recording (1553) by some twenty years.

An unusual instance is the noun *glum*, which *Lesclarcissement* describes as follows:

**Glumme a sower loke** rechigne s fe.

The *OED* has three citations of the word, the first dating from 1523, the second, also from Skelton's work, from 1529, and the last is from Palsgrave.

None of the neologisms discussed so far represent linguistic borrowings from French. In the following examples, the English headword clearly corresponds to the lexical item in French, and

Palsgrave's postlemmatic appositions look like English explanations of the respective item newly taken over from French:

> **Cressent the newe mone as long as it is nat rounde** cressant s ma.

Palsgrave's entry is the first citation in the *OED*. The same holds for the following entries:

> **Fayle an vpparmost garment of a woman** faille s fe.
> **Somersault a lepe of a tombler** sobersault x ma.

These examples are not the results of a systematic check. It was rather the postlemmatic expansion in each case that prompted me to look the headword up.

In other instances, there is a match between the French equivalent and the English headword, but the latter is not followed by a full English meaning paraphrase. Instead, the new English borrowing from French is described in terms of 'a kind of . . .':

> **Nauquayre a kynde of instrument** naquair s fe.

The corresponding entry in the *OED* provides us with the following information: '†**na'quaire**. *Obs. rare*. . . . A naker, kettledrum. **1523** LD. BERNERS *Froiss*. I.cxlvii, 176 The kyng . . . entred into the towne with trumpets, tabours, nakquayres & hornyes'. The only other citation is from *Lesclarcissement*.

> **Prune a kynde of frute** prune s fe.

Palsgrave's entry is the first attestation in the *OED* of this sense of the noun.

> **Sorbe a kynde of frute** sorbe s fe.

The *OED* defines *sorb* as 'the fruit of the service-tree . . . a service-berry'.

And, finally, there are complex lemma entries where the whole English noun phrase constitutes a free syntactic unit which looks like the description of a semantic unit that is lexicalized in French. Examples are:

> **Boke that sheweth the actes and order in a iourney.** uoyagier s ma.
> **Finesse of golde or syluer at the touche** karas ma.
> **Outar lyne or parte of a cercle** circumference s fe.
> **Syde of a boke that is written** pagee z fe.

*Voyager* does not occur in the *OED* in the meaning given by Palsgrave, though, of course, *carat*, *circumference*, and *page* do. The first *OED* attestations for *carat* and *page* are post-1530. The case of *circumference* is slightly more complicated. Palsgrave's lemma entry includes two senses of circumference, the line itself and a part of it. In the sense of a whole circle the word is recorded as early as 1393 (Gower). Palsgrave's second sense is also the *OED*'s sense **2**, 'In looser use: †**a**. A part of the circumference, an arc. *Obs.*', but, unaware of Palsgrave's use, the *OED* dates the first and only citation from 1656.

What is the lexicographical significance of Palsgrave's pairing of English free syntagmas with French lexicalized items? In view of Palsgrave's own statement that his lexicographical orientation was from English to French, one might suggest that he was trying to achieve something that is ignored in most modern bilingual dictionaries: to make lexicalizations in the foreign tongue recoverable for which the mother-tongue expressions are not lexicalized. Such an approach would imply that the word list in an alphabetical dictionary could include onomasiological clusters. One such onomasiological cluster is, for instance, 'someone having to do with something' or 'someone doing something'. Thus *Lesclarcissement* has a number of unlexicalized English headword entries with *man*. Examples are:

| | |
|---|---|
| **Man that vseth magicke** | magicien s ma. |
| **Man that loketh a squynt** | lovche s ma. |
| **Man with a morres pike** | picquier s ma. |

In the case of *man*, the onomasiological cluster was not prompted by a morphological pattern in the target language, French. The same would hold for *thing*, for which there are a number of unlexicalized lemma entries, as well as for *great*. Examples are:

| | |
|---|---|
| **Thyng beyond the mountaygne** | transmontaigne s ma. |
| **Thyng by it selfe** | particularite fe. |
| **Thyng layd vp in store** | repostaille s fe. |
| **Great eater** | glovtton s ma. briffre s ma. |
| **Great drinker** | biberon s ma. |
| **Great rude clothe** | bureau x ma. |

If the foreign language has a morphological pattern for a certain concept, then such onomasiological devices might be expected. Such a pattern exists in French for the female counterpart of a noun denoting a male. No wonder, therefore, that *Lesclarcissement* includes a set of lemma entries headed by *woman*. Derivational patterns may also lead to the clustering of lemma entries. French has a number of suffixes to indicate youngness and/or smallness—e.g. *-eau/-ceau*, *-et/-ette*, *-on/-onne*, and so on. The young aspect is reflected in the following entries from *Lesclarcissement:*

| | |
|---|---|
| **Yongman a seruaunt** | ualeton s ma. |
| | ualleton s ma. iouuenceau x ma. |
| **Yonge lyon a beest** | leonceau s. ma. |
| **Yonge leke** | porreau. porret s ma. |
| **Yonge haare** | leuereau s ma. |
| **Yonge rabbet** | laperiau s ma. |
| **Yonge rauyn** | corbineau s ma. |

The case of *lytell* is of particular interest, and the items are worth listing in full:

| | |
|---|---|
| **Lytell streame** | undette s fe. |
| **Lytell bell** | sounette campane s fe. |
| **Lytell bell for a horse trapper/** | clochette s fe. |
| **Lytell broke** | rvisselet s ma |
| **Lytell chese** | fromaige dengelon s fe. |
| **Lytell bagge** | sachet z ma. |
| **Lytell vyne that beareth grapes** | uignette s fe. |
| **Lytell fynger** | petit doigt z ma. |
| **Lytell serpent** | serpenteav x ma. |
| **Lytell porcyon of any thynge** | tantinet z ma. |
| **Lytell coffre a focer** | cofret z ma. |
| **Lytell shelde** | targette s fe. |
| **Lytell visage** | troignette s fe. |
| **Lytell vermyne** | ueminette s fe. |
| **Lytell ryuer** | riuierette s fe. |
| **Lytell table** | tableau x ma. |
| **Lytell Pares balle** | estevf z ma. |
| **Lytell chery** | cerisette s fe. |
| **Lytell lambe** | aignelet z ma. |
| **Lytell lane** | alee, ruellette s fe. |
| **Lytell cornar** | anglet z ma. |
| **Lytell bowe** | archelet z ma. |
| **Lytell guyrdell** | ceincturette s fe. |
| **Lytell songe** | chansonnette s fe. |
| **Lytell pratye thyng** | chosette s fe. |
| **Lytell boke** | libelle, liuret z ma. |
| **Lytell lodge** | logette s fe. |
| **Lytell house** | maisonnette s fe. |
| **Lytell teate** | mamellette s fe. |
| **Lytell flye** | mouchette s. fu. [*sic*] |
| **Lytell bote** | nasselleté s fe. |
| **Lytell goddes** | nim hette s fe. |
| **Lytell byrde** | oyselet z fe. |
| **Lytell spangle** | paillette s fe. |
| **Lytell sheparde** | pastoureau x ma. |

| | |
|---|---|
| **Lytell woode** | petit bois ma. |
| **Lytell fether** | plnmette s fe. [*sic*] |
| **Lytell fysshe** | poissonnetté s fe. |
| **Lytell boughe** | rainceau x ma. |
| **Lytell rayne for a horse** | regnetté s fe. |

*Little finger* is among the few of these *little*-items that are lexicalized in English. Some, like *little lamb* and *little house*, may be colloquial, as perhaps another headword entry: *Goodly yonge man* in the meaning of *beau fils*.

There is no doubt that the part of these entries which determines their place within the word list is the item *lytell*. Since Palsgrave specified that the English items of his list were arranged according to the order of the *ABC*, one might expect that it would be the nouns premodified by *lytell* that were given in alphabetical order, but this is not the case. However, the French translations from *aignelet* onwards encompassing the last twenty-two items, are indeed in alphabetical order. This does not mean that Palsgrave's approach was so different from modern lexicographical practice that he observed alphabetical order for the translation equivalents and not the English lemmata. There are two possible explanations. One might be that Palsgrave had compiled a little list of French diminutives for teaching purposes and that he brought this list into *Lesclarcissement*. The other possibility would be that this set of twenty-two French items in alphabetical order stems from a still unidentified source of *Lesclarcissement*, perhaps a French–English word list. Palsgrave would then simply have inverted the order of the lemmata and their equivalents. This would hold equally for a word list as a part of a little language book that had a section on word-formation or on the suffixes *-eau*, *-et*, *-ette*, for most of the French items are diminutives with these endings. The source could equally have been one that matched French with Latin or Dutch. In that case Palsgrave would have translated the French lemmata into English and then inverted lemmata and equivalents. It thus looks as if this small section of alphabetized French equivalents in *Lesclarcissement* might lead us to one of Palsgrave's ultimate sources.

Before tackling the lemma structure of the next word class, adjectives, a final word has to be said about the macro-structure of the noun list. Palsgrave himself describes it as alphabetical, but in early English dictionary-making alphabetical order does not yet mean that it is consistently alphabetical throughout. The question that arises is whether postlemmatic expansions which are printed in the same fount as the lemma are taken into account for the alphabetical arrangement. This is difficult to resolve where alphabetical order itself is not systematic. In addition, one has the impression that alphabetical order is occasionally superseded by pronunciation. A sequence such as *Flag or baner of a felde*, *Flagge that groweth*, *Flaget*, *Flagon* seems to disregard the double consonant and final *e* in *flagge*. Other typical cases are the spelling variants of *y* and *i*—for example, *Mayden a louer*, *Mayde of the mankynde*, *Maide of the woman kynde*, *Mayde a seruaunt*—etc., the alternation between *c* and *s* for /s/—e.g. *Pensell a lytell baner*, *Pencell to paynt with*, *Pensyfenesse*, etc.—between *o* and *ou*—e. g. *Priour*, *Prioresse*, *Priore*, and the alternation between *c* and *k* for /k/, e. g. *Pariury*, *Parke for dere*, *Parcar a man*, *Parlyament*, etc. In the still rather unsystematic order that seems to take into account spelling and pronunciation, postlemmatic expansions are as unsystematically considered for the macro-structure as other lemma entries.

## ADJECTIVES

The table of adjectives is much smaller than that of nouns. In the list of nouns, clashes between the word class purported to be recorded and that actually occurring in the lemma are rare, but in the list of adjectives there are more of such questionable instances. In some cases Palsgrave's material seems to have been mixed up, as in

> **Awkwarde men rynge aukewarde** on sonne enbrasle.

Others suggest lemmatization difficulties on Palsgrave's part. Thus lemma entries with *he* and *thyng* as the lemma proper are grammatically nouns, whereas the French equivalents are adjectives. They typically represent non-lexicalized lemma entries in English:

> **He that hath but one hande** ma.
> manquet s. fe. manquette s. ma.
> manchet s. fe. manchette s.
> **Thyng at the ordre of an other thyng**
> ma. subiect z. fe. subiecte s.

An odd instance is the entry

> **Weddyng/ belongyng to maryage**
> ma. nuptial x. fe. nuptialle s.

The noun *wedding* has an adjectival explanation, and one may wonder whether Palsgrave had *wedding* in a premodifying function in mind, as in *wedding ceremony*, *wedding house*, etc. The lemma would then be a first instance in an English dictionary where a premodifying noun is lexicographically given a quasi-adjective status.

And, finally, there are cases where the lemma proper in English is an adjective, but the following postlemmatic explanation incorporates a noun head so that the whole functions grammatically as a noun phrase:

> **Bonysshe/ one that hath great bones/** ma. ossu s. fe ossue s.
> **Fearfull a thyng that dothe make one afrayed** ma. terrible s. ma. et fe. redoutable s. ma. et fe. espouentable s.
> **Nauygable/ a water able to be sayled or rowed in** ma. et fe. nauigable s.

*Formal aspects and reference point*

With nouns, we noted several 'doublets'—that is, lemma entries which list the same lemma either in a different alphabetical place, or in a varying spelling, or with another postlemmatic expansion. This phenomenon is rare with adjectives, as in:

> **Olde or aged** ma. ancien s. fe. ancienne s. ma. et fe. antique s. ma. et fe. anticque s. ma. vieul x. fe. vieulle s.
> **Olde** ma. viel z. fe. vielle s. ma. vieulx fe. vieuse s. ma. ancien s. fe. ancienne s.

The pairing of spelling variants in one lemma entry, as in *Hyghe or hye*, is very rare. Unlike the *Catholicon*, but as in the noun list, there is no cross-reference system for adjectives. The following pair is exceptional, including a Latin cross-reference which relates to the French equivalents:

> **Mortall deedly** ma. mortel z. fe. mortelle s.
> **Mortell** idem.

In general, the use of an adjective is not illustrated, but exceptions include:

> **Disceassed** ma. feu s. fe. feue s.
> **Kyng Henry late disceased** le feu roy Henry.
> **Uery good/** fort bon, **veryest foole/** le plus fol, **to the very herte/** ou fyn cueur.

This last example might, however, be interpreted as a dictionary entry with idiomatic expressions of *very*. It would then constitute an exception because the adjective list consists of main entries only.

As with nouns, the authorial reference point is the third-person singular, predominantly with the form *one* for 'someone, a person' as in:

> **Bleare eyed as one is where the reed skynne apereth outwarde** ma. raillieux fe. raillieuse s.
> **Chypped as ones face or handes is ẇ the marche wynde** ma. et fe. gerce s.

The use of *man* in the meaning of 'someone, a person' is exceptional, and is generally used in contrast to *woman* or *beest*, as in:

> **Fayre as a woman or man is of their vysage** ma. specieux fe. specieuse s.
> **Croke backed as a man or beest is** ma. courbe fe. courbee.

*Person* is rare:

> **Priuate/ belõgyng to a persons owne selfe** ma. priuat s. fe. priuatte s.

In two cases, *folks* is used:

> **Murmuryng/ grutchynge as folkes that be nat contented** ma. murmuratif z. fe. murmuratifue s.
> **Pytyfull or pytuouse as a chaũce that moueth folkes to pytie** ma. et fe. piteable s. ma. et fe. miserable s.

*Types of headword structure*

Let us now have a closer look at the structure of the adjective lemma entries. An adjective lemma entry may consist of a single lexical item, a simple adjective (including both participles), a derived adjective, or a compound adjective. It may also be more complex and have a postlemmatic expansion. We may distinguish the following restrictive postmodifications.

1. The lemma is followed by a prepositional phrase:

> **Absẽt from a place.** m. absẽt s. f. absẽte s.
> **Desyrouse of honour or promocyon** ma. ambicieux fe. ambicieuse s.

2. The lemma is followed by an infinitive (plus complement) clause:

> **Harde to vnderstande** ma. difficil s. fe. difficille s.
> **Pleasante to beholde** ma. grcieux [*sic*] fe. gracieuse s.

3. The lemma is followed by a clause of comparison introduced by *such as* or *as*:

> **Brittle as a thyng ẏ wyll soone breke in sõdre** ma rompant s. fe. rõpante s.
> **Heary as one is vpon his handes or body.** ma. vellu s. fe. vellue s.
> ma. poilu s. fe. poilue s.

In general, the noun of which the adjective is predicated in such ostensive comparisons has the generic singular form, but occasionally the plural occurs:

> **Full/ heaped full as busshelles be with corne or salte** comble

These three types of restrictive postmodification are structurally the same as those outlined for nouns (see pp. 200–1,207).

Some postlemmatic expansions are appositional and we might distinguish the following types, many of which occur in combination:

1. The lemma proper is followed by another adjective which may be a participle:

> **Fayre/ beautyfull** ma. beau or bel. fe. belle s.
> **Obedyent obeyeng** ma. obedient s. fe. obediente s.
> **Pylled scalled** ma. tigneux fe. tigneuse s.

2. The lemma is followed by more than one adjective:

> **Clobysshe boystous onweldy** ma. lourt s. fe. lourde.

3. The lemma proper is followed by the coordinator *or* plus another adjective:

> **Hye or talle** ma. hault s. fe. haulte s.
> ma. bel, as bel homme.

4. The lemma proper is followed by two coordinated adjectives, the last conjoined by means of *or*:

> **Myserable wretched or myserouse** ma. et fe. miserable s.

5. The lemma proper is followed by a premodified simple or complex adjective phrase. The premodifier is predominantly a negative:

**Crafty craftely wrought** ma. artificieux fe. artificieuse s ma. fyn s. fe. fyne s.
**Hole nat broken** ma. entier s. fe. entiere s.
**Newe fangled/ nat cõstante and stedy of purpose** ma. et fe. muable s.

The negative premodifier is a characteristic in the glossing of adjectives.

6. The lemma proper is followed by a complex adjective phrase, having a present participle as head:

**Abydyng contynuyng in a place** ma. resident fe. residente s.

An interesting subgroup comprises adjective phrases introduced by 'belonging to':

**Musycall/ belongyng to musycke** ma. musical x. fe. musicalle s.

7. The lemma proper is followed by a complex adjective phrase, having a past participle as head:

**Baudy soyled with fylthe** ma. sally s. fe. sallye s.

8. The lemma proper is followed by a relative clause:

**Blynd that can nat se** ma. aueugle s.
**Daungerouse wherof daunger maye ensewe.** ma. dangereus fe. dangreuse s.

9. The lemma proper is followed by a prepositional phrase which is not a restrictive postmodification of the lemma:

**Glasye/ of the nature of glasse** ma. voiorreux fe. voierreuse s.
**Inordynate whout ordre or measure** ma. onordonne fe. onordonnee s.

For nouns we distinguished a third syntactic–semantic relationship between the lemma and the postlemmatic expansion: polysemous coordination by means of *or*. Coordination occurs with adjective lemma entries, but the polysemous nature of adjectives makes it more difficult to identify such cases. The adjective phrase following the conjunction *or* is usually a synonym of the headword. When *Eldyst*, for instance, is followed by *first begotten* (corresponding to

French *aisne*), we regard the two as clearly synonymous and therefore interpret the relationship as an appositive one. In other cases, full synonymy is more doubtful, making coordination a more likely relationship. For example:

> **Demure or sobre of countenance** ma. rassis fe. rassise s. ma. et fe. simple s.
> **Forked or braunched** ma. branchu s. fe. branchue s.

A clear case of coordination, though within the postlemmatic adjective phrase, is the example

> **Mylky of ẏ colour or nature of mylke** ma. lacteux fe. lacteuse s.

'Of the colour of milk' and 'of the nature of milk' are two different senses of the adjective *milky*.

Postlemmatic expansions joined by *and* are rare. The conjoined member constitutes a restrictive postmodification—that is, without this coordinated element we would have a different lemma. An example for nouns is

> **Pennar and ynkehorne** escriptoire s fe.

and for adjectives:

> **Large wyde ⁊ brode** ma. spacieux fe. spacieuse s. ma. et fe. ample s.

### *A comparison with the* Catholicon *and the* Promptorium

We turn now to the question of how innovative *Lesclarcissement* was in comparison with the *Catholicon Anglicum* and the *Promptorium parvulorum* in respect of adjective description.

The headword structure of adjectives in the *Catholicon* is very basic. In general, the headword entry consists of one lexical item. There are some restrictive postmodifications (types 1, 2, and 3). Occasionally, the adjective lemma is followed by a synonym, preceded by the coordinator *or*. A special feature of the *Catholicon Anglicum* is the lemma entry *like to* + *v* for Latin gerunds, as in:

> like to **Die**; *moribundus*.
> like to **Gruche**; *fremundus*.

In the *Promptorium parvulorum* (1499) the three types of restrictive postmodification occur:

> **Couetous of great Wordly goodes or ryches** Auarus ra rum.

**Heuy to bere.** Ponderosus sa sũ. Grauis ne.
**Drye as nete ẏͭ yeue no mylke** Exuberis re.

In addition, there are a number of restrictive coordinations by means of *and*. Most commonly, two English adjectives together capture the sense of the Latin adjective:

**Sly and fals togeder.** Subdosus sa sũ. Dolosus sa sũ. Versutus ta tũ. Versipellis le . . .

But there are also three and even four adjectives joined by means of *and*:

**Payed and quemed ⁊ pleased.** Placatus ta tũ.
**Large hye longe and semely.** Procerus ra rũ

We find examples for most of the adjective apposition types in the *Promptorium*. Syndetic coordination by means of *or* is common, but all the other types are rare. A characteristic of this dictionary (1440 and 1499) is to use the adverb of degree *somewhat* in paraphrasing adjectives:

**Dolled sumwhat hote.** Tepefactus ta tum

Two other features are worth noting because they are more fully developed in *Lesclarcissement*. There are three instances where the semantic paraphrase of a derived adjective has the form 'of *x*':

**Erthen or of erthe.** Terreus a um.
**Glasy or glasyn of glasse.** Vitreus a vm.

Adjectives ending in *-ly*, *-ous*, *-some*, and *-y* tend to be glossed as 'full of . . .' when they are given an English paraphrase:

**Lightsum or full of light.** Luminosus sa sũ
**Lyuely or quycke or full of life.** Uiuax cis . . .
**Pitiuous or full of pyte.** Pietitus ta tũ . . . Compassiuus a um.
**Wattry or ful of watyr.** Aquosus sa sum.

Compared to its predecessors, Palsgrave's list of adjectives reveals a systematic attempt at glossing the meaning of adjectives according to certain patterns. The wording of these postlemmatic glosses corresponds exactly to what modern monolingual English dictionaries would give as part of a description of the meaning of the adjectives in question. The following patterns are recurrent:

1. 'of the nature of':

**Aerysshe of the nature of the ayer**
ma. aerin s fe. aeryne s.
**Corallyke of the nature of corall.**
ma. coralin s fe. coraline s.

2. 'belonging to . . .':

> **Feldysshe belongynge to the feld** ma. et fe. champestre s.
> **Fraternall belongyng to a brother** ma. fraternel z. fe. fraternelle s.

Under *B* we find in addition a number of headwords beginning with 'belonging to'—as, for instance, *Belongyng to a mannes byrth*, *Belongyng to a shyppe*, *Belongyng to wytte of smellyng*, etc.

3. 'resembling':

> **Frosty/ resemblyng to the froste** ma. geleux fe. geleuse s.
> **Godly/ belongyng or resemblyng to god.** ma. et fe. deificque s. ma. deuin s. fe. deuine s.

Many derived adjectives in *-full*, *-ish*, *-ly*, *-ous*, and *-y* are glossed as 'full of . . .':

> **Thoughtfull/ full of thought or heauynesse** ma. soucieux fe. soucieuse s. ma. pencif z. fe. pencifue s.
> **Knottysshe knorrishe or full of knotes** ma. neueux fe. neueuse s.
> **Lyuely full of lyfe** ma. vif z. fe. vifue s. ma. vital x. fe. vitalle s.
> **Pompouse full of pompe or pride** ma. pompeux fe. pompeuse s.
> **Fylthy/ full of fylthe or vnclenlye** ma. villain s. fe. villaine s.

Unparalleled in the *Catholicon* and *Promptorium* are Palsgrave's adjective glosses in the form of a relative clause:

> **Blynd that can nat se** ma. aueugle s.
> **Paynefull/ that may endure payne** ma. et fe. penible s.

For adjectives ending in *-able*, *-ible* Palsgrave has the following paraphrases:

1. 'able/not able':

> **Flexyble/ able to be bowed** ma. et fe. flexyble s.
> **Ineuytable nat able to be auoyded** ma. et fe. ineuitable s.

2. 'apte/mete to':

> **Corrumpable apte or mete to be corrupted** ma. et fe. corrumpable s.

3. 'that may/can':

**Excusable that may be excused** ma.
et fe. excusable s.
**Inuysible that can nat be sene** ma.
et fe. inuisible s.

4. 'worthy to':

**cõmendable worthye to be cõmended**
cõmendable s.

Yet Palsgrave's pioneering methodological approach does not only manifest itself in the English explanations of the meaning of adjectives. It also emerges from his treatment of colours and, here again, reveals his independence from his two predecessors. One of the difficulties for lexicographers in describing colours is to decide whether the noun or the adjective is to be made the basic word. In the *Catholicon* and the *Promptorium*, the Latin equivalent tells the user whether the headword entry is a noun or an adjective. The majority of words denoting colours are treated as adjectives. In *Lesclarcissement* most colour words are also entered as adjectives, but some are entered as nouns. The only double listing is the colour *crimson*. The postlemmatic expansion, however, is often the same. Thus under the nouns we have *Byce a colour*, *Crane colour*, *Crymosin colour*, *Horse flesshe colour*, *Kenet coloure*, etc., and among the adjectives we find *Blewe colour*, *Browne a colour*, *Cramosyn colour*, etc. A more adjective-like form of postlemmatic expansion is 'of colour', as in *Reed of colowre*, or 'coloured', as in *Gray coloured as ones eyes be*.

The *Catholicon* and the *Promptorium* (1440 and 1499) include colour words which we do not find in *Lesclarcissement*—for instance, *Synoper* and *Vermiloun*. The Mayhew edition of the *Promptorium* lists *Ruddy* and *Tuly*, which do not occur in the *Catholicon*, the printed 1499 edition of the *Promptorium*, or *Lesclarcissement*. Both versions of the *Promptorium* include *Gaude grene*, but the printed edition is unique in having *Burnet* (Palsgrave has *burned blacke*) and *Syse*. Colour terms which occur only in *Lesclarcissement* include *Crane colour*, *Crymosin colour*, *Horse flesshe colour*, *Kenet coloure*, *Lyght grene*, *Popyniaye colour*, *Naturall colour*, *Puke coloure*, *Roselyke of the coloure of a rose*, *Saddle tawney coloured*, and *Safronnysshe of y coloure of safrone*.

Since the *Catholicon* tends to group word families, there are some verbs like *to be Grene*, *to be White*, *to mak White*, *to be ȝalowe*, as well as noun derivatives in *-ness* such as *Whittnesse* and *ȝalownes*. The *Promptorium*, too, lists some derived nouns, as *Blacknesse*, *Greynes*,

*Grenehede*, *Swartnesse*, *Whytnes* and *ȝelownesse*. In view of these precedents, it comes as a surprise that Palsgrave does not list abstract colour nouns in *-ness*, though, unlike his predecessors, he has a number of derived adjectives in *-ish*:

**Blackysshe** ma. et fe. noyrastre.
**Blewisshe** ma. azurin s fe. azurine s.
**Doskysshe**
**of colour** ma. subz brun.
**Grenysshe** ma. et fe. verdastre s.
**Swarte or Swartysshe/**
**burned blacke** ma. et fe. noyrastre s.
**Whytysshe** ma. et fe. blanchastre s.
**Yelowysshe** ma. et fe. iaunastre s.

As we can see, most of these formations correspond to a similar French pattern with *-astre*, confirming once more Palsgrave's awareness of word-formational structures.

### *The function of postlemmatic expansions*

We come to the function of the postlemmatic expansions for adjectives. In the case of nouns I suggested that there is a complex of interrelated functions. One of them is the discrimination of homographic sets. With adjective lemmata, this function is also prominent, although the overall number of actually co-occurring homographs is much smaller than that for nouns. Examples are:

**Dull of wytte** ma. lourt s. fe. lourde s.
**Dull at the spurre as a horse is** ma. restif z. fe. restifue s.
**Dull of edge** ma. et fe. agasse z.

Another possible function with nouns was that the postlemmatic expansion might help to explain the meaning of a neologism or an archaism. This could be illustrated for adjectives with the following examples collected from the sample check of the letter *C*:

**Clammy as breed is nat through baken** ma. pasteux fe. pasteuse s.

In the *OED*, this is the first record of *clammy* in the sense **I.b.** 'Of bread: Doughy . . .'.

**Clobysshe boystous onweldy** ma. lourt s fe. lourde.

The *OED* adduces Palsgrave's dictionary entry as the first record of *clubbish* in the sense of 'Clownish, boorish, rough, rude . . .'.

**Close or darke as the wether is**
ma. et fe. sombre s.

The sense of *close* that comes closest to Palsgrave's dictionary entry in the *OED* is '†5. Enclosed with clouds or darkness'. The earliest record dates from 1532, two years after the publication of the *Esclarcissement*.

**Cokbraynde lyght fole hardye**
ma. et fe. saffre. s.

This is the first record of the item in the *OED*.

**Crompled togyther**. ma. et fe. ronille s.

In the *OED* the first instance of the past participle is from 1535 (Coverdale), sense 3, 'Crushed into creases and folds; crushed out of shape, out of smoothness or tidiness . . .'.

Other entries under *C*—as, for instance, *chargefull* and *comprehensyble*—seem to go back to French influence and are first recorded in the *OED* for 1529.

This takes us to the third function suggested for Palsgrave's postlemmatic expansions (as well as for unlexicalized English headwords). The semantic specifications and/or subdivisions of the lemma adjectives are oriented towards the target language French. This could be illustrated with the dictionary entries for *fresh*. The first entry is the *OED*'s first record of this sense and it is particularly striking because of its two long *or*-phrases by means of which Palsgrave is trying to express in English the meaning of French *fade*:

**Fresshe or lussyouse as meate ẏis nat well seasoned/ or that hath an vnplesante swetnesse in it.** ma. et fe. fade s.
**Fresshe/ gorgyouse gay or well besene** ma. gorgias fe. gorgiase s. ma. et fe. frisque s. ma. gaillart s. fe. gaillarde s.
**Freshe nat salte nor stale** ma. frays fe. freche s.
**Fresshe newly kylled or newly gathered** ma. recent s. fe. recente s.
**Fresshe newe** noueau.
**Fresshe as water is** ma. frays s. fe. frayse s.

## VERBS

### *Normal aspects and reference point*

Palsgrave's table of verbs is not only the longest of the three lists but also the most interesting lexicographically. Dictionary entries for verbs include references to French grammar, to English and French language usage, and to English and French authors. The translation equivalents are given more explicit treatment and the use of the headword is illustrated in example sentences. In addition, there are cross-references.

In general, Palsgrave's verb headwords have a prelexemmatic part, the first person pronoun *I*. The following lemma proper is then given with an initial capital. Under the letter *I* we notice an interesting different practice. Having listed verbs beginning with the letter *is* (**I yssue**), Palsgrave does not continue with verbs beginning with the letter *I*, but with entries whose first element is the third-person pronoun *it* (**It yrketh** . . .). Nearly all of the lemma entries begin with *it*, mostly followed by *is*, so that one might assume that Palsgrave tried to list all *is*-lemmata. In no case is the item *is* capitalized, nor is any other word of the lemma entry. There thus seems to be no obvious lemma, since the word *it* which begins the line, just as all other line beginnings, has a capital letter.

These *it*-items are followed by headword entries which in most cases begin with existential *There is*. Again, none of the items within the headword entry has been singled out as lemma and printed with an initial capital. The fact that Palsgrave lists these entries under the letter *I* and not the letter *T* seems to suggest that *there* was regarded as the prelemmatic expansion analogous to impersonal *it*, with *is* as the relevant verb.

Palsgrave records quite a number of spelling variants for the verbs, but these are rarely listed within one single headword entry as in the *Catholicon* and the *Promptorium parvulorum*. They are usually recorded in separate entries.

The fact that Palsgrave makes use of cross-referencing in his table of verbs does not preclude the occasional occurrence of doublet entries. In the cases in which the respective lemmata are spelled differently without cross-reference, such double listings may result from oversight on the part of the compiler. An example is

> **I Groyne I grutche or murmure agaynst a thyng/** Ie grongne. prime cõiuga. **and** ie grõmelle. prime cõiu. **I loue hym nat he groyneth at euery thynge I do:** Ie ne layme pas, car il grongne, **or** grommelle a tout tant que ie fays.

This is immediately followed by the entry

> **I Groone I grutche/** Ie grongne, **and** ie gromelle, **and** ie gemys, iay

> gemy, gemir. secunde cõiuga. **Thou gronest euer whã I com in a dores** Tu grongnes, or tu grom̃elles tousiours quant ie entre a la mayson.

Publication pressure on Palsgrave may have been so strong that he did not have enough time to check his work and this would also account for those instances where the double listing cannot even be justified by a difference in spelling.

From the treatment of nouns and adjectives, we might expect that the reference point in the postlemmatic expansions of verbs is the third person, as indeed it is. We find *one*, *man*, as well as *person*:

> **I Bring a thyng to one that can nat go/** Iaporte. prime. **Bringe me some wyne:** Apportez moy du vyn.

> **I Caste awaye as a man dothe a thyng that he setteth no store by/** Ie deiecte. prime coniu. . . .

> **I Chere or I comforte a person that is in sycknesse or trybulacion/** Ie conforte. prime coniuga . . .

Palsgrave seems to use all three forms for indefinite human reference, but *man* can also be opposed to *beest* as in

> **I Cary as a man or beest caryeth a thyng that they beare/** Ieporte. pri me cõiu. . . .

Similarly, *person* can be opposed to *thing*:

> **I Cere a thyng or person in a cere clothe/** Ie enuelope en toylle de cire.

If we compare the table of nouns, adjectives, and verbs from this point of view, we note some further differences. First, Palsgrave also uses the pronouns *he*, *his*, or *him* in lemma entries that have no preceding *man*, *one*, or *person* to which they could refer:

> **I Cast downe from a hygh place to make hym haue a greuouse fall:** Ie trebusche . . .

Secondly, there are instances where the singular pronoun *one* or *person* is already paired with the plural possessive pronoun *their*:

> **I Chyppe as ones handes do or their lyppes w<sup>t</sup> the Marche wynde:** Ie garsche . . .

> **I Enheryte a person I am their heyre in their goodes or landes/** Ie herite . . .

Thirdly, in numerous instances the indefinite first-person plural pronoun occurs instead of *he*, *man*, *one*, or *person*:

**I Breake my faste as we do in the mornynge for the ayre**/ Ie desieune [*sic*] . . .

**I Darke I make darke as clowdes make darke the wether whan they hange bytwene the sonne and vs**/ Ie obnubule . . .

Palsgrave's headword entries for verbs are from this point of view well developed. In the *Catholicon Anglicum*, instances that include indefinite reference are extremely rare. An example is

to **Breke as a man brekis his fast;** dissoluere.

There are more such instances in the *Promptorium parvulorum* (1499), but the form used is not *man*, *person*, or *one*. The typical item used is *another*, as we can see from the following examples:

**Be buxum or bedient to another.** Obedio dis diui ire tum . . .

**Make token to another or bekkyn.** Nuo is nui nutũ. Annuo is similiter . . .

*Types of headword structure*

The structure of lemma entries for verbs is very complex and we might distinguish the following postlemmatic expansions which function as postmodifications:

1. The verb is followed by an adjective/participle complement. This type is common for entries with **I Am**, **I Make**, and **I Waxe**:

   **I Am pleased**/ Ie suis content, iay esté content, estre content, **and** il me plaist bien . . .

   **I Make certayne**/ Ie certifie. prime cõiuga. **or** ie certiore. prime cõiu. **and** ie assertaine. prime cõiu . . .

   **I Waxe reed**/ Ie menrougis. verbũ mediũ. secũde cõiu . . .

   The adjective/participle complement may also be postmodified:

   **I Am ware of a thyng ỷ I newly spye**/ Ie aduise. prime . . .

   **I Make wery by ouermoche studye or occupacyon of the mynde**/ Ie tanne. prime cõiu. . . .

   **I Waxe reed for shame**/ Ie me rougis. verbũ mediũ. secunde cõiu. . . .

2. The verb is followed by an adverbial phrase. These include adverbials of manner and place:

   **I Come out hastyly**/ Ie sauls, nous saillons, ie saillis, iay sailly, ie sailleray, que ie saille, saillir. tercie . . .

   **I Confeder togyther in amytye by promesse or treatye**/ Ie cõfedere. and ialye. prime coniuga . . .

3. A very common type is that of the verb followed by an object:

> **I Breake my superiours cõmaun demẽt/** Ienfrayns, nous enfraygnõs . . .

> **I Broche a wyne vessell/** Ie perce prime cõiuga . . .

The object itself may also be postmodified. Very common postmodifications are relative clauses, as in

> **I Catche a thyng that I reache after/** Ie happe. prime coniu. . . .

So too, infinitive clauses as in

> **I Carue a cockerell to make hym a capon.** Ie chastre. pri. cõiu.

In such cases, the object is further postmodified because the meaning of the lemma entry is not otherwise completely rendered by the verb–object combination, but the meaning of the lemma can also be more precisely described by providing several objects. By this means, Palsgrave may be trying to capture the verb's typical objects. A further step in the attempt at pinpointing the typical class of objects that the meaning of a verb encapsulates are generic characterizations of the type '. . . or suche lyke . . .'. Both cases can be illustrated as follows:

> **I Brewe ale or beere/** Ie brasse. pri me coniu . . .

> **I Borowe money or any other thynge that I haue nede of vpon a pledge or seurtye/** Iemprunte. prime coniuga . . .

4. In order to narrow down the meaning of the lemma, the verb–object sequence may also be followed by a clause of comparison:

> **I Feder a shafte as a fletcher doth whan he gleweth on the fethers/** Ie empenne. prime coniuga . . .

5. The verb can be followed by both an object and an object complement. Lexicographically, this type is interesting because Palsgrave varies with respect to the positioning of object and object complement if the latter is an adjective:

> **I Make my selfe a relygyouse man/** Ie me rends religieux. **coniugate in I yelde** . . .

> **I Make faste one thyng to a nother with a nayle or some other lyke thyng/** Iatache. prime cõiuga . . .

With the foregoing, contrast:

> **I Make one sure of a thynge by my promesse/** Ie affie. prime coiuga. [*sic*]

> **I Make one wery by trauaylyng of his bodye/** Ie lasse. prime cõiu . . .

If we make allowances for some exceptions, Palsgrave seems to have favoured the order V–$C_o$–O when the object itself was a complex noun phrase and V–O–$C_o$ when the object consisted of a simple pronoun. Relative 'weight' (Quirk *et al.* 1985: 1361–2) is clearly the determinant, and so in the case of a postmodified pronoun the sequence becomes again V–$C_o$–O:

> **I Make styll one that is angry/** Ie apayse. prime cõiu.

6. The verb plus object may be followed by a prepositional phrase which can have a number of different functions:

> **I Bring thynges with me/** Ie a-porte. prime coniu . . .
>
> **I Call one by his name/** Iappelle prime coniuga . . .

7. A rarer type is the one where the verb is followed by an indirect and direct object as in:

> **I Gyue a man an appetyte to his meate/** Ie entalente. prime cõiu . . .
>
> **I Graunte one ẏͤ vse of any thing that is myne as frely as thoughe it were his owne:** Ie abandonne. . . .

8. The postlemmatic expansion that gives *Lesclarcissement* its particular liveliness and picturesqueness are the ostensive comparisons introduced by means of *as* or *like*. Most of the structural types outlined so far can also co-occur with such ostensive comparisons. Examples are:

> **I Bring vp dayntely as some mothers do their chyldren whan they fede them with daynety meates:** Ie affriande. prime cõiu. **and** ie affriolle.
>
> **I Caste in to ẏͤ see as men do letters that they wolde shulde nat be sene/** Iemmarre. prime cõiuga . . .

For verbs that denote emitting a sound, such comparisons are often predictable:

> **I Cacle as a henne dothe whan she is aboute to laye/** Ie cacquette. prime cõiuga . . .
>
> **I Hysse as adders do/** Ie ciffle. prime coniuga . . .

We come to those postlemmatic expansions that constitute appositive semantic glosses of the verb lemma. Again, these structures are very complex, but we might distinguish the following basic types:

1. The simplest structure is the verb lemma followed by a verbal synonym, as in

> **I Bicker I skyrmysshe/** Ie escarmouche. prime coniu . . .

Both elements may also be conjoined by means of *or*, as in

> **I Lede or bringe to/** Iaconduis, aconduire, and reconduire . . .

or separated by a comma:

> **I Am cladde/ I am clothed/ Ie suis vestu . . .**

2. The postlemmatic gloss may also consist of two added synonyms. There are three styles:

> **I Attempt I enterprise I take in hande/** Ie attempte. prime coniuga . . .

> **It becometh/ it happeneth/ it chaũseth/** Il aduient . . .

> **I Chastyse I correcte or punysshe** Ie chastie. prime coniuga . . .

3. Whereas postlemmatic glosses for adjectives include at most two glosses, those for verbs may have three. We find a number of varying coordination devices, as in:

> **I Boke or prouoke or set a worke or moue a man to anger/** Iaposte. pri me coniuga . . .

> **I Encombre I trouble/ vexe/ or disquyete/** Iencombre. prime cõiuga.

4. Instead of a synonym, the postlemmatic gloss may present a full explanation of the meaning of the verb lemma:

> **I Iuste I ronne with speares/** Ie iouste. prime cõiu . . .

> **I Katche a thyng I laye handes on it to holde it faste/** Ie happe prime coniu . . .

I have deliberately chosen simple examples in order to highlight the different structural realizations of postlemmatic glosses. But the verb lemma as well as its English gloss may of course be much more complex, and in the following example the English gloss which paraphrases the verb lemma consists of a verb–object combination to which is added an ostensive *as*-clause:

> **I Clatter I make a noyse as harnesse dothe or dysshes or any thynges of metall/** Ie clicquette. prime. . . .

Other complex examples include:

> **I Ennewe I set the laste and freshest coloure vpon a thyng as payn ters do whan their worke shall remayne to declare their connyng.** Ie renouuelle. prime cõiu . . .

> **I Gagge one I put a gagge in his mouthe that he shulde nat speke nor krye/** Ie embaillonne. prime cõiu. . . .

The example *lyghten* illustrates another structural feature:

**I Lyghten I fyll or store a place with lyght/** Ie enlumine. prime cōiu.

The two glossing verbs *fyll* and *store* are coordinated to share the same object and adverbial. The effect is that the gloss is perceived as one unit and not as two separate glosses of the lemma *lyghten*. In other cases the object or adverbial, for instance, seems to hold together the lemma and its gloss:

**I Catche or holde faste with an hoke or croke/** Iaccroche. prime cōiu.

**I Choppe or cutte or hewe any thyng in to small peces/** Ie dehache. prime coniuga . . .

These few examples may suffice to demonstrate that, unlike the noun and the adjective tables, Palsgrave's verb lemmata cannot always unambiguously be separated into lemma proper and postlemmatic gloss. The two are syntactically and semantically interwoven and in so being the elements combine into one semantic unit which is matched by its French equivalent. The verb lemma entries thus call for the setting-up of an additional mixed class of postlemmatic expansions involving pronominalization, as in

**I Beare one company I entretayne him/** Ientretiēs, iay entretenu . . .

As with nouns and adjectives, there are also instances where the verb lemma entries include the expression of polysemy through coordination. The postlemmatic expansion which paraphrases the lemma includes two senses which are rendered by one French verb. In the following two cases, both the concrete and the abstract sense of the verb are illustrated by an example:

**I Enclyne I applye my mynde to a purpose or I bowe downe with my bodye or make one lowe reuerence/** Ie mencline, ie me suis encliné encliner. verbū mediū. prime coniu. **you shall neuer get hym to enclyne in this matter**: Iamays ne le ferez encliner en ceste matiere. **He dyd enclyne to do hym reuerēce so farre of as he myght se hym:** Il se enclinoyt pour luy faire la reuerence aussi loing de lui quil le pouuoyt choysir de veue or de loye, or quil le pouuoyt veoir.

**I Fyxe I set my mynde on a thing or I fasten a thynge in the grounde or otherwyse/** Ie affiche. prime cōiu.

**If I fyxe my mynde vpon a thynge ones I shall sone get it:** Si ie affice mon intencion sur quelque chose vne foys ie lattaindray biē tost. **I can nat remoue it/ it is fyxed in ẙ grounde:** Ie ne le puis remouuer il est affiché en terre.

*A comparison with the* Catholicon *and the* Promptorium

How pioneering and how original are Palsgrave's lemma entries for verbs? Of the types of postlemmatic expansions outlined above, some occur in the *Catholicon Anglicum.* The first three types of postmodification may be said to be quite common, except that there are no cases of verb lemma entries where the object is followed by a relative clause or an infinitive clause. There are some instances of type 6, but they are nearly all renderings of a specific Latin verb formation, as we can see from the following examples:

> to **Folowe y^e moder in maners**; *matrizare.*
> to folowe **Pepylle in maneres**; *plebere, plebescere.*
> to folow þe **syster jn maners**; *sororitare.*

There are about a dozen instances of type 8. Example entries from the *Catholicon* and *Lesclarcissement* are shown in Table 6.8.

Not all the verbs recorded in the *Catholicon* are included in *Lesclarcissement.* The differences between these two dictionaries are striking. The verb lemma entries of the *Catholicon Anglicum* are restricted to the basic comparison. Many of Palsgrave's entries reveal not only subtler observation and analysis but also a conscious endeavour to illustrate the meaning of the verb with a good example.

Before we turn our attention to the structure of the verb entries in the *Promptorium parvulorum*, we should mention some such structures in the *Catholicon* which are clearly prompted by the Latin equivalents and which cannot therefore be expected to occur in this form in the other two dictionaries.

First, we have subject complements consisting of a noun phrase, as in

> to be a **Bischope;** *pontificari.*
> to be **Medwyfe;** *obstetricare.*

Secondly, there are instances where two phrasal verbs are lumped together, as in

> to **Drawe oute or vp;** *educere, elicere, extrahere, euaginare, euellere, excerpere, eximere, vellere, re-, e-, con-, vellicare, eradicare, explantare, extirpare.*

Thirdly, in some cases, the verb lemma entry includes the negative *not,* and the compiler varied between making the verb or the negation the lemma under which to list the item:

TABLE 6.8. *Lemma entries for verbs which include a comparison:* Catholicon *and* Lesclarcissement

| *Catholicon Anglicum* | *Lesclarcissement* |
|---|---|
| to **Barke as a dog;** *latrare, debaulare* | **I Barke as a dogge dothe/** Iaboye. prime coniuga. **I fynde also in this sense/** ie latre. prime coniugati. **This dogge barketh agaynste the moone:** Ce chien aboye, or ce chien latre contre la lune. |
| to **Chatir as byrdis;** *cornicari, corniculari, garrire.* | **I Chatter as byrdes do or they begyn to speake or parfetly to synge their note:** Ie gariolle. prime coniu. **but the parisyens chaunge R/ in to S/ or Z/ and saye** ie gasoille, **as I haue in the first boke touched.** |
| | **I Chatter as byrdes do whan many be togyther/** Ie iargonne. prime. **Harke howe these byrdes chatter:** Escoutez comment ces oyseaulx iargonnent. |
| to **Chiter os byrdis dose;** *garrire, mimurire.* | **I Chytter I make a charme as a flocke of small byrdes do whan they be togyther/** Ie iargonne. prime con. **Byrdes chytter faster in Marche thã in any other season:** Les oyseletz iargonnent plus en Mars quen nulle aultre season. |
| | **I Chytter as a yonge byrde dothe byfore she can synge her tune/** Ie patelle. prime coniu. **This lytell byrde begynneth to chitter/ but she can nat synge her tune out playnly yet:** Ce petit oyselet cõmẽce a pateller, mays, il ne scayt pas encore chanter sa lay tout a playn. |

to not **Knawe;** *ignorare, nescire vel quod factum est non recordari, obliuisci, nescire omni noticia carere, ignoscere,* & *cetera; vbi* to forgett
to **Nott moghe;** *nequire, non posse.*
to not **Thryfe;** *devigere.*

We come now to the *Promptorium parvulorum.* The structural make-up of its verb entries occupies an intermediate position between the *Catholicon* and *Lesclarcissement.* Six of the eight types of postmodification distinguished occur, types 1, 2, 3, and 8 being quite common. Examples from the 1499 edition are:

1. The verb is followed by an adjective/participle complement:

   **Be besy** Solicitor taris tatum sum. prime coniugacionis. Deponens.

2. The verb is followed by an adverbial phrase:

   **Closen streytly.** Detrudo dis trusi trusũ. tercie coniugacõis. actiuũ.
   **Cenden by message.** Mitto tis misi missum. tercie coniugacõis. Actiuũ.

   The prepositional phrase may be more complex as in:

   **Chargen with burden or other thinges.** Que/ro ras. pri g. actiuũ.

3. The verb is followed by an object:

   **Crusshen bones.** Ostillo las. pri. . neutrũ.

   The direct object may consist of a more complex noun phrase, and, in order to specify the typical objects the verb can take, the compiler lists two objects; in addition, there may be such phrases as 'or other like', 'or other such thinges'. Examples are:

   **Clout disshes pottes pãnes.** Crusco as. p. q' n
   **Barre dores or other suche thinges like.** Pessulo las. prime coniugacionis. neutrum.

   There are sporadic instances where the object is followed by a relative clause, as in

   **Amende thinges that ar fauty.** Corrigo gis, exi ere di rectũ. tercie coniuga. actiuũ.

   The structural types (object + object complement; indirect and direct objects) do not occur.

Examples of type 8, postmodifying ostensive comparisons, are more numerous in the *Promptorium* than in the *Catholicon*. Interestingly enough, there is little overlapping. In the following comparison of the *Promptorium* and *Lesclarcissement* in Table 6.9, we restrict ourselves to instances which do not denote the sound or noise produced by a certain animal since otherwise the *Promptorium* entries would be too lengthy. As with the *Catholicon*, comparing *Lesclarcissement* with the *Promptorium* reveals striking independence, and Palsgrave excels in more discriminatory descriptions.

TABLE 6.9. *Lemma entries for verbs which include a comparison:* Promptorium *and* Lesclarcissement

| *Promptorium parvulorum* (1499) | *Lesclarcissement* |
|---|---|
| **Blase as doth the seme of a fyre.** Flammo mas maui mare di. prime coniugacionis. Neutrum. | **I Blase as yͤ fyre dothe/** Ie flãme. prime coniuga. **This fyre blaseth to light/ outher throw on a lytle water or els take awaye some of yͤ styckes:** Ce feu flãme or flãbe trop clere, iectez vng peu deaue dessus, ou oustez aulcuns des tysons. |
| **Cloderyn as blode or other lyke.** Coagulo as prime ꝯiugacionis neutrũ. | **I Clodder lyke whaye or bloode whan it is colde or any moyst thing dothe yͤ rõneth togyther on a heape/** Ie congele. prime coniu. **The bloode of any beest wyll clodder whan it waxeth colde:** Le sang de quelque beste que se soyt se congele quãt il deuient froyt. |
| **Crackyn as salt in fyre or other lyke.** Crepito tas. prime coniugacõis. Neutrũ. | **I Cracke as drye wodde dothe whan it is burned/ or drye styckes otherwyse/** Ie crespe. prime coniuga. **These styckes cracke a pace:** Ces ba stons crespent fort. **Herke howe his slyppers cracke:** Escoustez comment ces pantouffles crespent. **I Cracke I make anoyse as great plentye of wodde or strawe dothe whan it is set afyre/** Ie bruis. secũde. **I here by the crackynge that it is heathe that yonder men of the countrey burne:** Ie os bien par le bruyt que cest bruyre q̃ ces paysãs la bruslẽt. |

The verb entries of the *Promptorium* are rich in postlemmatic glosses. This is one of the main differences between the *Catholicon* and the *Promptorium.* The typical form is an appositive coordination by means of *or*, adding either one or two synonymous verbs to the verb lemma or a full semantic paraphrase. Examples are:

> **Abownden or haue plente.** Habũdo das aui re di datum. Prime coniugacõis neutrum.
> **Blabyr or speke oute of reason.** Blatero ras aui. prime ꝯiugacionis. Neutrũ. Catho.

Among the verbs that are fully glossed we find many denominal and deadjectival verbs, e.g. *Bare or make bare*, *Bladen or taken away the blades*, *Blaken*, *or make blacke*, *Bowlen or play with bowles*, and so on.

We conclude this comparison with the mention of two features characteristic of the *Promptorium*. It has already been noted (p. 238) that its compiler did not use *man*, *person*, or *one* to refer to an indefinite person, the preferred form being *another*. When a verb is reflexive, this is indicated by the phrase 'by the selfe':

> **Brenne by the selfe** Ardeo des si sũ. scd'e coniugacõnis, actiuum.

*The function of postlemmatic expansions*

We turn finally to the function of Palsgrave's postlemmatic expansions in verb entries.

The three basic functions outlined for nouns and adjectives seem to hold also for verbs, though possibly with a slightly different emphasis. Homograph differentiation seems to be less prominent than for nouns. Examples are:

> **I Barke as a dogge dothe/** Iaboye. prime coniuga. **I fynde also in this sence/** ie latre. prime coniugati. **This dogge barketh agaynste the moone**: Ce chien aboye, **or** ce chien latre contre la lune.
>
> (III, fo. c.lvii$^{v}$)

> **I Barke a tree or pyll of ẙ rynde or barke of it/** Iescorche. prime con. **He is a foole that wyll sell his okes for fuell afore they be barked**: Il nest qung fol qui veult vendre ses chesnes pour en faire du fuaille auant quil les escorche.
>
> (III, fo. c.lvii$^{v}$)

> **I Mete a man as I go or ryde by the waye/** Ie rencontre. prime coniu. **I mete him:** Ie luy rencontre, **and** ie encontre. prime cõiu. . . . **Hylles do neuer mete but acquayntaunce dothe often** . . .
>
> (III, fo. ccc)

> **I Mete clothe or sylke by ẙ yerde** Ie aulne. prime cõiuga. **Who mette this clothe you haue skante mesure:** Qui vous aulna ce drap a peyne auez vous vostre mesure.
>
> (III, fo. ccc)

It looks as if orientation towards lexicalization in French is much more conspicuous for the verb lemma entries than for noun and adjective lemmata. A good example of this is the verb *to depart*, for which there are sixteen different French verbs:

> **I Departe I deuyde thynges a sonder/** Ie depars, nous departons, ie departis, iay departy, que ie departe departir. tercie cõiu. **coniugate lyke his symple** ie pars. **I parte. and** ie desassemble. prime cõiuga. **Departe this meate a sonder:** Departez, **or** separez, **or** desassemblez ceste piece de viande.

**I Departe I distrybute/** Ie distribue. prime coniuga. **Departe to euery man a lyke:** Distribuez a chascun sa portion esgalle.

**I Departe thynges a sonder that be ioyned togyther/** Ie separe. prime coniuga. **No man can parte them:** Nul ne les peult separer.

**I Departe I distrybute the partes of a thynge to dyuers persons/** Ie mespars. **coniugate lyke his symple** ie pars. **I parte. He hath quartered an oxe and departed him vnto foure persones:** Il a escartellé vng beuf et la mesparty a quatre persõnes.

**I Departe or deuyde thynges a sonder that were myxed or medled togyther/** Ie desmesle. prime cõiuga. **and** ie desioings. **coniugate lyke his symple** ie ioings. **I ioyne. Departe this skayne of threde we can nat els wynde it vp:** Desmeslez ceste piece de fil ou autrement nous ne scaurions la deuider.

**I Departe from a place or from a person/** Ie me pars, nous partons, ie me partis, ie me suis party, ie me partiray, que ie me parte, de me partir. verbũ mediũ. tercie coniu. **Whan departed he frõ his lodgyng:** Quãt se departist il de son logys. **They wyl departe without your knowledge and you be nat ware:** Ilz se partiront sans le sceu, **or** le congé de vous se vous ny prennez garde.

**I Departe from a place to gyue a nother man place/** Ie cede. prime coniuga. datiuo iũgitur, **and** ie pars **coniugate in I parte. I am content to departe to gyue him place:** Ie suis content de luy ceder, **or** ie suis contẽt de me partyr pour luy faire place.

**I Departe farre out of ones companye/ properly in displeasure outher to hym that so dothe departe or to the persons he so departeth from/** Ie mesloigne, ie me suis esloigné, esloigner. verbũ mediũ. prime coniuga. **whiche I fynde written somtyme/** ie me aloigne, ie me suis aloigné, aloigner, verbũ mediũ. prime coniuga. **O the sorowes that I haue for my louer whiche is departed from me:** O les regretz que iay de mamye qui sest esloignée de moy.

**I Departe forthe of my lodgyng/** Ie me desloge, ie me suis deslogé, deslo ger. prime coniuga. verbũ medium. **Whan wyll you departe out of this lodgynge:** Quant vous deslogerez vous.

**I Departe from my wyfe by the lawe/** Ie me diuorse. **I haue naught to do with her we be departed:** Ie nay riens a fayre auec elle nous sommes diuorsez.

**I Departe from my wyfe or deuorce my selfe without the order of the lawe/** Ie me demarie, ie me suis demarié, demarier, verbũ mediũ. prime cõiuga. **He is departed from his wyfe and kepeth a nother woman:** Il se est desmarié et entretiẽt vne aultre fẽme. **She is departed from her housbande:** Elle se est desmarieé.

**I Departe out of the worlde/ I dye or lete my lyfe/** Ie trespasse. prime cõiu. **and** ie desuie. prime cõiuga. **and** ie vas de vie en trespas, ie men suis allé de vie en trespas, aller de vie entrespas. **Whan departed he:** Quãt trespassa il, quãt desuia il, quant alla il de vie a trespas, **and** ie me meurs. **They departed in ye towne twenty on a daye:** Ilz sen moururent en ceste ville la vingt pour vng iour.

Some postlemmatic expansions may have the function of explaining the meaning of an archaism, as can be illustrated with an example from those instances for which Palsgrave explicitly states that the item in question is no longer in use:

**I Queme I please or I satysfye/ Chauser in his Caũterbury tales/ this worde is nowe out of vse.**

There is no similar explicit statement for neologisms, which can thus be detected among Palsgrave's verbs only by an item-for-item check. Our concern here is not a complete list of English verbs lexicographically first recorded by Palsgrave but only a sample check to demonstrate the issue.

Let us begin with a sample of phrasal verbs. Palsgrave gives no French equivalent for *to put up*, as in

**I Put vp a hare I starte a hare.**

Perhaps Palsgrave did not know the corresponding hunting term in French, and/or it may be that *to put up* as a hunting term in English was new. The *OED* provides the following information under entry **56** of the verb *to put*:

**b.** (*a*) *Hunting.* To cause (game) to rise from cover; to rouse, start.
? *c* 1475 *Hunt. Hare* 112, Y wylle ryde and putt her vp. 1575 TURBERV. *Falconrie* 131 Let him which hath the Hearoner (that is the make Hawke) put up the Hearon . . .

The first record of this special sense of *to put up* stems from a metrical romance, the second from George Turberville's *Booke of faulconrie or hauking*. Palsgrave's entry thus is the first recording of the specialized sense in a general dictionary.

Other phrasal verbs listed under *put* are *to put asunder*, *to put forth*, *to put out*, *to put out of*, *to put together*, and they are worth comparing in Palsgrave and the *OED*:

**I Put a sonder I departe a sonder folkes/** Ie desioyncts. **coniugate lyke his symple** ie iongs. **I ioyne. Sythe they be ones put togyther by ẏͤ lawes of holy churche I wyll neuer put them a sonder:** Puis quilz sõt mys ensẽble par les loys de saincte esglise ie ne les desioyndray iamays.

(III, fo. ccc.xxiii (= ccc.xxvii))

OED **put 38: put asunder.** trans. To separate.
**1526** TINDALE *Matt.* xix 6 Let not man therfore put asunder, that which god hath cuppled togedder.
**1530** [see 54b] = [a quotation from Palsgrave for *to put together*, the very example from the entry given above].

**I Put forthe as a tree dothe whan it burioneth/** Ie boute hors, or ie bourionne. prime cõiu. **This eglantyne tre putteth forthe very tymely:** Cest eglantier boute hors, or bourionne bien matyn.

(III, fo. ccc.xxiii$^{v}$ (= ccc.xxvii$^{v}$))

OED **put 43. put forth . . . g.** (*a*) Of a plant: To send out (buds or leaves). Also *intr.* or *absol.*: To shoot, sprout, burst forth into bud, leaf or blossom . . .
**1530** palsgr. 672/1 this eglantyne tre . . .

Another sense of *put forth* is the following:

> **I Put forthe or expulse one out of a place/** Ie boute hors, iay boute hors bouter hors, prime cõiuga. **and** ie expoulse, iay expoulsé, expoulser. prime coniu. **I shall put hym forthe at all aduentures/ put hym in afterwarde who wyll:** Ie le bouteray dehors, **or** ie lexpoulseray vne fois mette le dedans apres qui vouldra.
>
> (III, fo. ccc.xxviii)

*OED* **put 43. put forth . . . † h.** (*a*) *trans.* To thrust out . . .
**1526** TINDALE *Matt.* ix 25 As sone as the people were put forthe a dores [**1611** put foorth].
**1530** PALSGR. 672/2, I shall put hym forthe . . .

> **I Put out a scripture or any thing that is put out with the weather or longe processe of tyme/** Ie oblittere. iay oblitteré, obliterer. prime coniu. **There was a writynge vpon his graue but the weather hath put it out:** Il y auoit quelque escripture sur sa tumbe mays le temps la oblitterée.
>
> (III, fo. ccc.xxix$^{v}$)

OED **put 48. put out . . . e. †** (*a*) To strike out or delete (a writing, drawing, etc.); to expunge, erase, efface. *Obs.*
**1530** PALSGR. 675/1 There was a writynge upon his grave . . .

Another sense of *put out* is the following:

> **I Put out fyre or a candell/** Iestayngs, nous estaindons, iestayndis, iay estaynct, iestaindray, q̃ ie estayngne, estayndre, tercie cõiuga. **I fynde also for to put out a candell/** Ie tue, iay tué, tuer. prime cõiu. **As/ I wyll put out the fyre:** Iestayndray le feu. **Put out ỷ candell:** Estayngs la chan delle, ⁊ tue la chandelle. **Rake vp the fyre and put out the candell or you come to bedde:** Mettez a poynt le feu, **or** couurez le feu et tuez la chãdeille auant que vous venez coucher.
>
> (III, fo. ccc.xxx)

*OED* **put 48. put out** . . . **e.** (*b*) To extinguish (fire or light, or a burning or luminous body) . . .
**1526** *Pilgr. Perf.* (W. de W. 1531) 40 No wynde ne rayne coude quenche it ne put it out.
**1530** PALSGR. 675/1 Rake up the fyre and put out the candell . . .

A yet further sense of *put out* is

> **I Put out of doute/** Ie mets hors de doubte. **To put you out of doute it is so in dede:** Pour vo⁹ mettre hors de doubte il est ainsi defait.
>
> (III, fo. ccc.xxx)

*OED* **put 49. put out of** . . . **e.** To remove from the region or sphere of; to cause to be out of the condition of.
**1530** PALSGR. 675/2 To put you out of doute it is so in dede . . .

And, finally, there is *to put together*:

> **I Put togyther/** Ie rassemble. pri me cõiu. **He can spell but he can nat put to gyther:** Il scait espeller, mays il ne peut pas rassembler.
>
> (III, fo. ccc.xxx^v^)

*OED* **put 54. put together** . . . **d.** To form (a whole) by combination of parts; to construct, compile, compose, compound.
**1530** PALSGR. 676/1 He can spell, but he can nat put to gyther. **1638** . . .

A similar check under *get*, *give*, and *go* yielded a similar result—that is, a good number of phrasal verbs with *get*, *give*, *go*, and *put* are, according to the *OED*, first recorded by Palsgrave.

The second group of verbs where one might suspect neologisms are denominal and deadjectival verbs, since the postlemmatic gloss of such entries is not a verbal synonym but an explanation that brings out the derivative nature of the word. Confirmation can be seen from the following examples.

1. *To gag*

> **I Gagge one I put a gagge in his mouthe that he shulde nat speke nor krye/** Ie embaillonne. prime cõiu. **Whan the theues had robbed hym of all that euer he had they gagged hym bycause he shulde nat speake:** Quãt les larrons luy auoyẽt derobbé tout tant quil auoyt ilz lembaillonne rent affyn quil ne parlast ne cryast.
>
> (III, fo. cc.xliii^v^)

The *OED* lists the transitive sense of the verb under **2.a.** *trans.* 'To stop up the mouth of (a person) with a gag in order to prevent speech or outcry; to put a gag into (the mouth) in order to keep the jaws distended.' The first attestations of use are:

**1509** HAWES *Past. Pleas.* xxxii. (Percy) 159 We saw men in great tormenting, With many ladies, that their mouthes gagged.
**1530** PALSGR. 559/2 I gagge one . . .

2. *To heighten*:

> **I Heyghten I set vp a heythe/** Ie exalse. prime cõiu. **and** ie eslieue plus hault. **This balke is heythened two foote:** Ce tref est exalsé, **or** eslieué plus hault de deux piedz.
>
> (III, fo. cc.lx[v])

The findings from the *OED* are: '**1.** *trans.* To give or add height to; to make high or higher; to elevate.' The first recording of this sense is '**1530** PALSGR. 582/2 This balke is heythened two foote'.

3. *To lubber*:

> **I Lubber I playe the lubber/** Ie loricarde. prime cõiuga. **You lubber as well as any knaue in this towne:** Vous lorricardez aussi bien que villayn de ceste ville.
>
> (III, fo. cc.lxxxv[v])

The *OED* describes the meaning of this intransitive verb as 'To behave as a lubber; to loaf about; to navigate a boat like a lubber', and the first attestation is from *Lesclarcissement*.

4. *To trumpet*:

> **I Trompet I blowe or sownde in a trompet/** Ie sõne vne trompette. **He trompetteth well:** li [*sic*] sonne bien la trompette.
>
> (III, fo. ccc.lxxxxiiii[v])

The *OED* gives as the first sense of the verb *to trumpet* its intransitive use: 'To blow or sound a trumpet.' The dictionary entry quoted from Palsgrave's dictionary is its first attestation.

5. *To whistle*:

> **I Whystell in a whystell or in my hande/** Ie ciffle, iay ciffle, ciffler. pri-

> me cõiu. **Dothe it yͤ horse any good trowe you whan yͤ carter whystelleth:** Fait il poynt de bien au cheual pencez vous quãt le charretton cyffle.
>
> (III, fo. cccc.viii)

Under sense 4 of the verb *to whistle*, the *OED* paraphrases the meaning as 'To blow or sound a whistle; to sound, as a whistle' and adduces the entry from *Lesclarcissement* as its first attestation.

6. *To white*:

> **I Whyte I make a thyng whyte/** Ie blanchis. secũde cõiu. **It is newe whyted:** Il est nouuellement blanchy.
>
> (III, fo. cccc.viii)

The *OED* gives as sense *c*: 'To bleach; to blanch . . .'. The first attestation is not the above example, but another occurrence of *to white* in *Lesclarcissement*:

> **I Bleche I whyte clothe/** Ie blanchis, iay blanchy, blanchir. tercie cõiuga. **I praye you gyue me leaue to bleche my naperye in your garden:** Ie vous prie de me donner congé de blanchyr mes toylles de lynen en vostre iardyn.
>
> (III, fo. c.lxvii$^{v}$)

The list of verb neologisms could be continued, but the examples provided will suffice to illustrate the explanatory function of postlemmatic glosses in the case of verbs that had been newly coined at the time.

# 7
# Networks and Structural Relations

The complexity of the lexicon of a language is such that no single ordering principle suffices to make a dictionary consultable. This is why all dictionaries are produced on the basis of a set of structural relations. Some examples from English may illustrate this. Compilers of purely alphabetical English dictionaries, for instance, will meet with problems when they come to decide on the order of such items as *(to) smoke*, *(a) smoke*; *(to) make up*, *(her) make-up*; *(to) throw away*, *(a) throw-away* (line); *reformation*, *Reformation*. Which member of these pairs of words should come first? Consistency-conscious lexicographers will make policy decisions for the whole of the work and avoid *ad hoc* solutions.

They could, for instance, opt for the following ordering practice:

1. If the alphabetical form of two or more lemmata is identical, nouns are listed before verbs, verbs before adjectives, etc.
2. If two or more lemmata have the same alphabetical form except for the presence/absence of a hyphen, the unhyphenated item is listed first.
3. If two or more lemmata have the same alphabetical form except for a lower-/upper-case initial, the one with the lower-case initial will be listed first.

With equal justification and no loss of general consistency, they might also have chosen the reverse order in all three cases. They could have done so, because they would have selected their criteria without taking care to recognize and represent the structural relations that hold between the items concerned. In all three cases one member of the pair of words is lexically derived from the other. Good lexicographers will always try to make their policy decisions reflect actual language processes, because these provide users with additional insights into, and information on, the structure of the lexicon.

It emerges from the examples that the lexicographical macrostructure may consist of a complex of formal, grammatical, and semantic relations and that this complex is a hierarchical one. We might say that the lexicographical macro-structure in our first example would be alphabetization followed by lexical basis followed by lexical derivation.

In a dictionary entry linguistic information of some sort, depending on the actual type of dictionary, is provided for the lemma. This information is typically broken down into information units. Thus in a monolingual English general-purpose dictionary, we may be given the pronunciation, the word class, the etymology, the subject field, the stylistic colouring, and the various senses of the lemma. These information units are usually set off by different founts, as well as brackets and numerals. The sequence in which they are displayed may vary from lexicographer to lexicographer or according to the envisaged public. In many countries with a long tradition in describing the language, conventions of lexicographical presentation have evolved. Thus, in some, the linguistic description of the lemma may begin with an example sentence showing the lemma in actual use; in others, illustrative examples occur only after the outline of the senses. We may refer to the arrangement and the sequencing of these linguistic information units as the formatting of the dictionary entry. What linguistic information units do display, how and where, are matters of entry formatting. A characteristic of the format units is that they are movable within the entry because they are not interdependent. The indication of the etymology of a word, for instance, does not depend on its pronunciation, nor does an example sentence necessarily depend on the indication of the meaning of the lemma. Formatted linguistic information units are thus cumulative in nature. The needs of the assumed user and/or the lexicographical convention characteristic of a particular country or publishing firm will decide the number of information units and the order in which they are presented.

From the formatting of a dictionary entry we have to distinguish its internal structures. These are made up of structural relations between the linguistic information units in terms of interdependencies. Thus, if a verb is described as intransitive, the sense description of the lemma obviously depends on this, and similarly, if it is described as transitive. A metonymic or metaphorical expansion of the meaning of a word depends on a relevant untransferred sense. But as well as structural relations within a dictionary entry, there are also structural relations between one dictionary entry and another or others. Such structural relations that link different dictionary entries may, for instance, be formal (spelling variants) or semantic (synonyms). Their signalling within a dictionary presupposes a lexicographical macro-structure. We might thus speak of primary structural relations in a dictionary (the macro-structure) and secondary structural relations, some of which are known as cross-references.

Whether and to what extent a specific dictionary marks structural relations within and across dictionary entries depends on various factors, of which depth of linguistic analysis provided, production time, and financial funding are just some. An alphabetical arrangement of a dictionary—as indispensable as it is—is an artificial processing of a natural language that does not relate to any ordinary use of language by its speakers, nor to any acquisition phase. Semantic differentiation, on the other hand, is common in everyday experience, along with the mental existence of partial associative word fields in the Saussurean sense. The communicative needs of dictionary users will, therefore, be better met by making apparent the structural relations between words such as similarities and dissimilarities in meaning, construction, sound, and spelling.

The more lexicographers have penetrated the intricate structural network of the word stock of a language, the more they will try to express these linguistic insights. The specific reference-book character of a dictionary precludes an entry from developing into a lengthy technical treatise. Compilers have, therefore, developed lexicographical devices to signal interlemmatic relations. If these are to achieve the purpose of providing users with further information on the entry words consulted, lexicographers have to make sure that the correlated units are easily and unmistakably identifiable, that their correlation is consistent, and that the structural relation linking two or more units is correctly understood. A dictionary with a well-handled cross-reference system is more demanding for the lexicographer than one without such an additional level. One may, therefore, expect that the inclusion of cross-references as well as their consistent handling will increase with the advance of lexicography.

## FIFTEENTH-CENTURY VOCABULARIES

With this in mind, let us look at the early English word lists and dictionaries and investigate whether or not structural relations within and across dictionary entries were already indicated, and, if so, which, and by what means they were made explicit. As before, we shall compare the most important lexicographical works preceding the publication of *Lesclarcissement* to assess Palsgrave's achievement in its proper historical context.

In the fifteenth-century Latin–English vocabularies edited by Wright, we can discern three relations, two of which are relations between different dictionary entries, and the first is the commonest. The lexicographical devices used for this structural relation vary, but they share the characteristic that the dictionary entries are contiguous. The first device is a linking of the entries concerned by means of the Latin phrase *idem est* (or just *idem*), as in the following example from the *English Vocabulary* (Wright 1884/1968: col. 636):

> *Hec mamma, A*$^{e}$ pappe.
> *Hec mamilla, idem est.*
> *Hoc vber, idem est.*

For the second, or the second and the third, member of the set there is no English equivalent. Instead, the Latin lemma is followed by the Latin specification *idem est*, which refers the reader to the English equivalent of the preceding entry, thus indicating that Latin *mamilla*, and *vber* correspond, like *mamma*, to English *pappe*. The identity relation between the first English equivalent and the second, or the second and the third respectively, establishes a synonymic relationship between *mamma*, *mamilla* and *vber*.

In the *Mayer Nominale* (see Stein 1985*a*: 57), we find two other lexicographical devices for the same relationship. The topical arrangement of the nominale enables its compiler to bring synonymous Latin lemmata together and to list them one after the other. They are then bracketed and for all of them one English equivalent is provided (Wright 1884/1968: cols. 720-2):

> *Hec ecclesia,*
> *Hoc templum,*
> *Hoc delubrum,* } a kyrk.
> *Hoc fanum,*
> *Hec basilica,*

A combination of these two devices occurs in the *Pictorial Vocabulary* (Wright 1884/1968: col. 745):

> *Hic crinis,*
> *Hic pilus,*
> *Hic capillus,* } *idem sunt, An*$^{ce}$ a here.
> *Hec coma,*
> *Hec sesaries,*

The notion underlying this identity relation varies, for, in the *Pictorial Vocabulary*, *idem est* is also used for nouns that denote the male and the female of an animal species (Wright 1884/1968: col. 759):

> *Hic ursus, A*$^{ce}$ a bere.
> *Hec ursa, idem est.*

Since the compiler explicitly differentiates between the male and the female by providing the corresponding English lexical items (*lion*, *lioness*, etc.) or equivalents (*wolf*, *female wolf*), it is not clear whether his use of *idem est* is meant to suggest the undifferentiated use of *bear* for both animals in English or whether he regarded the lexical core of the words as identical, with the sex specification merely as a grammatical feature.

The second structural relation occurs in the *Mayer Nominale* only. Two contiguous entries are linked in the second entry by an anaphoric reference to the first. From the viewpoint of English grammar we have to distinguish two different types. Each is found with two semantic types.

In the first case, the anaphoric relation is expressed by a pronoun, Latin *eius*:

Hic leopardus, $A^{cce}$ a leberde.
*Hec leoparda, uxor ejus.*

*Hic lupus*, $A^{cce}$ a wolffe.
*Hec lupa, uxor ejus.*

As we can see, the first semantic type is the one where the female animal is referred to the male animal in the preceding entry. There is no English equivalent.

The second semantic type is also based on a morphological pattern, as was the correlation between *-us*/*-a* for the male and the female animal. This can be illustrated with the following examples:

*Hec morus*, a fylberdtre.
*Hoc morum, fructus ejus.*

*Hec mespulus*, a meltre.
*Hoc mespulum, fructus ejus.*

The morphological pattern is a masculine noun ending in *-us* correlating with a neuter noun ending in *-um*. Semantically, the product (fruit) is referred to the producer (tree).

The other type of anaphoric reference is shown in the following examples:

*Hic flos, -ris*, a flowre.
*Hoc floretum, locus ubi crescunt.*

*Hoc pirum*, a pere.
*Hoc piretum, est locus ubi crescunt.*

The lemma in the second entry is a Latin noun derivative in *-etum* defined in Latin as 'locus ubi crescunt . . .'. The subject noun phrase of the relative clause is missing, but it can be supplied from the first entry: flowers or pears. Semantically, therefore, the place of production is referred to the product (the plant). Instead of Latin *crescere*, we also find *abundare*:

*Hec corulus*, a hesyltre.
*Hoc coruletum, ubi habundant.*

The third type of relation is of a different kind and it is met with only sporadically.

*Hic dipsas, -dis, i. quidam serpens.*
*Hec filago, quedam herba.*

For some Latin nouns denoting an animal or a plant, the compiler has not provided an English equivalent, as in the previous anaphoric cases. Instead, a Latin explanation is given which does not, however, refer back to a preceding lexical item. The explanations tell us that the words denote a serpent and a herb, respectively—that is, the *genus* is indicated, but not the *differentia specifica.* For the latter, an appeal is made to the reader's knowledge of the world to supply it (*quidam, quedam, quoddam*). We thus have a relation from language to the extralinguistic world.

## THE *ORTUS VOCABULORUM*

The lexicographical metalanguage in the fifteenth-century vocabularies is Latin and this also holds for the *Ortus vocabulorum.* That the *Ortus vocabulorum* is a very early bilingual English dictionary is manifest from its many dictionary entries that are glossed in Latin with no English equivalent at all. One cannot help feeling that this is a work halted in the process of compilation: that is, a monolingual Latin dictionary was converted into a bilingual Latin–English one by providing the Latin lemmata and the Latin glosses with English equivalents.

From the period of compilation, we might expect that the compiler may have indicated the same structural relations as we find them in the topical Latin–English vocabularies. But the *Ortus vocabulorum* is a full-sized dictionary of about 25,000 entries, and we may therefore wonder whether it was this that prompted the compiler to indicate other structural relations.

The common characteristic of all the synonymous and anaphoric relations included in the Latin–English vocabularies is the contiguity of the dictionary entries involved. This overall feature also holds for the *Ortus vocabulorum.* There are only a few exceptions where the correlated items are separated by other dictionary entries. These exceptions are also the only ones in which the dictionary user is directly addressed by means of *vide* and in which the adverbs *infra, prius,* and *supra* are used:

**Anphora vide supra in amphora.**

which is matched by

**Amphora e. est olla vel vas cũ duabus**
**ansis.** a kane or tankarde.

In the following example we have *vide infra*:

**Boglosa e. vide infra in buglosa.** f.p.

which is matched by

**Buglosa e. quedam herba.** an oxe tonge

In the examples two different forms of the lemma are linked. The number of instances is too small to reveal any lexicographical policy in the treatment—as, for example, a tendency to provide the lemma to which the other lemma is referred with the meaning explanation and an English equivalent.

The other lexicographical device to relate spelling variants and other types of variants is *vel*. The variants so linked, whether Latin or English, occur within one and the same dictionary entry, as can be seen from the following examples:

**Ancela vel ancesa. i. vasa circũpicta.** anglice paynted vessell. f.p.

**Basterna est theca manualis: vl'itinerȝ** a carre or a charre. f.p.

The practice of correlating lexical items regarded as synonyms is well in evidence in the *Ortus*. The Latin identity markers are, as in the Latin–English vocabularies, *idem est* (*idem sunt*) or simply *idem*. In addition, we find *in eodem sensu*, *in eadem significatione*. Examples are:

**Britannus. i.** a man of bretayne o.s.
**Britannicus a. um. idem.**

**Cubicularius. idest camerarius vel lecti custos vel factor vel preparator.** an.[e] chamberlayne m.s.
**Cubicularia e. idem est in eadem significatione.** f.p.

As we can see from these instances, occasionally more than two lemmata may be linked. If the Latin lemma has more than one meaning, as in the case of *cubilarius*, the specification in the following lemma that it has the same meaning remains ambiguous, because the user does not know whether the statement refers to all the senses.

Since dictionary entries in the *Ortus vocabulorum* may include a run-on entry, synonym relations may not only link different dictionary entries but also occur within them. What is common, however, is that in both cases there is a contiguity of the lemmata and the structural relation is interlemmatic. Examples that illustrate identity relations within dictionary entries are:

**Ante prepositio.** befor. **Antea idẽ.**

**Bibo onis. q̇ multũ bibit.** a grett drynker. **Bibulus idẽ est.** f.t.

Such word pairs as *Britannus/Britannicus*, *Ante/Antea*, and *Bibo/Bibulus* illustrate the formal richness of Latin, where one and the same lexeme may be the basis for various formal derivatives that belong to the same word class and are very similar in meaning. Although the examples given do not include any verbs, the same principle holds for this part of speech. The *Ortus vocabulorum* has a number of instances where an active verb and its deponent variant are equated, as in:

**Lectito as. idest frequenter legere.** angl'. to rede oft. **a.p.**
**Lecto as. idem.** an.[e] to rede ofte. **a.p.**
**Lector aris. deponẽs idem est.**

The compiler's notion of 'identical meaning' embraces more than the examples quoted so far. It also covers cases in which the derived form of the pair differs in meaning because of that added by the suffix. Here are three sets of typical examples:

1. Simple verbs and the corresponding inchoative/frequentative verbs:

**Innoteo es.** to note. **n.s.**
**Innotesco cis. idẽ est.** **n.t.**

2. Nouns denoting a male and a female human being:

**Malefactor oris.** an euyll doere. **m.t.**
**Malefactrix cis. idẽ est.**

3. Simple nouns and derived diminutives:

**Furtum ti.** angl.' thefte **n.s.**
**Furtulũ li. diminutiuũ idem est.** **n.s.**

The practice seems to suggest that the compiler regarded the shared lexical basis of the two words as criterial and that the separate meaning component contained in the suffix, added by a morphological process, was not taken into account for the establishing of a synonym relationship.

Anaphoric relations are expressed by pronouns only. The second type of anaphoric relation found with Latin noun derivatives in *-etum* in the Latin–English vocabularies does not occur because we are given the derivational basis which functions as the subject of the explanatory paraphrase in Latin—for example:

**Pyretum ti. quedã herba vel locus vbi crescunt piri** **n.s.**

As to the pronoun forms used, we find *eius* as well as *ille*-forms, which seem to have a systematic distribution. *Eius* tends to occur in the same cases as in the Latin–English vocabularies, with the modification that the male/female distinction also relates to human beings, not only to animals. Examples for this semantic group are:

> **Cenodochiarius. i. elemosinarius.** a hos-
> pyteler. **m.s.**
> **Cenodochiaria est vxor eius vel elemosi-**
> **naria. f.p.**
> **Draco onis.** a dragon. **Draconia vxor**
> **eius. m.t.**

As we can see, such an anaphoric relation may link two dictionary entries or occur within a dictionary entry that includes a main and a run-on lemma. Nouns of relationship pose the special problem of the reference point adopted by the compiler. The following examples illustrate the vacillation:

> **Abauus. i. pater aui.** my granusyris fa-
> ther. **m.s.**
> **Abauia eius uxor** hys wyf. **f.p.**

No possessive pronoun corresponding to *my* occurs in the Latin explanation, yet it slipped in with the English translation. It does not relate to a lemma in the dictionary but to the compiler (or the user of the dictionary). Other instances with a first-person possessive pronoun are found under *Abamita* and *Auũculus.*

The anaphoric relation from the name of a fruit back to the noun denoting the tree which produces it can be illustrated as follows:

> **Malogranatus ti. quedã arbor.** anglice
> a pome garnet tre. **f.s.**
> **Malogranatum ti. est fructus eius.**

The use of *illius* instead of *eius* is rare:

> **Picemus.** a blauncharde tree **f.s.**
> **Picemũ mi. fructus illius arboris.** an^e^.
> a blaunche **n.s.**

One might generalize and say that *eius* and *illius* are the predominant anaphoric pronouns when the semantic relation between the two items concerned is that of part and whole, as in

> **Crassula le. est quedã herba f.p.**
> **Crassulago inis. est semen eius f.t.**

> **Fiber eris. i. castor.** angl. a brokke. **m.t.**
> **Fibrinus a. um. ꝛ hoc fibrinum ni. lana**
> **illius aĩalis. o.s.**

Sporadically, a noun denoting the dignity or power of an office is referred back to the noun denoting the office:

> **Diacon onis.** an.$^{e}$ a dekyn m.t.
> **Diaconatus tus tui. est eius digni-
> tas.** m.q.

*Ille*-forms are used for anaphoric references to a *civitas*:

> **Bisantiũ ciuitas tracie que vocatur nũc
> constantinopolim.** n.s.
> **Bisantius a. ũ. aliq̃s de illa ciuitate.** o.s.
> **Bisantia. ẽ: est moneta ciuitatʒ** illiꝰ. f.p.

*Talis*-forms seem to be used to refer back to *regio*:

> **Anglia e. quedã regio.** Englonde. f.p.
> **Anglicus a. um. dicitur anglicanꝰ. et an
> gligenus aliq̃s de tali regione.** o.s.

Structural relations which are not yet in existence in the bilingual topical vocabularies but quite well represented in the *Ortus vocabulorum* are word-formation structures. A distinction has to be made between those that explicitly establish a structural link between the basis and the derivative (our concern here) and those that do so only by implication. To the latter belong all the cases with metalinguistic terms, usually occurring after the lemma, specifying that a word is a diminutive formation, an inchoative or frequentative verbal derivative, a deverbal noun in *-tio*, *-tor*, *-trix*, or a participle in *-atum*.

> **Excurso as. frequentatiuũm.** to renne
> hastely or to renne out
> **Flecto is. xi.** to bowe downe to knele or
> declyne. a.t.
> **Flectito as. frequẽtatiuũ.** a.p.
>
> **Damno as.** to damne or harme. **Tor
> trix et tio verbalis.** a.p.

The implied word-formational relationship is found within a dictionary entry and also between two entries.

The same types of derivative structures may also be described explicitly as one being derived from the other:

> **Estacula le. diminutiuũ de estas** f.p.
> **Estas estatis. quarta pars anni.** an$^{e}$.
> somer f.t.
>
> **Capio pis.** to take a.t.
> **Capisco cis. inchoatiuũ de capio.** to be
> gyñ to take. a.t.

Another lexicographical device to indicate word-formational structures is by means of the adverbs *inde* and the rarer *unde*. They usually occur within a dictionary entry and introduce a sublemma:

> **Ciliũ ij.** angl.' a ye lede or browe. **inde ve nit suꝑciliũ ⁊ interciliũ.** **n.s.**
>
> **Coeternus coeterna coeternum.** euerla-stynge togyder. **i. simul eternus.** **o.s.**
> **Inde Coeternitas atis.** **f.t.**

In Chapter 8 we will discuss the equivalent part in the French vocabulist and show that the compiler of the *Ortus vocabulorum* occasionally indicates meaning transfers by drawing attention to the literal meaning of a word. The lexicographical device used is the adverb *proprie*. We shall, therefore, not dwell further on these semantic relations except to show that attempts at providing the (assumed) literal meaning of a word and assessments of semantic developments shade into each other:

> **Exartuo as. i. diuidere et ꝓprie secare artus ad inuicem.** to karue **a.p.**

A very common feature in the *Ortus vocabulorum* is the appeal to the readers' knowledge of the world. This holds especially for the many lemmata that are proper names. Such encyclopedic entries are difficult to describe—for example, *Ethna ne. quidã mons sicilie qui semper in se ardet*—and therefore the compiler has often only indicated the general class to which a proper name belongs (*Aristoteles . . . philosophus*), enough perhaps to call up the full particulars of the cultural knowledge which he assumes the readers to share with him (i.e. replacing the lexicographer's pronoun *quidam* by the appropriate information). Such generic categories are, for instance, civitas (*Argos*), provincia (*Arragonia*), terra (*Equitania*), regio (*Egiptus*), insula (*Carpatos*), fluvius (*Ganges*), and mons (*Garganus*). Names of natural kinds (animals, birds, fish, plants), equally difficult to describe lexicographically, are also often given in this way. So, too, nouns denoting containers, sciences, games, figures of speech, and so on:

> **Astronomia e. est quedã sciẽtia.** angl.' a astronomye. **f.p.**
>
> **Capis dis. ẽ quoddã vas aquaticũ.** **f.t.**

At the basis of a substantial part of the structural relations outlined in the *Ortus vocabulorum* are the richness and productivity of Latin morphology. The compilers of the first English–Latin dictionaries both decided to dispense with this wealth of linguistic information in their respective works, just as they greatly reduced the encyclopaedic entries which they found in the Latin reference sources they consulted. The structural relations explicitly indicated in the *Promptorium parvulorum* and the *Catholicon Anglicum* thus differ in interesting ways from those of the *Ortus vocabulorum*. One feature which both the English–Latin dictionaries have in common, in sharp contrast to the *Ortus*, is that there is a cross-reference system that pervades the whole of the dictionary. If such a system is handled reliably, and establishing this is a goal of the present chapter, it puts on the compiler a much higher burden of control over the whole work. The predominant structural relation type of the *Ortus* which is based on the contiguity of the dictionary entries concerned (and therefore always a locational *ad hoc* feature) is rare.

## THE *PROMPTORIUM PARVULORUM*

A close study of the cross-references in the *Promptorium parvulorum* suggests that the compiler tried to outline five different types of relations. In four cases we have structural relations between linguistic items, in one case the relation is that between a lexical item and its source text. There are some marked differences in the treatment of these structural relations between the manuscript edition and the earliest printed edition. We shall, therefore, first look at the edition provided by Mayhew and then the 1499 print.

Functionally, the most prominent structural relation in the *Promptorium parvulorum* is that between the different forms of a linguistic sign, clearly reflecting the compiler's awareness and concern for linguistic variation. He goes beyond linking dictionary entries with different spellings for the same lexical item. He draws his users' attention to spelling correspondences between words. These observations are made in Latin, just as his lexicographical linking devices are all cast in Latin. Correlations between *C* and *S*, and between *K* and *C* are discussed under the respective letters. Thus after the last entry for the sequence *Ce* in the *nominale* part (col. 76) the compiler tells his users: 'Quere plura vocabula habencia in prima sillaba hunc sonum C in s littera vbi E sequitur immediate s,' and so he does in the *verbale* section after the last verb recorded with the spelling *Ce* (col. 109). These instructions are matched by similar ones under the letter *S* referring users back to the letter *C*. There the compiler even provides us with a reason for his cross-reference practice: 'Alia sunt plura habencia in principio huius littere C scriptum cum S que causa breuitatis non scribuntur, set require ea in C littera vbi in principio Diccionis E sequitur C immediate' (col. 409). Users are thus not only warned that the compiler has not always listed spelling variants at the respective alphabetical places, but are also told why (for brevity's sake) he has not. Similar notes are found after the last verb entry beginning with *Se* (col. 457), and the last noun entry with the initial sequence *Cy* (col. 84) and *Sy* (col. 413).

*Ce-/Cy-* and *Se-/Sy*-items are thus doubly cross-referred. In the case of spelling correlations between the initial sequences *Ca-*, *Co-*, *Cu-* and *Ka-*, *Ko-*, *Ku-*, the cross-reference is unilateral only. Under the letter *K* we are told that other items are listed as *C*-spellings (cols. 245, 251; see also the comment for the sequence *sk-* (col. 414)). The brevity argument is repeated.

There are quite a few lexicographical devices used to indicate spelling variants. Common adverbial phrases are *supra in*, *infra in*, or just *in*, as in:

> **Abul**, *supra in* **able**.
> **Ancle**, *infra in* **ankyl**.
> **Elmesse**, *in* **almosse**.

A further device is the one where the two variant forms are said to be identical (*idem quod supra in/infra in*):

> **ffurbyschour**, *idem quod* **fforby-schowre**, *supra*.

In a completely consistent cross-reference system, both terms will cross-refer to the other. That is, if the adjective *able* also occurred as *abul* in fifteenth-century English, there should not only be a cross-reference entry '**Abul**, *supra in* **able**' but the entry for *able* should also indicate that there is the variant spelling *abul*. If we assume that the cross-referred item is the less common variant—though there is no evidence for such an assumption in early English dictionaries—we would have to expect an entry where the standard lemma *able* is followed by the variant *abul*. The actual entry in the *Promptorium parvulorum* reads as follows:

> **Able**, or abul: *Abilis*, *-le*; *omnis generis*, *3^e^ decli*[*nacionis*].

It is one of the few instances where spelling variants are doubly cross-referred and where both items are both times spelt in the same way. At a time when English spelling was far from being fixed, such a correspondence is by no means general, as can be seen from the following examples:

> **Baker**, or baxter: *Pistor*, *-ris*; *Masc.*, *3*: *Pannicius*; *Masc.*, *2*, '*catholicon*': *Panifex*; *commune*, *3*, '*catholicon*': *Panificator*, *-ris*; *Masc. gen. 3 decl.*

> **Bakestare**, *supra in* **bakar**.

This lack of consistency in spelling holds for all types of cross-referred items, as we can see from the linking of the two nouns *bramble* and *brier*:

**Brerre**, or brymmyl: *Tribulus, -i, -o; Masc., 2: vepris, -pris; fem., 3.*

**Brymbyl**, *supra in* **brere**.

A user who had been cross-referred to *bakar* would not have found *bakar*, but *baker*, and if remembering the other form he originally looked up, *bakestare*, and wondering whether this *baker* was the item looked for, he would have been confronted with *baxter*. The modern scholar wonders whether the cross-references will have fulfilled their purpose, in view of such disparities.

As we can see from the examples quoted, when the structural relation concerns the form of the lemmata, the cross-reference usually occurs after the item which is referred to another lemma, and this very lemma is mentioned. The Latin translation equivalents are listed in the dictionary entry to which the reader was referred.

The second structural relation indicated in the *Promptorium parvulorum*, the (assumed) identity between two items, does not only occur with spelling variants. More characteristically, it is outlined in cases where the compiler regarded two or three items as having the same meaning (with the reservations made above (pp. 261–2) for the notion of identity). In a number of instances two abstract nouns are described as identical which are either a simple and a derived noun, or two derivatives with different suffixes:

**Gladsumnesse**, *idem quod* **gladness**, *supradicitur.*

**Hastynesse**, *idem quod* **haste** *supra.*

Such identity relations are indicated not only for nouns, but also for verbs and adjectives:

**Dyggyn**, *idem quod* **delvyn** *supra.*

**Sott**, *idem quod* **folt**, *supra in f.*

In the very few instances in which an identity relation is pointed out for two contiguous lexical items, the second term of the relation may not be expressed. After the lemma of the second dictionary entry, the indication is then simply *idem* or *idem est*:

**Chaston**, ffrute: *Castanea, -e; fem.*
**Chestyntre**, *idem est.*

Yet when there is contiguity between two dictionary entries, the cross-reference may also be *idem quod* . . . in the case of an identity relation, or *supra* (*in*) . . . if the exact relationship between the two lemmata is left open:

**ffor-ȝevenesse**: *Venia, -e; fem., prime*: *Remissio, -is; fem., 3*.

**ffor-ȝevyng**, *idem quod* **for-ȝevenesse**, *supra*.

In the dictionary entries linked by an identity relation, the compiler assumes that two English lexical items are synonymous. With the third structural relation openly indicated in the *Promptorium parvulorum*, the compiler's attention focuses on the relation between the English lemma and its possible Latin translation equivalents. In accordance with the rhetorical precepts of the Renaissance, he is trying to provide *copia* of expression. At the end of an entry, users may therefore be alerted to the fact that there are still further ways of rendering the English lemma in Latin, and, if they are interested in these, they should look up the item given. The lexicographical devices used are expressions like *alia supra/infra in*, *et nota alia infra in . . .*, *quere plura in . . .*, *et alia quere infra in*, and so on. In one case we even find *nota omnia in . . .*:

> **Pleyynge thynge**, or thyngis þat men or chyldyrne play with: *adluricum, -ci; neut., 2, vgucio in adri uel dros uel adros, nota omnia in* **laykyn**.

Under *laykyn* there are two further Latin equivalents besides *adluricum*:

> **Laykyn**, or thyng þat chylder pley with: *ludibile, -is; neut., 3, vgucio in ludo; ludibulum, -i, neut., 2*: *Adluricum, -i; neut., 2, vgucio in adri et adros*.

In general, there is at least one translation equivalent which is common to both the cross-referred entries. Latin *accipere* thus occurs under *nymmyn* and *takyn*:

**Nymmyn**, or takyn: *Accipio, -pis, -cepi, -re; 3 con., act., et alia supra in* **takyn**.

**Takyn**, or resevyn: *accipio, -is, -cepi, -re, -ceptum*: *Capio, -is, -cepi, -re, captum*: *apprehendo, -is, -di, -re, -sum*: *Sumo, -is sumpsi, -re, -sumptum*: *Tollo, -is, -tuli, -re, -latum*: *prendo, -is -didi, -re, -prensum, vgucio in prendo; omnia predicta verba sunt 3 con., act.*

At the end of the entry for *takyn*, we have a statement that embraces all the six Latin verbs provided as equivalents for the English verb: 'omnia predicta verba sunt 3 con., act.'. In order to avoid lengthy repetitions, the compiler gives the full grammatical description after all the members of the same class have been listed. The explicit indication that a particular number of verbs share the same grammatical features is an obvious expression of the structural relation that holds between them. It is the only structural relation type in the *Promptorium parvulorum* where both terms occur in one and the same dictionary entry.[1] All the others outlined above connect two different entries. Instead of the encompassing phrase 'omnia sunt' we may also encounter the specification 'similiter declinatur'.

We come to the last type of relation indicated in the *Promptorium*. This links a Latin translation equivalent to source material consulted for the compilation of the English–Latin dictionary. Here we have not a structural relationship that holds between specific features of some linguistic signs but rather an explicit declaration of a unidirectional lexicographical dependency of one work from the other. In general, the author or the title of the source work is given and occasionally the specific place within the work is mentioned:

> **Elf,** spyryt: *lamia, -e; fem., prime,*
> *'catholicon' et vgucio in lanio et*
> *'vgucio versificatus' in t.*

We come to the first printed edition of the *Promptorium parvulorum* (1499). In this later version of the work, the compiler's concern for linguistic variation is much less conspicuous. The instances where spelling correspondences between different letters were pointed out have shrunk considerably.

Apart from an exceptional *quere supra in* (*Tunneur*), all the cross-references linking different spellings of headwords have been standardized to an adverbial *supra/infra in . . .*, where the specific relation between the items concerned is not expressed but left to the users' interpretation or insight. There are no instances where two spellings are paired by an *idem quod supra/infra in . . .*

The compiler's practice of indicating structural relations where one item is said to be the same as another by means of *idem quod . . .*, as found in Mayhew's edition of the Winchester Cathedral MS, is not carried over into the Pynson edition.

[1] This leaves aside the sporadic instances where two Latin equivalents within one dictionary entry are described as being the same, as in

> **A-rayn,** or make honest: *Orno, -as,*
> *-aui; Adorno, -as, -aui, -are;*
> *honesto, -as; Decuso, -as: Decoro,*
> *-as; idem sunt; 'campus florum',*
> *kylwarbi, omnia prime con., act.*

See also *Brawnch of a tre* and *Buffyn of hondis ffolwyng here pray.*

What holds for the singling out of identity relations also holds for the practice of providing *copia* of expression in Latin. The lexicographical device of linking two different synonymous headwords by means of a simple *supra in* . . . or *infra in* . . . and not specifying the exact nature of this relationship, already well in evidence in the manuscript edition, has been generalized.

The other types of relation discussed for Mayhew's edition are unchanged in the Pynson edition.

The compiler's lexicographical metalanguage is Latin with two noteworthy exceptions in the vernacular. In both cases the same wording is used although the first example points out the more common spelling and the second provides another name for a specific kind of metal:

**Bysshell.** Modius dii. mas. ge. secunde d'. **otherwyse called busshell.**

**Blawmblũb. other wyse called whyte lede.** Albũ blumbũ albi plũbi, neu. ge. secũde d'.[2]

## THE *CATHOLICON ANGLICUM*

The second English–Latin dictionary, the *Catholicon Anglicum*, combines some of the structural relations indicated in the *Ortus vocabulorum* and the *Promptorium parvulorum*. At the same time it has a number of distinctive features of its own.

The most salient characteristic of the *Catholicon Anglicum*, we recall, is the compiler's endeavour to provide his users with a rich choice of Latin expressions that may render a particular English headword. In Chapter 8 we shall see that as many as several dozen Latin equivalents may be given. It will also be shown that there are excellent attempts at differentiating the meaning of some of them. A cross-reference component in the dictionary that relates entries with similar meanings would evidently still further increase the thesaurus-like wealth of expression. And this is exactly what the compiler of the *Catholicon Anglicum* did to ensure maximum effectiveness of his work.

Although in number of headwords the *Catholicon Anglicum* amounts to only two-thirds of the *Promptorium parvulorum* (some 8,000 entries compared to some 12,000 entries), it has nearly three times as many cross-references. That is, about one-tenth of the *Catholicon Anglicum* entries are cross-linked dictionary entries. One of the obvious consequences of this ambitiously planned lexicographical device is that sequences of cross-references are not unusual.

[2] In Mayhew's edition the headword is *Blanke plumb*.

When readers follow up a cross-reference in an entry, they may come across a further cross-reference inviting them to look up a third item. Thus from the adjective *cele*, for instance, the reader is sent to *happy*, and from there to *blissed*:

**Cele**; *vbi* happy.
**Happy**; *beatus, faustus, felix*, & *cetera*; *vbi* blissed.

**Blyssyd**; *beatus, beatificatus, beatulus, faustus, fortunatus, felix*, gloriosus.

And similarly, from the noun *costrelle* the reader is referred to *flakett*, and under *flaket* a consultation of the entry *a potte* is suggested:

a **Costrelle**; *oneferum, & cetera*; *vbi* a flakett.

a **Flaket**; *flacata, obba, vter, & cetera*; vbi A potte.

a **Potte**; *olla, ollula, orca, sania, seria, vrna, vrnula, testa, i. Argilla cocta, vnde versus*:

¶ *Vrceus, vrceolus est vrna vel Amfora, testa.*
*Olla vel idria, vas vini dic esse lagenam:*
*Obba vel onoferum, simul orca fidelia vas est*
*Ampullas, fiolas, hijs bullas Associamus.*

From these examples some conclusions may be drawn. One is that the Latin equivalents provided in an earlier entry of the sequence may be included in the next entry (e.g. *beatus, faustus*, and *felix* under **Happy** and **Blyssyd**). The case of *costrelle* and *flaket* illustrates that none of the Latin translation equivalents may be shared by both entries. The other is that circular cross-references are on the whole rare.

A corollary of the compiler's intent on bringing out the differences of meaning between the Latin items listed is that one single dictionary entry may invite the user to look up two other headwords. For the English noun *crime*, for instance, two semantic strands are suggested in the Latin equivalents, *trespass* and *sin*:

A **Cryme**; *delictum, crimen & cetera*; *vbi* trespas or syn̄.

a **Trespace**; *delictum, demeritum, forisfaccio, preuaricacio, transgressio*; *reatus, preuaricatorius, & cetera* [*vbi*] syn̄.

**Synne**; *Admissum, delictum quasi derelictum quod fieri debuit, peccatum cum committimus quod non licet, crimen, culpa, flagicium, flagiciosus, facinus, fomes, limus, noxa, noxius, sanguis, nox, pectamen, piaculum, reatus, vicium, viciolum, tradux, scelus est quod fit contra hominez ut rapina vel oppressio, jniquitas quasi non equitas & fit irridendo, detrahendo vel paciendo, vel scelus est quicquid non oportet, nephas est quicquid non licet.*

In a similar way, the Latin equivalents for the English verb *to grant* are divided into an *affirm*-branch and a *give*-branch:

to **Graunte**; *concedere, & cetera;*
*vbi* to afferme, *& vbi* to gyffe.

to **Afferme**; *Astruere, affirmare testimonio, confirmare officio, asseuerare, assentire, asserere, assertire, annuere, accensum prebere, Autorizare, concedere, adquiescere, ascribere.*

to **Gife**; *committere, donare, conferre, con-, dare, duputare, duere, exhibere, inpendere, inpensare, largiri, numerare, re-, prebere, reddere, rependere, soluere, delargiri, tradere, tribuere.*

Variation in linguistic expression to fit a particular context and style will naturally transgress the formal constraints imposed by grammatical word classes. In a number of instances the Latin equivalents provided for an English word therefore include items of a different part of speech. Often there is a derivational relationship between such members of a different word class so that in such entries different lexicographical principles pursued by the compiler may meet.

The entry for *an Alde man*, for instance, does not refer the reader to another noun lemma but to the adjective entry *Alde*. Readers may thus turn from their original idea of rendering the English headword by one single noun in Latin to an adjective + noun phrase and for this an ample number of adjectives is supplied. The ease with which an adjective may be used in a nominal function in Latin will undoubtedly have been an important factor for the compiler in setting up such links between lexical items belonging to different parts of speech:

an **Alde man**; *gerion; vbi* alde; *geronta, silicernus.*

**Alde**; *priscus qui fuerunt priores; antiquus, qui fuerunt ante nos; annosus, jnveteratus, decrepitus, vetulus o. g. a multitudine annorum emeritus, senilis, longeuus, pristinus, vetustus, senex, veteranus geronceus, gerontecus.*

We note that, unlike the *Promptorium parvulorum*, the *Catholicon Anglicum* refers to further Latin translation equivalents by means of *& cetera* (occasionally also *& cetera alia*). This phrase is quite frequent within the dictionary and usually occurs at the end of the entry, after a number of Latin equivalents.

The priority given to *copia* of expression in Latin and to semantic differentiation in the *Catholicon Anglicum* does not leave much room for other relations indicated in the *Ortus vocabulorum* and the *Promptorium parvulorum*. Spelling variants of English headwords play a very subordinate role. This is a sharp contrast between the *Promptorium parvulorum* and the *Catholicon Anglicum*. There are instances where this relation in the formal make-up is explicitly expressed—for example:

a **Censure**; *vide in S. littera.*

a **Sensure**; *batillus, thuribulum, cicendium.*

But the ubiquitous wording of cross-references in the *Catholicon* is the Latin adverb *ubi.* In the case of the adverbs *infra* and *supra* a conscientious compiler would have had to check the actual place of the cross-referred items. Since alphabetical order was not yet systematically observed and since standard forms of English spelling were not yet established, there was no automatic prediction for an *infra-* or a *supra-*position of a lexical item in an alphabetical list as it would be common in our days. The accuracy in this respect in the *Promptorium parvulorum* is impressive.

The choice of *ubi* instead of *infra* and *supra* enables the compiler to dispense with the additional burden of checking whether a cross-referred item has already been mentioned or whether it is still to come in the alphabetical list. All he would have had to ascertain was that the item was listed. Both the *Promptorium parvulorum* and the *Catholicon Anglicum* are remarkable for the insignificant number of cases where a cross-referred item has inadvertently been omitted in the word list.

With a mere *ubi*, the exact relationship that holds between cross-referred items is left unexpressed:

a **Buke**; *liber, & cetera*; *vbi* a boke.

a **Boke**; *carta, cartula, codex, codicillus, liber, libellus, volumen, pagina, pagella, sceda.*

As we can see from these examples, the dictionary entry with the fuller lexicographical treatment to which a variant is referred does not list the two different spellings. This is a characteristic which the early bilingual English dictionaries have in common. The beginnings of a double listing, side by side, the variant regarded as less common after the more common one, are made in the *Promptorium parvulorum.*

No attempt is made to single out identity relations. The instances which occur are odd occurrences. The formal means is always Latin *idem* or *idem est.* In the case of *Perys* and *Perkyn* the two entries are contiguous:

**Perys**; *petrus, nomen proprium.*
**Perkyñ**; *idem est.*

In the other examples two Latin equivalents within one and the same dictionary entry are said to be the same:

A **Wechecrafte**; *Sortilegium, veneficium idem est.*

As has been pointed out earlier, dictionary entries in the *Catholicon Anglicum* occasionally include suffixal derivatives of the Latin equivalents supplied. Two different kinds have to be distinguished. The one consists in the mere addition of one (or more) derivative(s), with or without a following specification of the grammatical class (diminutivum, participium), as illustrated below:

> a **Madyn**; *Ancilla, Ancillula; Ancillaris participium; Abra, puella, puellula; puellaris; virgo, virguncula; virginalis, virgeneus participia.*

These, we have suggested, may help users to vary the Latin translation in grammatical or stylistic form as required by the context. In the other case, the Latin derivative is provided with an explanation of its meaning in Latin. The explanatory paraphrase may then include an anaphoric reference—for example:

> **A Townesange**; *Commedia; Comedus scriptor earum.*

A *comedus* is someone who writes comedies. All the instances of anaphoric relations found in the *Catholicon Anglicum* link two items occurring within the same dictionary entry. Thus they do not bridge contiguous entries, as in the early vocabularies and the *Ortus vocabulorum*. Explicit anaphoric relations are expressed by forms of the Latin pronouns *is, ille, talis*. What becomes clear from the examples retrieved is that with one exception there is no systematic policy to include a particular type of derivative. The examples look like gleanings from a source text taken over *in toto*:

> a **Crab tre**; *arbitus, macianus, macianum est fructus eius.*[3]

> **Perman tre**; *volemus, volemum fructus eius.*[4]

[3] The corresponding entries in the *Ortus vocabulorum* are:

> **Macianũ ni.** a wylde appyll or a crabe.
> **Macianus ni.** a crabe tre. **f.s.**

[4] The corresponding entries in the *Ortus vocabulorum* are:

> **Volemus mi. est quoddã genus piri que facit pira adeo magna ꝙ vix in vola possunt includi. et plene implent illam** anglice a wardon tree **f.s.**
> **Volem mi. est fructus eius.** a wardon

a **Sturtre**; *Duracenus, Duracenum fructus eius.*[5]

a **Soldañ**; *soldanus; soldana vxor eius.*[6]

The Latin nouns concerned belong to the semantic groups outlined for anaphoric relations in the topical vocabularies and the *Ortus vocabulorum*: a fruit tree and its product, a male and a female human being.

The exception, where one has the impression that the compiler seems to have been intent on supplying one particular derivative, is the name of an affliction to which the noun denoting the person so afflicted is added:

> **þe Falland Euylle**; *epilencia, comicius vel comicialis, morbus caducus, noxa, gerenoxa, epilensis; epilenticus qui patitur illam infirmitatem.*

In the *Ortus vocabulorum* the name of the condition is listed as well as that of the person afflicted, in each case as separate entries, either linked by an anaphoric pronoun or by a repetition of the word for the condition.

Entries for names of plants or trees and animals may include a Latin derivative in *-etum* paraphrased as 'locus ubi crescunt' or 'locus ubi abundant'.

From a syntactic point of view these explanations are quite unsystematic. The basic noun may be repeated:

> a **Flee**; *musca, muscula, musco, cinifes, indeclinabile; muscetum, muscarium, muscularium, musceletum, sunt loca vbi habundant musce . . .*

It may not be present at all and then we have an implicit anaphoric relation:

> A **Violett**; *viola, violarium locus vbi crescit.*

The verb form of the meaning paraphrase may be in the singular, in which case there is agreement between the simple noun and the anaphoric reference:

[5] The corresponding entries in the *Ortus vocabulorum* are:

> **Durascenus ni.** a sture tree **f.s.**
> **Durascenũ ni.** a sture appell **n.s.**

[6] The corresponding entries in the *Ortus vocabulorum* are:

> **Soldanus.** a sawdyne. **m.s.**
> **Soldana e. vxor illius. f.p.**

an **Esche**; *fraxinus*; *fraxinus*, *fraxineus*; *fraxinetum est locus vbi crescit.*

Yet we may also have the plural form, which semantically is more adequate for *-etum*-derivatives:

an **Ellyrtre**; *Alnus*; *alnicetum est locus vbi crescunt.*

Just as the majority of instances in which an anaphoric relationship is expressed seems to have been prompted by a source text, so the dozen or so examples where an appeal is made to the users' knowledge of the world seem to have been copied from another reference source. They typically include a form of the Latin pronoun *quidam*—for example:

an **Ostyr**; *ostreum*, *peloris*: *ostreum quidam piscis qui in ostra lactitat.*

Where the *Catholicon Anglicum* stands clearly apart from the *Ortus vocabulorum* and the *Promptorium parvulorum* is in the treatment of word-formation for the mother tongue.

We recall from the description of the word list that the compiler made it his policy to bring together in one place members of word families. Alphabetical order may therefore be interrupted. This holds above all for the recording of negated adjectives and verbs prompted by a lexeme in Latin. Thus the English lemma to **Kepe**, for instance, is followed by the non-lexicalized lemma entries *to yif to* **Kepe**, and *thynge yifen to* **Kepe** because of Latin *commendare*, *deponere* for the former, and *commendatum*, *depositum* for the latter. The policy adopted by the compiler for the listing of adjectives prefixed by *un-* is stated at the beginning of the words headed *V ante N*. We read:

**Vn Abylle**; *inabilis.*

*Regula* { ¶ *Nota quod omnia huiusmodi idiomata jncipiencia ab* vn *sunt requirenda ad sua simplicia*; *verbi gratia* **vnabylle** *vbi* abylle.

The following lexical item is *unbuxom*, where a general remark to the effect of the above rule is made:

**Vn boxum**; *vbi* buxum *& sic de similibus.*

Finally, we draw attention to two aspects in the actual form of cross-references where the *Catholicon* differs from the preceding bilingual English dictionaries. English lemma entries in the *Catholicon* have a specific form: verbs are preceded by the particle *to*; for nouns we find the indefinite article, e.g. *a Gowrde*, the definite article, e.g. *þe Gowte*, and a zero article, e.g. *Gramary*. These elements tend to be maintained in cross-references.

In both the English–Latin dictionaries the English lemma entries may be complex. The lemma proper may be followed by a postlemmatic gloss or a postmodification. In cross-references it is usually the lemma proper to which users are directed. In the *Promptorium*, we also find instances where the item to which users are referred is already mentioned as a postlemmatic gloss in the headword entry, as *forhede* in the following example:

**Front or forhede.** supra in **forhede.**

In the *Catholicon*, there are instances of more complex structures, as is exemplified by *to dra on longe* and *to take hede*:

to **Differ**; *differre, prolongare, & cetera*; *vbi* to dra on longe

to **Drawe on longe or on lenght**; *crastinare, pro-, longare, differe, protelare, prorogare, protrahere, protendere*; *versus*: . . .

to **Study**; *studere, vacare, & cetera*; *vbi* to take hede.

to **Take hede**; *Ascultare, Attendere, jntendere, jndulgere, Assidere, jnsistere, vacare, operam dare, jnvigilare.*

## *LESCLARCISSEMENT*

Having reviewed the different types of structural and non-structural relations as well as their functions in the lexicographical works for English that preceded the publication of *Lesclarcissement*, we are now in a position to assess Palsgrave's own achievement. He has developed a cross-reference system with some striking features. It is the dictionary user's mother tongue that is used as the metalanguage. *Lesclarcissement* thus illustrates the shift of linguistic emphasis away from the classical languages towards the vernaculars of the time which is so characteristic of the Renaissance period. His French vocabulist is the first full-length dictionary in which English is matched with another vernacular, French, and the source language English has penetrated so far into the dictionary itself that it has replaced Latin in one area of the lexicographical metalanguage. Secondly, unlike the *Ortus vocabulorum*, but similar to the *Promptorium parvulorum* and the *Catholicon Anglicum*, *Lesclarcissement* provides cross-references between different lexical items through the whole of the alphabet, not restricting them to contiguous dictionary entries. Yet there is a further striking difference between *Lesclarcissement* in this respect and the two English–Latin dictionaries. Not all the parts of Palsgrave's dictionary are provided with a cross-reference system. Its use varies according to the word classes recorded. Of the nine parts of speech described by Palsgrave, it is only entries for pronouns and verbs that are cross-referred, though there are a few odd instances in the tables of adjectives, adverbs, and conjunctions. This seems to suggest that the idea of correlating lemmata under certain conditions came to Palsgrave rather late during the compilation process of the work, after he had already completed the tables of nouns and adjectives. It may also, and more plausibly, suggest that there is something word-class specific about pronouns and verbs that prompted Palsgrave to introduce lexicographical correlative devices. The mastery of the pronominal system of an inflecting language is often notoriously difficult to acquire because of the morphological irregularities. This may account for Palsgrave's decision and the particular nature of the cross-references used in the table of pronouns. They do not correlate different items of the pronoun table but refer the user to the grammar sections of *Lesclarcissement*, where the item in question is explained in more detail and subsumed under certain grammatical rules. Consider the following example:

> **Some**/ les vngz, les aulcuns, les aultres, les aulcunes, quelque, de, **or** tel. capi. xxix. regu. iii.

We note that the user is given the chapter reference and the number of the rule which applies to the particular item. The metalinguistic terms used are the Latin nouns *capitulum* and *regula* (or their abbreviations). The table of pronouns takes up five pages altogether and the type of cross-reference illustrated directs the user to a text other than the dictionary, which is therefore of little interest for the development of lexicographical method and practice. In what follows we shall thus concentrate on Palsgrave's table of verbs.

There are three stereotyped expressions which Palsgrave uses to refer his readers to another dictionary entry: *conjugate in*, *declared in*, and *look in*, of which the latter is the least frequent. Whereas *look in . . .* is a straightforward command for the user and purely directional, *conjugate in* is more complexly cross-referential. It tells the user how to conjugate the French verb in question and where to find the pattern displayed. *Declared in* (a shortening of *I have declared* or *it has been declared*) suggests that the user will be given more explanation on the verb item concerned in another entry. Like the compilers of the *Ortus vocabulorum* and the *Promptorium parvulorum*, Palsgrave uses adverbs of location in their relation to the particular lexical item dealt with. So there is no *where . . . is* which would correspond to Latin *ubi* in the *Catholicon Anglicum*, but an *here after* (*in . . .*) or a (*here*) *afore* (*in . . .*). In the case of references to contiguous dictionary entries, *next* is added (e.g. *declared here next afore*). None of the three cross-reference devices indicates the nature of the relation that holds between the items linked. This is also the case for some of the fuller lexicographical statements like *loke in . . . where I make mention of it* (**I Am colde**), *and how he is conjugate shall herafter apere in . . .* (**I Am skylled**). Two of the three devices may occasionally co-occur, as *conjugate* and *look* in the entry **I Defende**:

> **I Defende/** Ie defens, iay defendu, defendre, **coniugate lyke his symple** ie fens. **I cleaue/ loke in I forbydde. God diffende it**: A dieu ne plaise. **I shall defende your quarell agaynst all men**: Ie defẽderay vostre querelle contre tous, ⁊ ie contregarde. prime. **This medecyne wyll defende you from the sycknesse**: Ceste medicine vous contregardera de la peste.
>
> (III, fo. cc.vi)

So too *look* and *declared* in **I Feynte**:

> **I Feynte (Lydgate) loke in I faynte for laboure or trauayle/** Ie suis vayn, and le cueur me fault, **declared afore in I faynte.**
>
> (III, fo. cc.xxxv)

And *conjugate* and *declared* in **I Soyle**:

> **I Soyle from synne/** Ie assouls. **cõiugate and declared in I assoyle.**
>
> (III, fo. ccc.lxvi)

The review of Palsgrave's predecessors has brought to light a number of different structural relations that may be expressed by cross-references. It might, therefore, be advisable to deal first with those relations where there is a link between *Lesclarcissement* and the works that were compiled earlier and then with those that appear for the first time in Palsgrave's table of verbs.

A cross-reference may tell the user that the English verb occurs also in a different spelling and that more information may be found under that other spelling. As the following examples show, all the three lexicographical devices, *loke in*, *conjugate in*, and *declared in* may link variant spellings:

**I Blanche almondes/** Ie pelle des amandes, **loke in I blaunche.**

(III, fo. c.lxvii)

**I Blaunche almondes/** Ic pelle. prime coniuga. **you haue eaten mo beanes than blaunched almondes:** Vous auez mange plus de feues que des amandes pellées.

(III, fo. c.lxvii^v^)

**I Bowlne or swell/** Ienfle. prime coniuga. **declared in I bolne.**

(III, fo. c.lxxi)

**I Bolne I swell/** Ienfle. prime coniuga. **Se howe this toode bolneth:** Agardez comment ce crapault senfle. **My hande is bolne sythe yesternyght as moche agayne as it is wonte to be:** Ma mayn cest enflée depuis hier au soyr presque double autant quelle souloyt.

(III, fo. c.lxix^v^)

**I Descryue I declare ẏ facyons or maners of a thynge/** Ie blasonne. prime coniuga. **and** ie descrips, **coniugate in I descrybe.**

(III, fo. cc.ix)

**I Descrybe I sette forthe the facyons or maners of a thyng/** Ie descrips, nous descripuons, ie descripuis iay descript, ie descripray, que ie descripue, descripre, **cõiugate lyke his symple** iescrips, **I write. Pholomye hath discryued ẏ worlde best of any one man afore our tyme:** Pholomye a descript le monde mieulx q̃ nul aultre deuant noz iours.

(III, fo. cc.ix)

Like his predecessors, Palsgrave highlights the lemma (proper) of a dictionary entry by a capital initial. Yet, when the lemma occurs as part of a cross-reference, it is printed in its normal unlemmatized form.[7] The examples also illustrate that the two correlated entries are not fully complementary in the sense that the entry with the fuller lexicographical treatment includes the other spelling variant as well. A further feature which *Lesclarcissement* shares with the *Promptorium parvulorum* and the *Catholicon Anglicum* is that the spelling of an item in a cross-reference does not always agree with the actual spelling of the same item as a lemma. In Palsgrave's table of verbs, we have a further variable: the spelling of the lexical item concerned in the example sentences. Such variation is well exemplified by the following two sets of dictionary entries:

[7] An exception, for instance, is *Mayntayne* in the entry **I Stande I am mayntaynyd or vpholdyn** (III, fo. ccc.lxxii^v^).

> **I Hamyne I mynte as one dothe to hytte a thyng (Lydgat) and reasonlesse gan hamyn at his heed/** Ie esme, or ie prens mon aduis, **declared in I eyme.**
>
> (III, fo. cc.lvii)

The other member of the correlated set is not listed under *eyme* but under *ayme*:

> **I Ayme/ I mente or gesse to hyt a thynge/** Ie esme. prime coniuga. **or** ie fays semblant. **Ayme to hyt yonder whyte:** Esmes a toucher ce blanc la.
>
> (III, fo. c.xxxix[v])

Whereas the structural relation between different spellings of a lexical item is not explicitly stated, the identity relation may be. Yet explicit instances linking two dictionary entries are rare. It is here that Latin as a metalanguage slips in again in the form of *idem*:

> **I Demeane or behaue my selfe or I order me in a mater/** Ie me porte, ie me suis porté, porter. verbũ mediũ. prime coniuga. **and** ie macquitte, ie me suis acquitté, acquitter. verbum mediũ. prime coniuga. **and** ie me demayne, ie me suis demayné, demayner. verbũ mediũ. prime cõiuga. **I neuer sawe man in my lyfe demeane him selfe better than he dyd:** Iamays en ma vie ne vis homme se porter mieulx sacquitter mieulx, se demayner mieulx quil fist.
>
> (III, fo. cc.vii[v])
>
> **I Demene (Lydgate)** idem.
>
> (III, fo. cc.vii[v])

> **I Disparke/** Iescarte, ie desempare, ie desassemble, **and** ie disparse. prime coniuga. **They be disparkled nowe many a myle a sõder:** Ilz sont desassemblez, ilz sõt disparsez maynte myle, **or** lieue densemble.
>
> (III, fo. cc.xiiii)
>
> **I Disparpyll (Lydgate)** idem.[8]
>
> (III, fo. cc.xiiii)

In both cases the two dictionary entries are contiguous. When this is not so, the identity relation may occur in an overt English wording as in the following example:

> **I Deceyue I begyle one/** Ie decoys, nous decepuons, ilz decoyuent, ie deceus, iay deceu, ie deceueray,

[8] There is an instance of an identity relation in the table of adjectives for which the same conditions hold as for verbs; the entries are contiguous:

> **Mortall deedly** ma. mortel z.
> fe. mortelle s.
> **Mortell** idem.

que ie decoyue, decepuoyr. tercie cõ. **If you trust me I wyll nat deceyue you:** Sy vous vous fiez en moy ie ne vous deceueray poynt. **I deceyue hym:** Ie luy decoys, **and for dyuers other verbes of this signyfycacion loke afore in I begyle/ and** ie bille, prime cõiuga.

(III, fo. cc.v)

But more typically identity relations are expressed within a dictionary entry. When Palsgrave provides more than one French equivalent for an English verb lemma, the latter may be listed in different ways: by means of a conjunction, *and* (see **I Passe I excede**) or *or* (see **I Play the foole**), or by means of a phrase of the type *I also fynde* (see **I Laye the blame of an offence to ones charge**), *in this sence I fynde* (see **I Lamente**), *I also fynde in this sence* (see **I Pyke a quarell or fynde maters to fall out with one for**), and *of lyke signyfycacion is* (see **I Appertayne**). These could be regarded as stylistic variations of enumeration which would be supported by the fact that they may occur in combination. Yet Palsgrave may have in mind a subtler distinction. An area where he totally differs from his predecessors is his lemmatization. In many cases the different senses of a lexical item are broken down into different lemmata, with French equivalents then provided for these senses. That is, Palsgrave often pairs senses of lexical items, not always lexical items *in toto*. If we take account of this basic insight into language, together with his keen awareness that words (and here more specifically verbs) in English as well as in French may encapsulate different senses, then a phrase like *I also fynde in this sence* could also mean something more specific. This may be illustrated with the following example. The English verb *to pierce* is lemmatized into two headwords:

**I Perce I enter in to a thyng or or passe thorowe it/** Ie perce. prime cõiu. **and in this sence I fynde also** Ie penetre. prime cõiuga. **I holde the a groote thou shalte nat perce thorowe it at one stroke:** Ie gaige vng gros que tu ne le perceras pas a vng coup.

(III, fo. ccc.xvii$^{r-v}$)

**I Perce a thynge thorowe bothe the sydes/** Ie transperce. prime cõiu. **and** ie trãcys oultre. secũde. **He persed hym thorowe bothe the sydes w$^{t}$ an arowe:** Il luy transperca les deux coustez dune fleche.

(III, fo. ccc.xvii$^{v}$)

What Palsgrave is saying is that the sense of 'to enter into a thing or pass through it' is rendered by French *percer* and by French *penetrer*. By implication then, French *percer* and French *penetrer* share this sense and in this respect have the same meaning.

Verbs of similar meanings are cross-referred, but there is no overt specification of the relationship between the cross-referred entries: nor does anything match the *et cetera, et alia, plura in* of the *Catholicon Anglicum*.

In Chapter 8 we shall see that Palsgrave occasionally indicates transferred senses of words, for both English and French. The lexicographical device used to distinguish between a basic and a derived sense of a word is the adverb *properly*.

For his very explicit word-formation analyses, the reader is also referred to Chapter 8. In contrasting word-formational patterns for English and French, thus including derivational structures for two vernaculars, he goes far beyond his predecessors.

References to a source text or writer as an authority for the linguistic use recorded occur, as we have seen in previous chapters.

As the only bilingual reference work comprising both a dictionary and a grammar, *Lesclarcissement* cross-refers the reader between these parts from time to time: as when the French translation equivalent is irregular in its grammar or when the English and the French expression differ in the perspective being the linguistic norm (e.g. a personal construction in the one language, an impersonal one in the other).

Some new features in *Lesclarcissement* reflect Palsgrave's endeavour to make his dictionary as explicit as possible for English learners so that they will be able to produce adequate and correct French utterances. As we shall see in the French equivalents which he puts at his learners' disposal, he frequently draws their attention to the fact that when one is speaking another language one is usually not matching a mother-tongue item and a target-language item, but rather senses with senses, and these may be distributed differently in two languages. Yet a real dictionary for encoding purposes cannot stop here but must go on to describe the meaning of lexical items and show how the latter are varied in sentence production. Grammar and exemplification become necessary components of a bilingual dictionary for productive use.

The grammatical information which Palsgrave provides for French verbs is often quite comprehensive. Apart from the specification of the conjugation class to which the verb belongs, irregular forms are listed, and occasionally there is an indication of the object case which the verb requires. All this information is given in Latin: that is, for grammar the metalanguage is Latin, and for cross-references it is English. In order to avoid the constant repetition of certain conjugation patterns, Palsgrave makes use of cross-references by means of *conjugate in*. The latter are quite complex and call for a close study if one is to detect Palsgrave's policy. Leaving aside inconsistencies, which are unavoidable in a work of this nature, there seem to be four different aspects of policy which he observed.

1. The French item links two different English lemmata because it is the translation equivalent for both which might be represented as

$$EL_1 \longleftrightarrow F \longleftrightarrow EL_2$$

*EL*₁ is usually more specific (*behest*, *cherne*, *close*) than $EL_2$ (*promess*, *beat*, *put*), which is the reason why the conjugation pattern is given under $E_2$. Thus:

**I Behest I promesse/** Ie prometz **coniugate herafter in I promesse. He behested hym many great thynges:** Il luy promyst maintes grans choses.

(III, fo. c.lx)

**I Cherne butter/** Ie bas le beurre iay batu le beurre, batre le beurre, **and howe** ie bas, **is cõiugate I haue afore shewed in I beate. you are no good housewyfe/ for you haue nat cherned your butter to daye:** Vous nestez pas bõne mesnaigiere, car vous naue pas batu vostre beurre, **or** le beurre au iourdhuy.

(III, fo. c.lxxxvii)

**I Close a precyous stone or any suche lyke thyng in golde or syluer /** Ie mets en oeuure, iay mys en oeuure mettre en oeuure, **and howe** ie mets, **is coniugate shall herafter apere in I put. If this antique were closed in golde it were a goodly thynge:** Si ceste antique estoyt mise en or ce seroyt vne belle chose.

(III, fo. c.xc)

2. The second type is best introduced by examples:

**I Baare I vncover a thynge or make it bare/** Ie denue. prime coniu. **and** ie descouuers, **cõiugate lyke his symple** ie couuers, **I couer. What barest thou his arse/ wenest thou he haue an eye there to se with:** Que denues tu **or** descouuers tu sõ cul, pen ces tu quil ayt la vng oeyl pour regarder.

(III, fo. c.lvi$^v$)

**I Bereue one of their speche/** Ie forclos la parolle, **cõiugate lyke his symple** ie clos, **I shytte. I haue bereued hym of his speche:** Ie luy ay forclos la parolle.

(III, fo. c.lxiii)

**I Breake out as one dothe that waxeth scabby/** Ie deuiens roigneux **coniugate lyke his symple** ie viens, **I come. Me thynke you breake out the wrestes:** Il mest aduis q̃ vous deuenez royngneux autor des poignetz.

(III, fo. c.lxxiii$^v$)

The characteristic of this type of cross-reference is that the French translation equivalents *decouvrir*, *forclore*, and *devenir* are etymologically speaking prefixal verbs, the simple verbs of which also exist in French: *couvrir*, *clore*, and *venir*. The cross-references provide the learner with a whole complex of information:

(a) there is a simpler form of the verb in question in French;
(b) this simpler form is given;
(c) there is a dictionary entry where this simple form is the translation equivalent;
(d) this entry provides information on the conjugation pattern;
(e) the English equivalent of the simple verb is provided so that the latter becomes retrievable.

The cross-reference system is thus not only explicit but also very elaborate, for Palsgrave could easily have used such a basic type as

**I Baare** . . . Ie denue prime coniu. and ie descouuers, **coniugate in I couer**.

**I Bereue one of their speche/** Ie forclos la parolle, **cõiugate in I shytte**.

Since he did not, it may be that his elaborate cross-reference system was meant to serve a further purpose at the same time. This can be demonstrated with the following example:

**I Make chere to one at my firste meting ẘ him/** Ie accueil **or** accueils **coniugate lyke his simple** ie cueils, **I gather/** . . .

(III, fo. cc.lxxxxix$^{v}$ = cc.lxxxix$^{v}$)

Under the letter *G* there are eight dictionary entries with the lemma **I Gather**. Adopting the simple cross-reference system would have put users at a loss to identify the right *gather* they were supposed to look up. The pairing of *ie cueils—I gather*, on the other hand, will help to eliminate the entries

**I Gather grapes** . . . Ie vẽdenge . . .
**I Gather my spyrites to me** . . . Ie mesuertue . . .
**I Gather my selfe togyther** . . . Ie me acueils . . .
**I Gather men togyther** . . . Ie assemble . . .
**I Gather thynges togyther** . . . Ie accumule . . .
**I Gather thynges togyther** . . . Ie amasse . . .
**I Gather vp thynges** . . . Ie amasse . . .

Where a simple verb does not exist in French, it is interesting that Palsgrave usually refers the learner to another prefixal verb of the same (Latin) family, as in

> **I Restrayne one of their lybertye** Ie restrains, **coniugate lyke** ie constrayns, **and** ie cohibe. **It is a sore thyng to restrayne a man of his lybertye:** Cest vne dure chose que de restraindre vng homme de sa liberté, **or** de le cohiber de sa liberté.
>
> (III, fo. ccc.xl)

3. Thirdly, we have the cross-reference type in which two structural relations are combined: the relation between the spellings and that between verbs of the same conjugation pattern. Thus:

> **I Dey (Lydgate) coniugat in I dye/ I parte my lyfe:** Ie meurs.
>
> (III, fo. cc.vi[v])

> **I Preese/** Ie prise. prime cõiu. **con iugate in I prayse.**
>
> (III, fo. ccc.xxi[v])

4. Fourthly, for the most irregular verbs in French, as pointed out earlier, Palsgrave refers the learner to the respective section in the grammar of *Lesclarcissement*, as in:

> **I Burye I lay a deed corse in the grounde/ or suche lyke/** Ienterre. pri me coniuga. **and the defectyue** ie ensepuelis, **whose cõiugating apereth in the seconde boke. He is buryed at the whyte freres in London:** Il est enterré, **or** ensepuely aux carmes a Londres.
>
> (III, fo. c.lxxix)

> **I Come as one thynge cometh/ groweth/ or procedeth of a nother/** Ie nays, **cõiugate in I am borne/ in the seconde boke. This dysease cometh of yuell dyet:** Ceste maladie vient, **or** nayst de mauuayse diette, **or** mauuays gouuernement.
>
> (III, fo. cc.i)

As we shall see in Chapters 9 and 10, Palsgrave generously supplied examples to show how the verbs are actually used, partly from his reading, but predominantly from his imagination. He may from time to time have felt this as an additional strain during the compiling of the table of verbs, since he sometimes does not give any examples at all and refers the learner instead to another entry where he has listed them. Thus:

> **I Am named/** Ie me fais nommer **or** ie me fais appeller, **or** iay nom, **or** iay a nom, **I haue shewed exemples in I am called.**
>
> (III, fo. c.xlvi)

This is matched under **I Am called or named** (III, fo. c.xliii) with two examples.

> **I Appese (Lydgate) loke in I appayse.** Ie apaise. prime coniuga. **and there be also exemples.**
>
> (III, fo. c.l^v^)

There are two dictionary entries for **I Appayse** (III, fo. c.l) and both are provided with examples.

> **I Set one a gogge to do a thyng or I set one a warke/ or I set one on to do a thyng: as/ who dyd first set hym on/ looke for exemple of these thre verbes afore in I prouoke.**
>
> (III, fo. ccc.lviii^v^)

Since this last entry does not give any translation equivalents, one may wonder whether Palsgrave's use of 'example' refers to equivalents as well. In this context, attention has also to be drawn to his use of the lexicographical device *declared in*. When he uses this as a cross-reference, does he really explain anything in the dictionary entry which the learner is invited to look up? In general, such entries include no metalinguistic comments which might be regarded as 'explanations'. Instead, there may be a fuller, more explicit lemma entry which interprets the lemma entry that was referred—for example:

> **I Bringe aboute my purpose/ declared in I bringe to passe/** Ie viens au bout de mon entente.
>
> (III, fo. c.lxxiiii)

In the dictionary entry **I Bringe to passe,** the postlemmatic gloss does not only paraphrase the meaning of **I Bringe to passe**; the wording *to bring . . . to effect* also explains the verb *to bring about*, because it is less idiomatic:

> **I Bring to passe I bring my purpose or entreprise to effecte/** Ie acheuis, iay acheuy, acheuir, ie viens au bout, ie suis venu au bout, ie viẽdray au bout, venir au bout, **coniugate in I come. I wyll bringe my mynde to passe:** Ie viendray au bout de ce que ientens, **and** ie viens au chief. **I can nat bringe my mynde to passe:** Ie ne puis poynt acheuyr de mon entente, ie ne puis venir a chief de mon entente.
>
> (III, fo. c.lxxvii)

In addition, the entry includes a further translation equivalent (*acheuir*), grammatical forms of the expression *venir au bout*, and an English example sentence with its French translation. Palsgrave's use of 'declared in' might thus be taken as 'given a fuller treatment which covers the meaning of the headword, the number of equivalents, the grammatical information provided and exemplification'. But this wide interpretation does not always hold, as can be seen from the following two pairs of examples:

**I Brise herbes or suche lyke in a morter/** Ie brise. prime cõiuga. **declared in I braye in a morter.**

(III, fo. c.lxxvii)

**I Braye in a morter/** Ie brise. prime coniu. **Braye all this spices in a brasen morter:** Brisez toutes ces espices en vng mortier darrayn.

(III, fo. c.lxxi$^{v}$)

**I Bubbyll vp as water dothe that ryseth out of a spring/** Ie bouillonne. prime coniuga. **declared in I bobyll.**

(III, fo. c.lxxviii$^{v}$)

**I Bobyll as water or any other lycour doth vpon yͤ fyre whan it setheth:** Ie bouillõne. prime coniu. **Whan the potage begynneth to bobyll it is a token the potte wyll ron ouer if one take nat hede:** Quant le potaige cõmence a bouillõner, le pot sen fuyra sy on ny prent garde.

(III, fo. c.lxix)

In the first pair of examples, the verb *brayer* does not provide further insights into the meaning of the verb *briser*: there is the same French equivalent, the same amount of grammatical information; the difference is the example sentences in English and in French.

In the second, related by the different spellings of the lemma, the headword entries describe different situations, while the equivalent and its grammatical specification are identical. Yet, again, the second entry is 'fuller' because it includes an example.

This then suggests that the expression 'declared in . . .' in its narrow sense always means 'an example is provided in . . .'. Thus, as early as 1530, John Palsgrave knew that a linguistic element was not fully explained unless its actual use had been illustrated in a syntactic construction.

In most of the examples quoted here as illustrations, the lemma to which learners are referred is a simple headword with no postlemmatic expansion. Yet there are instances with such expansion. The *Catholicon Anglicum* was the only other early dictionary in which we had encountered this feature before, albeit on a much smaller scale. This may relate to the complexity of the headword structure in both works and the need to include adequate lexicographical devices to disambiguate homographic entries. Occurrences with postlemmatic postmodifications are more frequent than those with postlemmatic glosses. We conclude this chapter with some examples for both types of entries.

The lemma entry in the cross-reference includes a postlemmatic postmodification:

**I Forthynke I bye the bargayne or suffer sinerte for a thyng/** Ie compare, **cõiugat in I bye a thing dere** . . .

(III, fo. cc.xli^v)

**I Bye a thynge dere I suffre domage and displeasure for a matter/** Ie compare, ie comparus, iay comparu, comparer, ⁊ comparoyr. prime coniu. **As I haue bought this pleasure dere:** Iay cherement comparu ce plaisir. **Thou shalte abye for it:** Tu le compareras.

(III, fo. c.lxvi)

**I Set in tune as mynstrelles do their instrumẽces of musyke/ as lute harpe/ virgynals/ or suche lyke/** Ie monte. prime cõiuga. **declared afore in I set an instrument.**

(III, fo. ccc.lviii)

**I Set an instrument of musyke/** Ientonne. prime cõiu. **and** iaccorde. prime cõiu. **and in this sence I fynde also** ie monte. prime cõiu. **Set my virgynalles:** Entonnez mes espinettes. **Set my clarycordes:** Accordez mes monocordes. **Set my lute:** Montez mon lux. **so ỷ euery of these verbes is proper for ỷ sence that I here gyue exemple/ but** accorder, **is cõmen the settyng of all maner instrumentes.**

(III, fo. ccc.lvi)

The lemma entry in the cross-reference consists of a lemma proper and a postlemmatic gloss:

**I Hosse as a bee or flye dothe/** Ie bruys. **It is a perylous noyse I tell you to here a bee busse in a boxe:** Ie vous dis que cest vng bruyt bien perilleux que douyr vne mouche a miel bruyre en vne boette, **coniugate in I hurle I make a noyse as the wynde dothe.**

(III, fo. cc.lxiiii^v)

**I Hurle I make a noyse as the wynde dothe/** Ie bruys, nous bruyons, nous bruyrõs. ie bruys, iay bruy ie bruyray, que ie bruye, bruyre. tercie cõiuga. N. **The wynde hurled so sore that none of vs coulde nat here an other:** Le vent bruyoyt si tresfort que nul de nous ne pouuoyt poynt ouyr lung laultre.

(III, fo. cc.lxv)

# 8
# The French Translation Equivalents

What does Palsgrave tell us about his aims in providing his English readers with French equivalents? How much information does he want to put at their disposal? At the end of the grammatical treatment of nouns in book III, he explains his aim and method as follows:

> I shall set forthe all the englysshe substantyues in our tong/ after the order of a/b/c/ and in the same lyne shewe what substantyues in the frenche tonge is of lyke signification.
>
> And fardermore/ for a more helpe and spedy forderyng of the sayd lernar/ if he be nat parfyte in my rules herafore declared/ I shall expresse in the same lyne/ what letter the sayd frenche substãtyues haue in their plurell nombres/ and what gendre they be of in the sayd frenche tonge: for if they be of the masculyne gendre/ the lernar shall fynde after ỷ letter of the plurell nombre *Ma*, if they be of the femyne gendre *Fe*. (III, fo. xvi)

After this general characterization, he then discusses a more specific case, the plural of French compounds consisting of a noun + a preposition + a noun. He argues that he will indicate the plural and gender for the first noun, since the rest of the compound remains unchanged.

### NOUNS

From this statement, we might expect him not to list the French equivalents with an article form, but to specify the gender after the item in question. This is, in fact, the general practice—for example, '**Budde** bovton, bourgon s ma.', '**Buffette** buffee s fe. covp de poing z ma.'. When the French equivalent consists of a complex noun phrase with a postmodifying prepositional phrase, practice varies: '**Maggotte** uer de chair s fe.' or '**Blacke of the eye** le noyr de loyl s ma.'. Both forms may co-occur in one entry: '**Calfe of a legge** pommeau de la iambe x ma, le mol de la iambe z ma'.

In some instances, the indefinite article has crept in: '**Globerde a flye** ung uer q̃ reluit de nuyt', '**Warehouse to shewe marchandise in** une monstre a marchandise s fe.'. Instances with the definite article are: '**Thyll of a carte** le lymon s ma.', '**Wydowe of the Frenche kyng** la royne blanche s fe.'.

The entries under the letter *Z* are rather exceptional. Palsgrave here lists a number of proper names which do not match in style and culture his occasional mention of English first names, as *Johan*, *Mary*, and so on. Equally exceptional are the French equivalents in occurring as encyclopedic entries with an article and in mostly having a full lexicographical explanation:

| | |
|---|---|
| **Zacharie a prophet** | ung prophete s ma. |
| **Zabulon** | estoyt filz de Iacob s ma. |
| **Zebedeus** | le pere de saint Iaques et de saint Iohan Leuangeliste s ma. |
| **Zodiake** | le cercle qui fait tourner le firmament par ou le soleil et les planettes font leur cours. |

It looks as if Palsgrave may have tried to fill the *Z* column thus, for without these items his *Z* list would have had three headwords only: *Zalandyne an herbe*, *Zele loue or frenshyp*, *Zephirus*. But they may result from a still unidentified French source, which may also explain the exceptional *article partitif* found with two French equivalents: '**Glewe** du glev de la gleve s fe.', '**Gottes lether** du baroquin [*sic*] s ma.'. In general, there is agreement in number between the English headwords and the French translation equivalents. Yet when the English or French word is lexicalized in the plural form, then there is no correspondence in number: '**Dregges** lie de biere ou deuin [*sic*] s fe.', '**Weddyng** nopces fe.'.

In view of the fact that the general practice assumed by Palsgrave is to indicate number and gender after the French equivalent, translations with the indefinite article in the plural are rather striking. We have already noticed Palsgrave's interest in these forms in Chapter 3, because they occurred with French nouns corresponding to English words that are preceded by 'a pair of'. In the noun list, we find the following French items predetermined by *unes*/*ungz*:

| | |
|---|---|
| **Almery to put meate in** | unes almoires fe. |
| **Aumbrye** | unes avlmoyres fe. |
| **Belowes** | ungz suffletz au fev ma. |
| **Byrlyng yron** | unes espinces. |
| **Bridall** | unes nupces fe z espousailles fe. |
| **Coupborde** | unes almoires fe. |
| **Grese a stayre** | ungz degréz ma. |
| **Indenture** | unes indenturez fe.[1] |

[1] Under *P*, *endenturez* is listed without *unes*:

| | |
|---|---|
| **Payre of indentures** | endenturez fe. |

| | |
|---|---|
| **Payre of burlettes** | une [*sic*] paces fe. |
| **Payre of pastes** | unes tables fe. iev de tables fe. |
| **Payre of balances** | unes balances fe. |
| **Paste for a lady or woman** | unes paces fe. |
| **Potte hokes** | unes ancestes fe. |
| **Primer boke** | unes hevres fe. |
| **Stewe a bath** | vnes esteuues ma. fe. |
| **Stewe a hotehouse** | vnes esteuues. |

In the grammar chapters of book III which precede the list of nouns, Palsgrave discusses substantives which in French occur in the plural only, and he provides an alphabetical list. Eleven of the plural nouns used with *unes/ungz* recorded in the French vocabulist are included in this list. *Unes espinces* (*Byrlyng yron*) is missing. Yet the list in the grammar section is much longer. Table 8.1 reveals that these additional items are not always given with the form *unes/ungz* in the dictionary section. Although Palsgrave was not as explicit in the dictionary as in the grammar section, the comparison reveals a nearly total agreement between the French words actually recorded in the two lists.

The majority of the French translation equivalents consists of one French noun, simple or complex ('**Cutpurse** coupevr de bourse', '**Fallyng sickenesse** la maladie caducque, le mal sainct Iehan'). Instances where we have a full explanation in French instead of a one-word translation are rare. A case in point was *Zodiake*, quoted earlier; other examples are:

| | |
|---|---|
| **Myre tree** | larbre qui porte la mirre |
| **Wayter** | qui baille attendance s ma. |

The indication of spelling variants is rare. Examples are: '**Flaget** flacon, flaccon s ma.', '**Wallet or poke** besasse s ma. besache s fe. besace s fe.'. As we can see from these examples, when multiple lexical items are given as French translation equivalents, they are usually listed one after the other, separated by a comma. Occasionally, a coordinating conjunction, English *or*, is found: '**Aunt** tante **or** ante s fe.', '**Weddercocke** cochet deglise s ma. **or** cochet auent s ma.'. French *ou* also occurs sporadically. When it does, it links postmodifications of the basic French equivalent, e.g. '**Fenestrall** chassis de toille ou de paupier'.

In a number of cases, the alternatives provided for French are merely different word-formations from the same French basis which well reflect the richness in derivational variants common at the time:

TABLE 8.1. *Plural nouns with the determiner* vnes/vngz

| *Book III—Grammar section (fos. xii–xiii)* | | *Book III—The noun list* | |
|---|---|---|---|
| vnes armes | **an armes of a noble man or gentyll man** | **Armes of a noble man** | armes fe. |
| vnes besaces | **a wallet** | **Wallet or poke** | besasse s ma. besache s. fe. besace s fe. |
| vnes brayes | **a payre of sloppes or a payre of breches** | **Payre of sloppe hoses** | braiettes a marinier s fe. |
| | | **Breche of hosen** | braiette, braie, braies. |
| vnes chausses | **a payre of hosen** | **Hose for ones legges** | chavsse s fe. |
| vnes cartes | **a payre of cardes to playe with** | **Payre of cardes to playe with** | cartes fe. |
| vnes cimballes | **a payre of symballes/ an instrument of musyke** | **Symball an instrument** | cimballes fe. |
| vngz siseletz | **a payre of barbours sheyres** | **Payre of sycers** | ciseletz ma. forces fe. |
| vnes decrottoyres | **a rubbynge brusshe to make clene clothes with** | **Rubbar for a gowne** | decrottoires fe. |
| vnes escourgez | **a scourge a whyppe** | **Scourge to beate with** | fouet z ma. |
| | | **Whyppe for a plowman** | fouet s ma. |
| vnes estricquoyres | **a payre of pynsons an instrument** | **Payre of pynsons** | pinces fe. estriquoires fe. |
| vness escriptoyres | **a pennar and ynke horne** | **Pennar and ynkehorne** | escriptoire s fe. |
| vnes entraues | **a payre of boltes of yron for a prisoner** | **Bolte or shacle** | entraue s fe. |

| | | | |
|---|---|---|---|
| vnes estovpes | **a locke of towe or hurdes** | **Heerdes of hempe** | tillage de chamure s. ma, estovpes fe. |
| vnes fainsayles | **an assuryng or hand-fastynge** | **Hande fastyng** | fiansailles fe. |
| vnes forceps | **a payre of shermans sheres** | **Shermans sheres** | forceps fe. |
| vngz govions | **a payre of fetters for a horse or a man** | **Payre of fettars**<br>**Fettar for a prisonar** | ceps ma.<br>govions ma. |
| vngz gietz | **a payre of gesses for a hauke** | **Gesses for a hauke** | getz ma. |
| vnes lvnettes | **a payre of spectacles** | **Payre of spectacles** | lunettes fe. |
| vnes lices | **a tylte to lerne to iuste at/ or the barres that compasse a iustyng place** | **Tylte for iustyng** | lisses ma. fe. |
| vne [*sic*] lettres | **a letter missyfe** | | |
| vnes monstres | **a mustre of men that shall go a warfare** | **Mustre of harnest men** | monstre s fe. |
| vnes orgues | **a payre of organs an instrument of musyke** | **Organs an instrument** | ogres [*sic*] s fe. |
| vnes obseqves | **an obit for a deed body** | **Obsequies dirige** | uigiles fe. |
| vnes patenostres | **a payre of beedes to praye with** | **Payre of beedes** | paternostres ma. |
| vngz piegz | **a payre of stockes to punysshe vacabundes** | **Payre of stockes** | piege, seps fe. |
| vnes tournettes | **a payre of wyndynge blades** | **Payre of wynding blades** | tournettes fe. |
| vnes teuaylles [*sic*] | **a payre of tonges** | **Payre of tonges** | tenailles fe. |
| vnes taylles | **a payre of taylles/ suche as folke vse to score vpon for rekeunyng** | | |
| vnes uerges | **a brusshe to brusshe with** | **Brusshe to brusshe with** | uerges a nettoyer s fe. |

**Fresshnesse** freschevr, freshete z fe.
**Pyllar a robber** pillevr s ma. pillart z ma.
**Rolle of paper** rovlet, rovleau z ma.

The problem of differentiating between a designation for a male and a female does not really arise for the French equivalents, because Palsgrave transferred it to the English headwords. Thus, instead of entries like '**Louer** amoureux ma, amourevse s fe', we have the sex specification in the English lemmata already: '**Louer a man** amoureux ma.', '**Louer a woman** amourevse fe.'.

Exemplification of the lexical item concerned is extremely rare for nouns. In the three instances that occur, the lexicographical practice varies. Under the lemma *Iack*, the postlemmatic English gloss is illustrated in an example sentence for which a French version is supplied:

**Iacke or whitte nicquet, as I wyll nat gyue you a whyt** ie ne uous donneray pas ung nicquet z ma.

For the English noun *Thanke*, two French translations are given, and for the second its use is shown in a sentence:

**Thanke** remercys s fe.
gre. as Ie uous en scay bon gré,
**I can you good thanke.**

And, finally, there is one instance where Palsgrave's knowledge of old French comes through:

**Hauthorne** aulbespĩn espine blãche s ma.
Ro. dessoubz ung aulbespin gisant.

This takes us to another issue, the indication of regional and temporal variants. There are a few such instances. Other French equivalents with the temporal marker *Romant* are:

**Cuppe to drinke in** covppe z ma.
hanap s fe. Ro.
**Hunter** braconnier Ro. chassevr,
uenevr s ma.
**Knyfe** covsteau x ma. covstel Ro. z ma.

As a regionalism, Palsgrave gives the noun *hantel*:

**Steale or handell of a staffe**
manche s fe. hantel s fe. Normant

The highest number of French equivalents occurs with abstract nouns. Under the noun *distresse* we are given seven different possible translations:

**Distresse** disette s fe. effort s ma. perplexe s fe. subuertion s fe. souffrãce s fe. destresse s fe. esmoy s ma, disette s fe.

Six equivalents occur for *debate*, *plenty*, *richesse*, and *warning*. There does not seem to be a semantic or formal principle in the listing of these alternatives:

**Debate** question s fe. contens s ma. sedition s fe. litige s ma. debat z ma. noyse s fe.

## *Comparison with the* Promptorium *and the* Catholicon

Palsgrave contrasted two vernaculars, an undertaking which no Renaissance lexicographer before him had attempted on the monumental scale that characterizes *Lesclarcissement*. Did he take the *Promptorium* or the *Catholicon* as his model? Let us, therefore, look at how their compilers dealt with the Latin equivalents. They could fall back on substantial lexicographical collections for Latin and thus had precedents in how to treat lexical items in a dictionary.

The manuscript version and the first printed edition of the *Promptorium parvulorum* have in common that the Latin equivalents are listed in the nominative form, followed by an indication of the genitive form and the declension class. Occasionally the source from which the item has been taken is indicated. These three types of lexicographical information are included in the following entry from the printed edition:

**Felawe in office.** Collega ge duoꝝ generum prime declinacõis, Catho.

*Catho* is the *Catholicon*. They also include a cross-reference component in the language of the translation equivalents, that is Latin:

**Cropp** of a byrd, *supra* in **craw**. (1440)
**Croppe or crawe of a birde.** supra in crawe (1499)

In some instances the Latin equivalents provided for an English headword are explicitly differentiated in Latin. Table 8.2 shows that there seem to be more such examples in the manuscript edition.

In the *Catholicon Anglicum* we have a number of interesting features, some of which are already found in the early vocabularies. A case in point is the occasional differentiation of several Latin translation equivalents by means of a verse:

Table 8.2. *Differentiation of Latin equivalents in the* Promptorium parvulorum

| 1440 | 1499 |
|---|---|
| **Cumpany**: *Comitiua, -e; fem., prime decl.*: *Contubernium, -i; neut.*, 2: *Agmen, -is; neut.*; 3: *Turba, -e; fem. prime*: *Cetus, -vs; Masc.*, 4: *Turma, fem., prime.* | **Cumpany.** Comitiua ue. Turba be. Turma me. omnia feminĩ generis prime declinacõis. Contuberniũ nii. Conuenticulum li. sed proprie maloꝝ. omnia neutri generis secunde declinacõis. Agmen nis neutri generis tercie declinacõis. Cetus tus. masculi ni generis quarte d'. |
| **ffayr speche**: *lepos, -ris, non lepus, -ris; Masc.*, 3, 'campus florum': *Rethorica, -e; fem., prime, et est differencia inter lepus, -ris, Media correpta anglice* an hare, *et lepos, -ris, Media producta, Rure fugo lepores, in verbis quero lepores.* | **Fayre speche.** Lepos oris. mas. ge. tercie declitõis. Rethorica ce. feminini generis prime declinacõis. |

a **Fischer**; *piscator, piscarius; versus*:
*Piscator prendit quod piscarius*
*bene vendit.*

There may also be a paraphrase in Latin of the meaning of the Latin equivalent: 'a **Bay**; *bacca, est fructus lauri* & *oliue*'. Such entries are evidently indebted to the monolingual Latin dictionaries available at the time.

The following examples illustrate further features:

an **Ake**: *quarcus, quarculus, ilex, quarcinus, querceus, quernus; ilicetum, quercetum, querretum sunt loca vbi crescunt quarcus.*

a **Balle**: *pila, alipatus qui iaculatur pilam.*

a **Fader**: *pater, paterculus, parens, genitor, propagator, abba grece,* abia: *paternalis, patrenus, patrius, patruelis, participia.*

After the Latin equivalents for the English noun we find Latin derivatives of the equivalent. They may be relational adjectives, other nouns, or verbs. These additional Latin items are not usually translated into English. In some cases (as under *an Ake*) we are given a Latin paraphrase of the meaning ('sunt loca vbi crescunt quarcus'). Although such a practice is geared towards the dictionary user, Palsgrave could not make use of it because of his decision to list his words according to the different parts of speech.

From the example *father* we can derive that occasionally forms that go back to Greek are given.

The compiler's metalanguage is Latin. Cross-references are therefore introduced by means of *vbi*, and alternatives may be linked by *vel*.

### *Comparison with the* Ortus vocabulorum

Although the headword language is not English, but Latin, we might also turn our attention to the *Ortus vocabulorum*, since its headword part corresponds to the equivalent part in the English–Latin dictionaries. The unknown compiler specifies in the colophon that his word list is indebted to the *Catholicon*, the *Breviloquus*, the *Cornucopia*, and the *Medulla grammatice*. These were the main sources from which he derived his lexicographical method. For many of the Latin headwords there are no English equivalents, and the Latin headword entries are in many cases quite complex monolingual dictionary entries because they consist of a Latin lemma followed by one or more Latin synonyms and/or meaning explanations.

One of the characteristic features of the *Ortus vocabulorum* is the indication of the Latin gender and declension/conjugation class after the English equivalent at the end of the line—for example, '**Cãpana e.** a bell **f. p.**', '**Capellatus a. ũ.** hattyde **o. s.**', '**Capicio as.** to hoode **a. p.**'.

The English noun equivalents are predominantly preceded by the indefinite article. Abstract nouns and uncountables tend to have no determiner, and English nouns of unique reference or those with a postmodifying prepositional phrase beginning with *of* often occur with the definite article:

| | |
|---|---|
| **Custos dis.** | an.[e] a keper **cõ. t.** |
| **Carnes bouine.** | angl.' beyffe. |
| **Damnũ ni.** | harme or scathe **n. s.** |
| **Colus coli.** the galle or the gutte or a tharme. | |
| **Firmamentum ti.** anglice the firmamente. | **n. s.** |

In some exceptional cases, nouns of relation show a first-person possessive pronoun not present in the Latin lemma:

> **Abamita est soror aui.** angl.' my fathers aunte. **f. p.**
>
> **Abauus. i. pater aui.** my granusyris father. **m. s.**
>
> **Auũculus. i. frater m is.** myn eame. **m. s.**

As we can see from these examples, the English equivalents are usually one word items or lexicalized combinations. Yet occasionally we also find full paraphrases of the meaning of the Latin lemma in English:

> **Faros grece.** the grettest toure besyde alysaunder
>
> **Frumen nis.** the ouer parte of the throte or the throte boll' of a mane. **n. t.**

Latin nouns referring to a (male) human being may be rendered by the English construction 'he that . . .', as in '**Equimanus.** he that can with bothe handes **m. s.**'. 'She that . . .' is exceptional: '**Gmellipa pe.** Sche that has two chylder att onys. **f. p.**'.

Frequently, however, these English explanations are renderings of the preceding meaning paraphrase in Latin:

> **Adulatorculus est diminutiuũ: paruus adulator.** a smael gloser. **m. s.**
>
> **Collibista e. dicitur qui recipit collibia vel qui vendit collubia.** a receyuer or a seller of theftes. **m. p.**

The Latin paraphrases of the meaning of the Latin lemma may be introduced by *idest*, *.i.*, *est* or *dicitur* (more rarely by *significat* or *interpretatur*), thus reflecting the monolingual dictionary aspect of the Latin lemma entries:

> **Cosmos mi idest mundus.** anglice the worlde. **m. s.**
>
> **Edes dis. i. domus.** an.[e] an house **f. t.**
>
> **Crater. est vas vinariũ.** an.[e] a pyece or a wyne coppe. **Cratera idem est. m. t.**
>
> **Fel lis. dicit a follis.** anglice the galle

The metalanguage in the *Ortus vocabulorum* is also Latin and it is generally used with reference to the Latin language, its grammar, or vocabulary. Metalinguistic comments relating to the English equivalents are extremely rare and are then given in English:

> **Dama ẽ qd'dã aĩal quadrupes. vt dicũt** caprea. both the bucke ꝛ ẏ doo **epi. p.**

An exception is the coordinator *or*, which is the common link for different English equivalents, but alternative English translations may be listed with no explicit linking element: '**Accola** neygbor dweller tylmane'. The commoner practice, however, is the one where the various translation equivalents are joined by means of appositive *or*. The number of equivalents offered may go up to four or five: '**Falanga ge**. an.[e] a satere a spere shafte a polle or a rynge tree **f. p.**'.

The English equivalent may be followed by a Latin sublemma, usually introduced by *inde*. These sublemmata are derivatives of the Latin lemma, as, for instance: '**Magistra tre**. angl.' maystres. **Inde magistercula dimi. ꝑua magistra. f. p.**'. Very exceptionally, they are translated into English.

Instead of a Latin sublemma, the English translation equivalent may also be followed by a different sense of the lemma, not rendered by the English item. Cases in point are the following:

> **Cancellus li.** a chansell. **vel fenestra ī nu muro.** or the batellyng of a toure. **m. s.**
>
> **Nodulus li.** a lytell knote a botoñ. **vel quedã auis.** a kaa. **m. s.**

More commonly, however, the English translations are followed by Latin synonyms or explanations of the lemma:

> **Auditoriũ.** a heryng place. **locus vbi cõsi lia ꝛ responsa audiũtur. n. s.**
>
> **Debitor oris.** a detter. **idest ille qui de- bet. m. t.**

In such cases, the *Ortus vocabulorum* has become a double dictionary. A user competent in Latin is told that the meaning of *auditorium* or *debitor* is 'a hearing place' or 'a debtor' in English. At the same time, English users are provided with a Latin interpretation of *hearing place* 'locus ubi consilia et responsa audiuntur' and of *debtor* 'ille qui debet'.

The English equivalent may also be followed by a *versus* in Latin in which the meaning of two or more Latin words is differentiated. An example is

> **Acus us. ui.** angl.' nedle. **qr. acuta f. q̇.**
> **Acus eris. palea.** angl.' chaff. **m. t. v⁹.**
>
> **Paruula pungit acus: gallinis spargit acus.**

Another device is the introduction of a comment slot introduced by *nota*, as in the following example:

**Imporcitor oris. qui porcas facit. i. sulcos in agro. Nota porca dicitur terra eminens inter duos sulcos.** m. t.

When different Latin lexical items that follow each other in alphabetical order have the same meaning, the equivalents are not repeated. Instead the phrase *idem* (*est*) or *in eodem sensu* is used:

**Facundia die.** fayrnes of speche f. p.
**Facunditas atis. idem est** f. t.

**Olimpias dis.** a feste of solempite playe.
**Olimpica ce. in eodem sensu. Inde olim picus ca. cũ. Et olimpiacus a. ũ.** f. p.

From the English noun equivalents, we have to turn briefly to the Latin lemma entries in the *Ortus vocabulorum*, because in them we find *in nuce* some features which may have inspired certain of Palsgrave's practices. The first printed edition of the *Ortus vocabulorum* came out in 1500, and, as the only Latin–English dictionary available in a printed form, it was repeatedly reprinted during the years when Palsgrave was compiling his dictionary. As a scholar and teacher, he must have known this early bilingual dictionary.

We leave aside the occasional indication of the pronunciation of the Latin headword, and we shall not dwell on the more encyclopaedically oriented descriptions of lemmata, as in

**Columba be** a douue. **auis quedã habens septem proprietatis. Caret felle. nullum ledit. alienos pullos nutrit. gemitum pro cantu emittit. iuxta fluuium moratur. granum eligit quod comedat. in foraminibus petre nidificat.**

In a few instances, the compiler of the *Ortus vocabulorum* provides additional information on the Latin lemma (entry): apart from the Latin word, the Greek and/or Hebrew form is given, a Latin word is said to be no longer in use, and the source author is mentioned. This may be illustrated by the following examples:

**Choeleth hebraice grece ecclesiastes latine cõcionator.** a. speker.

**Angliũ ꝙ non est in vsu sed suũ cõopositũ. sed euãgeliũ in annũciatio.** m. s.

The Latin lemma may be followed by synonyms, synonymic expressions, or full explanations of the meaning of the lemma. But there are also numerous cases where the compiler of the *Ortus* specifies the semantic range of the Latin lemma. The beginning of a different sense is usually explicitly marked by such an item as *vel*, *et*, or *etiam*. The same holds for different senses listed after the English translation equivalent:

> **Aries tis. dr̃ veruex nõ castratus.** weder.
> **quia primo in ara ĩmolatus fuit. Et etiã**
> **instrumẽtũ bellicosum quo muri quatiũ**
> **tur ꝙ impugnat murũ admodũ arietis**
> **impugnãtiũ. Est etiam quodã signũ in ce**
> **lo.**

In some cases, the compiler felt the need to add a comment on what he regarded as the proper meaning of the Latin headword. For such specifications the adverb *proprie* is used:

> **Hiatus tus. tui. fissura vel apertio terre.**
> **Sed proprie hiatus est oris hominis ap**
> **ertio.** angl.' gapynge. **m. q.**

## ADJECTIVES

With this we conclude the section on noun equivalents and turn to adjectives and their translations in *Lesclarcissement de la langue francoyse*. Palsgrave's practice in the listing of French translation equivalents for English adjectives is the same as for nouns. He specifies the forms for the masculine and the feminine as well as the plural. Irregular forms are given, as, for instance, *bel* in the following example:

> **Beautyfull** ma. beau or bel, beaulx fe.
> belle s. ma. et fe. venuste s.

In general, the French equivalents are also adjectives, either simple or derived ones. Other linguistic structures are extremely rare, but in two cases we have a prepositional phrase which renders an English adjective:

> **Shamelesse** sans honte.
> **Well wylled** de bonne voulenté s.

If *non*, *bien*, and *mal* are not to be interpreted as prefixal elements, then we also have some adjective phrases as equivalents:

> **Neglygent or recklesse** ma. mal-
> soigneux fe. mal soigneuse s. ma. non-
> chalant s. fe. nonchalante s. ma. ne-
> glygent s. fe. neglygente s
>
> **Un maryed.** ma. nõ marié. f. nõ mariée

> **Well spoken** ma. bien enlangaigé. fe. bien enlangaigée. ma. bien emparlé. fe. bien emparlée. ma. disert. fe. diserte.

Different French spellings are occasionally given: '**Fewe in nombre** pou or peu'.

French *et* occurs when the French adjective has only one form and the grammatical specifications *ma.* and *fe.* are joined together, as in:

> **Comprehensyble able to be comprehẽded**. ma. et fe. cõprehensible. ma et fe. copable s. ma. et fe. comprehensible s.

French translation alternatives are listed one after the other without any further differentiation. One or two French equivalents are common, but we may have as many as five or six suggested translations:

> **Feate or proper of makyng** ma. godin s. fe. godyne s. ma. godinet z. fe. godinette s. ma. coint z. fe. cointe s. ma. mignon s. fe. mignonne s. ma et fe. fade s. ma. faicty s. fe. faictye s.
>
> **Quycke or delyuer of ones lymmes** ma. agil z. fe. agile s. ma. et fe. deliberé s. ma. apert s. fe. aperte s. ma. et fe. deliure s. ma. prompt s. fe. prompte s. ma. et fe. habylle s.

Among the adjective equivalents, we also encounter sporadic instances of illustrations of use and of earlier French use. Again, because there is no developed practice for adjectives to show their use in example sentences, the style varies in the few instances that occur. For the adjective *disceased*, Palsgrave felt the need to illustrate its postnominal use:

> **Disceassed** ma. feu s fe. feue s.
> **Kyng Henry late disceased** le feu roy Henry.

The French adjective form *bel* instead of *beau* is also shown in an example. This time, Palsgrave does not give an English sentence which is put into French; he simply shows *bel* with an appropriate French noun:

> **Hye or talle** ma. hault s. fe. haulte s. ma. bel, as bel homme.

In a third case, one has the impression that Palsgrave lists idiomatic expressions of the English lemma for which he then supplies French equivalents:

**Uery good**/ fort bon, **veryest foole**/ le
plus fol, **to the very herte**/ ou fyn cueur.

In two instances (**Gladde merye** and **Nyse**), Palsgrave provides both French equivalents current at his time and also forms current in Old French. In both cases, the older adjectives are listed at the end of the dictionary entry.

*Comparison with the* Promptorium, *the* Catholicon, *and the* Ortus

The picture which emerges from a comparison of *Lesclarcissement* with the earlier English–Latin dictionaries is similar to the one found for nouns. In the *Promptorium parvulorum*, the Latin equivalent of the English adjective is given in the masculine form, and the feminine and neuter forms are added. In the case of adjectives of the third declension, the declension class is indicated. In general, the Latin equivalent is formally speaking also an adjective or participle. Entries with other formal units that function as a translation equivalent of an English adjective are rare.

The lexicographical metalanguage is the language of the target language, Latin. For adjectives, there are also cross-references: '**Clensyd**, as lycowr, *supra* in **syed**' (1440).

In the *Catholicon Anglicum* the number of Latin equivalents provided may vary from one or two up to more than a dozen:

**Besy**; *argumentosus, anxius, assiduus, attentus, procliuus, procliuis, diligens, freque*[*n*]*s, instans, intentus, jndustris, jugis, sollicitus, solicitudinarius, studiosus, solers, efficax, vigilans, ardens, perseuerans, occupatus, officiosus, sedulus, susspensus.*

The various Latin equivalents may also be explicitly differentiated, as we can see from the examples *alde* and *blak*:

**Alde**; *priscus qui fuerunt priores; antiquus, qui fuerunt ante nos; annosus, jnveteratus, decrepitus, vetulus o. g a multitudine annorum emeritus, senilis, longeuus, pristinus, vetustus, senex, veteranus geronceus, gerontecus.*

**Blak**; *Aquileus, Ater, subater, Abnominabilis coloris est qui dicitur funereus, fuscus, neque album neque nigrum sed medij coloris est, niger est albo contrarium, nigellus, teter, pullus,* & *cetera; vbi* myrke.

The semantic differentiation may also take the form of a verse:

**Blynde**; *cecus, orbus: versus:* -
¶ *'Lumine priuatus violenter dicitur orbus,*

*Cecus invtiliter gerit instru-*
*menta vivendi'.*

The cross-reference system in the *Catholicon* also embraces adjective entries: '**Balde**; *Audax*, & *cetera*; *vbi* hardy'.

The clustering together of formally and semantically related words in the *Catholicon* leads to the listing of the positive and negative adjective one after the other, as in:

> **Chaste**; *castus corpore, pudicus animo, nuptus, continens.*
> vn **Chaste**; *inpudicus. jncontinens.*

Derivatives of the adjective lemma may also be listed within the same dictionary entry: '**Bare**; *vbi* nakyd: to bare, *vbi* to nakydun . . .'.

In the *Catholicon*, too, the metalanguage is the target language, Latin. Exemplification, introduced by Latin *ut*, is rare: '**Bothomles**; *pertusus, vt saccus pertusus*'.

We come to the *Ortus vocabulorum* and its English translation equivalents. Here, too, the picture is similar to that found for nouns.

When the Latin adjective lemma is followed by an explanatory relative clause, the Latin relative pronoun *qui* may be rendered by English *he that*, which strictly speaking makes the English equivalent grammatically a noun explanation. Examples are:

> **Aquilus a. um. q̀ curuñ habet nasum vt aquile rostrũ.** he that hath a hokyd nose. **o. f**
>
> **Lunaticus a. um. q̀ singulis lunationib⁹ vexa.** an.ᵉ he that ys wode. **o. s.**

Yet *he that* also occurs when there is no Latin explanation at all: '**Colicus a. um.** he that suffres gryndynge in the guttes. **o. s.**'.

Adjective translations in English are predominantly also adjectives, and the number of equivalents joined together may go up to four: '**Felix cis**. anglice happi sely holy or blesfull'. In general, the last member is conjoined by means of the coordinator *or*, but occasionally all the equivalents are linked in this way: '**Amenus dicitur ab amo. i. pnlcher** [*sic*] **delectabilis**. anglice swete or fayr or mery. **o. s.**'.

The translation equivalent in English may also consist of a prepositional phrase: '**Exspinis et hoc ne.** ẘout thorne **o. t.**'. This prepositional phrase may also be a rendering of a corresponding Latin prepositional phrase: '**Exermis et hoc me. idest sine armis**. without wepens **o. t.**'.

In addition, we find full semantic explanations of the Latin adjective in English. As in the previous instances, such paraphrases may be translations of a preceding explanation in Latin or they may be self-standing explanations:

> **Conspicuus a um. idest clarus vel luminis receptiuus.** Clere or apte to receyue lyght. **o. s.**
>
> **Fetans tis.** anglice bryngyng forth fruyt. **o. s.**

The present participle in English occurs in the *-ing* form, as in the example given. Yet we also encounter forms in *-and(e)* and *-ende*: '**Occidens tis**. an.[e] falland', '**Vigilans tis**. anglice wakende **o. t.**'.

In a very small number of cases, the English explanation contains a phrase of comparison—a type of explanation in which Palsgrave excels. Again, the comparison may be prompted by a Latin original or be an independent rendering of the meaning of the Latin adjective lemma. Examples are:

> **Erisonus a um. qui sonat cũ ere.** that soundes as brasse **o. s.**
>
> **Garrul⁹ la lũ.** ianglande as a iaye. **o. s.**

Exemplification of the Latin lemma in a phrase or sentence is found exceptionally, as in

> **Abrogatus.** anglice destroyd. **vt lex illa abrogata est.** **o. s.**
>
> **Effectiuus a. um.** spedfull. **vt medicina est effectiua sanitatis** **o. s.**

Most of these exemplificatory illustrations are introduced by means of *ut* and they are never translated into English.

In some of the preceding examples, the Latin adjective is first explained in Latin before the English-translation equivalent is added. Frequently the Latin paraphrase is explicitly introduced by means of *idest*, *.i.*, or *dicitur*, as was the practice with nouns:

> **Imbutus a. um. idest perfusus doctus informatus.** anglice tauht. **o. s.**
>
> **Mancus ca. cum. dicitur quasi manu carens.** anglice handles. **Vel cui aliquid deest.** **o. s.**
>
> **Prelustris et hoc tre. i. preclarus nobilis altus qui pre alijs lustratur et amatur** anglice well noble **o. t.**

Latin synonyms or explanations of the lemma may also follow the English equivalent, so that there is a double dictionary entry: Latin–English as well as English–Latin:

**Pinnosus a ũ.** hyghe or proude. **altus superbus** **o. s.**

**Preciosus a um.** a fayre **.i. multum valens** **o. s.**

The dictionary may also include Latin derivatives of the lemma, which may be given before or after the English equivalent and, in general, are not then translated into English: '**Grandis et hoc de .i. magn**[9]. angl.' grete. inde grantitudo inis. et grãditas tis **o. t.**'.

With nouns, it is difficult to detect what might be taken as a pattern of a semantic paraphrase to explain the meaning of the Latin lemma. One such that seems to emerge from a number of entries is 'a maner of . . .'. Yet the *of*-phrase does not describe an action or activity as we might expect in present-day English (*a manner of speaking*, *a manner of writing*, etc.). Its meaning is non-verbal and for this *a kind of* is the usual present-day phrase, as with Palsgrave, *a kind of fruit*, *a kind of instrument*. Examples from the *Ortus vocabulorum* are: '**Ruscus ci**. a maner of buske **m. s.**', '**Socellus li**. a maner of schone. **m. s.**'. It looks as if this paraphrase style is a lexicographical device when words denoting a people or a manner of speaking or arguing are not further explained: '**Saxon onis**. a maner of folke **m. t.**', '**Silogismus mi**. a maner of argumente. **m. s.**'.

With adjectives, however, we find some interesting paraphrase patterns. Latin relational adjectives, as, for instance, those expressing appurtenance to a place or material, may be paraphrased in English by means of 'of': '**Oppidanus a. um. i. castellanus in oppi do manens.** of the town. **o.s.**', '**Argenteus a. um. i. de argento existens** of syluer. **o.s.**'.

Latin adjectives ending in *-osus* and *-ulentus* tend to be paraphrased in English by 'full of':

**Frigorosus a. um.** full of colde **o. s.**
**Gratiosus a. um.** full of grace **o. s.**
**Corpulentus a um.** anglice full of body or corcy **o. s.**
**Florulentus a. um.** anglice full of flours. **o. s.**

When they are paraphrased, Latin adjectives in *-bilis* are rendered by 'able to', 'unable to', 'apte'. The paraphrase may be a translation of a preceding Latin explication:

**Cruciabilis et hoc le. qd' est dignũ vl' ap tũ cruciari.** apte to torment **o. t.**

**Habitabil' ꝛ hoc le. qd' habitari põt.** abyll to wõn or duell. **o. t.**

**Inexpugnabilis et hoc le. i. inuincibilis.**
not abyll to be ouercome. **o. t.**

An interesting paraphrase is that for Latin adjectives in *-bundus*:

**Fremebundus a. um. i. similis frementi.**
angl.' lyke to qwake. **o. s.**

**Hesitabundus a. um.** lyke to dowte. **o. s.**

Approximation in degree, for which Latin uses the suffixes *-aster*, *-ellus*, and *-ulus*, is in English rendered by 'a little', 'somewhat', 'somedeal':

**Caluaster a. ũ.** lyttyll ballyde. **o. s.**
**Rubellus a. um.** a lytyll redde. **o. s.**

'Somewhat' often corresponds to Latin *aliquantulum*: '**Curracul⁹.** somdele lyght to reñe **o. s.**'.

The comparison of the translation equivalents for adjectives yields an interesting insight. The first printed edition of the *Ortus vocabulorum* dates from 1500, but its manuscript versions reach back to the early fifteenth century (Stein 1985*a*: 75–7), thus preceding the compilation of the *Promptorium parvulorum* and the *Catholicon Anglicum*. It is widely assumed that the first English–Latin dictionaries are to a large extent inverted Latin–English dictionaries. We can now demonstrate this more concretely. In the *Ortus vocabulorum*, we have for adjectives some types of translation-equivalent structure which occur in the *Promptorium parvulorum* and the *Catholicon Anglicum* as headword structures. In Chapter 6 we noted for the *Promptorium* the modification of an adjective gloss by means of *somewhat* and for the *Catholicon* the rather striking adjective lemmata beginning with *like to* . . ., then matched by Latin adjectives in *-bundus*. And some of the types of translation equivalents found in the *Ortus vocabulorum* are also encountered in *Lesclarcissement*: glosses of the adjective lemmata in 'full of . . .', 'of . . .', 'able/apte to . . .'

## VERBS

### *The* Ortus vocabulorum

We come to the third word class, the verb. We shall begin with the lexicographical practice of translating Latin verbs into English, then discuss the translation of English verbs into Latin, and conclude with the translation of English verbs into French. That is, the order of discussion is chronological; we begin with the *Ortus vocabulorum* and conclude with Palsgrave's word list.

On the whole, the lexicographical practice of translating verbs into English is the same as that encountered for nouns and adjectives. In the *Ortus vocabulorum* there is thus conformity of style throughout the dictionary. We shall look at the more interesting features in some detail.

The translation equivalent may be one simple verb in English or more. When three equivalents are provided, the last or all three are linked by *or*:

> **Expolio is iui.** to pollysshe forbysshe or graue. **Expolitus a ũ. pert.** **a. q.**
>
> **Dirupio pis.** to wast or rynde or breke.

The number of equivalents suggested may go up to four or five:

> **Folleo es.** to madde or dote to bolne/ or to be proude. **n. s.**
>
> **Exploro as. inquirere vel inuestigare.** anglice to spye or to seke or open or trase or to bek handes. **Tor trix et tio. at⁹ a um. pert.** **a. p.**

The English equivalent may also be a paraphrase of the meaning of the Latin verb lemma. As with nouns and adjectives, this semantic explanation may itself translate a preceding explanation in Latin or be a rendering without such prompt: '**Constabulo as. i. ponere equos in stabuto** [*sic*]. to put horses in to the stable **a. p.**', '**Cõplodo is.** to Joy wᵗ yᵉ handȝ or to clap'.

The Latin verb lemma may be followed by one or more Latin synonyms, which then precede the English-translation equivalent. In such cases the Latin part of the dictionary entry thus resembles a monolingual Latin dictionary entry, and this becomes emphasized by such items as *idest*, *-i.*, *significat*, etc., inserted between lemma and synonym or explanation in Latin:

> **Adclino as. idest valde multum clino.** to boo doune. **a. p.**
>
> **Adoro as. significat venerari penul. ꝓdu cta. o. tor trix tio.** to honore. **a. p.**

In other cases, the proper sense of the lemma may be indicated or another sense of the lemma may be listed. This may be done after the Latin lemma or after the English translation. The lexicographical device is the same for both positions. Additional senses are introduced by *etiam*, *vel.* In order to draw attention to the proper sense of the word, the adverb *proprie* is used. Examples are:

> **Exstinguo guis stinxi. i. mortificare et ꝓprie ignem. an.ᵉ** to slacke or cesse **a. t.**

> **Latro as. are. angl.'** to barke **et proprie**
> **est canū.** **n. p.**

As with nouns and adjectives, there are numerous entries where we have, so to speak, a double dictionary, with the English equivalent followed by another Latin equivalent, as in '**Existimo as.** to wene. **i. putare a. p.**'. Derivatives of the verb, usually the deverbal abstract noun and the agent noun, may be given, often introduced by *inde*: '**Intelligo gis. exi.** to vnderstande. **Tor trix ⁊ tio. a. t.**'.

With a few exceptions, derivatives or additional senses of the verb lemma in entry-final position are never translated into English: '**Blandior iris. i. adulari.** to glose. **Blandiens. i.** glosynge'. The same holds for where the use of the Latin verb is illustrated. Such instances are rare, but more frequent than those occurring with nouns and adjectives. Examples are:

> **Labifacio cis. idest euellere concurrere: fe**
> **rire labē facere labare vel labi.** an.ᵉ or to
> smytte out. **vt ego labifaciā dētes tuos.**
> **actiui gn̄is tertie ꝯiuga.**
>
> **Liquefio fis. factussum.** to melt. **vt lique-**
> **facta est aīa mea.**

Instead of an illustration of use, there may be a metalinguistic comment on the currency of the lexical item in question. In such cases, the simplex is usually said to be no longer in use, and common prefixal derivatives are listed: '**Sidero as. non est in vsu sed sua cōposita vt cōsidero desidero**'. It is interesting to note that for these Latin items which are said to be no longer in use, there are no English equivalents.

Let us now look more closely at the wording of the English equivalents. Comparative phrases introduced by *as* are fairly regular for verbs denoting sounds, noises produced by animals:

> **Balare. i. clamare admodū ouis.** to crye
> as a scheepe. **n. p.**
>
> **Fritino as.** to synge as a swalo/ or as
> other smalle burdys. **n. p.**

We note, again, that comparative phrases of this type occur as part of the lemma entries in the *Promptorium parvulorum*, the *Catholicon Anglicum*, and *Lesclarcissement*. But apart from occurrences with this semantic group of verbs, *as* comparisons are rare: '**Grecisco as. i. loqui more grecorū.** to speke as a greyk. **n. p.**'. Latin inchoative verbs tend to be paraphrased in English as 'to begin to . . .': '**Capisco cis. inchoatiuū de capio.** to begyñ to take. **a. t.**'. Very occasionally, the English rendering includes the verb *to wax*: '**Brumesco cis.**

**ĩchoatiuũ**. to wax wynter'. Latin frequentative verbs are rendered with the help of 'often', 'oft': '**Nato as. frequentatiuũ de no as**. angl.' to swym oft. **a. p.**'. And finally, for some *verba deponentia* the English translation equivalent includes an active as well as a passive form: '**Criminor aris**. to blame or to be blamed. **Tor trix et tio**. **cõ. p.**'.

## *The* Promptorium parvulorum

The compiler of the *Promptorium parvulorum* was still much indebted to the medieval tradition of the nominalia and verbalia. He therefore listed the nominalia and the verbalia separately under the respective letters of the alphabet. The nominalia, including nouns, adjectives, and adverbs, are given first, then all the verbs in alphabetical order. There are even chapter headings of the type *Incipit littera B. Nomina*, ¶ *Incipiunt verba. B*. In the *Ortus vocabulorum*, the citation forms for verbs are those of the first-person singular, present tense, for which, in English, the infinitive form is given. In accordance with this lexicographical tradition, we have in the *Promptorium* the infinitive form of the verb as the English lemma and the first-person singular form, present tense, as the corresponding Latin. In the case of impersonal verbs, the English infinitive is matched to the Latin third-person singular, present tense, as in '**Behoue**. Oportet bat tuit erat bit tere. secũde coniugacõnis ⁊ Imꝑonale'.

In the *Ortus vocabulorum*, there is vascillation between the third-person singular and the infinitive form, as we can see from the example: '**Accidit bat. i. ꝯtingit**. to hape. **imꝑsõale**' and '**Decet bat. imꝑsonale**. an.ᵉ it semed'.

As appears from these examples, the first translation equivalent is then provided with its range of grammatical forms. They are usually the second-person singular, present tense, the first person singular, perfect tense, the infinitive, the past participle. They are followed by an indication of the conjugation class and a specification of the type of voice of the verb, *actiuum*, *neutrum*, *deponens*. When there are variant grammatical forms, these are given and linked by means of *vel*.

When the entry provides several Latin translation equivalents which belong to the same conjugation class, the latter is not always repeated. Instead, a cross-referential device is used, such as *eodem modo coniugatur* or overridingly *similiter*, *similiter declinatur* or *coniugatur*:

> **Beware**. Caueo ues ui uere cautũ. secunde cõiugacionis. actiuũ. Catho. Precaueo es ui ere. similiter declinatur ⁊ est. actiuum.

The last part of the preceding example illustrates a further device, that of subsuming the various verbs under one grammatical specification.

In the *Promptorium* the Latin adverb *proprie* is not used as in the *Ortus vocabulorum* for the proper sense of a Latin word, but rather its use is restricted to the following type of grammatical information:

> **Boylen ouer as pottes on the fyre.** Ebullio lis liui lire. quarte cõiugacionis neutrũ. sed proprie est in tercia ꝑsona tm̃.

> **Spyryn as corne or other lyke.** Spico as. pri. con. neu. Cath. sed ꝑprie in tercia ꝑsona tm̃.

In general, the English verb lemma is rendered by one or more one-word Latin verbs. The number of translation equivalents offered may go up to six or seven:

> **Takyn or receyuyn.** Accipio pis cepi ceptũ Ca pio pis cepi captũ. Apprehendo dis di hensũ Sumo mis sũpsi sũptũ. Suscipio pis cepi ceptũ. Tollo lis sustuli tollere sublatũ. oĩa sunt tercie coniugacionis. actiua.

As we can see from this example, the translation equivalents are simply listed one after the other, without further discrimination.

Equally rare in the *Promptorium* are translation equivalents which paraphrase in Latin the meaning of the English lemma. If one assumes that early English–Latin dictionaries are to a large extent inverted early Latin–English dictionaries, this does not come as a surprise. What appears as a lemma in Latin is usually a lexicalized item. When it occurs as a translation equivalent, it is a one-word match, not a semantic paraphrase: '**Fermyn.** Firmo as. prime con. actiuũ. vel ad firmã accipio'.

What is common to all the instances in which there is a Latin paraphrase of the meaning of the English verb is that these explanations are never the first translation equivalent provided. Instead, they come after a Latin translation equivalent that consists of one verb only. That is, they exactly correspond to postlemmatic glosses in a Latin–English dictionary and lend further support to the 'inversion theory'.

The Latin verbs provided as translations of the English headword are not illustrated in a sentence or phrase. There are no indications that a Latin item is no longer in use and that it has been replaced by one of its derivatives, nor does the *Promptorium* have a word-formational component as we have in the *Ortus vocabulorum*. An exception is the entry for *Ben aqueynt*, where the Latin verb *noscor* is described as a passive form of *nosco*:

> **Ben aqueynt or knowen.** Noscor ceris notus
> sũ ci notũ. tercie coniugacõnis. Passiuum.
> de Nosco cis.

The occurrence of a Latin verse at the end of an entry to differentiate two or more of the Latin equivalents is as rare as in the *Ortus*. But, unlike the *Ortus*, the *Promptorium* commonly cites the Latin source from which the item has been compiled. Occasionally, not only the name but also the place within the author's work is given:

> **Budden as trees.** Pampino nas prime con-
> iugacõnis. neutrũ. vel Gẽmo as. Pululo
> las oĩa prime ꝯiugacionis/ ⁊ neutra. C. f,
> Frondeo des. secunde. ꝯ. H. in Fores.

The *Promptorium* compiler also makes use of a cross-reference system in which, as for all other lexicographical comments, the metalanguage is Latin. An exception is the English word *or* used to introduce glosses of the English headword.

### *The* Catholicon Anglicum

We come to the verb equivalents in the *Catholicon Anglicum*. They share some features outlined for the *Ortus* and the *Promptorium*, but others are specific to this second English–Latin dictionary within the history of English lexicography. As to the different word classes described in the dictionary, there is uniformity of style, as for the *Ortus* and the *Promptorium*.

In the *Catholicon*, the English verb lemma is given in its infinitive form, usually preceded by the particle *to*, spelt in lower case and extraneous to the alphabetical arrangement. The English infinitive is matched with a Latin infinitive, but exceptions and vacillations are found in those cases where the Latin verb tends to be used in the third-person singular only. This might be illustrated with the following examples:

> to **Behove**; *oportet*, *conuenit*.

> to **Happyñ**; *Accidere malarum re-*
> *rum est*, *contingere bonarum re-*
> **rum est**, *euenire bonarum &*
> *malarum rerum est*, *fortunare*,
> *est*, *erat verbum jnper-*
> *sonale*.

A characteristic feature of the *Catholicon* is its concentration on providing *copia* of expression and on trying to differentiate this wealth of translation equivalents. One might say that, where in the *Ortus* and the *Promptorium* it is the grammatical description of the Latin items recorded that prevails, in the *Catholicon* it is lexical variety and semantic discrimination. The number of translation equivalents provided may be more than twenty, and in the case of *to show* and *to cry* more than sixty.

Under the verb *to cry*, the compiler has brought together all the various sounds produced by animals:

> **to Cry**; *clamare, Ac-, con-, re-, clamitare, clangere; canum est baulare & latrare, boum mugire ranarum coaxare, coruorum crocare & crocitare, caprarum vehare, anatum vetussare, Accipitrũm pipiare, Anserum clingere, aprorum frendere, apum bombizare vel bombilare, aquilarum clangere, Arietum lorectare, asinorum rudere, catulorum glatire, Ceruorum nigere, cicadarum firmitare, ciconiarum croculare, cuculorum cuculare, elephantum barrire, grabarlarum fringulare, equorum hinnire, gallinarum crispiare, gallorum cucurrire, gruum gruere, hedorum vebare, hircorum mutire, hirundinum mimurrire & mimerire est omnium minutissimarum Auicularum, leonum rugire, luporum vlulare, leperorum & puerorum vagire, lincum aucare vel nutare, miluorum pipire, murium pipare vel pipitare, mulorum zinzare, mustelarum driuorare, noctuarum cubire, olerum densare, onagrorum mugerilare, ouium balare, panterarum caurire, pardorum folire, passerum tinciare, pauorum paupeilare, porcorum grunnire, serpentum sibilare, soricum disticare, Tigridum rachanare, turdorum crucilare vel soccitare, verris quiritare, vrsorum vercare vel seuire, vulpium gannire, vulturum palpare, vespertilionum blaterare.*

By mentioning the animals themselves within the entry, the compiler has achieved a semantic differentiation for the many Latin verbs that may render the English verb *to cry*. The usual device adopted to indicate differences in meaning between semantically related words is an explicit wording which may have the form of a verse:

to **Drynke**; *bibere, con-, potare, con-e-, haurire; versus:*
¶ *Poto, do potum; poto, sumo michi potum.*
*Calicare; bibit qui aliquid re-linquit, ebibit qui totum bibit. bibimus ex necessitate, Pota-mus ex voluntate. Sebibere est seorsum bibere.*

to **Pray**; *deprecari, flagitare, ef-, impetrare, jmplorare est auxilium cum miseracioni petere, jnteruen-ire, jntercedere, jnterpellare, or-are, ex-, per-, obsecrari, precari, de-, procumbere, procubare, queso, quesumus, rogare, rogitare, sup-plicare, precatur qui rogat. qui eciam orat precatur, qui autem precatur non vtique orat, quia jnperiti ad preces descundunt.*

In the *Catholicon* much more use is made of the insertion of verses than in the *Ortus* and the *Promptorium*.

Translation equivalents where the meaning of the English verb is paraphrased in Latin are rare. The *Catholicon* here resembles the *Promptorium*. Examples are: 'to **Awntyr**; *jn euentu ponere*', 'to **Blawe**; *flare, suf-, cornare est cornu flare*'.

Unlike the *Promptorium*, however, the *Catholicon* has some instances where the Latin paraphrase constitutes the whole translation equivalent and where it does not explain a preceding Latin verb.

Illustrations of verbs in example phrases or sentences are less rare in the *Catholicon* than in the *Ortus* and the *Promptorium*. Yet they do not really meet the users' needs. The *Catholicon* is conceived as a productive dictionary for English learners of Latin. There are no instances where an example sentence in English is translated into Latin. The illustrations all have one of the Latin verbs given as a translation equivalent as their basis and are never provided with an English equivalent:

to **Forbed**; *Abdicare, abnuere, argu-ere, ut: arguo te ne maleficos imi-teris; jnhebere jmperio, prohibere iure, interdicere, vetare, euetare, dehortare.*

to **Plese**; *libere, -bescere, placere, per-, vacare, vt vacat michi scrib-ere.* i. *placet.*

As we can see from these examples, illustrations are variably placed but follow that translation equivalent, the use of which they show in a sentence. Among the illustrative examples in the *Catholicon*, we find one that also occurs in the *Ortus*:

to **Smyte oute**; *labifacere, vt: ego labifaciam dentes tuos.*

The corresponding entry in the *Ortus vocabulorum* reads:

**Labifacio cis. idest euellere concurrere: ferire labē facere labare vel labi.** an.[e] or to smytte out. **vt ego labifaciā dētes tuos.**

Thus, either the compiler of the *Catholicon* had a manuscript of the *Ortus* in front of him when he worked on his dictionary, or the compilers of both these dictionaries consulted the same Latin source. The instance itself is apt to lend further support to the theory that early English–Latin dictionaries are to a large extent inverted Latin–English dictionaries.

Other features of the *Ortus* also occur in the *Catholicon*, yet they look more like random instances of where something that was in the sources consulted was inadvertently copied and not discarded, as in the majority of the other cases.

## Lesclarcissement

With this we conclude our review of the translation equivalents for verbs in the bilingual dictionaries that preceded the publication of *Lesclarcissement*, to which we now return.

There are a number of unique features in the table of verbs that make *Lesclarcissement* an unparalleled work in the history of English lexicography: verb illustrations of the lemma in English with French translations, the authorial *I* observing and recording language use, and explicit contrastive analyses of English and French grammar and vocabulary. The practice of distinguishing different types of linguistic information by different founts, not yet found in the printed editions of the *Promptorium parvulorum* and the *Ortus vocabulorum*, but used for Palsgrave's tables of nouns and adjectives, is further developed for verb entries, which are much more complex than those for nouns and adjectives. And then there are features that occur sporadically in the earlier bilingual Latin–English and English–Latin dictionaries, but always in relation to Latin, for which there was already a long tradition of linguistic description. In *Lesclarcissement* these observations are made for two vernaculars, and the pioneering achievements concern differences of language use (temporal, regional, stylistic), variations in spelling, analyses of word-formation patterns, and attempts at etymologies.

In order to make the linguistic information provided for verbs easily accessible to his readers, Palsgrave uses a basic entry format which may then be expanded. This basic format has five information units: the English lemma entry, the corresponding French translation equivalent, the grammar of the French verb, an example sentence in English, and its full translation into French. A typical example is the following:

> **I Coole I make a hote thynge colde/** Ie refroydis, iay refroydy, refroydir. secũde coniuga. **Coole your potage or you eate them/ they be to hote:** Refroydissez vostre potage auant q̃ le humer, car il est trop chault.
>
> (III, fo. c.xci)

As we can see, there is agreement in grammatical form between the English lemma (*I Coole . . .*) and the French equivalent (*Ie refroydis*). Palsgrave will undoubtedly have resorted to citing the first-person, singular, present tense, because there were precedents, above all for highly inflecting languages as Latin. Grammatical treatises, too, listed certain stem forms from which the other forms for person and tense could be derived, and the first-person singular, present tense, was one of them. Yet, because of the lack of inflectional forms in the English verb system, the retention of the first-person singular, present tense, may not make much sense. But Palsgrave seems to have given priority to the agreement in grammatical form, which is confirmed by his matching third-person forms when the verb is impersonal:

> **It Becometh as a countenaũce or condycion becometh one/** Il aduiẽt. **This countenaunce becometh hym as well as of any man that euer I sawe:** Sa contenance luy aduiẽt aussi bien que a hõme que ie vis iamays, construitur cum datiuo, **bothe** il siet **and** il aduient.
>
> (III, fo. c.lviii[v])

In some cases, particularly when the verb is predominantly used in the third person, the first-person form strikes one as bizarre:

> **I Budde I blossome as a tree dothe/** Ie boutonne. prime coniuga. **This tree buddeth all redye:** Ceste arbre boutonne desia.
>
> (III, fo. c.lxxviii[v])

But the example that follows in each case immediately offsets the oddity of the lemma form. In a dictionary intended for productive use, first-person forms obviously have an immediate appeal for the users, putting at their disposal the form that comes naturally as the speaker's own expression.

The grammatical information which Palsgrave provides for the French verb equivalent varies. In general, the minimum specification is the conjugation class to which the French verb belongs. The metalinguistic terms are given in Latin: *prime coniuga.*, *secunde coniugatio*, *tercie cõiuga.* Other odd and very rare Latin indications, as *construitur cum datiuo* in the example *It Becometh*, are clearly inadvertent slips of compilation. Whatever is in Latin is printed in the small type also used for the French equivalents. This is fully in accordance with the whole printing style of *Lesclarcissement.* In the grammar parts, Latin has a very minor role and is literally banished to the margins where guide elements of the text passage are set out—for example, *Exceptionae duae*, *regula tertia*, and so on.

Irregular verb forms are usually listed, and they are given in full with the accompanying pronoun form. The irregular forms typically listed depend on the conjugation class to which the verb belongs. In book II (see fos. xli$^{v}$, xliii$^{v}$, xlvii), Palsgrave discusses at some length which grammatical forms he will indicate in the table of verbs so that his readers are left in no doubt. He distinguishes five classes of verbs (*Diuisio uerbi* (II, fo. xxxvii)): active, mean, passive, personal, and impersonal. Mean verbs are difficult to identify for a learner and therefore Palsgrave decided to mark these in the table of verbs, whereas the other classes are not usually indicated. Distinctions are based on linguistic criteria, which Palsgrave outlines as follows:

> vnto whom [verbes meanes] I haue gyuen this name for. ii. causes: One/ for so moche as determynatly they betoken neyther action nor passion: for where as the doar and sufferer ought to be distinct parsons/ the acte of these verbes retourneth euer to the doar agayne. An other/ for where as of euery verbe/ whiche signifieth an acte to be done without forth/ may be circumlocuted a passiue with the tenses of *ie svis* and theyr participle preterit: whiche shal in dede betoken sufferyng by the act of some parson without forth: in suche verbes as be meanes we can nat do so: but these thynges shal in the thirde boke in this place more playnly appere. Howe be it some thynge more playnely here to shewe the lernar/ howe he shall knowe suche verbes as in the frenche tong be vsed as meanes. In maner generally all suche verbes as signifie a parsone to do au [*sic*] acte eyther with his mynde/ hole body/ or any part therof/ of whiche the dede retourneth to the doars selfe agayne/ and betoken none acte to passe frõ hym without forth/ al suche verbes in this tong be vsed as meanes. (II, fo. xlvi$^{v}$)[2]

Palsgrave then exemplifies the three semantic groups of mean verbs and admits that there are exceptions. We cannot expect an early lexicographer to be totally consistent in his work, but the results of the

[2] See also the delimitations of mean verbs in *The Introduction of the author*, Cii$^{v}$–Ciii, book II, fo. xxxvii, and book III, fos. c.xxxii$^{v}$–c.xxxiii. In book I, he outlines three criteria which distinguish mean verbs: meaning, as described in the quotation given, the formation of the perfect tense by means of *être* instead of *avoir*, and the 'double' pronouns before the inflected verb, as in *Ie me maruaille.*

checks carried out are quite impressive. Of the thirteen verbs signifying 'actes of the mynde', nine are marked as mean verbs in the table of verbs, the others are either not included or not specified. Of the ten verbs signifying 'the actes of the hole body', five are marked as mean verbs, and so are six of the eight verbs given to exemplify verbs that signify 'particular actes of the partes of ones body'.

The number of French equivalents provided for an English verb may go up to ten. In such cases the grammatical information may be reduced, and the same may hold for the examples:

> **I Uexe I greue/** Ie vexe, iay vexé vexer. prime cõiu. ⁊ ie greue. prime. **and** iabire, ⁊ iattayne, ⁊ iangoysse, **and** ie infeste, ⁊ ie ressoigne, **and** ie persecute, ⁊ ie solicite, ⁊ ie moleste, prime cõiuga. **This mañ vexeth me sore euery daye:** Cest homme icy me vexe fort, **or** me greue fort, **or** me abire fort, **or** me attayne fort, **or** me angoysse fort, **or** me infeste fort, **or** me ressoigne fort, **or** me persecute fort, **or** me solicite fort, **or** me moleste fort tous les iours.
>
> (III, fo. ccc.lxxxxvi$^{v}$)

Compare also **I Hyde** with ten French equivalents and **I Ordayne** and **I Set at naught** with eight. In the above example, the French equivalents are joined by *and*, which corresponds to *et* in the bilingual dictionaries having Latin as one of the languages described. Instead of the coordinator *and*, other devices are used, such as *lykewyse*, *otherwyse*, *of lyke signyfycacion*, *they vse also*, but the most striking device is 'I fynde also'. In an entry that suggests eight French translations for the English verb **I Bewray**, it reoccurs five times:

> **I Bewray I vtter or shewe ones counsayle/** Iaccuse. prime coniuga. **in whiche sence I fynde also/** Ie descouuers, iay descouuert, ie ne le descouuriray point, descouuris, tercie coniuga. **coniugate lyke his symple** ie couuers, **I couer. I fynde also** ie reuele. prime coniuga. **I fynde also** ie chaleme, Romant. **I fynde also** ie defecte. prime coniuga. **I fynde also** ie recele. prime coniuga. **and** ie diuulgue. prime. **and** ie retrays, **Coniugate lyke his symple** ie trays, **I**

> **drawe. What so euer I knowe by hym it is nat my parte to bewraye it:** Quoy que ie saiche de luy il nest pas seant a moy de laccuser, de le descouuryr, de le reueler, de le receler, de le diuulguer, **as for** ie chaleme, **is used of the Romant by fygure.**
>
> (III, fo. c.lxv)

The 'I' is plainly authorial, and Palsgrave assumes in his dictionary the role of a language observer and recorder. The 'I find also', instead of a mere *also*, which would exactly correspond to the Latin *etiam* found in the earlier dictionaries, sounds less personal and more conventionally descriptive. It is an expression of the different approach which he had had to take compared to the compilers of the *Ortus*, the *Promptorium*, and the *Catholicon*. The compilers of these could all fall back on what other Latin scholars had achieved, and their compilations had become authoritative. Palsgrave's authorities were the French authors he had read, from whose works he had collected his French words and phrases and brought them together in his tables. The 'I find also' conveys the scholar's position embraced by Palsgrave to record only what is found in the texts. In this spirit, he also occasionally confesses to not having the necessary evidence available:

> **I Am wonte I am accustomed to do a thynge/** Ie seulx, nous soulons, vous soulez, ilz soulent, ie souloye, ie soulus, **and the same tence in ẏ subiũctyue mode shulde be/** ie soulusse, souloir, **I do nat remembre that I haue redde it/ ⁊ howe he is a verbe defectyue and hath no mo tenses of him selfe/ and howe the other tenses be circũmlocuted I haue all redy shewed in the seconde boke/ for I haue be wont/ they say** iay aprins, **I haue be wonte to ryse erly/** Iay apprins de me leuer matin, **or** ie souloye de me leuer au matin. **He was wonte to come euery daye:** Il souloyt venir tous les iours.
>
> (III, fo. c.xlviii$^{v}$)

The strongest confirmation of this attitude as a meticulous observer who describes language use as he has experienced it himself comes from those instances in which Palsgrave discusses an individual writer's use, sometimes even a particular work and the occurrence in a specific place. This is what Palsgrave repeatedly does in the sections where he describes French grammar and French pronunciation. And he does it in the table of verbs, as we can see from some examples:

> **I Make blynde/** Ie aueugle. prime cõiu. **or** ie aueuglis. secunde cõiu. **so that in ỹ olde romant tonge they vse this verbe of their fyrste coniugacion/ but Johan le Mayre vseth hym of their seconde. Wene you to make me blynde with your wyles:** Pencez vous de me aueuglyr de voz ruses.
>
> (III, fo. cc.lxxxxix (= cc.lxxxix))

> **I Shyne as any bright thynge shyneth/** Ie resplendis. secunde cõiu. **but Johñ le Mayre vseth/** ie resplẽs tu resplens, il resplend, aussi replend [*sic*] la ducalle baniere, **but all other tenses be euer vsed of the seconde coniugacion/ ⁊ in his first booke. capi. xxii.** Et la noble cõqueste de Iason en Colcos prent son fondemẽt dung mou ton a la toison dor qui resplend maintenant au ciel faisant lung des douze signes du zodiacque. **His victoriouse actes shyned thorowe all ỹ worlde:** Ses actes victorieux resplendissoyent par tout le monde.
>
> (III, fo. ccc.l$^{\mathrm{r}}$)

We have already discussed Palsgrave's use of French writers and the astonishing degree to which his command of French encompassed the earlier stage of the language in Chapters 3 and 5. What the above quotations illustrate at the same time is that for the French equivalents Palsgrave lists variations in spelling and grammatical use, and he usually draws his readers' attention explicitly to them.

In a few instances, the part which deals with the grammar of the French equivalent includes a puzzling capital letter. They are three in number: *A*, *M*, and *N*. Examples are:

> **I Se a thynge with myne eyes/** Ie voys, nous voyons, ie vis, iay veu, ie verray voyrra. A. voyent. N. veysmes. A. que ie voye, **or** voy, que ie vesse. A. veoir. tercie cõiu. vise. imperatiue. A. **I se or beholde a thyng:** Ie vise. prime cõiu. **For se or beholde in the imperatyue they vse/** Tenez. **As/ se these women wepe downe ryght:** Tenez ses femmes pleurent a grosses larmes . . .
>
> (III, fo. ccc.liii$^{\mathrm{v}}$)

> **I Pouruaye I prouyde:** Ie pouruoye iay pouruoyé, ie pouruoiray. M. ie pouruoierray. M. melius pouruoier. pri. con. . . .
>
> (III, fo. ccc.xxi)

One might think of them as abbreviations for active, mean, and neuter, though Palsgrave explicitly excluded the term 'neuter' from his grammar for French: 'The acte of the mean verbes passeth nat from the doar/ but retourneth to the doars selfe agayne/ or is done within the parsone of the doars selfe/ so that cõmenly all suche verbes as be vsed in the latin tong/ lyke neuters or deponentes be vsed in this tong lyke mean verbes' (I, C ii[v]). As we can see from the above examples, the capital initial is not always located where this kind of grammatical information is inserted, after the indication of the conjugation class. The letters may also co-occur in a dictionary entry:

**I Socour one that is towardes a daunger/** Ie secours, nous secourons, ie secouris, iay secouru, ie secourray, que ie secoure, secourir. A. secourre. N. **So god socour me:** . . .

(III, fo. ccc.lxvi)

**I Take awaye a thyng from one/** Ie oste. prime cõiu. ie priue. **I take awaye his offyce:** Ie luy oste son office, or ie le priue de son office, ⁊ ie toles, nous tolons, ie tolus, iay tollu, ie touleray. A. que ie tollisse. N. elle luy tolut, que ie tolle, tollyr. tercie cõiu. datiuo iũgitur . . .

(III, fo. ccc.lxxxiii)

It is not always clear whether the initial capital refers to what precedes or what follows. In the case of *Socour*, the form *secourir* would then have to be regarded as an active verb, the form *secourre* as a neuter verb. Or is Palsgrave recording that a source *A* has the infinitive form *secourir*, source *N* the form *secourre*, just as the sentence *elle luy tolut* was inserted from source *N*? The instances for *M* are similar:

**I Drinke wyne or ale or any other lycour/** Ie boys, nous beuvons, vous beuvez ilz boyuent, ie beus, iay beu, (Phil) ie buray, **or** ie boyray, que ie boyue, boyre, tercie. coniuga. **and** ie bus, M. **Bringe vs some drinke:** Ap portez nous a boyre. **He that drĩketh well and pysseth well shall neuer be greued with ỷ stone:** Qui boyt bien et pisse bien ne sera iamays greué de la grauelle.

(III, fo. cc.xxi)

**I Go/** Ie men vas, **coniugate in the seconde boke/ ⁊ note ỷ lyke as it is comenly vsed in our tonge to put this verbe/ I go/ byfore our verbes/ where we vse no mouynge to a place/ so vse they to put ỷ tenses of** ie men vas, **byfore their partyciples of the present tence/ as the Romant/** Et vont chantans, **for** chantãt, et lors va deprisãt les dames, **for** lors desprise les dames, & c. M. il alla mourir.

(III, fo. cc.l[v])

In the entry for *drink*, '(Phil)' looks like an abbreviation from a literary text, and *ie bus* like an alternative form in *M*. for *ie beus*. The verb *boire* itself is grammatically not a mean verb. In the entry for *pouruaye*, two forms for the future tense are given: *ie pouruoiray* and *ie pouruoierray*. The latter is attributed to *M*, and *M* is then regarded as the better form. The entry for *go* is very interesting. The French translation *s'en aller* is a mean verb, but this information has been overlooked in the section that deals with the grammar of the verb.

There is no such specification. Palsgrave then singles out two particular constructions with this verb. One is the use of *aller* + a present participle, illustrated by *vont chantans* and *va deprisant*, in Old French, which he equals with the simple verb forms *chantant* and *desprise*. The other construction is given only in the sentence *il alla mourir*; it is not explained. As an example, it does not fit Palsgrave's description of *aller* + participle and in the form *alla* it is not reflexive, therefore not a mean verb. The sentence *il alla mourir* is preceded by *M,* which seems to suggest that it occurs in or with *M*, and its occurrence at the end of the entry might indicate that Palsgrave was aware that there was another interesting use of *aller* + *infinitive* which he had not yet explained.

If the abbreviations *A*, *M*, and *N* do not relate to the grammatical terms active, mean, and neuter, they might stand for source texts or their authors. Alexis? Meschinot? The most puzzling remains *N*.

We come to Palsgrave's comments on spelling. In some instances, his observation of French usage seems to be the basis of what he takes as the more common form:

**I Gyrde a man or a woman with a gyrdell.** Ie ceings, no[9] ceyndons, ilz ceyndent, ie ceingnis, iay ceyngs, ie ceyndray, que ie ceigne, ceingdre. tercie cõiu. **but** ie saings, **is wronge written . . .**

(III, fo. cc.xlviii$^{r-v}$)

**I Make vyle/** Ie aduile, **and** ie aduilene. prime cõiu. **Uyle condyscyons make a man vyle:** Viles condiscions aduilleront, **or** aduilenerõt vng hõme, **but the trewe orthographye is** auile, **and** auilener.

(III, fo. cc.xcvii$^{v}$)

There are attempts at explaining differences in spelling:

**I Belche I voyde wynde out of my stomake/** Ie routte, iay routté, routter. prime coniuga. **Harke howe the churle belcheth:** Escoutez cõment le vilayn routte, **or** roucte, **bycause of** ructo, **in latyn.**

(III, fo. c.lx$^{v}$)

**I Burgen I put forthe as a tree dothe his blossomes/** Ie bourgonne. prime cõiuga. **whiche I fynde somtyme written** ie bourgeonne, **lest the reder shulde sounde the G/ amysse. These trees Burgen a moneth soner thã I loked for:** Ces arbres bour gonnent vng moys plus tost que ie ne pensoye.

(III, fo. c.lxxix)

Spellings which are closer to their Latin original and common forms are distinguished, and the more common form may be given preference:

**I Cõprehende I parceyue a thing in my mynde/** Ie comprens, nous cõprenons, ie comprins, iay comprins, ie comprendray, que ie compreingne

> comprendre. tercie coniu. **coniugate lyke his symple/** ie prens, **I take/ thoughe that after the ryght latyn formacyon it shulde be/** Ie comprehens, nous comprehennons & c. **but suche orthographye is neuer vsed.** . . .
>
> (III, fo. c.xciii)

Homographs present special problems for learners, and so Palsgrave gave them particular attention, as we have already seen in Chapter 2. This concern also becomes evident in the table of verbs. As we can see from the following examples, occasionally the language observer in Palsgrave is overtaken by the language corrector:

> **I Flye from myne enemye or I flye for feare I haue of any daũger:** Ie men fuys, nous nous fuions, ie men fuys, ie men suis fuy, ie men fuyray, que ie men fuye fuyr, **or** fouyr. verbũ mediũ. tercie coniu. **whiche thoughe I haue written with U/ only in the seconde boke to put a difference in orthographye bytwene the tenses of** ie fouys, **I dygge. yet Alayne Char tier and Johan le Mayre confoũde the orthographye in these verbes.** . . .
>
> (III, fo. cc.xxxvii[v])

> **I Growe as herbes and trees do or any lyuely thyng ỷ waxeth greater in quantyte/** Ie croys, il croyst, nous croyssons, il creus, iay creu, ie croystray, que il croysse, croystre. ter cie cõiuga. **and in the thyrde persone synguler he hath S/ to differ in writyng from** il croyt, **He byleueth** . . .
>
> (III, fo. cc.lv)

The observational stance adopted by Palsgrave makes him comment on contemporary French usage. Thus under **I Beheed a man,** *coupper la teste* is described as being more used than the verb *decoller*, or under **I Smell** he maintains that *sentir* is more common than *oler*. In other cases he points out that the French verb is not very common: for example, *abstraindre* for 'to constrain' (**I Constrayne** . . .), and *engreger* for 'to increase' (**I Encrease** . . .). He distinguishes already between a word that is obsolescent and one that is falling out of use because its referent is no longer common:

> **I Turne as a man dothe in a daunce/** Ie me renuoyse. prime cõiu. **and** ie me vire. prime cõiu. **and** ie me reuire. pri. cõiu. **This terme waxeth out of cõmen spetche bycause the maner of daunsynge is chaũged/ howe be it/ it is somtyme vsed.** . . .
>
> (III, fo. ccc.lxxxxv[v])

Occasionally, he specifies, as did the compilers of dictionaries involving Latin, that a compound verb is more common than its simple—for example, *remplir* is said to be commoner than *emplir* (**I Fyll an emptye vessell** . . .), *emouvoir* commoner than *mouvoir* (**I Moue I styre my bodye**), and *reluire* commoner than *liure* (**I Shyne as the sonne dothe** . . .). And, finally, there are instances where he distinguishes between a demotic and a hieratic use of language:

**I Go as softe as foote maye fall/** Ie men vas mon beau bas trac, ie men suis alle mon beau bas trac, aller mon beau bas trac [note the orientation towards the first person *mon* instead of *son*], **vsed in comen lãgage**.

(III, fo. cc.lii$^{v}$)

**I Rauysshe a mayde or wyfe I take them by force/** Ie rauys, iay rauy, rauyr. secũde cõiuga. **and** ie entaille. prime cõiuga. **and** ie viole. pri me cõiuga. **Some sayd she was rauysshed with her wyll:** Les aulcuns disoient quelle estoyt rauie, **or** quelle estoyt violée, **or** efforcée de son bon gre. **As for ientaille,** as pour entailler la gracieuse Helayne, **thoughe I fynde it in the estypell** [*sic*] **of Oenone to Parys it is nat vsed in comen spetche.**

(III, fo. ccc.xxxiii$^{v}$)

From the verb examples quoted so far, it is clear that most of the translation equivalents for English verbs are one-word verbs in French. Occasionally such a French verb is paired with a phrasal expression—for example, *mettre en effect* and *executer* for 'to execute' (**I Execute** . . .), *voler* and *aller a la volée* for 'to go hawking' (**I Go a haukyng** . . .), and *fouetter* and *donner du fouet* for 'to whip' (**I Whyppe** . . .). Translation equivalents which are longer turn out to be either French idiomatic one-word lexical units or renderings of the whole English lemma entry. Examples are:

**I Aduertyse him of a daũger that is towardes/** Ie luy aduertis dung danger qui est aduenir . . .

(III, fo. c.xxxviii$^{v}$)

**I Am compelled to do a thynge/** Il mest force de faire vne chose, **or** ie suis efforcé . . .

(III, fo. c.xliii$^{v}$)

**I Gyue vp the goste (Lydgate)** Ie rends mon ame, **or** ie rends mon esperit . . .

III, fo. cc.xlix$^{v}$)

**I Go a wrie as one dothe y$^{t}$ treadeth nat their shoe a tyght/** Ie marche de coste . . .

(III, fo. cc.li$^{v}$)

If the idiomatic rendering of the English verb requires a different grammatical form, it takes precedence over the functional match between lemma and equivalent. In such cases the English first-person lemma is paired with an impersonal construction in French:

> **I Etche as a man ỳ rubbeth hymselfe/** Il me cuit, il me cuisoyt, il me cuisyt, il me cuit, il me cuira, quil me cuise, quil me cuisist, cuire, verbũ imparsonale. secũde coniuga. **whan I ytche I can nat chose but I muste rubbe it:** Quant il me cuyt ie ne me puis contenir que ie ne le frotte.
>
> (III, fo. cc.xxii)

> **I Force nat I care nat for a thing** Il ne men chault, **coniugate in I care nat/ and** ie ne tiens compte de, **and** ie ne donne riens de. **I force nat for the:** Il ne men chault de toy, ie ne tiens compte de toy, ie ne donne riens de toy.
>
> (III, fo. cc.xl)

There are really no semantic paraphrases of English verbs, naturally enough, in view of Palsgrave's lemma structure and his explicit metalinguistic comments. In several places in his work, he stresses that what in one language may be expressed by one lexical item may have to be expressed in the other by a phrase, and vice versa. He therefore tends to verbalize such differences when the French translation of an English verb is not a straightforward verb. An example is the following:

> **I Fetche a thyng that I or other haue nat/ for this worde they haue no propre verbe but vse to ioyne the tenses of** ie men vas, **coniugate in the secõde boke to** querir, **as/** ie men vas querir, ie men suis allé querir, ie men iray querir, aller querir. **I wyll go fetche hym:** Ie le veulx aller querir. **Go set me my sworde at ones I shall teache the knaue good:** Va me querir mon espée a coup ie apprẽdray le villayn de mesmes.
>
> (III, fo. cc.xxxv)

On the other hand, such paraphrases may not be necessary because they are already anticipated in the postlemmatic expansions in English, as with *to grope*, for instance, where Palsgrave offers the translations *tãter* and *aller à tãtons*. Dictionaries like our modern bilingual ones are based on the lexical item *to grope*, and they would therefore have entries of the following type (taking into account Palsgrave's treatment of the item):

**grope** *vt* tãter . . .
*vi* aller à tãtons

Modern learners are left with the difficult task of working out which sense of *grope* corresponds to which French equivalent. If the modern bilingual dictionary provided a full grammatical description as well as illustrative examples, these might help users in the decoding task. Palsgrave's verb lemmata are very often based on senses of the lexical item. In order to delimit the sense of a lexical item taken as a lemma, he expands it—that is, there is a postlemmatic expansion. His lemmata thus take the form

**I Grope a thyng that I do nat se or proue a thyng . . .**

**I Grope as one dothe the wall or place whan he gothe darkelyng . . .**

The decision what to make a sense and thus a lemma may be prompted by the linguistic behaviour in English or by the knowledge that French has a word for it.

Yet the postlemmatic expansion does not only have the effect of identifying each respective sense. Since it is cast in the users' mother tongue, the postlemmatic expansion differentiates at the same time the native vocabulary for its users. From this point of view, postlemmatic expansions, above all those which are full semantic glosses of the headword, contribute to the linguistic education of the dictionary users. It is clear from the introduction to the *Comedy of Acolastus* that Palsgrave was strongly interested in the development of the mother-tongue skills in all those young clerks who had received teaching in Latin.

The postlemmatic expansions, whether prompted by the language facts of English or of French, mentally work as semantic paraphrases of the translation equivalent. They thus relate to the lemma as well as to the translation equivalent.

Palsgrave's table of verbs includes in part a highly sophisticated bilingual learner's dictionary. Some modern publishing houses have developed monolingual English learner's dictionaries like the *Advanced Learner's Dictionary of Current English* or the *Longman Dictionary of Contemporary English* into bilingual learner's dictionaries by providing for the English lemma a foreign-language equivalent and/or by translating the English explanation or examples into the foreign language. In such works the language of the lemma entries is English, the target language, which is matched with the users' mother tongue, the source language. These bilingual learner's dictionaries are for receptive use. With Palsgrave we have in his verb table a bilingual learner's dictionary for productive use.

There is one lexicographical device that shows very clearly the bilateral relation between the postlemmatic expansion and its lemma, on the one hand, and the French equivalent on the other. This is the adverb *properly*, used as Latin *proprie* in the earlier bilingual dictionaries, to indicate the proper sense of a word. It occurs as part of postlemmatic expansions and helps in this position to narrow down the sense of the English verb which is to be translated into French. Examples are:

> **I Bende I bowe ꝑperly a yonge spring or suche lyke thynge that is plyante/** Ie flechis, iay flechi. flechir. secũde coniuga. **I fynde also** Ie plessie. prime cõiuga. **and** ie ploye. prime. **A man may bende a wande while it is grene ⁊ make it strayght though it be neuer so croked:** On peult flechyr or plessier vne gaulle nouuellement cueillie et la faire droycte tant soyt elle tortue de soy.
>
> (III, fo. c.lxi)

> **I Fyll vp to the brimme or brinke as we do vessels or measures properly with drye thynges as corne or spyce or any suche lyke thyng/** Ie accõble. prime cõiu. **Fyll your busshell heape full you maye well ynoughe for you sell dere:** Accomblez vostre boysseau vous le pouez bien assez car vous vendez chier.
>
> (III, fo. cc.xxxvi)

This adverb *properly* also occurs in the equivalent part of the dictionary entry when Palsgrave differentiates between French equivalent verbs—for example:

> **I Constrewe as a grammaryen dothe a sentẽce whan he ioyneth the partes of speche in order/** Ie cõstruis nous cõstruisons, ie construis, iay construit, ie cõstruiray, que ie construise, que ie cõstruiisse, cõstruire. tercie con. **I shall be beaten if I can nat constrewe my lesson whan my mayster cometh:** Ie seray batu si ie ne puis con struyre ma lecon quant mon maistre vient, **but herin I folowe yͤ comen vse of speaking/ for** ie ordine, **is pro perly to constrewe on this maner. As cannest yͧ constrewe thy lesson:** Scays tu ordiner ta lecon.
>
> (III, fo. c.xcv$^{v}$)

> **I Gather vp thynges that befallen/** Ie amasse. prime coniu. **but more properly is** ie recueuilx, **coniugate lyke his symple** ie cueuils, **I gather as a man gathereth floures. Gather vp my beades my stryng is broken:** Amassez or recueillez mes patenostres ma corde est rompeue.
>
> (III, fo. cc.xliiiiv$^{v}$)

> **I Smyte/** Ie frappe, **and** ie fiers, nous fierons, ie ferus, iay feru, ie ferray, que ie fiere ferir. & c. **you smyte to harde:** Vous frappez trop fort, **but** frapper, **is properly with the hande or with a thing that dothe me great hurte/** ferir, **is to stryke with a weapen or to gyue a greuouse stroke/ but I fynde them ofte confounded.**
>
> (III, fos. ccc.lxiiii$^{v}$–ccc.lxv)

With these last examples, we have already come to Palsgrave's explicit attempts at describing the meaning of the French equivalent more fully or at differentiating the meaning of equivalents provided. This can naturally also be done without using *properly*, as for instance in:

> **I Throwe in to yͤ see/** Ie emmarre. prime cõiuga. **Rather than our en-**

> **nemyes shall se our letters lette vs throwe them in to ẏͤ see:** Plustot que noz ennemys verront noz lettres emmarrons les. **So ẏͤ** emmarrer, **signyfyeth to throwe a thyng in to the see that hath a heauy thynge tyed to it lest it shulde flete any more aboue the water.**
>
> (III, fo. ccc.lxxxx)

The semantic differentiation may also encompass English, so that we have in Palsgrave's verb table the beginnings of contrastive lexicology for two vernaculars, as in the following examples:

> **I Hoorde as a man hordeth golde or appels or any thyng in heapes to spare for store/** Ie entasse. prime cõiu. **but many tymes this verbe is named after the thyng that men horde vp thynges in. As/ I hoorde in cofers:** Ie encoffre. **I hoorde in tõnes:** Ie entonne. &c. **Hoorde nat vp your monay in your cofer/ lende it rather to poore men:** Ne entassez pas vostre argẽt en voz coffres, **or** nencoffrez pas vostre argent prestez le plustost a voz poures voysyns.
>
> (III, fo. cc.lxiiii^v^)

> **I Take peper in ẏͤ nose/ they vse no suche maner of speakyng/ but in the stede therof vse/** Ie me courouce, **or** ie me tempeste, **or suche lyke. you maye nat take pepper in the nose for a worde speakyng:** Il ne vous fault poynt courroucer pour vng mot ou deux.
>
> (III, fo. ccc.lxxxv^v^)

There are numerous verb entries where Palsgrave indicates the sociolinguistic and pragmatic conditions under which a verb is used. These will be investigated in more detail in Chapter 9, since they, just as the illustrative examples, provide us with glimpses of contemporary society and life. Two further examples may therefore suffice here to illustrate such differentiations of meaning:

> **I Am content/** Ie suis cõtent, **and whan we suppose in comunycacion a thyng to be so/** Ie le veulx bien: **as touchyng that I am content:** Quãt a cela ie le veulx bien.
>
> (III, fo. c.xli^v^)

> **I Come vp apon a stayres or ladder or any hye thyng/** Ie monte. prime coniuga. **and** ie viens en hault, ie suis venu en hault, venir en hault, cõiugate **in I come. I wyll come vp to you by and by:** Ie mõteray a vous tout asteure. **But he that is aboue al redy if he saye to one come vp/ for that they say/** Venez en hault, **or** montez en hault.
>
> (III, fo. cc.ii^v^)

With this we come to the examples by means of which Palsgrave shows his readers how the French verb in question is used. His general policy (not adopted where there are cross-references) is to supply examples which are usually full English sentences, though occasionally we find phrases or subordinate clauses not linked to a main clause. Since the French vocabulist is intended for productive use, the English example sentences come first, followed by a French translation.

There are, however, many entries where the illustrations may consist of six or seven examples, perhaps the random fruits of Palsgrave's fertile mind:

> **I Stuffe a podyng or suche lyke** Ie farce. pri. cõiu. **and** ie farcie. M. **or** ie espessis. secũde coniu. **Stuffe this podyng:** Farces ce boudyn. **Stuffe this breste of veale and make a podyng in it:** Farces ceste poictrine de veau et faictez vng boudyn dedens.
>
> (III, fo. ccc.lxxviii^v)

Both examples have the form of an imperative, both have a following object noun phrase, and both are translated by the French verb *farcer*, and none specifies the substance to be used for the stuffing.

A close study of the examples, however, reveals that Palsgrave may have had a specific purpose in providing more than one example sentence. When he offers several French translation equivalents, he tends to provide an example for each:

> **I Stablyshe/** Ie establys. secũde. **and** ie afferme, **and** ie prefixe. prime. **Whan a thyng is ones stablyschyd it is hard to change it:** Mays q̃ vne chose soyt vne foys establie cest forte chose que de la chãger. **What so euer he saye I wyll stablysche it:** Quoy quil die ie le veulx establir, **or** ie le veulx affermer. **The tyme is stablyschyd all redy:** Le temps est prefixé desia.
>
> (III, fo. ccc.lxxi^r–v)

> **I Steppe a syde out of the way/** Ie me desmarche. ie me desroye. pri me coniu. **Let them lay to my charge what they lyste I wyll neuer steppe a syde for it:** Quilz me enchargent tãt que leur playra iamays ne me desmarcheray pour tãt. **Nowe that you be ĩ good order loke you steppe nat a syde:** Mayntenant q̃ vous estez mys en bon ordre ne vous desroyez point.
>
> (III, fo. ccc.lxxiii^v)

If the English lemma entry includes two senses and both are rendered by one particular verb in French, the two examples illustrate that the same French verb covers these senses. The lemma entry for the verb *to conceive*, for instance, includes the concrete sense as well as the abstract one. Both are rendered by French *concevoir*:

> **I Conceyue as a woman dothe that is gotten with chylde/ or as a**

**man conceyueth or vnderstandeth a mater/** Ie concoys, nous cõcepuons, vous concepuez, ilz cõcepuent, ie con ceus, iay conceu, ie cõcepueray, que ie concepue, concepuoyr. tercie cõiu. **It is a wõdrouse thing ỷ she shulde cõceyue and is aboue threscore yere olde:** Cest vne chose estrange quelle deust concepuoyr et elle passe soyxante ans. **I can nat conceyue this thing it is to harde for my capacite:** Ie ne puis pas concepuoyr ceste chose elle est tresdifficille pour ma capacité.

(III, fo. c.xciii$^{v}$)

And similarly, under *supply*, the two senses specified in the lemma entry are, according to Palsgrave, rendered by French *supplier* and each is illustrated:

**I Supplye I praye or I fulfyll a space or a romme/** Ie supplie. prime cõiu. **I shall supplye hym the humblest that I can:** Ie luy supplieray le plus humblement que ie pourray. **If he be deed an other shal supplye his place:** Sil est mort vng aultre suppliera a sa place.

(III, fo. ccc.lxxx)

In addition to providing an example sentence for each French equivalent, thus differentiating them and showing their area of application, Palsgrave supplies further examples when he contrasts a positive and a negative expression. In the entry for *smell*, for instance, he opposes *smell swete* and *smell nat very well*, and under *I Set by one* an example with *much* is contrasted with one including *naught*:

**I Set by one I estyme him or regarde hym/** Ie tiens compte, iay tenu compte, tenir compte, ⁊ ie donne garde, ⁊ ie accompte. **I set moche by him:** Ie tiens grant compte de luy, ie donne beaucoup de luy, **I Set naught by hym:** Ie ne tiens compte de luy, **or** ie ne donne riens de luy.

(III, fo. ccc.lvii$^{v}$)

**I Smell I sauour well or yuell/** Ie ole. prime cõiu. **but they vse more comenly in this sence** ie sens, **coniugate in I fele/ and** ie fleure. prime. **Smell at my coler ⁊ you shall parceyue whether it be I that stynke or nat:** Sentez a mon collet et vo[9] apercoyuerez si cest moy qui put ou non. **You smell swete this mornynge you haue good rose water:** Vous sentez bien, **or** vous fleurez bien ce matin, vous auez de bonne eaue rose. **Take away this fysshe it smelleth nat ve-**

**ry well:** Ostez ce poison il ne sent pas trop bien. **Proue howe this gylowfloure smelleth:** Tastez comment cest oyllet sẽt bon, or fleure bien. **It smel leth well:** Il ole bien.

(III, fo. ccc.lxiiii)

A further reason for giving more than one example may lie in illustrating different verb forms (with respect to person, tense, or mood) or different complementation, the two often going together with a particular French verb:

**I Shriue me of my synnes/** Ie me confesse. verbũ mediũ. prime cõiu. **I wyll shriue me this lente at the Augustyne fryres for there is pardon:** Ie me confesseray aux Augustyns ce quaresme car il ya du pardon. **Go shriue you for you had nede:** Allez vous confesser, or allez a confesse car vous eu [*sic*] auez mestier.

(III, fo. ccc.lii^v)

**I Truste I hope/** Iespere, ie me fie, ie me confie, ⁊ ie maffie. **I truste to se hym a man or I dye:** Ie espere de le veoyr hõme auant que ie meure. **I truste in you:** Ie me fie en vous, ie maffie en vous. **It is nat good to truste to all men:** Il nest pas bon de se confier a tous hommes.

(III, fo. ccc.lxxxxv)

In the last example under *I Shriue*, another translation equivalent has cropped up besides *confesser*: *aller a confesse*. This is by no means the only instance. It looks as if there was not enough revision time to insert the additional French equivalent in its right place at the beginning of the entry. Another such example is the following:

**I Understande I haue knowledge of a thyng/** Ie entens, nous entendons, ie entendis, iay entendu, ie entenderay, que ie entende. entẽdre. tercie. cõiu. **They vnderstande it no more than a maynye of oxen:** Ilz ny entendẽt non plus q̃ vng tas de beufz. **I vnderstãde:** Ie me cõgnoys. **I vnderstande no latyn:** Ie ne me cõgnois pas en latin.

(III, fos. ccc.lxxxxvii^v–ccc.lxxxxviii)

And, finally, it is perhaps the case that, whenever an entry becomes more complicated by the inclusion of idiomatic uses of the verb lemma, further exemplification is called for. This is well documented by the following two examples, the second of which includes an interesting comparison between English and French:

**I Playe the wyse man/ the foole/ the dethe man/ the drõken man and suche lyke/ I cotrefayte or handell**

**I Saue one from daũger as harnesse dothe ones persone/ or as medecyne or preseruatyue dothe ones**

**my selfe lyke a wyse man/ a foole/ a dethe man/ a dronken man/** Ie fays le saige, or du saige, le fol, **or** du fol, le sourt, **or** du sourt, liuroigne, **or** de liuroigne, **ioynyng the tenses of** ie fais, **to ẏ wordes folowyng. I play the lorde:** Ie fais du seignieur. **Dothe he nat playe the calfe well that is escaped:** Ne fait il pas bien le veau eschappé. **He played the deefe man:** Il fist la sourde oreille. **But I shulde nat play but the wyse man:** Mays ne feroye ie point que saige. **you played the stoute man so hyghly:** Vous faisiez si fort du vaillant. **He that hath money ynoughe may well play the great man:** Qui a de largent assez peult bien faire du grant.

(III, fo. ccc.xvii[v])

**helth/** Ie contregarde. prime cõiuga. **This medecyne taken fastyng shall saue you from the pestylence:** Ceste medicine prinse a ieun vous contregardera de la peste. **Sauing your re uerence:** Sauf vostre grace, **or** saulue vostre grace, **for I fynde bothe/ but** saulue, **is trewer written. God saue the kyng:** Viue le roy. **God saue all good drinkers:** Viuẽt tous bons beuueurs, **But where we vse sauynge your reuerence whan we speke of a vyle thyng in the presence of a great man/ in frenche they saye:** Ne vous desplaise, **but they vse** saulue vostre grace, **whan they wolde contrarye the sayeng of their superyour/ and meane that it is nat so.**

(III, fo. ccc.xlvii)

A verb entry in Palsgrave's table of verbs may thus already show the lexicographical arrangement that we have in modern monolingual English dictionaries: idiomatic phrases or expressions are listed after the lemma and its exemplification, towards the end of the entry. Here Palsgrave's command of spoken idiomatic French is most impressive. His dictionary, and above all his table of verbs, is a treasure trove for further studies in sixteenth-century lexicology. We conclude this section on his verbal illustrations with an example that includes a description of the spoken language:

> **I Stande vpon my fete/** Ie me tiens debout, ie me suis tenu de bout, tenir debout, verbũ mediũ. prime cõ. **coniugate in I holde. but for stande in the imperatiue mode whan it is spoken to an enemy or in haste they saye** debout, **only and leue out the ꝟbe I fynde also vsyd in thys sens** Ie me mets sus mon estant, ie me suis mys sus mon estant, estre mis sus mon estant. **but where as we vse this ꝟbe in our tong for I tary as stãde their or tary theyr tyll I come they vse** ie me tiens, **coniugate in I holde. As stande theyr tyll I come agayn:** Tenez vous la tant que ie men reuiẽgne.
>
> (III, fo. ccc.lxxii)

*Word-formation*

We turn finally to Palsgrave's word-formation analyses. When we were discussing his assessments as to the frequency of occurrence of some forms, it was pointed out that he occasionally specifies that the simple verb is less common than a derived verb (see p. 326). The terms he uses are *simple* and *compound*. When the French equivalent for an English verb is a derived verb and Palsgrave does not want to repeat its grammar because he has already described it under the simplex, he usually refers the user to the entry with the simple verb:

> **I Fynissh I make a full ende and**
> **conclusyon of a thynge/** Ie parfays,
> iay parfait, parfaire, **coniugate lyke**
> **his symple** ie fays, **I do/ and** ie ter-
> mine. prime cõiu. **and** ie accomplis.
> secũde cõiu . . .
>
> (III, fos. cc.xxxvi$^{\mathrm{v}}$–cc.xxxvii)

Palsgrave's treatment of word-formation does not stop at such general analyses. He describes the meaning of the French prefix *re-* as 'again' and the formative process under the entry **I Come agayne**:

> **I Come agayne/** Ie reuiens, **con-**
> **iugat lyke** ie viens, **I come/ by put-**
> **tyng of** re, **byfore** ie viens, **for** re, **in**
> **cõposycion byfore a verbe in frẽche**
> **signyfyeth agayne.**
>
> (III, fo. c.xci$^{\mathrm{r-v}}$)

In other entries he contrasts French verb prefixes and their corresponding English prefixes. Under **I Mysagre**, English *mys-* and French *mes-* are matched:

> **I Mysagre/** Ie mesagrée. pri. cõiu.
> and ie discorde. prime cõiu. **I neuer**
> **wyst them misagre afore in my lyke:**
> Ie ne les cõgnus iamays deuant a ma
> vie mesagreer, or discorder. **So that**
> **where we vse mys/ byfore our ver-**
> **bes in our tonge/ they vse mes, by-**
> **fore their verbes of lyke sence.**
>
> (III, fo. ccc.i)

The English prefix *un-* is discussed in two verb entries. The first is very similar in structure to the one for *mys-*. At the end of the entry, a summarizing comparison is made:

> **I Onbynde.** Ie desli e. pri. coniu-
> **He maye do and vndo/ bynde ⁊ vn-**

> **bynde in that house.** Il peult faire et
> defarie [*sic*], lier et deslier en ceste mayson
> la. **So that for on/ in our tonge put**
> **before our verbes: They vse** de **put**
> **before their verbes for the most ꝑte.**
>
> (III, fo. ccc.viii)

Under the entry **I Unaglet**, the contrast is widened. It is not only *de-* that corresponds to English *un-* but also *des-*, and he describes the meaning of *un-* in front of a verb as 'an vn doynge of a dede or the contrarye acte that yͤ verbes selfe syngnyfyeth':

> **I Unaglet a poynte or lace/** Ie
> defferre. prime coniu. **Here it**
> **is to be noted where we vse vn/ by-**
> **fore our verbes betokennyng an vn-**
> **doynge of a dede or the contrarye**
> **acte that yͤ verbes selfe syngnyfyeth**
> **the frenche men for the moste parte**
> **vse to put** de, or des, **byfore their ver**
> **bes of lyke sence. As/ I pray you vn**
> **aglet this poynt:** Ie vous prie deffer-
> rez ceste esguillette.
>
> (III, fo. ccc.lxxxxvii)

The fourth prefix described is *over-*. French has a similar word-formation pattern, but when there is no corresponding verb in French, then the meaning of the English prefix is best rendered by the adverb 'trop':

> **I Ouerbye/ I bye a thynge**
> **aboue the price it is worthe.**
> Ie surachapte. prime cõiu. **There is**
> **nothing so good/ but it may be ouer**
> **bought.** Il ny a ryen si bon quil ne
> peult estre surachapté. **But where**
> **as we in our tonge vse often to com**
> **pounde our verbes with ouer/ if I**
> **haue nat expressed the verbe here in**
> **order/ it may be coũtreuayled with**
> sur, **put before the Frenche uerbe/ or**
> trop, **after him/ as I ouer worke my**
> **selfe.** Ie besoigne trop.
>
> (III, fo. ccc.ix)

In one instance, a diachronic perspective is added to the synchronic description of verb prefixation in French:

> **I Out beare one in his dede.** Ie
> supporte. prime coniu. **Who so euer**

> **saye the contrary/ I wyll out beare the.** Quiconque die le contraire, ie te veulx supporter. **But where as in som frenshe verbes I fynde** for **ad-did byfore them whiche cõtreualith owt/ whan he is thus cõpownde ẇ verbes in our tõg as where we saye I owt crye/ I owt eate/ I owttake/ I owt cept/ in Alayne Chartiers tyme they vsed** Ie forcrie Ie forman-geus Ie forprens Ie forcepte: **nowe ẏ frenshe tonge leueth syche maner of composition sauyng in one or two here expressed/ and for owt they vse oultre/ or** plus **as the sentence shall require.**
>
> (III, fo. ccc.xi)

The treatment of word-formation in the table of verbs here follows that in book II, where Palsgrave draws attention to differences in the use of some word-formation patterns between his own time and the time when the *Roman de la Rose* was written and when Alain Chartier flourished (II, fo. xlv^v^).

Deadjectival verb formation is also discussed in book II, and is taken over into the table of verbs. It is described under **I Waxe**, one of the English verbs that renders such French derivations:

> **I Waxe/ I begyn/ I become or I make fayre/ foule/ wyse/ foolysshe / great/ lytell/ or suche lyke: so that in our tonge we haue none other ma-ner to expresse inchoacion suche as the latynes call verbes inchoatyues but by puttyng one of these verbes/ I waxe/ I begyn/ I become/ or I make byfore our adiectyues/ but the french men in maner for euery suche verbe forme a verbe out of their ad-iectyues selfe/ whiche is of their se-conde coniugacyon and vsed lyke meane verbes. As/** Ie embellys, ie enlaydis, ie assaygis, ie enfollys, ie agrandys, ie appetisis, **and so of the resydue/ but for the more suertye to the lernar I shall expresse suche ver bes of this sorte as be moste vsed in the frenche tonge after the order of A. B. C. notynge here that some in our tonge write/ I waxe fayre:** Ie deuiens bel, **cõiugate lyke his symple**

ie viens, **I come. And the substantyue/ as for I waxe folysshe:** Ie deui ens fol. **or the adiectyue/ as I waxe wyse:** Ie deuiens saige.

(III, fo. cccc.ii)

# 9
# How Things were Done with Words

The examples used by Palsgrave in his table of verbs tell us much about sixteenth-century life as well as language use. When reading the table of verbs we cannot but feel transposed into a Renaissance society, with its people, their daily preoccupations, their beliefs, their worries, their pastimes. The picture provided by Palsgrave is so immensely rich and colourful that here we shall be able to get only some selective glimpses. We shall focus on the example sentences together with Palsgrave's metalinguistic comments on language use. Occasionally, the whole dictionary entry may be taken into account. References to the grammar and the tables of the other parts of speech may complement the insights gained from the verb illustrations.

In Chapter 9 we shall look at what an Englishman or a Frenchman actually said or was expected to say in a specific situation, Chapter 10 will provide a picture of Palsgrave's world and thus sixteenth-century society as it emerges from the verb illustrations.

Let us briefly visualize Palsgrave at work. In order to catch as adequately as possible the meaning or particular sense of a verb to be matched by a French equivalent, he paraphrases the English lemma in English or describes it in such a way that it becomes unambiguous. His first achievement is thus the linguistic analysis of his mother tongue. Very often, as we have seen, this analysis is not a simple listing of synonyms or a straightforward linguistic analysis of the type **I Moyst a thing I make it moyst**. Rather, his creative imagination tried to call up typical situations or contexts in which the meaning was used, to make it unmistakable—for example, **I Latche I catche a thyng that is throwen to me in my handes or it fall to the grounde, I Leche I heale one of a sore woũde as a cyrurgyen dothe**. For the English lemma a corresponding French equivalent was then given. This may have triggered off a metalinguistic comment on how to use it properly, and thus, depending on the particular item provided, have influenced his mind in his search for an appropriate example, or determined his choice in those few cases where he seems to have remembered something from his reading of French literature. But in most cases he must just have depended on his imagination to supply good examples, some doubtless pure inventions of his imagination, some reflecting his own personality. We might expect that his personal preoccupations and reactions, his professional beliefs, his moral principles, and his general knowledge may have informed these illustrations. They might also show how his mind occasionally followed tracks already used, when very similiar examples were provided, or that his thinking and general behaviour were characterized by a certain attitude towards his fellow creatures and life.

The concern for his learners, their linguistic and moral needs and education, may also have guided his mind in its inventiveness. His word tables were conceived as a productive dictionary. We know from various passages in *Lesclarcissement* that he was intent on helping his learners to *speak* French, to use the spoken language correctly. To this end he not only described the pronunciation of French in book I but illustrated the difference between the spelling and sounding of it by transcribing some text passages of prose and poetry at the end of book I.

From the context of Palsgrave's compilation situation we might assume that the actual language of his examples will be the contemporary English idiom and, to the best of his knowledge, the French idiom of the time. He refers to the latter as the 'comen speech', the 'vulgar speech', the 'vulgar tongue', terms used to designate ordinary vernacular language. We have already shown, in sample quotations, but above all in Chapters 3, 4, and 5, that he was aware of all the five parameters of language variation: region, social group, medium, field of discourse, and attitude. As we have already seen in presenting regional aspects in Chapter 3, these parameters are all closely intermeshed.

The situations and the human behaviour depicted in Palsgrave's illustrative examples are so close to real everyday life and experience, often so deeply typical of human nature, that they immediately engage the reader. The sharpness and detail of observation and the descriptive tone and attitude adopted make one sense a very human and sensitive personality that was well familiar with the demands, weaknesses, and pleasures of the human body and the mind. All this is expressed in a form that immediately appeals to the reader.

## FORMAL ASPECTS

Palsgrave's examples, in general, consist of full sentences, not snippets of syntactic constructions as we find them so often in modern

English dictionaries for foreign learners, who have to figure out how to use such units and supply a proper context to understand them. Palsgrave's example sentences may consist of a main and a subordinate clause, allowing for argumentation, reasoning, comparisons, and a sense of humour, as in the following examples:

**I Aryse I sette my selfe vpright where I laye afore alonge/** Ie madresse sur mon seant. **I can nat ryse a lone whan I am layed alonge with out I haue some body to helpe me I am so fatte:** Ie suis si gras que ie ne me puis poynt dresser quant ie suis chouché tout plat si ie nay quelqun pour me aider.

(III, fo. c.lii$^{v}$)

**I Boste or cracke of my dedes/** Ie me vante, ie me suis vãté, vanter. verbum mediũ. prime coniu. **and in this sence I fynde also** ie me groye, ie me suis groyé, groyer. prime cõiuga. **He bosteth him as moche for kyllyng of a snayle as some man wolde do for kyllyng of a lyon:** Il se vante autant pour auoyr tué vng limacon que aulcun feroyt pour auoyr tué vng lion.
. . .

(III, fo. c.lxx$^{v}$)

When he thinks that more context is needed, two sentences may be combined:

**I Bomme as a bombyll bee dothe or any flye/** Ie bruys. secũde cõiuga. **This waspe bommeth about myne eare/ I am afrayed leste she stynge me:** Ceste mouche guespe bruyr [*sic*] autour de mon oraille, iay paour quelle ne me picque.

(III, fo. c.lxix$^{v}$)

**I Bring out of order I vnsorte thynges that be sette in their ryght order/** Ie desempare. prime coniuga. **These bokes laye in very good order/ who so euer hath brought them thus out of order:** Ces liures estoyẽt mys en fort bon ordre, quicõque soit qui les a aynsi desempares.

(III, fo. c.lxxvi$^{v}$)

Palsgrave seems to have suffered the nuisance of having his books and papers interfered with, for under **I Bring out of order** (III, fo. c.lxxvi$^{v}$) the illustration is '*These bokes laye in very good order/ who so euer hath brought them thus out of order*', under **I Disorder** (III, fo. cc.xiiii) the example is '*Who hath disordered my bokes and I badde no body shulde touche them tyll I came agayne*', and the first example under **I Set thynges out of order or out of their place** (III, fo. ccc.lix$^{v}$) is '*Who hath set my bookes out of order on this facyon sythe I went*'.

Another disturbance which he may have experienced, or with which he sympathized through the experience of others, seems to have been noise that prevents one from sleeping. The theme recurs in his examples. The example under **I Iumbyll I make a noyse by remouyng of heauy thynges** (III, fo. cc.lxx) reads '*They haue iombled so ouer my heed to nyght I coulde nat slepe*'. Anger is expressed in '*I beshrewe you/ you lumbred so ouer my heed I coulde nat slepe for you* *to nyght*', the example under the entry **I Lumber I make a noyse aboue ones heed** (III, fo. cc.lxxxv$^{v}$). Further complaints about the noise from the room(s) above (him) are '*They make suche a noyse ouer my heed yͭ I can nat take my rest at nyghtes*' (III, fo. ccc.lxxxiiii$^{v}$: **I Take my rest**) and '*The boyes trampell so ouer my heed yͭ I can nat slepe*' (III, fo. ccc.lxxxxiii: **I Trampell** . . .). Lack of sleep may also have been caused by a howling dog: '*I wolde gladly yonder dogge were hanged he neuer ceased whowlyng all nyght*' (III, fo. cccc.x$^{v}$: **I Whowle as a dogge dothe**).

Grammatically, the examples may be declarative, interrogative, imperative, or exclamative sentences, corresponding to the discourse functions of statements, questions, directives, and exclamations. The subject of the sentence may be in the first, second, or third person, in each case either in the singular or in the plural. It is the distribution of these formal possibilities that distinguishes Palsgrave's illustrations from those in modern English dictionaries, where third-person statements with rather factual information predominate.

In Chapter 8 attention was drawn to Palsgrave's use of the first-person singular, present tense, as the lemma form of his verb entries. This enables him to cite as the first form of the French equivalent a form which is not only the first in the conjugation patterns usually memorized but also the very grammatical form learners trying to use the French language would most immediately need.

The use of the first person in the example sentences serves the same communicative need, but it achieves still more. The English *I* (French *ie*) form gives the impression that someone is speaking, that the learner is participating in a talk. The same effect is produced by the use of the second person. Learners may feel directly addressed, entrusted with some personal information or opinion, and have the impression that they are listening to direct speech. This effect is heightened and may even become more imposing when questions and directives are used. Here are some examples:

> **Thou deefest me with thy kryeng so loude:**
> Tu me assourdys par ton hault crier
>
> (III, fo. cc.vi: **I Deeffe** . . .)

> **Departe this skayne of threde we can nat els wynde it vp:** Desmeslez ceste piece de filou autrement nous ne scaurions la deuider.
>
> (III, fo. cc.viii: **I Departe or deuyde** . . .)

> **Who wolde haue thought yͭ euer he coulde haue deuysed suche a mater:** Qui eust pēcé quil sceust ymaginer, **or** machiner vne telle chose.
>
> (III, fo. cc.x: **I Deuyse I discryue** . . .)

> **Wyll you dyne so soone/ it is nat yet an houre sythe you brak your fast:** Voulez vo$^{9}$ diner si tost, il nya pas vne heure encore de puis que vous auez disieuné.
>
> (III, fo. cc.xi$^{v}$: **I Dyne . . .**)

Deictic elements like *this* and *yonder* again contribute to create a presence of speech for the reader/learner, and, when combined with directives, as *See yonder . . .*, they become invitations to follow the compiler's eyes. Exclamations enhance the liveliness of the examples: '*Howe these women cackyll nowe they haue dyned*' (III, fo. c.lxxix$^{v}$: **I Cakyll . . .**), '*The dyuell choke hym/ he hath eaten all the appels a lone*' (III, fo. c.lxxxvii$^{v}$: **I Choke with meate . . .**), '*Combe thy heed for shame*' (III, fo. c.xci: **I Combe ones heed**), '*What a foole was he to entreprise suche a mater ⁊ dyd nat forcaste what shulde come after*' (III, fo. cc.xxxix$^{v}$: **I Forcaste . . .**). Emotions are given full vent, and exclamatory sentences often include a rich array of interjections: *alas, by my faith/on my faith, by the faith of my body, by my truth, by God, by Saint Mary, fie for shame, fie on . . ., thank God, for God's sake, in God's name, good Lord.* Thus:

> **By the faythe of my bodye ⁊ you make moche a do I wyll take my fyste from your cheke:** Par la foy de mon corps si vous harcellez trop les gens ie partiray mon poyng dauec vostre ioe.
>
> (III, fo. cc.xciii: **I Make a do . . .**)

> **Good lorde howe you be sonne brunde for thre or foure dayes rydynge in the sonne:** Iesu que vous estez hasle pour auoyr cheuauché ces troys ou quatre iours au soleil.
>
> (III, fo. c.xlvii: **I Am sonne brunde . . .**)

> **Ha ha are you suche a one/ wolde you embesyll my thynges from me:** Ha ha estez vous tel, voulez vous celer mes choses de moy.
>
> (III, fo. cc.lxvi)

On other occasions, sharpness of observation is paired with an eye for detail and evokes an utterance of delight and enthusiasm:

> **In Aprill it is a pleasaũt syght to se the yonge herbes bedewed:** En Apuryl il fait beau veoyr comment les herbettes sont entousées.
>
> (III, fo. c.lix: **I Bedewe . . .**)

> **It reioyseth my herte to walke in my gardayne in Maye y$^{e}$ floures smell so swete:** Il me resiouyt tout le cueur

de me promener en mon iardyn au
moys de May les fleurs reflagrent, **or**
redolent, **or** sentent si bien.

(III, fo. ccc.lxiiii[v]: **I Smell swete . . .**)

**It is a fayre syght of a woman whan she is well tyred:** Il faict beau veoyr vne femme quant elle est bien habillée, **or** bien accoustrée.

(III, fo. ccc.lxxxxi: **I Tyer with garmentes**)

## LANGUAGE VARIATION IN WRITING

As to language variation in speech and writing, Palsgrave clearly recognized that the use of the one or the other medium might entail different rules. A basic distinction which is recurrent in *Lesclarcissement* is that between authors writing in prose and those writing in verse. Syncope and apocope in verbs, for instance, is said to be more common with writers using rhymes (III, fo. c.xxx). The difficulties in specifying the exact rules for the use of pronominal *en* in French made Palsgrave admit that 'it lyeth in the choyse of an accustomed eare to vse *en*, or leaue him out as he shall thynke good. So that of suche auctours as write in ryme I fynde hym more vsed than in comen speche/ rather to supplye their iuste syllables than for any necessyte' (III, fo. c.xxx[r–v]). He argues that French has no inchoative verbs and that inchoation is therefore expressed by verbal paraphrases with *aller*. A characteristic of poets is that they 'vse ỷ tenses of *ie vas*, with the actyue partyciple of a verbe for ỷ verbes selfe onely/ as *que vous yroye deuisant*, for *que vous deuiseroye*, *Amours va ses plaisirs doublãt*, for *amours double ses playsirs*, *et vont chantans a voix iolye*, *que bien leur pert de leur folye*, for *et chantent* &c.' (III, fo. c.xxxiii[v]; but see III, fo. cc.l[v]: **I Go**).

The language used by poets is sometimes closer to that common during the earlier stage of the language, *olde Rommant*. Palsgrave draws attention to two differences in adverbial use. An answer to a question **Sythe whan**, *Depuis quant* may be *from hence forth*, for which three French equivalents are given, each provided with an example. Of the three, *doresenauant*, *desormays*, and *des or*, this last is said to occur in rhyme only (III, fo. cccc.lviii[r–v]). A question seeking information on how something is done may elicit an answer where the adverbial is a prepositional phrase headed by *with/auec*. Under this entry, Palsgrave tries to differentiate between the use of French *de* and *a*, pointing out at the same time that the preposition *o* is *olde Rommant* and only used by authors writing in rhyme:

Where as it happenneth often tyme in our tonge that this preposycion with/ and his substãtyue/ or els his substantyue and an adiectyue ioyned vnto hym/ maye serue to make answere to this questyon howe/ demaũded of a verbe: as if I demaũde howe I dyd a thyng/ I maye be answered/ with payne or with great payne/ with al his might/ and suche lyke/ the frenche men vse for within this maner *a*, or *de*, with this difference/ whan the substantyue betokenneth ỹ instrumẽt wherwith the dede is doone/ they vse *a*, ⁊ els they use *de*, but this is nat thorowe generall/ ⁊ therfore exemple must chefely helpe/ and also bycause the wordes do oft tymes differ/ as shall here cosequenly apere by dyuerse: notyng first ỹ by cause *o*, for with: as/ *Bien võt o elle vng tas doiseaulx rapteurs.* and *Et vint maistre argus o ses dix figures.* bycause it is olde Rommant and nat vsed but of suche auctours as write in ryme/ I haue nat accõpted *o*, for with in ỹ preposycion amongest the other: *Auec, a toute, a de, ensemble.* (III, fo. cccc.xlvi$^v$)

Language may also vary with use in histories and farces. Writers of farces may attempt to imitate speech as commonly heard. An example provided in *Lesclarcissement* is the pronunciation of *que est ce* and *que est ce cy*: 'But as for *quesse* for *que est ce*, and *quessy* for *que est ce cy*, where in writtyng the letters be chaunged/ that is nat vsed of any proued auctor/ but onely of suche/ as writte farcis/ and contrefait the vulgar speche' (I, fo. vii). Other instances where Palsgrave specifies a particular language use concern letter-writing. One reference relates to formal letters—as a member of the duke of Richmond's household Palsgrave will have been familiar with this style of writing—the other describes a linguistic change in the signing of letters. It is found among the conjunctions. Palsgrave lists *whereas* in a sense which the *OED* gives as '[i]n view or consideration of the fact that; seeing that, considering that, forasmuch as, inasmuch as'. He characterizes the use of *whereas*, French *comme*, in this sense as follows:

**Where as/ by whiche wordes we vse to dylate our maters ⁊ vse them comenly in letters missyues or commyssyons/ or suche lyke:** Comme, as Comme nostre sire le roy a esté deuemẽt informé de ce. &c, Il est pour tant deliberé pour y mettre ordre et remede. &c. (III, fo. cccc.lxxii)

As for the style of signing a letter in French, a typical example would be 'Escript a Londres de par vostre amy Andrieu Bayntõ', but, according to Palsgrave 'this maner of subscribyng waxeth nowe out of vse/ for nowe they vse onely to write *vostre amy*' (III, fo. cccc.xv$^v$).

From letter-writing we move to the writing of 'accounts and books'. At the outset, an author may want to specify what the document is going to deal with. In English this could be done by the phrase 'Here follows'. Palsgrave therefore distinguishes different senses of the verb *to follow* and characterizes this particular use as follows:

**I Folowe one I come after hym**
**or I folowe as one thynge ensueth**
**after another/** Ie suis, nous suiuons,

> ie suyuis, or suyuy, iay suyuy, ie suy-
> ueray, q̃ ie suyue, suyure. tercie. cõiu.
> **but for here foloweth/ which we vse at the begynnyng of bookes or accountes or suche lyke. As/ here foloweth the lyue of saynte Margarete/ here foloweth the charges of the house for this yere/ they say:** Sen suyt la vie sainte Margarite, sensuyt les despẽs de lhostel pour ceste année, **vsynge the thyrde persones of this verbe onely with** sen, **afore them** . . .
>
> (III, fo. cc.xxxviii[v])

THE SPOKEN VERNACULAR

From all the instances outlining specific uses in the written medium, it emerges that Palsgrave was very perceptive to varying linguistic contexts. As early as 1530, he singled out characteristic features of different text types and judged them important enough to describe them for his learners.

The assessment of the spoken medium is not as easy as the written one, because *vulgar speech*, *common speech* may refer to ordinary language in writing as well as in speech. We shall, therefore, have to study his observations on language use very closely.

In the case of the Parisians' substitution of /z/ for intervocalic /r/ (see III, fo. c.lxvii: **I Blaber**; III, fo. c.lxxxv[v]: **I Chatter**) a particular feature of pronunciation is described. Three of the Normandy features recorded in *Lesclarcissement* are typical instances of the spoken language. A speaker from Normandy is recognized by asking in a personal encounter not '*Cõment vous portes vous* (*Howe fare you*)' but '*Cõment te va* (*Howe farest thou*)' (III, fo. cc.xxxiii[v]). When someone shows his agreement with another person's opinion by uttering '*ouy da*', this betrays him as a speaker of Norman French (III, fo. cccc.lx[r-v]), as does a reply '*douen danten*' in answer to a question '*Combien de temps*' (III, fo. cccc.liii[v]).

Many of Palsgrave's examples strike one as actual speech. They depict situations of common everyday experience with which learners/readers can identify. They can just hear themselves saying those words and the utterances ring true. The most impressive side of Palsgrave's power of imagination may be his acute sense for situations and what to say in them. He himself may have been a learner who had an immediate grasp on communicative situations and their characteristic language use. Yet, lacking a linguistic description of French, specifying speech-act situations and how to handle them linguistically, he will have needed—in his social position—to acquire a command of French that was not only grammatically correct and lexically comprehensive, but also socially and situationally adequate and appropriate. The *manières de langage*, the little conversation booklets, provided a certain precedent, exemplifying some speech-act situations like arriving at an inn, asking for a meal, making conversation at table, etc., but their range was restricted. Research into the history of spoken French has highlighted the fictitious model dialogues in these early conversation guides as source texts that come very close to the spoken language (Ernst 1980; Schmitt 1980; Radtke 1994). The difficulty of reconstructing the spoken language of earlier times and the scarcity of adequate source material have repeatedly been commented upon. For Ernst (1980) historical investigations into spoken French might be based on

- historical transcriptions of the spoken language,
- model dialogues of fictitious speech in didactic texts,
- fictitious direct speech in plays,
- fictitious direct speech in narrative texts,
- metalinguistic texts,
- developments of spoken French in geographical areas outside France.

These potential sources are beginning to be explored, but Schmitt (1980) has deplored the fact that the early conversation guides have not been studied systematically and shown what wealth of still unexplored material they contain. Radtke (1994) has undertaken just such a systematic study for seventeenth-century conversation booklets but gives only a cursory glance at the period from the invention of printing up to the end of the sixteenth century.[1]

Palsgrave's explicit descriptions of and comments upon what people actually said at his time could be covered by Ernst's category of 'metalinguistic texts'. His example sentences for verbs might be added as a further source of text for the study of sixteenth-century spoken English and French. Though invented by Palsgrave in order

[1] Radtke's list of works studied begins with an edition of the *Dictionario/coloqvios/o dialogos en qvatro lengvas* of 1580. A rich source for the sixteenth century would be the dialogues of Claude Desainliens (alias Claudius Holyband): his *French school-master* of 1573 includes familiar talks in English and French, and so does *The French littelton* (1576). In his *Campo di fior or else the flovrie field of fovre langvages* (1583) four languages are contrasted in the dialogues: Italian, Latin, French and English.

to illustrate the use of a particular verb, the form and content of these examples seem very close to actual speech: this holds for the situations described as well as those features that are characteristic of the spoken medium: the combination of deictic elements and commands or requests, vocatives, greetings and leave-takings, exclamatory phrases such as interjections and swearings that reveal the speakers' attitude towards the topic of discourse or its partners. In what follows we shall see that Palsgrave's command of French ranged over a whole array of speech-act situations, which he characterizes explicitly and illustrates with examples. The participants in the linguistic encounter are taken into account, their relation towards each other, the topic of discourse, their information needs, and their intended speech meanings.

*Meeting and greeting*

Let us begin with when people meet. Under the entry **I Make chere** Palsgrave describes what he regards as the typical behaviour of Frenchmen in a first encounter among friends:

> **I Make chere to one at my firste meting ẇ him/** Ie accueil, **or** accueils **coniugate lyke his symple** ie cueils, **I gather/ and** iaccueils **signyfyeth properly I gather vp/ for it is the maner of the frenchmen whan frendes mete and the one maketh curteysie to the other/ he that maketh lowest curteysie they wyll lyfte hym vp/ ⁊ that is** accueillyr, **but it is vsed for all the curtesye vsed to a person at his first comyng. He made me the greatest chere ẙ euer I had in my lyfe:** Il me accueillit le plus haultement que ie fus oncques, **or** il me fit le plus grãt accueil que il eus oncques.
>
> (III, fo. cc.lxxxxix^v=cc.lxxxix^v)

There are three further relevant entries:

> **I Receyue one I welcome a frẽde I take hym vp whan he cometh to make me reuerence after ẙ maner of Fraunce/** Ie accueuilx, iay accueuilly, accueuillyr, **coniugate lyke his symple** ie cueuilx, **I gather. He receyued me after ẙ gentyllest maner that euer you sawe:** Il maccueuillit

> **I Welcome I take one vp or receyue hym with myn armes ẙ maketh courtesye to me/ as the frenche men vse to do/** Ie accueuls, iay accueilly, accueyllir, **cõiugate lyke his symple** ie cueulx, **I gather/ and** ie recueulx, **cõiugate lyke his symple** ie cueuls, **I gather. Let hym come**

de la meilleure sorte que vous vistez iamays.

(III, fo. ccc.xxxiiii)

**I Take up as a man taketh vp his frende that maketh hym curtesye/ as the frenche men vse to do/** Ie acueuls, iay acueilly, acueillir, **coniugate lyke his symple** ie cueuls. **I gather . . .**

(III, fo. ccc.lxxxvi)

**whan he wyll he shall be welcomed on the best facyon:** Viengne quant il vouldra il sera recueilly, or accueilly de la meilleure sorte. **I fynde also in this sence/** ie recoys, **coniugate in I receyue.**

(III, fos. cccc.vi$^{v}$–cccc.vii$^{r}$)

The word *courtesy* as used in this last entry is defined in the *OED* as the 'customary expression of respect by action or gesture, *esp.* to a superior; the action of inclining, bowing, or lowering the body' and it is said to be usually used in the phrase *to make courtesy* or *to do courtesy*. The first quotation dates from 1513. The phrase *to make low courtesy*, as it occurs in Palsgrave's description 'he that maketh lowest curteysie', is not regarded by the *OED* as lexicalized, though it occurs in one of the citations (later than *Lesclarcissement*) for *to make courtesy*.

Courteous behaviour is something that children have to be taught; no wonder that it is stressed in *Lesclarcissement*:

> **I Make courtesye as a yonge childe doth whan he is first taught/** Ie fais le petit, iay fait le petit, faire le petit. &c.[2] **Make courtesye Iacke and thou shalte haue a fygge:** Fays le petit iacquet et tu auras vne figue. **O that is a fayre mayde se howe pre tyly she can make courtesye:** O voiez la que cest vne belle fille, agardez cõment elle faict le petit gentyment.
>
> (III, fo. cc.xc)

This sense of *to make courtesy* is distinguished from when it is merely a token of respect:

> **I Make courtesye to a person to reuerence hym/** Ie fais la reuerence, iay fait la reuerẽce, faire la reuerẽce. **What man he is your father/ you ought to make courtesye to hym all though you shulde mete hym twenty tymes a daye:** Cõment cest vostre pere, vous luy deueriez faire la reue-

[2] In the sense of 'saluer, faire la révérence', the expression *faire le petit*, *faire la petite* is attested by Huguet.

rence et le deussiez vous rencontrer
vingt foys pour vng iour.

(III, fo. cc.xc)

The French idiom *faire le petit* occurs in another example:

**I Inclyne I bowe downe or I applye my mynde to do a thyng/** Ie me encline. prime coniu. **If you wyll nat make courtesye inclyne you like a religiouse man:** Se vous ne voulez poynt faire le petit enclinez vous au moyns a la mode des religieux.

(III, fo. cc.lxvi$^{r-v}$)

There is a further idiomatic expression of *courtesy*, *to pinch courtesy*, which, according to the *OED*, is first documented in *Lesclarcissement*. The sense given, 'to insist too much on, be over-punctilious in, the observance of courtesy; to stand upon ceremony', does not quite catch the meaning and tone of Palsgrave's entry with the French equivalent *faire le nyce*:

**I Pynche courtaysye as one doth that is nyce of condyscions/** Ie fays le nyce. **What you pynche courtesye me thynke:** Comment vous faictez le nyce ce me semble.

(III, fo. ccc.xvi$^{v}$)

Respectful behaviour towards one's master requires that one takes off one's headwear:

. . . **Howe oft tymes haue I cõmaded ẏ to take of thy cappe whan thou metest thy mayster:** Quantes foys tay ie cõmandé de oster ton bonnet quant tu rencontres ton maistre.

(III, fos. ccc.lxxxiiii$^{v}$–ccc.lxxxv$^{r}$: **I Take of** . . .)

Yet Palsgrave does not only describe the ritualized behaviour when two people meet; he also tells his readers the proper words to use. The usual forms of greeting described by Palsgrave are given under the entry **I Gyue**:

**I Gyue/** Ie donne. prime cõiuga. **God gyue you good morowe:** Dieu vous doynt bon iour, **but lyke as we vse to leaue out the verbe in suche maner of salutyng/ and saye: Good morowe/ good euyn/ good nyght/**

> **so do they in comen language ⁊ saye:**
> Bon iour, bon vespre, bonne nuyct,
> **and as for** bon soyr, **betokeneth god**
> **sende you a good fore parte of the**
> **nyght/ ⁊ this may be vsed at length**
> **as/** dieu vous donne bon vespre.
>
> (III, fo. cc.xlvi$^{v}$)

As to who greets whom first, the examples under **I Salue** may have a personal background. One can easily imagine a caring priest and teacher saying 'I loue to salue the people or euer they salue me: Iayme bien de saluer les gens auant quilz me saluent' (III, fo. ccc.xlvi). With respect to any other person such a statement would not make much sense.

From these general forms of greeting, Palsgrave distinguishes forms that take into account the social standing of the person addressed. An undistinguished commoner should be greeted '*Dieu vous gart*' when first met, and someone of a high social standing '*Honneur a vous*':

> **I Saue I kepe/** Ie saulue. prime
> coniu. **God saue you/ whiche sayeng**
> **we vse whan we come firste to ones**
> **presẽce/ if it be a meane person they**
> **saye:** Dieu vous gart, **if it be a great**
> **personage:** Honneur a vous, **vnder-**
> **standynge/** dieu doynt . . .
>
> (III, fo. ccc.xlvii)

Löfstedt (1978: 208) has shown that this social difference in linguistic use is confirmed in literary works.

Further expressions of greeting are to be found at the end of the table of adverbs. Having exhausted the procedural framework adopted for the description of adverbs—twelve different questions eliciting answers that grammatically qualify as adverbials—Palsgrave adds five short lists of adverbs, assembled on the basis of semantic criteria and displayed in alphabetical order. Such a semantic arrangement had a certain precedent in Latin grammar. We have such a list in Thomas Linacre's *Rudimenta grammatices*, for instance, one of the earliest attempts at composing a systematic basic grammar of Latin, written in English and published at the time when Palsgrave was compiling *Lesclarcissement*. Yet the semantic groups established vary greatly. Those in *Lesclarcissement* are:

- The maners of sayeng ye or affermyng of a thyng,
- The maners of sayeng nay or denyeng of a thyng,

- The maners of blessynge and salutyng and wysshyng well to one,
- The maners of cursyng,
- Maners of exhortynge to do a dede (III, fos. cccc.lx–cccc.lxi).

The first has a match in groups 7 and 8 of the *Rudimenta* ('Of answeryng affirmatiuely', 'Of affirmyng'), the second in group 9 ('Of denyeng'). There is no match for adverbs of saluting and blessing, but there are adverbs of 'wysshyng' (group 13). Palsgrave's fourth class has a parallel in Linacre's adverbs 'of swerynge' and so has class 5 in adverbs 'of callyng on'.

Under the verb *to give*, Palsgrave had commented on a short and a long form of greeting for the time of day: the long form with the religious beginning *God give you . . . Dieu vous doynt . . .* and the short one consisting of the noun denoting the particular time of day premodified by the adjective *good/bon*. Both are regarded as equally current. In the list of adverbs of saluting and blessing he first adduces for English as well as French the short form and then the full form. Here, too, there is no indication of a difference in use:

**Good morowe:** Bon iour.
**God gyue you a good morow:** Dieu vous doynt bon iour.

**God gyue you a good morowe and well to fare:** Dieu vous doynt bon iour et bonne sancté.

**Good euyn/** Bon vespre.
**God gyue you a good euyn:** Dieu vous doynt bon vespre.

**Good nyght.** Bon soyr et bonne nuyct.

**God gyue you god nyght and good rest:** Dieu vous doynt bon soyr et bon repos.

(III, fo. cccc.lx$^{v}$)

Du Wes in his *Introductorie* outlines a third possibility in greeting. He does not oppose the full and the short form like Palsgrave but maintains that salutations in French 'may be tourned two maner wayes/ as whan ye saye in Englysshe/ God gyue you good morowe/ ye may saye/ Good morowe gyue you god' (D iii$^{v}$). He therefore presents his greetings in a sentence frame:

| | | |
|---|---|---|
| | Good morowe | |
| | **Bon iour** | |
| | Good yere | |
| | **Bon an** | |
| God hym gyue | Good euenyng | him gyue god. |
| **Dieu Luy doït** | **Bon vespre** | **Luy doït dieu.** |
| | Good euyn | |
| | **Bon soir** | |
| | Good nyght | |
| | **Bonne nuyt** | |
| | . . . | |

Palsgrave and du Wes thus complement the picture drawn up by Ewald Stange (1900) after a close study of sixteenth-century plays and literary texts: the full forms were in common use in the sixteenth century. Salmon (1967/1987: 43) draws attention to the full forms in Florio, since the Falstaff plays studied by her contain short forms only.

There is an interesting difference between Palsgrave and du Wes. Palsgrave equates *good euyn* and *bon vespre* as well as *good nyght* and *bon soyr* (twice) and *bonne nuyct.* For du Wes the only equivalent of *good night* is *bonne nuit,* and for *good euenyng/good euyn* he says the French use *bon vespre* and *bon soir.*

In the texts studied by Stange, occurrences of *bon vespre* are rare (1900: 19-20) and so are instances of *bonne nuyct* (ibid.: 21). He draws attention to Palsgrave's and du Wes's use of *bon vespre* and comments on *bon soir* functioning as a night greeting. H. C. Wyld in his *History of modern colloquial English* was certainly right when he pointed out that it was 'not until the appearance of plays that we find the actual forms of greeting recorded with frequency' (1956: 378). But he was obviously not aware that these forms received attention from du Wes and Palsgrave in connection with teaching Englishmen the French language well before the plays in question.

On meeting a stranger, one might ask '*Que demandez vous*' or '*Apres qui demandez vous*', corresponding to English '*For what seke you*' and '*For whome seke you*' (III, fo. ccc.liiii: **I Seke** . . .)

The habit of shaking hands is mentioned three times. First in a general way, as the custom when one meets another person:

> **I Gyue one my hande as one dothe ỷ wolde be holpen or lyfte vp or as men do whan they welcome one a nother or wolde make a bargen/** Ie tens la mayn, iay tendu la mayn. tendre la mayn. **cõiugat in I bende. Gyue me thy hande:** Tens moy ta mayn. **Gyue me thy hande ⁊ I wyll helpe the vp:** Tens ycy ta mayn et ie tayderay a mõter. **Gyue me thy hãde nowe by this hande I lay in thyne:** Tens ta mayn, or par ceste mayn que ie te baille.
>
> (III, fo. cc.xlviii)

Before a bargain is settled by a shaking of hands, the offer made by the one side has to be accepted by the other. Palsgrave gives us the proper wording for this process in the second example:

> **I Holde it as we saye whan we make bargen/** Ie le tiẽs. **Lay downe your monaye I holde it:** Sus boutez vostre argent ie le tiens.
>
> (III, fo. cc.lxiii$^{v}$)

In the third example Palsgrave shows how the idiom *to strike hands* is used in the verbal completion of a bargain:

> **I Stryke handes as men do that agre apon a bargen or cõuenant/** Ie touche la. **Stryke handes:** Touche la. **And thou wylt kepe thy promesse stryke handes:** Si tu veulx tenir promesse touches la.
>
> (III, fo. ccc.lxxvii)

This third example illustrates the third function of shaking hands: the settling of a promise.

*Agreeing and disagreeing*

From the speech-act situation of meeting and greeting someone, we have gradually moved on to what may actually be said at a verbal encounter. Palsgrave was very much aware that questions may contain different expectations on the part of the speaker and that it was important for learners to recognize these and to give pragmatically adequate answers. *Lesclarcissement* includes an interesting passage on conducive and non-conducive questions and how to reply to them affirmatively. It occurs in the section that describes the use of negation in French by means of *pas* and *point*. Having outlined the general rules and warned the learner not to use the old form *mie*, Palsgrave continues:

> Here is also to be noted that whan we aske a questyon in our tonge which we doute nat but the answerer muste confesse/ bycause we knowe our selfe it is so in dede/ in suche questyons thoughe we adde nat/ byfore our verbes: as dyd I nat tell you/ lo is he nat hurte nowe/ dyd nat I se the there yesterdaye. In suche questyons ẏ frenche tonge dothe nat vse to put *ne*, byfore their verbes/ but yet they adde *pas*, or *poynt*, after the verbe/ sayeng: *vous dis ie pas*, *agardez est il pas blessé mayntenãt*, *te vis ie pas la hyer*. But if we aske one a question whiche he hymselfe shewed vs/ and haue no farther knowledge but his owne reporte/ in such questyons we vse nat to put/ nat/ byfore ẏ verbe/ but yet in frenche they haue *pas*, or *poynt*, after the verbe. (III, fo. c.xxxii$^{r-v}$)

Since Palsgrave's basis of explanation is the lexical verb, not the verb form that carries the inflection, he was bound to perceive a difference in the position of the negative particle *nat*/*pas* in English and in French. The examples which he then provides and discusses, however, do not include a negative in English:

> Can he playe these pagentes well/ *Sayt il pas bien faire as tours,*
> hath he made you good chere than? *vous a il faict bonne chiere donc.*

> But in the frenche tonge vnto these two dyuerse questyons they haue dyuerse maners to answere/ for to the first they answere/ *sy fistes, si est,* or suche lyke: and to the other they answere *ouy* playnely/ and also I note this maner of demaundyng a questyon: you haue solde the asse haue you nat? *vous auez vendu lausne aues pas,* but for questyons demaunded to know the thyng they be vtterly ingnorante in/ there is no dyuersyte in wordes bytwene our tonge and theirs . . . (III, fo. c.xxxii^v).

The two example sentences are structurally not the same. In the context given, '*Can he playe these pagentes well?*' has to be interpreted as a positive exclamation '*Can he play these pageants wèll!*' where the speaker expects agreement (as in modern colloquial English). The more usual conducive modern English question would include a negative, just as in French: '*Can't he play these pageants well*?' An answer showing agreement with the speaker's opinion would be '*Yes indeed*', '*Yes*', '*As you say*', '*Certainly*', '*I agree*', matching the French answers given by Palsgrave '*Sy fistes*', '*Si est*'. The second example does not have a negative in either language, but includes a conjunct, *than* for English, *donc* for French.

Different types of questions calling for different types of affirmation also preoccupied Pierre Valence in his *Introductions in frensshe*. His differentiation between affirmation and consent is given in Table 9.1.

It looks as if all the three authors who, around the 1530s, had written introductory works for learning French and who had all had employment with the nobility, were shrewdly aware of the social importance of showing agreement with a discourse partner. They have all compiled a list of adverbs expressing affirmation. Valence and Palsgrave use a form of the verb to *affirm* as their term, du Wes calls them adverbs of 'sweryng'. Palsgrave has a further paragraph on adverbs of affirmation in book II. In addition, there are his example sentences in the verb list.

If we follow Koskenniemi's semantic classification of affirmative phrases, imprecations, and oaths (1962: 76–89), most of the phrases in Valence's *Introductions* contain nouns denoting human virtues—for example, *for soth—pour certain, in trouthe—en verite, in good faythe—en bõne foy, in good ernest—a bon etiant, without fayle—sans faulte.* Du Wes's list is both longer and more varied. Nearly half of the phrases provided relate to general expressions of certainty:

| | | |
|---|---|---|
| in earnes | of certayne | for sothe |
| **a certes** | **de certain** | **pour vray** |
| for earnes | certaynly | of truthe |
| **pour certes** | **certainement** | **de veritę** |

TABLE 9.1. *Pierre Valence: Expressions of affirmation and consent*

| | |
|---|---|
| **Nota. that there is two maners to answere in frẽsshe** | Nota quil y a deulx manieres de respõdre en frãcois |
| **Wherof one affermeth/ ⁊ ẙ other cõsẽteth/ after ẙ** | dont lũgne afferme/ et laultre cõsẽt/ selõ la demãde |
| **questyon.** | |
| **As who sholde say. Go fetche me my boke.** | Cõme qui diroit. Alles moy querir mon liure. ou, |
| **Come speke with me to morowe/ or/ teche me my** | venez demain parler a moy. ou/ apprenez moy ma |
| **lesson/ or/ bye me some newe thynge/ and** | lecon, ou/ achattez moy quelq; chose de nouuiau. et |
| **a thousande other. The answere to suche locucyons.** | Mille aultres Responce a telles locutions |
| **So wyll I do/ or well/ or I wyll well.** | Aussi feray ie. ou. bien, ou. Ie le veulx bien, |
| **yf ẙ speker say wͭout byddynge/ he shall be answered** | Se le parleur dit sãs cõmãder, On respõd aultremẽt |
| **otherwyse/ as who sholde say. My lady ẙ quene is a** | cõe qui diroit. Ma dame la Royne est vne gracieusse |
| **gracyous lady.** ***Re.*** **ye say true/ or so she is. So shal ye** | dame. ℞ vo$^{9}$ dictez vray ou. Cest mon Ainsi feres |
| **do of all other persones/ of this verbe/ I am. Thus.** | par toultes aultres personnes de ce ꝟbe Ie suis. ainsi |
| **It is not well done/ answere. Nomore it is truely.** | Cest bien faict. Responce. Cest mon vrayment |

Valence draws the learner's attention to the fact that there has to be a correspondence between the grammatical tense forms in the question and those in the answer:

| | |
|---|---|
| **Nota. yf the speker chaunge tyme/ chaunge in lyke-** | Nota/ se le parleur/ chãge temps. changez sẽblable |
| **wyse your answere/ as. She hath ben in her tyme a** | ment vostre respõce. Cõme/ Cestoit en son tẽps vne |
| **fayre woman. Re. So she hath/ or ye say treuthe.** | belle femme. ℞, Cestoit mon. ou/ vo$^{9}$ ditez vray. |
| **It hath ben a grete folysshenesse. Re. So hath it ben** | Ce a este vne grand follie, Respõce / ce a este mon, |
| **It hath bẽ by ẙ kynges comaũdemẽt. Re. So it hath** | Ce eust este extortion. Respõce. Ceust este mon |
| **It shall be almesse to do hym good. Re. So it shall be.** | Ce auoit este ꝑ le cõmãdemẽt du roy. ℞ ce auoit mõ |
| [Qi$^{v}$/Qii] | Ce sera aulmosue de luy bien faire. ℞. ce sera mon. |

| | | |
|---|---|---|
| of earnes | in trewth | of sothe |
| **de certes** | **en veritę** | **de vray** |
| in certayne | in sothe | trewly |
| **a certain** | **en vray** | **vrayment** |
| for certayne | for truthe | veritably |
| **pour certain** | **pour veritę** | **veritablement** |

(E iii$^{v}$)

From these we have to distinguish those that invoke a personal virtue:

| | |
|---|---|
| in my trewth | in my worthynesse |
| **en ma veritę** | **en ma prudõmie** |
| in my loyaltie | by my holynesse |
| **en ma loyaultę** | **par ma saĩctetę** |

(E [iiii])

These, as well as first-person assurances, have no match in Palsgrave's list: *I you assure* [*sic*]—**ie vous asseure,** *I promyse you*—**ie vo$^{9}$ promectz,** *I certifye you*—**ie vous certifie.**

There is only one invocation of God: '*in my god*—**en mon dieu**'. Unparalleled are: '*in good lucke*—**en bon omen**' and '*by the fayth of fayre women*—**par la foy de belles fẽmes**'. The arrangement of du Wes's list of adverbs of swearing is manifestly based on the form and meaning of the elements described. The overall arrangement in Palsgrave's list is alphabetical, and for some phrases we are given examples or metalinguistic comments. The independence of the three lists is obvious if we compare with the foregoing Palsgrave's 'maners of sayeng ye or affermyng of a thyng':

**Allgates it is so:** Toutesfoys il est aynsi.
**Certaynly it is so:** Certes il est aynsi.
**For a treuth it is so:** De vray il est aynsi, **as/** Saichez de vray quant ie louis grandement me resiouis.

**For a very truthe:** Pour tout fin vray
**For sothe:** Certes, pour certayn.
**Ye/** Ouy, **as/** Ie voy que ouy, ⁊ voyre, **as/** Il surmonte le roy Arthus voyre Alexandre.

**Good ynoughe: Bien assez.**
**Ye suerly:** Voyre certes.
**Ye trewly:** Voyre vrayement, **but as for** voyre vraymecques, **it is but a coutrefayte terme for nycenesse . . .**

**It dothe so:** Ce fait mon que chascun se taise.
**It is so:** Cest mon sans comparaison.
**It is suerly so:** Sans poynt de fault, **or** sans faulte nulle, pour tout certayn il est aynsi, **or** pour tout vray il est aynsi.

> **Yes that do you/ yes that haue you/**
> **Yes that dyd you/ yes yͭ had you, ⁊c.**
> Si faictez si, si auez si, si fistez si, si auiez
> si, **or** si faictez, **or** si auez. &c.
>
> **In faythe**: Par foy.
> **In good faythe**: En bonne fay.
> **It is so suerly**: Il est aynsi certainement.
> **Juste**: Tout iuste par mon ame.
> **Suerly**: Certes.
> **Sykerly**: Vrayement.
> **That shall you**: Si ferez si.
> **That shal nat skyll**: De cela ne peult riens
> chaloyr.
> **Their of no force**/ De cela ne vous chaille.

There are two phrases invoking god. '**So god helpe me**—*Si mayt dieu*' in its rather unemotional tone matches the other relatively neutral expressions of consent and asseveration. The other constitutes an instance of swearing and includes a contrastive analysis of the tabooed name of God:

> **By my sowle/ by god**/ Par mon ame,
> par dieu. **But as we vse by cockes**
> **body by cockes flesshe/ they saye**:
> Par le corps bieu, par le chair bieu,
> par la mort bieu.
>
> (III, fo. cccc.lx)

Swearing, as is well known, was very common at the time. This is also manifest from Palsgrave's examples illustrating the use of verbs. There is no clear-cut borderline between asseverations and swearings that emphasize the truth of what has been said. We shall return to them in more detail in the context of exclamations, interjections, and exhortations.

Agreement does not have to be prompted by a conducive negative question or a positive exclamation. Palsgrave tackles this speech, act situation in two different entries. The first is under **I am content**:

> **I Am content**/ Ie suis cõtent, **and**
> **whan we suppose in comunycacion**
> **a thyng to be so**/ Ie le veulx bien: **as**
> **touchyng that I am content**: Quãt
> a cela ie le veulx bien.
>
> (III, fo. c.xli^v)

The same French reply '*ie le veux bien*' is the equivalent of the English lemma **I Wyll well**:

> **I Wyll well whiche sayeng we**
> **vse whan we suppose in comunyca-**

**cion a thyng to be so**: Ie le veulx bien,

. . .

(III, fo. cccc.viii[v])

In a situation where we are concerned about the words we have used, we might say, in order to express that we did not mean any offence, '*No displeasure taken: Sauf vostre grace*', for which Palsgrave's comment is rather obscure (III, fo. ccc.lxxxii: **I Take I vnderstãde**).

We turn from positive to negative replies. Under the entry for *not* (III, fo. cccc.lxix) Palsgrave describes what the proper negative answer is in French: 'But here is to be noted that whan so euer we make answere by not/ vnto any preposycion or any questyon of aduerbes/ ẏͤ frenchmen vse for not/ *pas*, as/ *Pas pour moy*, *pas en moy*, *pas asteure*, *pas icy*. &c. as/whan cometh he? not yet: *pas encore*. Where is he/ nat here: *Pas icy* . . .' (see also III, fo. cccc.xxiiii[v]: **Not**). Other ways of saying 'no' or denying something are listed under the adverbs 'of sayeng nay or denyeng of a thyng' (III, cccc.lx[v]):

**Naye**: Non.
**Nay truely**: Non certes, non vrayement.
**Alas naye**/ Helas nenny.
**But why nat**/ Mays pour quoy non.
**Naye**: Nenny.
**Nay nay**/ Nenny non.
**Nay nay**/ Non non ceste responce est faulce.
**Sauyng your reuerence**: Sauf vostre grace.
**Nor no more I do**/ Aussi ne fais ie.
**No more can I**: Aussi ne scais ie moy.
**No more be we**: Aussi ne sommes no⁹ pas.

To these we might add '*ia* in nowise', '*riens* nothynge', and '*iamays* neuer' from the enumeration in book II (fo. lviii).

Under the entry **I Saue** (III, fo. ccc.xlvii) Palsgrave explains the situational context when the French expression *sauf vostre grace* is used more explicitly:

> **But where we vse sauynge your reuerence whan we speke of a vyle thyng in the presence of a great man/ in frenche they saye**: Ne vous desplaise, **but they vse** saulue vostre grace, **whan they wolde contrarye the sayeng of their superyour/ and meane that it is nat so.**

The use of the English expression '*no displeasure taken*' corresponding to French '*ne vous desplaise*' is shown under the entry **I say naye** (III, fo. ccc.xlvi):

> . . . **My lorde no displesure taken I say nay therto:** Monsieur mays que ne vous desplaise ie me y oppose . . .

A deferential attitude will be expressed by '*By your leaue*' or '*Ne vous desplaise*':

> **but whan we passe nere by one or do any thynge that we stande in doute whether our better wolde be cōtented with it or nat/ they saye for by your leaue/** Ne vous desplaise, **as/** Ne vous desplaise si ie passe si hardiement deuant vous. **But commenly they saye but** Ne vous desplaise, **and no more.**
>
> (III, fos. cccc.xxxix$^{v}$–cccc.xl)

*Forms of address*

Who addressed whom and in what form obviously depended on the social rank of the speaker. Under *I say naye* we have just encountered an example where a superior is addressed '*My Lord*'/'*Monsieur*' by the inferior. A good number of Palsgrave's examples include a form of address. According to the situational context described, the personal address may be just a vocative or it may be combined with a request to do something, advice not to do a certain thing, an expression of pity or comfort. It may also show impatience, indignation, and then contain a phrase of swearing.

We might distinguish the following groups:

1. The general form of address for a male is *Syr, Sir/Monsieur.* In the singular, the French equivalent usually is *Monsieur*, occasionally *Syre* (III, fo. cc: **I Crye**). For the plural form *Syrs, Sirs* three French forms occur: *Messieurs, mes sieurs*, and *gallans*:

> . . . **Nowe sirs pull a good** Or messieurs tyrez, or hallez a bon escient.
>
> (III, fo. ccc.xxv$^{v}$: **I Pull** . . .)

> **Make mery syrs we shall go hence to morowe:** Faictez bonne chiere mes sieurs nous partirons demayn.
>
> (III, fo. cc.xc.ii$^{v}$: **I Make mery** . . .)

> . . . **Plucke syrs for shame be nat you syxe able to plucke a iade out of ỹ myer:** Tyrez, or hallez gallans nauez vous poynt de honte que vo⁹ six ne pouues tirer vne charoigne hors de la fange.
>
> (III, fo. ccc.xix: **I Plucke** . . .)

In the plural the English form of address corresponding to French *messieurs/mes sieurs* is occasionally *maysters*:

. . . **Maysters make no noyse my lorde is a slepe**: Messieurs ne sonnez mot monsieur dort, or monsieur sen dort.

(III, fo. cc.xc.iii^v: **I Make no noyse** . . .)

. . . **Make romme maysters here cometh a player**: Faictez place mes sieurs voicy venir vng ioueur.

(III, fo. cc.xc.v: **I Make rome** . . .)

An interesting case is the English vocative *man* in the singular.[3] The *OED* first records this use from 1400, and the second attestation is from Palsgrave. In general, Palsgrave gives no French equivalent, merely the second-person pronoun corresponding to the normal English *thy*-form. In those cases where the French verb is reflexive *man* is then matched by *toy*:

**Aryse man thou lyest a beed al day:**
Lieue toy tu te tiẽs au lict toute iour.

(III, fo. cc.lxxxi: **I Lye a bedde**)

As a match of English *man*, we sometimes find French *mon ami*:

. . . **Synge out man why fayne you:** Chãtez a plaine voix mon amy pour quoy chantez vo⁹ a basse voix.

(III, fo. ccc.lxi^v: **I Synge out** . . .)

*Man* may also be premodified by an adjective, and then the adjective and the noun have a French equivalent:

. . . **Alas good man thou haste combraunce ynough I pray god vncombre the:** Helas poure homme tu as de lencombrance assez ie prie a dieu quil te desencombre. or quil te descombre.

(III, fo. ccc.lxxxxvii^v: **I Uncombre** . . .)

2. The polite forms for addressing a female are *damoysell* and *good ladye*, which co-occur with *you-forms*, French *vous*-forms:

. . . **In dede damoysell you be dagged:** En verité damoyselle vous estes crottée.

(III, fo. c.lix: **I Be dagge** . . .)

**Good ladye how you be sonne burned for one dayes rydynge:** Nostre dame que vous estez haslé pour auoyr cheuaulché au soleil vng iour seullement.

(III, fo. ccc.lxvi^v: **I Sonne burne** . . .)

[3] There are no occurrences of *men* in the plural, as Salmon (1967/1987: 50) records them for the Falstaff plays.

By contrast, the vocative *woman* co-occurs with *thou*-forms (confirming Salmon's findings for Elizabethan English (1967/1987: 50) and corresponds to *femme* and *tu*):

> **Skumme the potte woman intendest thou to poyson vs:** Escume le pot femme, as tu intencion de nous enpoysonner.
>
> (III, fo. ccc.lxiii: **I Skumme . . .**)

But *woman* may also be rendered by *mamye* in French—for example:

> **. . . Take hym in thyne armes woman he is thy housbande and thou sawest him nat many a day:** Embrasses le mamye cest ton mary et tu ne las point veu de long temps.
>
> (III, fo. ccc.lxxxiiii: **I Take one in myn armes**)

3. Instances where the form of address is a name are very rare in Palsgrave's examples:

> **. . . Come hyther Kate and I wyll set yͤ on my lappe and daũce the:** Viens ca Katheline et ie te engeronneray et te feray dancer.
>
> (III, fo. ccc.lvii: **I Set a thynge . . .**)[4]

> **. . . Frier Nycolas whan wyll you synge masse:** Frere Nicolas quant voulez vous celebrer, or quant chanterez voꝰ messe.
>
> (III, fo. ccc.lxi$^{v}$: **I Synge masse**)

4. As a fourth group we might regard those terms that belong to the family in the wider sense: friends, neighbours, children's nurse. Examples are:

> **Come hyther good sonne lette me stroke thy heed:** Ca bon filz que ie te applanye la teste.
>
> (III, fo. ccc.lxxviii: **I Stroke . . .**)

> **Cease cease my frende from this folysshe lyfe/ it is tyme and more than tyme:** Cesses cesses mon amy de ceste folle vie, il est temps et plus q̃ temps.
>
> (III, fo. c.lxxxiiii: **I Cease**)

> **. . . Gossyppe whan your catte kytelleth I praye you let me haue a kytlynge:** Voysine quant vostre chat chatonnera ie vous prie que iaye vng de voz chattons.
>
> (III, fo. cc.lxxii$^{v}$: **I Kyttell . . .**)

> **. . . Fede your chylde nouryce you knowe he hath no tethe yet:** Apastellez vostre enfant nourrice vous scauez biẽ quil na pas des dens encore.
>
> (III, fo. cc.xxxiiii: **I Fede . . .**)

[4] Under the verb entry **I Coll I take aboute the necke** we find a second example referring to a Kate: '*Come colle me Kate and thou shall haue a gaye thyng*: *Viens moy accolier Catelyne et tu auras ie nescay quoy*' (III, fo. c.xci). Palsgrave may thus have had a real Kate in mind.

5. Quite common in Palsgrave's example sentences are vocatives of occupational terms. The only noun referring to a female occupation is *nourrice*, *nourice*. Among the vocatives for men we have *page* as well as *hosteller*, *feryeman*, *mariner*, *hosyer*, *spurryer*. They are all used in the singular with the exception of *mariner*, which occurs also in the plural. In the majority of instances the vocative goes together with *thou*/*tu*-forms:

> **Curry my horse hosteller I praye the/ I wene the iade hath nede of it:** Estrille mon cheuall hostellier ie te prie, ie pence que la charoigne en a bien mestier.
>
> (III, fo. cc.ii$^{v}$: **I Curry a horse** . . .)

> **Ferye man what shal I gyue the to set me ouer the water:** Passeur que te donneray ie pour me passer.
>
> (III, fo. ccc.lix: **I Sette one ouer** . . .)

But *pilot* always occurs with a second person plural form in French (see also *chaussetyer*):

> **Sownde mariner let vs se what water we haue to spare:** Pilotez marinier voyons combien deaue nous auons dauantaige.
>
> (III, fo. ccc.lxvii: **I Sownde**)

> . . . **Stryke my hosen hosyer/ they be to shorte yet bytwene yͤ legges:** Amontez mes chausses chaussetyer, car elles sont encore trop courtes entre les iambes.
>
> (III, fo. ccc.lxxvii$^{v}$: **I Stryke vp** . . .)

Although the large number of example sentences might have contained a wide range of occupational terms used as vocatives, in fact the few that do occur, rather strikingly, predominantly refer to just those professional people a traveller would have had to deal with. From what we know of Palsgrave's life they might therefore well reflect his personal experience.

6. The last group of nouns used as vocatives are terms abusing folly, cowardice, idleness, vileness. In general the objectionable aspect is conveyed by a noun, but an exception is *lewd person*/ *méchante créature* (III, fo. cccv: **I Murmure**), where the opprobious feature occurs in the premodifying adjective. Palsgrave's English abusive vocatives are *coward*, *knaue*, *lourdayne*, *villayne*, and *wretche*, and their French equivalents are *couart*, *lourdault*, *villayn*, and *chétif*. Illustrations are:

> **Fye coward gyuest thou ouer for so small a mater:** Fy couart te succũbes tu, or te rens tu pour si peu de chose.
>
> (III, fo. cc.xlvii$^{v}$: **I Geue ouer**)

> . . . **Ha wretche you go a borowyng in tauernes:** Ha chetif vous allez a croyre en tauernes.
>
> (III, fo. cc.l$^{v}$: **I Go a borowyng** . . .)

. . . **Fye on the villayne thou gnawest thy mete with thy tethe lyke a dogge:** Fy villayn tu ronges ta viande de tes dens cõme se tu fusses vng chien.

(III, fo. cc.l[v]: **I Gnawe**)

. . . **Holde thy peace lourdayne:** Tays toy lourdault . . .

(III, fo. cc.lxiii[v]: **I Holde my peace**)

Not a vocative but a disparaging reference to a female is the use of *olde trot* in the following example:

. . . **Se yõder olde trot howe she mumbleth:** Auisez ceste vielle a refondre cõment elle, masche en belyn.

(III, fo. ccc.v: **I Mumbyll as an olde persone** . . .)

According to the *OED*, the English noun is first recorded in the fourteenth century and then in an *a*-form. The form with the vowel *o* is first documented in *Lesclarcissement.*

Some of the above examples include an exclamatory *fye* of reproach. Before we review utterances that contain interjections and exclamations, thus revealing surprise, impatience, indignation, and other feelings on the part of the fictitious speaker, we shall look at more neutral argumentative ways of talking as they emerge from Palsgrave's descriptions.

### *Discussing*

How does one put a case in an argument? Palsgrave tells his learners that the wording should not be *I put the case/ je mets le cas, je pose le cas,* but rather that the first person plural imperative should be used: '*Let vs put the case it be so/ what than*: *Posons, or mettons le cas quil soyt ainsi, quoy donc*' (III, fo. ccc.xxx[v]: **I Put as men put a case**).

When a person with whom we are engaged in a conversation says something we find disappointing, Palsgrave offers an ironic way of reacting:

**I Serue one well or I serue one fayre/ whiche kynde of spekyng we vse whan one hath dispoynted vs or done vs a displeasure/** Ie luy baylle belle, **you haue serued me wel or you haue serued me fayre:** Vous maues baillé belle . . .

(III, fo. ccc.lv[v])

In the turn-taking of conversation, conclusions may be drawn and assumptions made. An element used in these situations is the conjunct *so*, already singled out in *Lesclarcissement*, which describes one of its discourse functions as follows:

> **So/ whiche we vse moche in tellyng of a tale at the begynnyng of a mater whiche foloweth vpon the thynges tolde a fore:** Si, **but yet the frenche tonge vseth this worde** si **very often and very differētly from our tonge/ so ẏᵗ somtyme** si, **semeth to signyfye nothynge with vs/ or at the leste we haue no worde to countreuayle it.**
>
> (III, fo. cccc.lxxᵛ)

The conjunct *now*, also listed in Palsgrave's table of conjunctions, is also aptly assessed in its discourse-initiating function and paired with French *et puis*:

> **Nowe/ as we vse to say to one whã we haue sent hym on our erande or els mete one that we be disposed to talke with:** Et puis, **as/ Nowe what tydynges:** Et puis que nouuelles, **or** et puis que dit on de nouueau, **and** et puis que dit on de bon.
>
> (III, fo. cccc.lxixᵛ)

Palsgrave draws his learners' attention also to the fact that the literal meaning of what is said may not be the intended meaning. Under the entry for **I Make**, for instance, he discusses the expression '*it maketh no mater*', translated into French as '*Cest tout vng*'. Depending on the context in which it is used, it could be used, '*in maner of a threate*: *Cest tout vng. It maketh no mater but I wyll quyte it you and I lyue*: *Cest tout vng mays ie le vous rendray si ie vis*' (III, fo. cc.lxxxviᵛ).

*Imprecations*

Where an emotional reaction or involvement needs to be vented in exclamatory language, Palsgrave provides a subtle gamut of expressions. Emphatic confirmations in the form of such phrases as *by my faythe/by my trouth*, *on my faythe*, rendered in French by *par ma foy/sur ma foy*, function as asseverations of what is being said. Whereas Palsgrave's list of adverbs specifying 'maners of sayeng ye or affermyng a thyng' has such prepositional phrases as *for sothe/certes*, *pour certayn*, *in faythe/par foy*, *in good faythe/en bonne foy*, it does not include instances of the abstract nouns *faith* or *truth* with a first-person singular possessive pronoun, as they occur in the verbal illustrations (see III, fos. cc.lxvi, cc.lxxiii$^{\mathrm{v}}$, cc.lxxv, etc.). Exclamatory phrases that combine a protestation of truth with a word referring to a part of the speaker's body might be regarded as co-occurring instances of asseveration and swearing. An example is:

> . . . **By the faythe of my body ⁊ you make moche a do I wyll take my fyste from your cheke:** Par la foy de mon corps si vous harcellez trop les gens ie partiray mon poyng dauec vostre ioe.
>
> (III, fo. cc.xciii: **I Make a do**)

The swearing instances recovered from Palsgrave's verb illustrations confirm Koskenniemi's statement (1962: 78) made for the language in English drama from 1550 to 1600 that the majority of oaths found in pre-Shakespearian drama refer to religion (for French, see Zöckler 1905). Those occurring most frequently include a reference to God. Instances where a saint or the soul are invoked are rare:

> . . . **By saynt Marye and he wyll nat do it he shall be enforced to it:** Par saincte Marie sil ne le veult poynt faire il y sera forcé **or** parforce de le faire.
>
> (III, fo. cc.xxv: **I Enforce**)

> **By my soule you be very slowe:** Sur mon ame vous tardes beaucop.
>
> (III, fo. c.xlvii: **I Am slowe . . .**)

The findings also confirm Salmon's point (1967/1987: 63) that *Christ* is not used as an expletive (H. Hoffmann (1894: 12) gives only one instance), yet *Jesus* is found:

> . . . **Iesus howe you be spronge sythe I sawe you:** Iesus que vous estez creu despuis que ie ne vous vis.
>
> (III, fo. ccc.lxx$^{\mathrm{v}}$: **I Spring**)

In some expressions of swearing, the English expression and French counterpart closely match each other. Cases in point are *by god—par dieu/pardieu, thanke god—dieu mercy, a goddes name—de par dieu.* In others we note some interesting variations. Thus *for goddes sake* is rendered in one example by *pour lamour de dieu*, in another by *pour dieu*:

> . . . **Plucke vp thy herte man for goddes sake:** Prens couraige pour lamour de dieu.
>
> (III, fo. ccc.xix$^{\mathrm{v}}$: **I Plucke vp**)

> . . . **Stoppe the thefe for godȝ** saake: Arrestez le larron la pour dieu.
>
> (III, fo. ccc.lxxv: **I Stoppe . . .**)

In one instance, *good lorde* is rendered by *Iesu*:

> . . . **Good lorde howe you be sonne brunde for thre or foure dayes rydynge in the sonne:** Iesu que vous estez hasle pour auoyr cheuauché ces troys ou quatre iours au soleil . . .
>
> (III, fo. c.xlvii: **I Am sonne brunde**)

*De par dieu*, which is normally given as the French equivalent of *a goddes name*, is also the translation for the only example that refers to the Passion and shows a euphemistic substitution of the name of God at the same time:

> . . . **Stryke for cockȝ body:** Chargez de par dieu . . .
>
> (III, fo. ccc.lxxvi$^{v}$: **I Stryke one**)

Unlike Palsgrave, Valence (1528) distinguishes adverbs that denote manners of swearing. He provides not only a brief list of adverbs of affirmation but also one for adverbs of swearing (Alston 1967*a*: O i$^{v}$). Not surprisingly, there is an overlap of items which might have prompted du Wes to treat both types as one group only. A comparison of the three authors shows that Valence mentions some expressions of swearing which we find neither in du Wes nor in Palsgrave. These include *by Saint N.—par saint N.* and *by myn othe/or sothe—par mon serment.*[5]

The strength of emotional reaction or involvement may lead to cursing. Palsgrave is the only one of the three authors who has a section on 'maners of cursyng'. They differ strikingly from the other adverbs listed at the end of the table of adverbs. No attempt is made at listing them in alphabetical or topical order. There are two sets, the second, consisting of three expressions, milder in content, in each case pairing a command or exhortation with 'villayn' as a vocative. None of them is accompanied by an English version. One may wonder whether the author, who was to become a chaplain to Henry VIII, sensed it as inappropriate to provide a list of curses in English. Here are Palsgrave's French expressions:

> La malle bosse le puisse estrangler.
> Le feu saint Anthoy ne larde. [*sic*]
> La malle mort le puisse abatre.

[5] It is to be regretted that G. Hughes's book on *Swearing* of 1991, which is described as a 'social history of foul language, oaths and profanity in English', does not mention du Wes, Valence, or Palsgrave. There is no reference either to relevant earlier studies by Sharman (1884), Swaen (1888), Koskenniemi (1962), and Salmon (1967/1987).

La fieure quartayne le puisse espouser.
Le grant diable luy rompe le col et les deux iambes si souldra.
Le diable lemporte corps et ame tripes et boyaux.
Dieu le met en mal sepmayne.
Dieu le met en mal an.
La mal encontre le puisse encontrer.
Tous les diables denfer le puissent emporter.

Allez villayn de par tous les diables.
Auant villayn cocqyn que vous estez.
Va villayn va.

An appeal is made to God, the devil, or another entity regarded as causing harm, such as an illness, to come down and afflict the person upon whom the curse has been called. The list can be enriched by two examples from the verb list where the English version and its French counterpart are given:

. . . **The dyuell burst him he hath eaten all ỷ creame with out me:** Le diable le crieue il a mangé toute la cresme sans moy, **or** le diable lacrauante, **or** laccreue.

(III, fo. c.lxxix: **I Burst**)

. . . **The dyuell choke hym/ he hath eaten all the appels a lone:** Le diable lestrangle, il a mengé toutes les põmes tout seul.

(III, fo. c.lxxxvii$^{v}$: **I Choke with meate . . .**)

We note that the strong feeling underlying both curses given by Palsgrave is the thwarted pleasure to enjoy a particular delicacy.

In another instance, Palsgrave provides an example and describes it as a manner of cursing. The French equivalent given is one of the curses listed above for which there was no English lemma:

. . . **God sende you yuell cheuyng/ whiche is a maner of cursing**
Dieu vous met en malle sepmayne.

(III, fo. ccc.liiii$^{v}$: **I Sende a thing . . .**)

*Interjections and exclamatory language*

Palsgrave singles out a number of situations and emotions in which exclamatory language is common. Among them are how to command silence, how to face danger, how to make someone hurry, and so on. They are described in the verb illustrations and they are also dealt with in the table of interjections at the end of book III. There is also a brief section on interjections in book II. In this context, it is worth mentioning that Palsgrave's description of interjections shares some features with earlier treatments of this part of speech, but at the same time it goes far beyond the earlier semantic classifications. Two of the French *Donatus* texts edited by Städtler, for instance, include a little dialogue for interjections (*Donat G* and *Donat M²*). In both, interjections are said to come in four meanings and these are exemplified: 'Les unes signefient leesce, si comme *evax*! "Dieu aide!", les autres douleur, si comme *heu*! "las!", les autres admiration, si comme *pape*! "quel merveille!", les autres poour, si comme *actat*! "hareu!"' (Städtler 1988: 125; see also 95). This semantic classification is also found in the corresponding Middle English grammatical treatises. Two of the *Accidence* texts edited by Thomson, for instance, mention four meanings for interjections. Whereas the A text simply enumerates them ('ioy', 'sorow', 'wondyr', and 'drede' (D. Thomson 1984: 8)), the D text provides both Latin and English examples: 'myrthe, as "to gooderhele", as *euax*; sorwe, as *heu*; drede, as "haa", id est *metum*; wondryng, as *pape*, id est *miror*, et cetera' (ibid.: 43). The C and the F text of the *Accidence* list five meanings, and again, one text, F, is without examples ('joy', 'woo', 'wondyr', 'dredre', and 'indignacion') (ibid.: 49), and the other, text C, includes them: 'joye or sorow or dred or wunderyng or indignacyon, as "aha", "alas", "welawey", "out out", "owgh", "so howgh", and soch oþer' (ibid.: 30). John Stanbridge in his *Accidence* gives the same five meanings (Alston 1969*b*: [B $_v$$^v$]). In his *Rudimenta grammatices*, Linacre also has five meanings, yet they differ. Instead of 'indignation' there is 'exclamation' (Alston 1971: [F $_i$]).

With this we come to Palsgrave. Interjections 'betokening sorowing' are mentioned in book II and book III. The only element given is *O*, which is illustrated by '*O ie meurs si on ne maide*'. Among the occurrences of *O* in the illustrations some denote sorrow (e.g. III, fo. c.xxxvi$^v$: **I Absente** . . .; III, fo. cc.viii$^v$: **I Departe farre** . . .), others pleasure (e.g. III, fo. cc.lxv$^v$: **I Iape**; III, fo. cc.xc: **I Make courtesye**). On the other hand, we also find *a* as an interjection of sorrow among the verb illustrations:

> . . . **A the thefe caryed a waye my bouget with hym:** A le lar ron emporte ma bougette auecques luy.
>
> (III, fo. c.lxxxi$^v$: **I Cary awaye**)

'Joy' as one of the meanings of an interjection is listed in book II, supported by *How*, but there is no example. 'Fear' as such does not occur in either book, but 'maruaylyng' is richly illustrated in the grammar as well as in the dictionary. In both places four interjections expressing wondering are listed, the dictionary providing an example for each:

| | |
|---|---|
| **Ha:** | Ha nostre dame de clery qui leust pencé. |
| **Oya:** | Oya vray dieu quest cecy a dire. |

| | |
|---|---|
| **Dieulx:** | Dieulx auoit il tout eschappé forsque cela et encore fut happé. |
| **Dea:** | Dea a il batu sa femme desia. |

(III, fo. cccc.lxxiii)

The dictionary mentions interjections expressing indignation and cites *trut*, as in '*Trut auant trut*', as an example (III, fo. cccc.lxxiii). 'Outcry' comes closest to Linacre's 'exclamation'. One interjection is given: *Haro*, and it is illustrated with the example: *Haro a larme trahy trahy* (II, fo. lix; III, fo. cccc.lxxiii). There is also an instance in the example sentences for verbs:

> . . . **My mother was a frayde there had ben theues in her house/ ⁊ she kryed out haroll alarome:** Ma mere auoit paour quil ny eust des larrons a la mayson, et elle sescria harol alarme.
>
> (III, fo. cc: **I Crye out** . . .)

Interjections commanding silence do not figure in any of the earlier grammatical treatises consulted. According to Palsgrave the use of the right word depends on who is to be silenced:

> **Holde peace/ whiche sayeng we vse whan we cõmaũde a multytude to kepe sylence:** Paix, or faictez paix.
>
> (III, fo. cc.lxiii^v: **I Holde one** . . .)

If *paix* is the word to calm down gatherings of people, by implication *houische* and *mom* cannot be used in such circumstances. All three, in sentence-initial position, are illustrated in the table of interjections without any English model:

| | |
|---|---|
| **Houische:** | Houische ne sõnez mot. |
| **Mom:** | Mom ne parlez plus. |
| **Paix:** | Payx paix monsieur vient. |

An instance of exhortation is found under the entry **I Get me hence**. For a situation where we would press someone to get away by '*Hence, hence*!', the French say hastyly '*Fuy, fuy*' (III, fo. cc.xlv^v). Other situations singled out by Palsgrave are: *Sus* 'come of', or 'haue done' and *Faictez ie covrt* 'be shorte' (II, fo. lviii) and at the end of the table of adverbs: *Viens auant* 'Come away', *Viens auant viste* 'Come away at ones', *Or ca mon amy* 'Come of my frende', *Sus dócques* [*sic*] or *mets sus donques* 'Come of than', *Tost* 'Shortly', *Viste* 'Anone', and *Acoup* 'At ones' (III, fo. cccc.lxi). Several adverbs of 'adhortynge' are also supplied by Valence (1528): *up—forwarde—hens—hey—thus—*

*that—do* and their French equivalents *sus—auant—hay—ainsi—la—faictez* (Alston 1967*a*: N[iiii]ᵛ—Oi).

An interesting entry in this connection is the following, where Palsgrave describes a stylistic construction to denote swiftness of movement:

> . . . **And he to go/ whiche sayeng we vse whan we signyfye a great haste in ronnynge awaye:** Et luy deuant.
>
> (III, fo. cc.lᵛ: **I Go**)

In a situation of danger, learners are given the relevant idiomatic French phrase under the verb entry for **I Helpe:**

> . . . **Helpe helpe/ as men krye that be in daunger of theues or any other peryll:** A layde alayde . . .
>
> (III, fo. cc.lxᵛ)

The interjection of warning of a danger *Ware*! *Garre*! is mentioned both in the grammar and the dictionary. The French form *garre* is even explained under the entry **I Am ware from a daũger:**

> . . . **Ware ware spoken in haste:** Garre garre, **for** garde . . .
>
> (III, fo. c.xlviiᵛ)

An imminent danger may call for a warning to stop. This has the following forms in English and in French: '*Stoppe there! Ho la*' (III, fo. ccc.lxxv) or '*Hola cest assez*!' *Ho* as in '*Ho de par le diable ho*' may also be heard (III, fo. cccc.lxxiii).

These semantic groups do not exhaust Palsgrave's table of interjections. In addition to those mentioned, we find interjections 'of callyng', 'of askyng', 'of parceyuing', 'of lamenting', 'of abhoryng', and 'of mocking'.

It is interesting to note that Lily's grammar, which was to become the official grammar of teaching Latin from the 1540s onwards, has an enlarged section on interjections compared to the earlier Latin treatises. Of the thirteen semantic groups distinguished, five were already mentioned in the earlier introductory works to Latin grammar produced in England. Two others are already discussed in 1530 by Palsgrave, 'silence' and 'callyng'. This latter group is particularly interesting because of Palsgrave's metalinguistic comments.

For attracting attention Palsgrave lists three interjections: *Hay*, *hau*, and *hola*. The first two are exemplified by '*Vienca hay lacquay hay*' and '*Dy hau fais tu le sourt*'. '*Hau pety Iehan apportez mon arc*'. Learners are then given the following differentiation:

> **. . . so that** hay, **is vsed whan they call one that is in their syght or nere them:** hau, **to one that is farther of or out of syght/ also whan they call at ones doore standynge without/ they saye** Hola, **and they within forthe answere:** Qui est la. **as I haue afore declared.**
>
> (III, fo. cccc.lxxiii)[6]

Thus, on the one hand, we are told that *hay*, *hau*, and *hola* are interjections of calling, and, on the other, we find *ho* and *hola* under the interjections betokening a warning to stop. The examples provided seem to suggest that the basic function of *hay*, *hau/ho*, and *hola* is to attract the attention of someone whose name one does not know or who is occupied in doing something else. This last case emerges from one of the examples given under interjections betokening mocking. The interjection *boo* is illustrated by '*Boo boo on le scait assez*' and '*Boo il suffit*'. The second interjection listed is *hay*, exemplified in use by '*Hay Iehan iennyn tu dis vray*'. *Hay* here clearly has an attention-catching function (see also Ramm 1902: 75–7).[7] An instance from the verb illustrations is:

> **Howe page rubbe my shoes a lytell with a cloute:** Hay page tordies mes souliers vng peu dung hallion.
>
> (III, fo. ccc.xliiii$^{v}$: **I Rubbe thynges**)

Asking a question may also be accompanied by an interjection. Palsgrave adduces *haa* as an interjection of asking and shows it in two different uses, in sentence-initial and in sentence-final position: '*Haa que dis tu*' and '*As tu dit cela haa?*'

An interesting group is the one which Palsgrave calls 'Interiections of parceyuing'. Three interjections are given: *haha*, *atat*, and *hadea*. They are illustrated as follows: '*Haha maistre chien vous auez mangé le lart.*' '*Haha villayn hantez vous la?*' '*Atat, cest cela.*' '*Hadea ie scauoye bien quil estoyt aynsi.*' Of the three, *haha* (in various English forms) is the only one that occurs in illustrations, suggesting that it was the more common one:

[6] This specific situation is not mentioned by Radtke, who discusses *hola* in its contact-establishing, attention-attracting function (1994: 77–8, 258).

[7] Although Valence (1528) lists *hey/hay* as an adverb of exhortation, he does not include the French form among his adverbs of calling: *Haye, come-heus, ça* (Alston 1967*a*: O i$^{v}$–O ii).

. . . **Ha wretche you go a borowyng in tauernes:** Ha che tif vous allez a croyre en tauernes.

(III, fo. cc.l$^{v}$: **I Go a borowyng**)

. . . **Ha ha are you suche a one/ wolde you embesyll my thynges from me/** Ha ha estez vous tel, voulez vous celer mes choses de moy.

(III, fo. cc.lxvi: **I Imbesell**)

**A ha you waxe reed/ there is somthynge a mysse:** Ha ha vous vous en rougissez il y a quelque chose qui va mal.

(III, fo. cccc.v: **I Waxe reed**)

The feature which all these examples share is that the speaker has noticed and recognized something, and rejoices at his grasp of the situation; clearly, therefore, this is the exclamation corresponding to modern English [ɑː'hɑː] and not the *haha* representing laughter [hɑ'hɑ], which Palsgrave ignores.

This then leaves us with two semantic groups of interjections in *Lesclarcissement* which are not listed in Lily's grammar: interjections of lamenting and of abhorring.

Interjections of lamenting are distinguished from interjections expressing sorrow. Palsgrave lists five interjections of lamenting and illustrates them as follows:

**Helas** *Helas que ferons nous poures gens darmes.*
**Las** *Las qui eut iamays cuydé que cela fust aduenu.*
**Lasse** *Lasse moy dolẽte creature.*
**Hee** *Hee moy miserable.*

*Hemy* is not illustrated with an example. Palsgrave regarded it as 'vsed rather in the doutche lande ⁊, where they speake rõmant and wallon than in Fraunce' (III, fo. cccc.lxxiii). As with the interjections of perceiving, only one of the set of elements given occurs in the example sentences that illustrate the use of verbs. This is *helas*, for which the English forms vary:

. . . **Alas to whome shall I complayne:** Helas a qui me playngdray ie? or complayng dray ie?

(III, fo. c.xciii: **I Complayne**)

. . . **Helasse poore woman howe she languyssheth:** Helas poure femme cõment elle languyst, or cõment elle sadoule.

(III, fo. cc.lxxvi: **I Languysshe**)

Utterances that express strong disapproval or loathing are introduced by the interjection *fie*, for which Palsgrave gives the French forms *fy* (II, fo. lix; III, fo. cccc.lxxiii) and *fuy* (II, fo. lix). The only example provided has the structural pattern *fy* + vocative + *que*: '*Fy, lourdault que vous estez villayn.*' Among the verb illustrations we find a good number of examples which show a range of construction patterns:

1. *Fye for shame/Fy de honte*:

> **Fye for shame howe thou haste defyled thy gowne:** Fy de honte comment tu as deturpé ta robe.
>
> (III, fo. cc.vi^v: **I Defoule**)

2. *Fye* + vocative/ *Fy* + vocative + question:

> **Fye coward gyuest thou ouer for so small a mater:** Fy couart te succũbes tu, or te rens tu pour si peu de chose.
>
> (III, fo. cc.xlvii^v: **I Geue ouer** . . .)

3. *Fye on* + NP/*Fy* + vocative/*Fy de* + NP:

> . . . **Fye on the villayne thou gnawest thy mete with thy tethe lyke a dogge:** Fy villayn tu ronges ta viande de tes dens cõme se tu fusses vng chien.
>
> (III, fo. cc.l^v: **I Gnawe as a dogge**)

> **Fye on hym villayne that he is/ he waxeth faynte herted ⁊ yet he seeth no bodye:** Fy de luy villayn quil est il se accouardit et si ne voyt ame.
>
> (III, fo. cccc.iii: **I Waxe faynte herted**)

4. *Fye that/Fy que*:

> . . . **Fye that thou arte waxen lothsome sythe I knewe the first:** Fy que tu tes affetardi de puis que ie te cogn⁹ premier.
>
> (III, fo. cccc.iiii: **I Waxe lothsome**)

5. *Fye howe/Fy commẽt*:

> . . . **Fye how you haue slubbred your geare for one dayes wearyng:** Fy commẽt auez vo⁹ barbouille voz habillemens pour les porter vng iour seullement.
>
> (III, fo. ccc.lxiiii: **I Slubber**)

Exclamatory language in *Lesclarcissement* may conclude with two instances provided among the list of verbs and adverbs. The first is listed under the verb entry **I yssue**, where Palsgrave tells his learners what one says when one is knocking at someone's door and what one may hear on that occasion:

> ... **Who is here/ as we saye whan we knocke at a doore:** Hola. **Who is there/ as they vse to answere that be with in:** Qui est la.
>
> (III, fo. cc.lxviii[v])

The description is repeated under the interjections of calling (III, fo. cccc.lxxiii).

The second is found under the adverbs of affirmation. The wish expressed in Palsgrave's time when someone sneezed was '*Christ helpe*' or '*Dieu vous soyt en ayde*' (III, fo. cccc.lx). The same French expression could also be used in a different context, as we can see from the following example:

> ... **God sẽde you/ as we vse to answere beggars whan we be nat mynded to gyue them almesse:** Dieu vous soit en ayde ...
>
> (III, fo. ccc.liiii[v]: **I Sende forthe** ...)

*Thanking and leave-taking*

We come to the speech act of thanking. The table of verbs has two lemma entries. The first provides the French translation equivalents *mercier*, *remercier*, and *regracier* (III, fo. ccc.lxxxviii[v]). The second is basically a dictionary entry with some typical examples:

> **I Thanke god/** Dieu mercy **with out a verbe. I thanke you:** La vostre mercy. **I thanke him:** La sienne mercy. **God be thanked:** La dieu mercy. **At the leste I am one of them god be thanked:** Aumoyns en suis ie vng de eulx dieu mercy.
>
> (III, fo. ccc.lxxxviii[v])

Under **I yelde**, another expression of thanks is given: '*God yelde you*', the meaning and use of which are explained as 'whiche we vse by maner of thankyng of a person' and translated as '*Grant mercy*' or '*grans mercy*' (III, fo. cccc.xi[v]).

Finally, there is the speech act on taking one's leave from one's discourse partner, which, for the earlier periods of English and French, has attracted some scholarly interest (see e.g. Stange 1900: 36–40; Ramm 1902: 13; Nyrop 1934: 35; Senge 1935: 80–7; Wyld 1956: 377 ff.; Salmon 1967/1987*b*: 43–4 Löfstedt 1978; Lewicka 1979; Radtke 1994: 199–211). Palsgrave explains to his learners that French *A Dieu* is very similar in use to English *Fare well*:

> **I Fare well/ whiche we vse to say whan we take our leaue of a person** A dieu, **in whiche wordes yͤ frenche men vnderstande/** Ie vous cõmande, **lyke as we do in fare well/ I praye you may fare well.**
>
> (III, fo. cc.xxxiii)

The verb entry is matched in the adverb list, where Palsgrave specifies 'maners of blessynge and salutyng and wysshyng well to one'. Here, too, the short form of the departing greeting is given: *Fare well*: *A dieu*. It is followed, as in the instances of day greetings, by the longer version: '*I betake you to god: Ie vous recommande a dieu*'. In all of Palsgrave's examples *a dieu* is spelled in two words (see Lewicka 1979: 286). The French verb used in the full form is *recommander*, no longer *commander*, as was common in Old French (see Stange 1900: 36–7; Senge 1935: 80–3). It is interesting to note that the only example which shows *farewell* in use has the short form followed by a vocative:

> . . . **Farewell good felowe I picke no matter to you:** A dieu compaignon ie ne vous demande riens.
>
> (III, fo. ccc.xvi: **I Pycke no mater**)

*Fare well* and *a dieu* are the actual words uttered in the situation itself, but what is the proper word referring to the action performed? In the special sense in which *to bid* is used in *to bid farewell*, it has to be translated by *dire* in French:

> **I Bydde one farwell/ as we do whan we departe out of his companye:** Ie dis a dieu. **Wyll you departe and nat bydde hym farwell:** Voulez vous partyr sans luy dire a dieu. **I wyll byd my mayster farewell and come by ⁊ by:** Ie diray a dieu a mon maistre et viendray tout incontinẽt. **So that for byd in this sence they vse dis, as bydde hym go hence:** Dy luy quil sen aille. &c. **Byd hym tarye a whyle:** Dy luy quil attẽde vng peu . . .
>
> (III, fo. c.lxv$^{v}$)

There is no metalinguistic comment in the other verb entry:

> **I Take my leaue/** Ie prens congé, and ie dis a dieu. **Wyll you go hence and take nat your leaue of vs:** Voulez vous partyr sans nous dire a dieu, or sans prendre congé de nous.
>
> (III, fo. ccc.lxxxiiii$^{v}$)

At the end of the table of adverbs *prendre congé de* is also listed among the manners of saluting:

> **I take my leaue of you:** Ie prens congié de vous.

Stange (1900: 39–40) has already commented upon this new form of taking leave by comparison to *dire adieu* and the fact that it is adduced by Palsgrave.

On parting a wish may be expressed to see the other person again. Senge (1935: 84) maintains that *adieu* could co-occur with *jusqu'au revoir* from the fourteenth century onwards. Lewicka (1979: 289), however, argues that for the texts investigated by her the verb *revenir* was more common: 'On émet aussi le voeu de voir les présents à nouveau réunis. L'expression la plus courante dans ce cas est *jusques au revenir.*' *Revoir* is said to be rare. There was one single instance in her material, believed to date from the beginning of the sixteenth century. She therefore concludes: 'Visiblement, l'expansion moderne de *au revoir* qui, plus tard, devait évincer (*jusques*) *au revenir* et remplacer *adieu* dans une grande partie de ses emplois, n'est pas encore entamée à notre époque' (ibid.). The period she studied is the Middle Ages. The order in which Palsgrave gives *revoir* and *revenir* in his example may be significant:

> **Farewell tyll I se you agayne or come agayn:** A dieu iusques au reueoyr, or a reuenir.
>
> (III, fo. cccc.lxi)

*Reueoyr* may have been given as the first choice because it was already more common than *reuenir*. But the order could also reflect the literal translation of English *see* and *come*.

Palsgrave lists *Good nyght—Bon soyr et bonne nuyct* at the end of his day greetings, not among the farewells (see in this respect Radtke 1994: 199–211). His arrangement may have been guided by the times of the day (*morowe, euyn, nyght*), because the list of adverbs expressing 'blessynge', 'salutyng', and 'wysshyng' shows a clear tri-partite structure: greetings containing nouns denoting times of the day are followed by expressions of wishing and blessing, and the latter by farewells. Du Wes in his list observes the same order. The expressions of farewell given by him are: '*I bydde you farwell—Adieu vous dis*', '*god be with you—adieu soiez*', '*I take my leaue of you—adieu sans adieu*', '*farwell tyll we se agayne—adieu iusques au reueoir*'. He, too, gives the verb *revoir*. The form '*adieu soiez*' (see also Lewicka 1979: 285) does not occur in Palsgrave.

What are these other wishes that might be offered to another person? Du Wes lists twice as many expressions as Palsgrave. What both lists have in common is that all the wishes either invoke God to watch over the person entrusted to his care or thank him for his protection. One set of du Wes's 'salutatyons' is embedded in a sentence frame:

*God gyue . . ./ Dieu doint: Good metyng—Bon encontre, Good ioye—Bon ioie, Good lyfe and longe—Bõne vie et lõgue, Good fortune—Bõne fortune, Good prosperyte—Bõne ꝑsperite, well to prospere—Bien prosperer, Good lucke—Bon heur, Good begynnyng—Bon cõmẽcement, Good meane—Bon moĩen, Good ende/ ⁊ well to fynisshe—Bon fin/ ou bien acheuer, well to lyue/ well to dye—Bien viure/ bien mourir, Good helthe—Bonne sante, Paradyse at the ende—Paradis en la fin, The hole/ or the fulfyllyng of your desyres—Letier* [*sic*]/ *ou la complissemẽt de vos desirs.* (D iii$^{v}$)

The other group includes the following wishes:

*God kepe you—Dieu vous gart, god blesse you—dieu vous benie, god saue you—dieu vous saue, god gyde you—dieu vous cõduyt, god be within—Dieu soit ceans, god be your helpe—dieu vous soit en aide, god be wyllynge to helpe you—dieu vous veuille aider, god kepe you from yuell and trouble—dieu vous garde de mal et dẽcombrier.* (D iii$^{v}$–D iiii)

Most of these expressions are not found in the texts studied by Stange, which made him conclude that they not only sound highly artificial but also cannot be regarded as forms of the colloquial idiom. In contrast, he says that the phrases listed by Palsgrave reflect more actual language use as it is found in contemporary literature (1900: 26-7). Here are the wishes formulated by Palsgrave which in style differ markedly from those expressed by du Wes:

**All myghty god preserue you:** Dieu vous vueille garder de mal.
**God kepe you:** Dieu vous ayt en sa garde.
**God kepe you from yll:** Dieu vous garde de mal.
**God blesse you and all your companye:** Dieu vous benie et toute la compaigne.
**God sẽde you good company:** Dieu vous doyent bon encontre.
**God sende you good spede:** Dieu vous doyent bon encontre.[8]
**God haue you in his kepyng:** Dieu vous ayt en sa garde, and dieu vous ayt en sa tuytion.
**God be thanked I am in good case:** Dieu mercy ie suis en bon poynt.
**God sẽde you good lyfe and longe:** Dieu vous doynt bõne vie et longue.
**God sende you the desyres of your herte:** Dieu vous doyent les desires de vostre cueur.

(III, fo. cccc.lx$^{v}$–cccc.lxi)

[8] This looks like a printing mistake because the French equivalent of the previous phrase is repeated. In the verb list there is a very close example: '*I praye god spede you*' which in French is '*Dieu vous conduye*' (III, fos. ccc.lxvii$^{v}$–ccc.lxviii: **I Spede me**).

In addition, there are three examples under the verb entry **I Sende** . . .:

> . . . **God sende you good lucke in your iourney:** Dieu vo⁹ dont bon encõtre. **God sende you good spede:** Dieu vo⁹ veuille cõduire. **God sende you helth:** Dieu vous doynt la santé.
>
> (III, fo. ccc.liiii^v)

Four of the wishes in Palsgrave's list are not found in the literary texts investigated by Stange: *Dieu vous doyent bon encontre*, *Dieu vous ayt en sa garde*, *Dieu vous ayt en sa tuytion*, and *Dieu vous doyent les desires de vostre cueur*. Palsgrave himself includes among the adverbs of saluting and wishing those of blessing. One may, therefore, wonder whether the phrases should not be taken as an autobiographical feature. In style, tone, and context, they could qualify, whether documented in the literature or not, as blessings typically uttered by a priest. *Lesclarcissement* was compiled for learners of French, intent on producing correct and appropriate French utterances. One cannot easily imagine that such learners would have had much occasion to use words of blessing, and surely the number of clergymen envisaged as potential users of the work would have been too small to require their special professional needs to be catered for.

In such a scene of a priest blessing his parting flock, the language chosen is manifestly adapted not only to the content of the message but also to the individuals involved and their social relationship. In many of the instances quoted to illustrate that a large part of Palsgrave's examples closely reflects the spoken language, several of the varietal parameters are co-present—for instance, the spoken medium, the social group, and the attitude displayed. Our focus so far has been on the medium. Yet we would not do Palsgrave justice if we were not also to turn briefly to the issues of social group and attitude.

## LANGUAGE VARIATION AND SOCIAL GROUPS

How language use varies according to the professional group using it has already been shown for poets writing in rhyme and in prose (see pp. 90, 344–5), merchants (see pp. 134, 354), the learned (see pp. 134–5), and servants (see p. 365). In Palsgrave's introduction peasants are characterized by their pronunciation:

> The whole reason of theyr accẽt is groũded chefely vpon thre poyntes/ fyrst there is no worde of one syllable whiche with them hath any accent/ or that they vse to pause

vpon/ and that is one great cause why theyr tong semeth to vs so brefe and so dayn and so harde to be vnderstãded whan it is spoken/ especially of theyr paysantes or cõmen people/ for thoughe there come neuer so many wordes of one syllable together/ they pronouce them nat distinctly a sonder as the latines do/ but sounde them all vnder one voyce and tenour/ and neuer rest nor pause vpon any of them/ except the cõmyng next vnto a poynt be the cause therof. (B ii$^{v}$)

Social class differences are worded in different ways. In the example describing a first meeting, 'a mean person' is said to be greeted 'Dieu vous gart', and a 'great personage' to be offered an 'Honneur a vous'. (III, fos. ccc.xlvi$^{v}$–ccc.xlvii). Under the adverb *by your leaue*, we have learned that the French expression '*Ne vous desplaise*' is appropriate when we are in doubt whether 'our better' will be content (III, fo. cccc.xxxix$^{v}$). A third way is the explicit opposing of *an inferior* and *a superior* as in the following instance:

**I Murmur I grutche or repyne as an inferior person dothe agaynst the actes of his superyor/** Ie murmure. prime cõiuga. **and** ie me argue. verbũ mediũ. prime cõiu. **Go lewde person nat so hardy thou murmure agaynst my doyng:** Va meschante creature si hardy que tu ne murmure contre mon faict.

(III, fo. ccc.v)

'Great man' and 'superior' occur in III, fo. ccc.xlvii.

That the difference in social standing also calls for a certain ritualized behaviour emerges from the following examples, where the 'better' or 'superior' is the 'master' or a 'gentilman':

. . . **Howe oft tymes haue I cõmaũded ẏ to take of thy cappe whan thou metest thy mayster:** Quantes foys tay ie cõmandé de oster ton bonnet quant tu rencontres ton maistre.

(III, fo. ccc.lxxxiiii$^{v}$–ccc.lxxxv)

. . . **Put of your cappe whan the gentylman speaketh to you:** Ostez vostre bonnet quant le gentilhomme parle a vous.

(III, fo. ccc.xxviii$^{v}$: **I Put of my cappe**)

The poor are mentioned in the context of the phrase *God sende you/ Dieu vous soit en ayde* as we gather from the entries **I Sende a thing** and **I Conforte**:

**God sẽde you/ as we vse to answere beggars whan we be nat mynded to gyue them almesse:** Dieu vous soit **en ayde . . .**

(III, fo. ccc.liiii$^{v}$: **I Sende a thing . . .**)

**But whan we vse to speke to poore men that aske almesse/ for god comforte you/ they say:** Dieu vous soyt en ayde . . .

(III, fo. c.xciiii$^{v}$: **I Conforte**)

In the case of a stranger or an enemy, the social status may not be obvious and then an address may be '*What seke you?—Que demandez vous*', or '*For whome seke you?—Apres qui demandez vous?*' (III, fo. ccc.liiii: **I Seke** . . .), or a brief directive may be given:

> . . . **but for stande in the imperatiue mode whan it is spokyn to an enemy or in haste they saye** debout, **only and leue out the ꝟbe . . .**
>
> (III, fo. ccc.lxxii: **I Stande vpon my fete**)

When he outlines the numerals, Palsgrave distinguishes several groups of language users: the vulgar people, merchants, learned men, history writers, and authors writing in rhyme. He has two lists of numerals, the first gives *septante*, *octante*, and *nonante* for seventy, eighty, and ninety, the second *soixante dix*, *quatre vingtz*, and *quatre vingtz et dix*. The second is headed by a title specifying those who use this way of counting: 'Here foloweth wherin ẏ voulgar people marchate men/ and suche as write hystories dyffer from the maner of nombring here afore rehersed' (III, fo. c.xv$^{v}$). This reiterates part of the earlier comment

> Note also that all be it the volgar people vse neuer/ *soixante, septante, octante,* and *nonante, as* I shall herafter playnly declare/ yet that the lerned men vse them and suche as nombre by aulgorisme appereth by the Romant of the Rose/ where he bringeth in nature workynge in her forge by these wordes/ *dix ans ou vingt, trent, ou quarante, cinquãte, soixante, ou septante, voire octante, nonante, ou cent.* (III, fo. c.xv$^{v}$)

As to the difference between *mil* and *mille* for a thousand, poetic licence in rhyme is said to favour *mil* when the following noun phrase begins with a vowel or *h* (III, fo. c.xvii).

*The language of sex*

We might illustrate the attitude displayed towards the topic and/or the discourse partner with some instances of what Palsgrave calls 'covert' language, some of which have already been mentioned. For instance, the use of *cock* or French *bieu* for God/Dieu in *by cockes body*, *by cockes flesshe—par le corps bieu, par le chair bieu, par la mort bieu*. Or the euphemism *demander pour dieu*, a fairer term in Palsgrave's words for French *belistrer* 'to beg' (III, fo. c.lix$^{v}$). A third example is the French expressions for 'to make love'. Under the entry **I Iape a wenche** we learn that the verb may be rendered in three different ways in French: by *foutre*, *bistocquer*, and *faire cela*. *Bistoquer* is explained in its proper sense and *faire cela* is described as covert language:

> **I Iape a wenche/** Ie fous, nous foutons, ie foutis, iay foutu, ie fou-

> teray, que ie foute, foutre. tercie cõ. **and** ie bistocque. prime cõiuga. **It is better to iape a wenche than to do worce:** Il vault mieulx foutre vne fille que de faire pis, **as for** bestocquer, **is but a fayned worde/ for it betokeneth properly to stabbe or to foyne/ also in more couerte langage they vse** ie fays cela. **As/ I iape her whan me lyste:** Ie luy fays cela quant il me playst. **Wyll you iape:** Voulez vous faire cela, ⁊ ie luy fays bien. **O that my louer pleaseth me well:** O que mon amy le me fait bien.
>
> (III, fo. cc.lxv^v^)

Another range of expressions, apart from *bistocquer*, is given under the entry **I Swyue a wenche**. They are also commented upon and put in relation to *foutre*:

> **I Swyue a wenche/** Ie bistocque prime cõiuga. ⁊ ie roussine. pri. cõiu. **and** ie houspille. prime coniu. **and** ie hosche. pri. coniu. **I wyll nat swyue her and she wolde pray me:** Ie ne la bistocqueray, ie ne la roussineray, ie ne la houspilleray, **or** ie ne la hoscheray ia si elle me vouloyt prier, **but all these word3 be but vsed of pleasure/ for the very worde is/** ie fous, **coniugate and declared in I sarde.**
>
> (III, fos. ccc.lxxxi^v^–ccc.lxxxii).[9]

Under **I Sarde a queene** the verb *foutre* is conjugated, and, contrary to the previous two entries, there is no metalinguistic comment:

> **I Sarde a queene/** Ie fous, nous foutons, ie foutis, iay foutu, ie fouteray, que ie foute, foutre. ter. **They say there was a lorde in Englande asked a spyrite of the ayre if she was nat well sarded:** Lon dit qung seignieur Dangleterre demãda a vne dia blesse aerine si elle nestoyt pas bien foutue.
>
> (III, fo. ccc.xlvi^v^)

[9] It is not clear why L. Sainéan (1922–3: ii. 302), in his discussion of the *verba erotica* in Rabelais's works, mentions that *bistocquer* occurs in Palsgrave, but not that this also holds for *roussiner*.

In the context of *to sard*, Palsgrave uses the word *quean*, not *wench*, as he did for *to jape* and *to swive*. He does the same for the lemma entry for *to frig*:

> **I Frygge ẇ the arse as a queene dothe whan she is in iapynge/** Ie fringue. **Frygge on hardly my lady dothe so to:** Fringez hardyment ma dame le faict aussi.
>
> (III, fo. cc.xlii^v^)

From the Middle Ages onwards, *quean* has been used as a disparaging term for a woman, a bold or impudent one, a strumpet. One may therefore wonder whether the verb *to sard*, the oldest of the three in this sense, was the coarser and more direct term, corresponding to French *foutre*, for, interestingly, the common English four-letter verb is not found in Palsgrave, although some sixty years later it is listed by John Florio in his dictionary. There seems to be a fine scale of distinctions in Palsgrave's use of verbs for 'to make love to' which is based on the social, emotional, and/or moral standing of the male and female involved. Thus under *to handle*, husband and wife are mentioned:

> **I Handell one plesaũtly as a hous bande dothe his wyfe in the nyght tyme/** Ie le luy fays bien. **My hous-bande handleth me pleasaũtly:** Mon mary le me fait bien.
>
> (III, fo. cc.lvii)

In the entry for *to have to do with—connaître charnellement*, the terms are *woman* and *maid*:

> **I Haue to do with a woman or mayde/** Ie congnoys charnellement. **I haue had to do ẇ her:** Ie lay cong-nue charnellement.
>
> (III, fo. cc.lx)

Both these words also occur under *to devour*:

> **I Deuoure a mayden or woman agaynst her wyll/** Ie rauis, iay rauy, rauyr, secunde cõiuga. **and** ie viole. prime cõiu. **He hath deuoured twẽty maydens and wyues agaynst their wylles in his dayes:** Il a rauy, **or** il a violé vingt filles et femmes contre leur gré en son temps.
>
> (III, fo. cc.x^v^)

The phrase *maid and/or wife* is repeated under *I ravish*:

> **I Rauysshe a mayde or wyfe I take them by force/** Ie rauys, iay ra-uy, rauyr. secũde cõiuga. **and** ie en-taille. prime cõiuga. **and** ie viole. pri me cõiuga. **Some sayd she was ra-uysshed with her wyll:** Les aulcuns disoient quelle estoyt rauie, **or** quelle estoyt violée, **or** efforcée de son bon gre. **As for ientaille,** as pour entail-ler la gracieuse Helayne, **thoughe I fynde it in the estypell** [*sic*] **of Oenone to Parys it is nat vsed in comen spet-che.**
>
> (III, fo. ccc.xxxiii^v^)

And, similarly, we have *wife and/or maid* in

> **I Take awaye a mans wyfe or a mayde byforce/** Ie rauis. secũde cõiu. **What meanest thou man wylt thou take away a mans wyfe:** Que veulx tu dire veulx tu rauyr la femme daul-truy.
>
> (III, fo. ccc.lxxxiii)

The generic term *woman—femme* occurs in **I Company with a woman bodily** (III, fo. c.xcii^v^) as well as in *to take against one's will*:

> **I Take a woman agaynst her wyll/** Ie force vne femme. prime cõiu. **What meanest thou man wylt thou take me against my wyl:** Que veulx tu dire me veulx tu efforcer.
>
> (III, fo. ccc.lxxxiii)

As we have seen, Palsgrave was familiar with sexual taboo language in English and in French. He also knew some of the folk wisdom in this area, as we learn from the example under the verb *to engender*:

> **If the comen people speake wysely/ so sure as froste engendreth hayle a lycorouse mouthe a lycorouse tayle:** Se les cõmunes gens parlẽt saigemẽt, aussi vray que de la gelée sengendre la gresle, qui est friant de bouche est aussi friant de queue.
>
> (III, fo. cc.xxv)

This clearly echoes a passage in the Prologue to the *Wife of Bath*'s tale, though Palsgrave may be quoting from memory, since Chaucer uses 'cold' not 'frost':

> And after wyn on Venus moste I thynke,
> For al so siker as cold engendreth hayl,
> A likerous mouth moste han a likerous tail.
>
> (Robinson 1983: 80, ll. 464–6)

The fact that Palsgrave illustrates the verbs for 'making love' with example sentences shows that he himself was relaxed about using expressions for the pleasures of the flesh. Indeed, some of his examples are positively risqué, as the one under the verb *to frig* and the other inserted under one of the entries for the verb *to stand*. The lemma entry is **I Stande vpon my legges without any helpe of staffe or thynge to lene by** and its French equivalent *se soutenir*. The first example is a good illustration: '*I can nat stãde vpon my legges: Ie ne me puis poynt soustenir sus mes iambes.*' And then we have:

> **I stande vpryght or I stande**
> **styfe as ones gere doth:** Ie me arri-
> ge. **My gere standeth:** Mon vit se
> arrige fort et ferme, or ie marrige
> . . .
>
> (III, fo. ccc.lxxii)

where the French translation in its explicitness goes far beyond the English *my yard standeth*.

# 10

# A Picture of Palsgrave's World

We shall in this chapter attempt to draw a tentative picture of Palsgrave and his world as they emerge from his choice of verbs and examples. This does not mean that we take the content of all his examples as autobiographical, and we need to be aware of the ambiguity created by the frequent use of first-person singular forms. We shall first outline examples that seem to relate to more general aspects of him as a chaplain to the king, a man of the Church, and a sixteenth-century individual with personal principles and views, and then look in more detail at various domains of life which, through the number and/or content of examples, appear more prominent in the work.

A recurrent theme that seems central in the verb illustrations and that reflects on the author of the work is the grace of God:

. . . **All thyng consumeth but the grace of god:** Toute chose se consume forsque la grace de dieu . . .

(III, fo. c.xcvi: **I Cõsume**)

. . . **All thynges come to naught sauyng ẙ grace of god:** Toutes choses deuiennẽt a riens forsque la grace de dieu.

(III, fo. cc.ii[v]: **I Come to naught**)

How could Palsgrave have seen his position in this world? The first example which he provides for the verb *longe* 'to belong' is rather striking:

. . . **I longe to the king:** Ie suis au roy, ⁊ ie appartiens au roy . . .

(III, fo. cc.lxxxiv[v]: **I Longe to one**)

His attitude toward his superiors may be reflected in the only example for *to disobey*:

. . . **I wyll neuer disobey my prĩce nor myársshoppe:** Iamays ne desobeyray a mon prince ne a mon euesque.

(III, fo. cc.xiiii: **I Disobey**)

The same absolute *never* renounces insubordination and quarrelling:

> . . . **I wyll neuer cõtende with my superyour nor stryue with my felowe:** Ie ne me cõtenderay iamays a mõ superieur, ne nestriueray a mon compaignon.
>
> (III, fo. c.xcvi: **I Contende**)

Palsgrave will undoubtedly have experienced the effect that a public recognition by the king could produce on rivals and courtiers. The only example for the verb *to becken* (an unusually long one) recalls such an instance:

> . . . **It dyd me more good than if one had gyuen me twenty poũde that ẏ kyng dyd becken on me with his heed as he passed by me to daye:** Il me fit plus grant bien que si vng meust donné vingt liures que le roy me fist signe de la teste ainsi quil passa par deuant moy au iourdhuy.
>
> (III, fo. c.lviii$^{v}$: **I Becken** . . .)

We know that Palsgrave received his first benefice, Portpool, in 1514, and that it was only under Cranmer as Archbishop of Canterbury that he became the master of the rich St Dunstan-in-the-East, having been ordained priest the same year (1533). We do not know why his promotion within the Church was so slow. If at the time of the publication of *Lesclarcissement* some fifteen years of professional disappointment had elapsed, the following examples might reflect personal experience:

> **It is a great synne to hynder a man that standeth vpon his promocyon vpon malyce:** Cest vng grant peché que de desauãcer vng homme par malice que est sur le poynt de sa promocion.
>
> (III, fo. cc.lxii$^{v}$: **I Hynder ones promocion**)

> . . . **This fyftene yere hath he kepte me backe god forgyue hym:** De ces quinze ans il ma desauãce dieu luy pardoynt.
>
> (III, fo. cc.lxxi$^{v}$: **I Kepe one a backe I hynder hym of his promocion**)

> . . . **Kursed be the priest of god that dyd apeche me wrongfully and without deseruyng:** Mauldit soyt le prestre de dieu qui maccusa a fort et sans riens desseruyr.
>
> (III, fo. c.l: **I Apeche**)

The total lack of resentment manifest in the above example would go together with the outlook on life that we find in the illustration of *to covet*, made absolute by the use of the adverbial *never*:

> . . . **I neuer couet more good but to haue ynoughe to paye euery man his:** Iamays ie ne desire, **or** ie ne couuoyte plus de biens que da uoir asses pour paier a chascun le sien.
>
> (III, fo. cc.iii^v^: **I Couet**)

As far as we know, Palsgrave's employment in the services of the duke of Richmond came to an end in 1526. The following example, which mentions seven years of financial difficulties, may also have an autobiographical resonance:

> **I Whysshe I couet or desyre a thyng/** Ie souhaicte. **For seuen yeres togyther I lyued in gret payne/ but nowe I lyue as well as I coulde wysshe:** Iay vescu sept ans tout du long en grant peyne, mays mayntenant ie vis aussi bien comme ie pourroye souhaitier, **or** souhaiter.
>
> (III, fo. cccc.viii)

A man at peace with himself and the world speaks through the example given under one of the senses of the verb *to love*:

> . . . **I take the worlde as it cometh and loue god of all:** Ie prens le monde ainsi cõme il va et loue dieu de tout.
>
> (III, fo. cc.lxxxiv^v^: **I Loue I prayse one**)

We know that Palsgrave spent some time studying in France and that he accompanied the king's sister there as well as Henry VIII himself. His memory may have gone back to those days when he was called upon to illustrate the use of the verb *to jeopard*:

> . . . **I coulde haue gotten a goodly botye one daye whan we were in Fraunce if I durst haue geoparded:** Ie eusse bien gaigne vng beau butyn vng iour quant nous estions en Frãce si ie eusse osé aduẽturer.
>
> (III, fo. cc.xlv: **I Geoparde**)

It might have been his moral integrity that held him back from seizing the opportunity, for under the verb *to esteem* we learn that the thing valued highest is personal honesty:

> **I estyme myne honestye aboue all the rychesse in ẏͤ worlde:** Ie prefere mon honneur par dessus toutes les richesses du monde, **and** ie estime mon honneur.
>
> (III, fo. cc.xxix: **I Esteme**; see also III, fo. ccc.vii^v: **I Offende my conscyence,** and III, fo. ccc.lxxx: **I Supporte**)

For a clergyman, abstinence should not have been unfamiliar. Palsgrave, as we shall see, was well versed in the cooking and preparing of food. To forgo the delights of the palate is regarded as a great pain:

> **. . . It is an easye thyng to speke of abstynẽce but it is a payne to contayne from meate:** Cest vne chose bien aysée que de parler dabstinence, mays cest vne grande peyne que de se contenir de manger.
>
> (III, fo. c.xcvi: **I Conteyne**)

There is one entry only for the verb *to study*, and Palsgrave illustrates the verb thus: '*I wolde fayne be a great clerke but I loue nat to studye*: *Ie vouldroye estre voulentiers vng grãt clerc mays ie nayme pas a estudier*' (III, fo. ccc.lxxviii^v). Is this the admission of a secret ambition and at the same time a confession?

The position taken with respect to fulfilling one's duty is very clear. '*He that wyll nat do his dutye with good wyll muste be corrected*: *Qui ne veult faire son debuoyr de bon gré fault quon le coarcte*, **or** *quon le constraigne*' (III, fo. c.xc^v: **I Coarcte**). So too the rejection of idleness, asserted twice with the same curious example:

> **. . . It is better to ryppe ones clothes ⁊ sowe them agayne than to be ydell:** Il vault mieulx quon decouse ses habillements et les recoutre que destre oyseux.
>
> (III, fo. ccc.xlii: **I Ryppe a seame . . .**)

> **. . . If thou haue naught to do ryppe thy clothes ⁊ sowe them agayn:** Si tu nas riens affaire descous tes habellements et les recous . . .
>
> (III, fos. ccc.lxvi^v–ccc.lxvii: **I Sowe**)

He even links idleness to angling:

> **. . . It is but a sory lyfe and an yuell to stande anglynge all day to katche a fewe fysshes:** Ce nest qune meschante vie et oyseuse que de pescher a verge toute iour pour vng peu de poissons.
>
> (III, fo. c.xlix: **I Angle**)

That idleness was a moral and educational issue at the time we also learn from Sir Thomas Elyot's *Book named the governor* (Alston 1970*d*: fos. 47, 95ᵛ).

Expressions involving gradability may well suggest a personal stance. *Backbiting* is regarded as the greatest fault in man, a vice worse than lechery:

**I knowe nat a greater faulte than to backbyte a mã:** Ie ne scayche plus grant crime quede diffamer vne parsõne, or que de remorder.

(III, fo. c.lvii: **I Backbyte**)

. . . **It is worse to be a backbyter than a leachour:** Il vault pis destre vng detracteur qung paillart . . .

(III, fo. cc.lxixᵛ: **It is worse**)

See also a related example under **I Dyffame** (III, fo. cc.xᵛ). Palsgrave does not put crucifixion in its Christian moral context: '*The most vyle dethe that coulde be was somtyme to crucifye one*: *La plus ville mort qui pouuoyt estre estoyt iadis de crucifier vng homme*' (III, fo. cc.i).

Some of Palsgrave's examples reflect political issues. This can be illustrated with examples from the verbs *to bring up a new custom or new law* and *to rebel as subjects do when they disobey their souvereign*:

. . . **Reformacions of misgydyng be very necessary in a comen welth/ but to bringe vp newe lawes is a perlous worke:** Reformacions des abus sont fort necessaires au bien publique, mays de mettre sus nouuelles loyx, cest vne dangereuse besongne.

(III, fo. c.lxxviiᵛ).

. . . **It is a pytuouse case and their owne distruction whan subiectes rebell a gaynst their naturall lorde:** Cest vng cas pitoyable et leur propre cõfusion quãt aulcuns subiectz se rebellent cõtre leur seignieur naturel.

(III, fo. ccc.xxxiiiᵛ)

We come to selected areas of sixteenth-century life and their representation in the verb list. A substantial part of the illustrations concerns eating and drinking, together with the physical effects of overindulgence and excesses. We learn that onions and garlic are peeled (III, fo. ccc.xviᵛ), that peas and saffron are pricked (III, fo. ccc.xvi), that beans and peas are shaled (III, fo. ccc.xlviii) and eaten (III, fo. c.lxvii), and that peas may be strained before serving (III, fo. ccc.lxxvi). Almonds are blanched (III, fo. c.lxvii, c.lxviiᵛ) and herbs are finely crushed in a mortar before being used for seasoning (III, fo. c.lxxviii)—for instance, sorrel and violet leaves (III, fo. ccc.lxxvii). Other specified preparations of cooking are the gilling of fish (III, fo. cc.xlviii), the scaling of 'roches' (III, fo. ccc.xlvii), the laying of saltfish in water (III, fos. cc.lxxv, ccc.lxxiiiᵛ: **I Stepe**), the beating of stockfish to soften it (III, fo. cc.xcvi), and the slitting of a pike's belly to take out the rivet (III, fo. ccc.lxix) (and his use of this word for 'the liver of a fish' is the first to be recorded in the *OED*).

Partridges obviously had to be plucked before cooking (III, fo. ccc.xix$^{v}$). The refinements of cookery included the larding of rabbits (conies) (III, fo. cc.lxxviii$^{v}$) and their basting to prevent them from becoming too dry (III, fo. c.lvi$^{v}$), the sticking of a shoulder of mutton with herbs (III, fo. ccc.lxxiiii$^{v}$), and the stuffing of a breast of veal or a pudding:

> **I Stuffe a podyng or suche lyke** Ie farce. pri. cõiu. and ie farcie. M. or ie espessis. secũde coniu. **Stuffe this podyng:** Farces ce boudyn. **Stuffe this breste of veale and make a podyng in it:** Farces ceste poictrine de veau et faictez vng boudyn dedens.
>
> (III, fo. ccc.lxxviii$^{v}$)

This second use and sense of *pudding*, 'a stuffing roasted within a part of an animal', clearly predates the one given in the *OED* (**pudding** . . . **I. 1. b.**) for Shakespeare.

For venison (III, fo. ccc.lxiiii$^{r-v}$), capons (III, fo. ccc.xxviii$^{v}$), swans (III, fo. cc.lxx$^{v}$: **I Karue meat**), quails (III, fos. c.lxxiii, ccc.xxviii$^{v}$), pheasants (III, fo. c.lxxiii), and sheep's feet (III, fo. c.lxxviii), no specific preparation is mentioned. Yet we learn that a sheep's foot is broiled on burning coals (III, fo. c.lxxviii), broiling on a gridiron has the disadvantage that what is broiled too much, will stick to it (III, fo. c.lxxviii), that capons and quails are put on spits (III, fo. ccc.xxviii$^{v}$), and so are pigs (III, fo. ccc.xliiii), and that venison and also other meat is 'parboiled' (III, fo. ccc.xii$^{v}$) or 'seethed' (III, fo. ccc.lix$^{v}$) before baking it in an oven. Beef may be soaked in brine (III, fo. cc.lxxvii$^{v}$: **I Ley in brine**; see also **I Ley in pyckell** (ibid.)) and in order to make a galantine one has to '*laye some breed in soke*' (III, fo. cc.lxxv$^{v}$: **I Lay in soke**). *Petrier*, the French equivalent for *lay in soke*, also renders the English verb **I Temper**:

> **I Temper I laye breed or other thynges in stepe/** Ie petrie. pri. cõiu. **you muste temper your breed in vynayger:** Il vous fault petrier vostre payn en vinaigre.
>
> (III, fo. ccc.lxxxviii)

Food may also be fried in oil or butter, and frying may be overdone and thus spoil fish (III, fo. cc.xlii$^{v}$: **I Frye hole meat**). Since the English verb *to fry* is rendered by two French verbs, *frire* and *fricasser*, we also learn that meat was hacked small and then fried in oil or butter:

> . . . **Frye this frycasse in all the haste for it shalbe first serued:** Fricassez ceste fricassée en toute haste possible, car on la mettera premierement a la table.
>
> (III, fo. cc.xlii^v^: **I Frye meate . . .**)

Bread and pastries are obviously baked in the oven (III, fo. c.lvi^v^) and liquids boiled (III, fo. c.lxix). '*Paste will be better if you use butter and eggs in making it*' (III, fo. cc.lxxiii: **I Knede paast**). As for choosing the best kind of pot: '*An erthen potte well anneled is the holsomest vessell ẏ can be to boyle meate in: Vng pot de terre quant il est bien plommé, or plõmié est la plus saine chose que peult estre pour cuire de la viande dedans*' (III, fo. c.xlviii^v^) (see also III, fo. cc.lxx^v^: **I Kanker . . .: This potte is kankred it is nat holsome . . .**).

Preservation of food was important, and how that might be achieved for venison is pointed out in two entries. The meaning of *to parboil* is paraphrased as follows: '*I Parboyle I sethe venyson or any other flesshe to sucke out ẏ blode of it that it maye be the lenger kept*' (III, fo. ccc.xii^v^). A further means was salting and peppering:

> . . . **Uenayson well poudred with pepper and salt wyll last longe on corrupted:** La venayson qui est bien pouldrée de poyure et de sel durera longuement auant que se corrumpre.
>
> (III, fo. ccc.xxi: **I Pouder with spyce**)

Oversalting may, of course, ruin the enjoyment of a roast (of beef, for instance: see III, fo. ccc.xxi: **I Pouder with salte**). Other complaints are the burning of the soup: '*I wyll eate no potage to day for the potte is burned to the bottome: Ie ne veulx poynt manger de potaige au iourdhuy, car le pot est aoursé*' (III, fo. c.lxx: **I Borne to the bottome as a potte dothe for want of lycour**). Palsgrave even provides his learners with an idiomatic expression to describe the taste of a burnt soup: '*This potage sauoureth/ which we vse whan the meate is sodden to the pottes bottome: Ie sens a ce potage que le pot est aoursé*' (III, fo. ccc.xlvii: **I Sauour**). A pasty of pigeons may not have been baked enough (III, fo. c.lvi^v^: **I Baake a pastye**), a woodcock may not have been roasted enough (III, fo. ccc.xliiii: **I Roste meat vpon a spytte**), an apple may be overcooked: '*Take awaye this appell from the fyre the beste is ronne out: Le meilleur de la pomme sen est en fuy, ostez la du feu*' (III, fo. ccc.xliii^v^: **I Ronne ouer**). Meat may be burnt, and Palsgrave uses a term for this, which according to the *OED*, is only found in *Lesclarcissement*:

**I Squarken I burne the vtter part of a thyng agaynst the fyer or roste meat vnkyndly/** Ie ars, coniugat in **I burne. This mete is nat rostyd it is squackynnyd:** Ceste viande nest pas rostye elle est arse.

(III, fo. ccc.lxxi)

That meat roasting requires skill and care becomes obvious from the following example:

. . . **Turne rounde you haue swarted this meate and yet it is nat halfe ynoughe:** Tournez rond vous auez gresille la viande encore elle nest pas a demy rostye.

(III, fo. ccc.lxxxi: **I Swart as a thyng dothe . . .**)

We are also given glimpses of how some foods were eaten. When guests were at table, bread was not offered as it had been baked, but should have the crust cut away:

. . . **Chyppe the breed at ones/ for our gestes be come:** Chappellez le payn viste, car noz inuitéez sont venus.

(III, fo. c.xxxvii^v: **I Chyppe breed**)

If a soup was too thin, '*Put more breed in your potage to make it thycke*: *Mettez plus de pain en vostre potaige pour lespessyr*' (III, fo. ccc.lxxxviii^v: **I Thycke a thĩg**). The first entry for *chafing-dish* in the *OED* dates from 1483 and Palsgrave commends its use:

. . . **Call for a chafyngdysshe for your potage wyll waxe colde els** Faictez venir vng reschauffoyr car vo stre potaige se refroydira aultremẽt.

(III, fo. cccc.ii^v: **I Waxe colde**)

Knives were precious, and, when invited out, you brought your own knife along and you had made sure it was well whetted:

. . . **I wyll sharpe my knyfe or I go to dynner/ for I intende to fede well to daye:** Ie aguyseray mon cousteau auãt que daller disner, car ie suis deliberé de bien briffer au iourdhuy.

(III, fo. ccc.xlix: **I Sharpen a knyfe**)

. . . **I loue better whettynge of knyues afore a good dyner than whettynge of swordes and bylles:** Iayme mieulx laguysement des cousteaulx auãt q̃ daller a vng bon disner que ie ne fais laguysement des espées et voulges.

(III, fo. cccc.vii^v: **I Whette a knyfe**)

And after eating: '*Your knyfe wyll ruste and you wype it nat after salte meates*: *Vostre cousteau senrouillera si vous ne le nettoiez apres dauoyr mangé viandes sallées*' (III, fo. ccc.xlv[v]: **I Ruste as a knyfe or weapon of yron**).

There are five examples where we may have expressions of Palsgrave's personal tastes: '*I hade as lefe stryke my breed with butter as with hony*: *Ie ayme aussi chier embeurrer mon pain que de lemmieller*' (III, fos. ccc.lxxvi[v]–ccc.lxxvii: **I Stryke a thyng with hony**). He seems to have preferred to salt his beef himself: '*I neuer salte my befe but in ẏ potte*: *Iamais ie ne salle mon beuf que au pot*' (III, fo. ccc.xlvi: **I Salte a thynge**). As to fish, the preference was for broiling it whole:

> . . . **Some splet their pyckes whan they broyle them/ but I wolde broyle them hole:** Les aucuns ouurẽt leurs brochetons quãt ilz les rotyssent sus le gryl, mays ie les rotiroye sur le gril tous entiers.
>
> (III, fo. ccc.lxix[v]: **I Splette a fysshe asonder**)

And he knew the culinary pleasures of a fish's head:

> . . . **He wolde haue me take out ẏ bones from this turbotes heed or euer I bake it/ and the bones be best of all:** Il vouldroyt que ie desarestasse ceste teste de tourbot auant que la mettre au four et les arestes vaillẽt mieulx q̃ toute la reste.
>
> (III, fo. ccc.lxxxv: **I Take out the bones**)

We might assume a sweet tooth from the following:

> . . . **I loue well a flawne/ but and it be well sugred I loue it the better:** Iayme bien vng flan, mays sil est bien sucré ie layme de mieulx.
>
> (III, fo. ccc.lxxix[v]: **I Suger**)

Of the beverages mentioned in the verb list there is, of course, water (III, fo. cc.xcix[v]: **I Meryte**), but also milk (III, fo. cccc.v: **I Waxe sowre**), beer and ale (III, fo. c.lxxiiii: **I Brewe . . .**), wine (III, fo. c.lxxiiii: **I Bring a thyng**), wine of Beaune (III, fo. c.xxxvi[v]: **I Abroche**), and other unspecified drinks which may go sour during heat (III, fo. cc.xcvi: **I Make sowre**), pall if left uncovered over night (III, fo. ccc.xii: **I Palle as drinke . . .**), need some sugaring (III, fo. cc.xcvi[v]: **I Make swete**), or be made bitter by adding wormwood (III, fo. cc.lxxxxix [*sic*]: **I Make bytter**).

Wine and water may be mixed (III, fo. cc.xcix$^{v}$: **I Mengle**) and so may ale and wine (III, fo. c.lxvii$^{v}$: **I Blenne**).

Ale may go off in the summer (III, fo. cccc.v: **I Waxe sowre**), and beer may be single or double (III, fos. c.lxxvii$^{v}$–c.lxxviii: **I Broche** . . .).[1] The former is recommended for slimming:

> **. . . you muste drinke syngle bere if you wyll waxe small:** Il vous fault boyre de la biere sengle si vous voulez appetisser.
>
> (III, fo. cccc.v: **I Waxe small**)

With this last example we have already moved to that area of life which is closely linked with a person's eating and drinking habits: health. Palsgrave clearly perceives the relevance of an adequate diet for a person's physical well-being (III, fo. ccc.xxii). In numerous examples, we are given interesting insights into the assumed effects and dietary beliefs of certain foods in sixteenth-century English society. Hoarseness, which Palsgrave as a teacher and preacher may well have endured, is mentioned in two instances:

> **I Make horse in the throte/** Ie en roue. prime cõiuga. **Drinke no reed wyne for it wyll make you horse:** Ne beuuez pas du vin vermeil car il vous enrouera.
>
> (III, fo. cc.xcii)

> **I Waxe hoorse in yͤ throte/** Ie me enroue. verbũ mediũ. prime cõiuga. **Soft chese is nat good for you that haue the coughe/ for it wyll make you waxe horse agayne:** Frommaige mol nest past bon pour vous qui auez la toux, car il vous fera enrouer de rechief.
>
> (III, fo. cccc.iii$^{v}$)

Coughing was commoner in winter than in summer (III, fo. c.xcix: **I Cough**) and one might catch cold through not covering the head:

> **. . . you haue the murre me thynke by my faythe you caught it yester-daye standyng bare heed:** Vous auez la catarre ce me semble, cela vous hap pa hier quant vous vous tinstez nude teste.
>
> (III, fo. cc.lx: **I Haue the murre**)

In the summer the consumption of butter is said to make one sweat (III, fo. ccc.lxxxi$^{v}$: **I Sweate** . . .). Chestnuts are likely to make one put on weight (III, fo. cc.xci: **I Make fatte**), and as for hot wine, it may enflame one's liver (III, fo. cc.xxv: **I Enflame**).

[1] The *MED* gives the meaning of *double ber* as 'strong beer, stout' with a first attestation for 1467. *Single beer* in the sense of 'weak beer, beer inferior in quality' is given by both the *OED* and the *MED*, again from the last decades of the fifteenth century.

Just as some foods may have an unhealthy effect, others may help to counteract or undo a physical state. The flesh of a hart is mentioned in two entries and it is purported to give back youth:

> . . . **Hartes flesshe wyll make one yong agayne if some men say trewe:** Chayr de cerf raieunyra vng homme si les aulcuns disent verité.
>
> (III, fo. cc.xcvii$^{v}$: **I Make yonge**; see also III, fo. cccc.vi: **I Waxe yonge**).

Loss of taste could be counteracted by eating prunes: '*Proynes be good for you if your mouthe be out of taste*: *Prunes de damas vous sont bonnes si vous estez degousté.*' (III, fo. c.xlvi$^{r-v}$: **I Am out of taste**).

A breakfast with toast and ale is said to be good for one's eye sight:

> . . . **Toste me this breed/ for a cuppe of ale and a toste is holsom in a mornyng for a mans syght:** Tostez moy ce pain, or faictez men vne tostée de ce pain, car vne couppe de goodalle a tout vne tostée est bonne et saine au matyn pour la veue dune personne.
>
> (III, fo. ccc.lxxxxii$^{v}$: **I Tooste breed**)

From some examples we also learn when people used to get up. Under **I Wake out of my slepe** (III, fo. cccc), for instance, we read: '*I wake euery daye at syxe of the clocke.*' Under the entry **I Beate with a hãmer**, a smith is praised as a good husband for having started hammering in his smithy before four o'clock (III, fo. c.lxiiii$^{v}$). Working from six o'clock in the morning until six o'clock in the evening, carding wool, is not enough to make ends meet (III, fo. c.lxxxi: **I Carde woll**).

The treatment for a drunkard calls for malmsey:

> . . . **Whan a drõken man swouneth there is no better medecyne to dawe hym with than to throwe maluesy in his face:** Quant vng hõme yure sespaume, il ny a poynt de meilleure medicine pour le reuiuer, reuigourer, or resusciter que de luy iecter de la maluaysie au visaige.
>
> (III, fo. cc.iiii$^{v}$: **I Dawe from swounyng**)

Malmsey was also recommended against worms:

> . . . **It is good for your sonne to drinke a courtesye of maluesye for he bredeth wormes:** Il est bon pour vostre filz de boire vng peu de maluaisye, car les vers luy viennent au ventre.
>
> (III, fo. c.lxxii: **I Brede wormes**)

Fish should not be eaten during spawning:

> **Neuer vse to ete fyschys whan they spawne for they be nat holsom than/** Ne acoustumez poynt a manger des poyssons quant ils frayent, or engendrent car doncques ne sont pas sayns.
>
> (III, fo. ccc.lxvii$^{v}$: **I spawne as fyshys do**)

Nor should meat be eaten when one had a high temperature:

> . . . **Though I haue the axis I wyll spare no metes that my hart standeth to:** Cõbien q̃ iaye les fieures si nespergneray ie nulles viandes, or si ne me garderay ie de nulles viandes ou iay le cueur.
>
> (III, fo. ccc.lxvii$^{v}$: **I Spaare**)

Many examples concern health more generally, and throw light on the prevailing ideas of the human body and the medical profession. For the cutting of a wound, for instance, the moon had to be in a favourable constellation:

> . . . **The cyrurgyen dare nat cutte me to day bycause the moone is nat in a good signe:** Le cirurgien ne me ose poynt ensciser au iourdhuy a cause q̃ la lune nest pas en vng bon signe.
>
> (III, fo. cc.iii: **I Cutte a woũde . . .**)

We also learn that '*Physicyens forbyd men to company with women some seasons of the yere: Les medecins deffendent aux hommes deulx habiter a fẽmes en aulcunes saisons de lannée*' (III, fo. c.xcii$^{v}$: **I Company with a woman**).

The potential danger and harm produced in a healing process is described in the following example:

> . . . **And you heale his legge vp afore you kyll the deed flesshe quyte**

> **you marre hym for euer:** Se vous luy parguerissez sa iambe auant quauoyr du tout mortifié, **or amorty** la chair morte vous le gastez a tout iamays.
>
> (III, fo. cc.lxxii$^{v}$: **I Kyll as any freatynge medecyne** . . ., see also III, fo. cc.xlii$^{v}$: **I Freete as a corrosyfe doth**)

A belief in the human humours emerges from the following instance:

> . . . **Bynde his legge fast lest yͤ humours fall downe to it:** Bendez sa iambe bien serrée, de paour que les humeurs ne se viennẽt cheoyr dedans.
>
> (III, fo. c.lxvi$^{v}$: **I Bynde with a clothe as a cirurgyen dothe his pacyentes sore**)

'Whealing' was taken as a symptom that you had either worms or something wrong with your liver:

> . . . **Outher you haue many wormes or els you be nat well in your lyuer for your handes wheale a pace:** Ou vous auez beaucoup de cyrons ou vous nestez pas bien en vostre foye car voz mayns vessient fort.
>
> (III, fo. cccc.vii$^{v}$: **I Whele as ones hãdes in sommer whan they brede wheales by ytchyng of wormes**)

Honey is said to help against scurf:

> . . . **There is nothynge better agaynst yͤ scorfe that cometh vpon yonge chyldrens heedes than to anoynte them with hony:** Il ny a riens meillieur contre la roigne que vient aux testes des petitz enfans que de les emmieller.
>
> (III, fo. c.xlix$^{r-v}$)

Boar's fat had healing qualities, but they are not specified:

> . . . **He hath anoynted his legge wͭ bores grease:** Il a oincte sa iambe de sain de pourceau.
>
> (III, fo. c.xlix: **I Anoynte with oyle**)

Cleanliness may keep away illness. Toothache for instance, will not plague you if you regularly clean your teeth:

> ... **Clense thy tethe often if thou wylt nat haue the tothe ake:** Nettoye tes dens souuent si tu ne veulx poynt auoyr de mal aux dens.
>
> (III, fo. c.lxxxix: **I Clense**)

Having a bath from time to time is regarded as wholesome (III, fo. c.lvii: **I Bayne**). Washing or bathing may even be a pleasure:

> ... **In the sõmer it is a great pleasure to bathe one in a fayre ryuer:** En temps desté cest vng grant playsir que de se baigner en vne belle riuiere.
>
> (III, fo. c.lviii: **I Bathe**)

But in order to keep healthy nothing is better than a good diet and exercise:

> **Nothing cõserueth a man better in helth than walking and good dyet:** Il nya riens qui mieulx conserue vng home en sa sancté que de se promener et viure sobrement.
>
> (III, fo. c.xcv: **I Conserue**)

In this very spirit it is interesting to see the example that came to Palsgrave's mind when he described the verb **I Custome I vse a thynge**:

> ... **I custome me to walke euery daye or euer I eate any meate:** Ie me accoustume de me promener tous les iours auant que ie mange quelque chose.
>
> (III, fo. cc.iii)

One of the great health fears will have been the plague. There is an interesting example where *the sicknesse* is the equivalent of French *la peste*:

> **Good dyet ⁊ great fiers do preserue a mã from the sickenesse:** Bonne diette et grant feu contre gardent vng homme de la peste.
>
> (III, fo. ccc.xxii: **I Preserue**)

That physical well-being was not something to be taken for granted emerges from other examples. Thus work and recreation should complement each other:

> . . . **A man muste recreate him selfe somtyme after his labour:** Il se fault recréer aulcunes foys apres ses labeurs.
>
> (III, fo. ccc.xxxiiii^v: **I Recreate**)

He even quotes Marcus Tullius Cicero as to what the best recreation pastime is:

> . . . **Tullye prayseth ẏͤ pastyme to labour the yerthe aboue all other exercyses:** Tullie loue le passetemps de cultiuer la terre pardessus tous aul tres exercises.
>
> (III, fo. cc.lxxiiii: **I Laboure the yerthe**)

Physical exercise was even regarded as an integral part of a gentleman's education by Palsgrave's contemporary Sir Thomas Elyot (in chapter 16 of *The book named the governor*):

All thoughe I haue hitherto aduaunced the cõmendation of lernyng/ specially in gentil men. yet it is to be cõsidered/ that continuall studie without some maner of exercise/ shortly exhausteth the spirites vitall/ and hyndereth naturall decoction and digestion/ wherby mãnes body is the soner corrupted ⁊ brought in to diuers sickenessis/ and finally the life is therby made shorter. where contrarye wise by exercise/ whiche is a vehement motion (as Galene prince of phisitions defineth) the helthe of man is preserued/ and his strength increased: for as moche as the membres by meuyng and mutuall touchĩg/ do waxe more harde/ and naturall heate in all the body is therby augmented. More ouer it maketh the spirites of a man more stronge ⁊ valiant: so that by the hardnesse of the membres/ all labours be more tollerable: by naturall hete/ the appetite is the more quicke: the chaunge of the substance receiued/ is the more redy: the nourisshĩge of all partes of the body/ is the more sufficient and sure. By valiaunt motion of the spirites/ all thĩges superfluous be expelled: and the condutis of the body clẽsed. wherfore this parte of phisike/ is nat to be contemned or neglected in the educatiõ of children ⁊ specially from the age of .xiiij. yeres vpwarde/ in whiche tyme strẽgth with courage increaseth. (Alston 1970*d*: fo. 62^r–v^)

A nimble body presupposes physical exercise (III, fo. cccc.iiii^v: **I Waxe nymble or delyuer of my ioyntz**) and for the older generation a nap after a meal is recommended as wholesome:

> . . . **It is holsome for olde men to nappe in a chayre after dyner:** Il est sayn aux vielles gens de eulx endormyr en vne chaiere apres disner.
>
> (III, fo. ccc.vi: **I Nappe**)

The illustrative sentence under *to nap* has taken us to the elderly and how they may preserve their strength. Ageing itself is a recurrent theme in Palsgrave's examples. If a good diet and exercise are contributory to good health, then one might expect that a poor diet could lead to illness, and illness will age a person. There is thus a considerable consistency in the prevailing opinions. No wonder that when Palsgrave had to think of an example to show the use of *to make old* that he comes up with

> . . . **Sycnesse and yuell fare wyll make a man olde at ones:** Maladie et mauluays manger enuieillera vng homme bien tost.
>
> (III, fo. cc.xciiii$^{v}$: **I Make olde**)

'*Age crepeth vpon vs or we be ware: Vieillesse nous surprent a despouueu auant que nous y donnons garde*' (III, fo. cc: **I Crepe**), and when man has crossed the threshold of adulthood he will decrease little by little: '*Whan a man is full growen he begynneth to grow downwarde agayne: Quant vng hõme est parcreu il commence a se descroystre*' (III, fo. cc.lv$^{v}$: **I Growe downewarde** . . .). Yet it is not only in the course of nature that we age; imprisonment and thought may make us old (III, fo. cc.lxxxvi$^{v}$: **I Make aged**). The traces that old age leaves upon us are pallour (III, fo. cccc.v$^{v}$: **I Waxe wanne**), wrinkles in the face (III, fo. cccc.xi: **I Wrinkell**), and a stouping walk (III, fo. ccc.lxxv$^{v}$: **I Stowppe forwarde**).

We also get some insight into the funeral rites of the time: '*Where haste thou ben so longe thy father is all redy wounde in his wyndyng shete and redye to be buryed: Ou as tu tant demouré ton pere est desia enseuely et prest a estre enterré*' (III, fo. cccc.ix: **I Wynde a man in a wyndynge shete**). The above example is a much better illustration of the use of the noun than the first citations in the *OED* (one from Lydgate and two from the sixteenth century).

Garments, their appearance, and their effect on the beholder are another constant theme in the verb illustrations. In a good number of cases it is pointed out that a coat, a gown, a pair of trousers, a cap, gloves, shoes, and so on are dirty, soiled, stained with blood, covered in dust or ashes, trailing in the mire, torn, or not properly worn or fastened. The contrast between the expected code of cleanliness and style in dress and sixteenth-century practical reality is well caught in Palsgrave's lemmatization of the verb *to wear*: **I Weare as a man weareth his garment clenly or lyke a slut vpon hym/ or any other thynge ẏͭ he weareth vpon him/** ie porte (III, fo. cccc.vii).

The examples not only show us a dress-conscious teacher and chaplain to the king; they also provide us with interesting insights into social differences as they are reflected in the provision of, and material used for, garments, as well as glimpses of how people in sixteenth-century England took care of their clothes.

Fitting his servants out with shoes and trousers was a costly duty for a master:

> **It costeth me monaye in the yere to hose and shoe my seruauntes:** Il me couste de largent par lan a chausscer mes seruiteurs.
>
> (III, fo. cc.lxiiii^v: **I Hose**)

Garments could be offered as a gift (*'As for my gowne I graunte it you/ but nat the furre: Quant a ma robbe ie la vous donne, mays non pas la fourrure'* (III, fo. cc.liiii^v: **I Graunte . . .**) or bequeathed:

> **. . . He hath be queythed me in his testamẽt his best gowne:** Il ma donné en son testament sa meilleure robbe.
>
> (III, fo. ccc.xxxi: **I Queythe**)

For Palsgrave, the wearing of clothes that had belonged to someone else seems to have been unacceptable unless they had been exposed to smoke to kill off whatever animal life there might have been hidden in them:

> **. . . I wyll medyll me with no garmẽtes that were his tyll they be well smoked:** Ie ne me mesleray point de nulz habillemens qui estoy-ent aluy tãt quilz soyẽt bien enfumez.
>
> (III, fo. ccc.lxv: **I Smoke a thyng**)

(On contemporary views of clothes carrying contagion, see Hole 1949*b*: 71.)

Since the quality of dress and its immaculate appearance were taken as an indication of a person's social rank, it was important that the fit and fall of a garment be perfect and that the shine of the fabric brought out fully. Some of the examples here reveal a very detailed expert knowledge of the art and skill of tailoring. A good fall of a garment, for instance, depends on the quality of its preparatory basting:

> **. . . This dublet was nat well ba-sted at ẙ first/ and that maketh it to wrinkle thus:** Ce pourpoynt nestoyt pas bien basty au cõmencemẽt, et cest cela que le fait ainsi froncer.
>
> (III, fo. c.lvi^v)

The verb *to cadge*, for which *Lesclarcissement* is the first documentation, is even listed twice. Under the letter *C* we find:

> **I Cadge a garment I set lystes in the lynyng to kepe ỷ plyghtes in order.** Ie metz des lisieres aux plies pour les tenir en ordre.
>
> (III, fo. c.lxxix^v^).

The entry under **I Kadge** has no postlemmatic gloss and is thus not as explicit as the foregoing, but there is an example:

> **I Kadge the plyghtes of a garment/** Ie dresse des plies dune lisiere. **This cote is yll kadged:** Ce sayon a ses plies mal dresses dune lisiere.
>
> (III, fo. cc.lxx^v^)

In the following example we learn that the fabric of a garment is coarsened if it rubs against wool:

> . . . **This rubbynge of your gowne agaynst the wolle wyll make it sture to the syght:** Ce frotter de vostre robbe contre la layne larudyra quant a la veue.
>
> (III, fo. cc.xcvi: **I Make sture**)

We are also informed of what tailors used to do with silk and velvet to prevent 'rivelling' or fraying. They were treated with wax:

> **I Ceare a garmẽt of sylke or veluet as a taylour doth with a ceryng candell/** Iencire. prime cõiuga. **This veluet was nat well ceared/ ⁊ that maketh it to ryuell out:** Ce vellours nestoyt pas bien enciré, et ce la le faict ainsi raueler.
>
> (III, fo. c.lxxxiiii)

According to the *OED*, the verb *to rivel out* (= 'ravel') (see also III, fo. ccc.xlii^v^) is first documented in English with Palsgrave's *Esclarcissement.*

Keeping one's clothes clean was not an easy matter. Coarse linen was subjected to 'bucking', a process which Palsgrave paraphrases as follows:

> **I Bucke lynen clothes to scoure of their fylthe ⁊ make them whyte/** Ie bue. prime cõiuga. and ie fays de la lessiue. **Bucke these shyrtes for they be to foule to be wasshed by hande:** Buez ces chemises, car elles sont trop sallies de les lauer a sauon.
>
> (III, fo. c.lxxviii^v^)

Compare in this respect also the two entries **Bouke of clothes** —*buee* (III, fo. xxi) and **Bucke to wasshe clothes in** —*cvuier* (III, fo. xxii) in the noun list, for which the first record in the *OED* is Palsgrave.

Another treatment was *chalking*:

> **I Chalke/ I marke or whyte a thyng with chalke/** Ie craye. prime. **It is good wearynge of whyte hosen/ for whã they be soyled they may be chalked ouer agayne:** Il fait bon vser de chauces blanches, car quant elles sont sallies on les peult crayer.
>
> (III, fo. c.lxxxiiii$^{v}$)

Despite Palsgrave, the *OED* just records this use of the verb for 1575.

Against moths, a constant threat to precious clothes, a springtime-airing was recommended:

> . . . **It shall be well done to weather your garmentȝ in Marche for feare of mothes:** Il sera bien faict de aerer voz habillemens au moys de Marche de paour de vers.
>
> (III, fo. cccc.vii$^{v}$: **I Wether a thyng**)

A rather humorous example further illustrates a preoccupation with the care of clothing:

> **He hath made my gowne so bare that a lowse can get no holde on it:** Il a si trestant vse ma robbe qua peyne y peult vng pouyl trouuer a quoy se tenir.
>
> (III, fo. cc.lxxxix: **I Make bare**)

What did the poorer people do with frayed clothes to make them last a little longer? They tried to 'list' them:

> . . . **I haue lysted my cote within to make it laste better/ am nat I a good housebande:** Iay bendé mon saion dune lisiere pur le faire plus lon guement durer, ne suis ie pas vng bon mesnaiger.
>
> (III, fo. cc.lxxxiii: **I Lyste a garment**)

Another possibility was to 'pink' them: '*He is outher a landed man or a foole yͭcutteth his garmẽtes*: *Il a des terres ou il est fol qui decouppe ainsy ses habillemens*' (III, fo. cc.iii$^{v}$: **I Cutte or iagge . . .**). See also the entry for **I Iagge or cutte a garment** (III, fo. cc.lxv).

There are other instances where the difference between rich and poor is highlighted. Whereas a rich gentleman would buy a new pair of boots, a poorer man would have to grease them:

> . . . **Whan a poore man greaseth his bootes if he were ryche he wolde bye a payre of newe:** Quant vng poure homme engresse ses houseaulx, sil estoyt riche assez il en aschapteroyt des nouueaulx.
>
> (III, fo. cc.liiii^v: **I Grease with grease**)

How a gown was furred also depended on the wealth of its owner:

> . . . **I wyll furre my gowne with buggye as for martyrs and sabyls be for great estates:** Ie fourreray ma robbe de rommenys, **or** de peaulx de lambardie, car martres et sables sõt fourreures pour gens de grãt estat.
>
> (III, fo. cc.xliii: **I Furre a gowne**)

*Buggye* is modern English *budge* 'a kind of fur, consisting of lamb's skin with the wool dressed outwards' (*OED*).

From clothes to housing, and a good number of examples contrast that of the rich and the poor:

> **I Daube with lome that is tempered with heare or strawe/** Ie placque. prime coniuga. **A wall well daubed wyll last lõge if it be kept drie:** Vne muraille bien placquée durera longuement si on la garde seiche.
>
> (III, fo. cc.iiii^v)

But instead of using lime, plaster, or loam, the poorer people had to be satisfied with clay:

> **I Daube with claye onely/** Iardille. prime coniuga. **I am a poore man. I muste daube my walles for I can make none other shyfte:** Ie suis vng poure homme, il fault que ie ardille mes murailles car ie ne puis aultrement cheuyr.
>
> (III, fo. cc.iiii^v)

*I am a poore man* is also the beginning of the example under **I Thacke a house**:

> . . . **I am but a poore man/ sythe I can nat tyle my house I muste be fayne to thacke it:** Ie ne suis que vng poure hõme, puis q̃ ie ne suis pas riche assez pour couuryr ma mayson de tuylles il fault q̃ ie la couure de chaulme.
>
> (III, fo. ccc.lxxxviii$^{v}$)

Yet at the same time we learn

> . . . **I wyll tyle all the barnes I haue for thacke wyll nat endure:** Ie couureray toutes les granches que iay de tuylles car le chaulme ne dure guayres.
>
> (III, fo. ccc.lxxxxi: **I Tyle a house**)

Having an azure roof is a sign of wealth: '*This roufe is costly/ for it is coloured with azure*: *Ce ciellement est fort coustagieux, car il est fort azuré*' (III, fo. c.xci: **I Colour with azure**).

Broken glass in windows might be repaired by paper: '*Make faste a paper here in ẏͤ wyndowe where ẏͤ glasse wanteth*: *Collez vng papier cy en la fenestre la ou la voyrrine fault*' (III, fo. cc.xc$^{v}$: **I Make faste a thyng**). One could not always afford to use lead in windows: '*I wyll leed no mo wyndowes it is to costely*: *Ie ne plommeray non plus de fenestres il couste trop, or ie ne couureray nõ plus de fenestres de plomb*' (III, fo. cc.lxxvii: **I Leede**).

Lighting was also costly, and good housewives might burn rushes instead of candles:

> **In wynter tyme good housewyues pyll risshes to burne in stede of candels:** En hyuer les bonnes mesnaigieres pillẽt des ioncz pour les brusler en lieu de chandelles.
>
> (III, fo. ccc.xvi$^{v}$: **I Pyll rysshes**)

Oak is said to burn clearer than elm (III, fo. c.lxx: **I Borne as the fyre**).

Houses were cold and cold floors a danger to health. For this reason it is suggested to use floorboards: '*Let your parlour be boorded for the colde grounde is nat holsome*: *Que vostre parloyr soit plãché car la terre nest pas sayne*' (III, fos. c.lxix$^{v}$–c.lxx: **I Boorde ẏͤ flouth**). Boards should not be used before they are dry enough, otherwise they would warp: '*These bordes wyll warpe bycause you occupye them or they be well seasonned*: *Ces ais se debifferõt pour ce que vous les occupes deuant quilz soient bien saisonnez*' (III, fo. cccc.i: **I Warpe as bordes do**).

What the cold and the supply of water will have been like emerges from the example: '*Sette the potte to the fyre to thawe the water*: *Mettez le pot aupres du feu pour fondre leaue*' (III, fo. ccc.lxxxviii$^{v}$: **I Thawe**). See also the example under **I Am frosyn** (III, fo. c.xliiii$^{v}$).

Another good piece of advice given by Palsgrave is that one should not move into a new house until the 'privy' is ready: '*Neuer come to your newe house tyll your seges or priuyes be fermed*: *Ne venez iamays a vostre nouuelle mayson tãt que vous ayez curé les orttrays*' (III, fo. cc.xxxv: **I Ferme a siege**).

How draughty sixteenth-century houses will have been emerges from the following confession under the entry **I Rocke**:

> **. . . I loue nat to lye in his house for if there be any wynde styrryng one shall rocke to ⁊ fro in his bedde:** Ie nayme pas coucher en sa mayson car sil fait aulcun vent on branslera de ca et de la en son lict.
>
> (III, fo. ccc.xliii)

As to some comfort in bed, the warmth and the softness of the mattress obviously depended on its stuffing. The example under **I Flocke** suggests that wool was expensive in the first part of the sixteenth century: '*Flocke your mattres for woll is dere*: *Estouppez vostre matras de bourre car la laine est chiere*' (III, fo. cc.xxxviii). The cost of living is also illustrated under **It is to my pay**, where Palsgrave says: '*I payde twelue pens to day for my dyner whiche was but lytell to my pay*: *Il me cousta douze deniers pour mon disner au iourdhuy ce que ne me vint guayres au gré* (III, fo. cc.lxix$^{v}$).

When guests were expected, rushes were strewn on the floors, a custom still common in the seventeenth century (see Hole 1949*b*: 4): '*Strawe rysshes agaynst his comynge in euery place of my house*: *Semez des ioncz contre sa venue tout par tout a ma mayson*' (III, fo. ccc.lxxviii: **I Strowe rysshes**). To welcome the king, however, floors were covered with carpets: '*Strowe al your chamber with carpettes agaynst the kyng come*: *Tapyssez vostre chambre tout par tout cõtre la venue du roy*' (III, fo. ccc.lxxviii$^{v}$: **I Strowe or laye floures**).

Easter was the time when whitewashing one's house was recommended: '*Whytelyme your hous against this Ester*: *Blanchissez vostre mayson de chaulx, or de plastre cõtre ces pasq̃s*' (III, fo. cccc.viii: **I Whytelyme**). It was not only the time when clothes were aired (see p. 404); it was also a time of scouring: '*Agaynst this Eester I wyll scoure all ẏ vessel in my house*: *Contre ceste Pasque ie veulx escurer toute la vaisselle de ma mayson*' (III, fo. ccc.liii: **I Scoore potte**).

Spring, or more precisely March, is judged to be the best time for setting young plants and grafting (III, fo. cc.liiii: **I Graffe a tree**). Working or relaxing in the garden recurs as a theme. Changes in nature are noted, phases of growth in plants, trees, and flowers are observed. A keen gardener's delight will be the fruit his plants bear. In order to make trees fruitful, Palsgrave recommends digging the area around the roots: '*To make your trees beare dygge them aboute the rootes*: *Pour faire porter voz arbres cerfouissez les*' (III, fo. cc.xi: **I Digge** . . .). '*If the yerthe be well eryed it bringeth forthe moche corne*: *Se la terre est biẽ labourée elle porte beaucoup de grain*' (III, fo. cc.xviii$^{v}$ (= cc.xxviii$^{v}$): **I Erye**). Again, '*Some saye that frutyers put their peeres in horse dunge to make them rype the soner*: *Les aulcuns disent que ces fruyctiers mettent leurs poyres en fiens de cheuaulx pour les ameurir plus tost*' (III, fo. cc.xcv: **I Make rype**).

Of the domestic animals, cats are ignored, while the dog and the horse, the latter as a means of transport, are frequently mentioned in the illustrations. Palsgrave notes the following characteristic of a dog's behaviour:

> . . . **It is the propertye of a dogge to burye his meate in the grounde whan he hath eaten ynoughe:** Cest la proprieté a vng chien denfouyr sa viande quant il en a mangé son soul.
>
> (III, fo. c.lxiii: **I Bery or hyde** . . .)

On hens, Palsgrave's learners are told: '*You maye knowe whan a henne is redye to laye egges/ for she is reed aboute the eyes and the byll*: *Vous pouez congnoistre q̃uãt vne geline est preste de pondre car elle deuient rougeastre au tour des yeulx et du bec*' (III, fo. cc.lxxiiii$^{v}$: **I Laye an egge**).

Some examples relating to birds make one rather wonder about some of Palsgrave's possible personal sports or culinary needs. Thus there is not only a headword entry **I Pull downe byrdes out of their nestes** but the illustration is

> . . . **It is a good sporte to pull down pyes nestes:** Cest vng bon passetemps que de denischer les pies.
>
> (III, fo. ccc.xxv$^{v}$)

Because of the thievish nature attributed to magpies, the manifest satisfaction obtained from this activity might be acceptable. Under the entry **I Fowle after byrdes/** *Ie vas a la pipée* we read in a similar vein:

> ... **It is a good sporte to fowle all day/ but a man may vse it longe or he be wyse:** Cest vng bon passetẽps daller a la pipée tout le iour, mays on le peult longuement vser auant quon deuiengne saige.
>
> (III, fo. cc.xlii)

A third entry is **I Clymme a nest I take the byrdes out of a nest.** Here the example is:

> ... **I haue clymmed twenty nestes to day/ and one dawes nest a mongest them:** Iay desniché vingt nydz doyseaux au iourdhuy, et entre eulx vng nyd de chouettes.
>
> (III, fo. c.lxxxix$^{v}$)

This is partly echoed under **I Clamer or clymme vp vpon a tree,** where the illustration is: '*I haue clamered vp on twenty trees to daye*: *Iay gryppé plus de vingt arbres au iourdhuy*' (III, fo. c.lxxxviii$^{v}$). The numeral *twenty* is here used to refer, not to a specific number, but merely a quantity bigger than what under the circumstances might be taken as a usual norm (see also III, fo. cc.xvii$^{v}$: **I Enter in to**). Further instances where *twenty* is used in this approximative sense occur under the following entries: **I Caste in the tethe** (III, fo. c.lxxxii$^{v}$); **I Deuoure a mayden** (III, fo. cc.x$^{v}$); **I Ensure I make one certayne** (III, fo. cc.xvii); **I Foryet** (III, fo. cc.xli$^{v}$). The use of *twenty* to indicate an indefinite larger number seems to be commoner than that of *hundred*, where the hyperbolical nature is stronger (see **I Forthynke I repente me,** III, fo. cc.xli$^{v}$)).

One may wonder whether the slightly unusual example under **I Salue I grete** is an expression of the overall attitude which Palsgrave showed towards his fellow human beings: '*I loue to salue the people or euer they salue me*: *Iayme bien de saluer les gens auant quilz me saluent*' (III, fo. ccc.xlvi). It reveals a welcoming disposition, an unassuming openness and kindness of character. The choice of *I love* instead of *I like* suggests a personal predilection that goes beyond the religious call of humbleness expected of a man of the Church.

Of the nouns of relationship, *father*, *grandmother*, *mother*, and *brother* occur in examples, the latter being ambiguous because it could also refer to a religious brother:

> ... **I pray the go chere my brother/ he is nowe well amended of his sycknesse:** Ie te prie

va reconforter mon frere, il est mayntenant bien amendé de sa maladie.

(III, fo. c.lxxxvi$^{v}$: **I Chere or I comforte** . . .)

The example needed to illustrate the verb *to bequeath* made Palsgrave say:

**My grant mother byquaythed me
a hundred pounde whan she dyed/
but her executours kepe it from me:**
Ma mere grant me delaissa, or ceda
en son testamẽt cent liures quant elle
mourut, mays les executeurs de elle
le me detiennent.

(III, fo. c.lxi)

The first clause would have been enough to show the use of *to bequeath*. One may wonder whether the antithetic clause has a personal background.

It has already been pointed out in Chapter I that some of the examples referring to 'my father' may have had foundations in Palsgrave's life. Under the entry **I Sekyn I waxe sycke** we learn '*My father syckened first vpon saynte Bartylmewes euyn*' (III, fo. ccc.liiii), and under **I Lette my lyfe** the death of a father is reported: '*My father let his lyfe vpon saynte Bartylmewes euyn*' (III, fo. cc.lxxix$^{r-v}$). The repetition of the same time of day is rather striking. There are two further instances that mention the death of the father. The verb *to resume* prompted him to the example sentence

**. . . I wyll resume
in to my handes agayne all the gyf-
tes that my father gaue two yere a
fore he dyed/** Ie resumeray entre mes
mayns tous les octroys que mon pere
fit deux ans auant quil mourut.

(III, fo. ccc.xl$^{v}$)

A will made by a father is mentioned under the verb *to register*: '*My fathers wyll is regystred in ẏ bysshops courte*: *Le testament de mon pere est registré, or enregistre en la court de lesglise, or de lesuesque*' (III, fo. ccc.xxxv$^{v}$). For a will to be registered in the bishop's court, the deceased must presumably have had a certain social position. There are two entries in which the reference to 'my father' is accompanied by a professional noun. Interestingly, in both the grammatical tense used is the past tense:

**. . . My father was chefe car-
uer with kyng Henry the seuenth:**

**. . . Am
nat I a great gentylman my father**

Mon pere estoyt premier escuyer tren chant au roy Henry septiesme.

(III, fo. c.lxxxii: **I Carue**)

**was a hosyer and my mother dyd heckell flaxe:** Ne suis ie pas vng grãt seignieur, mon pere estoyt vng chaussetyer et ma mere habilloyt du lyn, or cerancoyt du lyn.

(III, fo. cc.lx$^{v}$: **I Heckell flaxe**)

For the mother, we do not only have the above past-tense reference; there is another example with a present tense: '*And you wyll speake with my mother she spynneth nowe at home*: *Si vous voulez parler a ma mere elle fille mayntenant a la mayson*' (III, fo. ccc.lxix: **I Spynne threde**). The illustrative examples referring to 'my father' and 'my mother' thus reveal an internal consistency; the father is dead, the mother still alive, and this increases the likelihood of a personal link. For further instances one might consult the entries **I Cõmende me** (III, fo. c.xci$^{v}$), **I Make cockes of haye** (III, fo. cc.xc), **I Receyue** (III, fo. ccc.xxxiiii), **I Stryke ones heed** (III, fo. ccc.lxxvii), **I Thresshe** (III, fo. ccc.lxxxix).

The Christian command that one should honour one's parents is stressed in the examples (e.g. III, fo. c.lxxxvii: **I Cherysshe**), and its non-observation is taken as predicting bad relations with one's master: '*If thou contemne thy father and mother it is a shreude signe that thou wylte obey thy master*: *Si tu cõtempnes tes parens, or pere et mere, cest mauluays signe q̃ tu veulx obeyr a ton maistre*' (III, fo. c.xcvi: **I Contemne**).

There is the possibility that Palsgrave may have adopted a little boy. We do not only have a verb entry for the process of adoption, we also have a very interesting illustration:

> **I Make of a frenned chylde my sonne by ẏ lawe/** Ie adopte. pri. cõiu. **I had neuer no wyfe nor chylde but I haue made this lytell boye my sonne by ẏ lawe whiche is nothyng a kyn to me:** Ie neus iamays ne fẽme ne enfant, mays iay adopté ce petit garcon qui ne mest riens . . .
>
> (III, fo. cc.xciiii)

The entry in the *OED* for the adjective **frenne, fren** explains the item as a 'corrupt form of *frend*, FREMD, influenced by etymologizing association with *forenne*, FOREIGN', and gives as its meaning 'strange, not related'. Not only does the form appear in *Lesclarcissement* with a final *d*. The entry also predates the only citation quoted in the *OED*.

As we have already seen from various quotations given, the attitude shown towards children is gentle and caring, with the occasional stricter tone of moral education. The recurrence of expressions in the examples promising rewards may have its origin in a grown-up's playful talk to children. The first type of these expressions contains a request and the granting of a reward if the request is fulfilled. The typical reward promised is a fig, the sixteenth-century equivalent of a sweet, or a coin:

. . . **Halse me aboute the necke my sonne and thou shalte haue a fygge:** Acollez moy mon filz et tu auras vne figue.

(III, fo. cc.lvii: **I Halse one**, cf. also III, fo. cc.lxxiii: **I Knele vpon bothe the knees**; fo. cc.xc: **I Make courtesye**)

. . . **Come double this same and I shall gyue the a grote:** Viens doubler cecy et ie te donneray vng gros.

(III, fo. cc.xviii: **I Double**)

The other type of expression is trifling bets, challenging a fact or truth, inviting participation to watch the speaker perform some 'deed' or to compete in an activity. The wager offered ranges from a penny to a groat to a noble; in one instance it even goes up as far as twenty nobles. Examples are:

. . . **I holde the a peny that I hurle this stone ouer yonder house:** Ie gaige a toy vng denier q̃ ie iecteray ceste pierre oultre ceste maison la.

(III, fo. cc.lxiiii[v]: **I Horle**)

. . . **Take as swyfte a geldynge as thou canste fynde/ ⁊ I holde the twenty nobles I out ryde the.** Prẽs aussi viste hõgre que tu peulx trouver et ie gaige a toy vingt angelotz que ie te surpasseray en cheuaulchant.

(III, fo. ccc.xi[v]: **I Out ryde**)

In another example the expression *twenty to one* occurs:

**And you sette hym at large nowe twẽty to one he is ondone for euer:** Si vous leffrenes, **or** si vous le mettez au large mayntenãt vingt contre vng il est gasté.

(III, fo. ccc.lvi[v]: **I Set at large**)

The *OED* misses this Palsgrave instance and credits Shakespeare (1591) with the first use of the phrase.

Verbal bragging and physical beating seem to have been quite common in sixteenth-century English daily life, to judge from Palsgrave's examples. Thus someone may be 'lulled' about the ears until they crack (III, fo. cc.lxxxiiii: **I Lolle one**). The example is the *OED*'s first record of the verb *to lull* in the sense of pulling someone's ears. The verb *to maul* is illustrated by '*If he mall you on the heed I wyll nat gyue a peny for your lyfe*: *Sil vous maille sur la teste ie ne donneray pas* *vng denier pour vostre vie*' (III, fo. cc.xcviii). Accidental injury is also graphically described: '*I knocked my heed agaynst the poste that the fyre starte out of myn eyes*: *Ie aheurtay de ma teste, or ie me heurtay la teste si fort cõtre le poste que le feu me sortissoyt des yeulx*' (III, fo. cc.lxxiii^v). Equally striking is the example accompanying the gnashing of teeth: '*He gnast with the tethe that a man myght haue herde him a stones caste*: *Il grynsoyt les dens de sorte quon leust bien ouy dung iect de pierre loing, or il grinchoyt les dẽs*' (III, fo. cc.l).

Physical appearance was important in social relations, to judge from Palsgrave's examples. A good number of Palsgrave's examples tell us what was the expected behaviour in certain interpersonal situations. Failure to meet the social expectations was regarded as shameful. One's outer appearance, for instance, was to be guided by cleanliness ('*Kepe thy selfe clenly for shame*: *Garde toy or tiens toy honnestement tu doybs auoyr honté*' (III, fo. cc.lxxi^v: **I Kepe I mayntayne**)) and orderliness in the wearing of one's clothes ('*Garter thy hose/ it is a shame to se the go so*: *Lye ta chause, or lye ton gertier, cest honte de te veoyr aller aynsi*' (III, fo. cc.xliiii: **I Garter**)).

Palsgrave seems to have had an eye for hair, because various examples describe a reaction produced by a well-kempt or a negligent hair style. Lack of combing ('*Combe thy heed for shame*: *Pigne ta teste, tu doys auoyr honte*' (III, fo. c.xci) and long, disorderly hair gave rise to reprimands:

. . . **Brayde your heare vp/ and let it nat hange downe aboute your eares:** Tortillez voz cheueulx, et ne les laissez pas pendre entour de voz oreilles.

(III, fo. c.lxxviii: **I Broyde heare**)

. . . **Shede your heare that hangeth so yuell fauouredly aboute your eares:** Desmesles voz cheueulx, **or** separez voz cheueulx qui vous pendent si mal a poynt autour de voz oreilles.

(III, fo. lx^v: **I Shede I departe**)

Well-maintained hair, on the other hand, prompted him to express his pleasure and delight in such admiring words as 'gorgeously', 'goodly', and a 'good sight':

. . . **your heare cryspeth gorgyously after this washyng:** Voz cheueulx se crespellẽt gor giasement apres ce lauemẽt, **or** apres que vous les, auez bien lauez.

(III, fo. cc.^v)

. . . **you are goodly coyfed this mornynge/ can you make your selfe redy so well?** Vous estes bellemẽt coyffée ceste matinée, scauez vo⁹ si bien habiller vous mesmes?

(III, fo. c.xc^v: **I Coyfe**)

Palsgrave's use of the verb *to not* 'to clip or cut short' is the first record in the *OED* ('*I haue notted my heed nowe that sõmer is come*: *Iay tousé ma teste mayntenant que lesté est venu*' (III, fo. ccc.vii^{r–v})). An echo of this example is the one under the verb *to poll* (*I shaue ẏ heares of ones heed*):

> . . . **I holde best to polle my heed nowe agaynste this sõmer that cometh in:** Ie pence quil sera pour le mieulx de raire ma teste contre ceste esté qui vient.
>
> (III, fo. ccc.xx)

One's walk should be upright:

> . . . **Fye for shame you go forwarde lyke one ẏ were broke backed:** Fy de hõte vous allez en cambrãt comme se ce fut vng qui eust les rayns rompus.
>
> (III, fo. cc.liii: **I Go stoupyng forwarde**)

Graceful carriage should be observed in dancing:

> . . . **Are you nat a shamed to skyppe thus in your daunsynge lyke a gyrle of the countray:** Nauez vous poynt de hõte de sauteller en ce poynt en dancant comme vne garce du pays.
>
> (III, fo. ccc.lxii$^{v}$: **I Skyppe as one dothe** . . .)

Calling upon people in their houses without being invited was regarded as improper:

> **I Come to a mans place on loked for/ on bydden/ on welcome/ as a ma lapert felowe dothe/** Iaccoquine. pri me cõiu. **If you vse to come to mennes houses on this facyon vnbydden/ other men wyll call you a bolde begger or a dysour.** Si vous vous acoustumez daynsi accocquiner, les gẽs vous tiendront pour vng belistre deshonté, or pour vng diseur.
>
> (III, fo. cc.ii)

Searching people's things in their absence is frowned upon: '*Me thynketh it is no good maners to serche ones cofer whan he is out of the waye*: *Il mest aduis q̃ cest contre bonnes meurs de fouiller en le coffre daultruy quant il est hors de voye*' (III, fo. ccc.lv: **I Serche a cofer**).

Many of the illustrations deal with behaviour at table. Someone who has just cleaned the privy, for instance, is asked to wash his hands before he eats: '*Thou shalte eate no buttered fysshe with me tyll thou wasshe thy handes/ for thou hast fowed a gonge late*: *Tu ne mangeras poynt de poysson beuré auecques moy tant que tu auras laué tes mayns, car tu as curé vng retrayt naguayres*' (III, fos. cc.xli$^{v}$–cc.xlii: **I Fowe a gonge**). Care should be taken not to spill one's soup and stain the tablecloth (III, fo. ccc.xlix: **I Shede**), nor should butter be spread with the thumb (III, fo. ccc.xviii$^{v}$: **I Platte with claye**). Greedy gobbling was reproved (see the entries **I Cramme meat** (III, fo. c.xcix$^{v}$), **I Manche** (III, fo. cc.xcviii)). Gnawing one's meat was regarded as reprehensible (see **I Gnawe as a dogge** (III, fo. cc.l$^{v}$)) and so was belching (see **I Rowte** (III, fo. ccc.xliiii$^{v}$)). And Palsgrave considered it '*a great shame for a mã to eate so moche y$^{t}$ he muste be compelled to caste his gorge*: *Cest grant honte a vng homme de tant manger que luy soyt force de vomyr, or de gomyr*' (III, fo. c.lxxxiii: **I Cast my gorge**).

Interrupting another person's talk was deemed discourteous:

> **. . . It is no good maner**
> **to take the worde out of my mouthe**
> **or I haue made an ende of my tale:**
> Ce nest pas bonne maniere de prendre
> la parolle hors de ma bouche auant
> que ie aye paracheué mon compte.
>
> (III, fo. ccc.lxxxvi: **I Take the worde . . .**)

In view of the undisputed importance of good manners in high society, it does not come as a surprise that *Lesclarcissement* includes a lemma entry for the verb *to bring up in manners/moriginer*. The illustration in the entry provides us with an insight into how young girls were taught manners:

> **. . . Some folkes**
> **sende their doughters to nõneryes**
> **to be well brought vp in maners:**
> Aulcunes gẽs enuoyẽt leur filles aux
> maysons des religieuses pour y estre
> bien moriginées.
>
> (III, fo. c.lxxvii$^{v}$)

We might expect that the example sentences called up by a man of the Church and a teacher would centre on bringing up boys and girls in the prevailing virtues of the time. This is indeed the case. The verb entries for **I Bolden** and **I Enbolden** prompted Palsgrave to similar statements, both beginning with an expression of opinion 'it is good . . .':

> **. . . It is**
> **good to bolden a boye in his youth/**
> **and to acustome a gyrle to be shame**

> **faste:** Il fayt bon danimer, or dẽhardyr vng garcon en sa ieunesse, et daccoustumer vne garce destre vergongneuse.
>
> (III, fo. c.lxix$^{v}$: **I Bolden**)

He draws attention to the ease with which young people may be incited to evil (III, fo. cc.lxvii$^{v}$: **I Intyse**) and condemns enticing young girls to vice (III, fo. cc.xvi: **I Entyce**). Dangers on the way of a virtuous life are, for both sexes, getting used to drinking wine (III, fo. c.lxxvi: **I Bringe one in vse**), and, for young girls, repeated exposure to shameless talk:

> . . . **Often speakyng of rybauldrye wyll make a yonge wenche shamelesse or paste shame anone:** Souuent parler de paillardise desuergondera vne ieune fille bien tost.
>
> (III, fo. cc.xciiii: **I Make one shamelesse**)

A recurrent theme is the influence on us of the company we keep. '*He ẏ haunteth honest mennes companye shall haue honestye of it . . .*' (III, fo. cc.lx: **I Haunte I resorte**), and a valiant captain will make his soldiers brave (III, fo. cc.xci$^{v}$: **I Make hardy**). Vile conditions or vile company are said to make a man vile (III, fo. cc.xcii: **I Make knauysshe**; fo. cc.xcvii$^{v}$: **I Make vyle**; fo. cccc.iiii: **I Waxe knauysshe**). Should things go too far:

> . . . **A woman can defende her selfe no better than to scratche and byte:** Vne femme ne se peult mieulx defendre que de gratigner et mordre.
>
> (III, fo. c.lxvi$^{v}$: **I Byte as a man**)

Company, on the other hand, is part of our pastime, and we might therefore next look at some sports and games in the illustrations under the verbs. Games are also listed under the nouns, and bringing together all the entries relating to them would make an interesting study in sixteenth-century lexicology. Suffice it here to point out that among the nouns there are some which, according to the *OED*, are first recorded in Palsgrave's *Lesclarcissement*: *rebound*, *somersault*, and *titter-totter*.

When discussing illustrations that relate to health, we found that Palsgrave regarded walking as a good exercise. He seems to have done quite a bit of it, and not only the daily walk. Unter the entry for *to avow*, for instance, we learn '*I haue auowed my pylgrymage vnto our lady of Walsynhã: Iay aduoué mon pelerinaige a nostre dame de vvalsingham*' (III, fo. c.lvi) (see also the example **I Offer my offryng** (III, fo. ccc.viii)). At a later place in the verb list we have an example suggesting that he carried out his promise and actually went to the famous Norfolk priory:

> **This iournaye to Walsyngham a foote hath made my legg3 so starke that I can nat styrre me:** Ceste iournée a pied a nostre dame de vvalsingham ma tant arroydy les iambes que ie ne me puis poynt contourner.
>
> (III, fo. cc.xcvi: **I Make stronge**)

The second-person pronoun in the example '*And you exercyse your body you shall waxe nymble: Si vous exercitez vostre corps vous vous assouplirez*' (III, fo. cccc.iiii$^{v}$: **I Waxe nymble**) appears to tell us that this was advice given to others, not necessarily practised by himself. This may also hold for the following case, which uses not the first-person pronoun but the general generic 'a man':

> . . . **A man shall neuer swym well except he lerne it in his youthe:** On ne nagera iamays biẽ si on ne lapprent en sa ieunesse.
>
> (III, fo. ccc.lxxxi$^{v}$: **I Swymme in ẏ water**)

The difficulty of learning to swim also emerges from the passage in Elyot's *Book named the governor* in the chapter on 'Exercises/ wherby shulde growe both recreation and profite': 'There is an exercise/ whiche is right profitable in extreme daunger of warres/ but by cause there semeth to be some perile in the lernynge therof: And also it hath nat bene of lõge tyme moche vsed/ specially amõge noble men: ꝑchance some reders wyll litle esteme it: I meane swymmynge' (Alston 1970*d*: fo. 64$^{v}$).

Though Thomas Elyot (1531) says it is 'seldom vsed' (Alston 1970*d*: fo. 99), tennis seems to dominate among Palsgrave's references to pastimes, and the game was certainly very popular with Henry VII and Henry VIII (cf. Strutt 1855: 93-4; Hole 1949*a*: 43). We learn that it was played not only by two players but also as doubles:

> **I Stoppe on ones syde as one ẏ is a stoppar in a tenes play or at the foote ball/** Ie garde. **I wyll stoppe on your syde:** Ie garderay de vostre costé.
>
> (III, fo. ccc.lxxv)

If you wanted your partner to watch for the ball you shouted: '*Stoppe there at ỹ tenys. Gardez la!* (III, fo. ccc.lxxv: **I Stoppe a hoole**). But two examples seem to suggest that tennis was not Palsgrave's favourite sport:

> . . . **I had as leue tosse a ball here alone as to play at ỹ tenys ouer ỹ corde with the:** Ie aymeroye aussi chier ballouetter [*sic*] icy a par moy que de iouer au tripot auecques toy.
>
> (III, fo. ccc.lxxxxii^v: **I Tosse a ball**)

Huguet in his dictionary lists the French verb as *ballonetter* and quotes Palsgrave as the only evidence. Whereas the lack of enthusiasm in the above example might have been caused by the imagined partner, the following example suggests that the game was too fast for Palsgrave's liking:

> **I Playe at ỹ tenys with a ball/** Ie ioue a la paulme. **I loue nat to playe at the tenys it chaffeth me to sore:** Ie nayme pas a iouer a la paulme car il me eschauffe trop.
>
> (III, fo. ccc.xvii^v)

The strong physical fitness required in the game of tennis prompted Thomas Elyot (1531) to regard it as more appropriate for the younger generation:

> Tenese . . . is a good exercise for yonge men/ but it is more violent than shoting: by reason that two men do play. wherfore neither of them is at his owne libertie to measure the exercise. For if the one stryke the balle harde/ the other that intendeth to receyue him/ is than constrained to vse semblable violence/ if he wyll retourne the balle from whens it came to him. If it trille fast on the groũde/ ⁊ he entendeth to stoppe: or if it rebounde a great distaunce from hym/ and he wolde eftesones retourne it: he can nat than kepe any measure in swiftnesse of mocion. (Alston 1970*d*: fo. 99)

Next we have bowling. Palsgrave differentiates between bowling as a game and bowling as throwing a bowl (cf. the entries **I Bowle I throwe a boule** and **I Bowle I play at the boules** (III, fo. c.lxxi)). For the former the French translation equivalent is *jouer aux boules*, for the latter it is *bouler*, for which Godefroy has a quotation from 1507 whereas Huguet cites Palsgrave's example. The illustration under the game, again, expresses in the form of the first-person pronoun a preference for one sport rather than another:

> . . . **I had leuer boule than shote:** Iayme plus chier iouer aux boulles que tirer de larc.
>
> (III, fo. c.lxxi)

From another instance we learn part of the game itself. There is one bowl that is first thrown to serve as a mark and aim for the players. For this Palsgrave uses *mayster boule*: '*Who shall caste the mayster boule*: *Qui boullera, or qui iectera la maistresse boulle*' (III, fo. c.lxxxiii: **I Cast or throwe a boule**). *Maistresse boulle* could be a translation of the English phrase, but equally well the English phrase could be a rendering of the French expression for the modern French term *cochonnet*, which, according to Godefroy and the *Trésor de la langue française*, is first documented in Rabelais's *Gargantua* (1534, slightly later than *Lesclarcissement*). *Master bowl* for the jack in bowling is first recorded by Palsgrave (*OED* **master sb**[1] . . . **9**.). The present-day term for this piece is *jack* in English. The *OED* has a quotation from Shakespeare as the first record of this sense of the noun *jack*.

Another game played is quoiting. The English verb *to quoit* is first recorded in the *Promptorium parvulorum* (1440) and Palsgrave's example sentence suggests that quoiting was for grown-ups: '*Let vs leaue all boyes games ⁊ go coyte a whyle*: *Laissons tous ieux de petitz garcons et iouons au palet vng peu*' (III, fo. c.xc[v]: **I Coyte**). The *Trésor de la langue française* credits Rabelais with the first record of the verb phrase *jouer au palet*, but in fact Palsgrave is earlier. The use of the verbal noun *quoiting* in combination, as in *quoiting stone*, is also first recorded in *Lesclarcissement*.

Elyot rather frowned on noblemen quoiting, and actually regarded bowling as liable to cause injury. For Elyot, all these pastimes were inferior to the double utility of shooting, and in his description of sports Elyot at the same time explains why noblemen should not play football:

> why shulde nat boulynge/ claisshe/ pynnes/ and koytyng: be as moche cõmended? Verily as for two the laste/ be to be vtterly abiected of al noble men/ in like wise foote balle/ wherin is nothinge but beastly furie/ and extreme violence: wherof procedeth hurte/ and consequently rancour and malice do remaine with them that be woũded. wherfore it is to be put in perpetuall silence.
>
> In classhe is emploied to litle strength: in boulyng often times to moche. wherby the sinewes be to moche strayned/ ⁊ the vaines to moche chafed, wherof often tymes is sene to ensue ache/ or the decreas of strẽgth or agilitie in the armes. where/ in shotyng/ if the shooter vse the strength of his bowe within his owne tiller/ he shal neuer be ther with grieued or made more feble. (Alston 1970*d*: fo. 99[v])

According to the *OED*, Palsgrave is also the first to use *to dart* in the sense of 'to throw a dart'. He gives two French equivalents *dardoyer* and *darder*, and, as we have seen, regards the Irish as specially skilled:

> . . . **These yrisshe men darte**
> **best or throwe a dart best of all mẽ:**

> Ces yroys, **or** ces yrlandoys dardent
> mieulx que nulz aultres.
>
> (III, fo. cc.iiii)

The game of faring is not illustrated by an example. '*I Fare I playe at a game so named at the dyse*: *Ie ioue aux dez*' (III, fo. cc.xxxiii). We do not know what game of dice this was. The noun *fare* as used by Palsgrave is the only record of the game in the *OED*, and the verb has one other sixteenth-century quotation after Palsgrave's instance.

Palsgrave illustrates the verb *to stake* with the example '*I wyll nat play except euery man stake*: *Ie ne ioueray poynt si chascun ny boute*' (III, fo. ccc.lxxi$^{v}$). Again, the first documentation of the intransitive use is from *Lesclarcissement*, and as the source of the corresponding noun, the *OED* quotes Palsgrave's later work, his translation of *Acolastus* (1540). The French equivalent is *bouter*. The *Trésor de la langue française* refers to Palsgrave's use of *bouter* only in the sense of 'to shoot, to sprout'.

Another pastime was casting or drawing lots. Palsgrave clearly distinguishes between its practice as a form of arbitration and as a game. For the former he adduces the English idioms *to cast lots*, *to draw lots*, or *to draw cuts*, which are rendered by French *sortir* and *iecter du sort*. For the game, the phrases used are the same as those for the arbitration sense, but in addition we have *to play at the lots* or *to cast at the lots*. What is common to all the expressions is the plural form in English. The French equivalent in all the game instances is *jouer au court festu*. The examples provided are direct invitations to a game and thus reflect the spoken idiom of the time: '*Here be fayre longe russhes/ let vs play or caste at ẏ lottes*: *Voycy de beaux iouncx et longz iouons au court festu*' (III, fo. c.lxxxiii: **I Caste lottes**) and '*Let vs drawe cuttes*: *Iouons au court festu*' (III, fo. cc.xix: **I Drawe lottes**). The expression *iouer au court festu* is mentioned neither by Godefroy nor by Tobler-Lommatzsch, though both list the phrase *tirer au festu*. Since the modern idiom includes the modifying adjective, *tirer à la courte paille*, one may wonder whether the form given by Palsgrave (*jouer*) *au court festu* represents an intermediate stage.

Instances relating to the game of chess are more numerous under the noun list. The interest of the illustration under the verb entry for *to mate* 'to checkmate' lies in the mention of the moves in the game, which are not included among the lemma entries for the verb *to draw*:

> . . . **He mated me or I coulde drawe thre draughtes:** Il me matta auant que ie peusse tirer troys foys.
>
> (III, fo. cc.xcix)

According to Palsgrave, the sport of jousting was beginning to be less practised during his time: '*The iustes begynne to weare out a pace nowe*: *Les ioustes se cõmencent fort a faillir mayntenant*' (III, fo. cccc.vii$^v$: **I Weare out as a terme** . . .). Some of the instances referring to hunting address one of the educational debates of the time, the conflict between studying and going on a hunt. Thus the first example under *to hunt* reads:

> . . . **I wyll go to scole/ I do no good here but hunte and hauke all day:** Ie yray a lescolle ie ne fays riẽ icy que chasser et voller toute iour . . .
>
> (III, fo. cc.lxv)

Given the choice between the two activities, learning is clearly regarded as the more valuable pastime. In the following example the assumed effect of hunting on studying is described and we are well reminded of Palsgrave's unhappy experience as the tutor to the duke of Richmond when some of the latter's attendants were more intent on distracting him from learning than on encouraging him:

> **It is a payne to lerne thynges/ but a man may unlerne by goyng a hun tyng:** Cest vne payne que daprendre, mays on peult desaprendre en allant a la chasse.
>
> (III, fo. ccc.lxxxviii$^v$: **I Unlerne**)

The *OED* quotes this example as the first instance in which the verb *to unlearn* is used in an absolute construction.

References to conjuring tricks and jugglery are also common. The example under **I Iogyll** appears to suggest that there was a certain Matthew whose juggling skills were highly regarded in Palsgrave's time. There are two verb entries. In the one, **I Play a caste of legyer demayne,** the French equivalent is *jouer un tour de passe passe* (III, fo. ccc.xvii$^v$). According to Godefroy, Palsgrave's entry is the first use of the noun *passe passe.* Under the entry **I Iogyll** the French equivalent is *jouer de pas pas.* The *Trésor de la langue française* gives an instance of 1420 that precedes Palsgrave's use.

Finally, a pastime enjoyed by children. In its French form, according to the *Trésor de la langue française,* it is first recorded in *Lesclarcissement*:

> **I holde ẏ a peny that I wyll tryll my whirlygyg longer about than thou shalte do thyne:** Ie gaige a toy vng

denier que ie pirouetteray de ma pirouette plus longuement que tu ne feras de la tienne

(III, fo. ccc.lxxxxiiii: **I Tryll a whirlygyg**)

Not surprisingly, numerous verb entries could be regarded as relating to Palsgrave's professional life. We might also expect that the scholar, the schoolmaster, and the man of the Church to come through in the verb illustrations. They do, but they are far from being a dominant theme. The interesting fact about Palsgrave's example sentences in the verb list is that they cover a whole range of fields without one being more strikingly prominent than the others. We have already mentioned that several examples express annoyance at books having been interfered with. Others draw attention to omissions in the writings of letters. Dates and addresses should not be forgotten. Still others deal with the drafting, dictating, and copying of letters or pieces of writing, with the compiling and printing of books, as well as their exposition.

School life, teaching practice, and educational standards become alive in the following selection of illustrations. Discipline in the classroom seems to have been a problem. The verb entry for *to make a noise* prompted Palsgrave to the example:

> . . . **They make so great a noyse in ẏ scoole that one can nat here a nother:** Ilz maynent, or menent si grant bruyt, or si grant noyse a lescolle que lung ne peult poynt ouyr laultre.
>
> (III, fo. cc.lxxxvii$^{v}$)

Under the verb entry **I Excercyse or vse tyrannye**, the example shows how a teacher should not behave:

> . . . **This skole mayster is a foole/ he exercyseth tyranny amongest a meynye of poore innocētes:** Ce maistre descolle est vng fol, car il tyrannyse entre vng tas de poures innocens.
>
> (III, fo. cc.xxx)

In the following fuller examples, we hear the voices of pupil and teacher:

> . . . **This auctour was so darke that I coulde nat vnderstande one worde in hym/ but my mayster hath made hym so clere ẏ I vnderstande**

> . . . **Now haue I shewed you in a generaltie the contentes of the chapiter/ but to set forthe the partyculers reguyreth a further layser:**

**hym parfytely:** Cest aucteur estoyt si tres obscur que ie ne pouoye entendre vng seul mot en luy, mais mon maistre la si tresbien delucidé que ie lentens asteure parfaictement.

(III, fo. cc.xxxxix$^{v}$)

Or vous ay ie compté en somme le contenu de ce chapitre, mays pour le singulariser demãdez vng plus grant loysyr.

(III, fo. ccc.lvii$^{v}$: **I Set forthe the qualyties**)

Spelling, reading, and writing were the achievements that one was to acquire at school. The following example suggests the progress expected in spelling:

> **He hath bene at scole thys halfe yere and yet he can nat spell his pater no ster:** Il a esté a lescolle vng demy an et encore ne peult il espeller sa pate-nostre.
>
> (III, fo. ccc.lxviii$^{v}$: **I Spell**)

Once you could spell, you had to combine the letters to read words. Palsgrave's verb entry for *to put together* in this sense is the first evidence in the *OED* (**put** *v.*[1], . . . 54. **put together** . . ., d.). His example is:

> . . . **He can spell but he can nat put to gyther:** Il scait espeller, mays il ne peult pas rassembler.
>
> (III, fo. ccc.xxx$^{v}$)

In order to further listeners' understanding, a true professional made adequate pauses in reading aloud, as we learn from the example under **I Poynte in redyng**:

> . . . **I Parceyue by his re-dyng that he is no clerke for he can nat poynte:** Ie voys bien a son lire quil nest pas clerc, car il ne scayt pas punctuer, or poynter.
>
> (III, fo. ccc.xix$^{v}$)

One of Palsgrave's verb illustrations tells us of the existence of writing-schools and indeed the first evidence in the *OED* for such institutions comes from *Lesclarcissement*. When Palsgrave was looking for an exemplification of the verb lemma **I Appayre or waxe worse**, the remet was:

> . . . **He goeth to the writyng scole/ but his hande appay reth euery daye:** Il va a lescole pour escripre, mays sa lettre sempire tous les iours.
>
> (III, fo. c.xlix$^{v}$)

Several illustrations specify the preparation of parchment or paper before one could write on them. In one case, we have a verb lemma which, according to the *OED*, is unique to Palsgrave:

> **you muste slecke your paper if you wyll write greke well:** Il vous fault faire vostre papier glissãt si vous vou lez bien escripre le grec.
>
> (III, fo. ccc.lxiii: **I Slecke**)

The practice of learning by rote is also described:

> **By that tyme that I haue repeted my lesson halfe a dosen tymes vpon the booke I haue it without booke:** Mays que iaye repete ma lecon vne demy douzayne de foys sur le liure ie lay par cueur.
>
> (III, fo. ccc.xxxviii$^{v}$: **I Repete**)

The scholarly aspirations were obviously learning and knowledge. Palsgrave highlights their merit and moral rewards:

> . . . **Connyng and vertue shall make the more noble than all the rychesse in the worlde:** Siẽce et vertu tanobliront plus, **or** tennobliront plus que toutes les richesses du monde.
>
> (III, fo. cc.xciii$^{v}$: **I Make noble**)

But he also draws attention to the moral dangers they may hold:

> **Connynge inflateth excepte a man haue grace with all:** Science enflese on na pas de grace aussi.
>
> (III, fos. cc.lxvi$^{v}$–cc.lxvii)

He seems to speak from experience when he describes the long way to learning as hard: '*Connyng is a great treasure/ but it is harde to come by*: *Cest vng grant tresor que de science*, *mays cest forte chose que de y paruenir*, *or yattayndre*' (III, fo. cc.i$^{v}$: **I Come by**).

Let us now turn to the names of people, writers, and places mentioned in the examples and the philosophical or scientific views expressed, and reconstruct some of the historical, geographical, and philosophical parameters of knowledge that made up his world.

What emerges very clearly from the examples is that the world of his examples centres on personal life experience, very much along the lines of his own professional activities, as we were able to retrace them in Chapter 1. The centre of this life, in a world where the '*ayer gothe rounde aboute the erthe and the water*' (III, fo. cc.liii) and where the '*power of yͤ sterres worketh secretly vpon vs*' (III, fo. cccc.x$^{v}$; see also the reference to Saturn in **I Applye** (III, fo. c.li)) is the place where he lives: London. No other place is mentioned as often as London.

All routes of trade lead to London in general. Yet we are also taken to specific places in the capital and we learn about the customs held dear or practised at his time. A man of the Church would wait for and meet someone in St Paul's (III, fo. cc.liii$^{v}$: **I Go vp and downe**), a place where events and news were publicly proclaimed: '*It is shewed openly at polles crosse*: *On la denoncé a la croyx saint de pol*' (III, fo. ccc.l). On our walk through London we pass St Magnus and St Martin's and hear the chiming of their bells (III, fo. c.lxxxvii$^{r-v}$). There are other brothers in the spirit, the White Friars (III, fo. c.lxxix: **I Burye**) and the Augustine Friars (III, fo. ccc.lii$^{v}$: **I Shriue me**), and there is the Guild of St Anthony's (III, fo. c.lix$^{r-v}$) in need of money (**I Begge for a churche**).

One place that appears to have made a more lasting impression on Palsgrave is London Bridge and the sound of the river there. The verb entries **I Make a noyse as yͤ water dothe that hath a great fall** (III, fo. cc.lxxxviii) and **I Roore as water dothe yͭ hath a fall** (III, fo. ccc.xliii$^{v}$) both made him call up London Bridge:

> . . . **The water at the lowe ebbe maketh suche a noyse at London bridge yͭ one can scarce here an other speke:** Ouãt leaue est presques tout aualée elle bruyt si fort soubz le pont de Londres qua peyne peult on ouyr lung laultre parler.
>
> (III, fo. cc.lxxxviii)

> **Harke howe yͤ water roreth at London bridge nowe:** Escoustez cõment leaue bruyt au pont de Lõdres mayntenant.
>
> (III, fo. ccc.xliii$^{v}$)

We learn about Charing Cross (III, fo. c.lxxi: **I Bowe**) and the 'Crosse in Cheape' (III, fo. ccc.lxxxvi$^{r-v}$: **I Take vp my horse**) and we are told which specific crafts and trades are plied where. The Tower of London is the place where money is coined (III, fo. c.xc$^{v}$: **I Coyne money**), at Tower Hill decapitation takes place (III, fo. cc.lx$^{v}$: **I Hedde a man**), those who curry leather live near the London Wall (III, fo. cc.ii$^{v}$ + cc.iii), and council is heard at Westminster (III, fo. c.lxxix$^{v}$: **I Call vpon a man**). Westminster could be approached by boat, rowing being one of the recreations of the time: '*I wyll out rowe the or thou cõe to westminster for. xii. d*' (III, fo. ccc.xi$^{v}$). Two places of royal residence, Greenwich and Richmond, are mentioned. The impression made by Greenwich on an observer is '[a]*ll the foreparte of Grenewiche is couered with blewe sclate*' (III, fo. ccc.lii$^{v}$: **I**

**Sclate a house**) and the location of Richmond has Palsgrave's admiration: '*Rychemonte is very well set in my mynde*' (III, fo. ccc.lvi$^{v}$: **I Sette as a place**).

After London the next most prominent place is Dover, from which he started his journeys to the Low Countries and France (III, fo. c.xlviii$^{v}$; c.lxx$^{v}$: **I Bowe or leane**; cc.ii$^{v}$; cc.lxxvii$^{v}$: **I Ley at anker**; ccc.xxi: **I Poursewe**; ccc.lxxxiiii: **I Take landyng**). After that comes York, where he was in the service of the duke of Richmond (III, fo. cc.lxxii: **I Kepe resydence**; cc.lxxxvii: **I Make a house**; ccc.xvii (= ccc.xv): **I Peplysshe**). Walsingham has already been mentioned in another context (see p. 417). There are two instances praising the richly adorned shrine of St Thomas of Canterbury, which suggests that Palsgrave may have made a pilgrimage to Canterbury (III, fo. c.xcviii$^{v}$: **I Couer ouer with golde**; ccc.lii: **I Shrine a saynte**). There is one very general mention of the plain of Salisbury (III, fo. cc.xxiiii: **I Encounter**).

The River Thames is part of Palsgrave's London. We hear of its flooding overnight (III, fo. ccc.lxx: **I Spredde a brode as a ryuer**). He compares the swiftness of its flow to that of the Severn, maintaining that the waters of the Severn move faster (III, fo. ccc.xliii$^{v}$: **I Ronne as the streame**), which suggests personal observation of the Severn. And he tells us: '*I haue sene the place where Temmes springeth ꝛ sene kyne drinke there*: *Iay veu la place ou la Tamise se sourt, et ay veu des vaches boyre la.*' (III, fo. ccc.lxx$^{r-v}$).

Mention should be made of the public feasts which Palsgrave tells us about, for example, All Saints. The need to illustrate the use of the verb *to celebrate* made him say: '*The feest of all hallowen is greatly celebrate* [*sic*] *in our towne*: *La feste de tous saynctz est gramment celebrée en nostre ville*' (III, fo. c.lxxxiiii). The illustration for *to hallow a day* is: '*They halowe or kepe saynte Iames day hye and holye at our towne*: *Ilz celebrent haultement le iour saynct Iacques a nostre ville*' (III, fo. cc.lvi$^{v}$). The phrase *high and holy* (compare German *hoch und heilig*) is not included among the phrases given in the *OED*. And we learn that: '*The bouchers in London solempnyse saynte Lukes daye aboue all feestes in the yere*: *Les bouchiers de Londres solempnisent le iour de sainct Luc par dessus toutes les festes de lannée*' (III, fo. ccc.lxvi: **I Solempnyse**).

A recurrent theme in Palsgrave's view of life is the lack of permanence, the pervasiveness of change. This evidently also holds for cherished customs. An insight into one such fading custom is the following:

> . . . **The maydens of London**
> **were wonte to tymber more than**
> **they do nowe:** Les filles de Londres

**souloyẽt plus tymbrer quelles ne font mayntenant.**

(III, fo. ccc.lxxxxi: **I Tymber, see also the entry I Playe vpon a tymbre**)

No reason for this change is offered, and it may have been common knowledge (for the practice of playing on the timbrel by the London maidens, see Strutt 1855: p. xxxv). For the verb *to timbre* in the sense of 'to play on the timbrel' the *OED* has two citations only, the first from *c.*1400 and the second the example from Palsgrave.

We move now to the Continent. Not surprisingly, the place mentioned most frequently is the port of Calais, then still in English hands and clearly familiar to Palsgrave. It sometimes co-occurs with Dover, both ends of the boat journey being mentioned (cf. III, fo. cc.ii$^{r-v}$: **I Come to lande**; ccc.lxxxiiii: **I Take landyng**), but we also learn of an envisaged journey by the king (III, fo. c.lxxxix: **I Clere the coste or the countrey**). The rocks of Brittany and Dover are compared (III, fos. c.lxx$^{v}$–c.lxxi: **I Bowe or leane**), a shipwreck at Dunkirk is mentioned (III, fo. cc.liii$^{v}$: **I Go to wrake**), and we are not told whether the journey scheduled for Bordeaux ever took off after the reported delay of fourteen days (III, fo. cc.xlii$^{v}$: **I Freyght a shyppe**). The example under **I Set a siege** appears to suggest that he also went to Tournai: '*It was a goodly syght to se whan the kynges good grace dyd set his siege byfore tournaye*: *Il faisoyt beau veoyr la bonne grace du roy quant il planta son siege deuant tournay*' (III, fo. ccc.lvi$^{v}$). The event Palsgrave is referring to is the siege of Tournai 1513. As we have seen in Chapter 1, 1513 is the very year for which we have evidence that Palsgrave was in the service of the king, being paid as schoolmaster to his sister Mary.

The verb list includes two other instances that we can date. We know that Palsgrave accompanied the king to Calais in 1520 to meet the French king. The splendour of the Field of Cloth of Gold is well recorded in contemporary accounts of the occasion. Temporary palaces and pavilions had been set up for the English and the French king. Henry VIII thus resided at Guînes and Francis I at Ardres. *Guynes* occurs in two verb illustrations. The first under the verb entry **I Break vp as a parlyament or an assembly of people/ or a iustes or tournay or suche lyke** (III, fo. c.lxxiii). The question '*Whan dyd ẏ iustes breake vp at Guynes*: *Quant faillerent les ioustes a Guynes*' calls up some of the extended entertainments during the festivities. The other forced itself on Palsgrave's mind when he was looking for an example to illustrate the verb lemma **I Put souldyers or men of armes out of wages**: '*All the crewe ẏ was at Guynes is put* *out of wages*: *On a cassé toute la creue qui estoit a Guynes*' (III, fo. ccc.xxx$^{r–v}$).

During the compilation of the French vocabulist, the days of his stay in Paris may have seemed to him remote, because the French capital is mentioned only twice. In one case, reference is made to the king's stay in Paris (III, fo. cc.lxxxi: **I Lye I rest**). The other focuses on Saint-Denis and the rich revenue obtained from it, a matter of obvious interest to a man of the Church struggling to make a good living: '*Saynt Denys in Frãuce is greatly endewed with reuenewes*: *Labbaye de sainct Denis en Frãuce est grandement rentée*' (III, fo. cc.xxiiii$^{v}$: **I Endewe a religyouse house**). Very little is said about Holland (III, fo. ccc.lxiii$^{v}$: **I Slyde as one . . .**), Artois and Picardy (III, fo. cc.lxviii: **I Ioyne as two countreys ioyne togyther**). Of more interest is another mention of Picardy under the entry **I Drawe to the borders**: '*What meane the burgonyons to drawe to the borders of Pycardye*: *Que veullent dire les bourgoignons de se aborder a la Picardie* (III, fo. cc.xix$^{v}$). (see also the example under **I Ouerronne** (III, fo. ccc.x))

Palsgrave's travels do not seem to have gone beyond France and the Low Countries. One of his unfulfilled ambitions may have been a journey to the Holy City, if it is not too fanciful to read autobiography into the first example given under the verb entry *to dream in one's sleep*:

> . . . **I dreamed to nyght that I was at Rome:** Ie songeay a nuyct que ie estoys a Romme.
>
> (III, fo. cc.xx)

The second reference to Rome also expresses an ambition to travel there—with a specific companion:

> **If thou wylte ryde with me to Rome/ I wyll paye thy costes/ it shall nat cost the a peny.** Si tu veulx cheualcher auecq̃s moy iusques a Rõme, ie te deffrayeray il ne te coustera pas vng denier.
>
> (III, fo. ccc.xii: **I Paye one his costes**)

Palsgrave's interest in rivers informs the sole reference to Spain:

> **They haue a great aduauntage in Spayne to temper their bladʒ well bycause of ẏ nature of their ryuers:** Ilz ont vng grant aduantaige en espaigne pour bien acierer leurs alumelles a cause de la nature de leurs riuieres.
>
> (III, fo. ccc.lxxxviii)

The instances of *Tournai* and *Guînes* have already put us into the middle of sixteenth-century political life. Other contemporary historical personalities or events mentioned in the examples include, of course, 'the King', Palsgrave's regular way of referring to Henry VIII. There are quite a number of references to him (e.g. III, fo. c.lviii$^{v}$: **I Becken**; III, fo. cc.i: **I Crowne**; III, fo. cc.xxii: **I Dubbe**; III, fo. cc.lxxxviii: **I Make a sermonde**), naturally enough from someone who moved in court circles. Within English lexicography, there can be no other English dictionary that includes as many references to the monarch as Palsgrave's French vocabulist. The king's predecessors are referred to as Henry VII and Henry VI. What seems to have astonished the religious Palsgrave with respect to the latter is that '[*t*]*hough kyng Henry the syxte were a holy man/ yet he is nat canonysed*: *Combien que le roy Henry le sixieseme estoyet vng sainct hõme il nest pas pourtant encore canonizé*' (III, fo. c.lxxxi: **I Canonyse**). Henry VII is mentioned several times. Two instances relate to his being deceased (III, fo. cc.v$^{v}$: **I Decease**; fo. cc.lxxxi: **I Lye as a corps**). Another provides an interesting insight into the practice of displaying the monarch in pictures:

> **I Offer a thyng to a saynt whiche cannot after be taken a waye/** Ie dedie. prime cõiu. **Kyng Henry yͤ. vii. offeryd vppe his picture armyd in harnesse of syluer in dyuers places of this realme.** Le roy henry septiesme dedia sõ ymage armée en harnoys dargent en plusieurs places de ce roiaulme.
>
> (III, fo. ccc.viii)

We are also given an assessment of the esteem in which the emperor was held: '*The Emperour yͭ is nowe is the moste spokyn of/ of any man that I knowe*: *Lempereur qui est mayntenãt est le plus reclamé homme que ie congnus iamays*' (III, fo. ccc.lxviii$^{r-v}$: **I Speke of one**).

The verb list contains one reference to Luther. Unfortunately, I have not been able to trace anything that could enlighten me on Palsgrave's example:

> **I haue sene the booke yͭ dyd pronostycate yͤ comyng of Luther twenty yere or he was borne:** Iay veu le liure qui pronostiqua laduenement de Luther vingt ans auant quil fut né.
>
> (III, fo. ccc.xxiiii$^{v}$: **I Pronostycate**)

The historic head of state that is most frequently mentioned after Henry VIII is the one who then struck terror in the whole of Western

Europe and who epitomised threat and hostility to Christendom: the head of the Ottoman Empire. It is quite revealing to see the types of verb entry that made Palsgrave refer to him. A first set of expressions denotes warfaring. Thus, under the lemma entry **I Warre I make or kepe warre agaynst one** Palsgrave states: '*The turke hath warred with christendome all my dayes*: *Le grant turc a guerroyé la chrestyenté*, **or** *a mené guerre contre la chrestienté toute sa* [*sic*] *vie*' (III, fo. cccc.i$^{v}$). The English term here is *the turke*, the French *le grant turc*. In all the other instances, he speaks of the *Great Turk*. Under the entry **I Crye open warre** the example is: '*The great turke hath kryed open warre agaynst thẽ of Hõgary*: *Le grãt turc a faict crier*, **or** *a fait sõner la guerre a feu et a sang contre ceulx de Hongerye*' (III, fo. cc.$^{v}$). As a further indication of how much war and cruelty in the first part of the sixteenth century were associated in the minds of the people with the belligerous Turks, we might take Rabelais's *Pantagruel*, where Panurge gives us a vivid account of his capture by, and escape from, the Turks.

The reference to Hungary enables us to monitor Palsgrave's progress in the compilation of *Lesclarcissement*: the Hungarians were severely defeated by Suleiman the Magnificent in 1526. Another example which allows us such an insight is the reference to the siege of Vienna, which took place in 1529. Yet under the entry **I Laye siege to a town** the Ottoman head himself is not mentioned (III, fo. cc.lxxv$^{v}$).

In another instance, the conquest of Egypt, the Great Turk is mentioned:

> . . . **The great turke hath domynacion vpon two empyres ⁊ thurty kyngdoms bysydes Egypt whiche was the Soldans**: Le grant turc do mine sur deux empires et trente royaulmes sans Egypte le quel estoyt au Soulden
>
> (III, fo. cc.lix: **I Haue domynacion**)

Palsgrave does not confine himself to mere factual statements in his comments relating to the Ottoman leader. With respect to those who change their allegiance and follow the Great Turk, he, as a Christian, wonders '*In what case stãde they in that renounce their faythe and go to the great turke*? *En quel estat sont ceulx qui regnient leur foy et vont au grant turc*' (III, fos. ccc.xxxviiv–ccc.xxxviii: **I Renounce**). And he expresses specific criticism: '*The great turke kepeth his subiectes to moche in thraldome or in subiection*: *Le grant turc subiecte trop*, **or** *soubtiue trop ses subiectz*' (III, fo. cc.lxxi$^{v}$: **I Kepe in thraldome**).

Yet wars were not only caused by the expansionist ambitions of Selim I and Suleiman the Magnificent. The Emperor, Charles V, and Francis I of France were fighting over their territorial possessions in Italy. For several decades Italy was subjected to the various struggles between the Habsburg and the Valois. The situation in Italy did not leave Palsgrave unconcerned. But as a man of the Church he assumed its fate to be the will of God (III, fo. ccc.liii: **I Scourge I punysshe as god punyssheth**). The city of Milan is singled out because of its rebellions: '*The cyte of Mylan hath rebelled dyuerse tymes in my dayes*: *La cite de Milan se est mutinée souuent foys en mon temps*' (III, fo. ccc.xxxiii^v: **I Rebell** . . .).

Nearer home, Palsgrave remembers another uprising:

> . . . **I remēber well ynough whan ẏ comens of Cornewall dyd ryse:** Il me souuient asses bien quant les communs de Cornovvaille se mutinerent.
>
> (III, fo. ccc.xlii: **I Ryse as cōmens**)

The appeal to his memory seems to suggest a rebellion during his younger years, before he ever started on *Lesclarcissement*. This could be the 1497 rebellion in Cornwall.

We conclude this section on recent and current politics as it may be glimpsed through Palsgrave's illustrations with an example that refers to the Scots, the meaning of which is not clear:

> . . . **Saynte Cutbertes banner was neuer yet displayed agaynst the skottes but they had the worse:** Iamays iusques a ores ne fut lestandart de saynct Cuthber desployé contre les escossoys quilz nen eussent du pire, **or** du pis.
>
> (III, fo. cc.xiiii^v: **I Displaye**)

We move on to those examples that show us the scholar: Palsgrave's absorption of classical knowledge and learning. The number of instances is relatively small, confirming the view that in the invention of his verb illustrations Palsgrave was guided by the events, experiences, sorrows, and pleasures of everyday life. He was not intent on disseminating scholarly learning.

There is a reference to Solomon and his legendary wisdom (III, fo. c.xcii^v: **I Compare two thynges**). Cicero's praise of '*ẏ pastyme to labour the yerthe aboue all other exercyses*' (III, fo. cc.lxxiiii: **I Laboure the yerthe**) has already been mentioned in another context (see

p. 400). The verb entry **I Descrybe** made Palsgrave quote Ptolemaeus, the great Greek astronomer, as having given the best description of the world (III, fo. cc.ix). We here have to remember that in 1530 Copernicus' famous work which was to challenge the ancient teaching that the earth was the centre of the universe, his *De revolutionibus orbium celestium*, was not yet available, since, although it was completed by 1530, it was not published until 1543. Palsgrave also reminds us that it was St Jerome who translated the bible out of Hebrew into Latin (III, fo. cc.lxvii$^{v}$: **I Interprete**).

We come across the names of three great rulers: Alexander the Great, Julius Caesar, and Charlemagne. To what aspects of these did Palsgrave draw attention in his examples? With respect to the former two, it was their heroic deeds and bravery. Alexander the Great not only beat all the enemy armies that dared to oppose him (III, fo. c.lxi$^{v}$: **I Beare or beate**); he is also credited with having caused the rebuilding of Troy (III, fo. c.lxxxiii$^{v}$: **I Cause or make**). Caesar is given praise for a specific feat: '*It was well doone of Cesar to swymme ouer a ryuer with one hande*: *Cestoyt bien fait a Cesar que de transnouer, ou de transnager vne riuere a vne mayn*' (III, fo. ccc.lxxxii: **I Swymme ouer a ryuer**). A fuller description of this is given in Elyot's *Book named the governor*, which well illustrates the degree to which classical knowledge was shared by the scholars in the service of Henry VIII:

> Howe moche profited the feate in swymmynge to the valiant Julius Cesar: who at the bataile of Alexandri/ on a bridge beinge abandoned of his people for the multitude of his enemyes/ whiche oppressed them/ whan he moughte no lenger sustaine the shotte of dartes and arowes/ he boldly lepte in to the see/ and diuynge vnder the water/ escaped the shotte/ and swamme the space of. CC. pasis to one of his shyppes/ drawynge his cote armure with his teethe after hym/ that his enemies shulde nat attayne it. And also that it moughte some what defende hym frõ theyr arowes: And that more maruaile was/ holdynge in his hande aboue the water/ certayne lettres/ whiche a litle before he had receyued from the Senate. (Alston 1970*d*: fos. 66$^{v}$–7)

There is one example in which Alexander the Great and Caesar are matched in order to disprove the educational views put forward by some writers and not shared by Palsgrave:

> . . . **Some thynke that lernynge dothe but make one cowardysshe/ but Alexanders and Cesars actes proue the contrarye:** Les aulcuns pencent que doctrine ne fait que accouardyr vng home, mays les actes Dalixandre et de Cesar preuuent le contraire.
>
> (III, fo. cc.xc: **I Make cowardysshe**)

Charlemagne is seen as a king who dubbed many a knight. The French version of the example, stylistically not a match of the English sentence, sounds rather poetic, and one may wonder whether it echoes a specific line of Palsgrave's reading of Lemaire de Belges: '*Charlemayne adoubbed many a knyght*: *Maynt cheualier adoubá Charlemaygne*' (III, fo. c.xxxviii$^{v}$: **I Adubbe**). The other instance calls up the earlier reference to the richly endowed church and abbey of Saint-Denis:

> . . . **Charlemayne endowed ẏ churche of Fraũce with many great gyftes:** Charlemaigne endoua lesglise de France de maynt riches dons.
>
> (III, fo. cc.xxiiii$^{v}$: **I Endowe**).

The example immediately precedes the one referring to Saint-Denis, thus nicely documenting how one's mind occasionally remains narrowly focused when one is looking for linguistic illustrations.

Troy has already been mentioned in the context of Alexander the Great. The verb entry **I Battayle** made Palsgrave think of the ten years of battle between the Trojans and Greeks (III, fo. c.lviii). The Romans also figure in his examples. There is a certain admiration: '*It was a maruaylouse syght to se the romaynes tryumphe whan they had the vyctorie of their ennemyes*: *Cestoyt vne chose esmerueillable que de veoyr les Romayns triumpher quant ilz auoyent la victoyre de leurs ennemys*' (III, fo. ccc.lxxxxiiii$^{v}$: **I Tryumphe**). But there is also explicit criticism:

> . . . **The romayns were called wyse men/ but they were shamelesse fletterers to deifye their emperours:** Les rommayns estoyent tenus pour saiges gens, mays ilz estoyent flatteurs sans toute honte de deifier leurs empereurs.
>
> (III, fo. cc.vi$^{v}$: **I Deifye**)

From classical mythology we have Proteus (III, fo. c.lxxxvi: **I Chaunge in to**) and Hercules (III, fo. ccc.xxvi: **I Pull vp by the roote**), and from Celtic mythology King Arthur (III, fo. c.xcv: **I Conquere**).[2]

We have seen that Palsgrave's examples quite naturally reflect

2 The following references seem to come from Palsgrave's literary reading: the Castle of Hedyn (III, fo. c.lxiii$^{r–v}$: **I Besege a castell**; the house of Melysyn (III, fo. cc.ix: **I Deryue**), Rockeley (III, fo. ccc.xxxi$^{v}$: **I Quod**).

aspects of his professional life as teacher and scholar without their dominating the whole body of the verb list. What still remains to be dealt with is his quality as a priest and chaplain to the king and how far this vocational side affected the choice of his examples. Reflections of Christian life, the Church, and its teachings constitute an integral part of the example sentences and they are well blended in with the other concerns and preoccupations of everyday life in early sixteenth-century English society. Some of the scenes evoked by the examples allow us to participate in the daily duties of a priest. We sense the care for the material objects in his church '*Touche nat the super altare there for it is halowed*: *Ne touchez poynt ce superaltaré la*, *car il est sacré*, or *consacré*' (III, fo. cc.lvi^v: *I Halowe a thyng*). We can share the proprietorial pride '*Nowe that my picture of the crucifyce is set in bordes it doth much better than it dyd afore*: *Mayntenant que iay enchassé mon ymaige de crucifix elle semble beaucoup plus belle quelle ne faysoyt par deuant*' (III, fo. ccc.lvi: **I Set a picture**). We can hear him talk to those who seek his assistance: '*I muste induct an abbotte to morowe or els I wolde wayte vpon you*: *Il me fault demayn confermer vng abbé ou aultrement ie entenderoye a vous*' (III, fo. cc.lxvi^v: **I Inducte**), or his comfort: '*Sythe I can do you none other seruyce at the leest I wyll pray for you*: *Puis que ie ne vous puis faire aultre seruice ie prieray dieu pour vous*' (III, fo. ccc.xxi^v: **I Pray for one**). When a young person of his congregation is in need of persuasion, he tries to sweeten the required effort with a reward: '*Knele downe ⁊ aske my blessyng and you shal haue a fygge*: *Agenouillez vous et me demãdez ma benediction et vo⁹ aurez vne figue*' (III, fo. cc.lxxiii: **I Knele vpon bothe the knees**). He assesses the keenness of people to come to Mass quite realistically when he says: '*Many men had leuer se a play than to here a masse*: *Mayntes gens aymeroyẽt plus chier*, *or auroyẽt plus chier de veoyr vng mistere iouer que douyr vne messe*' (III, fo. cc.lix^{r–v}: **I Haue leuer**). His disapproval of people's spitting and retching during a sermon is unmistakable:

> . . . **It is a foule thyng at a sermonde to here people spytte ⁊ retche or rough as they do:** Cest vne layde chose que de ouyr les gens a vng sermon cracher comme ilz font.
>
> (III, fo. ccc.lxix: **I Spyt spittell**)

For the English triad of verbs, *to spit*, *to retch*, and *to rough* there is only one French item, *cracher* 'to spit'. *To retch* in the sense of 'bring up phlegm, clear one's throat' in *Lesclarcissement* is earlier than the first citation in the *OED*. The last citation for the verb *to rough* 'to cough, to clear one's throat' in the *OED* is 1529 for Palsgrave's contemporary John Skelton.

The particular use of religious language is explained to the readers: '*Bycause ẏ oyle that prĩces ⁊ bysshops be anoynted with is halowed their noyntyng is called sacrynge: A cause que lhuylle dont les princes et les esuesques sont oynctz est consacrée on appelle leur oyngnement consecracion*' (III, fo. c.xlix: **I Anoynt with holy oyle**).

Palsgrave seems to have been well aware of weaknesses among the clergy. One of the problems was the vow of chastity:

> . . . **Wolde to god euery man ẏ professeth chastyte coude kepe it well:** Pleut a dieu que tout homme qui professe chasteté la sceut bien garder.
>
> (III, fo. ccc.xxiii$^{v}$: **I Professe as a relygyouse man dothe**)

As mentioned above (p. 386), the spiritual foundation of Palsgrave's attitude towards life and his fellow human beings appears to have been his Christian belief in the grace of God. A message equally reiterated is that man should trust in God and not despair (III, fo. cc.vii: **I Delyuer I helpe out**; fo. cc.ix$^{v}$: **I Despayre**; fo. cc.xiii: **I Dispayre**; fo. cc.xiiii: **I Dispayre**). When he comes to look for an example for the verb *to abound* his mind travels to the place of eternal abundance: '*Paradyse aboũdeth in all ioye and comforte*: *Paradys abonde or afflue de toute ioye et comfort*' (III, fo. c.xxxvi$^{v}$).

Examples relating to the text of the Bible encompass the creation (III, fo. c.lxxvi$^{v}$: **I Bringe to naught**; fo. cc.: **I Create**), the prophesying of the coming of Christ (III, fo. ccc.xxiiii$^{v}$: **I Prophesye**), his coming (III, fo. cc.i$^{v}$: **I Come downe**; fo. cc.xlviii: **I Gyue an answere**), the passion of Christ (III, fo. ccc.xxii: **I Prefygurate**), his descent to hell (III, fo. ccc.ix: **I Descende**), his transfiguration (III, fo. ccc.lxxxxiii: **I Transfygure**) and our redemption (III, fo. ccc.xxxv: **I Redeme**). The reader confronts the fall of Lucifer (III, fo. ccc.lxxxix$^{v}$: **I Throwe downe**), the transformation of Lot's wife (III, fo. ccc.lxxxxii$^{v}$: **I Transforme**), the stoning of St Stephen (III, fo. ccc.lxxv: **I Stone**), and the resurrection of Lazarus (III, fo. ccc.xxxvi: **I Reyse from dethe**). And there is the doctrine of predestination (III, fo. ccc.xxi$^{v}$: **I Predestynate**; fo. ccc.xlvi$^{v}$: **I Santifye**).

As we have seen, the grammatical form which Palsgrave has chosen for his verb entries is generally the first-person singular, present tense. Many of his example sentences occur in this form too, but they amply alternate with illustrations showing a second-person or third-person form in the singular or plural. In view of this variation, the fact that there are three instances which relate to an appearance before a spiritual court and which are all couched in the first-person singular makes one suspect an autobiographical link. We remember from the State Papers of Henry VIII that Palsgrave's place was searched several times (see pp. 16–19). The three examples occur under the entries **I Adiourne I monisshe or warne one to apere afore a iudge at a daye certayne** (III, fo. c.xl), **I Cyte a person to apere in a spyrytuall courte** (III, fo. c.lxxxviii), and **I Warne a mã to apere at a courte in iudgement** (III, fo. cccc.i).

Punitive action obviously depended on the severity of the offence and the social status of the member of the clergy concerned. A religious man, such as Palsgrave, could be '*corrected in the chapter house for breakyng of his order/ discipliné au chapitre pour auoyr offencé contre sa religion*' (III, fo. c.xcviii$^{r-v}$: **I Correcte**), or worse: '*A preest may do so great a faulte ẏ he shal be disgraded*: *Vng prestre peult cõmettre si grant crime quil sera degradé*' (III, fo. cc.xiii$^{v}$: **I disgrade** [*sic*]). In addition, there was excommunication:

> . . . **Medyll nat with**
> **hym he is a cursed out of ẏ churche**
> **with boke bell and candell:** Nayez
> point affaire a luy il est anathematizé.
> (III, fo. cc.iii: **I Curse out**)

The *OED* records the phrase as *to curse by bell, book, and candle* and explains its origin as 'referring to a form of excommunication which closed with the words, "Doe to the book, quench the candle, ring the bell!"' (**bell** *sb.*[1] 8.). There is one citation, the first from the *Cursor Mundi*, with the sequence *candell*, *book*, and *bell*, none for the order we find in Palsgrave. Since the 'bell, book and candle' order is first documented for Shakespeare, Palsgrave's version, like the *Cursor Mundi* one, seems to be interesting testimony of variation before the phrase was finally lexicalized.

The verb list includes a number of punishments, administered by both secular and spiritual courts. In some instances the offence or crime committed is indicated as well as the punishment. Cutpurses had their ears cut off:

> . . . **His eares be cutte of**
> **it is a signe he hath ben a cut purse:**
> Il est desoreillé, or on luy a couppé
> les oreilles, cest signe quil a esté vng
> couppeur de bources.
> (III, fo. cc.iii$^{v}$: **I Cutte of ones eares**)

Torture was applied in order to get confession:

> **I Brake on a brake or payne bauke as men do mysdoers to confesse the trouthe/** Ie gehynne. prime coniuga. **whiche I fynde also written/** ie gehēne. prime cōiu. **The false murdrer was braked thrise or euer he wolde confesse the trouthe:** Le faulx meurdrier fust par troys foys gehenné auant quil voulut confesser la verité.
>
> (III, fos. c.lxxi$^{v}$–c.lxxii)

This occurrence of the verb *to brake* in the sense of 'to torture on the brake or rack' is the only citation of its use in the *OED*, and a *brake* as an instrument of torture is also first recorded in Palsgrave's *Lesclarcissement* (*OED* **brake** *sb.*[6] 3.). The verb entry for *to geld* prompted the example: '*Gelde hym for gettynge of fooles*: *Chastrez le, or escouillex le afin quil nengendre poynt de folz*' (III, fo. cc.xliiii$^{v}$). Prisoners could be chained: '*The offence of ẏ man was so horryble that he was iudged to be boũde in chaynes*: *Loffence de cest homme estoyt si execrable quil estoyt adiugé destre en chayné or destre pendu en chaynes*' (III, fo. c.lxvi$^{v}$: **I Bynde in a chayne**). Or they could be fastened in the stocks (III, fo. c.lxxxvi$^{v}$: **I Cheyne**). An offence that could carry a death sentence was the clipping of the king's coin (III, fo. c.lxxxix$^{v}$: **I Clyppe as one doth money**). The offender could be dismembered by wild horses (III, fo. cc.xiiii: **I Dismember**), beheaded (III, fo. cc.lx$^{v}$: **I Hedde**), or sacked:

> . . . **He shall nat be hãged/ but he shall be sacked and throwen in to Seyne:** Il ne sera pas pendu, mays il sera ensacqué et iecté dedans seyne.
>
> (III, fo. ccc.xlv$^{v}$: **I Sacke**)

Someone sentenced to the gallows, a sentence usually inflicted upon traitors, would be '*ledde thorowe ẏ towne vpon a hardell ⁊ so to the gallowes*: *On le traynoyt trauers le ville sur vne herce et de la au gibet*' (III, fo. cc.lxxvii: **I Lede a man or thynge**). We are also told what could be part of a hangman's job:

> . . . **The hange man hath cutte hym a sonder in to foure quarters:** Le bourreau la detrenché en quattre quartiers.
>
> (III, fo. cc.iii: **I Cutte a sonder**)

And there could be a post-mortem penalty:

> . . . **It shulde seme that he hath done some great offence that they vnbury hym nowe:** Il fault dire quil ayt fayct quelque grant offence quilz le vont de terrer mayntenant.
>
> (III, fo. ccc.lxxxxvii: **I Unberye**)

The schoolmaster, the scholar, and the priest are evidently only professional sides of Palsgrave the man. They feed on the mental and moral predispositions that make up his personality. We know from the facts that we were able to establish for his life, as well as from *Lesclarcissement* itself and his translation of *Acolastus*, that he was a dedicated teacher. His works include several passages that document his commitment to serve God and his country, but the examples which he contrived to illustrate the use of verbs have also revealed a very creative and lively imagination. The quality and topicality of the examples further attest to a sharp linguistic mind able to grasp what was typical and essential and to put this into words. In addition, they have laid open aspects of Palsgrave the human being. He abhors backbiting and regards crucifixion as the vilest form of death. He marvels at the wonders of creation and in doing so he subjects his readers to the experiences of his senses. We see a chicken breaking free of its shell: '*It is a straũge syght to se a chycken howe it cralleth first out of ỷ shell: Cest vne chose estrange que de veoyr vng ieune pouceyn comment il crosle premierement hors de lescalle*' (III, fo. cc.: **I Crawle**). We hear the flapping wings of a soaring swan: '*What a noyse a swan maketh with her wynges whan she flyeth: Commẽt vng cygne bruyt de ces esles quãt il vole*' (III, fo. cc.lxxxvii$^{v}$: **I Make noyse**), and we catch the scent of spring flowers: '*It reioyseth my herte to walke in my gardayne in Maye ỷ floures smell so swete: Il me resiouyt tout le cueur de me promener en mon iardyn au moys de May les fleurs reflagrent, or redolent, or sentent si bien*' (III, fo. ccc.lxiiii$^{v}$: **I Smell swete**). He does not want young children to be spoiled, he points out bad manners and outlines correct behaviour, and he stresses again and again that the company which we keep will influence our moral bearing.

The last page of *Lesclarcissement* tells us that he intended to compile a book of proverbs.[3] These adages are '*darke sentẽces comprehẽdyng great wysdome*' (III, fo. cccc.lxxiii$^{v}$). Let us now, to conclude, look at the wise advice and sayings which this close observer of human nature offers to his readers. The moral lessons included confirm the wide

[3] Palsgrave's use of *adage* antedates the *OED*, whose first record is 1548.

range we have seen, with no particular bias in Palsgrave's verb illustrations. What makes them so readable and enjoyable is the presence of all the ingredients singled out so far and their excellent blending.

Here is a selection of the wisdom that we find in the verb list. Some observations link up with similar ones so that we have something like a theme, others do not. To this latter group belong the following:

> . . . **A man is soone ledde out of the waye by a crafty ypocryte**: Vng hõme est bien tost seduit ꝑ vng caulleux ypocript.
>
> (III, fo. cc.lxxvii: **I Lede one**)

> . . . **If a vyce be ones rooted in a man it is harde to get it away:** Mais qung vice soit vne fois habitué on aura fort afaire de loster.
>
> (III, fo. ccc.xliiii: **I Roote in custome**)

> . . . **Whan a man is throwen vnder the foote ones than euery man gothe vpon hym:** Quant vng hõme est vne foys suppedité tout le monde a donc luy court sus.
>
> (III, fo. ccc.lxxxx: **I Throwe vnder foote**)

> . . . **Whan a man is deed ones he is sone put out of mynde:** Quant vng hõme est mort il est bien tost mys en oubly.
>
> (III, fo. ccc.xxx: **I Put out of mynde**)

> . . . **You maye haunte dysynge and cardyng longe ynough or euer it make you ryche:** Vous pouez hanter les dez et les cartes longuement assez auant que cela vous enrichira.
>
> (III, fo. cc.xcv: **I Make ryche**)

People should have a realistic and sound appreciation and control of themselves, with self-knowledge: '*Whan a man mysknoweth hymselfe it is a daungerouse thyng for hym*: *Quãt on se mescongnoist cest vne chose dangereuse pour luy*' (III, fo. ccc.ii: **I Mysknowe**). One's temper should be under control: '*He that can nat refrayne his anger at a tyme muste nedes haue moche busynesse*: *Celui qui ne peult refrayndre, or refrenyr son yre, or qui ne se peult refraindre de son ire en temps fault quil ayt beaucoup a faire*' (III, fo. ccc.xxxv$^{r-v}$: **I Refrayne**). Liberality should not be taken too far: '*It is good to be lyberall but euer reserue somwhat to yourselfe*: *Il fait bon estre liberal mais reseruez tousiours quelque chose pour vous mesmes*' (III, fo. ccc.xxxix: **I Reserue**). It is no use hankering after something that cannot be undone: '*To waxe sorowfull for the thing that is paste remedye it is but a folye*: *De vous contrister pour la chose qui est sans remede ce nest que folye*' (III, fo. cccc.v: **I Waxe sorowfull**), and when something is unavoidable, it should be faced gladly: '*The thynge that a man can nat shonne it is wysdome to take it in good worthe*: *La chose quon ne peult poynt escheuer*, *or euiter cest saigesse que de la prendre en bon gré*' (III, fo. ccc.li: **I Shonne I auoyde**).

Relying on oneself includes relying on one's judgement of others: '*Kepe your hert your selfe or els you haue but a fooles heed*: *Gardez vostre cueur vous mesmes ou aultremẽt vous nauez que la teste dung fol*' (III, fo. cc.lxxi: **I Kepe a thyng in my custody**). Distrust eyes that do two things at once: '*He that wynketh wͭ one eye and loketh with the tother I wyll nat trust hym and he were my brother*. *Qui clyngne dung oeil et regarde de laultre ie ne me fieray pas en luy et fut il mon frere*' (III, fo. cccc.ix: **I Wynke I shytte**). A very clear warning paired with a description of the inevitable outcome is the example under **I Ouercome**: '*Truste neuer a cowarte for if he can ouercome the he hath no mercy*: *Ne te fie iamays a vng couart car sil te peult vaincre il na poynt de mercy*' (III, fo. ccc.ix^v). For further examples see the verb entries **I Geue credence** (III, fo. cc.xlvii) and **I Sweare I make an othe** (III, fo. ccc.lxxxi^v). To know someone else is almost impossible, but there is one situation that will reveal a person's character: when he is put in power. Under the verb entry **I Auctorise** and the entry **I Put one in auctorite**, the same idea is expressed: '*A man is nat knowen tyll he be auctorized*: *Len ne peult cognoystre que cest que dung homme iusques a tant quil soyt auctorisé*' (III, fo. c.lv^v) and '*A man is neuer knowen tyll he be put in auctorite*: *On nest iamays congnu iusques autant quon soyt auctorisé, or mys en auctorité*' (III, fo. ccc.xxix^r–v).

Maintaining friendship is therefore all the more important: '*Fall nat out with your frẽdes for a thing of naught*: *Ne prẽnez poynt de noyse a voz amys pour vne chose de rien*' (III, fo. cc.xxxii^v: **I Fall out with one**; see also the example under **I Altercate** (III, fo. c.xli)).

Attention is given to the ethics of work and craftsmanship:

> . . . **He shall neuer thriue that asshameth wͭ his crafte:** Iamays ne sera son prouffit qui se ahontist de son mestier.
>
> (III, fo. c.liiii: **I Ashame me**)

No one is born an expert and therefore '[*i*]*t behoueth a man first to be a scoler and than a maister*: *Il conuient, il fault, il affiert a vng homme premierement estre vng escolier et puis apres vng maistre*' (III, fo. c.lx^r–v: **It Behoueth**). Recognition of one's achievement will not come with beginning a task but with seeing it through to its completion:

> **It is nat they that begyn well but they that perseuer/ that shall come to honour:** Ce ne sont pas ceulx qui

cõmencent bien qui paruiendront a honneur mays ceulx qui perseueront.

(III, fo. ccc.xv[v]: **I Perseuer**)

Palsgrave promotes the interesting view that the behaviour adopted towards one's parents predicts behaviour to a superior:

. . . **If thou contemne thy father and mother it is a shreude signe that you wylte obey thy mayster:** Si tu cõtempnes tes parens, or pere et mere, cest mauluays signe q̃ tu veulx obeyr a ton maistre.

(III, fo. c.xcvi: **I Contemne**)

**He that disobeyeth his father ⁊ beateth his mother/ and betrayeth his mayster muste nedes come to an yuell ende.** Celuy qui desobeyt a son pe re et bat sa mere, et trahyt son maistre il fault quil viengne a mauuayse fin.

(III, fo. c.lxiiii[v]: **I Betray**)

In the two examples quoted Palsgrave uses the word *master*; the use of *superior*, which would go more with a clerical occupation, is much less common. This could be taken as further evidence for his envisaged readership. That one has to obey whoever is in authority, however, also occurs with the noun *superior*: '*He that is a subiecte muste obey to his superyours*: *Qui est subiect fault quil obtempere a ses superieurs*' (III, fo. ccc.vii[v]: **I Obey**). One's master may not always be to one's liking, but if one is to get on well, one must adjust and submit: '*He ẏ wyll haue his mayster good to hym muste conferme hym selfe to his maners*: *Qui veult gaigner la grace de son maister se doybt confermer a ses condiscions*' (III, fo. c.xciiii[v]: **I Conferme**). And with respect to any faults detected in one's master, Palsgrave firmly enjoins:

. . . **What so euer faute you knowe by your mayster/ loke you bewraye it nat:** Quelque faulte que vous sachiez de vostre maistre, gardez vous de le retrayre.

(III, fo. c.lxv: **I Bewray ones coũsayle**)

A wise man will always try to anticipate the consequences of actions: '*A wyse man wolde thynke byfore what shall come after*: *Vng saige hõme precogiteroyt la chose qui pourroyt aduenir*' (III, fo. ccc.lxxxviii[v]: **I Thynke byfore**), and: '*It is a wise mans parte to prouyde for daũgers or euer they come*: *Cest le faict dung saige homme dobuehir aux inconueniens auant quilz aduiengnent*' (III, fo. ccc.xxv: **I Prouyde a remedye**). A wise man should not talk too much (III, fo. c.lxxxviii[v]: **I Clatter I babell**) and should dress soberly (see **I Appartayne** (III, fo. c.l[v])).

The wisdom and moral advice imparted to the readers in the examples selected so far are straightforward and explicit in their linguistic form. Yet the verb list also includes a good number of cases where form and meaning are more condensed, where there is linguistic parallelism in structure or even end rhyme. These would be more the 'darke sentẽces comprehẽdyng great wysdome' which Palsgrave wanted to collect and describe in his next book. In some instances, he himself calls them an adage or a proverb. Thus he says of the entry **I Serue one of the same sauce** that it is used 'in maner of a prouerbe' (III, fo. ccc.lv$^{v}$). The French equivalent is *Ie fays de tel pain souppes*. Under the entry **I Contracte matrymonye with one** (III, fo. c.xcvi$^{v}$) the English form in the example is not 'of the same sauce' but 'on the same sauce', perhaps through a misprint. The preferred form in the *OED* has the preposition *with*, and the meaning of the expression could be paraphrased as 'to inflict upon someone the same treatment that one has suffered'. The first citation (with the preposition *of*) dates from 1523 and occurs in Lord Berners' *Froissart*.

An example that is referred to as a French adage is the following:

> . . . **Thou nyest for an others otes/ whiche we expresse by these wordes. Thou lokest after deed mens shoes:** Tu te hannys pour lauoyne daultruy, **it is an adage in the frenche tonge.**
>
> (III, fo. ccc.vi$^{v}$: **I Nye**)

The recorded form in the *OED* is *to wait for dead men's shoes* 'to wait for the death of a person with the expectancy of succeeding to his possessions or office', first quoted in one of John Heywood's works (1546).

Under **I Purpose**, the illustration is '*Man purposeth and god disposeth*: *Homme propose et dieu dispose*' (III, fo. ccc.xxvi$^{v}$). The proverb is an English translation of the Latin *Homo proponit, sed Deus disponit* in Kempis *De Imitatione* (*OED*). Under **I Plye or bowe**, the advice is given: '*Better plye than breake*: *Il vault mieulx se plier que de rompre*' (III, fo. ccc.xviii$^{v}$). According to the *OED*, the closest source for '*Foule wordes corrupte good maners*: *Layz motz corrompẽt bonnes meurs*' (III, fo. c.xcviii$^{v}$: **I Corrupt**) seems to be Tindale's 'malicious speakinges corrupte good manners' (1526–34).

An end rhyme occurs in the saying listed under **I Dyght**:

> **A foule woman rychly dyght/**
> **semeth fayre by candell lyght:**
> Vne fẽme richemẽt acoustrée, or habillée
> semble belle a la chandeille.
>
> (III, fo. cc.xi$^{r-v}$)

Palsgrave even quotes the socio-cultural question raised by John Ball at the outbreak of the Peasants' Revolt of 1381:

> **Whan Adam delueth ⁊ Eue span/**
> **who was than a gentylman.**
> Quant Adam fouissoyt, **or** beschoyt,
> **or** tournoyt la terre, **or** houet et
> Eue filoit, qui estoyt alors gentil-
> homme.
>
> (III, fo. cc.vii$^v$: **I Delue**)

The *Oxford Dictionary of Quotations* ($^2$1956: 235) describes this as an altered form of the piece in verse by Richard Rolle de Hampolle:

> When Adam dalfe and Eve spane
> so spire if thou may spede,
> Whare was than the pride of man,
> That nowe merres his mede?

We conclude this chapter with some examples that reveal still another side of Palsgrave, his sense of humour. This quality may have appeared as an accompanying feature in many of the illustrations already quoted. Yet there are also clear cases, with example sentences surely inserted for the fun of it. Some of them ring so universally human that many readers may recall making similar jocular remarks themselves.

The entry **I Moyst a thing I make it moist** is illustrated as follows:

> **. . . I dyd nat drinke to day**
> **I dyd but moyste my lyppes with a**
> **quarte of wyne:** Ie nay poynt beu au
> iourdhuy ie ne fys que mouiller mes
> leures dune quarte de vin.
>
> (III, fo. ccc.iii$^v$)

In similar vein, Palsgrave continues in the very next entry **I Molde as breed dothe for stalenesse**:

> **. . . I do**
> **some good in ẏ house I kepe breed**
> **from moldyng ⁊ drinke from sow-**
> **ryng:** Ie fays quelque peu de bien a
> la mayson ie garde le payn de moysir
> et le boyre de seurer.
>
> (III, fo. ccc.iii$^v$)

A third comic irony is where the *I*-figure says under the lemma entry **I Set a house a fyre**:

> **. . . I can do some thyng for I**
> **can set a house a fyre ⁊ ronne awaye**
> **by the lyght whan I haue done:** Ie

scay faire quelque chose, car ie scay
bouter le feu en vne mayson et men
fuyr par la clarté.

(III, fo. ccc.lvi)

In perhaps similar style is the euphemism for *steal*:

**I Pull awaye a thyng out of the waye by sleyght/** Ie substrays, **coniugate lyke his symple/** Ie trays, **I drawe. He dothe nat steale it he dothe but pull it out of the waye:** Il ne lemble poynt il ne le fait q̃ substraire.

(III, fo. ccc.xxv^v)

Nor does Palsgrave draw back from the comically absurd:

**. . . Stycke me full of fethers ⁊ you shall se me flye:** Empennez moy et vous me verrez voller.

(III, fo. ccc.lxxiiii)

# 11
# Palsgrave in Perspective

In the preceding chapters we have closely studied Palsgrave's vocabulists, their word lists, their headword structure, the French equivalents, the verb illustrations, and the interlemmatic relations. We have compared his linguistic descriptions and his lexicographical methods of presentation with earlier and contemporary works in order to show where he stays within lexicographical practice as it had developed by the early sixteenth century and where he goes beyond it. The insights gained are little short of startling. John Palsgrave was a teacher and a scholar who understood his mother tongue profoundly, who had a superb command of French, and beyond English and French a remarkable grasp of the nature of language and language pedagogy. The picture of his personality drawn from the few existing records and documents in Chapter 1 was complemented by the human and moral views and attitudes displayed in his verb illustrations in Chapters 9 and 10. He was well acquainted with Thomas More, who introduced him to Erasmus. In order to serve his king best, as Latin tutor to the king's son, he sought the professional advice of leading contemporary scholars and teachers. William Gonell, William Horman, and John Rightwise are named in his letter to More. He has also given us the names of those of his contemporaries who, like himself, were engaged on writing an introduction to the French language: Alexander Barclay, Pierre Valence, and Giles du Wes. All four knew of each other's endeavours, and *Lesclarcissement de la langue francoyse*, as well as the *Introductions in frensshe* and *An introductorie for to lerne to rede to pronounce and to speke Frenche trewly*, openly express what their respective authors thought of the work of their competitors. All four moved in court circles, and we might assume that they will have been acquainted with the leading men of letters and learning. In view of the fact that he was on good terms with Thomas More, it is very likely that Palsgrave will have come to know More's close friends, Colet and Lily. One may even wonder whether he had become acquainted with Johannes Ludovicus Vives, who lectured for a period at Louvain and who became a Latin tutor to the Princess Mary. He might also have been introduced to

Thomas Linacre, who imparted his knowledge of Greek to Thomas More.

There is a further possible acquaintanceship: that with John Skelton. One link may be Louvain. According to the *DNB* (xviii. 327), Whittington, in 1519, mentioned that Skelton had become poet laureate in the university of Louvain. Another may be Skelton's denunciations of Cardinal Wolsey. His *Colyn Cloute* was such an attack, and, although it seems that efforts were made to prevent its publication, copies of it circulated. Could these have been the reason for the three searches of Palsgrave's personal affairs?

In the introduction to *The Comedy of Acolastus* we are given a very clear account of Palsgrave's educational views. He regards a reform in the teaching of languages as necessary. For him, the main task of a language teacher consists in the exposition of the differences between two languages. That is, he advocates explicit contrastive teaching. This presupposes a competent command of the mother tongue. He provided literal and more idiomatic translations of the Latin text in order to further the teachers' competence and accuracy in English. Systematic exposure to good renderings in the mother tongue, he believed, might achieve two things: a use of a more uniform English, which in turn might contribute to a longer preservation of the perfect state which English had reached for him (see in this respect Jones 1966: 265–6, where attention is drawn to similarities between Palsgrave and William Bullokar). The idea that language variation may promote further differentiation whereas uniformity may favour linguistic preservation may have been prompted by a knowledge of the development of the Greek language and its *koine*.

Another pedagogical measure welcomed by Palsgrave was the imminent standardization of grammar teaching which would benefit the teacher as well as the pupil.

In *Lesclarcissement*, published ten years earlier than *The Comedy of Acolastus*, his educational views recur throughout its three books. He criticizes earlier educational policy stipulating that Latin and French be taught at the same time, because this practice impaired the pronunciation of Latin. A foreign language should, therefore, not be taught through another foreign language. What holds for the teaching of different languages also holds for the teaching of the best form of a language and its relation to regional variants. Learners should not be confused by the variety of regional pronunciations but be introduced to whatever is deemed the best form of pronunciation.

Palsgrave repeatedly stresses the self-study value of *Lesclarcissement*. For whoever wants to learn true French without a teacher, his monumental work will be an unparalleled help. We are even told how self-study is achieved. He distinguishes between different types of learners. The beginner should follow the rules (III, fo. c.xxxv) and not the usage of those authors who break the rules. Then there are the learners who will be satisfied with a 'lytell study': they should read the introduction carefully, learn by heart 'the conjugation of the thre parfyte verbes in the seconde boke *Ie parle/ ie conuertis/* and *ie sais/* and the thre verbes anomales *Ie ay/ ie suis/* and *ie men vas*', then, with the help of his word lists, they will be able to translate anything into French (*The Introduction of the authour*, C [vi]). From these learners we have to distinguish a third set, who want to excel in their command of French. They are expected to 'rede ouer all ỷ thre bokes by order' (*The Introduction of the authour*, C [vi]), be intent on 'redyng and dilygent obseruyng of suche authours/ as in the sayd tong be moost excellent' and 'note well the styles of suche secretaries/ as in the fayt of enditung be most approued' (III, fo. i).

He distinguishes between a receptive and a productive use of the foreign language, and, since his word lists are predominantly English–French, but partly also French–English, his assertion is justified that, with the help of his vocabulist, learners will not only be able to translate into French but also read French authors.

But it was also necessary to make explicit in the book the kind of instruction that a teacher in the classroom would make orally. These must include not only what to say but what not to say in the foreign language. Thus Palsgrave gives repeated warnings not to imitate Old French usage (e.g. *mye* (III, fo. c.xxxii)) or Chartier's use of French.

For the self-studying learner the presentation should be as clear and explicit as possible. Palsgrave is very concerned that his readers should find their way about *Lesclarcissement*. References to ease the readers' burden thus occur in the context of alphabetical order and the table of contents. And it is quite indicative that he voices his concern for the readers/learners and their understanding when he is dealing with intrinsic problems of French grammar (whether verbs are preceded by *le/la* or *lui*, whether they are mean verbs, the use of *en*, and the adverbials).

Attention is also given to the way the linguistic material might be presented in a learner-oriented fashion. We know from a letter to the king that he had thought of supporting his teaching by visual illustrations of selected items provided by an artist.

Another aspect of presentation is the formulation of rules for the learner; better still are rules with accompanying examples. The high value Palsgrave attached to exemplification is expressed in 'every exemple is as vayllable to ỷ lerner as thoughe I gaue a rule' (III, fo. cccc.xv).

Both in his endeavour and in the magnitude of his achievement to provide a comprehensive linguistic description of the pronunciation, grammar, and vocabulary of a vernacular, and to contrast it with another vernacular, Palsgrave is unparalleled at the beginning of the sixteenth century. As early as 1492, it is true, Antonio de Nebrija had compiled a grammar as well as a dictionary for Spanish, but the language of contrast was Latin, not another vernacular.

For his reduction of French to rules, probably no better title could have been chosen than *Lesclarcissement de la langue francoyse*, but this very title may have prevented it from going into a second edition. A title specifying that the work was a grammar as well as a dictionary would have been more explicit had both terms been current at the time.

*Lesclarcissement* is a unique work of early linguistic scholarship which investigates the pronunciation, and the grammar as well as the vocabulary, of a sixteenth-century vernacular and contrasts it with another vernacular. Its very comprehensiveness precludes any classification into well-established traditional categories. If this was already the case at Palsgrave's time, it is still more so in our times. The monumental character of the work both in coverage and in sheer size may have made linguistic historians a little hesitant to attempt a full-scale assessment. Though admittedly very difficult, such an assessment is quite vital, since for both the languages, French and English, the sixteenth century is of prime importance in their respective development. It is true that Palsgrave's work has received some more scholarly attention in recent years (see, above all, D. A. Kibbee's work), yet there is still the danger of giving his work a mere cursory mention and of neglecting serious investigation of it in its proper historical and linguistic context because it does not fit conventional categories. Some of what has just been said may even apply to Lindemann's book *Die französischen Wörterbücher von den Anfängen bis 1600*, which takes stock of the lexicographical works involving French up to 1600. The comprehensiveness of coverage, the wealth of individual descriptions given, and the range of affiliations traced between different word lists make Lindemann's work an invaluable research tool for all studies of early French lexicography. But Palsgrave does not emerge from her study with the credit he deserves or with the depth of treatment we have the right to expect. For example, it simply will not do to go on regarding Palsgrave as a mere glossarist (as though supplying only the necessary lexical information to understand French texts) when he plainly makes the pioneering claim to present the lexicon of English and French as a whole.

Palsgrave's French vocabulist has demanded the extensive investigation that has been attempted in my Chapters 3 to 10. My study is on the lexicographical side of his work. We have seen it in comparison with earlier and contemporary word lists involving English and/or French to highlight his contribution to English and French lexicography and to demonstrate to what extent he was dependent on the tradition of dictionary-making as it had evolved by then and how far he was ahead of his time.

Let us here recapitulate some of the major findings. We have no definite proof that Palsgrave used specific word lists compiled by his predecessors or contemporaries. Yet, given the scholarliness of his approach and his conscientiousness as a teacher of Latin and French, it is very likely that he was familiar with the *Promptorium parvulorum* and the *Ortus vocabulorum*, the printed English–Latin and Latin–English dictionaries available at the beginning of the sixteenth century. We have not been able to identify a definite source for his French equivalents.

Definite proof of Palsgrave's sources comes only from those works and authors which he himself has given us by name. Our checking of his linguistic attributions has revealed that they are in the majority of cases reliable.

In resorting to the works of those French writers held in the highest esteem and excerpting from them his word material, he applied a method to vernacular lexicography that was well established for the classical languages. Since he is the first English lexicographer whose name is known, we might even say that English dictionary-making with a known authorship begins with the compilation of words from literary texts in the vernaculars.

Palsgrave's overriding attitude towards the linguistic uses he is describing is that of an objective language recorder (see his frequent 'I fynde . . .' in the list of verbs). Occasionally, he takes sides for or against the actual use encountered. Contrasting different scholarly views on a particular linguistic issue in a dictionary entry was also something that he will have been familiar with from dictionaries describing Latin.

His comments on temporal and regional restrictions in the use of lexical items anticipates the modern lexicographical practice of usage labels in dictionaries. Since his attributions seem to be reliable, historians of the English language will have to take account of his findings. This will have to be done in two ways: the data will have to be incorporated into the body of historically recorded forms. In addition, the fact that these forms were commented upon as early as 1530 will have to be part of the metahistory of English. Historical dialectologists will thus have to assess Palsgrave's contribution to the historiography of English dialects, and, similarly, linguistic historians will have to assign Palsgrave his due place in an English linguistic historiography. For example, Palsgrave's functional description of adverbs with its explicit test frames is a major achievement in early vernacular grammatical analysis and thus deserves a special chapter in a history of English grammar-writing. His verb illustrations offer a treasure trove for historical studies on spoken English and his characterizations of quite a number of speech-act situations will be valuable facets in any description of English pragmatics that embraces earlier stages of the language. In modern English dictionary-making the inclusion of such pragmatic indications is a recent feature in learners' dictionaries which emphasize the productive use of the dictionary. Here again, then, Palsgrave was centuries ahead of vernacular lexicographical practice.

Since the French vocabulist was meant as a learning tool for self-studying English speakers, Palsgrave had to make sure that learners would understand his presentations and descriptions. We might regard the verb table as that part of Palsgrave's English–French dictionary in which a combination of features contributes to create a pioneering productive learner's dictionary. First there is the frequent double function of the postlemmatic expansions: they describe the headword in the mother tongue of the learner and at the same time provide a full semantic description of the following translation equivalent in French. Metalinguistic comments in the learners' mother tongue are a further help. The verb illustrations are fully translated into French, so that no puzzles are left for the learners. If necessary, additional comments on the use of the item are given in the learners' mother tongue and cross-references are provided too. The verb list may thus be regarded as a first attempt at a bilingual vernacular learner's dictionary.

Many of Palsgrave's postlemmatic expansions make his dictionary an excellent monolingual English dictionary at the same time. His explicit and very discriminating semantic descriptions of English words constitute an invaluable field of research for historical lexicologists. There is a wealth of information for historical semantics, but also on neologisms, archaisms, borrowings, idioms, and word-formations.

The French vocabulist also includes a number of close comparisons between English and French usage, so that in *Lesclarcissement* we also have the beginnings of contrastive linguistics in the vernaculars. These beginnings are made for contrastive grammar and contrastive lexicology, with its subfields contrastive semantics, contrastive word-formation, contrastive phraseology, and contrastive pragmatics. The sections in Chapter 9 on social differences in the use of sixteenth-century English and French illustrate that Palsgrave's *Lesclarcissement* also holds valuable insights into linguistic variation for the historical sociolinguist.

That Palsgrave's work constitutes an almost inexhaustible linguistic source for the description of the English and French languages during the first decades of the sixteenth century can be demonstrated with two examples from the fields of grammar and lexicology.

Let us consider his recording of neologisms, (*a*) for French and (*b*) for English. Future research will have to assess Palsgrave's achievement as a mere recorder of sixteenth-century English and French as well as the quality of his semantic descriptions. A close study of his neologisms may also reveal their status—that is, whether, for instance, he tended to compile common central items of the English and French lexicon or more specialized items from particular subject fields, and whether the items recorded by him were to become integral parts of the vocabulary of English and French or whether they were rather ephemeral in nature. Future research may also focus on Palsgrave's achievement as a 'word recorder' in relation to other contemporary lexicographers or earlier and later ones.

We already have the beginning of such research in Kesselring's *Dictionnaire chronologique du vocabulaire français. Le XVI*[e] *siècle* (*DCVF*). The *DCVF* is based on the seven volumes of the *Grand Larousse de la langue française* of 1971–78 and it arranges in chronological order all the lexical and semantic neologisms recorded in this edition of the *Grand Larousse.* Unless superseded by more recent research, the first datings given are thus from this work.

For language historians as well as specialists of the history of European culture, this type of dictionary is a most welcome research tool. In order to show what insights we may gain from Kesselring's work I have studied (for obvious reasons) all the entries included for 1530. We are first given the sources and abbreviations used, and then the lexical and semantic neologisms are listed in alphabetical order. For each instance Kesselring has supplied a source, e.g. PA (= Palsgrave), MA (= C. Marot), S.G. (= Saint-Gelais).

For 1530, we have a total of 684 new lexical items or new senses of items already recorded in the language. I was interested not only in assessing the share of these owed to *Lesclarcissement de la langue francoyse* but also in its grammatical make-up. I therefore analysed the data in the four major word classes, nouns, verbs, adjectives, and adverbs. All the other parts of speech are subsumed under the category 'other'. Within each of these word classes I then distinguished between Palsgrave's contribution and those by all other authors. The respective figures are shown in Table 11.1.

TABLE 11.1. *French neologisms for 1530*

| Letter | Nouns | | Verbs | | Adjectives | | Adverbs | | Other | | Total | |
|---|---|---|---|---|---|---|---|---|---|---|---|---|
| | *Palsg.* | *Others* | *Palsg.* | *Others* | *Palsg.* | *Others* | *Palsg.* | *Others* | *Palsg.* | *Others* | *Palsg.* | *Others* |
| A | 1 | 3 | 4 | 1 | 1 | 1 | — | — | — | — | 6 | 5 |
| B | 4 | 4 | 1 | 2 | — | — | — | — | — | — | 5 | 6 |
| C | 15 | 16 | 11 | 6 | 3 | — | 3 | 1 | — | — | 32 | 23 |
| D | 5 | 2 | 10 | 8 | — | 3 | 1 | — | 1 | 1 | 17 | 14 |
| E | 9 | 10 | 11 | 6 | 1 | 3 | — | 3 | 1 | 2 | 22 | 24 |
| F | 2 | 11 | — | 4 | — | 5 | 1 | — | 1 | — | 4 | 20 |
| G | 6 | 6 | 8 | 2 | 1 | 4 | — | — | — | — | 15 | 12 |
| H | 8 | 6 | — | 1 | — | 2 | — | — | — | 1 | 8 | 10 |
| I | 5 | 7 | 5 | 1 | — | 8 | — | 1 | — | 1 | 10 | 18 |
| J | 2 | 3 | 1 | — | 1 | 1 | — | — | — | — | 4 | 4 |
| L | 20 | 6 | 8 | 2 | 3 | 2 | — | 1 | 5 | 1 | 36 | 12 |
| M | 20 | 9 | 3 | 5 | 1 | 6 | 4 | 2 | — | 1 | 28 | 23 |
| N | 2 | 2 | 1 | 1 | 1 | — | 2 | 1 | — | — | 6 | 4 |
| O | 4 | 5 | 2 | 6 | 1 | — | — | — | 1 | 1 | 8 | 12 |
| P | 33 | 16 | 13 | 6 | 5 | 9 | — | 2 | 2 | 2 | 53 | 35 |
| Q | — | 3 | 1 | — | — | — | — | — | 2 | — | 3 | 3 |
| R | 20 | 9 | 20 | 9 | 1 | 2 | — | 2 | 1 | 1 | 42 | 23 |
| S | 16 | 8 | 11 | 5 | 4 | 7 | 1 | 2 | 4 | — | 36 | 22 |
| T | 16 | 5 | 4 | — | 1 | 7 | 1 | 1 | 3 | 3 | 25 | 16 |
| U | 1 | 2 | 2 | — | 1 | — | — | — | — | 1 | 4 | 3 |
| V | 11 | 5 | 4 | 2 | 2 | — | — | 1 | 1 | 3 | 18 | 11 |
| Z | — | — | — | — | — | — | — | — | — | 2 | — | 2 |
| TOTAL | 200 | 138 | 120 | 67 | 27 | 60 | 13 | 17 | 22 | 20 | 382 | 302 |
| | 338 | | 187 | | 87 | | 30 | | 42 | | 684 | |
| | 59.1% | 40.8% | 64.1% | 35.8% | 31.0% | 68.9% | 43.3% | 56.6% | 52.3% | 47.6% | 55.8% | 44.1% |

The findings of this analytical table are:

1. Of all the French neologisms recorded for 1530 more than a half (55.8 per cent) occur in *Lesclarcissement*.
2. As to the different parts of speech, the order from the highest to the lowest number of all the additions is:

| | | |
|---|---|---|
| nouns | 338 | 49.4% |
| verbs | 187 | 27.3% |
| adjectives | 87 | 12.7% |
| others | 42 | 6.1% |
| adverbs | 30 | 4.3% |

3. Words in the French language first recorded in the work of Palsgrave are especially numerous among verbs (64.1 per cent). For example: *ravauder*, *renifler*, *rôler*, *singulariser*. But he is also the first to document new senses of numerous verbs. To illustrate again from among the verbs (and again restricting examples to a small section of the alphabet), we have: *ramoner* v. tr., *se rapporter* v. pr., *se rasseoir* v. pr., *rebondir* v. intr., *rejeter* v. tr., *répéter* v. tr. et absolu, *représenter* v. tr., *se retirer* v. tr., *retrousser* v. tr., *revenir* v. tr., *rimer* v. intr., *rincer* v. tr., *semer* v. tr., *sentencier* v. tr., *sentir* v. tr. et intr., *servir de* v. tr., *solliciter* v. tr., *songer de* v. tr., *sonner* v. intr., *surpasser* v. tr. In some further cases, *Lesclarcissement* has a transitive sense instead of an intransitive one or vice versa: *renier* v. intr., *rôder* v. intr., *souffrir* v. intr.

   Nouns (with 59,1%) have the second highest figure for first attestations. Among these we have not only one-word lexical items, such as *balançoire*, *ménagerie*, and *noisetier*, but also adjective + noun compounds, as in *une mauvaise herbe*, *une mauvaise langue*, and *une nouvelle lune*; noun + adjective compounds, as in *un écuyer tranchant*, *une ortie blanche*, and *un savon noir*; and noun + noun compounds, as in *un homme de guerre*, *une tête d'ail*, and *le trou du cul*.

   In third position (52.3 per cent) we have the parts of speech other than verbs, nouns, adjectives, and adverbs. This category ('others') includes prepositions, conjunctions, and idiomatic expressions. For example:

| | |
|---|---|
| prepositions | *au-dessous de*; for *loin de* and *selon* Palsgrave records a new sense. |
| conjunctions | *si ce n'est* ('sinon'), (*tant et*) *si bien que*, *en tant que*. |
| idiomatic expressions | *prendre sur le fait*, *il vaut mieux se plier que de rompre*, *ronger son frein*, *tout d'un même trait*, *se tenir au large*, *du vivant de*. |

Adverbs score 43.3 per cent and first attestations by Palsgrave include *à la fois*, *à sec*, *de long en large*, *de moins en moins*, *nonobstant*, *par milliers*, and *quelque peu*.

Adjectives—not surprisingly if one looks at the relatively small size of the adjective table—have the lowest percentage (31.0 per cent). *Jaunâtre*, *pluvial*, and *prêt à* are among those first recorded by Palsgrave, while *lourd*, *poilu*, *prompt*, *sombre*, *subtil*, and *superflu* are among the instances for which *Lesclarcissement* provides a sense not previously recorded.

The examples quoted amply demonstrate that Palsgrave's keen observation of what was new in the French language (words and senses of words) focused predominantly on the central core of the French lexicon (some are more specialized, e.g. *un caneton*, *une langue-de-boeuf*, *un lérot*). This has already been noted in Chapters 9 and 10 for his word lists and above all his verb illustrations. This co-presence of everyday words and more technical or specialized items in Palsgrave's word lists has already emerged from the discussion of his sources (Ch. 4), the structure of his headwords (Ch. 6), his French translation equivalents (Ch. 8), and the characterization of Palsgrave's picture of the world (Ch. 10).

So much for the French lexical items first attested in Palsgrave.

There is no chronological dictionary for English that focuses on writers of one particular century only.[1] It is, however, possible to extract from the *OED* all those words or senses of words for which Palsgrave's *Lesclarcissement* is the first source of attestation. This is what I have done. Leaving aside those instances where a lexical item is well documented before 1530 and where *Lesclarcissement* provides a variant spelling of this item only, we have a total of 1,923 first instances in the *OED*. In order to provide at least a limited comparison with the data from Kesselring's study, the total was then broken down into the four word classes—nouns, verbs, adjectives, and adverbs. All the other remaining first attestations (idiomatic phrases, prepositions, conjunctions, interjections) were subsumed under the category 'others'. The result of this breakdown for the letters of the alphabet is shown in Table 11.2.

Since we do not have comparative figures for neologisms recorded for 1530 by other authors, we can compare the relative sizes for the word classes only. These are given in Table 11.3. The corresponding

[1] The *Chronological English dictionary* does not specify authorial sources; it indicates source dictionaries only.

TABLE 11.2. *First attestations from* Lesclarcissement de la langue francoyse *according to the* OED

| *Letter* | *Nouns* | *Adjectives* | *Verbs* | *Adverbs* | *Other* | *Total* |
|---|---|---|---|---|---|---|
| A | 28 | 9 | 40 | 5 | 1 | 83 |
| B | 72 | 17 | 32 | 1 | 7 | 129 |
| C | 92 | 15 | 48 | 2 | 9 | 166 |
| D | 60 | 24 | 53 | 2 | 3 | 142 |
| E | 17 | 2 | 10 | — | — | 29 |
| F | 30 | 9 | 21 | 1 | 7 | 68 |
| G | 29 | 3 | 20 | 1 | 7 | 60 |
| H | 48 | 13 | 16 | 1 | 10 | 88 |
| I | 17 | 12 | 12 | 5 | — | 46 |
| J | 9 | 1 | 5 | — | — | 15 |
| K | 9 | 2 | 6 | — | 1 | 18 |
| L | 38 | 6 | 24 | 4 | 15 | 87 |
| M | 55 | 16 | 29 | 2 | 14 | 116 |
| N | 23 | 2 | 5 | 4 | 4 | 38 |
| O | 15 | 4 | 16 | — | 1 | 36 |
| P | 77 | 19 | 51 | 2 | 5 | 154 |
| Q | 4 | — | 6 | — | — | 10 |
| R | 46 | 12 | 45 | 1 | 5 | 109 |
| S | 131 | 39 | 104 | 11 | 21 | 306 |
| T | 39 | 11 | 23 | 2 | 5 | 80 |
| U | 6 | 12 | 21 | 3 | — | 42 |
| V | 14 | 3 | 3 | — | — | 20 |
| W | 36 | 14 | 18 | 3 | 6 | 77 |
| X | — | — | — | — | — | — |
| Y | — | 3 | 1 | — | — | 4 |
| Z | — | — | — | — | — | — |
| | 895 (=46.5%) | 248 (=12.8%) | 609 (=31.6%) | 50 (=2.6%) | 121 (=6.2%) | 1,923 (=100%) |

percentages are given in Table 11.4. As we can see, the percentage of noun neologisms is higher for French, while the percentage of adjective neologisms is higher for English. For both languages the figures reveal an interesting, rather similar distribution of the various word classes.

Lexicological studies to come will have to investigate the nature and status of Palsgrave's neologisms. First insights which we gain from a brief check of the noun neologisms in the *OED* are that slightly less than 6 per cent have a subject-field label. Since there is no clear dividing line between the common core and specialized vocabularies, this figure can provide only a preliminary impression and has to be taken with caution. We note, for instance, that such items as *compound*, *phrase*, *pronoun*, *semi-vocal*, *semi-vowel*, *sense*, and *termination*

TABLE 11.3. *Neologisms according to language and word class*

| *Word class* | *French* | *English* |
|---|---|---|
| Nouns | 200 | 895 |
| Verbs | 120 | 609 |
| Adjectives | 27 | 248 |
| Adverbs | 3 | 50 |
| Others | 22 | 121 |
| TOTAL | 382 | 1923 |

TABLE 11.4. *Neologisms according to language and word class (%)*

| *Word class* | *French* | *English* |
|---|---|---|
| Nouns | 52.3 | 46.8 |
| Verbs | 31.4 | 31.1 |
| Adjectives | 7.0 | 12.8 |
| Adverbs | 3.4 | 2.6 |
| Others | 5.7 | 6.6 |
| TOTAL | 99.8 | 99.9 |

in their grammatical/linguistic sense are left unmarked, whereas many other items are clearly labelled *Gram.* The subject field with the highest number of occurrences is *Gram.* which calls for a separate study of Palsgrave's contribution to grammatical terminology in English.

For verbs I have undertaken another check. In order to assess the type of verbs recorded by Palsgrave in his tables I have chosen two relatively short alphabetic sets, those for *N* and for *W*, and then checked the verb entries against the *OED*. Under *N* we have thirty-five dictionary entries for verbs and six of them are first attested in Palsgrave. The items in question are: *to nail up* (III, fo. ccc.vi: **I Nayle in a thynge**), *to newfangle* (III, fo. ccc.vi: **I Newefangyll**), *to nick* 'to make a nick or notch in' (III, fo. ccc.vi$^{v}$: **I Nycke**), *to nuzzle* 'to burrow or dig with the nose' (III, fo. ccc.vii: **I Nosyll as a swyne**), *to nuzzle* 'to accustom (a dog or hawk) to attack other animals or birds' (III, fo. ccc.vii: **I Nosyll a yonge thing**), *to not* 'to clip or cut short (the hair or beard)' (III, fo. ccc.vii$^{r-v}$: **I Notte ones heed**).

If we subtract the misplaced verb *to upbraid*, there are 288 verb entries under the letter *W*. Of these, 104 are constructions with the verb *to wax* in the sense of 'become' or 'grow'. Leaving these aside, we have a total of 184 verb instances. The *OED* credits Palsgrave with being first to record seventeen of them. They are:

*to weaken* — *OED*: **I.4.** 'to lessen (authority, influence, power, credit) . . .'
**I Wayken a thynge** (III, fo. cccc)

*to weaken* — *OED*: **I.1.a.** 'to steep (salt meat) in water, so as to remove the salt . . .'
**I Wayken salte meates** (III, fo. cccc)

*to wall* — *OED*: **3.** 'to shut up (a person or thing) within walls . . .'
**I Wall I shyt vp or close vp with in walles** (III, fo. cccc$^{v}$)

*to warble* — *OED*: **2.a.** intr. 'to modulate the voice in singing . . .'
**I Warbell with the voyce as connyng syngers do** (III, fo. cccc.i)

*to water* — *OED*: **II.12.a.** 'Of the mouth: To secrete abundant saliva in the anticipation of appetizing food or delicacies . . .'
**I Water a horse . . . My tethe waters to se yonder fayre appels** (III, fo. cccc.i$^{v}$)

*to wave* — *OED*: **I.4.a.** 'Of water, the sea: To move in waves, undulate'
**I Waue as ẙ see dothe** (III, fo. cccc.i$^{v}$)

*to wear away* — *OED*: **III.14.b.**: The entry from *Lesclarcissement* is the first with *away* as an intensifier.
**I Weare awaye as a scrypture or thyng made for remembraũce** (III, fo. cccc.vii)

*to wedge* — *OED*: **2.a.** 'To cleave or split by driving in a wedge'
**I Wedge a blocke** (III, fo. cccc.vi)
**I Wedge I lay in pledge** (III, fo. cccc.vi$^{r-v}$)

*to welter* — *OED*: **I.** *intr.* **1.b.** 'To roll about (*in* the mire, etc.) . . .'
**I Welter** (III, fo. cccc.vii)

*to whistle* — *OED*: **I.4.** 'To blow or sound a whistle . . .'
**I Whystell in a whystell or in my hande** (III, fo. cccc.viii)

*to wind out* — *OED*: **13.** *intr.* and *refl.* **a.** 'With *out*: To extricate or disentangle oneself from a state of confinement or embarassment'
**I Wynde out as one wyndeth him out of busynesse** (III, fo. cccc.ix)

*to whinny* — *OED*: 1. *intr.* 'Of a horse: To neigh . . .'
**I Whynye as a horse dothe** (III, fo. cccc.viii)

*to whip* — *OED*: I.11. *fig.* 'To vex, afflict, torment, to punish, chastise . . .'
**I Whyppe with a shrode tourne** (III, fo. cccc.viii)

*to wont* — *OED*: 2. *trans.* 'To use habitually'
**I Wonte or vse** (III, fo. cccc.x)

*to wrench* — *OED*: **I.5.** 'To injure or pain (a person, the limbs, etc.) by undue straining or stretching . . .'
**I Wrenche my foote or any lymme** . . . (III, fo. cccc.xi)

*to wreathe* — *OED*: **I.1.b.** 'To wind or turn (some flexible object) about or over something . . .'
**I Wrethe one thyng aboute an other** (III, fo. cccc.xi)

*to wrinkle* — *OED*: **1.b.** 'Of person, the face, etc.: To become creased or puckered . . .'
**I Wrinkell as ones face dothe** (III, fo. cccc.xi)

But for some of Palsgrave's 184 *W* entries the *OED*'s first citation is the year 1528 or 1529. One can plausibly add these to the Palsgrave first attestations, since they clearly testify to his early acquaintance with recent additions to the vocabulary. Cases in point are: *to wamble* 'of the stomach or its contents: to be felt to roll about', for which Skelton *c.*1528 and More 1533 and 1534 are cited; *to winch* 'to hoist or draw up', where Palsgrave's entry is preceded by a 1529 citation, and *to wrinkle* in the sense of 'to suffer or undergo contraction or puckering into wrinkles or small folds', where the entry from *Lesclarcissement* is second after a 1528 quotation from Paynell.

Our checking of *W* verbs in the *OED* yielded, in addition, a number of instances where either the items or senses in Palsgrave were not included in the *OED* at all or citations of them are later than 1530. This applies to the following items:

*to warn* — **I Warne a mã to apere at a courte in iudgement/** Ie sõme, ie adiourne, and ie semons . . .
(III, fo. cccc.i)

*to warn* — **I Warne one of a mater in processe/** Ie intime . . .
(III, fo. cccc.i)

*to watch* — **I Watche for a thynge in vayne/** Ie me amuse . . .
(III, fo. cccc.i$^{v}$)

*to worry* **I Wery a persone by speakynge or by shewyng of any thyng that is displeasaunt to the eare or to ẏͤ eye/** Ie fache . . .

(III, fo. cccc.vi[v])

The *OED*'s sense **6.a.** under *to worry* is 'to vex, distress, or persecute by inconsiderate or importunate behaviour; to plague or pester with reiterated demands, requests, or the like', and the first citation is from Milton (1671).

*to write out* **I Write out any thynge I copye it out/** Ie transcrips . . .

(III, fo. cccc.xi[v])

The first citation in the *OED* (*to write*—**17. write out**) dates from 1548 (Elyot).

It would seem that the words and senses for which Palsgrave's *Lesclarcissement* is actually our first source of citation are, on the whole, items that belong to the common core of the language, and most of them have acquired a permanent place in the English vocabulary. As noted in earlier chapters, the *OED* can be credited with a good coverage of the lexical material from Palsgrave's work, but for an adequate description of the English vocabulary in the sixteenth century scholars would need a revised database. This would involve a reassessment not only of Palsgrave's contribution but of other sixteenth-century dictionaries. Already the *OED* has borne eloquent testimony to Palsgrave's importance in English lexicography—as had earlier dictionaries (see Smalley (1948) on Cotgrave). My purpose in this book has been broader: to show his importance in vernacular language description and language-teaching, where his remarkable achievements have been much less acknowledged. This is perhaps most notable with respect to grammar. So far as English is concerned, we may consider for example the second-person pronoun. The inherited formal system in Middle English distinguished between number and case. In the singular the subject form was *thou*, the object form *thee*. In the plural the subject form was *ye*, the object form *you*. During the Middle English period the number contrast began to change into a contrast in status, which Baugh and Cable summarize as follows:

In the thirteenth century the singular forms (*thou*, *thy*, *thee*) were used among familiars and in addressing children or persons of inferior rank, while the plural forms (*ye*, *your*, *you*) began to be used as a mark of respect in addressing a superior. In England the practice seems to have been suggested by French usage in court circles, but it finds a parallel in many other modern languages. In any case, the usage spread

> as a general concession to courtesy until *ye*, *your*, and *you* became the usual pronoun of direct address irrespective of rank or intimacy. By the sixteenth century the singular forms had all but disappeared from polite speech . . . (Baugh and Cable 1978: 242)

Finkenstaedt in his Habilitationsschrift on *You and Thou* investigates the semantic development of the shift and therefore does not focus on the formal distinction between *ye*/*you* and its persistence. Yet some of the examples adduced for colloquial English and taken from the 1567 collection of jests, *Tales and quicke answers*, include *ye* forms: '*Ye* speak now too late', '*ye* shall have it' (Finkenstaedt 1963: 113–14).

A study of the use of these forms by Palsgrave and a comparison with his contemporaries, Pierre Valence and Giles du Wes, yield some interesting findings. In his discussion of the various verb forms Valence regularly uses *ye* for the subject and *you* for the object, whether singular or plural, irrespective of whether he is addressing his readers or citing examples. I have noticed only two exceptions: both, significantly enough, in the examples rather than the more formal address to readers: *Wherfore speke you not?—Que ne parles vous?* ([P ii$^{v}$]), *You wynkle with your eye.—Vous borgues de loiel.* ([Q ii$^{v}$]).

Du Wes prescribes the same system as Valence. In his lists of tense forms the French form *vous* in subject function is systematically matched by English *ye*. In addressing his reader(s) he uses *ye* as the subject form and *you* in non-subject function. The same holds in general for his examples and dialogues, whether the subject or non-subject is singular or plural. Yet there are some interesting exceptions.

The exceptions found in the verb illustrations seem to be related to questions or dependent clauses:

howe do you / ꝛ howe do ye fare ([Q i$^{v}$])
Howe do you ([Q ii])

o yf I knew . . . yf you . . . knew
**O se ie cogneusse . . . se vo$^{9}$ cogneussies** ([N iiii$^{v}$])

whan I shall se . . . you . . .
**Mais Que ie voie . . . q̃ vous voiez** ([Q i])

Three other exceptions seem to suggest that for du Wes the English reflexives and reciprocals were uncertain territory or that there was a more general tendency for a blurring between these sets of pronouns. In one instance the object form *you* may have prompted the use of *you* in subject position:

howe shall you beare you.
**Comẽt . . . Vous porteres vous.** (Q ii)

In the other, the French verb is *sengenouller* (*s'agenouiller*). The English verb is not reflexive, but the French reflexive may have triggered off a *you* for English: *you kneele* for *vous vous angenoulles*.

Instead of finding *you* in place of *ye*, the co-occurrence of subject and object may occasionally yield the converse *ye* where *you* would be expected:

do ye nat vnderstande ye . . .
**ne vous entendes vous pas** . . . (S ii)

We note again the apparent relevance of the examples being questions.

There are about a dozen exceptions in the second book of du Wes's *Introductorie* (the dialogue passages) and they fall into three groups:

1. *You* as subject in questions:

From whens come you my frende.
**Dou venes vous mon amy.** (T ii)

Do nat you bring me some remembraunce or token from them.
**Ne maportęs vous q̃lque souuenãce ou enseigne de par eulz.** (T ii)

whan pretende you or purpose you to retourne toward the court . . .
**quant pretendęs vo⁹ quant proposęs vous de retournęr deuers la court . . .** (T iii)

2. *You* as subject in dependent clauses:

That you dyd speke ryght good frenche
**Que vous parlięz tres bon francois** (T iii^v^)

For if it dyd please our lorde [t]hat you might ones cõme to
**Car sil plaisoit nostre seigneur [q]ue vous peussięz ia paruenir**

where your hert hath his desire
**Ou vostre coeur a son desir** ([T iii^v^–iiii])

how be it I loue better that for this tyme you do declare vnto me what it is of peas.
**toutesuoies iayme mieulx / que pour le presẽt vous me declaręs q̃ cest que paix.** (Aa ii)

And if you aske me of what substaunce she is . . .
**et sy vous me demãdęs de q̃l matięre elle est** (Cc ii^v^)

3. *You* as subject preceded by *you* as non-subject:

Trewly I am ryght glade to here you / and you haue gyue me
**En bonne veritę Giles ie suis tresioieuse de vo⁹ auoir ouy et maues donnęs**

in your words solas and recreation.
**en vos parolles soulas et recreation.** ([Cc iiii^v^])

but for to shew you how you ought to maintene you at the masse . . .
**que pour vous monstręr coment vous vous debuęs contenir a la messe** . . . (Dd ii^v^)

To sum up, both Valence and du Wes observe in general the singular and plural use of *ye* as subject, *you* as non-subject. But for both, though especially du Wes, there seems to be a growing tendency in non-formal language (i.e. the colloquial examples) to use *you* as a general second-person form, unmarked for case or number.

This tendency is strikingly conspicuous in Palsgrave, who, unlike Valence and du Wes, seems to have no use for *ye* at all.

His overriding form of address, for the singular as well as for the plural, is *you*. He does not even list *ye* among the personal pronouns in book II:

Ie—**I**
tu—**thou**
il—**he**
élle—**she**
len lon or on—**a man betokenyng a parson vncertayne**
se—**hym or her**
nous—**we**
uous—**you**
ilz—**they men**
élles—**they women**
se—**them men or women**

(II, fo.xxxiiii)

When he discusses the declension of these pronouns, he subsumes *len*, *lon*, *on*, *nous*, and *vous* under one paragraph, maintaining

> [a]nd as for *Len*, *lon*, and *on*: *Novs* and *vovs* remayne vndeclyned/ ꝛ without any chãgyng/ serue for all maner of spekyng/ wherby apereth that sythe we haue in our tonge we/ whiche serueth for the nominatyue case/ and vs/ whiche serueth for an accusatyue case or oblyque case/ As we lone [*sic*]/ he loueth vs/ for vs in this worde our tong is more parfyte. (II, fo. xxxv)

Although in Palsgrave's system of personal pronouns *you* has its place in the plural set between *we* and *they* and he thus opposes it to the singular forms *thou/thee*, it seems clear that number *per se* is not involved. Rather his system is already the one that became generalized in Modern English: *you* is second person, without number or case distinction.

Just as *you* is his general form of address for his learners, so it is also the predominant form in his verb illustrations. Occurrences of *thou/thee* are certainly singular but they are marked not primarily for number but for the speaker's attitude towards the discourse partner and/or his or her behaviour. Some of the examples could be interpreted as expressing familiarity or intimacy, paired with well-meaning advice:

. . . **If thou dispende thy good3** on this facion **thou shall**

. . . **What nedest you to iotte me with thyne el-**

**sone be poore:** Si tu despens tes biens en ce poynt tu seras bien tost poure.

(III, fo. cc.xiiii[v]: **I Dispende**)

**bowe/ thou arte disposed to pyke a quarell:** A quoy est il besoing de me hercer, or de me heurter de tõ coulde tu es deliberé de prendre noyse aux gens.

(III, fo. cc.lxviii[v]: **I Iotte**)

Others seem to be addressed to a child or a young person:

**Come of come of/ and thou mayest lyngar behynde thou arte safe:** Sus sus vien auant, si tu peulx targer, or faire la queue tu te trouues bien.

(III, fo. cc.lxxxiii: **I Lyngar**)

**. . . I pray the mo lest me nat I haue ben troubled y-noughe to daye:** Ie te prie ne me molestes poynt iay esté assez empesché au iourdhuy.

(III, fo. ccc.iii[v]: **I Molest**)

Displeasure or anger may also be cast in a *thou*-form:

**. . . Thou gronest euer whã I com in a dores:** Tu grongnes, or tu grõmelles tousiours quant ie entre a la mayson.

(III, fo. cc.lv: **I Groone**)

**. . . By god thou shalt go from they worde or thou shalte se that it shall displease me:** Pardieu tu ten desdiras ou tu voyras quil men desplaira.

(III, fo. cc.lii[r–v]: **I Go from a thynge**)

In quite a number of examples we find a reprimand, as in

**Aryse man thou lyest a beed al day:** Lieue toy tu te tiẽs au lict toute iour.

(III, fo. cc.lxxxi: **I Lye a bedde**)

**. . . Fye on the villayne thou gnawest thy mete with thy tethe lyke a dogge:** Fy villayn tu ronges ta viande de tes dens cõme si tu fusses vng chien.

(III, fo. cc.l[v]: **I Gnawe as a dogge**)

The vocatives in the last two examples show that the *thou*-forms are addressed to people regarded as inferior in rank.

Though such affective reactions are often found together with forms of the second person singular, *thou/thee/thy*, this does not mean that displeasure or anger cannot be expressed with *you*-forms, as we can see from the following two examples:

**. . . Haue you nat doone yet on my faythe you do but loyter:** Nauez vous pas fait encore, sur ma foy vous ne faictez que truander, or vous ne faictez que desbaucher.

(III, fo. cc.lxxxiii[v]: **I Loyter**)

**. . . You lubber as well as any knaue in this towne:** Vous lorricardez aussi bien que villayn de ceste ville.

(III, fo. cc.lxxxv[v]: **I Lubber**)

The fact that Palsgrave, as early as 1530, uses *you* alone where Valence and du Wes distinguish between *ye* as subject and *you* as object calls for an explanation which is not easy to give. Both were speakers of French and as such (despite the fact that *vous* was both subject and object) they might have observed the perceived grammatical distinction between subject and object more closely than the native Englishman Palsgrave. At any rate, since *ye* in subject function was still quite common in the second half of the sixteenth century, it is Palsgrave's use of one single form that is exceptionally modern.

For French grammar, we may consider negation. Language historians have pointed out that in sixteenth-century French the negative particle *ne* could be omitted in certain linguistic contexts. These are described by Gougenheim in his *Grammaire de la langue française du 16ᵉ siècle* (1974) as interrogative sentences. The question may be a main clause, as in 'Sont ce *pas* des songes de l'humaine vanité de faire de la lune une terre céleste?' (Gougenheim 1974: 242), or a subordinate one, as in 'Je ne sçay si ce fut *point* ce mesme singe dont nous parlions tant maintenant' (ibid.).

The beginnings of this usage are by no means clear. If one assumes that the construction may have originated in the spoken language, one is again confronted with the problem of the textual bases which we have for early spoken French. C. Schmitt has repeatedly stressed that scholars have not really yet begun to tap the rich linguistic material contained in sixteenth-century *manières de langage* and practical treatises to teach a language. For the French vocabulary his study of du Wes's *Introductorie* has 'brought to light' a considerable number of lexical and semantic neologisms and archaisms. With respect to French grammar, he has investigated Abraham La Faye's *Linguae gallicae et italicae hortulus amoenissimus* of 1608. This work has an appendix with dialogues in French and Italian which may well be regarded as rather close to the spoken idiom of the time. A careful study of all the sentences in these dialogues revealed a relatively high percentage of interrogative negations without *ne*; indeed, according to Schmitt's knowledge (1980: 26), they constitute the highest relation (15:68) for longer texts of the period.

Let us, therefore, look at Palsgrave's description of negation in French to see whether he was already aware of the possibility of omitting the particle *ne* under certain conditions. Let us also look at his verb illustrations to see whether they include interrogatives which have no *ne*.

It is in book III that Palsgrave provides his learners with an explicit account of how one negates a sentence or a phrase in French. The most detailed section is the part which precedes the table of verbs and explains the use of *pas*, *poynt*, and *mye* (III, fo. c.xxxii). Further insights are given under the table of adverbs and conjunctions (*not*:

III, fo. cccc.xxxi[v] and III, fo. cccc.lxix; *without*: III, fo. cccc.xlvii).

The overall pattern of sentence negation is described as follows:

Whan the sentence is negatyue in our tonge/ that is to saye that the verbe hath nat after hym/ as I wyll nat/ I se nat/ I wotte nat whyther to go/ and all suche lyke: the frenche tonge remoueth the negacion and putteth hym byfore the verbe/ and immedyately after the verbe putteth *pas*, *poynt*, or *mye*, especially if the verbe be indycatyue/ and the laste worde in the sentence. So that *pas*, *poynt*, or *mye*, be vsed for a more clere expressyng of negacion/ and as though the speker wolde byde by ẏ thing whiche he denyeth: in so moche that if ẏ speker do but fayntly denye a thyng/ they vse than to leaue out *pas*, *poynt*, or *mye*. (III, fo. c.xxxii)

Three sets of examples are provided, the shorter form preceding the longer one. The verbs in the sentences are *savoir*, *pouvoir*, and *faire*. He admits, however, that there may be other factors involved which he cannot reduce to rule ('But herin also is requyred a farther iudgement than can be gyuen by any rule'), but two things are more clearly statable: *mye* should not be used by the learner because it is no longer common usage, and *iamays*, *onques*, *riens*, *plus*, *moyns* in sentences have to co-occur with *ne*.

Palsgrave then focuses on questions as a particular sentence type, and he describes French usage as follows:

Here is also to be noted that whan we aske a questyon in our tonge whiche we doute nat but the answerer muste confesse/ bycause we knowe our selfe it is so in dede/ in suche questyons thoughe we adde nat/ byfore our verbes: as dyd I nat tell you/ lo is he nat hurte nowe/ dyd nat I se the there yesterdaye. In suche questyons ẏ frenche tonge dothe nat vse to put *ne*, byfore their verbes/ but yet they adde *pas*, or *poynt*, after the verbe/ sayeng: *vous dis ie pas*, *agardez est il pas blessé mayntenãt*, *te vis ie pas la hyer*. But if we aske one a questyon whiche he hymselfe shewed vs/ and haue no farther knowlege but his owne reporte/ in such questyons we vse nat to put/ nat/ byfore ẏ verbe/ but yet in frenche they haue *pas*, or *poynt*, after the verbe. (III, fo. c.xxxii[r–v])

As we can see, Palsgrave is not only aware that *ne* can be dropped in sentence negation; he is even able to identify the specific sentence type in which this is possible—conducive questions—and he provides examples. This is striking proof of Palsgrave's superb command of French and his sharp linguistic and analytic faculties. As early as 1530, he has explicitly and correctly described, in a vernacular of the time, his mother tongue English, a particular syntactic pattern in another vernacular, French.

Such conducive questions without *ne* occur also among the examples in his verb table. For example:

> . . . **Haue I nat acquit me lyke a man?** Me suis poynt acquité cõme vng homme?
>
> (III, fo. c.li[v]: **I Aquyte or demeane**)

> . . . **Haue I nat sene the begge from doore to doore/ and nowe thou arte as prowde as if thou were a lorde:** Tay ie poynt veu blistrer or coquiner dhuys en huys, et mayntenant tu es aussi fier cõme se tu fussez vng seignie^r^.
>
> (III, fo. c.lix^v^: **I Begge as a begger**)
>
> **Wenest thou I can nat lyue ẘout her:** Pẽses tu que ie men puis pas passer sans elle.
>
> (III, fo. cc.lxxxiii^r–v^: **I Lyue without a thyng**)

The brief account of two grammatical issues in English and French illustrates the way in which *Lesclarcissement de la langue francoyse* constitutes an invaluable source for the study of these languages in the sixteenth century[2] as well as being a treasure trove for early linguistic analyses of these two vernaculars.

[2] Since the studies on spoken French by Schmitt and Radtke concentrate on the period from 1600 onwards, it might be worthwhile drawing attention to the earlier works by Claude Desainliens (alias Claudius Holyband) and their dialogues. *The French school-master* (1573) and *The French littelton* (1576) include familiar talks in English and French, the *Pronuntiatione linguae gallicae* (1580) has a French–Latin dialogue part, and in the *Campo di fior or else the flovrie field of fovre languages* (1583) Italian, Latin, French, and English are contrasted. From the latter work, for instance, is the following *ne*-less question:

It.: O fanciulli, vi desterete vi oggi?
Fr.: Or sus enfans, vous reveillerez vous point au-iourdhuy?
(Desainliens 1583: 3)

# Bibliography


Aarsleff, H., Kelly, L. G., and Niederehe, H.-J. (1984) (eds), *Papers in the history of linguistics* (ICHoLS 3; Amsterdam and Philadelphia: Benjamins).

Abélard, J. (1982), 'Une contribution au dictionnaire du moyen français: le glossaire des *Illustrations de Gaule de Jean Lemaire de Belges*', in P. Wunderli (ed.), *Du mot au texte. Actes du III^e Colloque International sur le Moyen Français. Düsseldorf, 17–19 septembre 1980* (Tübinger Beiträge zur Linguistik, 175; Tübingen: Narr), 89–102.

Allen, P. S. (1910) (ed.), *Opus epistolarum des. Erasmi Roterdami. Denuo recognitum et auctum*, ii. *1514–1517* (Oxford: Clarendon Press).

Alston, R. C. (1964), 'The *Introductions in frensshe* of Pierre Valence and the Lambeth Fragment 1528', *Studia Neophilologica*, 36: 101–10.

——(1967*a*) (ed.), *Pierre Valence. Introductions in Frensshe* [1528] (English Linguistics 1500–1800; A collection of facsimile reprints, 38; Menston: Scolar Press).

——(1967*b*) (ed.), *A very necessary boke* [*1550*] (English linguistics 1500–1800; A collection of facsimile reprints, 43; Menston: Scolar Press).

——(1968*a*) (ed.), *Ortus vocabulorum. 1500* (English Linguistics 1500–1800; A collection of facsimile reprints, 123; Menston: Scolar Press).

——(1968*b*) (ed.), *Promptorium parvulorum. 1499* (English Linguistics 1500–1800; A collection of facsimile reprints, 108; Menston: Scolar Press).

——(1968*c*) (ed.), *Thomas Linacre. De emendata structura Latini sermonis libri sex. 1524* (English Linguistics 1500–1800; A collection of facsimile reprints, 83; Menston: Scolar Press).

——(1969*a*) (ed.), *John Palsgrave. Lesclarcissement de la langue francoyse. 1530* (English Linguistics 1500–1800; A collection of facsimile reprints, 190; Menston: Scolar Press).

——(1969*b*) (ed.), *John Stanbridge. Accidence* [*ca.1496*] (English Linguistics 1500–1800; A collection of facsimile reprints, 134; Menston: Scolar Press).

——(1970*a*) (ed.), *Claude Desainliens. The French littleton* [*1576*] (English linguistics 1500–1800; A collection of facsimile reprints, 220; Menston: Scolar Press). [See also Holyband.]

——(1970*b*) (ed.), *Claude Desainliens. De pronuntiatione linguae gallicae. 1580* (English Linguistics 1500–1800; A collection of facsimile reprints, 212; Menston: Scolar Press). [See also Holyband.]

Alston, R. C. (1970*c*) (ed.), *William Lily and John Colet. A short introduction of grammar. 1549* (English Linguistics 1500–1800; A collection of facsimile reprints, 262; Menston: Scolar Press).

——(1970*d*) (ed.), *Thomas Elyot. The book named the governor. 1531* (English linguistics 1500–1800; A collection of facsimile reprints, 246; Menston: Scolar Press).

——(1971) (ed.), *Thomas Linacre. Rudimenta grammatices* [*1523*?] (English Linguistics 1500–1800; A collection of facsimile reprints, 312; Menston: Scolar Press).

——(1972*a*) (ed.), *Claude Desainliens. The French school-master. 1573* (English linguistics 1500–1800; A collection of facsimile reprints, 315; Menston: Scolar Press). [See also Holyband.]

——(1972*b*) (ed.), *Giles du Wes. An introductory for to learn to read, to pronounce, and to speak French.* [1532?] (English Linguistics 1500–1800; A collection of facsimile reprints, 327; Menston: Scolar Press).

——(1974), *A bibliography of the English language from the invention of printing to the year 1800* (corrected repr. of vols. i–x; Ilkley: Janus Press).

——(1985), *A bibliography of the English language from the invention of printing to the year 1800*, xii. *The French language: grammars. miscellaneous treatises. dictionaries* (Otley: Smith Settle).

Ames, J. (1749), *Typographical antiquities: being an historical account of printing in England: with some memoirs of our antient printers, and a register of the books printed by them, from the year M CCCC LXXI to the year MDC. With an appendix concerning printing in Scotland and Ireland to the same time* (London: W. Faden).

——(1816/1969), *Typographical antiquities; or the history of printing in England, Scotland and Ireland: containing memoirs of our ancient printers, and a register of the books printed by them. Begun by the late Joseph Ames . . . considerably augmented by William Herbert . . . and now greatly enlarged by . . . Thomas Trognalf Dibdin*, iii (London: John Murray, 1816; repr. as Anglistica & Americana, 19; Hildesheim: Olms, 1969).

Anderson, J. D. (1978), *The development of the English–French, French–English bilingual dictionary: a study in comparative lexicography* (supplement to *Word*, 28/3 (December 1972), Monograph 6).

Angelis, V. de (1977–80), *Papiae Elementarium. Littera A.* (Testi e documenti per lo studio dell'antichità 58; 3 vols; Milan: Cisalpino-Goliardica).

Anon. (1499), *Incipit prologus in libellũ qui dicitur promptorius puerorum . . .* (London: Pynson).

Anon. (1500), *Ortus vocabulorum* (London: de Worde).

Anon. (1508), *Promptorium paruulorum clericorum quod apud nos Medulla grammatice appellatur . . .* (London: Notary).

Anon. (1509), *Ortus vocabulorum . . .* (London: Pynson).

Anon. (1510), *Promptorium paruulorum clericorum quod apud nos Medulla grammatice appellatur . . .* (London: de Worde) (later edns: 1516, 1528).

Anon. (1511), *Ortus vocabulorum . . .* (London: de Worde) (later edns: 1514, 1518, 1528).

Anon. (1517), *Ortus vocabulorum . . .* (Rothomagi: Hardy).

Anon. (1520), *Ortus vocabulorum . . .* (*s.l.*: Cousin).

Arber, E. (1875–94) (ed.), *A transcript of the registers of the company of stationers of London; 1554–1640. A.D.* (5 vols.; London: privately printed).

Aries, P. and Margolin, J.-C. (1982) (eds.), *Les jeux à la Renaissance. Actes du XXIII° colloque international d'études humanistes, Tours—juillet 1980* (De Pétrarque à Descartes, 43; Paris: Vrin).

Arnold, I. D. O. (1937), 'Thomas Sampson and the *Orthographia Gallica*', *Medium Aevum*, 6: 193–209.

Arnould, E. J. (1939), 'Les sources de *Femina nova*', in *Studies in French language and medieval literature presented to Professor Mildred K. Pope by pupils, colleagues and friends* (Manchester: Manchester University Press), 1–9.

Arveiller, R. (1982), 'Lexicologie (XVI^e^–XVII^e^ s.): quelques difficultés', in M. Höfler (ed.), *La lexicographie française du XVI^e^ au XVIII^e^ siècle. Actes du Colloque International de Lexicographie dans la Herzog August Bibliothek Wolfenbüttel (9–11 Octobre 1979)* (Wolfenbüttel: Herzog August Bibliothek), 81–101.

Asbach-Schnitker, B. and Roggenhofer, J. (1987) (eds), *Neuere Forschungen zur Wortbildung und Historiographie der Linguistik. Festgabe für Herbert E. Brekle zum 50. Geburtstag* (Tübingen: Narr).

Atkins, B. T., *et al.* (1987) (eds), *Collins Robert French–English English–French Dictionary* (London, Glasgow, and Toronto: Collins; Paris: Dictionnaires Le Robert).

Atkinson, W. E. D. (1964), *Acolastvs. A Latin play of the sixteenth century by Gulielmus Gnapheus. Latin text with a critical introduction and an English translation* (University of Western Ontario Studies in the Humanities, 3, London and Ontario: Humanities Department of the University of Western Ontario).

Aubert, M. (1909), 'Les anciens Donats de la bibliothèque nationale', *Bibliographie moderne*, 13: 220–40.

Ayres-Bennett, W. and Carruthers, J. (1992), '"Une regrettable et fort disgracieuse faute de français?": The description and analysis of the French *surcomposés* from 1530 to the present day', *Transactions of the Philological Society*, 90/2: 219–57.

Bacon, R. (1266/1961), *The Opus majus of Roger Bacon* (1266), a translation by Robert Belle Burke), i (Philadelphia: University of Pennsylvania Press, 1928; microfilm repr., Ann Arbor: University Microfilms Inc., 1961).

Baker, D. E. (1782), *Biographia dramatica, or, a companion to the playhouse*, a new edition, carefully corrected, greatly enlarged, and continued from 1764 to 1782, i (London: printed for MSS. Rivingtons, T. Payne & Son).

Baker, J. H. (1989), 'A French vocabulary and conversation guide in a fifteenth-century legal notebook', *Medium Aevum*, 58: 80–102.

Balbus, J. (1460), *Incipit summa quae vocatur Catholicon . . .* (Mainz).

Baldinger, K. (1951), 'Autour du «Französisches etymologisches Wörterbuch» (FEW). Considerations critiques sur les dictionnaires français, Aalma 1380—Larousse 1949', *Revista Portuguesa de Filologia*, 4: 342–73.

Baldinger, K. (1957), 'Contribution à une histoire des provincialismes dans la langue française', *Revue de linguistique romane*, 21: 62–92.

——(1974) (ed.), *Introduction aux dictionnaires les plus importants pour l'histoire du français* (Paris: Klincksieck).

——(1979), 'Le Catholicon de Jehan Lagadeuc, ed. Christian-J. Guyonvarc'h', *Zeitschrift für romanische Philologie*, 95: 186–8.

——(1982*a*), 'Séance de clôture. Le colloque dans le cadre de la lexicologie historique du français', in M. Höfler (ed.), *La lexicographie française du XVI^e au XVII^e siècle. Actes du colloque international de lexicographie dans la Herzog August Bibliothek Wolfenbüttel (9–11 Octobre 1979)* (Wolfenbütteler Forschungen, 18, Wolfenbüttel: Herzog August Bibliothek), 149–58.

——(1982*b*), 'Estienne 1531 et son importance pour l'histoire du vocabulaire français', in M. Höfler (ed.), *La lexicographie française du XVI^e au XVIII^e siècle. Actes du colloque international de lexicographie dans la Herzog August Bibliothek Wolfenbüttel (9–11 Octobre 1979)* (Wolfenbütteler Forschungen, 18, Wolfenbüttel: Herzog August Bibliothek), 9–20.

——(1986), 'François Rabelais: son importance pour l'histoire du vocabulaire français', in S. Cigada (ed.), *Le moyen français. Actes du V^e colloque international sur le moyen français. Milan, 6–8 mai 1985*, ii (Milan: Vita e Pensiero), 163–79.

Bale, J. (1557), *Scriptorvm illustriū maioris Brytannie, quam nunc Angliam & Scotiam uocant*: Catalogus . . . (Basileae: apud Ioannem Oporinum).

Banner, M., Curtis, F. J., and Friedwagner, M. (1912) (eds), *Festschrift zum 15. Neuphilologentage in Frankfurt am Main 1912* (Frankfurt: Gebrüder Knauer).

Bateson, M. (1903) (ed.), *Grace book B, Part I, containing the proctors' accounts and other records of the University of Cambridge for the years 1488–1511* (Cambridge: University Press).

Baugh, A. (1959), 'The date of Walter of Bibbesworth's *Traité*', *Festschrift für Walther Fischer* (Heidelberg: Winter), 21–33.

Baugh, A. C. and Cable, T. (1978), *A history of the English language* (3rd edn., London: Routledge & Kegan Paul).

Baynes, T. S. (1894), *Shakespeare studies and essay on English dictionaries*, with a biographical preface by Professor Lewis Campbell (London: Longmans, Green & Co.).

Beaulieux, C. (1927), 'Les dictionnaires de la langue française du seizième siècle', *Revue internationale de l'enseignement*, 5: 155–67.

——(1972), 'Liste des dictionnaires, lexiques et vocabulaires français antérieurs au «Thresor» de Nicot (1606)', in *Mélanges de philologie offerts à Ferdinand Brunot* (Geneva: Slatkine Reprints; repr. of the 1904 edn.), 371–98.

Beer, J., Ganelin, C., and Tamburri, A. J. (1992) (eds), *Romance languages annual 1991*, iii. *French, Italian, Portuguese, Spanish* (Purdue Research Foundation).

Bell, A. (1962), 'Notes on Walter de Bibbesworth's *Treatise*', *Philological Quarterly*, 41: 361–72.

Beloe, W. (1807–12), *Anecdotes of literature and scarce books*, i, v, vi (London: Rivington).

Bement, N. S. (1928), 'Petrus Ramus and the beginnings of French grammar', *Romanic Review*, 19: 309–23.

——(1947), 'A selective bibliography of works on the French language of the sixteenth century', *Philological Quarterly*, 26: 219–34.

Bennett, H. S. (1947), 'The production and dissemination of vernacular manuscripts in the 15th century', *The Library*, 5th ser., 1: 167–78.

——(1950), 'Notes on English retail book-prices, 1480–1560', *The Library*, 5th ser., 5/1: 172–8.

——(1970), *English books & readers, 1475 to 1557* (repr. of 2nd edn., Cambridge: University Press) (1st edn. 1952, 2nd edn. 1969).

Benoist, A. (1877), *De la syntaxe française entre Palsgrave et Vaugelas* (Paris: Thorin; repr. Geneva: Slatkine, 1968).

Bergen, H. (1906–35) (ed.), *Lydgate's Troy Book. A.D. 1412–20*, edited from the best manuscripts with introduction, notes and glossary. Part I: *Prologue, Book I, and Book II* (with side-notes by Dr Furnivall) (Early English Text Society, extra series, 97; London: Kegan Paul, Trench, Trübner & Co., 1906). Part II: *Book III* (with side-notes by Dr Furnivall) (Early English Text Society, extra series, 103; London: Kegan Paul, Trench, Trübner & Co., 1908). Part III: *Books IV and V, completing the text* (with side-notes by Dr Furnivall) (Early English Text Society, extra series, 106; London: Kegan Paul, Trench, Trübner & Co., 1910). Part IV: *Bibliographical Introduction, Extracts from Guido Delle Colonne's Historia Troiana, notes, glossary and index to Lydgate's text* (Early English Text Society, extra series, 126; London: Milford, 1935).

——(1927) (ed.), *Lydgate's Fall of Princes*. Part IV: *Bibliographical introduction, notes and glossary* (Early English Text Society, extra series, 124; London: Early English Text Society).

Besterman, T. (1942), 'On a bibliography of dictionaries', *The Proceedings of the British Society for International Bibliography*, 4: 63–75.

Bischoff, B. (1961), 'The study of foreign languages in the Middle Ages', *Speculum*, 36: 209–24.

Blake, N. (1992) (ed.), *The Cambridge history of the English language*, ii. *1066–1476* (Cambridge: Cambridge University Press).

Blake, N. F. (1965–6), 'The vocabulary in French and English printed by William Caxton', *English Language Notes*, 3: 7–15.

Bloch, O. (1904), 'Étude sur le dictionnaire de J. Nicot (1606)', in *Mélanges de philologie offerts à Ferdinand Brunot* (Paris), 1–13; repr. Geneva: Slatkine, 1972).

——(1927), 'L'assibilation d' R dans les parlers gallo-romans', *Revue de linguistique romane*, 3: 92–156.

Bloch, O. and Wartburg, W. v. (1975) (eds), *Dictionnaire étymologique de la langue française* (Paris: Presses Universitaires de France).

Blondheim, D. S. (1909), 'Le glossaire d'Oxford', *Reone des études juives*, 57: 1–18.

Boase, C. W. (1885), *Register of the university of Oxford*, i. *1449–63; 1505–71* (Oxford: Clarendon Press).

Bolland, W. C. (1912), 'Of a treatise on medieval French orthography', *Eyre of Kent 6 & 7 Edward II, 1313–14* (The Publications of the Selden Society, 27; The Year Books Series, 7), pp. xliii–li.

Bonin, T. and Wilburn, J. (1977), 'Teaching French conversation: a lesson from the fourteenth century', *The French Review*, 51: 188–96.

Bourciez, É. (1946), *Éléments de linguistique romane*, revised 4th edn. (Paris: Klincksieck).

Bovelles, C. de (1533/1973), *Sur les langues vulgaires et la variété de la langue française. Liber de differentia vulgarium et gallici sermonis varietate (1533)*, texte latin—traduction française et notes par Colette Dumont-Demaizière (Paris: Klincksieck).

Bradley, H. (1900), *Dialogues in French and English. By William Caxton*, adapted from a fourteenth-century book of dialogues in French and Flemish, edited from Caxton's printed text (about 1483), with introduction, notes, and word-lists (Early English Text Society, extra series, 79; London: Kegan Paul, Trench, Trübner & Co.).

Brasart, G. (1945), 'La vie des écoliers au XVIe siècle d'après deux comptes de tutelle', *Bibliothèque d'Humanisme et Renaissance*, 7: 273–81.

Bray, L. (1989), 'Consultabilité et lisibilité du dictionnaire: aspects formels', in F. J. Hausmann *et al.* (eds), *Wörterbücher, dictionaries, dictionnaires*, i (Berlin and New York: de Gruyter), 135–46.

——(1990), 'La lexicographie française des origines à Littré', in F. J. Hausmann *et al.* (eds.), *Wörterbücher, dictionaries, dictionnaires*, ii (Berlin and New York: de Gruyter), 1788–1818.

Breitinger, H. (1868), *Zur Geschichte der französischen Grammatik 1530–1647* (Programm der thurgauischen Kantonsschule für das Schuljahr 1867/68; Frauenfeld: Huber).

Brewer, J. S. (1859), *Fr. Rogeri Bacon Opera quaedam hactenus inedita*, i. *Containing* I.—*Opus tertium*. II.—*Opus minus*. III.—*Compendium philosophiae . . .*, ed. J. S. Brewer (with facsimiles) (London: Longman, Green, Longman & Roberts).

——(1864/1965) (ed.), *Letters and papers, foreign and domestic, of the reign of Henry VIII*, ii, pt. II (London: Her Majesty's Stationery Office; repr. Vaduz: Kraus, 1965).

——(1867/1965) (ed.), *Letters and papers, foreign and domestic, of the reign of Henry VIII*, iii, pts. I and II (London: Her Majesty's Stationery Office; repr. Vaduz: Kraus, 1965).

——(1870/1965) (ed.), *Letters and papers, foreign and domestic, of the reign of Henry VIII*, iv, pt. I (London: Her Majesty's Stationery Office; repr. Vaduz: Kraus, 1965).

——(1872/1965) (ed.), *Letters and papers, foreign and domestic, of the reign of Henry VIII*, iv, pt. II (London: Her Majesty's Stationery Office; repr. Vaduz: Kraus, 1965).

——(1876) (ed.), *Letters and papers, foreign and domestic, of the reign of Henry VIII*, iv, pt. III (London: Longman & Co.).

——(1920) (ed.), *Letters and papers, foreign and domestic, of the reign of Henry VIII*, i, pt. II (2nd edn. rev. and greatly enlarged by R. H. Brodie, London: His Majesty's Stationery Office).
Bridges, J. H. (1266/1964), *The 'Opus majus' of Roger Bacon*, ed. with introduction and analytical table (2 vols.; unchanged repr. of the Oxford edn.) (Oxford: Clarendon Press, 1897–1900) (Frankfurt a.M.: Minerva GmbH).
Brown, M. C. (1911), *Mary Tudor, Queen of France* (London: Methuen & Co.).
Bruneau, C. (1958), *Petite histoire de la langue française*, i. *Des origines à la révolution* (2nd edn.; Paris: Colin) (1st edn. 1955).
Brunner, K. (1961), 'Sprachlehrbücher im Mittelalter', in *Language and Society. Essays presented to Arthur M. Jensen on his seventieth birthday* (Copenhague: Det Berlingske Bogtrykkeri), 37–43.
Brunot, F. (1894), 'Un projet «d'enrichir, magnifier et publier» la langue française en 1509', *Revue d'histoire littéraire de la France*, 1: 27–37.
——(1905/1966), *Histoire de la langue française des origines à 1900*, i. *De l'époque latine à la Renaissance* (Paris: Colin) (new edn., 1966).
——(1906/1967), *Histoire de la langue française des origines à 1900*, ii. *Le XVIe siècle* (Paris: Colin) (new edn., 1967).
Buridant, C. (1986*a*), 'Lexicographie et glossographie médiévales. Esquisse de bilan et perspectives de recherche', *Lexique*, 4: 9–46.
——(1986*b*) (ed.), *La lexicographie au moyen âge* (= *Lexique*, 4) (Lille: Presses Universitaires de Lille).
Burke, R. B. (1928/1961), *The Opus majus of Roger Bacon* (1266), a translation by Robert Belle Burke, i (Philadelphia: University of Pennsylvania Press, 1928; microfilm repr., Ann Arbor: University Microfilms Inc., 1961).
Cable, T. (1984), 'The rise of written standard English', in A. Scaglione (ed.), *The emergence of national languages* (Speculum artium, 11; Ravenna: Longo), 75–94.
Carver, P. L. (1937), *The comedy of Acolastus. Translated from the Latin of Fullonius by John Palsgrave*, with an introduction and notes (Early English Text Society, original series, 202; London: Oxford University Press).
Casley, D. (1734), *A catalogue of the manuscripts of the King's library: an appendix to the catalogue of the Cottonian library . . .* (London: printed for the author).
Catach, N. (1968), *L'Orthographe française à l'époque de la Renaissance (Auteurs—imprimeurs—ateliers d'imprimerie)* (Genève: Droz).
Catach, N. and Mettas, O. (1972), 'Encore quelques trouvailles dans Nicot', *Revue de linguistique romane*, 36: 360–75.
Chassant, L.-A. (1857), *Petit vocabulaire latin-français du XIIIe siècle, extrait d'un manuscrit de la bibliothèque d'Évreux* (Paris: Aubry).
Chevalier, J.-C. (1968), *Histoire de la syntaxe. Naissance de la notion de complément dans la grammaire française (1530–1750)* (Publications romanes et françaises, 100; Geneva: Droz).

——*et al.* (1976), *Grammaire transformationelle: syntaxe et lexique* (Villeneuve-d'Ascq: Université de Lille).

Chevalier, J.-C. (1976), 'Le jeu des exemples dans la théorie grammaticale: étude historique', in J.-C. Chevalier *et al.*, *Grammaire transformationelle: syntaxe et lexique* (Villeneuve d'Ascq: Université de Lille), 233–63.

——(1986), 'Le problème des données dans deux grammaires anglaises du français: *Lesclarcissement* de John Palsgrave (1530) et *The French Schoolmaster* de Cl. Sainliens dit Holyband (1609)', in C. M. Grisé and C. D. E. Tolton (eds), *Crossroads and perspectives: French literature of the Renaissance* (Geneva: Droz), 65–75.

Childe-Pemberton, W. S. (1913), *Elizabeth Blount and Henry the Eighth with some account of her surroundings* (London: Nash).

Cigada, S. (1985) (ed.), *Les grands rhétoriqueurs. Actes du Ve colloque international sur le moyen français. Milan, 6–8 mai 1985* (Milan: Vita e Pensiero).

——(1986) (ed.), *Le moyen français. Actes du Ve colloque international sur le moyen français. Milan, 6–8 mai 1985*, ii (Milan: Vita e Pensiero).

Cigada, S. and Slerca, A. (1991) (eds.), *Le moyen français: recherches de lexicologie et de lexicographie. Actes du VIe colloque international sur le moyen français. Milan, 4–6 mai 1988*, i (Milan: Vita e Pensiero).

Claes, F. (1973), 'L'influence de Robert Estienne sur les dictionnaires de Plantin', *Cahiers de lexicologie*, 23/2: 109–16.

Clément, L. (1899/1967), *Henri Estienne et son œuvre française. Étude d'histoire littéraire et de philologie* (repr. Geneva: Slatkine).

Cohen, D. (1970) (ed.), *Mélanges Marcel Cohen. Études de linguistique, ethnographie et sciences connexes offertes par ses amis et ses élèves à l'occasion de son 80ème anniversaire* (The Hague: Mouton).

Cohen, G. (1931), *Geofroy Tory. Champ fleury ou l'art et science de la proportion des lettres*, reproduction phototypique de l'édition *Princeps* de Paris 1529, précédé d'un avant-propos et suivie de notes, index et glossaire (Paris: Bosse).

Collinson, R. L. (1982), *A history of foreign-language dictionaries* (London: Deutsch).

Colon, G. and Kopp, R. (1976) (eds), *Mélanges de langues et de littératures romanes offerts à Carl Theodor Gossen* (Bern: Francke; Liège: Marche romane).

Cooper, C. H. and Cooper, T. (1858), *Athenae Cantabrigienses*, i. *1500–1585* (Cambridge: Deighton, Bell & Co., and Macmillan & Co.; London: Bell & Daldy).

Cotgrave, R. (1611/1968), *A dictionarie of the French and English tongues*, reproduced from the 1st edn., London, 1611, with introduction by William S. Woods (Columbia: University of South Carolina Press, 1950; 2nd printing 1968).

Counson, A. (1922), 'Le français en belgique et les «écoles wallonnes» à l'époque de la Renaissance', in *Mélanges offerts par ses amis et ses élèves à M. Gustave Lanson* (Paris: Hachette), 98–102.

Curtis, F. J. (1912), 'A 16th century English–French phrase-book (Hollyband's *French Littelton*)', in M. Banner, F. J. Curtis, and M. Friedwagner (eds), *Festschrift zum 15. Neuphilologentage in Frankfurt am Main 1912* (Frankfurt: Gebrüder Knauer), 229–67.

Cytowska, M. (1973) (ed.), *Opera omnia Desiderii Erasmi Roterodami: Recognita et adnotatione critica instructa notisque illustrata*, iv. *De recta latini graecique sermonis pronuntiatione* (Amsterdam and Oxford: North-Holland Publishing Company).

Dainville, F. de (1947), 'Librairies d'écoliers toulousains à la fin du XVI$^e$ siècle', *Bibliothèque d'Humanisme et Renaissance*, 9: 129–40.

Daly, L. W. (1967), *Contributions to a history of alphabetization in antiquity and the Middle Ages* (Collection Latomus, 90; Brussels: Latomus).

Danielsson, B. (1959), 'La prononciation du français au XVI$^e$ siècle d'après John Hart (1551, 1569, 1570) et G. Ledoyen de la Pichonnaye (1576)', in *Mélanges de linguistique et de philologie, Ferdinand Mossé in memoriam* (Paris: Didier), 75–86.

Darmesteter, A. (1872), 'Glosses et glossaires', *Romania*, 1: 146–76.

—— and Hatzfeld, A. (1887), *Le seizième siècle en France. Tableau de la littérature et de la langue* (3rd edn., rev. and corrected; Paris: Delagrave).

Dauzat, A. (1930), *Histoire de la langue française* (Paris: Payot).

Dees, A. (1985) (ed.): *Actes du IV$^e$ colloque international sur le moyen age* (Amsterdam: Rodopi).

Delbouille, M. (1959), 'A propos de la genèse de la langue française', in *Atti dell' VIII° Congresso Internazionale di studi romanzi (Firenze, 3–8 Aprile 1956)*, ii. *Communicazioni*, pt. 1 (Florence: Sansoni), 151–3.

—— (1970), 'Comment naquit la langue française?', in *Phonétique et linguistique romanes. Mélanges offerts à M. Georges Straka*, i (Lyon and Strasbourg: Centre National de la Recherche Scientifique), 186–99.

Delcourt, M. (1936), 'L'amitié d'Érasme et de More entre 1520 et 1535', *Bulletin de l'Association Guillaume Budé* (Janvier), 7–29.

del Re, A. (1936) (ed.), *Florio's first fruites. Facsimile reproduction of the original edition* (Memoirs of the Faculty of Literature and Politics, Taihoku Imperial University, III, 1) (Formosa, Japan: Taihoku Imperial University).

Demaizière, C. (1983), *La grammaire française au XVI$^e$ siècle: les grammairiens picards* (2 vols.; Paris: Didier).

Desainliens, C. (1583), *Campo di fior or else the flovrie field of fovre languages* (London: Vautroullier). [See also Holyband.]

Dibdin, T. F. (1969) (ed.), *Joseph Ames: Typographical antiquities or the history of printing in England, Scotland, and Ireland* (Anglistica & Americana, 19; Hildesheim: Olms).

*Dictionary of national biography*, vols. iii, xiii, xviii, and xix, ed. L. Stephen; vol. xxv, eds L. Stephen and S. Lee; vols. xxxiv and xliii, ed. S. Lee (London: Smith, Elder, & Co., 1885, 1888, 1889, 1891, 1893, 1895).

Diez, F. (1856), *Grammatik der romanischen Sprachen*, pt. 1 (2nd edn., Bonn: Weber).

—— (1865), *Altromanische Glossare, berichtigt und erklärt* (Bonn: Weber).

Dobson, E. J. (1956), 'Early Modern Standard English', *Transactions of the Philological Society*, 25–54.
Dodd, C. (1737–42), *The church history of England, from the year 1500 to the year 1688* (3 vols.; Brussels).
Dolet, E. (1540/1972), *La manière de bien traduire d'une langue en aultre* (1540) (Lyon: Chés Dolet mesme; repr. Geneva: Slatkine, 1972).
Doucet, R. (1956), *Les bibliothèques parisiennes au XVI^e siècle* (Paris: Picard).
Doutrepont, G. (1934), *Jean Lemaire de Belges et la Renaissance* (Brussels: Lamertin).
Dowling, M. (1986), *Humanism in the age of Henry VIII* (London: Croom Helm).
Dubois, C.-G. (1972), *Celtes et gaulois au XVI^e siècle. Le développement littéraire d'un mythe nationaliste avec l'édition critique d'un traité inédit de Guillaume Postel* (Paris: Vrin).
Dubois, J. [Sylvius] (1531/1971), *Iacobi Sylvii Ambiani in linguam Gallicam Isagoge, una, cum eiusdem grammatica latinogallica ex hebraeis, graecis et latinis authoribus* (Paris: Estienne) *1531* (repr. Geneva: Slatkine, 1971).
Duff, E. G. (1905), *A century of the English book trade* (London: The Bibliographical Society).
——(1907), 'A bookseller's accounts, circa 1510', *The Library*, NS 8: 256–66.
——Greg, W. W., McKerrow, R. B., Plomer, H. R., Pollard, A. W., and Proctor, R. (1913), *Hand-lists of books printed by London printers, 1501–1556* (London: Blades, East & Blades).
Duraffour, A. (1946), 'Dictionnaires français à mettre à jour ou au jour', in *Études romanes dédiées à Mario Roques par ses amis, collègues et élèves de France* (Paris: Droz).
Dutko, Z.-E. (1935), 'Contribution chronologique à l'étude du vocabulaire du XVI^e siècle', *Français moderne*, 3: 356–62.
du Wes, G. (1532/1972), *An introductorie for to lerne, to rede, to pronounce and to speke French trewely (1532)* (repr. Geneva: Slatkine, 1972).
E. . . [Escallier], E.-A. (1851), *Remarques sur le patois, suivies du vocabulaire latin-français de Guillaume Briton (XIV^e siècle)* (Douai: d'Aubers).
Eccles, M. (1957), 'Bynneman's books', *The Library*, 5th ser. 12/2: 81–92.
——(1986), 'Claudius Holyband and the earliest French-English dictionaries', *Studies in Philology*, 83: 51–61.
Ellis, A. J. (1871*a*), 'John Hart's phonetic writing, 1569, and the pronunciation of French in XVIth century', in A. J. Ellis, *On Early English pronunciation, with especial reference to Shakspere and Chaucer*, iii. *Illustrations of the pronunciation of the XIVth and XVIth centuries: Chaucer, Gower, Wycliffe, Spenser, Shakspere, Salesbury, Barcley, Hart, Bullokar, Gill. Pronouncing vocabulary* (London: Asher & Co.; Berlin: Trübner & Co.), 794–838.
——(1871*b*), *On early English pronunciation, with special reference to Shakspere and Chaucer . . .*, pt. III (Early English Text Society, extra series, 14; London: The Philological Society).
Ellis, H. (1846), *Original letters, illustrative of English history; including numerous royal letters . . .* (3rd ser., 2; London: Bentley).

Emden, A. B. (1974), *A biographical register of the University of Oxford A.D. 1501 to 1540* (Oxford: Clarendon Press).

*The English dialect dictionary* (*EDD*) (1898/1970), ed. J. Wright (Oxford: Oxford University Press).

Erasmus, D. (1973), *Opera omnia Desiderii Erasmi Roterdami: Recognita et adnotatione critica instructa notisque illustrata*, iv. *De recta latini graecique sermonis pronuntiatione*, ed. M. Cytowska (Amsterdam and Oxford: North Holland Publishing Company).

——(1981), *Opera omnia Desiderii Erasmi Roterdami: Recognita et adnotatione critica instructa notisque illustrata*, v, eds F. Heinimann and E. Kienzle (Amsterdam and Oxford: North Holland Publishing Company).

Erdmann, A. (1911) (ed.), *Lydgate's Siege of Thebes. Edited from all the known manuscripts and the two oldest editions, with introduction, notes and glossary*. Part I: *The Text* (Early English Text Society, extra ser., 108; London: Kegan Paul, Trench, Trübner & Co.).

——and Ekwall, E. (1930) (eds), *Lydgate's Siege of Thebes. Edited from all the known manuscripts and the two oldest editions*. Part II: *Introduction, notes, rhyme-lists, and a glossary, with an appendix* (Early English Text Society, extra ser., 125; London: Humphrey Milford).

Ernst, G. (1980), 'Prolegomena zu einer Geschichte des gesprochenen Französisch', in H. Stimm (ed.), *Zur Geschichte des gesprochenen Französisch und zur Sprachlenkung im Gegenwartsfranzösischen*. Beiträge des Saarbrücker Romanistentages 1979 (*Zeitschrift für französische Sprache und Literatur*, NS 6; Wiesbaden: Steiner), 1–14.

Escallier, E.-A. (1856), *Remarques sur le patois suivies d'un vocabulaire latin-français inédit du XIV^e siècle. Avec gloses et notes explicatives pour servir à l'histoire des mots de la langue française* (Douai: Wartelle).

Ewert, A. (1934), 'A fourteenth-century Latin-French nominale (St John's College, Oxford, MS. no. 178)', *Medium Aevum*, 3: 13–18.

——(1957), 'The Glasgow Latin–French glossary', *Medium Aevum*, 25: 154–63.

Erzgräber, W. (1989) (ed.), *Kontinuität und Transformation der Antike im Mittelatter* (Sigmaringen: Thorbecke).

Fabri, P. (1521/1972), *Cy ensuit le grant et vray art de pleine rhétorique, utille, proffitable et nécessaire a toutes gens qui désirent a bien élegamment parler et escrire* (Rouen: Rayer; repr. Geneva: Slatkine, 1972).

Finkenstaedt, T. (1963), *You and thou. Studien zur Anrede im Englischen* (*Mit einem Exkurs über die Anrede im Deutschen*) (Quellen und Forschungen zur Sprach- und Kulturgeschichte der germanischen Völker, NS 10 (134); Berlin: de Gruyter).

——Leisi, E., and Wolff, D. (1970), *A chronological English dictionary* (Heidelberg: Winter).

Finoli, A. M. (1991), 'Italien et français dans l'*Utilissimo Vocabulista*', in S. Cigada and A. Slerca (eds), *Le moyen français: recherches de lexicologie et de lexicographie. Actes du VI^e colloque international sur le moyen français, Milan, 4–6 mai 1988*, i (Milan: Vita e Pensiero), 61–82.

Fiorelli, P. (1950), 'Pour l'interprétation de l'ordonnance de Villers-Cotterets', *Français moderne*, 18: 277–88.

Fisher, J. H. (1977), 'Chancery and the emergence of standard written English in the fifteenth century', *Speculum*, 52: 870–99.

Florio, J. (1578), *His firste fruites: which yeelde familiar speech, merie prouerbes, wittie sentences, and golden sayings* (London: Dawson for Woodcocke).

——(1591), *Florios second frvtes* (London: Woodcock).

Ford, F. (1882), *Mary Tudor. A retrospective sketch* (Bury St Edmunds: Barker).

Förster, M. (1902), 'Ein englisch-französisches Rechtsglossar', in *Beiträge zur romanischen und englischen Philologie. Festgabe für Wendelin Förster zum 26. Oktober 1901* (Halle: Niemeyer), 205–12.

Förster, W. (1911), 'Lateinisch-französisches Glossar von Tours', in W. Förster and E. Koschwitz (eds), *Altfranzösisches Übungsbuch* (*Die ältesten Sprachdenkmäler mit einem Anhang zum Gebrauch bei Vorlesungen und Seminarübungen*) (4th augmented and rev. edn., Leipzig: Reisland), 206–14.

Foster, J. (1968), *Alumni Oxonienses: the members of the university of Oxford, 1500–1714: their parentage, birthplace, and year of birth, with a record of their degrees*, iii (Nendeln, Liechtenstein: Kraus Reprint Ltd.).

Fought, J. G. (1961–2), 'Sigmatism in French', *Romance Philology*, 15: 7–11.

François, A. (1959), *Histoire de la langue française cultivée des origines à nos jours* (Geneva: Jullien).

Françon, M. (1957), 'La question de la langue, en France, au XVI$^{e}$ siècle', *Studi francesi*, 1: 257–9.

*Französisches etymologisches Wörterbuch* (*FEW*) (1928–1983), ed. W. v. Wartburg *et al.* (24 vols.; Bonn: Klopp, *a.o*).

Fries, U. and Heusser, M. (1988) (eds.), *Meaning and beyond. Ernst Leisi zum 70. Geburtstag* (Tübingen: Narr).

Furnivall, F. J. (1867), 'Pynson's contracts with Horman for his *Vulgaria*, and Palsgrave for his *Lesclarcissement*, with Pynson's letter of denization', *Transactions of the Philological Society*, 362–74.

——(1899–1904) (ed.), *The pilgrimage of the life of man. Englisht by John Lydgate, A.D. 1426, from the French of Guillaume de Deguileville, A.D. 1330, 1355, with introduction, notes, glossary and indexes by Katharine B. Locock* (Early English Text Society, extra ser. 77, 83, 92; (London: Kegan Paul, Trench, Trübner & Co.).

Gairdner, J. (1880) (ed.), *Letters and papers, foreign and domestic, of the reign of Henry VIII*, v (London: Longmans & Co.).

——(1882), *Letters and papers, foreign and domestic, of the reign of Henry VIII*, vi (London: Longmans & Co.).

——(1883), *Letters and papers, foreign and domestic, of the reign of Henry VIII*, vii (London: Longmans & Co).

——(1892/1967), *Letters and papers, foreign and domestic, of the reign of Henry VIII*, xiii (London: Her Majesty's Stationery Office; repr. Vaduz: Kraus, 1967).

——and Brodie, R. H. (1896) (eds), *Letters and papers, foreign and domestic, of the reign of Henry VIII*, xv (London: Her Majesty's Stationery Office).

——(1908) (eds.), *Letters and papers, foreign and domestic, of the reign of Henry VIII*, xxi, pt. 1 (London: His Majesty's Stationery Office).

Gamillscheg, E. (1969), *Etymologisches Wörterbuch der französischen Sprache* (2nd edn., Heidelberg: Winter).

Gaufinez, E. (1902), 'Notes sur le vocalisme de Meigret', in *Beiträge zur romanischen und englischen Philologie. Festgabe für Wendelin Förster zum 26. Oktober 1901* (Halle: Niemeyer), 363–420.

Gebhardt, K. (1982), 'L'apport des dialectes d'oïl (surtout entre 1300 et 1600) au lexique de la langue commune (d'apres le FEW)', in P. Wunderli (ed.), *Du mot au texte. Actes du III^e^ colloque international sur le moyen français. Düsseldorf, 17–19 septembre 1980* (Tübinger Beiträge zur Linguistik, 175; Tübingen: Narr), 31–48.

Geckeler, H., Schlieben-Lange, B., Trabant, J. *et al.* (1981) (eds.), *Logos semanticos. Studia linguistica in honorem Eugenio Coseriu 1921–1981* (Berlin and New York: de Gruyter; Madrid: Gredos).

Gemmingen-Obstfelder, B. v. (1982), 'La réception du bon usage dans la lexicographie du 17^e^ siècle', in M. Höfler (ed.), *La lexicographie française du XVI^e^ au XVIII^e^ siècle. Actes du colloque international de lexicographie dans la Herzog August Bibliothek Wolfenbüttel (9–11 Octobre 1979)* (Wolfenbütteler Forschungen, 18; Wolfenbüttel: Herzog August Bibliothek), 121–36.

Génin, F. (1852) (ed.), *L'Éclaircissement de la langue française par Jean Palsgrave, suivi de la grammaire de Giles du Guez, publiés pour la première fois en France* (Collection de documents inédits sur l'histoire de France publiés par les soins du ministère de l'instruction publique, deuxième série, Histoire des lettres et des sciences; Paris: Imprimerie nationale).

Gernetz, H. J. (1981), 'Die Bedeutung der Gesprächsbücher des Rußlandhandels im 17. Jahrhundert für die Entwicklung der Lexikographie', *Kopenhagener Beiträge zur germanistischen Linguistik*, 17: 63–93.

Geschiere, L. (1968), 'L'Introduction des phonèmes vocaliques nasaux en français et le témoignage de Jehan Palsgrave', *Word*, 24: 175–92.

Gessler, J. (1931), *Le livre des mestiers de Bruges et ses dérivés. Quatre anciens manuels de conversation* (6 vols.; Bruges: Imprimerie Sainte-Catherine).

——(1933), *Fragments d'anciens traités pour l'enseignement du français en Angleterre* (New York: Publications of the Institute of French Studies at Columbia University).

——(1934), *La manière de langage qui enseigne à bien parler et écrire le français. Modèles de conversations composés en Angleterre à la fin du XIV^e^ siècle* (new edn. with introduction and glossary; Paris: Droz).

——(1941*a*), *Deux manuels de conversation imprimés en Angleterre au XV^e^ siècle* (Brussels: Édition de la Librairie Encyclopédique).

——(1941*b*), 'Deux manuels de conversation imprimés en Angleterre au XV^e^ siècle par deux élèves de William Caxton', *Leuvensche Bijdragen*, 33: 93–126.

Giard, L. (1987), 'La mise en théorie du français au XVI^e siècle', *Schifanoia*, 2: 63–76.

Glatigny, M. (1989), 'Norme et usage dans le français du XVI^e siècle', in P. Swiggers and W. van Hoecke (eds), *La langue française au XVI^e siècle: usage, enseignement et approches descriptifs* (Louvain: Leuven University Press), 7–31.

Glauning, O. (1900) (ed.), *Lydgate's minor poems. The two nightingale poems. (A.D. 1446), edited from the mss. with introduction, notes and glossary* (Early English Text Society, extra series, 80; London: Kegan Paul, Trench, Trübner & Co.).

Godefroy, F. (1881–1902/1982), *Dictionnaire de l'ancienne langue française et de tous ses dialectes du IX^e au XV^e siècle* (10 vols.; Paris: Vieweg & Bouillon; repr. Geneva: Slatkine, 1982).

Goetz, G. (1923), *De glossariorvm latinorvm origine et fatis*, i (Leipzig and Berlin: Teubner).

Görlach, M. (1994), *Einführung ins Frühneuenglische* (2nd augmented edn., Heidelberg: Winter).

Gorog, R. P. de (1968), 'Notes on Old French lexicology and historical phonetics', *Word*, 24: 193–206.

Gossen, C. T. (1957), 'Die Einheit der französischen Schriftsprache im 15. und 16. Jahrhundert', *Zeitschrift für romanische Philologie*, 73: 427–59, 485.

Gougenheim, G. (1949), 'Notes sur le vocabulaire de Rabelais', *Word*, 5: 147–50.

——(1974), *Grammaire de la langue française du 16^e* siècle (Connaissance des langues, 8; new edn., completely reset, Paris: Picard).

Goyens, M. and Swiggers, P. (1989), 'La grammaire française au XVI^e siècle. Bibliographie raisonnée', in P. Swiggers and W. van Hoecke (eds), *La langue française au XVI^e siècle: usage, enseignement et approches descriptives* (La pensée linguistique, 2; Louvain: Leuven University Press), 157–73.

Green, M. A. Everett (1854), *Lives of the princesses of England, from the Norman conquest*, v (London: Colburn).

Greg, W. W. (1967) (ed.), *A companion to Arber: being a calender of documents in Edward Arber's 'Transcript of the registers of the company of stationers of London, 1554–1640', with text and calendar of supplementary documents* (Oxford: Clarendon Press).

Greg, W. W. and Boswell, E. (1930) (eds), *Records of the court of the stationers' company 1576 to 1602 from register B* (London: The Bibliographical Society).

Greimas, A. J. and Keane, T. M. (1992), *Dictionnaire du moyen français. La Renaissance* (Paris: Larousse).

Grimarest, J.-L. le Gallois (1712/1973), *Éclaircissemens sur les principes de la langue françoise (1712)* (Paris: Florentin Delaulne; repr. Geneva: Slatkine, 1973).

Guarinus Veronensis (1478), *Vocabularius breviloquus* . . . (Basel).

——(1486), *Breuiloquus vocabularius* . . . Colonie (BL IB. 4527; for IB. 10761 the date 1485 is queried).

Guildhall Library MS 9531, vol. 9 (1507–21/2), fo. 166$^{v}$, vol. 10 (1522–30), fo. 163$^{v}$, vol. 11 (1530–9), fo. 129$^{v}$, Diocese of London, bishop's registers.

Gunn, S. J. (1988), *Charles Brandon, Duke of Suffolk, c.1484–1545* (Oxford: Blackwell).

Gwyn, P. (1990), *The king's cardinal: the rise and fall of Thomas Wolsey* (London: Barrie & Jenkins).

Haas, S. W. (1979), 'Henry VIII's *Glasse of Truthe*', *History*, 64: 353–62.

Handover, P. M. (1960), *Printing in London from 1476 to the modern times* (London: Allen & Unwin).

Hanks, P. (1979) (ed.), *Collins dictionary of the English language* (London and Glasgow: Collins).

Hartmann, R. R. K. (1986) (ed.), *The history of lexicography* (Amsterdam studies in the theory and history of linguistic science, 3; Studies in the history of the language sciences, 40; Amsterdam: Benjamins).

Hasenohr, G. (1984), 'Note sur un lexique technique monolingue de la fin du XV$^{e}$ siècle', *Romania*, 105: 114–29.

Hausmann, F.-J. (1980*a*), *Louis Meigret. Le traité de la grammaire française (1550). Le menteur de Lucien—Aux lecteurs (1548)* (Lingua et traditio, 5; Tübingen: Narr).

——(1980*b*), *Louis Meigret. Humaniste et linguiste* (Lingua et traditio, 6; Tübingen: Narr).

——(1991), 'La lexicographie bilingue anglais-français, français-anglais', in F.-J. Hausmann *et al.* (eds), *Wörterbücher, dictionaries, dictionnaires*, iii (Berlin and New York: de Gruyter), 2956–60.

Hausmann, F.-J. *et al.* (1989–91) (eds), *Wörterbücher, dictionaries, dictionnaires* (3 vols.; Berlin and New York: de Gruyter).

Hayashi, T. (1978), *The theory of English lexicography, 1530–1791* (Amsterdam studies in the theory and history of linguistic science, 3; Studies in the history of linguistics, 18; Amsterdam: Benjamins).

Heim, W.-D. (1984), *Romanen und Germanen in Charlemagnes Reich. Untersuchung zur Benennung romanischer und germanischer Völker, Sprachen und Länder in französischen Dichtungen des Mittelalters* (Münstersche Mittelalter-Schriften, 40; Munich: Fink).

Heinimann, F. and Kienzle, E. (1981) (eds), *Opera omnia Desiderii Erasmi Roterodami: Recognita et adnotatione critica instructa notisque illustrata*, v. *Adagionum chilias tertia* (Amsterdam and Oxford: North-Holland Publishing Company).

Hennessy, G. (1898), *Novum repertorium ecclesiasticum parochiale Londinense, or London diocesan clergy succession from the earliest time to the year 1898* (London: Swan Sonnenschein & Co.).

Henry, A. (1965), *Wallon et Wallonie. Esquisse d'une histoire sémantique* (Études d'histoire wallonne, 1; Brussels: Fondation Plisnier).

——(1973), 'Jean Wauquelin et l'histoire du mot WALLON', *Travaux de linguistique et de littérature*, 11/1: 169–75 [= *Mélanges de linguistique française et de philologie et littérature médiévales offerts à Paul Imbs par ses collègues, ses élèves et ses amis à l'occasion de son soixante-cinquième anni-*

*versaire* (le 4 mai 1973) *et publiés par Robert Martin and Georges Straka* (Strasbourg: Klincksieck)].

Héron, A. (1889/1969) (ed.), *Le grant et vrai art de pleine rhétorique de Pierre Fabri* (Rouen: Imprimerie Espérance Cagniard; repr. Geneva: Slatkine, 1969).

Herrtage, S. J. H. (1881) (ed.), *Catholicon Anglicum, an English–Latin Wordbook, dated 1483*, edited, from the MS. no. 168 in the Library of Lord Monson, collated with the Additional MS. 15,562, British Museum, with introduction and notes, with a preface by Henry B. Wheatley (Early English Text Society, 75; London: Trübner & Co.).

Heymann, W. (1903), *Französische Dialektwörter bei Lexikographen des 16. bis 18. Jahrhunderts* (diss. Gießen) (Gießen: von Münchow'sche Hof- und Universitätsdruckerei (Kindt)).

——(1909), 'Wortgeschichtliches. Ausdrücke der Pariser Sprache, die von Lexikographen des 16. bis 18. Jahrhunderts als solche besonders kenntlich gemacht werden', *Zeitschrift für französische Sprache und Literatur*, 35: 306–24.

Hoffmann von Fallersleben, A. H. (1854) (ed.), *Altniederländische Sprichwörter nach der ältesten Sammlung. Gesprächsbüchlein romanisch und flämisch* (Horae belgicae, 9; Hanover: Rumpler).

Hoffmann, H. (1894), *Über die Beteuerungen in Shakespeare's Dramen* (diss. Halle-Wittenberg) (Halle: Kaemmerer & Co.).

Hoffmann, M. (1965), 'A general linguist's view of word-formation in middle French', *Romance Philology*, 18: 54–63.

Höfler, M. (1982) (ed.), *La lexicographie française du XVI^e^ au XVIII^e^ siècle. Actes du colloque international de lexicographie dans la Herzog August Bibliothek Wolfenbüttel (9–11 Octobre 1979)* (Wolfenbütteler Forschungen, 18; Wolfenbüttel: Herzog August Bibliothek).

——(1989), 'L'Étude historique des régionalismes français', *Revue de linguistique romane*, 53: 111–29.

——and Vernay, H. (1979) (eds), *Festschrift Kurt Baldinger zum 60. Geburtstag*, i (Tübingen: Niemeyer).

Hofmann, C. (1868), 'Das zweitälteste unedirte altfranzösische Glossar', *Sitzungsberichte der königl. bayer. Akademie der Wissenschaften zu München*, 1/1: 121–34.

Hogrefe, P. (1959), *The Sir Thomas More Circle. A program of ideas and their impact on secular drama* (Urbana, Ill.: The University of Illinois Press).

Hole, C. (1949*a*), *English sports and pastimes* (London: Batsford).

——(1949*b*), *English home-life 1500 to 1800* (2nd edn.; London: Batsford).

Holmér, G. (1964), 'Fragment d'un glossaire latin-ancien français', *Vox Romanica*, 23: 85–103.

Holtus, G. (1991), 'Zum Stand der Erforschung der historischen Dimension gesprochener Sprache in der Romania', *Zeitschrift für romanische Philologie*, 107: 547–74.

Holtz, L. (1981), *Donat et la tradition de l'enseignement grammatical* (Documents, études et répertoires publiés par l'Institut de Recherche et d'Histoire des Textes; Paris: Centre national de la recherche scientifique).

Holyband, C. (1580), *The treasurie of the French tong* (London: Bynneman). [See also Desainliens.]

Hooykaas, R. (1958), *Humanisme, science et réforme. Pierre de la Ramée (1515–1572)* (Leyden: Brill).

Horner, P. J. (1977), 'The use and knowledge of spoken French in early fifteenth-century England', *Notes & Queries*, 24: 488.

Hughes, G. (1991), *Swearing. A social history of foul language, oaths and profanity in English* (Oxford: Blackwell).

Huguet, E. (1925–67/1989), *Dictionnaire de la langue française du seizième siècle* (7 vols.; Paris: Champion and Didier; repr. Geneva: Slatkine, 1989).

Hulbert, J. R. (1968), *Dictionaries. British and American* (rev. edn.; London: Deutsch).

Humpers, A. (1921), *Étude sur la langue de Jean Lemaire de Belges* (Bibliothèque de la Faculté de Philosophie et Lettres de l'Université de Liège, 26; Liège: Vaillant-Carmanne; Paris: Champion).

Hunt, R. W. (1958), 'The "lost" preface of the Liber Derivationum of Osbern of Gloucester', *Proceedings of the Southeastern Institute of Medieval and Renaissance Studies: Medieval and Renaissance studies*, 4: 267–82.

Hunt, T. (1979*a*), 'Les gloses en langue vulgaire dans les manuscrits du *De nominibus utensilium d'Alexandre Nequam*', *Revue de linguistique romane*, 43: 235–62.

——(1979*b*), 'Les gloses en langue vulgaire dans les mss. de L'*Unum Omnium* de Jean de Garlande', *Revue de linguistique romane*, 43: 162–78.

——(1979*c*), 'The vernacular entries in the *Glossae in Sidonium* (MS Oxford Digby 172)', *Zeitschrift für französische Sprache und Literatur*, 89: 130–50.

——(1979*d*), 'Vernacular glosses in medieval manuscripts', *Cultura Neolatina*, 39: 9–37.

——(1980), 'The Anglo-Norman vocabularies in MS Oxford, Bodleian Library, Douce 88', *Medium Aevum*, 49: 5–25.

——(1981), 'The trilingual vocabulary in MS Westminster Abbey 34/11', *Notes & Queries*, 28: 14–15.

——(1989), *Plant names of medieval England* (Cambridge: Brewer).

Huntsman, J. F. (1973), *Pepys MS 2002' Medulla Grammatice: an edition* diss., Austin, Texas) [University of Texas microfilm 1990] (xerox copy).

——(1980), 'The state of lexicography and lexicology in Plantagenet England: a data base', in J. Raben and G. Marks (eds), *Data bases in the humanities and social sciences* (Amsterdam: North Holland Publishing), 197–201.

Huth, G. (1899), *Jacques Dubois, Verfasser der ersten latein.-französischen Grammatik (1531)* (Programm des königl. Marienstifts-Gymnasiums zu Stettin für das Schuljahr Ostern 1898 bis Ostern 1899; Stettin: Herrcke & Lebeling).

Imbs, P. (1971–94) (ed.), *Trésor de la langue française. Dictionnaire de la langue du XIX^e^ et du XX^e^ siècle (1789–1960)* (16 vols.; Paris: Centre national de la recherche scientifique).

Isidore (of Seville) (?1470), *Incipit epistola Isidori iunioris hispalensis episcopi ad Braulionem Cesaraugustanum episcopum . . . liber ethimologiarum Isidori Ispalensis Episcopi* ([Strasburg: Mentelin]).

Jerdan, W. (1842), *Rutland papers: original documents illustrative of the courts and times of Henry VII and Henry VIII*, selected from the private archives of his Grace the Duke of Rutland, &c. (London: Camden Society).

Johnson, F. R. (1950), 'Notes on English retail book-price, 1550–1640', *The Library*, 5th ser. 5/2: 83–112.

Johnston, R. C. (1987) (ed.), *Orthographia gallica* (Anglo-Norman Text Society, Plain texts series, 5; London: Anglo-Norman Text Society).

Johnston, S. H., Jr. (1977), *A study of the career and literary publications of Richard Pynson* (diss., University of Western Ontario).

Jones, R. F. (1966), *The triumph of the English language* (Stanford: Stanford University Press).

Joret, C. (1875), 'Changement de *r* en *s* (z) et en *dh* dans les dialectes français', *Mémoires de la Société de linguistique de Paris*, 3/2: 155–62.

Joseph, J. E. (1987*a*), 'Case study: the elaboration and control of French in the sixteenth century', in J. E. Joseph, *Eloquence and power: the rise of language standards and standard languages* (London: Pinter), 132–59.

—— (1987*b*), *Eloquence and power: the rise of language standards and standard languages* (London: Pinter).

Julien, M. (1988), 'La terminologie française des parties du discours et de leurs sous-classes au XVIe siècle', *Langages*, 92: 65–78.

Jusserand, J. J. (1901), *Les sports et jeux d'exercices dans l'ancienne France* (Paris: Librairie Plon).

Kachru, B. B. and Kahane, H. (1995) (eds), *Cultures, ideologies, and the dictionary: studies in honor of Ladislav Zgusta* (Lexicographica, Series maior, 64; Tübingen: Niemeyer).

Kastovsky, D. and Szwedek, A. (1986) (eds), *Linguistics across historical and geographical boundaries*, ii. *Descriptive, contrastive and applied linguistics* (Berlin, New York, and Amsterdam: Mouton de Gruyter).

Ker, W. P. (1901), 'Panurge's English', in *An English miscellany presented to Dr Furnivall in honour of his seventy-fifth birthday* (Oxford: Clarendon Press), 196–8.

Kesselring, W. (1981), *Dictionnaire chronologique du vocabulaire français. Le XVIe siècle* (Heidelberg: Winter).

Kibbee, D. A. (1984), 'Bilingual lexicography in the Renaissance: Palsgrave's English–French lexicon (1530)', in H. Aarsleff, L. G. Kelly, and H.-J. Niederehe (eds), *Papers in the history of linguistics* (ICHoLS 3) (Amsterdam and Philadelphia: Benjamins), 179–88.

—— (1985*a*), 'John Palsgrave's "*Lesclarcissement de la langue francoyse*" (1530)', *Historiographia Linguistica*, 12/1–2: 27–62.

—— (1985*b*), 'Progress in bilingual lexicography during the Renaissance', *Dictionaries*, 7: 21–31.

—— (1986), 'The humanist period in bilingual lexicography', in R. R. K. Hartmann (ed.), *The history of lexicography* (Amsterdam studies in the theory and history of linguistic science, 3; Studies in the history of the language sciences, 40; Amsterdam: Benjamins), 137–46.

——(1989), 'Enseigner la prononciation du français au XV$^{e}$ siècle', *Documents pour l'histoire du français langue étrangère ou seconde*, 3: 15–20.

——(1990*a*), 'French grammarians and grammars of French in the 16th century', in H.-J. Niederehe and K. Koerner (eds), *History and historiography of linguistics: papers from the fourth international conference on the history of the language sciences* (ICHoLS 4), *Trier, 24–28 August 1987*, i (Amsterdam studies in the theory and history of linguistic science, ser. 3, 51; Amsterdam and Philadelphia: John Benjamins), 301–14.

——(1990*b*), 'Language variation and linguistic description in 16th-century France', *Historiographia Linguistica*, 17/1–2, 49–65.

——(1991), *For to speke Frenche trewely. The French language in England, 1000–1600. Its status, description and instruction* (Amsterdam studies in the theory and history of linguistic science, ser. 3: Studies in the history of the language sciences, 60; Amsterdam and Philadelphia: Benjamins).

——(1992), '16th-century bilingual dictionaries (French–English): organization and access, then and now', *CCH Working Papers*, 2: 33–68.

Kipling, G. (1977), *The triumph of honour: Burgundian origins of the Elizabethan Renaissance* (Leiden: Leiden University Press).

Koll, H.-G. (1958), *Die französischen Wörter 'langue' und 'langage' im Mittelalter* (Kölner romanistische Arbeiten, NS 10; Geneva: Droz; Paris: Minard).

Koskenniemi, I. (1962), *Studies in the vocabulary of English drama 1550–1600: excluding Shakespeare and Ben Jonson* (Annales Universitatis Turkuensis, ser. B, 84; Turku: Turun Yliopisto).

Kremos, H. (1955), *Höflichkeitsformeln in der französischen Sprache. Aufforderungs- und Bittformeln. Dankesbezeugungen (mit historischem Rückblick bis ins 16. Jahrhundert)* (diss. Zurich) (Zurich: Schipper).

Kristol, A. M. (1989), 'Le début du rayonnement parisien et l'unité du français au moyen âge: le témoignage des manuels d'enseignement du français écrits en Angleterre entre le XIII$^{e}$ et le début du XV$^{e}$ siècle', *Revue de linguistique romane*, 53: 335–67.

Kukenheim, L. (1932), *Contributions à l'histoire de la grammaire italienne, espagnole et française à l'époque de la Renaissance* (Amsterdam: Noord-Hollandsche Uitgevers-Maatschappi).

Kurath, H., Kuhn, S. M., and Lewis, R. E. (1954–) (eds), *Middle English dictionary* (*MED*) (Ann Arbor: Michigan University Press).

Labarre, A. (1975), *Bibliographie du Dictionarium d'Ambrogio Calepino (1502–1779)* (Bibliotheca Bibliographica Aureliana, 26; Baden-Baden: Koerner).

Lagadeuc, J. (1499), *Le Catholicon de Iehan Lagadeuc. Dictionnaire breton, français et latin.* Publié par R. F. Le Men d'après l'édition de M. Auffret de Quoetqueueran. Imprimé à Tréguier chez Iehan Caluez (Lorient: Corfmat).

——(1499/1975), *Le Catholicon de Jehan Lagadeuc. Dictionnaire breton-latin-français du XV$^{eme}$ siècle.* Publié et édité avec une introduction par Christian-J. Guyonvar'ch. Réproduction de l'édition de Jehan Calvez

(Tréguier 1499) (Supplément à Ogam—tradition celtique 27, Celticum 22) (Rennes: Ogam—tradition celtique).

Laing, M. (1989) (ed.), *Middle English dialectology: essays on some principles and problems by Angus McIntosh, M. L. Samuels and Margaret Laing* (Aberdeen: Aberdeen University Press).

Lambley, K. (1920), *The teaching and cultivating of the French language in England during Tudor and Stuart times* (Publications of the University of Manchester, 129; Manchester: Manchester University Press).

Lancashire, I. (1992), 'Bilingual dictionaries in an English Renaissance knowledge base', *CCH Working Papers*, 2: 69–88.

Lange, H. (1892), *Die Versicherungen bei Chaucer* (diss. Halle) (Berlin: Meyer).

Langenfelt, G. (1933), *Select studies in the colloquial English of the late middle ages* (Lund: Ohlsson).

—— (1956), 'Notes on English interjections', *Studier i Modern Språkvetenskap Utgivna av Nyfilologiska Sällskapet i Stockholm*, 19: 63–8.

Lanusse, M. (1893/1977), *De l'influence du dialecte gascon sur la langue française, de la fin du XV^e^ siècle à la seconde moitié du XVII^e^* (Paris: Maisonneuve; repr. Geneva: Slatkine, 1977).

Laurent, P. (1940/1972), 'Une source retrouvée du «Champ Fleury» de Geofrey Tory', in *Mélanges de philologie et d'histoire littéraire offerts à Edmond Huguet par ses élèves, ses collègues et ses amis* (Paris: Boivin), 184–93 (repr. Geneva: Slatkine, 1972).

Lebrija, A. de (1492), *Esta tassado este vocabulario por los muy altos ꝛ muy poderosos principes el Rey ꝛ la Reyna . . .* (Salamantice).

—— (1492/1517/1969), *Grammatica castellana. 1492. El orthografia castellano. 1517* (European Linguistics 1480–1700; A collection of facsimile reprints, 11; Menston: Scolar Press, 1969).

Lebsanft, F. (1988), *Studien zu einer Linguistik des Grußes. Sprache und Funktion der altfranzösischen Grußformeln* (Beihefte zur Zeitschrift für romanische Philologie, 217; Tübingen: Niemeyer).

—— (1989), 'Kontinuität und Diskontinuität antiker Anrede- und Grußformen im romanischen Mittelalter. Aspekte der Sprach- und Gesellschaftskritik', in W. Erzgräber (ed.), *Kontinuität und Transformation der Antike im Mittelalter* (Sigmaringen: Thorbecke).

Lee, S. (1893) (ed.), *Dictionary of national biography*, xxxiv (London: Smith, Elder & Co.).

—— (ed.) (1895), *Dictionary of national biography*, xliii (London: Smith, Elder & Co.).

Lefèvre, Y. (1973), 'De l'usage du français en Grande-Bretagne à la fin du XII^e^ siècle', in *Études de langue et de littérature du moyen âge. Offertes à Felix Lecoy par ses collègues, ses élèves et ses amis* (Paris: Champion), 301–5.

Legge, M. D. (1961), 'Some notes on Anglo-Norman vocabulary', in *Studies in medieval French: presented to Alfred Ewert in honour of his seventieth birthday* (Oxford: Clarendon Press), 214–31.

—— (1963), *Anglo-Norman literature and its background* (Oxford: Clarendon Press).

Legros, E. (1965–7), 'Sur «wallon» et «Wallonie»', *La vie wallonne*, 39 (1965), 118–26, 185–96, 253–71; 40 (1966), 50–3; 41 (1967), 35–40.

Leip, J. (1921), *Provenzalisches und Frankoprovenzalisches bei französischen Lexikographen des 16. bis 18. Jahrhunderts* (Gießener Beiträge zur romanischen Philologie, 6; Gießen: Meyer).

Lemaire de Belges, J. (1510–13), *Les illustrations de Gaule et singularitez de Troye. Auec les deux epistres de Lamant Vert* (Lyon: Baland), *Le second livre* (Lyon: Baland), *Le tiers livre* (Paris: de Marnef).

Le Neve, J. (1854), *Fasti ecclesiae Anglicanae, or a calendar of the principal ecclesiastical dignitaries in England and Wales, and of the chief officers in the universities of Oxford and Cambridge, from the earliest time to the year M.DCC.XV.*, corrected and continued from M.DCC.XV to the present time by T. D. Hardy, 3 vols., ii (Oxford: Oxford University Press).

Léon, P. R. and Perron, P. (1985) (eds), *Le dialogue* (Ottawa: Didier).

Le Ver, F. (1440/1994), *Firmini Verris Dictionarius = Dictionnaire latin-français de Firmin Le Ver*, édité par Brian Merrilees et William Edwards (Corpus Christianorum continuatio mediaevalis, series in 4°, 1; Lexica latina medii aevi, 1) (Turnholti; Brepols).

Lewicka, H. (1961), 'L'emploi stylistique des dialectes dans le théâtre comique français au XV^e^ et au début du XVI^e^ siècle', *Kwartalnik Neofilologiczny*, 8: 161–9.

——(1970), 'Les types d'unités nominales composées d'après le témoignage de J. Palsgrave', in D. Cohen (ed.), *Mélanges Marcel Cohen. Études de linguistique, ethnographie et sciences connexes offertes par ses amis et ses élèves à l'occasion de son 80ème anniversaire* (The Hague: Mouton), 171–6.

——(1976), 'Les formules de salutation dans le théâtre français du moyen âge', in G. Colon and R. Kopp (eds), *Mélanges de langues et de littératures romanes offerts à Carl Theodor Gossen* (Bern: Francke; Liège: Marche romane), 497–504.

——(1979), 'Les formules pour prendre congé dans le théâtre profane français du moyen âge', in M. Höfler and H. Vernay (eds), *Festschrift Kurt Baldinger zum 60. Geburtstag*, i (Tübingen: Niemeyer), 283–92.

Lindemann, M. (1982), 'Les apports du *Thesaurus theutonicae linguae* dans la lexicographie du XVI^e^ siècle', in M. Höfler (ed.), *La lexicographie française du XVI^e^ au XVIII^e^ siècle. Actes du colloque international de lexicographie dans la Herzog August Bibliothek Wolfenbüttel (9–11 Octobre 1979)* (Wolfenbütteler Forschungen, 18; Wolfenbüttel: Herzog August Bibliothek), 33–47.

——(1985), 'Le *Vocabularius nebrissensis* latin-français et les débuts de la lexicographie française', in A. Dees (ed.), *Actes du IV^e^ Colloque International sur le Moyen Age* (Amsterdam: Rodopi), 55–86.

——(1994), *Die französischen Wörterbücher von den Anfängen bis 1600. Entstehung und typologische Beschreibung* (Lexicographica, Series maior, 54; Tübingen: Niemeyer).

Littré, E. (1895), 'Glossaires', in *Histoire littéraire de la France XXII*, reproduction facsimilée publiée avec l'autorisation de l'Institut de France (Paris: Welter), 21–38.

Livet, C.-L. (1859/1980), *La grammaire française et les grammairiens au XVIe siècle* (Paris: Didier; repr. Geneva: Slatkine, 1980).
Löfstedt, L. (1978), 'A propos des formules de salutation au moyen âge', *Neuphilologische Mitteilungen*, 79: 193–215.
Loiseau, A. (1866/1969), *Étude historique et philologique sur Jean Pillot et sur les doctrines grammaticales du XVIe siècle* (Paris: Thorin; repr. Geneva: Slatkine, 1969).
——(1875), *Histoire des progrès de la grammaire en France depuis l'époque de la Renaissance jusqu'à nos jours* (Paris: Thorin).
——(1881), *Histoire de la langue française, ses origines et son développement jusqu'à la fin du XVIe siècle* (Paris: Thorin).
Longden, H. J. (1941), *Northamptonshire and Rutland clergy from 1500*, x (Northampton: Archer & Goodman).
Lörscher, W. and Schulze, R. (eds) (1987), *Perspectives on language in performance. Studies in linguistics, literary criticism, and language teaching and learning. To honour Werner Hüllen on the occasion of his sixtieth birthday* (Tübingen: Narr).
Lowndes, W. T. (1861), *The bibliographer's manual of English literature* (new edn. revised, corrected and enlarged; with an appendix relating to the books of literary and scientific societies by Henry G. Bohn, 6 vols.); iv, pt. VII (London: Bohn).
Lusignan, S. (1986), *Parler vulgairement. Les intellectuels et la langue française aux XIIIe et XIVe siècles* (Montréal: Les Presses de l'Université de Montreal).
Lütgenau, F. (1880), *Jean Palsgrave und seine Aussprache des Französischen* (diss. Bonn) (Bonn: Carthaus).
McConica, J. K. (1965), *English humanists and reformation politics under Henry VIII and Edward VI* (Oxford: Clarendon Press).
McIntosh, A., Samuels, M. L., and Benskin, M. (1986), *A linguistic atlas of late medieval English* (4 vols.; Aberdeen: Aberdeen University Press).
Madden, D. H. (1897), *The diary of Master William Silence: a study of Shakespeare & of Elizabethan sport* (London: Longmans, Green & Co.).
Magnin, M. (1849), 'Rapport au comité des publications historiques, sur le projet de réimpression de la plus ancienne grammaire française' (séance du 5 février 1849), *Journal des Savants* (Feb.), 115–19.
Mai, A. (1836), *Classicorum auctorum e vaticanis codicibus editorum*, viii. *Thesaurus novus latinitatis, sive lexicon vetus e membranis nunc primum erutum* (Rome: Typis Collegii Urbani).
Marc'hadour, G. (1963), *L'univers de Thomas More. Chronologie critique de More, Erasme, et leur époque (1477–1536)* (Paris: Vrin).
Marchello-Nizia, C. (1979), *Histoire de la langue française aux XIVe et XVe siècles* (Paris: Bordas).
Marsden, W. (1796), *A catalogue of dictionaries, vocabularies, grammars, and alphabets* (2 parts; London: privately printed).
Martin, R. (1982), 'Pour un dictionnaire du moyen français', in P. Wunderli (ed.), *Du mot au texte. Actes du IIIe colloque international sur le moyen*

*français. Düsseldorf, 17–19 septembre 1980* (Tübinger Beiträge zur Linguistik, 175; Tübingen: Narr), 13–24.

Martin, W. (1988), 'Variation in lexical frequency', in P. van Reenen and K. van Reenen-Stein (eds), *Distributions spatiales et temporelles, constellations des manuscrits. Études de variation linguistique offertes à Anthonij Dees à l'occasion de son 60ème anniversaire* (Amsterdam and Philadelphia: Benjamins), 139–52.

Massebieau, L. (1878/1968), *Les colloques scolaires du seizième siècle et leurs auteurs (1480–1570)* (Paris: Bonhoure; repr. Geneva: Slatkine, 1968).

Matoré, G. (1968), *Histoire des dictionnaires français* (Paris: Larousse).

Matzke, J. E. (1905–6), 'Some examples of French as spoken by Englishmen in old French literature', *Modern Philology*, 3: 47–60.

Mayhew, A. L. (1908) (ed.), *The promptorium parvulorum. The first English-Latin dictionary. c.1440 A.D., edited from the manuscript in the Chapter Library at Winchester, with introduction, notes and glossaries* (Early English Text Society, extra ser., 102; London: Kegan Paul, Trench, Trübner & Co.).

Merrilees, B. (1985), 'Le dialogue dans la méthodologie du français langue seconde au moyen âge', in P. R. Léon and P. Perron (eds), *Le dialogue* (Ottawa: Didier), 105–15.

——(1986), 'Teaching Latin in French: adaptations of Donatus' *Ars minor*', *Fifteenth Century Studies*, 12: 87–98.

——(1987), 'An aspect of grammatical terminology in insular French', *Cahiers de lexicologie*, 51: 193–201.

——(1988*a*), 'Les débuts de la terminologie grammaticale en français: à propos de quelques travaux récents', *Romania*, 109: 397–411.

——(1988*b*), 'The Latin–French *dictionarius* of Firmin Le Ver (1420–1440)', in M. Snell-Hornby (ed.), *Zürilex '86 Proceedings* (Tübingen: Francke), 181–8.

——(1990), 'Prolegomena to a history of French lexicography: The development of the dictionary in medieval France', *Romance Languages Annual 1989*, 1: 285–91.

——(1991), 'Métalexicographie médiévale: la fonction de la métalangue dans un dictionnaire bilingue du moyen âge', *Archivum Latinitatis Medii Aevi (Bulletin Du Cange)*, 50: 33–70.

——(1992), 'The organization of the medieval dictionary', in J. Beer, C. Ganelin and A. J. Tamburri (eds.), *Romance languages annual 1991*, iii. *French, Italian, Portuguese, Spanish* (Purdue Research Foundation), 78–83.

——and Edwards, W. (1989), 'Le statut du français dans le *dictionarius* de Le Ver (1420–1440) et dans un imprimé dérivé (*c*.1494)', in G. di Stefano and R. M. Bidler (eds), *Du manuscrit à l'imprimé. Actes du colloque international Université McGill, Montréal, 3–4 Octobre 1988* [= *Le Moyen Français* 22], 37–50.

————(1994) (eds.), *Firmini Verris Dictionarius = Dictionnaire latin-français de Firmin Le Ver*, édité par Brian Merrilees et William Edwards

(Corpus Christianorum continuatio mediaevalis, series in 4°, 1; Lexica latina medii aevi, 1) (Turnholti: Brepols).

—— ——and Megginson, D. (1992), 'The *Dictionarius* of Firmin Le Ver (1440)', *CCH Working Papers*, 2: 9–19.

Meyer, P. (1866), 'Bribes de littérature anglo-normande', *Jahrbuch für romanische und englische Literatur*, 7: 37–8.

——(1873), 'La manière de langage qui enseigne à parler et à écrire le français. Modèles de conversations composés en Angleterre à la fin du XIVe siècle, et publiés d'après le ms. du musée britannique Harl. 3988', *Revue critique d'histoire et de littérature*, 8: 373–408.

——(1875), 'Du passage de *z*, *s* à *r* et d' *r* à *z*, *s* en provençal', *Romania*, 4: 184–94, 464–70.

——(1876), '*R* pour *s*, *z*, à Beaucaire', *Romania*, 5: 488–90.

——(1884), 'Notice et extraits du MS. 8336 de la bibliotèque de Sir Thomas Phillipps à Cheltenham', *Romania*, 13: 497–541.

——(1886), 'Les manuscrits français de Cambridge. II. Bibliotèque de l'université', *Romania*, 15: 236–357.

——(1903), 'Les manuscrits français de Cambridge. III. Trinity College', *Romania*, 32: 18–120.

——(1907), 'Les manuscrits français de Cambridge. IV. Gonville et Caius College', *Romania*, 36: 481–542.

——(1908), 'Notice du MS. Bodley 761 de la bibliotèque Bodléienne (Oxford)', *Romania*, 37: 509–28.

Michael, I. M. (1970), *English grammatical categories and the tradition to 1800* (Cambridge: Cambridge University Press).

Michael, J. (1987), *The teaching of English from the sixteenth century to 1870* (Cambridge: Cambridge University Press).

Michaud, M. (1843–7) (ed.), *Biographie universelle ancienne et moderne . . .* (Nouvelle édition, revue, corrigée, et considérablement augmentée d'articles inédits et nouveaux, 45 vols.) (Paris: Thoisnier Desplaces).

Michelant, H. (1875) (ed.), *Le livre des mestiers.—Dialogues français flamands composés au XIVe siècle par un maître d'école de la ville de Bruges* (Paris: Tross).

*Middle English dictionary* (*MED*) (1954–), eds H. Kurath, S. M. Kuhn, and R. E. Lewis (Ann Arbor: Michigan University Press).

Millet, A. (1933), *Les grammairiens et la phonétique ou l'enseignement des sons du français depuis le XVIe siècle jusqu'à nos jours* (Paris: Monnier).

Milroy, J. C. (1992), 'Middle English dialectology', in N. Blake (ed.), *The Cambridge history of the English language*, ii. *1066–1476* (Cambridge: Cambridge University Press), 156–206.

Möhren, F. (1982), 'Remarques concernant les bases philologiques d'un dictionnaire du moyen français', in P. Wunderli (ed.), *Du mot au texte. Actes du IIIe colloque international sur le moyen français. Düsseldorf, 17–19 septembre 1980* (Tübinger Beiträge zur Linguistik, 175; Tübingen: Narr), 49–56.

Monfrin, J. (1986), 'Lexiques latin-français du moyen âge', in O. Weijers (ed.), *Actes du 'workshop' Terminologie de la vie intellectuelle au moyen âge*,

*Leyde/La Haye 20–21 septembre 1985* (= CIVICIMA. Études sur le vocabulaire intellectuel du moyen âge 1) (La Haye, 19–26; cf. pp. 26–36 in Weijers 1988).

Moore, J. L. (1910), *Tudor-Stuart views on the growth, status and destiny of the English language* (Studien zur englischen Philologie, 41; Halle: Niemeyer; repr. College Park, Md.: McGrath Publishing Company, 1970).

Morgan, W. (1982), '"Who was then a gentleman?": Social, historical and linguistic codes in the *Mystère d'Adam*', *Studies in Philology*, 79: 101–21.

Morley, C. (1936), 'Catalogue of beneficed clergy of Suffolk, 1086–1550', *Proceedings of the Suffolk Institute of Archeology and Natural History*, 22: 29–85.

Mulholland, J. (1967), '"Thou" and "you" in Shakespeare: a study in the second person pronoun', *English Studies*, 48: 34–43.

Mynors, R. A. B. and Thomson, D. F. S. (1977), *The correspondence of Erasmus: Letters 446 to 593. 1516 to 1517*, trans. R. A. B. Mynors and D. F. S. Thomson, annotated by J. K. McConica (Toronto, Buffalo, and London: University of Toronto Press).

——(1979), *The correspondence of Erasmus. Letters 594 to 841. 1517 to 1518*, trans. R. A. B. Mynors and D. F. S. Thomson, annotated by P. G. Bietenholz (Toronto, Buffalo, and London: University of Toronto Press).

Naïs, H. (1959), 'Réflexions sur le dictionnaire de la langue française du XVI^e siècle d' E. Huguet', *Français moderne*, 27: 45–64.

——(1986), 'Présentation d'une future concordance de l'Aalma', *Lexique*, 4: 185–96.

Nebrija, A. de see Lebrija.

Neumann, S.-G. (1959), *Recherches sur le français des XV^e et XVI^e siècles et sur sa codification par les théoriciens de l'époque* (Études romanes de Lund, 13; Lund: Gleerup; Copenhagen: Munksgaard).

Newcourt, R. (1708), *Repertorium ecclesiasticum parochiale Londinense: an ecclesiastical parochial history of the diocese of London*, i (London: Motte).

Nichols, J. G. (1846) (ed.), *The chronicle of Calais in the reign of Henry VII and Henry VIII to the year 1540* (London: Camden Society).

——(1855), *Inventories of the wardrobes, plate, chapel stuff, etc. of Henry Fitzroy, Duke of Richmond, and of the wardrobe stuff at Baynard's Castle of Katherine, Princess dowager.* Edited with *A memoir and letters of the Duke of Richmond. The Camden Miscellany*, iii (London: Camden Society).

Niederehe, H.-J. (1968), review of Claus Riessner, *Die «Magnae Derivationes» des Uguccione da Pisa und ihre Bedeutung für die romanische Philologie* (Temi e testi, 11; Rome: Edizioni di storia e letteratura), in *Romanistisches Jahrbuch*, 19: 163–6.

——(1982), 'Les vocabulaires techniques dans la lexicographie française du 16^e au 18^e siècle', in M. Höfler (ed.), *La lexicographie française du XVI^e au XVIII^e siècle. Actes du colloque international de lexicographie dans la Herzog August Bibliothek Wolfenbüttel (9–11 Octobre 1979)* (Wolfenbütteler Forschungen, 18; Wolfenbüttel: Herzog August Bibliothek), 65–79.

——and Koerner, K. (1990) (eds), *History and historiography of linguistics: papers from the fourth international conference on the history of the language sciences* (ICHoLS 4), *Trier, 24–28 August 1987*, i (Amsterdam studies in the theory and history of linguistic science, ser. 3; vol. 51) (Amsterdam and Philadelphia: Benjamins).

Nobel, P. (1986), 'La traduction du *Catholicon* contenue dans le manuscrit H 110 de la bibliothèque universitaire de Montpellier (section médicine)', *Lexique*, 4: 157–83.

Noble, W. M. (1914), 'Incumbents of the county of Huntingdon', *The Transactions of the Cambridgeshire and Huntingdonshire Archaelogical Society*, 3: 50–6, 97–104, 117–40, 157–72, 189–204, 251–66, 271–86, 327–38.

Norton, G. P. (1984), *The ideology and language of translation in Renaissance France and their Humanist antecedents* (Geneva: Droz).

Nugent, E. M. (1956) (ed.), *The thought & culture of the English Renaissance: An anthology of Tudor prose 1481–1555* (Cambridge: Cambridge University Press).

Nyrop, C. (1904), *Grammaire historique de la langue française, Tome I* (2nd edn., rev. and enlarged; Copenhagen: Gyldendalske Boghandel—Nordisk Forlag).

—— (1934), *Linguistique et histoire des mœurs. Mélanges posthumes*, Traduction par E. Philipot (Paris: Droz).

Oates, J. C. T. and Harmer, L. C. (1964) (eds), *Vocabulary in French and English: A facsimile of Caxton's edition c.1480* (Cambridge: Cambridge University Press).

Oizumi, A. (1991) (ed.), *A complete concordance to the works of Geoffrey Chaucer in ten volumes* (Alpha–Omega. Lexika—Indizes—Konkordanzen. Reihe C. Englische Autoren; Hildesheim, Zurich, and New York: Olms–Weidmann).

Omont, H. (1891), 'Les manuscrits français des rois d'Angleterre au château de Richmond', in *Études romanes dédiées à Gaston Paris le 29 décembre 1890 (25e anniversaire de son doctorat ès lettres) par ses élèves français et par ses élèves étrangers des pays de langue française* (Paris: Bouillon), 1–13.

Orme, N. (1973), *English schools in the Middle Ages* (London: Methuen & Co.).

Östergård, Ö. (1953), 'Une manière de parler. MS. Cambridge, Bibliothèque de l'université, I i.6.17', *Neuphilologische Mitteilungen*, 54: 201–25.

Owen, A. (1929/1977), *Le traité de Walter de Bibbesworth sur la langue française. Texte publié avec introduction et glossaire* (Paris: Les Presses Universitaires de France; repr. Geneva: Slatkine, 1977).

*The Oxford dictionary of quotations* (1941; 2nd edn., London: Oxford University Press, 1956).

*The Oxford English dictionary* (*OED*) (1989), eds J. A. Simpson and E. S. C. Weiner (20 vols.; Oxford: Clarendon Press).

Padberg, W. (1912), *Der Vocabularius Breviloquus und seine Bedeutung für die Lexikographie des ausgehenden Mittelalters* (diss., Münster) (Münster).

Padley, G. A. (1985–8), *Grammatical theory in Western Europe, 1500–1700* (Trends in vernacular grammar; 2 vols.; Cambridge: Cambridge University Press).

Palmer, C. J. and Tucker, S. (1878), *Palsgrave family memorials* (Norwich: Miller & Leavins).

Palsgrave, J. (1530), *Lesclarcissement de la langue francoyse* (London: Iohan Haukyns). Facsimile reprint: (English linguistics 1500–1800; A collection of facsimile reprints, 195; Menston: Scolar Press, 1969); Slatkine facsimile reprint (Geneva: Slatkine, 1972; microfiche edition: Paris: Archives de la linguistique française, 309).

Percival, W. K. (1975), 'The grammatical tradition and the rise of the vernaculars', in T. Sebeok (ed.), *Current trends in linguistics*, xiii (The Hague: Mouton), 231–75.

Pirenne, H. (1929), 'L'instruction des marchands au moyen âge', *Annales d'histoire économique et sociale*, 1: 13–28.

Piron, M. (1964), 'Note sur le sens de *wallon* dans Shakespeare', *Bulletin de l'Académie Royale de Langue et de Littérature Françaises*, 42: 177–85.

Pits, J. (1619), *Relationvm historicarvm de rebus Anglicis*, i (Paris: Thierry & Cramoisy).

Place, E. B. (1962), 'The first French grammar', *The French Review*, 35: 578–82.

Plomer, H. R. (1900), *A short history of English printing 1476–1898* (London: Kegan Paul, Trench, Trübner & Co.).

——(1909), 'Two lawsuits of Richard Pynson', *The Library*, NS 10: 115–33.

Pocock, N. (1870) (ed.), *Records of the Reformation: the divorce 1527–1533* (Oxford: Clarendon Press).

Pollard, A. F. (1929), *Wolsey* (Westport, Conn.: Greenwood Press; repr. London: Longmans, Green & Co.).

Pollard, A. W. and Redgrave, G. R. (1976–91), *A short-title catalogue of books printed in England, Scotland & Ireland and of English books printed abroad, 1475–1640* (2nd edn., rev. and enlarged), i (London: The Bibliographical Society, 1986); ii (London: The Bibliographical Society, 1976); iii (London: The Bibliographical Society, 1991).

Pope, M. K. (1910), 'The "*Tractatus orthographiae*" of T. H. Parisii studentis', *The Modern Language Review*, 5: 185–93.

Priebsch, J. (1905), 'Ein anglonormannisches Glossar', *Bausteine zur romanischen Philologie. Festgabe für Adolfo Mussafia* (Halle: Niemeyer), 534–56.

Quemada, B. (1967), *Les dictionnaires du français moderne 1539–1863. Étude sur leur histoire, leurs types et leurs méthodes* (Paris, Brussels, and Montreal: Didier).

Quirk, R. (1974*a*), *The linguist and the English language* (London: Arnold).

——(1974*b*), 'Shakespeare and the English language', in R. Quirk, *The linguist and the English language* (London: Arnold), 46–64.

——*et al.* (1985), *A comprehensive grammar of the English language* (London and New York: Longman).

Rabelais, F. (1962), *Pantagruel*, publié sur le texte définitif, introduction et présentation de V. L. Saulnier, texte établi et annoté par Pierre Michel (Paris: Club du Meilleur Livre).

Raben, J. and Marks, G. (1980) (eds), *Data bases in the humanities and social sciences* (Amsterdam: North Holland Publishing).

Radtke, E. (1984), 'Le français parlé au XVII^e siècle et l'analyse de la conversation', *Actes du XVII^e congrès international de linguistique et philologie romanes (Aix-en-Provence, 29 août 1983–3 septembre 1983)*, v. *Sociolinguistique des langues romanes* (Aix-en-Provence: Université de Provence), 133–47.

—— (1994), *Gesprochenes Französisch und Sprachgeschichte.* Zur Rekonstruktion der Gesprächssituation in Dialogen französischer Sprachlehrbücher (Beihefte zur Zeitschrift für romanische Philologie, 255; Tübingen: Niemeyer).

Ramm, R. (1902), *Beiträge zur Kenntnis der französischen Umgangssprache des 17. Jahrhunderts* (diss. Kiel) (Kiel: Fiencke).

Read, M. K. and Trethewey, J. (1976), 'Two Renaissance contributions to the semantic analysis of language', *Vox Romanica*, 35: 1–12.

Reenen, P. van and Reenen-Stein, K. van (1988) (eds), *Distributions spatiales et temporelles, constellations des manuscrits. Études de variation linguistique offertes à Anthonij Dees à l'occasion de son 60ème anniversaire* (Amsterdam and Philadelphia: Benjamins).

Remacle, L. (1948), *Le problème de l'ancien wallon* (Liège: Faculté de Philosophie et Lettres).

Repogle, C. (1973), 'Shakespeare's salutations: a study in stylistic etiquette', *Studies in Philology*, 70: 172–86; repr. in V. Salmon and E. Burness (eds), *A reader in the language of Shakespearean drama* (Amsterdam studies in the theory and history of linguistic science, ser. 3; Studies in the history of the language sciences, 35; Amsterdam and Philadelphia: Benjamins, 1987), 101–15.

Rheinfelder, H. (1935), review of *Le livre des mestiers de Bruges et ses dérivés. Göttingische gelehrte Anzeigen*, 10: 402–8.

—— (1937), 'Das mittelalterliche Sprachbüchlein der Stadt Brügge', *Zeitschrift für deutsche Geistesgeschichte*, 3: 175–93.

Richardson, H. G. (1939), 'An Oxford teacher of the fifteenth century', *Bulletin of the John Rylands Library*, 23: 436–57.

—— (1941), 'Business training in medieval Oxford', *The American Historical Review*, 46: 259–80.

Richardson, M. (1980), 'Henry V, the English chancery, and chancery English', *Speculum*, 55: 726–50.

Richardson, W. C. (1970), *Mary Tudor: The white queen* (London: Owen).

Rickard, P. (1968), *La langue française au seizième siècle. Étude suivie de textes* (Cambridge: Presses Universitaires).

—— (1983), 'Le «Dictionarie» franco-anglais de Cotgrave (1611)', *Cahiers de l'association internationale des études françaises*, 35: 7–21.

Riessner, C. (1965), *Die «Magnae Derivationes» des Uguccione da Pisa und ihre Bedeutung für die romanische Philologie* (Temi e Testi, 11; Rome: Edizioni di storia e letteratura).

Rigolot, F. (1972), *Les langages de Rabelais* (Études Rabelaisiennes, 10; Geneva: Droz).

Ritter, E. (1897), 'Le grammarien Louis Meigret, Lyonnais', *Revue de philologie française*, 11: 136–40.

Robert, U. (1873), 'Un vocabulaire latin-français du XIV^e siècle, suivi d'un recueil d'anciens proverbes', *Bibliothèque de l'école des Chartes*, 34: 33–46.

Robinson, F. N. (1983) (ed.), *The works of Geoffrey Chaucer* (2nd edn., Oxford: Oxford University Press).

Rogers, E. F. (1947), *The correspondence of Sir Thomas More* (Princeton: Princeton University Press).

——(1961), *St. Thomas More: selected letters* (New Haven and London: Yale University Press).

Roques, G. (1982), 'Les régionalismes dans Nicot 1606', in M. Höfler (ed.), *La lexicographie française du XVI^e au XVIII^e siècle. Actes du colloque international de lexicographie dans la Herzog August Bibliothek Wolfenbüttel (9–11 Octobre 1979)* (Wolfenbütteler Forschungen, 18; Wolfenbüttel: Herzog August Bibliothek), 81–101.

——(1987), 'Pour la constitution d'une banque de données lexicales sur le français mediéval. Réflexions autour du glossaire des glossaires du moyen français', in H. E. Wiegand (ed.), *Theorie und Praxis des lexikographischen Prozesses bei historischen Wörterbüchern. Akten der internationalen Fachkonferenz Heidelberg, 3.6.–5.6.1986* (Lexicographica, Series maior, 23; Tübingen: Niemeyer), 55–70.

Roques, M. (1935), 'Un modèle de conversation pour le réception d'un envoyé royal au XV^e siècle', *Festschrift für Ernst Tappolet* (Basel: Schwabe), 261–6.

——(1936), 'Travaux collectifs. Recueil général des lexiques français du moyen âge', *Romania*, 62: 248–55.

——(1936–8), *Recueil général des lexiques français du moyen âge (XII^e—XV^e siècle)* (2 vols.; Paris: Champion; repr. Paris, 1970).

Rothwell, W. (1968), 'The teaching of French in medieval England', *Modern Language Review*, 63: 37–46.

——(1978), 'A quelle époque a-t-on cessé de parler français en Angleterre?', *Mélanges de philologie romane offerts à Charles Camproux*, ii (Montpellier: Centre d'Estudes Occitans), 1075–89.

——(1982), 'A mis-judged author and a mis-used text: Walter de Bibbesworth and his *Tretiz*', *Modern Language Review*, 77: 282–93.

——(1983), 'Language and government in Medieval England', *Zeitschrift für französische Sprache und Literatur*, 93: 258–70.

——(1985), 'Stratford atte Bowe and Paris', *Modern Language Review*, 80: 39–54.

——Stone, L. W., and Reid, T. B. W. (1992) (eds), *Anglo-Norman Dictionary* (London: The Modern Humanities Research Association).

Royster, J. F. (1928), 'The first edition of de la Mothe's *French Alphabeth* and of Hollybrand's [sic] *French Schoolemaister*', *Philological Quarterly*, 7: 1–5.

Rye, W. (1898), *An account of the church and parish of Cawston, in the county of Norfolk* (Norwich: privately printed).

Sainéan, L. (1922–3), *La langue de Rabelais* (2 vols.; Paris: de Boccard).

Salmon, V. (1965/1987), 'Sentence structures in colloquial Shakespearean English', *Transactions of the Philological Society*, 105–40 (repr. in V.

Salmon and E. Burness (eds), *A reader in the language of Shakespearean drama* (Amsterdam studies in the theory and history of linguistic science, ser. 3; Studies in the history of the language sciences, 35; Amsterdam and Philadelphia: Benjamins, 1987, 265–300).

Salmon, V. (1967/1987), 'Elizabethan colloquial English in the Falstaff plays', *Leeds Studies in English*, 1: 37–70 (repr. in V. Salmon and E. Burness (eds), *A reader in the language of Shakespearean drama* (Amsterdam studies in the theory and history of linguistic science, ser. 3; Studies in the history of the language sciences, 35; Amsterdam and Philadelphia: Benjamins, 1987, 37–70).

——and Burness, E. (1987) (eds), *A reader in the language of Shakespearean drama* (Amsterdam studies in the theory and history of linguistic science, ser. 3; Studies in the history of the language sciences, 35; Amsterdam and Philadelphia: Benjamins).

Scaglione, A. (1984) (ed.), *The emergence of national languages* (Speculum artium, 11; Ravenna: Longo).

Scheler, A. (1865) (ed.), *Glossaire roman-latin du XVe siècle (MS. de la bibliotèque de Lille, annoté par M. Aug. Scheler)* (Anvers: Buschmann) [= *Extrait des annales de l'Académie d'archéologie de Belgique*, xxi; 2nd ser., 1].

——(1886) (ed.), *Le Catholicon de Lille. Glossaire latin-français publié en extrait et annoté par A. Scheler.* [Présenté à la Classe des lettres dans la séance du 1er juin 1885] (Brussels: Hayez).

Schellenberg, G. (1933), *Bemerkungen zum Traité des Walter von Bibbesworth* (Nach der Ausgabe von A. Owen, Paris 1928) (diss., Berlin) (Berlin: Liebheit & Thiesen).

Schick, J. (1891) (ed.), *Lydgate's temple of glass. With introduction and notes* (Early English Text Society, extra series, 60; London: Kegan Paul, Trench, Trübner & Co.).

Schmidt, P. (1952), 'Die Interjektion im Englischen', *Die Neueren Sprachen*, 1: 492–8.

Schmitt, C. (1977), 'La grammaire française des XVIe et XVIIe siècles et les langues régionales', *Travaux de linguistique et de littérature*, 15/1: 215–25.

——(1979), 'La grammaire de Giles du Wes. Étude lexicale', *Revue de linguistique romane*, 43: 1–45.

——(1980), 'Gesprochenes Französisch um 1600', in H. Stimm (ed.), *Zur Geschichte des gesprochenen Französisch und zur Sprachlenkung im Gegenwartsfranzösischen. Beiträge des Saarbrücker Romanistentages 1979* (= *Zeitschrift für französische Sprache und Literatur*, NS 6) (Wiesbaden: Steiner), 15–32.

Schulte-Herbrüggen, H. (1965), 'A letter of Dr. Johann Eck to Thomas More', *Moreana*, 8: 51–8.

——(1966), *Sir Thomas More: Neue Briefe* (Neue Beiträge zur Englischen Philologie, 5; Münster: Aschendorff).

——(1967), 'Ein unbekannter Brief an St. Thomas More', *Moreana*, 15–16: 241–7.

——(1983), 'Three additions to More's correspondence', *Moreana*, 79–80: 35–41.

——(1990*a*), 'A hundred new humanists' letters: More, Erasmus, Vives, Cranevelt, Geldenhouwer and other Dutch humanists', *Bibliothèque d'Humanisme et Renaissance*, 52: 65–76.

——(1990*b*), 'Seven new letters from Thomas More', *Moreana*, 103: 49–66.

Schulze-Busacker, E. (1985), *Proverbes et expressions proverbiales dans la littérature narrative du moyen âge français. Recueil et analyse* (Geneva and Paris: Editions Slatkine).

Schwartze, R. (1875), *Die Wörterbücher der französischen Sprache vor dem Erscheinen des "Dictionnaire de l'Académie française", 1350–1694*, ein Beitrag zur Geschichte der französischen Lexikographie (Jena: Ratz).

Sebeok, T. (1975*a*) (ed.), *Current trends in linguistics*, xiii (The Hague: Mouton).

——(1975*b*) (ed.), 'L'instruction des marchands au moyen âge', *Annales d'histoire économique et sociale*, 1: 13–28.

Senge, M. (1935), *Französische Grußformeln* (diss. Bonn) (Lippstadt: Blömeke).

Sharman, J. (1884), *A cursory history of swearing* (London: Nimmo & Bain).

Shirley, F. A. (1979), *Swearing and perjury in Shakespeare's plays* (London: Allen & Unwin).

Simon, J. (1966), *Education and society in Tudor England* (Cambridge: Cambridge University Press).

Simonini, R. C. (1951), 'Language lesson dialogues in Shakespeare', *Shakespeare Quarterly*, 2: 319–29.

——(1952), 'The Italian pedagogy of Claudius Holyband', *Studies in Philology*, 49: 144–54.

Simpson, J. A. and Weiner, E. S. C. (1989) (eds), *The Oxford English dictionary* (*OED*) (20 vols.; Oxford: Clarendon Press).

Skeat, W. W. (1873–7), 'A bibliographical list of the works that have been published, or are known to exist in ms., illustrative of the various dialects of English', *English Dialect Society Publications*, Section I.–General. (A.) Dictionaries, 3–17.

——(1903–6) (ed.), 'Nominale sive verbale', *Transactions of the Philological Society*, suppl. 1–50 (repr. Hertford: Austin & Sons, 1906).

Sledd, J. H. (1947), *The Alvearie of John Baret* (diss., Austin, Texas).

Slerca, A. (1985), 'A propos des néologismes des rhétoriqueurs', in S. Cigada (ed.), *Les grands rhétoriqueurs. Actes du V^e colloque international sur le moyen français. Milan, 6–8 mai 1985*, i (Milan: Vita e Pensiero), 61–82.

Smalley, V. E. (1948), *The sources of 'A dictionarie of the French and English tongues by Randle Cotgrave (London, 1611)* (The John Hopkins studies in Romance literatures and languages, extra volume, 25; Baltimore: The John Hopkins Press).

Smith, P. M. (1980), 'Henri Estienne et Cotgrave: Les deux dialogues du nouveau langage françois Malianisé et le dictionnaire of the French and English tongues', *Le Français moderne*, 48: 246–55.

Snell-Hornby, M. (1988) (ed.), *Zürilex '86 Proceedings* (Tübingen: Francke).

Södergård, Ö. (1953), 'Une manière de parler. MS. Cambridge, University Library I.i. 6.17', *Neuphilologische Mitteilungen*, 54: 201–25.

——(1955), 'Le plus ancien traité grammatical français', *Studia Neophilologica*, 27: 192–4.

——(1973), 'La langue médicale française. Quelques nouvelles datations', in *Études de langue et de littérature du moyen âge. Offertes à Felix Lecoy par ses collègues, ses élèves et ses amis* (Paris: Champion), 541–50.

Sofer, J. (1930), *Lateinisches und Romanisches aus den Etymologiae des Isidorus von Sevilla. Untersuchungen zur lateinischen und romanischen Wortkunde* (Forschungen zur griechischen und lateinischen Grammatik, 9; Göttingen: Vandenhoeck & Ruprecht).

Soulié, E. and Barthélemy, E. de (1868) (eds), *Journal de Jean Héroard sur l'enfance et la jeunesse de Louis XIII (1601–1628). Extraits des manuscrits originaux* (2 vols.; Paris: Firmin Didot Frères et Cie).

Spillebout, G. (1985), *Grammaire de la langue française du XVII^e^ siècle* (Paris: Picard).

Städtler, T. (1988), *Zu den Anfängen der französischen Grammatiksprache. Textausgaben und Wortschatzstudien* (Beiträge zur Zeitschrift für romanische Philologie, 223; Tübingen: Niemeyer).

Stange, E. (1900), *Beiträge zur Kenntnis der französischen Umgangssprache des 16. Jahrhunderts* (diss. Kiel) (Kiel: Peters).

Starnes, D. T. (1937), 'Bilingual dictionaries of Shakespeare's day', *Publications of the Modern Languages Association*, 52: 1005–18.

——(1954), *Renaissance dictionaries. English–Latin and Latin–English* (Austin: University of Texas Press).

——and Noyes, G. E. (1946/91), *The English dictionary from Cawdrey to Johnson, 1604–1755*, new edition with an introduction and a select bibliography by Gabriele Stein (Amsterdam and Philadelphia: Benjamins).

St Clare Byrne, M. (1930) (ed.), *The Elizabethan home: Discovered in two dialogues by Claudius Hollyband and Peter Erondell* (2nd rev. edn., London: Cobden-Sanderson) (1st edn. 1925).

Stecher, J. (1969) (ed.), *Jean Lemaire de Belges. Œeuvres* (4 vols.; Geneva: Slatkine Reprints).

Stefano, G. di and Bidler, R. M. (1989) (eds.), *Du manuscrit à l'imprimé. Actes du colloque international Université McGill, Montréal, 3—4 octobre 1988* (= *Le Moyen Français*, 22).

Stein, G. (1981), 'The English dictionary in the 15th century', in H. Geckeler, B. Schlieben-Lange, J. Trabant, *et al.* (eds), *Logos semanticos. Studia linguistica in honorem Eugenio Coseriu 1921–1981*, i (Berlin and New York: de Gruyter; Madrid: Gredos), 313–22.

——(1985*a*), *The English dictionary before Cawdrey* (Lexicographica Series maior, 9; Tübingen: Niemeyer).

——(1985*b*), 'Forms of definition in Thomas Elyot's *dictionary*', in *Kontinuität und Wandel. Aspekte einer praxisoffenen Anglistik. Festschrift für Leonard Alfes zum 8. Februar 1985* (Siegen), 195–205.

——(1986*a*), 'Definitions and first person pronoun involvement in Thomas

Elyot's *Dictionary*', in D. Kastovsky and A. Szwedek (eds), *Linguistics across historical and geographical boundaries*, ii. *Descriptive, contrastive and applied linguistics* (Berlin, New York, and Amsterdam: Mouton de Gruyter), 1465–74.

——(1986*b*), '16th-century English vernacular dictionaries', in R. R. K. Hartmann (ed.), *The history of lexicography* (Amsterdam and Philadelphia: Benjamins), 219–28.

——(1987*a*), 'Peter Levins: a sixteenth-century English word-formationalist', in B. Asbach-Schnitker and J. Roggenhofer (eds), *Neuere Forschungen zur Wortbildung und Historiographie der Linguistik. Festgabe für Herbert E. Brekle zum 50. Geburtstag* (Tübingen: Narr), 287–302.

——(1987*b*), 'Reference point and authorial involvement in John Palsgrave's *Esclarcissement de la langue francoyse*', in W. Lörscher and R. Schulze (eds), *Perspectives on language and performance: Studies in linguistics, literary criticism and language teaching and learning to honour Werner Hüllen on the occasion of his sixtieth birthday* (Tübingen: Narr), 530–46.

——(1988*a*), 'Problems of affinity in early polyglot word lists', in U. Fries and M. Heusser (eds), *Meaning and beyond: Ernst Leisi zum 70. Geburtstag* (Tübingen: Narr), 93–114.

——(1988*b*) 'The emerging role of English in dictionaries of Renaissance Europe', *Folia Linguistica Historica*, 9: 29–138.

——(1995), 'Chaucer and Lydgate in Palsgrave's *Lesclarcissement*', in B. B. Kachru and H. Kahane (eds), *Cultures, ideologies, and the dictionary: Studies in honor of Ladislav Zgusta* (Lexicographica, Series maior, 64; Tübingen: Niemeyer), 127–39.

[Stengel, E.] (1878), 'The earliest French grammars', *Athenaeum*, 5 October, no. 2658: 433.

Stengel, E. (1879), 'Die ältesten Anleitungsschriften zur Erlernung der französischen Sprache', *Zeitschrift für neufranzösische Sprache und Literatur*, 1: 1–40.

——(1888), 'Zur Abfassung einer Geschichte der französischen Grammatik, besonders in Deutschland', *Zeitschrift für französische Sprache und Literatur*, 10: 184–201.

——(1890*a*), 'Anhang zum Verzeichnis französischer Grammatiken', *Zeitschrift für französische Sprache und Literatur*, 12/1: 284–90.

——(1890*b*/1970), *Chronologisches Verzeichnis französischer Grammatiken vom Ende des 14. bis zum Ausgang des 18. Jahrhunderts, nebst Angabe der bisher ermittelten Fundorte derselben* (Oppeln: Francks Buchhandlung; repr. Amsterdam: Grüner, 1970).

——(1890*c*), 'Plan einer Geschichte der französischen Grammatik, besonders in Deutschland (mit Beschreibung der *Institutio* Pilot's)', *Zeitschrift für französische Sprache und Literatur*, 12: 257–83.

——(1896), 'Über einige seltene französische Grammatiken', in *Mélanges de philologie romane dédiés à C. Wahlund* (Mâcon: Protat), 181–95.

——(1976), *Chronologisches Verzeichnis französischer Grammatiken vom Ende des 14. bis zum Ausgang des 18. Jahrhunderts nebst Angabe der bisher ermittelten Fundorte derselben*, neu herausgegeben mit einem Anhang von

Hans-Josef Niederehe (Amsterdam studies in the theory and history of linguistic science, ser. 3; Studies in the history of linguistics, 8; Amsterdam: Benjamins).

Stephen, L. (1885) (ed.), *Dictionary of national biography*, iii (London: Smith, Elder & Co.).

——(1888) (ed.), *Dictionary of national biography*, xiii (London: Smith, Elder & Co.).

——(1889) (ed.), *Dictionary of national biography*, xviii (London: Smith, Elder & Co.).

——(1889) (ed.), *Dictionary of national biography*, xix (London: Smith, Elder & Co).

——and Lee, S. (eds) (1891), *Dictionary of national biography*, xxv (London: Smith, Elder & Co.).

Stevenson, W. H. (1901), 'The introduction of English as the vehicle of instruction in English schools', in *An English miscellany presented to Dr Furnivall in honour of his seventy-fifth birthday* (Oxford: Clarendon Press), 421–9.

Stimm, H. (1980) (ed.), *Zur Geschichte des gesprochenen Französisch und zur Sprachlenkung im Gegenwartsfranzösischen. Beiträge des Saarbrücker Romanistentages 1979* (= *Zeitschrift für französische Sprache und Literatur*, NS 6) (Wiesbaden: Steiner).

Stone, L. C. (1962), 'English sports and recreations', in L. B. Wright and V. A. La Mar (eds), *Life and letters in Tudor and Stuart England* (Ithaca, NY: Cornell University Press), 427–79.

Streuber, A. (1914), *Beiträge zur Geschichte des französischen Unterrichts im 16. bis 18. Jahrhundert. Die Entwicklung der Methoden im allgemeinen und das Ziel der Konversation im besonderen. I* (Berlin: Ebering).

——(1962–4), 'Die ältesten Anleitungsschriften zur Erlernung des Französischen in England und den Niederlanden bis zum 16. Jahrhundert', *Zeitschrift für französische Sprache und Literatur*, 72: 37–86, 186–211; 73: 97–112, 189–209; 74: 59–76.

——(1964–9), 'Französische Grammatik und französischer Unterricht in Frankreich und Deutschland während des 16. Jahrhunderts', *Zeitschrift für französische Sprache und Literatur*, 74: 342–61; 75: 31–50, 247–73; 77: 235–67; 78: 69–101; 79: 172–91, 328–48.

Strutt, J. (1838), *The sports and pastimes of the people of England*, a new edition, with a copious index, by William Hone (London: Tegg & Son).

——(1855), *The sports and pastimes of the people of England: including the rural and domestic recreations, maygames, mummeries, shows, processions, pageants, & pompous spectacles from the earliest period to the present time*, a new edition, with copious index, by William Hone (London: Tegg).

Stürzinger, J. (1884), *Orthographia gallica. Ältester Traktat über französische Aussprache und Orthographie* (Altfranzösische Bibliothek, 8; Heilbronn: Gebr. Henninger; repr. Darmstadt: Wissenschaftliche Buchgesellschaft, 1967; repr. Wiesbaden: Sandig, 1968).

Swaen, A. E. H. (1888), 'Figures of imprecation', *Englische Studien*, 24: 16–71, 195–239.

Swiggers, P. (1984), 'La plus ancienne grammaire du français', *Medioevo romanzo*, 9: 183–8.

——(1986), 'Le Donait françois: la plus ancienne grammaire du français. Édition avec introduction', *Revue des langues romanes*, 89: 235–51.

Swiggers, P. and Hoecke, W. van (1989) (eds), *La langue française au XVIe siècle: usage, enseignement et approches descriptives* (La pensée linguistique, 2; Louvain: Leuven University Press).

Tatlock, J. S. P. and Kennedy, A. G. (1927), *A concordance to the complete works of Geoffrey Chaucer and to the Romant of the Rose* (Carnegie Institution of Washington Publication, 353; Washington: The Rumford Press Concord).

Tell, J. (1874/1967), *Les grammairiens français depuis l'origine de la grammaire en France jusqu'aux dernières œuvres connues. Ouvrage servant d'introduction à l'étude générale des langues* (Paris: Firmin Didot; repr. Geneva: Slatkine, 1967).

Thomas, A. (1877), 'Du passge d' *s z* à *r*, et d' *r* à *s z* dans le nord de la langue d'oc', *Romania*, 6: 261–6.

Thompson, C. R. (1962), 'Schools in Tudor England', in L. B. Wright and V. A. La Mar (eds), *Life and letters in Tudor and Stuart England* (Ithaca, NY: Cornell University Press), 285–334.

Thomson, D. (1977), *A study of the Middle English treatises on grammar.* (diss., Oxford).

——(1979), *A descriptive catalogue of Middle English grammatical texts* (Garland Reference Library of the Humanities, 171; New York and London: Garland Publishing).

——(1984) (ed.), *An edition of the Middle English grammatical texts* (Garland Medieval Texts, 8; New York and London: Garland Publishing).

Thomson, R. L. (1981), 'Aelfric's latin vocabulary', *Leeds Studies in English*, NS 12: 155–61.

Thurot, C. (1881–3/1966), *De la prononciation française depuis le commencement du XVIe siècle d'après les témoignages des grammairiens* (2 vols.; Paris: Imprimerie Nationale; repr. Geneva: Slatkine, 1966).

Tilley, M. P. (1950), *A dictionary of the proverbs in England in the sixteenth and seventeenth centuries* (Ann Arbor: University of Michigan Press).

Tobler, A. and Lommatzsch, E. (1925–93), *Altfranzösisches Wörterbuch* (11 vols.; Berlin: Weidmannsche Buchhandlung; Wiesbaden: Steiner Verlag).

Tory, G. (1529), *Champ fleury auquel est contenu lart et science de la deue et vraye proportion des lettres . . .* (Paris: de Gourmont).

——(1529/1927), *Champ fleury*, trans. into English and annotated by George B. Ives (New York: The Grolier Club).

Trapp, J. B. (1991), *Erasmus, Colet and More: The early Tudor humanists and their books* (The Panizzi Lectures 1990; London: The British Library).

Trudeau, D. (1992), *Les inventeurs du bon usage (1529–1647)* (Paris: Les Éditions de Minuit).

Vorlat, E. (1975), *The development of English grammatical theory 1586–1737 with special reference to the theory of parts of speech* (Leuven: University Press).

Wagner, R. L. (1967–70), *Les vocabulaires français* (2 vols.; Paris: Didier).

Wakelin, M. F. (1982), 'Evidence for spoken regional English in the sixteenth century', *Revista Canaria de Estudios Ingleses*, 5: 1–25.

Wartburg, W. v. *et al.* (1928–83) (eds), *Französisches etymologisches Wörterbuch* (*FEW*) (24 vols.; Bonn: Klopp, *a.o.*).

Watson, F. (1968), *The old grammar schools* (London: Cass).

Way, A. (1843) (ed.), *Promptorium parvulorum sive clericorum. Lexicon Anglo-Latinum princeps, auctore fratre Galfrido grammatico dicto, e predicatoribus lenne episcopi, Northfolciensi A. D. circa M.CCCC.XL.* Olim e prelis pynsonianis editum, nunc ab integro, commentariolis subjectis, ad fidem codicum recensuit (London: Sumptibus Societatis Camdensis).

Weijers, O. (1988) (ed.), *Terminologie de la vie intellectuelle au moyen âge* (Turnhout: Brepols).

——(1989), 'Lexicography in the Middle Ages', *Viator*, 20: 139–53.

——(1990*a*), 'Les dictionnaires et autres répertoires', in O. Weijers (ed.), *Methodes et instruments du travail intellectuel au moyen âge. Études sur le vocabulaire* (CIVICIMA Études sur le vocabulaire intellectuel du moyen âge, 3; Turnhout: Brepols), 197–208.

——(1990*b*), *Methodes et instruments du travail intellectuel au moyen âge. Études sur le vocabulaire* (CIVICIMA Études sur le vocabulaire intellectuel du moyen âge, 3; Turnhout: Brepols).

Wendel, H. (1875), *Die Aussprache des Französischen nach Angabe der Zeitgenossen Franz I* (*Vocalismus*) (Plauen: Hohmann).

West, A. G. B. [1923], *The church and parish of St. Dunstan in the East, Great Tower Street, E.C.* (London: Simpkin, Marshall, Hamilton, Kent & Co.).

Wey, F. (1848), *Histoire des révolutions du langage en France* (Paris: Firmin Didot Frères).

Whalley, P. (1791), *The history and antiquities of Northamptonshire. Compiled from the manuscript collections of the late learned antiquary John Bridges, Esq.* (2 vols.; Oxford: [no printer given]).

Wheatley, H. B. (1865), 'Chronological notices of the dictionaries of the English language', *Transactions of the Philological Society*, 218–93.

Wiegand, H. E. (1987) (ed.), *Theorie und Praxis des lexikographischen Prozesses bei historischen Wörterbüchern. Akten der internationalen Fachkonferenz Heidelberg, 3.6.-5.6.1986* (Lexicographica, Series maior, 23; Tübingen: Niemeyer).

Wildermuth, J. (1857), *Die drei ältesten süd- und nordfranzösischen Grammatiken* (Programm des Gymnasiums in Tübingen zu der Feier des Geburtstagsfestes Seiner Majestät des Königs Wilhelm von Württemberg; Tübingen: Laupp).

Woledge, B. (1956), 'The plural of the definite article in old French', *Modern Language Review*, 51: 17–32.

Wolf, L. (1969), *Texte und Dokumente zur französischen Sprachgeschichte, 16. Jahrhundert* (Tübingen: Niemeyer).

Wood, A. A. (1813/1967), *Athenae Oxonienses, an exact history of all the writers and bishops who have had their education in the university of Oxford, to which are added The Fasti or Annals of the said university*, i (New York and London: Johnson Reprint Corporation, 1967 (a facsimile of the London edn. of 1813)).

Woolridge, T. R. (1977), *Les débuts de la lexicographie française. Estienne, Nicot et le Thresor de la langue francoyse (1606)* (Toronto, Buffalo, and London: University of Toronto Press).

—— (1982), 'Projet de traitement informatique des dictionnaires de Robert Estienne et de Jean Nicot (TIDEN)', in M. Höfler (ed.), *La lexicographie française du XVI^e au XVIII^e siècle. Actes du colloque international de lexicographie dans la Herzog August Bibliothek Wolfenbüttel (9–11 Octobre 1979)* (Wolfenbütteler Forschungen, 18; Wolfenbüttel: Herzog August Bibliothek), 21–32.

Worcester, J. E. (1860), *A dictionary of the English language* (Boston: Hickling, Swan, & Brewer).

Wright, J. (1898/1970) (ed.), *The English dialect dictionary* (*EDD*) (Oxford: Oxford University Press).

Wright, L. B., and La Mar, V. A. (1962) (eds.), *Life and letters in Tudor and Stuart England* (Ithaca, NY: Cornell University Press).

Wright, T. (1857–73/1882) (ed.), *A volume of vocabularies, illustrating the condition and manners of our forefathers, as well as the history of the forms of elementary education and of the languages spoken in this island, from the tenth century to the fifteenth* (London: privately printed; repr. 1882).

—— (1884/1968), *Anglo-Saxon and Old-English vocabularies* (2nd edn.; ed. and collated by Richard Paul Wülcker), i. *Vocabularies*, ii. *Indices* (London: Trübner & Co.; repr. Darmstadt: Wissenschaftliche Buchgesellschaft, 1968).

—— and Halliwell, J. O. (1841), 'Glossary of names of plants', *Reliquiae antiquae*, 1: 36–8.

Wright, W. A. (1903) (ed.), *Femina. Now first printed from a unique MS. in the library of Trinity College Cambridge* (Cambridge: Cambridge University Press).

Wunderli, P. (1982) (ed.), *Du mot au texte. Actes du III^e colloque international sur le moyen français. Düsseldorf, 17–19 septembre 1980* (Tübinger Beiträge zur Linguistik, 175; Tübingen: Narr).

Wyld, H. C. (1956), *A history of modern colloquial English* (3rd edn., with additions; Oxford: Blackwell).

Zachrisson, R. E. (1914), 'Notes on some early English and French grammars', *Beiblatt zur Anglia*, 25: 246–53.

Zöckler, R. (1905), *Die Beteuerungsformeln im Französischen* (diss. Gießen) (Berlin, Chemnitz, and Leipzig: Gronau).

# Index